Perspectives in Medical Sociology

Perspectives in Medical Sociology

Edited by
Phil Brown
Brown University

Wadsworth Publishing Company
Belmont, California
A division of Wadsworth, Inc.

I dedicate this book to my daughter, Liza Littenberg-Brown.

Printed in the United States of America
1 2 3 4 5 6 7 8 9 10 DO 93 92 91 90 89

Library of Congress Cataloging-in-Publication Data

Perspectives in medical sociology / edited by Phil Brown.

    p. cm.

   Bibliography: p.

   ISBN 0-534-11100-9 (pbk.)   88–25714

   1. Medical sociology. I. Brown, Phil.   CIP

RA418.P435 1989

362.1'042—dc19

Preface

Perspectives in Medical Sociology is centered around the theme that health and illness cannot be understood by simply looking at biological phenomena and medical knowledge. Rather, it is necessary to situate health and illness in the framework of larger political, economic, and cultural forces. This approach to medical sociology is a modern and critical one that offers a more structural perspective than do traditional analyses of health and illness. This new viewpoint arises from the dramatic intellectual growth and expanded breadth of medical sociology in recent years and also from the need to situate the American health care system's deepening problems in a fresh perspective.

Although *Perspectives in Medical Sociology* contains much recent scholarship, it also includes a sufficient number of classic works. Further, the book encompasses all the areas of medical sociology that an instructor expects to find, regardless of the points of view.

This collection employs a macro-level approach that views medical sociology as influenced by political-economy, institutional structures, and professionalism. The book also presents a micro-level approach that focuses on interaction between patients and providers. In addition, emphasis is placed on integrating the macro- and micro-levels. There is one other theme—the role of social movements in health care—a development that is increasingly visible and important. This theme not only is presented in an entire part of the book but is also developed throughout the introductions and selections in other parts. Another feature of the book is the inclusion of many international and cross-national comparative contributions. This volume also presents the student with articles that utilize a broad range of research methods, and introductory material points these out.

Part I, "The Social Context of Health and Illness," contains sections titled "Social Factors in Health and Illness," "Environmental and Occupational Health," "Perspectives on Health and Illness," and "Becoming Patients and Experiencing Illness." Part II, "The Health Care System," contains the sections "Structures," "Institutional Settings," "Policies," and "Emerging

Impacts on Health Care and Policy." In Part III, "The Health Care Work Force," there are sections on "Physicians" and "Nonphysician Providers." Part IV, "Relations between Patients and Providers," offers sections on "Interaction and Negotiation" and "Rights, Responsibilities, and Social Control." The last part—"Social Movements, Social Change, and Health"— has two sections: "Reform and Change within Medicine" and "Reform and Change in the Larger Society."

Perspectives in Medical Sociology offers a compilation that is as inclusive as possible, enabling the instructor to use this collection as a basic text for medical sociology courses. The material has been tested and refined in actual medical sociology courses. Although the book is intended to be used in the order in which it is presented, it can be used selectively or in another sequence.

This book is intended for both undergraduate and graduate students. Students are guided through the material by a comprehensive Introduction to the Book, by introductory essays for each of the five parts, and by an introduction to each section within each part. Graduate students and advanced undergraduates are aided by research aids in two appendixes: "Sources of Data" points the student to locations of basic data on health and illness; and an "Annotated Bibliography of Journals in Medical Sociology and Related Fields" directs students to where to look for material for research papers, class presentations, and general interest.

Most selections in this volume are written by sociologists, but a number are the product of experts in other fields, such as public health, medicine, epidemiology, psychology, political science, history, and anthropology. This reflects the diversity of material employed by medical sociologists, and it also makes the book accessible for courses in other health-related disciplines. Some selections are complete articles or book chapters, while others are edited; edited selections contain no ellipses in order to prevent the reader from being distracted. Introductory material does not contain references; this serves to entice students into reading the introductions, and in many cases these references would simply be repeating references made in the selections.

Medical sociology is a tremendously exciting field. My intent throughout is to make it interesting, accessible, and challenging to the student as well as to the instructor who teaches the material. I will be pleased to hear instructors' and students' comments on their use of the book.

ACKNOWLEDGMENTS

Susan Bell, Catherine Kohler Riessman, and Irving Kenneth Zola spent a great deal of time in personal discussions and in written comments and suggestions concerning the style and selections. They were always willing to have yet one more discussion, and their wise counsel and intelligent help are greatly appreciated. Their input to this book has been not merely to help in the selection of articles, but to foster a deeper understanding of the nature of and the important issues in the field of medical sociology. David Himmelstein, Susan Reverby, and Steffie Woolhandler also helped out in discussions about the selections. Catherine Kohler Riessman and Ronnie Littenberg, my wife, carefully read the introductions and gave valuable feedback. Charles Bonjean and several anonymous reviewers offered many useful suggestions for improving the collection. Paul O'Connell of The Dorsey Press urged me to prepare a collection of readings in medical sociology, in pursuit of my long-standing interest in doing so. He has been immensely helpful in shaping the book as it has undergone many developments. Students in my courses in medical sociology have been important sources of reaction to the topics and selections in the book. I offer my appreciation to the authors of the selections, particularly those with whom I had contact in the process of revising and editing articles. Carol Walker was very helpful in handling reprint permissions and other technical details. Sandra Yeghian helped with clerical preparations of the manuscript. The Faculty Development Fund of Brown University facilitated my work with a grant, and I offer my sincere appreciation.

Phil Brown

Contents

Introduction to the Book

A new killer epidemic—AIDS—strikes the world and alters patterns of disease and death, affects sexual practices, threatens legal rights, and overwhelms health care institutions. Toxic wastes create illness, death, and fear in workplace and community. Millions of Americans find themselves without medical insurance in a society where medical care is a valuable, but scarce, commodity. Public hospitals close their doors, while private profit-making ones expand without apparent limits. Medical technology offers unheard-of hope in the form of organ transplants and surgery, yet proliferates in a context of unclear expectations about the ethics and the allocation of resources. Age-old patterns of doctors' status and practices are altered by government regulation, insurance companies, and public challenges. Health policy and universal health insurance become central points of political debate, and health issues take on the character of social movements.

These and many other health issues affect each of us every day of our lives. Many less dramatic features of health and illness also play a role in our daily existence: our complaints about illness, our interactions with doctors, how illness affects our work.

Why study medical sociology? In a way, it's all quite simple: we are conceived, we are born, we live in sickness and in health, and we die. These are fundamental elements of human existence, and we seek to understand them better and, increasingly, to better control them. Typically, we grasp only some of the issues involved in health and illness, and we are unable to understand the whole picture. There is, therefore, a need for a perspective that can link together many components: biomedical data; professional practice; institutional structures; economics and financing; demographics of disease and death; and the individual experience of health, illness, and medical care. Medical sociology offers a way to make the linkages, to compose and focus the whole picture, to make social sense of the varied manifestations of health and illness.

In earlier periods, religious leaders might have been consulted on matters of health and illness. In modern societies, doctors are the more likely source. Increasingly, other authorities have entered the contest for expert knowledge on health affairs: philosophers, economists, bioethicists,

1

psychologists, and political scientists. But in neither traditional nor modern civilizations do any of these sources typically provide a strong link between health and illness on the one hand and social structure on the other. Social structure includes a society's forms of political organization; economic structure; hierarchy of status, power, and wealth; family and kinship networks; value systems; forms of social interaction; and formal and informal institutions of education, health, welfare, and punishment.

Indeed, those who often speak with the authority of their society on medical matters are those with self-interests of one sort or another that make it hard for them to go beyond their particular view of the world. That is where sociology steps in, and more specifically, where medical sociology steps in. As a discipline, sociology seeks to provide an understanding of social structures, ranging from the smallest interactions (such as interpersonal communication) to the largest world-size affairs (such as diplomacy and war). Further, sociology attempts to do so by providing theoretical linkages between levels of social structure so that individual entities are not studied in isolation from their surroundings. For example, the particular set of attitudes to health held by members of an ethnic group are related to the ways that such members seek medical care and interact with providers. At the same time, the ethnic group as a whole must be seen in light of its history of immigration and acculturation; its standing in the hierarchies of status, power, and wealth; and public and professional attitudes toward the group.

As a specialty area of sociology, medical sociology seeks to make connections and linkages as mentioned above, with particular attention to the domains of health and illness. Medical sociology is concerned with the distribution of disease and how that differs on the basis of class, race, sex, ethnicity, education, and other social factors. It is concerned with the different ways that people conceptualize disease and illness, with reference to the above categories. Medical sociology is also interested in conceptual differences based on conflicts between lay and professional beliefs. Medical sociology looks at the sources of morbidity (disease) and mortality (death) as stemming from political, economic, cultural, and professional forces, as well as from biomedical factors. Medical sociology is also interested in how people experience illness and how they make their way to various providers and institutions to seek care. It is likewise interested in the interaction between help-seekers and help-providers. As a further interest, medical sociology examines the backgrounds, structures, and functions of health care providers and institutions. From this, it is a logical next step to examine issues of health policy and to investigate how basic social structures relate to illness, treatment, and health policy. Since the societal determinants of health and illness are paramount, medical sociology increasingly emphasizes the interactions between health and social change.

This nutshell view of the scope of medical sociology sets the stage for what we study in this subdiscipline. Some readers, however, may be aware of recent discussions about the appropriateness of using the term *medical so-*

ciology to identify the field as I have just described it. These discussions argue that the term *medical sociology* is old-fashioned and traditional, in that it represents an older school of thought in which sociology served as a handmaiden of medical practitioners and providers, that is, it was really *sociology in medicine*. Newer and more critical approaches have expanded the scope of the field to include what is conceived of as *sociology of medicine*, a broader realm of concern that covers the wide range of topics noted earlier in this introduction. Why then do I retain the term *medical sociology*, instead of, say, *sociology of health and illness*? I do so because medical sociology is a familiar and less cumbersome term and because many adherents of the more modern view still find it a useful term.

Why raise this issue of terminology now? Because medical sociology is a vital and growing field—in fact, it is the largest section in the American Sociological Association—and it is undergoing many significant debates, alterations, and reformulations of its scope, theory, methods, and audience. It is useful for the reader to know that these changes are occurring and that this book represents the broader and more modern perspective that is emerging in the field of medical sociology. At the same time, though, I have included a number of readings that represent more traditional perspectives in order to provide an adequate background for understanding both older and more modern approaches.

CENTRAL THEMES

Perhaps the single most overarching theme of *Perspectives in Medical Sociology* is that health and illness cannot be understood with reference to biological phenomena and medical knowledge alone. Rather, it is necessary to bring to bear a variety of political, economic, and cultural forces. This focus on large-scale social structural factors is often termed a *macro-level approach*. We can consider medical sociology to be influenced by three major categories of social structure. First, political-economy deals with the class, race, and sex differentials so central to the social order. Political-economy also includes the overall economic order and political system. Second, professionalism concerns the development of the medical profession, its present value systems and practices, and the conflicts between lay and professional perspectives. Third, institutional structures include health institutions, health regulatory bodies, and related institutions and agencies. Some social structural factors—such as class, sex, and race—play major roles in health status, in how people and caregivers view health, how and when they seek help for illness, and how they interact with health institutions and providers. Help-seeking and interaction, in turn, are affected by the structure of the health care system and its major professional grouping, doctors.

The exploration of *interaction between people and their health providers*, or a *micro-level approach*, is the second theme. A belief in the social nature of health and illness does not imply a monolithic view of the health care system. For example, despite what an emphasis on professionalism tells us about the extraordinary social power of physicians, patients' expectations of physicians' behavior are a complementary part of medical interaction. Individuals bring to medical encounters their own backgrounds and agendas, and these are involved in an interplay with professional and institutional frames. Even if one party (the doctor) is dominant, the impact of the weaker party (the patient) is nevertheless significant. As with other parts of society, *social interaction* in medical settings is a fundamental part of the social fabric that is necessary for understanding health and illness.

A third theme, which ties together the first two, is that medical sociology should *link both micro- and macro-levels of analysis*. Too many scholars focus on only one level and lose much understanding. For example, if we want to understand what goes on in the interaction between client and health provider, we cannot simply analyze the language, information exchange, and power relationships in that encounter. After all, the encounter is influenced by the larger context—including issues of professional, institutional, sociocultural, political, and economic factors. Likewise, suppose we want to examine the effects of a major new federal reimbursement program, diagnosis-related groups for Medicare patients. We cannot look only at aggregate data on hospital length of stay. We must explore also the policy's impacts on particular interchanges between providers and consumers, such as doctor-patient discourse concerning potentially premature hospital discharge.

The *role of social movements* in health care is a fourth central theme of this book. Social movements include formal and informal organizations, as well as more general social trends, that seek to change some element of the social structure. While the focus on social movements is clearly indicated by the material in the final Part V—"Social Movements, Social Change, and Health"—the theme crops up throughout the book. Nearly all changes in the social structure result from social movements that are characterized by varying degrees of cohesiveness and formal organization. The democratic freedoms we may take for granted today, for example, are all products of social movements. Products of such struggles include the abolition of slavery and the outlawing of segregation, women's suffrage and equal rights for women, Social Security, the right to organize labor unions, and workers' compensation. Of course, not all of these rights are firm and complete, and this fact engenders continuing social movement efforts.

Since health and illness are pivotal elements of society, it is not surprising that social movements play major roles in the health care system. Witness, for example, the history of efforts at food and drug regulation, occupational safety and health organizing, environmental activism, the women's health movement, the enactment of Medicare and Medicaid, consumer efforts to eradicate disease, self-help movements, endeavors to expand access to care, struggles to keep public hospitals open, campaigns to expand informed consent, drives to correct substandard conditions in mental hospitals and other institutions, and efforts to curtail unlimited expansion of profit-making hospital chains. Not only have these social movements aimed to achieve specific goals, but in the process they have often altered our perspectives on the very definitions of health and illness and the proper ways to create and sustain a healthy society.

The four themes mentioned above recur throughout the book, not only in sections that are specifically dedicated to them. Keeping the themes in mind will allow you to make better use of the book's selections. More importantly, focusing on these themes will give you a better sense of what the field of medical sociology as a whole is all about.

FORMAT AND SPECIAL FEATURES OF THE BOOK

My intent is to provide a selection of articles that is as inclusive as possible. This is important because I view this collection as a basic text for medical sociology courses. The material has been tested and refined in actual medical sociology courses, and it is designed for use in the order in which it is presented, although it certainly can be used selectively or in another order.

Although the majority of the selections are by sociologists, you will find many articles by others in the fields of public health, medicine, epidemiology, psychology, political science, history, and anthropology. This is because medical sociology has been successful at integrating much material from those other disciplines. Students reading this book for courses in other fields (e.g., public health, health education, health and public policy) will find therefore that they are not totally surrounded by a discipline different from their own.

Besides its organizing themes, *Perspectives in Medical Sociology* is concerned with health and illness in other countries. Thus, the reader will find articles about other societies, both developed and developing. Also, seven articles deal with *comparative analysis* of health and illness, so that you can see differences in the same issue (e.g., health status, women physicians) across societies.

I also have worked to provide the reader with a sample of many different *methods of research* and *sources of data*. It is important to understand how researchers obtain their information and how they analyze it. Each section of the book will include varied data sources and methodologies, and introductory essays will note this. Even if this is the student's only medical sociology course, such knowledge will be useful in learning how scholars locate and use data and in seeing the bases on which conclusions and inferences are drawn. For the student who will go on to further study, and for the graduate student, this may be even more significant, for the information can be applied to the student's own research in the field.

I have provided further *research aids* in two appendixes. First, "Sources of Data" is a valuable compilation of information on where to get basic data on health and illness. Even if students do not consult these sources, they may find it quite informative to read over the appendix just to get a sense of where researchers obtain data. Second, an "Annotated Bibliography of Journals in Medical Sociology and Related Fields" offers assistance in figuring out where to look for material for research papers, class presentations, and general interest. Students may find it very informative to spend some time in the library simply leafing through the last year or two of various journals in order to see what topics and areas have sparked recent scholarly interest.

    With all these preliminary remarks in place, let's move on to explore the exciting field of medical sociology.

The Social Context of Health and Illness

INTRODUCTION

A core conception of this book is that *health and illness must be understood in a social context*. In the creation of disease and death, biomedical factors are often eclipsed by social factors. For instance, modern sanitation and improved living conditions are widely acknowledged to have been more important than medical advances in the modern decrease in the death rate. Even when biomedical factors are of primary importance, social factors—such as race, class, and access to care —often result in differential rates of disease and death. Nor does medical knowledge alone provide sufficient understanding of the underlying causes of morbidity (disease) and mortality (death). For example, medical practitioners and researchers often fail to take into account environmental variables such as workplace and community toxic wastes. Nor do practitioners and researchers tend, for example, to focus on such phenomenon as the correlation between military spending and mortality. Even social concepts that have arisen in part from within medicine— for example, the role of stress in illness—are generally underutilized by medical professionals in explaining health status.

Part I includes four sections. In "The Health of the People: Social Factors in Health and Illness," we examine social epidemiology, the distribution of disease and death in various parts of the population (e.g., sex, race, class, and ethnic group) and in relation to various social factors (e.g., stress, unemployment, social inequality). In the next section, "Environmental and Occupational Health," we take a look at how community and workplace hazards play major roles in health. These areas have long been overlooked but are increasingly coming under closer scrutiny. The section "Perspectives on Health and Illness" provides a number of conceptual frameworks on health and illness. The selections demonstrate a broad range in viewpoints (some of them compatible, others less so) that are brought to bear on an understanding of health and illness. The final section, "Becoming Patients and Experiencing Illness," emphasizes the personal encounter between patient and provider. These articles examine the diverse forms of patients' experience of illness, sometimes as a result of an individual's particularities and sometimes as a result of a person's membership in a certain social group.

The Health of the People: Social Factors in Health and Illness

We start with *social epidemiology* because it is useful to understand the key social variables that affect health status. The readings in this first section familiarize us with overall statistics and with a framework for situating them in a social context. It is not enough to know that rates of disease and death are different; sociologists want to know why they are different and what this means for health care and for other social institutions.

As a field, epidemiology has not always been as politically conscious as medical sociology. As we will see later in the topic on environmental and occupational issues, epidemiology often falls short because its demand for statistically significant levels of proof are different from those needed for social policy applications, and because it does not generally conceive of health and illness with reference to political, economic, and institutional structures. Thus, medical sociologists have applied their insights to epidemiological questions, not in the interests of furthering epidemiology per se, but as a means of improving sociological analysis.

Epidemiological background allows us to examine some central forces in health and illness. Class, race, and gender are generally the key social variables in any sociological area. Social class (people's position in the hierarchy of economic wealth and political power) is fundamentally related to basic political and economic structures of the society, especially in terms of the unequal distribution of wealth and power. Likewise, race (at least in the United States) is tied up with unequal relations and a particularly brutal history of slavery and segregation. In addition, race plays a major role in the relations between the developed and underdeveloped countries. Gender involves a core disparity in social power between two halves of the human species. The readings in this first section aim to introduce you to the key social factors, and you will continue to encounter these social factors throughout the rest of the readings.

9

The health of the people might be a result of their wealth, or so we might think. Since the United States is such a wealthy and powerful nation, we might expect its citizens to have a health status consistent with that position. When we hear of a heroic new surgical or drug treatment with astounding results, we might be tempted to say, "Yes, our health system is the finest." But in much of the routine day-to-day life of most Americans, health status and access to health care are not so perfect.

A country's wealth *should* relate to the public's health, but the United States falls behind many industrialized nations that spend less money on health care. This point is made in an excerpt from Victor Sidel and Ruth Sidel's book, *A Healthy State*. The authors inform us that key measures of a nation's health (such as life expectancy, infant mortality, and maternal mortality) show the United States to rank fairly low. The Sidels' data show that America's health conditions are far less perfect than is commonly believed and provide clear evidence for a growing crisis of American health care.

Diana Dutton's contribution, "Social Class, Health, and Illness," provides us with a summary of essential information on the health ramifications of social class. Because of the high correlation between class and race, she is often compelled to offer data on race differences as well.

Dutton shows that there is no single explanation for poorer health status in poor and nonwhite people. She points to multiple causes: environmental hazards, stress and social isolation, individual behavior, and inadequate medical care. This article raises some key themes that have preoccupied medical sociologists: whether or not medical care matters to health status, how social policies can improve health or even to reverse improvements (as in the 1980s), and how important is preventive care in reducing disease.

In "Sex, Illness, and Medical Care," Constance Nathanson uses cross-national data from Europe and North America to show how gender affects health status, attitudes toward illness, and use of health services. Women generally have more illness than men (except in chronic illness). They make greater use of health services, are more likely to be hospitalized, and tend to have a regular source of care. Men, however, have a higher mortality rate.

Besides presenting these basic data, Nathanson's article is useful for other reasons. She introduces the idea of bias in both interviewer and respondent in health surveys. As does Dutton, Nathanson also discusses how medical researchers use different types of outcome measures to explain health and illness, depending on their orientation. She concludes with a discussion of several perspectives for explaining sex differences regarding illness and medical care.

Steffie Woolhandler and her colleagues, in "Medical Care and Mortality: Racial Differences in Preventable Deaths," employ a useful method of separating preventable and nonpreventable causes of death. They found the black/white mortality ratio to be higher for preventable causes, except in persons over seventy-five. The researchers interpret their data as evidence of racial disparity in health care delivery. The methodology of this study is instructive in showing how medical researchers can attempt to unravel complex questions by a retrospective study of medical records.

Ronald Angel's article on "The Health of the Mexican Origin Population" provides basic data on the nation's largest and most rapidly growing ethnic minority group. He points out that ethnicity alone does not determine health status, but that it interacts with social class and with characteristics of the health care system itself. Angel's article is also useful in pointing to inaccuracies and biases in various sources of health data, such as errors in accounting for mortality rates. Angel also emphasizes the importance of the cultural and language gap between interviewer and subject in health surveys. Angel's points concerning data biases are relevant to *all* sources of health data.

In recent years, we have come to understand that *stress* is a significant factor in producing ill health. We have also learned that people's *social supports* and the ways in which people *cope* with stress are important influences on how stress affects their health and help-seeking. The growing importance attached to stress is manifested in current approaches toward health education, corporate wellness programs, and stress reduction courses. Leonard Pearlin and Carol Aneshensel's article, "Stress, Coping, and Social Supports," points to four major ways in which coping and social supports affect stress: preventing the stressful condition, altering the stressful condition, changing the meaning of the situation, and managing stress symptoms.

1 THE HEALTH OF THE PEOPLE

Victor W. Sidel and Ruth Sidel

By most comparable measures of health status the people of the United States are less healthy than are people in other technologically developed, wealthy countries. Most of the factors influencing the health of a people lie outside what is conventionally defined as the responsibility of "medical care," and many of the most important ones lie outside the responsibility of conventionally defined "health care." These factors include individually inborn characteristics such as genetic inheritance and socially determined characteristics such as housing, nutrition and life-style. Nonetheless, since one of the generally accepted purposes of a health-care and medical-care system is promotion and protection of health, it may be relevant to begin by reviewing some comparative data on health and illness. A look at four commonly used criteria will suffice

SOURCE: From *A Healthy State: An International Perspective on the Crisis in United States Health Care* by Victor W. Sidel and Ruth Sidel. Copyright © 1977 by Victor W. Sidel and Ruth Sidel. Reprinted by permission of Pantheon Books, a Division of Random House, Inc.

to make the point that health in the United States is poorer than it needs to be.

Death Rates and "Life Expectancy"

Death rates are the ones most often used for comparisons of health status between, and within, countries. The relative clarity of the definition of death (despite, in the case of a few dying people, a problem in defining the precise moment of "death") and the completeness of reporting of deaths (despite lapses in some of the poorer countries) make death rates much more reliable and comparable than rates of illness, disability, malnutrition or poor physical fitness, and infinitely more comparable than rates of positive good health. Death rates, in other words, may not be—and in some respects are probably not—the most important measures of the health status of a country, but they are by far the most reliable and comparable indicators.

Death rates in the United States at every age level except for the very oldest groups in the population are higher than in other comparably developed countries. Since the total death rate (technically known as the "crude death rate") of a country is more a reflection of the number of its older people than of the death rate at each age, "age-specific death rates" are used for comparison, as shown in Tables 1 and 2. Except for the oldest age groups, for 1973, the most recent year for which the World Health Organization has published comparable statistics, U.S. rates are consistently higher, for both males and females, than are those for England and Wales or Sweden. In all three countries the death rates for males are considerably higher than the rate for females; in the United States the difference is particularly pronounced.

If one examines the tables for each sex separately one finds, for example, that girls one to four years old in the United States had almost twice the chance of dying during 1973 that Swedish girls of the same age had. A 15-to-24-year-old in the United States, of either sex, had almost twice the chance of dying that an English young person had at the same age. A 25-to-34-year-old U.S. male had over twice the chance of dying that his English counterpart had, and a 45-to-54-year-old U.S. male had almost twice the chance of dying of one in Sweden. Only at the oldest ages were the "age-specific" rates in the United States at approximately the same levels as, or lower than, those in Sweden or England.

Similar differences may be found between areas within countries. In the United States startling differences occur between states, between areas within states, and even between contiguous sections of cities. Victor Fuchs has recently analyzed in detail the fact that, even though the states are contiguous, age-specific death rates in Nevada are considerably higher at all ages than in Utah. Fuchs's attribution of the differences almost exclusively to lifestyle and the conclusions he draws —which we would term "blaming the victim"—may be arguable, but the fact of the enormous differences in death rates of groups of people

TABLE 1 Age-Specific Death Rates for Males, 1973 (deaths per 1,000 population per year)

Age	Sweden	England and Wales	United States
Less than 1 year	10.8	18.9	19.9
1–4	0.5	0.8	0.9
5–14	0.3	0.4	0.5
15–24	1.0	1.0	1.9
25–34	1.2	1.0	2.1
35–44	2.4	2.3	3.8
45–54	5.5	7.2	9.2
55–64	14.3	20.4	22.1
65–74	38.2	51.5	47.3
75+	117.3	136.4	118.4
All ages ("crude death rate")	11.6	12.4	10.7

SOURCE: From *World Health Statistics Annual, 1973–1976, Vol. 1, Vital Statistics and Causes of Death* (Geneva: World Health Organization, 1976).

within a few miles of each other is not.

Age-specific death rates are often converted, by what can only be termed a statistical trick, into the widely reported indicator called "life expectancy," usually given as "life expectancy at birth," "life expect-ancy at age 40," or at some other specific age. The calculation of life expectancy, however, is based on an assumption that is clearly incorrect: that current age-specific death rates will remain constant for the remaining life of the group of people for whom the prediction is made.

TABLE 2 Age-Specific Death Rates for Females, 1973 (deaths per 1,000 population per year)

Age	Sweden	England and Wales	United States
Less than 1 year	8.9	14.7	15.4
1–4	0.4	0.6	0.7
5–14	0.3	0.2	0.3
15–24	0.4	0.4	0.7
25–34	0.6	0.6	0.9
35–44	1.3	1.6	2.2
45–54	3.2	4.3	4.9
55–64	7.3	10.2	10.8
65–74	21.5	26.8	24.5
75+	88.6	101.0	86.4
All ages ("crude death rate")	9.4	11.5	8.1

SOURCE: From *World Health Statistics Annual, 1973–1976, Vol. 1, Vital Statistics and Causes of Death* (Geneva: World Health Organization, 1976).

Therefore the calculation is flawed— and it may in fact be almost meaningless—if one is calculating life expectancy at birth or at some other young age.

An even more important problem, at least in the popular interpretation of widely publicized change in life expectancy, is the little-mentioned fact that in recent years almost all the improvement in "life expectancy at birth," the most commonly used figure, has been due to decreases in the death rate in the first year of life; "life expectancy" at later ages has improved little because the death rates at later ages have fallen little.

In short, "life expectancy" is an inadequate and often misleading shorthand for a series of age-specific death rates at every age. Since age-specific death rates for young and middle-aged Americans—particularly males—are considerably higher than in Sweden, Britain and other industrialized countries, their "life expectancy" is consistently lower, and little information and less insight is gained by citing it. Nonetheless, since it is often cited, for the record let it be said here too that "life expectancy at birth," and at all ages up to age 65, is lower in the United States than in most comparably developed countries and that within the United States, although the gap has been narrowing somewhat in recent years, life expectancy at birth for nonwhite males is six years shorter than for white males, and five years shorter for nonwhite females than for white females. The differences in life expectancy at birth for males and females in selected countries are shown in Figure 1.

Far more important than "life expectancy" in making comparisons are more specific, and therefore more comparable, death rates. It is for this reason that the most widely internationally compared death rate is the infant mortality rate—the number of live-born babies dying in their first year of life per 1000 live births. The U.S. infant mortality rate, despite recent declines, remains almost double that of the country with the lowest rate (Sweden) and 50 percent higher than the rates in countries like the Netherlands, Japan and Switzerland.

It has often been noted—usually by apologists for the relatively high rates in the United States—that there are problems with comparisons of infant mortality among different countries. Indeed there are. It is not clear, for example, that all countries use similar criteria in distinguishing between babies born alive and then dying shortly after birth, and babies already dead at birth. Most countries, including the U.S., attempt to include in the statistics all babies alive at the time of birth. France and Spain, however, beginning in 1973, have excluded live-born infants dying before registration of birth from both the live-birth data and the infant-death data. The USSR excludes infants of less than 28 weeks, less than 1000 grams (two pounds) in weight and less than 35 centimeters (14 inches) in length who die within seven days of birth.

These problems of comparison are relatively small, however, compared with the overall rates and with the differences in rates among countries.

FIGURE 1 Life Expectancy at Birth for Selected Countries in the Early 1970s

Rank	Males	
1	Sweden (1973)	72.12
2	Norway (1971-72)	71.24
3	Netherlands (1973)	71.20
4	Denmark (1971-72)	70.70
5	Japan (1972)	70.49
6	Israel (1973)	70.23
7	Switzerland (1969-72)	70.16
8	Spain (1970)	69.69
9	Canada (1970-72)	69.34
10	Italy (1970-72)	68.97
11	England and Wales (1970-72)	68.90
12	German Democratic Republic (1969-70)	68.85
13	Bulgaria (1965-67)	68.81
14	France (1972)	68.60
15	Ireland (1965-67)	68.58
16	New Zealand (1965-67)	68.19
17	Belgium (1965-72)	67.79
18	Australia (1965-67)	67.63
19	United States (1973)	67.56
20	Greece (1960-62)	67.46

Life expectancy at birth in years

Rank	Females	
1	Sweden (1973)	77.66
2	Norway (1971-72)	77.43
3	Netherlands (1973)	77.20
4	France (1972)	76.40
5	Canada (1970-72)	76.36
6	Switzerland (1969-72)	76.17
7	Denmark (1971-72)	76.10
8	Japan (1972)	75.92
9	United States (1973)	75.27
10	England and Wales (1970-72)	75.10
11	Spain (1970)	74.96
12	Italy (1970-72)	74.88
13	Austria (1973)	74.70
14	New Zealand (1965-67)	74.30
15	Belgium (1968-72)	74.21
16	Finland (1971)	74.21
17	German Democratic Republic (1969-70)	74.19
18	Australia (1965-67)	74.15
19	U.S.S.R. (1971-72)	74.00
20	Federal Republic of Germany (1970-72)	73.83

Life expectancy at birth in years

Prepared by the National Center for Health Statistics, from data in the *United Nations Demographic Yearbook 1974*, for testimony before the U.S. Senate Health Subcommittee on March 31, 1977. Note that the scales begin with a life expectancy of 60 rather than 0 years; the figure therefore shows *absolute* differences rather than *relative* differences in life expectancy between countries.

Even if one counts only countries of over one million population and with "complete" counts of live births and infant deaths as defined by the United Nations, 14 countries, as shown in Figure 2, some of them— such as East Germany or Finland— considerably less affluent than the United States, had lower infant mortality rates than ours in the most recent year for which comparable data are available.

Even if one limits the comparison to white babies, the United States was no better than the tenth among the countries of the world in infant mortality in 1974. More alarming, the United States, which 25 years ago ranked much higher among the world's countries, has steadily lost its position—even as its infant mortality rate has fallen—as other countries reduced their infant mortality rates at a far faster rate. There have

FIGURE 2   Infant Mortality Rates for Selected Countries in the Early 1970s

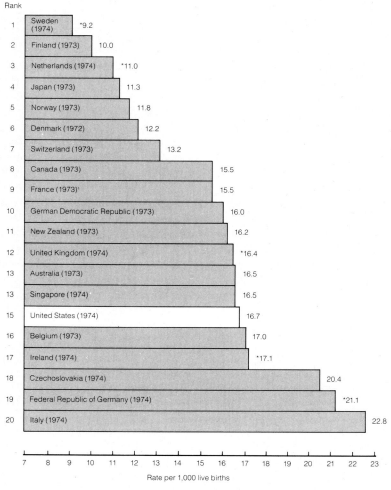

The rates marked by an (*) were provisional. The 1974 rate of 12.1 for France was not used because it includes live-born infants dying before registration of birth. Note that the scale begins with a rate of 7 rather than a rate of 0; the figure therefore shows *absolute* differences rather than *relative* differences in rate between countries.

SOURCE: See Figure 1.

been further declines in the U.S. infant mortality rate in the past few years, and the U.S. position relative to other countries may now be beginning to improve—although that is not yet clear—but that still cannot make up for the thousands of infant deaths that might have been prevented over the past two decades.

Even more disturbing than the international differences are the differences in death rates between groups within the United States. Since the possible underlying causes of these differences are closely related to each other, the differences are difficult to assign to single causes. Poverty is certainly a critical component. Not by accident, however, the wealth, income, education, job classification—or other direct measures of social class—during the life of the deceased is not usually recorded on death certificates in the United States. "Race" and residence address at the time of death are recorded, though, and these are the data used in most analyses.

Analyzed by "race," the 1974 infant mortality rate among "white" infants in the United States was 14.8 deaths in the first year of life per 1000 live births; among "nonwhite" infants it was 24.9 deaths per 1000 births, almost twice the rate. Analyzed geographically, U.S. infant mortality ranged from a low of 11.3 (in a "health service area" in Massachusetts) to a high of 27.1 (in an area in South Carolina), the highest rate more than double the lowest.

Special studies are needed to examine the effects of poverty directly. One such study, performed by the U.S. National Center for Health Statistics of infant mortality in poverty and nonpoverty areas of 19 large cities of the United States from 1969 to 1971, showed that "whites" living in poverty areas had an infant mortality rate almost 50 percent higher than that of "whites" living in nonpoverty areas, and that "blacks," while having a higher rate than the "whites" in either type of area, also have a far higher infant mortality rate in poor areas than in nonpoor areas. In short, all three factors—poverty, "race" and residence—seem associated with greater numbers of dead babies.

If one looks specifically at those infant deaths which would appear to be preventable, the differences are even more disturbing. A small number of infant deaths seem unpreventable; some babies are born with such severe physical defects that their lives can't—and, some would say, shouldn't—be saved. If we assume that the infant mortality rate in Sweden, the country with the lowest rate (11 deaths per 1000 births), was the minimum one achievable in 1969–71 with the then current state of knowledge of how to care for pregnant women and their babies, then the "excess" deaths among babies born in nonpoor areas in the United States in those years was 6 per 1000 births and the "excess" deaths among babies born in poor areas was 13 per 1000 births. In other words, the probably preventable deaths in poor areas were over 100 percent higher than those in the nonpoor areas rather than "merely" 50 percent higher. Analyzed the same way, the "excess" deaths among "non-white" infants born in 1974 (15.7 per 1000) was almost three times as great as the "excess" deaths among "white" infants (5.6 per 1000). Furthermore, while deaths among infants after one month of age ("postneonatal infant deaths") are especially susceptible to preventive actions, during 1969–73 the rates for these deaths among health-service areas in the United States varied from a high of 13.6 per 1000 live births (in Arizona) to 2.9 per 1000 (in Connecticut), a ratio of over four to one.

There is, as we have noted, considerable controversy over the international comparability of infant mortality rates. But there is relatively little controversy over the comparability of maternal mortality rates —the number of mothers dying due

to complications of childbirth per 100,000 live births.

The United States in 1950 had the lowest maternal mortality rate in the world (70 deaths per 100,000 births). But although the maternal mortality rate has fallen even lower since 1950, it has fallen considerably faster in many other countries; as shown in Table 3, the percent decrease in maternal mortality from 1960 to 1971 was lower for the United States than for any of the other countries listed. As a result, by 1971 at least nine other countries had lower maternal mortality rates than did the United States. The 1971 U.S. rate (20 deaths per 100,000 births) was two and a half times that of Sweden (8 per 100,000) and almost four times that of Denmark (5.3 per 100,000). In

TABLE 3   Maternal Mortality in Selected Countries, 1960–1971 (deaths due to childbirth per 1,000 live births)

1960		1971		Percent Decrease 1960–1971
Australia	52.5	Australia	18.5	65
Belgium	40.7	Belgium	20.4 (1970)	50
Canada	44.9	Canada	18.3	59
Denmark	30.2	Denmark	5.3	82
England and Wales	39.5	England and Wales	16.9	57
Finland	71.8	Finland	8.1	89
Japan	130.8	Japan	45.2	65
Netherlands	39.4	Netherlands	12.1	69
Norway	42.0	Norway	19.6	53
Sweden	37.2	Sweden	7.9	79
Switzerland	57.2	Switzerland	27.0	53
U.S.A.	37.1	U.S.A.	20.5	45

From Robert Maxwell, *Health Care: The Growing Dilemma* (New York: McKinsey & Co., 1975), Table 5, drawn from the *World Health Statistics Reports* published regularly by the World Health Organization, Geneva.

other words, in proportion to the number of births, four women died as a result of pregnancy and birth in the United States for every one who died of similar causes in Denmark. There has been a further reduction of maternal mortality in the United States since 1971—in part because of liberalized abortion laws—but our rates remain higher than those of other industrialized countries.

Preventable deaths, of course, occur at ages other than infancy and at times other than childbirth. Among the problems in international comparisons of such deaths is that death rates due to specific illness vary considerably from country to country and, perhaps even more important, the standards of reporting by physicians of cause of death on death certificates vary enormously from country to country.

Nevertheless, it appears, for example, that U.S. men aged 35–44 appear to be almost three times as likely to die of cardiovascular disease or of respiratory diseases as Swedish men of the same age. Death rates in this age group from cancer or from accidents, poisoning or violence are, on the other hand, only slightly greater in the United States. In the other direction, although reporting may be particularly unreliable for this cause of death, the Swedish rate for suicide (for the entire population) is almost double that of the United States.

A recent U.S. study identified some 70 medical conditions that can and should, in the present state of knowledge, be successfully prevented or managed. Yet in 1974 there were, exclusive of infant

deaths, over 200,000 deaths from these 70 conditions, which include several different types of cancer, respiratory diseases and accidents.

Lung cancer, for example, is the most common type of cancer among men and the fastest rising type of cancer among women. It has been reliably estimated that some 90 percent of lung cancer could be prevented by abstinence from cigarette smoking. The U.S. Department of Health, Education and Welfare unequivocally states that "cigarette smoking remains the largest single preventable cause of illness and early death" in the United States. Yet attempts to induce people to give up cigarette smoking or, better still, to make sure they never start smoking are pitifully inadequate compared to the resources that are spent on cigarette advertising.

The rate of deaths from accidents, suicides and homicides in the United States is almost double that of the United Kingdom. Automobile accidents are the leading cause of death among Americans from age 1 through 38. There are some 50,000 deaths (and two million injuries) caused by the automobile each year, more than the number of deaths among U.S. troops in the entire 15 years of our involvement in Indochina. Other countries, such as Sweden, have materially reduced the deaths (and injuries) from automobiles by making the use of seat belts mandatory and by imposing heavy penalties—including imprisonment—on drivers with even a small amount of alcohol in their bloodstreams.

In 1975 almost 12,000 people died

as a result of fires, the highest fire-death rate of all industrialized nations in the world.

In short, there is good evidence that a significant number of people in the United States, particularly men, die at an earlier age than the experience of other countries or the experience of other groups within the United States suggests they need to; and that those who are poor, who are "nonwhite," or who live in certain areas of the country are more likely to die an early—and probably preventable—death than are their fellow citizens.

Illness Rates

Rates of illness are far harder to compare cross-nationally than deaths. Not only do definitions of what constitutes, for example, a "common cold" or a "mild stroke" differ, but capabilities of reporting vary widely from country to country. Many U.S. doctors do not bother to report even those illnesses they are required by law to report.

While some argument may be made for maintenance of confidentiality in the case of socially stigmatized illnesses such as venereal disease (although even here the general feeling among public health workers, as contrasted with the feeling of many practicing physicians, is that the positives which come out of case-finding, treatment and prevention outweigh the negatives of disclosure), there would appear to be no excuse whatever for not reporting cases of a preventable and "socially acceptable" disease such as measles. Yet the U.S. Center for Disease Control estimates that only 10 percent of the measles cases in the United States are reported; a study in New York State showed that fewer than 5 percent of general practitioners and pediatricians reported any measles cases at all in 1971, a year of relatively high incidence of measles.

Even worse, there are large differences in reporting among areas within the United States. Thus, for the incidence of illness—as, to a lesser extent, for the exact causes of deaths—there is not even adequate information on which to base precise statements of health status.

Nonetheless, it is clear that preventable illnesses such as measles still unnecessarily strike down our children, leading in some cases of measles to encephalitis or other complications, to permanent disability or even death. A vaccine to prevent measles has been available since 1963, and there is no need for another child ever again to have measles, yet over one-third of American children one to four years of age have not been immunized against the disease. In the slums of our cities the rate of immunization is unknown but is certainly even lower than the overall rate; in parts of the South Bronx well over 50 percent of the preschool children, perhaps as many as three-fourths of them, are unprotected.

It is no surprise that those who are poor have a far greater chance of becoming sick—particularly a greater chance of becoming sick from preventable illness—than those who are not. Recent outbreaks of measles in the United States have concentrated among the poor and the nonwhite: In outbreaks in Los

Angeles, Houston, Dallas and Little Rock, the reported rates among black children were three to *fifty* times as high as the rates among white children.

Rates of tuberculosis and venereal disease—in fact, rates of almost all forms of communicable disease and of injury and death due to accidents and violence—are far higher in poor areas than in affluent ones. The study by the National Center for Health Statistics of poverty and nonpoverty areas of 19 large U.S. cities, which we cited in connection with infant mortality, showed that "whites" living in poverty areas have a far higher rate of these illnesses than do "whites" living in nonpoverty areas, and that "nonwhite" people living in poverty areas have similarly higher rates than "nonwhite" people living outside such areas.

Furthermore, many forms of preventable illness in the United States are associated with medical care itself. For example, it is estimated that 20,000 to 30,000 patients receiving blood transfusions in the United States contract hepatitis. As Richard Titmuss pointed out in *The Gift Relationship*, in countries where blood donations are truly voluntary rather than paid for in some way, there is far less incentive for a donor to lie about a history of hepatitis before giving blood. Excessive health risks in the United States are also associated with high rates of use of medications, particularly antibiotics, and with high rates of elective surgery, such as hysterectomies and tonsillectomies.

In short, although the evidence is less precise and reliable than that for deaths, rates of certain preventable illnesses seem to be high in the United States, probably higher than in other industrialized countries and certainly far higher among the poor and the nonwhite than among the affluent.

Disability Rates

Surveys using standard definitions, done regularly by the U.S. Public Health Service, consistently show that the poor have much more chronic illness and disability than do those who are not poor. While it is not clear to what extent one is cause and the other is effect, people ages 17–44 with family incomes under $5000 in the early 1970s had a 30 percent higher prevalence rate of chronic conditions such as arthritis and heart conditions, and a 50 percent higher rate of diabetes, hypertension, hearing impairments and vision impairments than do those with incomes higher than $15,000.

The poor in this age group also lose 50 percent more days from work each year and have 100 percent more (twice as many) days of restricted activity and days of bed disability than do the wealthy; while 2.5 percent (1 in every 40) of those in this age group with low incomes had limitation of mobility (defined as "confined to the house, needs help in getting around, or had trouble getting around alone"), only 0.4 percent (1 in every 250) of those in the high-income category had similar limitations.

Similar differences occur in other age groups. In short, although the extent to which poverty causes illness and illness causes poverty is still debated, what is unquestionable is that the poor in the United States are much sicker and more disabled than are the wealthy.

Malnutrition and Poor Physical Fitness

The rates of less clearly definable characteristics of ill health are hardest of all to measure, but may in the long run be the most important. Some 20 percent of the people in the United States—particularly among the poor and the elderly—have inadequate amounts or types of food to meet their bodily needs. It has been estimated that 26 million Americans cannot afford an adequate diet and that, in 1973, when the report was prepared, almost half of them received no help whatever from any federal food program.

More subtle but in some ways even more telling, the average height of ten-year-old children of families with incomes below poverty level is significantly less than that of the ten-year-olds of families with incomes above poverty level. While American children have, on the average, been growing taller over the past century, the average height for poor children lags behind that for nonpoor children by more than a generation. This is not due to a difference in height associated with race, for the average height of black children is slightly more than that of white children of the same income level. Sweden in comparison has in recent years managed to eliminate

growth differences between social classes, so far as is known the first country in the world to do so.

Furthermore, study after study has demonstrated the poor physical fitness of the American people. It was found in the early 1960s that one-third of all young men in the United States failed to meet the standards for induction into the armed forces, about one-half of these because of disease and disability and about one-half through inability to qualify on the mental test. The president's Task Force on Manpower Conservation found that "although many persons are disqualified for defects that probably could not be avoided in the present state of knowledge, the majority appear to be the victims of inadequate education and insufficient health services."

Summary

Despite the highly publicized drop in U.S. death rates—and specifically in infant mortality rates—and despite the dramatic and even more highly publicized improvements in medical technology in recent years, the health status of the American people on the whole remains unsatisfactory. This is true whether viewed in absolute numbers of people dying, sick, disabled or unfit, compared by commonly accepted measures of illness in other affluent countries, or measured internally by comparing the health of some groups in the population with the health of others.

2 SOCIAL CLASS, HEALTH, AND ILLNESS

Diana B. Dutton

In the early 1960s, the rediscovery of poverty amid plenty—and the devastating effects of poverty on health—helped launch the federal government's War on Poverty. Medicaid and Medicare were established to reduce economic barriers to health care, while Neighborhood Health Centers and other public programs tried to reduce geographic barriers. With increasing access, however, came rising medical costs and a new policy agenda; the dominant concerns shifted from equity to cost-effectiveness, and from increasing access to controlling medical costs.

Improved access led to some gains in health status, yet for most measures there is still a large gap between rich and poor. This persisting gap is given short shrift in the policy agenda of the 1980s. Indeed, cutbacks involve the very programs that have been most successful over the last two decades in improving access and reducing inequalities in health. The government contends that the most needy will not be affected. Some analysts question the continued importance of income per se as a determinant of health in our society. Others argue that medical care will not solve the health problems of the poor, whatever their causes. Such arguments belie a wealth of data on the relationship between social class and health and the factors responsible for that relationship.

This essay describes socioeconomic differences in morbidity and mortality and various possible causes, including adverse environmental conditions, psychological stress, social alienation, unhealthy lifestyles, and inadequate medical care. I briefly discuss the impact on health of programs such as Neighborhood Health Centers and conclude with a discussion of the likely impact of recent policy trends. Special attention is given to children since they are disproportionately involved in—and affected by—the problem of poverty. In a very real sense, moreover, the future well-being of any society depends on its children's health.

Social Class and Health

Whether social class is measured by income, education, or occupation, much the same picture emerges: those at the bottom have the highest rates of death and disease. Race is strongly correlated with social class; although two-thirds of the poor (people below the official poverty level) are white, almost half of all blacks are poor (Price 1984). The poor are heavily concentrated in the South, where public assistance is least adequate. Half of the poor are

SOURCE: From "Social Class, Health, and Illness" by Diana B. Dutton in *Applications of Social Science to Clinical Medicine and Health Policy*, Linda H. Aiken and David Mechanic, Editors. Copyright © 1986 by Rutgers, The State University. Reprinted with permission of Rutgers University Press.

children and young adults under age twenty-two. In 1983 one out of four children in America—and nearly one out of two black children—lived in poverty (Demkovitch 1984). During the last decade the proportion of poor children has increased steadily (Preston 1984).

It should be noted that the relation between illness and income—unlike that between either race and illness or education and illness—involves a two-way effect: being poor often leads to worse health, and, in turn, worse health may also lead to diminished earning capacity and hence reduced income. We must bear in mind both effects when interpreting comparisons by income for working age adults. For children, however, and for comparisons involving race or prior educational attainment, inequalities may be attributed largely or entirely to the impact of relative deprivation on health. That comparisons by income, education, and race all tend to show roughly the same pattern, even for working age adults, suggests that gradients by income also reflect primarily the adverse effects of poverty on health rather than vice versa.

Mortality

The United States ranks sixteenth in the world in infant mortality, mainly due to high rates of infant mortality among the poor and minorities. Infant mortality rates are highest in the South, which has the lowest per capita personal income (U.S. Congress, House of Representatives 1979). Data on infant mortality by family income are not routinely collected; the closest approximation is a comparison of poverty and nonpoverty areas of nineteen large cities in 1969–1971, in which infant mortality rates were 50 percent higher in the poverty areas (U.S. Department of Health, Education, and Welfare, Public Health Service 1977). Differentials by race are even more pronounced: nonwhite babies continue to die at roughly twice the rate of white babies, despite improvements for both (U.S. Congress, House of Representatives 1984b). This differential is not confined to any single cause but is reflected in all listed causes of death (U.S. Department of Health, Education, and Welfare, Public Health Service 1979b). Moreover, it shows no signs of disappearing. Between 1950 and 1980, in fact, the overall decline in infant mortality was proportionately greater for whites than nonwhites (National Center for Health Statistics 1982).

The racial gap in mortality does not end with infants but continues on into adulthood. As seen in Table 1, death rates for nonwhites are substantially greater than for whites in all age groups up to sixty-five, with a more than twofold difference in the thirty-five to forty-four year age group.[1] A 1983 study in Maine found that children in low-income families had a death rate over three times higher than that of other children (Maine Department of Human Services 1983). This finding is consistent with a major epidemiological investigation by Kitagawa and Hauser (1973), which found that age-sex-race-adjusted mortality ratios in 1960 were from 31 to 105 per-

TABLE 1   Death Rates in the United States by Age and Race, 1980

| Age Group | Death Rate per 100,000 Population | | Ratio of Nonwhite/White |
	White	Nonwhite	
< 1 year	1,088	2,070	1.90
1–4	58	91	1.57
5–14	30	35	1.19
15–24	112	134	1.19
25–34	120	236	1.97
35–44	197	411	2.08
45–54	540	965	1.79
55–64	1,273	2,008	1.58
65–74	2,885	3,597	1.25
75–84	6,601	6,940	1.05
85 and over	15,915	12,674	.80

SOURCE: National Center for Health Statistics 1982a, 16–18.

cent higher among individuals with the least education compared to those for individuals with the most education. Mortality ratios by income generally followed a similar pattern, although differential mortality among working-age men was greater for income than for education, reflecting the impact of poor health in reducing the income of male wage earners. A study of the elderly in Massachusetts estimated that for every age group, the poor had a shorter active life expectancy than the nonpoor, with differences ranging from less than a year for the oldest group to 2.4 years for those aged sixty-five to sixty-nine (Katz et al. 1983).

Acute Conditions

Great strides have been made against infectious diseases in this century, but they are still a threat to many of the disadvantaged. Figure 1 shows trends in age-adjusted death rates from influenza and pneumonia (the fifth leading cause of death) for whites and nonwhites. Although the death rate for nonwhites has declined markedly since 1950, it was still 50 percent higher than for whites in 1975. The greatest reductions have occurred since 1968, probably as a result of the improved medical care—earlier detection and better treatment—provided by Medicaid and other publicly funded programs.

The prevalence of acute conditions, as reported in national household interviews, is somewhat higher among upper- than lower-income individuals (U.S. Department of Health, Education, and Welfare, Health Resources Administration 1979). However, "acute conditions" are defined as those requiring medical attention or resulting in restricted activities; these requirements probably tend to reduce reporting among

FIGURE 1   Age-adjusted Death Rates in the United States for Influenza and
Pneumonia, by Color, 1950–78

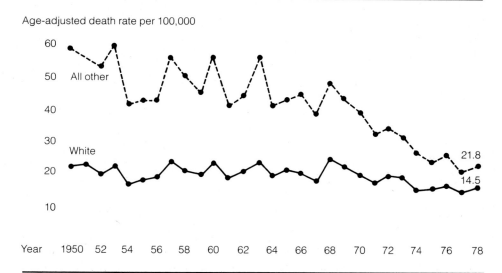

Age-adjusted death rate per 100,000

SOURCES: U.S. Department of Health, Education, and Welfare, Health Resources Administration 1979; National Center for Health Statistics 1982b.

the poor, who may be less likely than the more affluent to seek care for a given illness because of limited income, and also less likely to forego wage-earning opportunities. Moreover, there is evidence that the afflu-ent report relatively mild conditions, while the poor are more likely to report only more severe conditions (U.S. Department of Health, Education, and Welfare, Health Resources Administration 1979). Significantly

TABLE 2   Hospitalization Rates in the United States by Income and Race, 1980

Family Income and Race	Discharges per 100 Persons per Year	Days per 100 Persons	Average Length of Stay
All persons	12.0	95.8	7.1
Income			
Under $7,000	15.8	145.8	8.4
$7,000 to $9,999	14.2	127.0	8.2
$10,000 to $14,999	12.0	96.0	6.9
$15,000 to $24,999	11.1	78.3	6.5
$25,000 or more	10.2	71.4	6.0
Race			
White	12.0	92.1	6.9
Nonwhite	13.0	136.6	9.2

SOURCE: U.S. Department of Health and Human Services 1982.

higher rates of hospitalization as well as longer lengths of stay for the poor and minorities (Table 2) are consistent with this interpretation, suggesting more severe illness, much of which may be acute. Differentials in children's hospitalization are even greater (U.S. Congress, House of Representatives 1979).

Certain infectious diseases appear to be more prevalent as well as more severe among the poor. In a diphtheria epidemic in San Antonio, Texas, poor and minority children suffered twelve times as much disease as children who were white and affluent (U.S. Congress, House of Representatives 1979). Tuberculosis has all but disappeared among the affluent but is still a serious problem for the poor and minorities, especially those living in urban poverty areas (U.S. Department of Health, Education, and Welfare, Health Resources Administration 1979).

Chronic Illness and Disability

Although chronic disease is sometimes thought of as the affliction of the well-to-do, in fact it now far outstrips acute illness in its disproportionate impact on the disadvantaged. For example, the prevalence of heart conditions, the leading cause of death, is more than three times as high among low-income persons as among the most affluent (114 versus 35 per 1,000) (U.S. Department of Health, Education, and Welfare, Health Resources Administration 1979). Age-adjusted death rates from four of the five major causes of death—heart disease, can-

cer, stroke, and diabetes—are also higher among the disadvantaged. Arthritis, the leading cause of disability after heart disease, is twice as common among the poor (Newacheck et al. 1980). Comparable prevalence differences are found across a wide range of chronic diseases (U.S. Department of Health, Education, and Welfare, Health Resources Administration 1979).

Restricted activity and other measures of disability reflect similar disparities. Restricted activity is more common among the poor than the nonpoor at all age levels, but the gap is greatest for persons aged forty-five to sixty-four; in 1980 poor people in this prime working-age category spent more than two months out of the year with restricted activity—more than four times as much time as those in the upper-income group (National Center for Health Statistics 1983b). There were comparable gradients in bed disability. Bed disability and restricted activity are good measures of the overall impact of health problems—their perceived severity as well as the resulting disruption of normal activities. Analyzing data from the 1977 National Health Interview Survey, Newacheck and colleagues (1980) found that about 75 percent of the gap in restricted activity and bed disability days between the poor and nonpoor was attributable to the greater prevalence and severity of activity-limiting chronic conditions among the poor.

Self-reported health status mirrors the same patterns. Nationally, the reported prevalence of most forms of impairment (including problems of speech, vision, and motor function) is two to ten times higher among the poor than the nonpoor (National Center for Health Statistics 1981c). More than three times as many low- as high-income people rate their health status as "fair or poor" (23 percent versus 7 percent in 1980), and there are similar differentials by education (U.S. Department of Health and Human Services 1982). Furthermore, both education and income exert an independent influence on perceived health: there are clear income gradients in self-rated health status at every educational level, and, likewise, clear educational gradients in health status at every income level (National Center for Health Statistics 1983a).

For many measures, the health gap between rich and poor increases with age, reflecting the cumulative effects of a lifetime of impoverishment. Yet there are substantial disparities even among children. Based on a comprehensive review, Egbuono and Starfield (1982) concluded that poor children are more likely than others to become ill, to suffer adverse consequences from illness, and to die. They found that poor children had a higher prevalence of many specific disorders, including cytomegalic inclusion disease (the most common congenital infection), iron deficiency anemia, lead poisoning, hearing disorders, and poor vision, and almost twice as many bed disability days and four times as many hospital days as their more affluent peers. Poor children are also more than twice as likely to be reported by their parents as having chronic conditions and only "fair or poor" health; these parental ratings are confirmed in physicians' clinical examinations (National Center for Health Statistics 1973). Whatever it is about poverty that is detrimental to health apparently takes effect very early in life.

The Cycle of Poverty and Illness

There has been a longstanding debate about whether the worse health of lower socioeconomic groups should be attributed primarily to the material conditions of poverty and the biological and emotional stresses they create or to aspects of the life-style of the disadvantaged (e.g., cultural values and individual behavior). There is surely no single explanation for socioeconomic differentials in health. Figure 2 portrays various factors that appear to reinforce and perpetuate the cycle of poverty and illness. This section will describe some of the evidence for each of these different mechanisms.

Environmental Conditions

One of the most concrete problems faced by lower-social-class groups is adverse conditions in both home and work environments. Lower-status jobs tend to be more hazardous, menial, and physically taxing (Berman 1978) as well as less rewarding emotionally and economically. They involve more accidents, even within similar occupational groupings. For example, within each of the seventeen job categories listed by the Census Bureau, work-related accidents were more common among

FIGURE 2   The Cycle of Poverty and Pathology

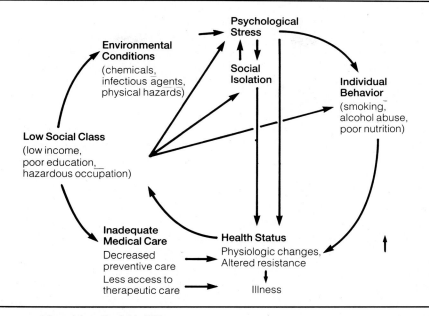

SOURCE: Adapted from Starfield, 1984.

workers earning under $10,000 than among those earning $10,000 or more; for farm laborers, the difference was almost fourfold (National Center for Health Statistics 1980). There is even evidence suggesting that children of workers occupationally exposed to certain chemicals are more likely to have some types of malignant brain tumors (Starfield 1984).

Higher mortality levels in poor neighborhoods are well documented (Nagi and Stockwell 1973; Kitagawa and Hauser 1973; Jenkins 1983). Urban poverty areas are plagued by chemical and air pollution, noise, accidents, and crime. Air pollution has been linked to higher rates of respiratory disease and increased hospitalization (Carpenter et al. 1979;

Whittemore 1981). National data show that lead poisoning is far more common among lower-income and minority children, probably because of their greater exposure to chips of lead-based paint, gasoline residues, and other environmental sources (Mahaffey et al. 1982). Exposure to constant noise produces physiological alterations suggesting generalized stress responses. Children living in noisy environments have blood pressure abnormalities and unusually high pulse rates as well as cognitive and behavioral problems; these effects did not appear to be attributable to other social factors, and some were not reversed when the noise abated (Starfield 1984).

Substandard housing conditions present various threats to health:

rats, poisons, fires, inadequate heat and plumbing, dangerous electrical wiring, trash, deteriorated structures, and crowding (Rainwater 1966). Research indicates that crowded housing leads to greater stress, less opportunity for rest and recuperation, and more susceptibility to infection, all of which may result in greater illness (Gove, Hughes, and Galle 1979).[2]

Psychological Stress and Social Isolation

Many of the physical and environmental conditions experienced by the poor probably also take a psychological and emotional toll on health. In an extensive review of environmental influences on health, Lindheim and Syme (1983) concluded that it is people's relative status in the social hierarchy—not their absolute position—that has the critical impact on health. They speculate that being "on the bottom" of any hierarchy involves not only specific physical hardships but also stigmatization and humiliation in the eyes of the world and a damaging loss of self-esteem and perceived control over one's life.

For example, unemployment appears to have psychological and emotional consequences at least as serious as the financial problems caused by loss of income. People who are unemployed are more likely to report being unhappy and dissatisfied with life, to suffer from insomnia and headaches, and to increase smoking and drinking (Schlozman and Verba 1978). Recent data from Wisconsin show a clear relation be-

tween unemployment and child abuse. In the fifty-one counties where unemployment increased between 1981 and 1982, 69 percent reported an increase in child abuse; in the twenty-one counties where unemployment decreased, in contrast, 71 percent reported a decline in child abuse (Mills 1984).

Social isolation is another potential source of psychological stress for lower socioeconomic groups. The importance of supportive social relationships was first demonstrated empirically in 1897 by Durkheim in his classic study of factors related to suicide. Cassel (1976) extended this notion to other health problems, noting that individuals without "meaningful social contacts" also tended to have higher rates of tuberculosis, schizophrenia, alcoholism, and accidents.

Data reported by Berkman and Syme (1979) suggest that social isolation is a special problem for the poor. In a nine-year study of mortality in Alameda County, California, they found that social support—ties to family and the community—reduced the age-adjusted relative risk of mortality, independent of initial health status, medical care, personal health practices, and socioeconomic status. But lower-income individuals were much less likely to have a large number of social contacts than their more affluent counterparts. There were also socioeconomic gradients in mortality even *within* groups with high and low social contacts.

In light of the extraordinary consistency of social class gradients in morbidity and mortality, Syme and Berkman (1976) have suggested that a more general process of break-down and vulnerability may be at work. Indeed, lowered resistance may heighten the effects of specific risk factors. In a study of 18,403 office-based civil servants in London, Marmot, Shipley, and Rose (1984) found threefold differences in mortality between men at the lowest and highest grades of employment, for all major causes of death. The authors attributed these remarkably consistent patterns to a combination of disease-specific factors along with a more general factor—related to the psycho-social stress experienced by lower-status workers—which increases susceptibility to all illness.

Exactly what causes increased susceptibility remains unclear, but psychosocial factors appear to play an important role. Stress and social isolation, for instance, appear to have a major influence on survival after heart attacks. Controlling for multiple clinical and prognostic indicators, Ruberman et al. (1984) found that men who were socially isolated and who had a high degree of life stress had a risk of dying during the three years postattack more than four times as high as men with low levels of both stress and isolation. Education was also a risk factor, but mainly because men with low education tended to have high levels of stress and isolation; controlling for psychosocial factors largely eliminated educational gradients in mortality.

Individual Behavior

Some aspects of the life-style of the disadvantaged may also contrib-ute to poor health. Alcohol consumption tends to be higher among lower socioeconomic groups (National Center for Health Statistics 1981b), as does cigarette smoking, at least for men (National Center for Health Statistics 1979).[3] Both may be seen as ways of coping with the stresses of relative deprivation. In addition, a more affluent life-style typically involves more leisure-time physical exercise and less obesity (Lambert et al. 1982). Yet these conventional risk factors do not appear to account for much of the health gap between rich and poor. In their study of London civil servants, Marmot, Shipley, and Rose (1984) still observed 50 to 100 percent differences in the relative risk of coronary heart disease mortality among men in different grades of employment, even after controlling for age, smoking levels, cholesterol, blood pressure, blood glucose, and height. Nor were these differences accounted for by leisure-time activity.

Poor and minority groups are also more likely to have an inferior diet. Data from the 1971–1975 National Health and Nutrition Examination Survey indicate that black children are consistently more likely to suffer from protein deficiency than white children. Likewise, about half of all low-income children under age four were below nutritional standards for vitamin A and C, a quarter were deficient in calcium, and 95 percent were deficient in iron (U.S. Department of Health, Education, and Welfare, Public Health Service 1979a). Eating habits are a likely cause; the daily diet of poor and minority children is much more likely to include candy, sweetened beverages, and salty snacks (Rice and Danchik 1979). Such habits may result not only from lack of proper dietary information but also from limited income and absence of parental supervision. Almost half of all children under six now living in poverty are members of female-headed households, and this number is projected to increase (U.S. Congress, House of Representatives 1983).

Inadequate Medical Care

The final link in the cycle of poverty and illness is inadequate medical care. Although utilization of services by disadvantaged groups has increased markedly over the last fifteen years (Robert Wood Johnson Foundation 1983), many inequalities remain. By a few measures—for example, hospitalization rates and annual number of physician visits—the poor now receive more care than the affluent. But such measures are misleading for they confound access with medical need; utilization is higher among the poor in large part because of their more prevalent and more severe illness (in fact, hospitalization rates are sometimes used as an indicator of illness severity). To determine whether the poor have adequate access to medical care, utilization must be measured in relation to the underlying level of illness, or medical need.

Measures that relate utilization to illness, such as the "use-disability ratio" (number of visits per one hundred disability days), indicate that the poor still receive significantly less care relative to illness than the

rest of the population. Data from the 1978 National Health Interview Survey (NHIS) show, for example, that lower-income people had only about half as many physician visits per disability day as the affluent (Davis, Gold, and Makuc 1981).[4] Another way to take medical need into account is to compare individuals with a specified level of illness. Analyzing 1976–1978 NHIS data, Kleinman, Gold, and Makuc (1981) found income gradients within most age and race subgroups among people reporting fair or poor health status. Overall, the age-adjusted rate of physician visits for upper-income whites was about 35 percent higher than for poor whites, and more than 50 percent higher than for poor blacks.

Even without adjusting for medical need, the proportion of the population with at least one visit in the last year remains slightly higher among the white and affluent (Robert Wood Johnson Foundation 1983). This is a better measure of access than total physician visits since it indicates how many people were able to make initial contact with the medical system; follow-up visits, a major component of total visits, are controlled largely by physicians rather than patients (Gertman 1974). And, despite higher illness levels, poor children receive less ambulatory care. In 1980 poor children under age five averaged 5.6 physician visits per year compared to an average of 7.5 visits for upper-income children (National Center for Statistics 1983c).

The poor tend to receive less preventive care—services that are viewed as "discretionary" regardless of their medical benefit. A third fewer low-income women receive prenatal care in the first trimester of pregnancy than high-income women (Aday, Anderson, and Fleming 1980). Likewise, four times as many low-income children as high-income children under seventeen had *never* had a routine physical examination in 1973 (20 percent versus less than 5 percent) (National Center for Health Statistics 1977). The consequences of undetected medical problems in children are potentially serious; regular health monitoring, especially during the early years of life, is widely recommended (Task Force Report 1976; Breslow and Somers 1977). Other clinically effective preventive services, including dental care, pap smears, breast exams, and childhood immunizations, are also less common among the disadvantaged (U.S. Department of Health and Human Services 1982; David, Gold, and Makuc 1981; Dutton 1981).

In part, these disparities stem from different patterns and sources of care; lower socioeconomic groups are much less likely to have a personal physician, or even a regular source of care. Nationally, three times as many low- as high-income children (18 percent versus 6 percent) had no regular source of care in 1974 (Dutton 1981). When the poor and minorities do see a physician, they are more than twice as likely as others to have visits in hospital clinics rather than in doctors' offices or by telephone (U.S. Department of Health and Human Services 1982). In addition, various structural barriers make the process of obtaining care more difficult for the disadvan-

taged. National data show that twice as many low- and high-income persons travel more than a half-hour to reach their regular provider (12 percent versus 6 percent), and wait more than an hour to be seen (21 percent versus 9 percent) (Aday, Anderson, and Fleming 1980). And, despite Medicaid and other public programs, out-of-pocket medical expenses remain a much greater burden for the poor relative to income. Annual out-of-pocket medical expenses consumed 17 percent of income among people in the lowest income group in 1977 compared with less than 2 percent in the highest income group (National Medical Care Expenditure Survey 1984). Moreover, this disproportionate burden was borne by more than two-thirds of the poor. In 1984, there were nearly 39 million Americans, or 19 percent of the total population, without health insurance ("Uninsured Increase, Study Shows" 1984). Lack of insurance coverage has been shown to be associated with significantly lower rates of ambulatory care utilization (Davis and Rowland 1983).

There are, in short, a number of persisting inadequacies in the amount and types of medical care received by the disadvantaged, especially relative to medical need. But what is the evidence that such disparities lead to worse health?

Does Medical Care Matter?

While obviously not all medical services are equally effective, there is substantial evidence that disadvantaged groups still go without basic forms of prevention and primary care that, when provided, yield real and measurable benefits to health (Starfield 1985; Brunswick 1984; Levine, Feldman, and Elinson 1983; Hadley 1982). One study which followed a group of California Medicaid recipients who lost their eligibility in 1982 showed that they had less access to ambulatory care and suffered significant deterioration of previously controlled hypertension and diabetes (Lurie et al. 1984). Preventive services have been particularly effective in counteracting prevailing patterns of illness. Periodic screening for breast cancer, for example, using mammography and palpation of the breast, was shown to eliminate the traditional racial differences in survival in a randomized trial of sixty-two thousand women in the Health Insurance Plan of New York. In the control group, which was not screened, nonwhite women with breast cancer had a lower five-year survival rate than white women, whereas there were no racial differences in survival among women who had been screened (Shapiro et al. 1982).

Childhood immunizations are another effective form of disease prevention where needs are unmet. In California, about 40 percent of low-income children did not have the immunizations required to enter school in 1983 (Children's Research Institute of California 1984). Immunization rates for measles and rubella are lower in poverty areas, and the prevalence of infections correspondingly higher (U.S. Congress, House of Representatives 1979). Measles and mumps immunizations are highly cost-effective, with an estimated savings of $7 to $10 in medical and social expenses for every dollar spent on vaccination (Witte and Axnick 1975; Wiederman and Ambrosch 1979).

Public programs such as Maternal and Child Health (MCH), and Early Periodic Screening, Detection, and Treatment (EPSDT) have sought to fill some of these needs. MCH services have been credited with higher levels of immunization among poor children and improved levels of hearing and vision (U.S. General Accounting Office 1979). The Alabama MCH program estimated savings of $5 to $10 in prevented illness for each $1 spent (National Health Law Program 1983). Evaluations of EPSDT in six state programs also showed cost-savings (Hiscock 1984). For example, a study of EPSDT in Pennsylvania found that children previously screened under EPSDT had almost 30 percent fewer abnormalities requiring care upon re-screening, and also significantly fewer abnormalities than a control group (Irwin and Conroy-Hughes 1982). A review by the Health Care Financing Administration of 150 studies on the effectiveness of preventive child health care concluded that the bulk of the evidence indicated preventive services did have a beneficial effect on health (Shadish 1981).

Many poor women do not receive appropriate prenatal care, another beneficial—and highly cost-effective—form of prevention. Most studies have demonstrated that prenatal care reduces the likelihood of low birth weight and other adverse outcomes, especially among high-risk women (Institute of Medicine 1985; Showstack, Budetti, and

Minkler 1984; Norris and Williams 1984; Kessner et al. 1973; Eisner et al. 1979; Dott and Fort 1975; Donaldson and Billy 1984). Findings from a study by Levy, Wilkinson, and Marine (1971) of a three-year demonstration program that provided nurse-midwives to a disadvantaged population in rural California were particularly dramatic. During the program, prenatal care doubled and prematurity rates fell by 40 percent, with no significant changes in these measures in the surrounding areas; after its termination, both rates returned to roughly their earlier levels. Precisely how prenatal care yields these benefits, however, is not well understood.

Nutritional supplements provided through the federally funded Supplemental Food Program for Women, Infants, and Children (known as WIC) have decreased the risk of low birth weight, and perhaps also reduced neonatal mortality (U.S. General Accounting Office 1984; Kotelchuck et al. 1984). There is also evidence that nutritional supplements for newborns may affect subsequent cognitive and behavioral development (Hicks, Langham, and Tanenaka 1982).

Neighborhood Health Centers: Broadening the Definition of Medical Care

Traditional forms of disease prevention and primary care have clearly helped ameliorate some of the health problems of the poor. But they do nothing to attack the roots of those problems—the social, economic, and environmental conditions of poverty that compromise health and exacerbate illness. As long as these conditions exist, the vicious cycle of poverty and illness will continue.

Recognizing the limits of conventional medical approaches in dealing with the needs of the poor, Congress launched the Neighborhood Health Center Program in the mid-1960s to provide accessible and appropriate health care to the most disadvantaged urban and rural areas, where existing medical services were sparse and where health problems were caused or confounded by general deprivation. The most ambitious health centers sought to improve health not only through direct medical care but also through community organizing efforts designed to change basic social and economic circumstances.

A good example is the center established in Mound Bayou, Mississippi, an extremely poor region in the Mississippi Delta with rates of infant and maternal mortality that were among the highest in the nation (Tokarz 1982; Geiger 1984). To meet this challenge, Mound Bayou offered a broad array of social and environmental services in addition to basic clinical care. Environmental services included protected wells, water and sewage line construction, and home improvements such as screens and sanitary outhouses. Social services ranged from bus transportation to legal services, day care, and continuing education. The center responded to nutritional problems not only with prescriptions of food and emergency food programs but also by organizing a cooperative vegetable farm. As part of the center's "community health action" program, ten local health associations were created to foster social and economic development (Geiger 1984). The hope was to create self-sustaining initiatives that would ultimately enable the community to lift itself out of impoverishment.

Not all of Mound Bayou's pioneering programs have survived. With growing concern about cost control in the early 1970s, the federal government significantly narrowed the scope of reimbursable services in Neighborhood Health Centers nationally and instituted rigid standards of physician "productivity." Such constraints have tended to force community health centers toward a more traditional medical model. Nonetheless, Mound Bayou can claim credit for some notable achievements. The infant mortality rate dropped 40 percent in the first four years of the center's operation. Hundreds of townsfolk have better housing and sanitary water thanks to the environmental improvement campaigns. By 1984 the health center was seeing several hundred patients a day—mostly those with neither public nor private insurance—and had become the major employer in the community. Over one hundred people obtained post-secondary-school degrees, including thirteen M.D.s, as a result of health center-sponsored programs—in a community where the average adult education level had been four years of school. Many of these people, like the health center's medical director, returned to live and work in Mound Bayou.

The Community Health Center Program, as it is now called, has grown dramatically during the last two decades, surviving various political challenges and professional assaults; by 1982, 872 centers around the country served 4.2 million people, mostly the poor and minorities (Geiger 1984). On the whole, these centers appear to have been remarkably effective. The quality of medical care is equal to or better than that of traditional medical settings (Morehead, Donaldson, and Servall 1971; Sparer and Johnson 1971), and center users have more appropriate and less costly patterns of utilization: reduced hospitalization, fewer operations, and more ambulatory and preventive care (Reynolds 1976; Davis and Schoen 1978). Studies have documented reductions in infant mortality of 25 to 40 percent in areas served by centers, with no change in surrounding areas (Anderson and Morgan 1973, Gold and Rosenberg 1974; Goldman and Grossman 1981). In Baltimore, low-income census tracts with comprehensive health centers[5] had a 60 percent reduction in the incidence of rheumatic fever over a ten-year period—a decrease attributed to early detection and treatment of streptococcal infections—whereas tracts without centers remained unchanged (Gordis 1973). And, as in Mound Bayou, many centers have led to improvements in the quality as well as quantity of life, with better housing, sanitation, and nutrition.

Starting from the premise that the primary determinants of health lie in the social order, Community Health Centers have attacked many different points in the cycle of poverty and illness, including nonmedical as well as medical factors.

Current Policy Trends: Impact on the Poor

The strengths of the Community Health Center model are notably absent from the current health policy agenda. Increasingly, people of all income levels are turning to hospital outpatient clinics and emergency rooms for regular care (Aday and Andersen 1983). Cost control has become the overriding goal of both the federal and state governments, leading to major contractions in most publicly funded health and social programs. In the 1980s, nearly every state reduced the scope of Medicaid services, eligibility, or both (National Health Law Program 1984). An estimated 700,000 children lost their Medicaid coverage in 1982, as did 567,000 old people between 1981 and 1984 ("Health Care Found in 'Deterioration'" 1984). Many poor, elderly, and handicapped people depend on public programs to meet their basic medical needs and have gone without care or suffered financial hardship because of the new restrictions (Scott 1982). In some groups, as noted previously, deteriorating health status has been reported (Lurie et al. 1984). These cutbacks cannot help but exacerbate existing inequalities in health status and service utilization.

Federal funding for Community Health Centers was also cut sharply, with revenue losses averaging 30 to 45 percent in 1982 (Brazda and Glenn 1984). As a result, 239 centers (28 percent of the total) had to limit their services or close (National Health Law Program 1983). A study of five Community Health Centers in Boston revealed that budget cuts had led to a 14 percent decline in obstetrics visits and a 12 percent decline in pediatric visits; there was also a substantial increase in infant mortality (Feldman 1984). In view of the demonstrated health benefits of Community Health Centers and their record of substituting ambulatory and preventive care for hospitalization and other costly medical interventions, these cutbacks could well end up increasing total health care expenses for society.

Another trend in health policy that may boomerang is the growing emphasis in both Medicaid and Medicare on patient "cost sharing" —money paid out-of-pocket toward medical bills. The equity of imposing additional cost sharing on low-income groups is questionable since, as noted previously, they already spend 17 percent of their income on medical care compared to less than 2 percent by the well-to-do (National Medical Care Expenditure Survey 1984). But cost sharing for the poor may not make economic sense either. Low-income groups are disproportionately affected by even small copayments (Beck 1974; Dallek and Parks 1981).[6] When a $1.50 to $2.00 charge was imposed on physician visits in Saskatchewan, for example, the reduction in utilization among the aged and poor was three times that of the 6 percent reduction overall (Barer, Evans, and Stoddart 1979). If reduced ambulatory care eliminates needed services, it does not necessarily save money. In California's

1972 "copayment experiment," which imposed a $1 charge on certain Medicaid recipients, physician visits declined by 8 percent—but hospitalization rose by 17 percent, resulting in a new increase in total program costs (Helms, Newhouse, and Phelps 1979).

Equally unsound, especially in the long run, are reductions in aid for needy children and pregnant women. Proposed cuts of $1.25 billion in the WIC program in fiscal 1985 would mean half a million fewer program participants (National Health Law Program 1984). Maternal and Child Health funds were cut 18 percent in 1981, leading to reductions in forty-four states in prenatal, delivery, and preventive services for pregnant women. Savings in reduced prenatal visits are trivial compared with the costs associated with inadequate prenatal care: prematurity, mental retardation, and various developmental disorders. (In 1981, neonatal intensive care for a single premature infant averaged $60,000 to $100,000, and the costs of institutionalizing a mentally retarded person ran about $25,000 per year; Los Angeles County Health Alliance et al. 1982). The Department of Consumer Affairs in California has estimated the state could save approximately $66 million annually in neonatal intensive care costs if all women received adequate prenatal care (Dallek 1982).

While poverty-related programs were being cut, poverty in the United States has been on the rise. Between 1980 and 1982, the number of poor children increased by 2 million (Price 1984). In 1983 the number of people living in poverty had risen to the highest level since 1965 (U.S. Department of Commerce, Bureau of the Census 1984). The gap between rich and poor has also been widening, reversing the gradual trend toward income equality that prevailed from the 1950s through the 1970s. Tax and benefit cuts enacted during 1983 further enlarged the gap: according to the Congressional Budget Office, families earning under $10,000 suffered a net loss of $390, while those earning over $80,000 enjoyed an overall gain of $8,270 (Demkovitch 1984). In a 1984 national survey, one out of every five adults reported that they could not always afford food for their families (Gallup 1984). With reduced funding for poverty-related programs, the swelling ranks of the poor warrant added concern.

Conclusion

Illness, in this country as in most, is disproportionately concentrated in the lower social class. There is a large gap between those at the bottom of the socioeconomic ladder and those at the top in nearly every measure of morbidity and mortality. Some of this gap may still be due to inadequate medical care: despite the increased access provided by public entitlement programs, the poor still have lower rates of utilization among children, fewer services at all ages relative to illness levels, less preventive care, more reliance on hospital-based clinics, and greater financial and organizational barriers to access. But much of the gap undoubtedly stems from a variety of nonmedical factors, including a hazardous environment, unsafe and unrewarding work, poor nutrition, lack of social support, and, perhaps most important of all, the psychological and emotional stress of being poor and feeling powerless to do anything about it.

Efforts to improve the health status of lower socioeconomic status groups must occur on many fronts. Health promotion efforts directed at individual behavior will solve only part of the problem. Changes are also needed in the multiple social, psychological, and environmental circumstances that reinforce and perpetuate the cycle of poverty and illness. Only through such broadly structured interventions is this vicious cycle likely to be broken.

Notes

1. The reversal of this racial differential in the oldest age group is probably due to the older average age of whites aged eighty-five or more and also to the "natural selection" effect of the higher death rates among nonwhites in all of the younger age groups.
2. These effects have also been documented in laboratory studies. Particularly striking is an experiment by Riley 1975, in which environmental circumstances significantly affected the onset of illness in groups of genetically equivalent mice, all infected with a virus that produces mammary tumors. One group, exposed to "standard" laboratory conditions, developed the tumors when the mice were middle-aged; a group raised in more desirable conditions (quiet and spacious cages, a nocturnal schedule, and minimal disturbance) did not de-

velop the tumors until the mice were near the end of their life span.
3. Smoking patterns among women differ depending on whether socioeconomic status is measured by education or income, and may be changing over time. In 1976 the proportion of women who smoked increased linearly with income, but exhibited a strong inverse U-shaped relationship with education (lowest proportion of smokers among the least and most educated women), (National Center for Health Statistics 1979, p. 22). Data for 1979 are available only by education and suggest a positive linear relation with education—higher rates of smoking among more educated women (National Center for Health Statistics 1981b, 15). For men, in contrast, the proportion who smoke is strongly inversely related to both income and education.
4. Using 1976 data from a different national sample with a different method of defining disability days, Aday, Anderson, and Fleming (1980) report a much smaller differential between the use-disability ratios of high- and low-income groups. However, for a variety of methodological reasons (Davis, Gold, and Makuc 1981, 166; Dutton 1981, 372), results based on the National Health Interview Survey appear to be more reliable.
5. These centers were funded by the Children and Youth Program but resembled Neighborhood Health Centers in the comprehensiveness of the care provided.
6. Results from the Rand Health Insurance Experiment indicate that people of different income levels had a similar reduction in utilization in response to cost sharing that was proportionate to income (Newhouse et al. 1981). In the real world, unfortunately, most forms of cost sharing (including copayments and deductibles) are not

proportionate to income but rather highly disproportionate. Furthermore, according to a subsequent Rand report, even income-related cost sharing was detrimental to the health of low-income people with high blood pressure (Brook et al. 1983).

References

Aday, Lu Ann, and Ronald M. Andersen. 1983. *National trends in access to medical care: Where do we stand?* Paper presented at the American Public Health Association meeting in Dallas, Texas.

Aday, Lu Ann, Ronald M. Andersen, and Gretchen Fleming. 1980. *Health care in the U.S.: Equitable for whom?* Beverly Hills, Calif.: Sage.

Anderson, R. E., and S. Morgan. 1973. *Comprehensive health care: A southern view.* Atlanta: Southeast Regional Council.

Barer, M. L., Robert G. Evans, and Glenn L. Stoddart. 1979. *Controlling health care costs by direct charges to patients: Snare or delusion?* Toronto, Ontario: Ontario Economic Council.

Beck, R. G. 1974. The effect of copayment on the poor. *Journal of Human Resources* 9(1):129–142.

Berkman, Lisa F., and S. Leonard Syme. 1979. Social networks, host resistance, and mortality: A nine-year follow-up study of Alameda County residents. *American Journal of Epidemiology* 109(2): 186–204.

Berman, Daniel M. 1978. *Death on the job: Occupational health and safety struggles in the U.S.* New York: Monthly Review Press.

Brazda, J. F., and K. Glenn. 1984. Block grant, part two: ADM and primary care. *Washington Perspectives*, July 16. McGraw-Hill.

Breslow, Lester, and Anna Somers. 1977. The lifetime health-monitoring: A practical approach to preventive medicine. *New England Journal of Medicine* 296(11):601–608.

Brook, Robert H., John E. Ware, Jr., William H. Rogers, Emmett B. Keeler, Allyson R. Davies, Cathy A. Donald, George A. Goldberg, Kathleen N. Lohr, Patricia C. Masthay, Joseph P. Newhouse. 1983. Does free care improve adults' health? *New England Journal of Medicine* 309(23):1426–1434.

Brunswick, Ann F. 1984. Effects of medical intervention in adolescence: A longitudinal study of urban black youth. *Youth and Society* 61(1):3–28.

Califano, Joseph A. 1984. U.S. must discipline health-care market. *New York Times*, May 6, p. E23.

Carpenter, Ben H., James R. Chromy, Walter D. Bach, D. A. LeSourd, and Donald G. Gillette. 1979. Health costs of air pollution: A study of hospitalization costs. *American Journal of Public Health* 69(12):1232–1241.

Cassel, John. 1976. The contribution of the social environment to host resistance. *American Journal of Epidemiology* 104(2):107–123.

Children's Research Institute of California. 1984. Capsule update. Sacramento, Calif.

Dallek, Geraldine. 1982. America's widening infant death gap. *Health & Medicine* (Summer/Fall):23–27.

Dallek, Geraldine, and Michael Parks. 1981. Cost-sharing revisited: Limiting medical care to the poor. *Clearing House Review*, March, pp. 1149–1158.

Davis, Karen, Marsha Gold, and Diane Makuc. 1981. Access to health care for the poor: Does the gap remain? *Annual Review of Public Health* 2:159–182.

Davis, Karen, and Diane Rowland. 1983. Uninsured and underserved: Inequities in health care in the United States. *Milbank Memorial Fund Quarterly: Health and Society* 61(2):149–176.

Davis, Karen, and Cathy Schoen. 1978. *Health and the War on Poverty: A ten-*

year appraisal. Washington, D.C.: Brookings Institution.

Demkovich, Linda E. 1984. Fairness issue will be campaign test of Reagan's record on budget policies. *National Journal*, September 8, pp. 1648–1653.

Donaldson, Peter J., and John O. G. Billy. 1984. The impact of prenatal care on birth weight. *Medical Care* 22(2): 177–188.

Dott, Andrew B., and Arthur T. Fort. 1975. The effect of availability and utilization of prenatal care and hospital services on infant mortality rates: Summary of the findings of the Louisiana Infant Mortality Study, part II. *American Journal of Obstetrics and Gynecology* 123(8):854–860.

Dutton, Diana B. 1981. Children's health care: The myth of equal access. In *Better health for our children: A national strategy*. Report of the Select Panel for the Promotion of Child Health, DHHS (PHS) Publication No. 79-55071. Washington, D.C.: Government Printing Office.

Egbuonu, Lisa, and Barbara Starfield. 1982. Child health social status. *Pediatrics* 69(5):550–557.

Eisner, Victor, Joseph V. Brazie, Margaret W. Pratt, and Alfred C. Hexter. 1979. The risk of low birthweight. *American Journal of Public Health* 69(9): 887–893.

11 die after losing aid: U.S. found them fit to work. 1982. *San Francisco Chronicle*, Sept. 18, p. 4.

Enthoven, Alain. 1978. Consumer choice health plan. *New England Journal of Medicine* 298:650–658 (pt. 1) and 709–720 (pt. 2).

Feldman, Penny Hollander. 1984. Study of the impact of changes in health programs for the poor on primary care centers and local health departments. Final Report to the Robert Wood Johnson Foundation, Princeton, N.J.

Freeman, Howard E., K. Jill Kiecolt, and Harris M. Allen. 1982. Community

health centers: An initiative of enduring utility. *Milbank Memorial Fund Quarterly* 60(2):245–267.

Gallup, George. 1984. One of every 5 adults in U.S. can't always afford food. *San Francisco Chronicle*, March 19, p. 7.

Geiger, H. Jack. 1984. Community health centers: Health care as an instrument of social change. In *Reforming medicine: lessons of the last quarter century*, ed. Victor W. Sidel and Ruth Sidel. New York: Pantheon.

Gertman, P. M. 1974. Physicians as guiders of health services use. In *Incentives for health care*, ed. S. J. Mushkin, pp. 362–368. New York: Prodist.

Gold, M. R., and R. G. Rosenberg. 1974. The use of emergency room by the population of a neighborhood health center. *Health Services Reports*.

Goldberg, Victor. 1976. Some emerging problems of prepaid health plans in the Medi-Cal system. *Policy Analysis*, pp. 55–68.

Goldman, Fred, and Michael Grossman. 1981. The responsiveness and impacts of public health policy: The case of community health centers. Paper presented at the American Public Health Association Annual Meeting, Los Angeles, Calif., November 1–5.

Gordis, Leon. 1973. Effectiveness of comprehensive-care programs in preventing rheumatic fever. *New England Journal of Medicine* 289:331–335.

Gove, Walter R., M. Hughes, and O. R. Galle. 1979. Overcrowding in the home: An empirical investigation of its possible pathological consequences. *American Sociological Review* 44:59–80.

Hadley, Jack. 1982. *More medical care, better health?* Washington, D.C.: Urban Institute Press.

Health care found in "deterioration." 1984. *San Francisco Chronicle*, Oct. 18, p. 14.

Helms, Jay, Joseph Newhouse, and

Charles Phelps. 1979. Copayments and demand for medical care: The California Medicaid experience. *Bell Journal of Economics*.

Hicks, Lou E., Rose A. Langham, and Jean Takenaka. 1982. Cognitive and health measures following early nutritional supplementation: A sibling study. *American Journal of Public Health* 72(10):1110–1118.

Hiscock, W. McC. 1982. Prevention, primary care, and cost containment: The early and periodic screening, diagnosis, and treatment (EPSDT) programs. Internal memo, U.S. Department of Health and Human Services, March 23. Cited in Glenn Austin, Child health-care financing and competition, *New England Journal of Medicine* 311(17): 1117–1120.

Institute of Medicine. 1985. *The prevention of low birthweight*. Report of the Committee to Study the Prevention of Low Birthweight. Washington, D.C.: National Academy Press.

Irwin, Patrick H., and Rosemary Conroy-Hughes. 1982. EPSDT impact on health status: Estimates based on secondary analysis of administratively generated data. *Medical Care* 20(2):216–234.

Jenkins, C. D. 1983. Social environment and cancer mortality in men. *New England Journal of Medicine* 308(7):395–398.

JRB Associates, Inc. 1980. Final report for community health center cost-effectiveness evaluation.

Katz, Sidney, Lawrence B. Branch, Michael H. Branson, Joseph A. Papsidero, John C. Beck, and David S. Greer. 1983. Active life expectancy. *New England Journal of Medicine* 309(20):1218–1224.

Kessner, David M., James Singer, Carolyn E. Kalk, and Edward R. Schlesinger. 1973. *Infant death: An analysis by maternal risk and health care, contrasts in health status*. Vol. 1. Institute of Medicine. Washington, D.C.: National Academy of Science.

Kitagawa, Evelyn M., and Philip M. Hauser. 1973. *Differential mortality in the United States*. Cambridge: Harvard University Press.

Kleinman, Joel C., Marsha Gold, and Diane Makuc. 1981. Use of ambulatory medical care by the poor: Another look at equity. *Medical Care* 19(10): 1011–1029.

Korenbrot, Carol C. 1984. Risk reduction in pregnancies of low income women: Comprehensive prenatal care through the OB access project. *Mobius* 4(3):34–43.

Kotelchuck, Milton, Janet B. Schwartz, Marlene T. Anderka, and Karl S. Finison. 1984. WIC participation and pregnancy outcomes: Massachusetts statewide evaluation project. *American Journal of Public Health* 74(10):1086–1092.

Lambert, Craig A., David R. Netherton, Lorenz J. Finison, James N. Hyde, and Sharon J. Spaight. 1982. Risk factors and life style: A statewide health-interview survey. *New England Journal of Medicine* 306(17):1048–1051.

Levine, Sol, Jacob J. Feldman, and Jack Elinson. 1983. Does medical care do any good? In *Handbook of health, health care, health professions*, ed. David Mechanic. New York: Free Press.

Lindheim, Roslyn, and S. Leonard Syme. 1983. Environments, people, and health. *Annual Review of the Public Health* 4:335–359.

Los Angeles County Health Alliance et al. 1982. Factual memorandum and argument in support of petition for rulemaking to declare prenatal care a public health service and establish standards for access to such care by low income women. Petition submitted to Beverly Myers, director of the State of Consumer Affairs, California.

Lurie, N., N. B. Ward, M. F. Shapiro, and R. H. Brook. 1984. Termination from Medi-Cal: Does it affect health?

New England Journal of Medicine 311(7): 480–484.

Mahaffey, Kathryn R., Joseph L. Annest, Jean Roberts, and Robert S. Murphy. 1982. National estimates of blood lead levels: United States, 1976–1980. *New England Journal of Medicine* 307(10):573–579.

Maine Department of Human Services. 1983. *Children's deaths in Maine*. America's Children Project, Office of the Commissioner, Maine Department of Human Services, State House Station 11, Augusta, Maine.

Marmot, Michael G., M. J. Shipley, and Geoffrey Rose. 1984. Inequalities in death: Specific explanations of a general pattern? *Lancet* 1:1003–1006.

Mills, David. 1983. Statement in *Impact of unemployment on children and families*. Hearing before the Subcommittee on Labor Standards of the Committee on Education and Labor, House of Representatives, 98th Cong., 1st sess. Washington, D.C.: Government Printing Office.

Morehead, Mildred A., R. S. Donaldson, and M. R. Servall. 1971. Comparison between OEO's neighborhood health centers and other health care providers of ratings of the quality of health care. *American Journal of Public Health* 61:1294–1306.

Nagi, M. H., and E. G. Stockwell. 1973. Socioeconomic differentials in mortality by cause of death. *Public Health Reports* 88(5):449–456.

National Association of Neighborhood Health Centers, Inc. N.d.a. Issue paper: The effectiveness of community-based primary health care centers. Xerox copy. 1625 I Street, N.W.–Suite 420, Washington, D.C. 20006.

———. N.d.b. Issue paper: The efficiency of community-based primary health care centers. Xerox copy. 1625 I Street, N.W.–Suite 420, Washington, D.C. 20006.

National Center for Health Statistics. 1973. Examination and health history findings among children and youths 6–17 years, United States. Series 11, no. 129. Public Health Service.

———. 1977. Use of selected medical procedures associated with preventive care, United States, 1973. Series 10, no. 110. Public Health Service.

———. 1979. Use habits among adults of cigarettes, coffee, aspirin, and sleeping pills, United States, 1976. Series 10, no. 131. Public Health Service.

———. 1980. Selected health characteristics by occupation, United States, 1975–76. Series 10, no. 133. Public Health Service.

———. 1981a. Height and weight of adults ages 18–74 years by socioeconomic and geographic variables, United States, 1981. Series 11, no. 224. Public Health Service.

———. 1981b. Highlights from Wave I of the National Survey of Personal Health Practices and Consequences: United States, 1979. Series 15, no. 1. Public Health Service.

———. 1981c. Prevalence of selected impairments, United States, 1977. Series 10, no. 134. Public Health Service.

———. 1982a. Annual summary of births, deaths, marriages, and divorces: United States, 1981. Monthly vital statistics report. Vol. 30, no. 13. Public Health Service.

———. 1982b. Vital statistics of the United States, 1978. Vol. 2, part A. DHHS Publication No. (PHS) 83-1101. Public Health Service.

———. 1983a. Americans assess their health: United States, 1978. Series 10, no. 142. Public Health Service.

———. 1983b. Disability days: United States, 1980. Series 10, no. 143. Public Health Service.

———. 1983c. Physician visits: Volume and interval since last visit, United States, 1980. Series 10, no. 144. Public Health Service.

National Health Law Program. 1983. Hard facts: The administration's 1984 health budget. Los Angeles, Calif.

————. 1984. In poor health: The administration's 1985 health budget. Los Angeles, Calif.

National Medical Care Expenditure Survey. 1984. Unpublished data provided by Dan Walden, National Center for Health Services Research, Hyattsville, Md.

Newacheck, Paul W., Lewis H. Butler, Aileen K. Harper, Dyan L. Piontkowski, and Patricia E. Franks. 1980. Income and illness. Medical Care 17 (12):1165–1176.

Newhouse, Joseph P., Willard G. Manning, Carl N. Morris, Larry L. Orr, Naihua Duan, Emmett B. Keeler, Arleen Leibowitz, Kent H. Marquis, M. Susan Marquis, Charles E. Phelps, and Robert H. Brook. 1981. Some interim results from a controlled trial of cost sharing in health insurance. New England Journal of Medicine 305(25): 1501–1507.

Norris, Frank D., and Ronald L. Williams. 1984. Perinatal outcomes among medicaid recipients in California. American Journal of Public Health 74(10): 1112–1117.

Orso, Camille L. 1979. Delivering ambulatory health care: The successful experience of an urban neighborhood health center. Medical Care 17(2):111–126.

Preston, Samuel H. 1984. Children and the elderly in the U.S. Scientific American 251(6):44–49.

Price, Deb. 1984. U.S. families face more poverty. San Francisco Examiner and Chronicle, March 11, p. A9.

Rainwater, Lee. 1966. Fear and the house-as-haven in the lower class. Journal of the American Institute of Planning 32:23–31.

Reed, Dwayne, Daniel McGee, and Katsuhiko Yano. 1984. Psychosocial processes and general susceptibility to chronic disease. American Journal of Epidemiology 119(3):356–370.

Reynolds, Roger A. 1976. Improving access to health care among the poor: The neighborhood health center experience. Millbank Memorial Fund Quarterly: Health and Society 54(1). 47–82.

Rice, Dorothy, and Kathleen Danchik. 1979. Changing needs of children: Disease, disability, and access to care. Paper presented at Institute of Medicine Annual Meeting, Washington, D.C.

"Richer, poorer, truer." 1984. New York Times, August 8, p. 20E.

Ricketts, Tom. 1983. How to make the poor die elsewhere. Washington Monthly, February, p. 43.

Riley, Vernon. 1975. Mouse mammary tumors: Alteration of incidence as apparent function of stress. Science 189:465–467.

Robert Wood Johnson Foundation. 1983. Updated report on access to health care for the American people. Special Report No. 1. Princeton: R. W. Johnson Foundation.

Ruberman, William, Eve Weinblatt, Judith D. Goldberg, and Banvir S. Chaudhary. 1984. Psychosocial influences on mortality after myocardial infarction. New England Journal of Medicine 311(9): 552–559.

Schlozman, Kay L., and Sidney Verba. 1978. The new unemployment: Does it hurt? Public Policy 26(3):333–358.

Schwarz, Rachel, and Paul Poppen. 1982. Measuring the impact of CHCs on pregnancy outcomes. Final Report, Contract No. 240-81-0041. Health Resources and Services Administration. Rockville, Md.: Government Printing Office.

Scott, Austin. 1982. County's poor seen delaying visits to doctor. Los Angeles Times, Dec. 19, pt. 2, p. 1.

Shadish, William. 1981. Effectiveness of preventive child health care. Health Care Financing Administration. HSS Publication, HCFA Publication No.

03099. Washington, D.C.: Government Printing Office.

Shapiro, Sam, Wanda Venet, Philip Strax, Louis Venet, and Ruth Roeser. 1982. Prospects for eliminating racial differences in breast cancer survival rates. *American Journal of Public Health* 72(10): 1142–1145.

Showstack, Jonathan A., Peter P. Budetti, and Donald Minkler. 1984. Factors associated with birthweight. An exploration of the roles of prenatal care and length of gestation. *American Journal of Public Health* 74(9):1003–1008.

Sparer, Gerald, and Joyce Johnson. 1971. Evaluation of OEO neighborhood health centers. *American Journal of Public Health* 61(May):931–942.

Starfield, Barbara. 1984. Social factors in child health. In *Ambulatory Pediatrics III*, ed. Morris Green and Robert J. Haggerty, pp. 12–18. Philadelphia: W. B. Saunders.

———. 1985. *Effectiveness of medical care: Validating clinical wisdom*. Baltimore, Md.: Johns Hopkins University Press.

Syme, S. Leonard, and Lisa F. Berkman. 1976. Social class, susceptibility, and sickness. *American Journal of Epidemiology* 104:1–8.

Task Force Report. 1976. Education and training of health manpower for prevention. In *Preventive Medicine USA*. New York: Prodist.

Tokarz, Wally. 1982. Controversy engulfs care project. *American Medical News*, February 12.

Uninsured increase, study shows. 1984. *Washington Report on Medicine and Health* 38:3.

U.S. Congress House of Representatives Committee on Interstate and Foreign Commerce. 1979. *Child Health Assurance Act of 1979*. Report No. 96-568. Washington, D.C.: Government Printing Office.

———. Select Committee on Children, Youth, and Families. 1983. Demographic and social trends: Implications for federal support of dependent-care services for children and the elderly. 98th Cong., 1st sess. Washington, D.C.: Government Printing Office.

———. 1984a. Children, youth, and families: 1983, a year-end report. 98th Cong., 2d sess. Washington, D.C.: Government Printing Office.

———. 1984b. Infant mortality rates: Failure to close the black-white gap. Subcommittee on Oversight. 98th Cong., 2d sess. Series no. 98-131. Washington, D.C.: Government Printing Office.

U.S. Department of Commerce. Bureau of the Census. 1984. Money income and poverty status of families and persons in the U.S., 1983. In *Current population reports*, p. 1. Series P-60, no. 145. Washington, D.C.: Government Printing Office.

U.S. Department of Health and Human Services. Public Health Service. 1982. *Health: United States, 1982*. National Center for Health Statistics. Hyattsville, Md.: Government Printing Office.

U.S. Department of Health, Education, and Welfare. Public Health Service. 1977. *Health of the disadvantaged: Chartbook*. DHEW Publication No. (HRA) 77-628. Office of Health Resources Opportunity. Hyattsville, Md.: Government Printing Office.

———. 1979a. Dietary intake source data: U.S., 1971–74. DHEW Publication No. (PHS) 79-1221. Hyattsville, Md.: Government Printing Office.

———. 1979b. *Healthy people: The surgeon general's report on health promotion and disease prevention, 1979*. DHEW Publication No. (PHS) 79-55071. Washington, D.C.: Government Printing Office.

———. Health Resources Administration. 1979. *Health status of minorities and low-income groups*. DHEW Publication

No. (HRA) 79-627. Washington, D.C.: Government Printing Office.

U.S. General Accounting Office. 1979. *Early childhood and family development programs improve the quality of life for low-income families.* Publication No. HRD-79-40. Washington, D.C.: Government Printing Office.

————. 1984. WIC evaluations provide some favorable but no conclusive evidence on the effects expected for the special supplemental program for women, infants, and children. Report to the Senate Committee on Agriculture, Nutrition, and Forestry. GAO/

PEMD-84-4. Washington, D.C.: Government Printing Office.

Whittemore, Alice S., 1981. Air pollution and respiratory disease. *Annual Review of Public Health* 2:397–429.

Wiederman, G., and F. Ambrosch. 1979. Costs and benefits of measles and mumps immunization in Austria. *Bulletin of the World Health Organization* 57(4):625–629.

Witte, J. J., and N. W. Axnick. 1975. The benefits from ten years of measles immunization in the U.S. *Public Health Reports* 90(30):205–207.

3 SEX, ILLNESS, AND MEDICAL CARE: A REVIEW OF DATA, THEORY, AND METHOD

Constance A. Nathanson

Introduction

"In all societies certain things are selected as reference points for the ascription of status. . . . *The simplest and most universally used of these reference points is sex*" [1, pp. 115–116]. There can be few more convincing demonstrations of this statement than to review the world's literature on mortality, morbidity, and medical care. Data collected by national and international administrative bodies, as well as by individual investigators, are almost universally tabulated by sex. As a consequence of this uniform practice, there exists an enormous wealth of statistical material on sex differences in almost every dimension of health, ranging from crude death rates to the frequency of home visits by a physician. The bulk of these data, however, have been collected with the aim of describing mortality and morbidity in selected populations. While sex has been used as a primary basis of more detailed classification, there has been relatively little sustained attention to the broad range of sex differences across a variety of health indices. The purpose of this paper is to focus the attention of social scientists on these sex differences in illness and medical care and on the problems of understanding and interpretation that they present.

SOURCE: Reprinted with permission from *Social Science and Medicine*, 11:13–25, Constance A. Nathanson, "Sex, Illness, and Medical Care: A Review of Data, Theory, and Method." Copyright 1977, Pergamon Journals, Ltd.

In carrying out this purpose, the paper is limited both by considerations of space and by the nature of the available data. While there are significant sex differences in patterns of mental illness, these differences have received somewhat more attention than have differences associated with physical disease [2–7]. Consequently, this paper will focus on physical rather than mental illness. Secondly, although reasonably reliable data on mortality are available from *developed* countries for much of the 20th century, comparable morbidity data have only recently begun to be collected. Since one aim of this paper is, wherever possible, to be international in scope, it will focus primarily on the *contemporary* picture of sex differences in health indices, although changes in mortality will be briefly considered. Furthermore, while mortality data are published for most countries of the world, indices of morbidity and the utilization of health services are not readily available, even for the majority of developed countries. This paper relies heavily on certain indices which have been employed in more than one country, but the overall description of sex differences in morbidity and mortality is strongly weighted with the United States experience. The limitations of this approach are recognized, and highlight the need for data collection on a more international basis. Finally, this paper is limited by the very nature of its subject matter. "Sex," "illness," and "medical care" are not coherent conceptual categories, but only indices to a bewildering variety of underlying biological, psychological, and so-

cial processes. No single theory or set of hypotheses will possibly encompass this variety. Consequently, while this paper has a certain descriptive unity of focus, it is conceptually and theoretically eclectic. In this sense, it reflects the state of the literature of sex differences in illness and medical care, in which *ad hoc* speculation concerning cause and effect relationships is the rule rather than the exception. One function of the present paper will be to define and order the alternative directions that speculation may take, with the hope that future investigation in the area of sex differences will be more precisely directed to the examination of specific alternatives.

The body of the paper is divided into four sections. The first section is entirely descriptive, and will summarize the current state of knowledge with respect to sex differences in mortality, morbidity, and medical care. The following two sections will consider, respectively, the methodological and the theoretical issues that arise in evaluating and interpreting these data. Finally, the last section will indicate some directions for future research into sex differences in health status.

Sex Differences in Illness and Medical Care

In a relatively short paper it is possible to do no more than call attention to the most salient and consistently reported sex differences in indices of health and medical care. Five topics will be covered in this section: first, the sources of data employed in this paper, secondly, overall sex differences in mortality, morbidity, and the use of health services, third, principal causes of differential mortality and morbidity, and finally, variations in the pattern of sex differences by age and by marital status.

Sources of Data

Mortality data both as to the cause of death and demographic characteristics of the deceased are based on information recorded on the death certificate, and classified as to cause by the International Classification of Diseases. Death registration is considered to be virtually complete in all the economically developed countries [8]. These data are compiled annually by the United Nations and by the World Health Organization, and are widely reported in a variety of secondary sources.

The morbidity data presented in this paper come from two principle sources, the United States Health Interview Survey and the British General Household Survey. The Health Interview Survey (HIS) is a continuing weekly household sample survey, conducted in the United States since July, 1957. In this survey, data are collected to describe the distribution in the population of chronic and acute illness, associated disability, and the use of health services. The General Household Survey (GHS) was inaugurated in 1971. Data are obtained, also from a national household sample, covering a wide variety of topics including current health status. While differences in question wording limit the direct comparability of health *levels* between the U.S. and British surveys, they are suffi-

ciently similar in the types of data collected to warrant the comparison of sex ratios for a variety of health indices. The World Health Organization reports "morbidity statistics" for a number of countries based on hospital inpatient data, but morbidity is here *completely* confounded with utilization of services, a problem inherent to some degree in almost all measures of morbidity that are currently employed.

The two most widely used indices of medical care are hospital discharge or separation rates and physician visit rates. Hospital in-patient data are compiled by WHO, as indicated, and are also available from several other sources. Data for the present paper were obtained from the Hospital Discharge Survey conducted annually by the U.S. National Center for Health Statistics, *Hospital Morbidity*, published by Statistics Canada, the British GHS, and several *ad hoc* research investigations carried out in the United States. (These investigations, as well as the other sources described will be cited specifically as the data are presented.) Both the HIS and the GHS report physician visits, and these data are also available from special research studies carried out in several other Western and Eastern European countries and in Israel. Data on more detailed aspects of medical care including preventive care, health expenditures, and the like, are limited almost entirely to the United States.

Overall Sex Differences

In all developed countries and for all ages the death rate for females is appreciably below that for males, and has been so at least since the beginning of the 20th century [8–10]. Sex ratios based on age-adjusted death rates for 18 countries of "low mortality" are presented in Table 1. In addition to the uniformly favorable mortality experience of women, two further points concerning sex differences in mortality should be noted. First, the variability of death rates among the countries listed in Table 1 is considerably greater for

males than females. (The standard deviation of male rates is about 1½ times that of female rates, and this difference is constant from 1930 to 1960.) Secondly, the difference between male and female death rates has increased markedly during the 20th century, due primarily to excess mortality in men [10–13].

The apparent contrast between male excess mortality and female excess morbidity—"women get sick and men die"—was observed in

TABLE 1 Sex Ratios (Female/Male) of Age-Adjusted Death Rates for Selected Countries of Low Mortality, 1960*†

Country	Ratio
U.S., white	0.61
England and Wales	0.63
Scotland	0.68
Australia‡	0.63
New Zealand§	0.67
Canada	0.67
Ireland	0.77
Netherlands	0.74
Belgium	0.65
France	0.60
Switzerland	0.69
West Germany	0.70
Denmark	0.78
Norway	0.73
Sweden	0.76
Finland	0.63
Portugal	0.74
Italy	0.71
Average—1960	0.68
1950	0.77
About 1930	0.85

*This table is adapted from Table 3.4, presented by Spiegelman and Erhardt [8].
†Age-adjusted on the basis of the age-distribution of the total population of the United States. Census of April 1950.
‡Excludes full blooded Aborigines.
§Excludes Maoris.
Note: The statistical measures for 1950 and about 1930 were taken from Spiegelman M. *An International Comparison of Mortality Rates at the Older Ages*. Proc. World Population Conference, Rome, Vol. 1, p. 289. United Nations Department of Economic and Social Affairs. New York, 1955.

England as early as 1927 [14] and has been exciting sporadic comment since that time [2, 15–18]. Sex differences in several indices of morbidity, as reported to household interviewers in Great Britian [19] and the United States [20] are shown in Table 2. Data are presented for adults (15 and above in Great Britain, 17 and above in the United States), and exclude illness and disability associated with pregnancy and its aftermath. Rates for each index were calculated on somewhat different bases in the two countries, and are not shown. However, the direction of the sex ratios is remarkably consistent. When morbidity is measured, as it is in these surveys, by behavioral indices (restriction or limitation of activity, medical consultation, going to bed, staying away from work) adult women almost invariably report more *acute* illness and associated disability than adult men. Unfortunately, it has not been possible to obtain comparable *morbidity* data for other countries.

With scattered exceptions, adult women also make more physician visits than adult men, and they do so in all countries where the relevant data have been obtained. Comparable data on physician visits were collected in seven countries as part of an international collaborative study of medical care [21]. Sex ratios based on two week physician visit rates as reported in this study are presented in Table 3. Age groups are those used in the published table from which these data were taken, with the omission of the age group 15–44. About 10–15% of physician visits by women in this age group are accounted for by pre- and postnatal care, and these were not excluded from the reported rates. Of the 24 sex ratios shown for age groups above 44, only seven reflect a higher rate of physician visits by men than by women. (Discussion of the differences in these ratios by age is reserved for a later section.) Surveys conducted in Israel and Finland [22, 23] have obtained identical results, and these differences persist in the United States, at least, when obstetrical visits *are* excluded [2, 15]. The obverse of these findings is ob-

TABLE 2   Sex Ratios (Female/Male) for Selected Morbidity Indices, United States and Great Britain, 1971*

Index	United States	Great Britain
Acute conditions	1.19	1.15
Chronic conditions	0.89	1.08
Days of restricted activity	1.28	1.14
Days of bed disability	1.34	1.17
Days lost from work	1.20	0.88

*Ratios calculated by the author from data presented in U.S. Department of Health, Education, and Welfare [20] and Office of Population Censuses and Surveys [19]. Ratios shown are for adults 17 and over in the United States, 15 and over in Great Britain. Pregnancy associated illness and disability have been excluded from these data.

TABLE 3 Sex Ratios (Female/Male) for Physician Visits, Ages 0–14, 45–64, and 65 and Above. Selected Countries*

Country	0–14	45–64	65 +
Canada			
Grande Prairie	0.94	1.72	2.14
Saskatchewan	0.60	0.56	0.97
Fraser	1.18	0.89	1.06
Jersey	0.83	1.67	1.03
United States			
Northwestern Vermont	0.67	1.31	0.83
Baltimore, Maryland	0.73	1.08	1.25
Argentina			
Buenos Aires	0.84	1.14	1.17
United Kingdom			
Liverpool	0.80	1.11	1.18
Finland			
Helsinki	0.83	1.82	1.18
Poland			
Lódź	0.63	1.32	1.85
Yugoslavia			
Banat	0.98	0.80	0.83
Rijeka	0.86	1.75	0.54

*Ratios calculated by the author from data presented in White [21].

tained in studies focused on low utilizers of physicians' services [24, 25]. This population of "nonattenders" is predominantly male.

Data describing more detailed aspects of ambulatory medical care are limited to the United States. Women are more likely than men to report a regular source of care [26, 27], and are much more likely to obtain various types of preventive care [15, 28, 29]. Evidence regarding a more basic dimension of preventive health care is reported by Andersen and Anderson [27]. Among men, they observe, the most prevalent reason for having a physical examination is that it is *required* for work or insurance purposes, while women are likely to be examined *voluntarily*, in response to symptoms or as a preventive measure. In perhaps related findings, women are reported to be generally better informed about disease than are men [30, 31].

Total rates of hospitalization are higher for women than for men, even when these rates are age-standardized and exclude obstetrical conditions [15, 19, 27, 32–34]. More detailed analyses of hospital data from Canadian [35] and United States [15, 36] sources report surgical procedure rates for women 1½ times the comparable rates for men. Sex differences in average length of hospital stay are less consistent in direction, although the majority of sources report longer hospital stays among men [19, 27, 32–35, 37].

In the United States the total cost of medical care is higher for women than for men [27, 38], hardly a surprising finding in view of women's greater use of medical services. Furthermore, this difference persists well beyond the child-bearing ages. Women are larger consumers of medicines than men, both in Great Britain [39] and in the United States [40]. This difference is reflected in drug expenditure data from the United States, both for prescribed and for nonprescribed medications [41].

This section has rapidly reviewed what are perhaps, by now, familiar statistics to most students of health and medical care. In all European countries and in North America, male mortality rates are higher than those of females. However, for all countries where the necessary data are available, women report more acute illness than men, and make substantially greater use of health services. In the following pages, these differences will be examined in more detail, by specific cause, and by age and marital status.

Causes of Death and Disease

Excessive mortality among adult males in recent decades, resulting in an increasing divergence of male and female death rates, has been attributed to three principle causes of death, cardiovascular disease, cancer, and bronchitis [13]. Of these, cardiovascular disease makes by far the largest contribution to mortality [10, 12, 13]. Other leading causes of death among adults in Europe and North America are diabetes, tuber-culosis, influenza and pneumonia, cirrhosis of the liver, suicide, and accidents [8]. Diabetes is the only condition among these major killers for which higher death rates are reported for women than for men. Particularly large differences in the sex ratio have been observed for those conditions (cirrhosis, suicide, accidents) which may be wholly or partially attributed to overt acts of the individual [9, 12, 18, 42].

In a recent paper, Verbrugge [18] has suggested that the apparent contrast between male mortality and female morbidity is due, in part, to the fact that women, while having more illness than men, have it in milder forms. This hypothesis is consistent with data on sex differences in morbidity rates for specific conditions. Women have higher rates than men for acute conditions and for the disability associated with these conditions, but they have lower rates of chronic conditions in almost all age groups. The specific acute conditions reported more frequently by females both in Great Britain and the United States are upper respiratory infections and influenza [19, 20] and, in the United States, genito-urinary disorders. Injuries are the only large group of acute conditions for which males have consistently higher rates; the same pattern is found in hospital morbidity data for all countries where this information is reported by sex [33, 34, 43–45]. While no data are available to compare case-fatality rates for these acute conditions, it is at least plausible that injury is more frequently associated with mortality than are the acute conditions predominant among females. Males have slightly higher chronic condition rates than females, and this difference is primarily accounted for by disease groups (heart disease, cerebrovascular disease, bronchitis) that are also frequent causes of mortality. In contrast to this pattern, women report fewer chronic conditions than men, and the specific conditions for which they do show an excess (principally arthritis and rheumatism) are relatively nonlethal [18–20].

Additional light on specific conditions which contribute substantially to morbidity among women is provided by detailed analyses of hospital morbidity statistics from Canada and the United States. This analysis, presented in Table 4, compares total hospital discharge rates for men and women, and then successively refines these rates, first, by excluding obstetrical conditions and, secondly, by excluding *all* conditions associated with the reproductive organs and therefore specific to one sex or the other. This procedure entirely eliminates the difference in hospi-

tal discharge rates between the two sexes. Among the total group of conditions specific to women, slightly over 70% (in both countries) represent obstetrical conditions, and this is not unexpected. However, almost 30% (accounting for 10% of all hospital discharges among women) are non-obstetrical "diseases of the female genital organs." Approximately 40% of these diseases fall into the two categories of disorders of menstruation and prolapsed uterus, lending some slight weight, perhaps, to the 19th century physician's view of woman as the "product and prisoner of her reproductive system" [46, p. 335]. However, 5% of all hospital episodes among men are similarly caused by conditions of the reproductive organs.

Variations by Age

From the standpoint of developing explanatory hypotheses, a description of overall sex differences in mortality, morbidity, and medical care does little more than whet the

TABLE 4   Hospital Discharge Rates by Sex and Condition, Canada, 1971, and United States, 1968

Discharge Rates per 1,000 Population	Canada*		United States†	
	Male	Female	Male	Female
Total discharge rate	1367.3	1950.3	1191.9	1658.2
Discharge rate excluding obstetrical conditions	1367.3	1477.2	1191.9	1245.4
Discharge rate excluding *all* sex specific conditions	1285.5	1289.3	1139.3	1084.6

*Rates calculated by the author from data presented in Statistics Canada [34].
†Rates drawn directly from U.S. Department of Health, Education, and Welfare [33, pp. 4–7].

appetite. Not only is an examination of variations in sex ratios among different population subgroups more likely to be fruitful in *generating* hypotheses, but any hypotheses that are advanced must be consistent with these variations. An analysis based on published data is limited, however, by the population characteristics that *other* analysts have thought important. The most frequently reported of these character-

istics, in addition to sex, are age and marital status.

Changes in the pattern of sex differences over the life span are shown in Figs. 1 and 2 for Great Britain and the United States. Sex ratios (female/male) for mortality and acute illness rates are presented in Fig. 1, and for chronic conditions and hospital episodes in Fig. 2. Ratios of less than 1.00 reflect higher male rates, while ratios above 1.00

FIGURE 1   Sex Ratios (Female/Male) for Mortality and Acute Illness by Age, Great Britain and the United States, 1971*†

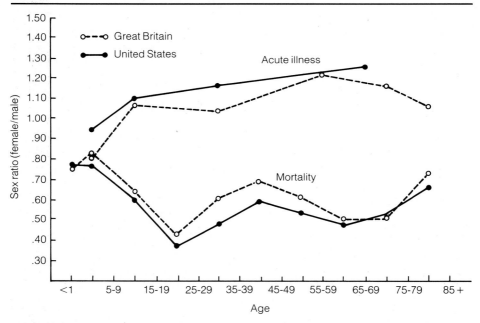

* Sex ratios calculated by the author using the following sources:
Mortality.
   World Health Organization. *World Health Statistics Annual, 1971.* Volume 1, Vital Statistics and Causes of Death. Geneva, 1974; U.S. Department of Health, Education, and Welfare. *Vital Statistics of the United States, 1971.* Vol. II, Mortality. Rockville, MD., 1975.
Acute illness.
   Office of Population Censuses and Surveys [19].
   U.S. Department of Health, Education, and Welfare [20].
   † Available data did not permit the calculation of mortality and acute illness sex ratios for exactly corresponding age-groups.

FIGURE 2   Sex Ratios (Female/Male) for Chronic Conditions and Hospital Episodes by Age, Great Britain and the United States, 1970–1971*†

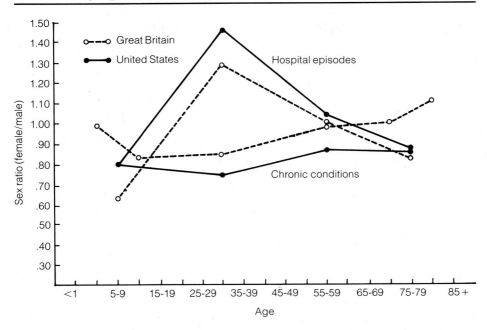

* Sex ratios calculated by the author from the following sources:
Chronic conditions.
    Office of Population Censuses and Surveys [19].
    U.S. Department of Health, Education, and Welfare [20].
Hospital episodes.
    Office of Population Censuses and Surveys [19].
    U.S. Department of Health, Education, and Welfare. *Utilization of Short-Stay Hospitals, Summary of Non-medical Statistics, United States, 1970. Vital and Health Statistics, Series 13, No. 14, 1973.*
    † Data did not permit calculation of all ratios for exactly corresponding age groups.

mean that rates are higher among females. Several points are dramatically illustrated by these figures. First, the patterns of change in sex differences by age are remarkably parallel in the two countries. Not only is this true of mortality as would be predicted from overall similarities in social and economic development, but it is also true for the much softer health indices based largely on household survey data. Differences between the United States and Great Britain in population composition and medical care organization, not to speak of differences in survey methods, make this parallelism all the more striking. The second point to note about these figures is the convergence of all sex ratios toward equality between the sexes both at the beginning and at the end of life. It is during the broad span of middle life, ranging from school entrance to retirement, that differences in the illness experience of the two sexes are most marked. Finally, these figures demonstrate graphically a point that has already been made verbally—over the age span during which sex differences are most profound, males have greater mortality and higher rates of chronic conditions, while females report more acute illness and make greater use of health services. Indices of illness *behavior*—activity restriction, days in bed, sickness absence from work—show the same general age specific pattern as acute illness, while the pattern for physician visits resembles that of hospital episodes.

A number of more detailed aspects of the variation in sex differences by age are illustrated by these figures, and confirmed by other sources. By *all* indices of health status, pre-school age boys are less well off than girls in this age group. Infant mortality among males is about one-half to one-third above that of females in all developed countries [9]. Commenting on the evidence of sex differences in illness during early childhood, the authors of the GHS remark that "small boys are not only more liable to acute sickness than small girls, but also . . . the nature of their sickness is more serious, or more seriously regarded" [19, p. 299]. Following the pre-school years, however, divergent trends in patterns of sex differences are quickly established. A marked increase in male relative to female mortality rates occurs in the age-group 15–24. This increase has been widely noted [9, 12], and is attributed primarily to deaths from acci-

dents among young men. Comparing Sweden and the United States, Fuchs [9] has commented that while infant mortality sex ratios in the two countries are very similar, the gap between male and female death rates in early adulthood is much larger in the United States. This difference is attributed to different life styles of Swedish and American youth.

It is during the prime of adult life that men and women differ most radically in their illness experience, as has already been observed. Women in the reproductive age-groups utilize both physician and hospital services at almost one and one-half times the rate of men in this age-group, exclusive of utilization associated with pregnancy. Men, on the other hand, show a second marked increase in their relative mortality, extending from ages 45–64, but there is no corresponding change in other health indices. The size of this increase in relative mortality varies both among countries, and between regions within the same country [9], and is due primarily to male mortality from heart disease [9, 12].

Beginning at about age 65, there are further changes in the illness experience of the two sexes. Chronic illness rates among women begin to approach or exceed those of men, although men in this, as in younger age-groups, are more likely to be rendered "unable to carry on" their major activity by chronic illness [47]. Finally, while women over 65 are less likely than men in this age-group to be hospitalized, when they do enter a hospital their length of stay is longer [17, 19, 33, 48].

This brief review has documented

wide variation over the life cycle in the pattern of sex differences in health indices. However, although sex ratios for mortality, morbidity, and use of health services are inconsistent among themselves, they vary in parallel fashion among several countries of Europe and North America. These observations suggest that variations in sex ratios are produced by common underlying processes and, furthermore, that these processes are probably social rather than biological in nature. Speculation as to the precise nature of these processes is reserved to a later section of this paper.

Variations by Marital Status

In all developed countries, the unmarried have significantly higher death rates than the married, and this differential is much greater for males than for females [9, 10]. A middle-aged unmarried man living in the United States has a probability of death about five times that of a married woman in the same age range, and similar, although somewhat less marked, differences are observed for other countries in Europe and North America. Based on a detailed analysis of sex mortality differentials by marital status, Gove [42] remarks that the differences between married and unmarried (single, divorced, separated, widowed) men are particularly large for those causes of death where "one's psychological state would appear to affect one's life chances" (suicide, homicide, accidents, cirrhosis of the liver, and several other conditions of less obvious social-psychological etiology.)

While sex *mortality* differentials by marital status are reasonably well established, this is much less true of differences in reported illness and in the use of health services. Data are not always cross-classified by marital status, marital status categories are not uniform among different sources of data, and the apparent effects of marital status, when this information is given, are not always in the same direction. Consequently, generalizations made in this paper concerning the influence of marital status on patterns of sex differences in illness and medical care are highly tentative, and subject to amendment or disproof by subsequent investigation.

The married of both sexes fare better than the unmarried in most studies of morbidity based on data collected in household surveys [19, 49–51]. It has been suggested, however, that, from the standpoint of health status, the married state is less advantageous to women than to men [3, 52, 53]. The relative protection that marriage affords to each sex may be examined by dividing morbidity rates of the unmarried by those of the married [42, 54]. If the ratios formed by this procedure are greater than 1.00, then married persons are better off. Furthermore, if marriage is, indeed, less advantageous to women, then their ratios should be consistently lower than the corresponding ratios for men.

Morbidity rates by marital status, age, and sex are published in the report of the General Household Survey [19], and these data have been used to calculate the ratios presented in Table 5. This table illustrates two points. First, of the 32

TABLE 5   Ratios Produced by Dividing Morbidity Rates of the Unmarried by the Rates of the Married, Great Britain, 1971*

Morbidity Index and Unmarried Category (Ratio)		Age			Average Ratio
		15–44	45–65	65+	
Limiting long-standing illness					
Single:	Male	0.97	1.13	—	1.05
	Female	0.95	1.36	0.95	1.09
Widowed, divorced, separated:	Male	1.30	1.22	1.07	1.20
	Female	1.66	1.42	1.14	1.41
Presence of restricted activity					
Single:	Male	1.03	0.83	1.16	1.01
	Female	1.09	1.10	1.21	1.13
Widowed, divorced, separated:	Male	—	1.16	1.43	1.30
	Female	1.01	1.15	1.15	1.10
Number of restricted days					
Single:	Male	0.87	0.84	—	0.86
	Female	0.97	1.37	1.17	1.17
Widowed, divorced, separated:	Male	—	1.17	1.66	1.42
	Female	1.41	1.22	1.03	1.22

*Ratios calculated by the author from morbidity rates presented in the General Household Survey [19].

ratios shown in this table, 26 are greater than one, again confirming that married people of both sexes report less illness and associated disability than the unmarried. The only exceptions to this generalization occur in comparing married with single persons, and these exceptions are equally frequent among men and women. Secondly, there is no basis in the data presented *here* for concluding that marriage affords more protection against morbidity to men than to women. On the contrary, in 10 of the 14 comparisons between the sexes made possible by this table, unmarried women report *more* morbidity relative to the married than do unmarried men. The reader should be cautioned, however, that these are data from a single source, and that both age and marital status are reported in very broad categories. The question of how marital status affects sex differentials in morbidity is an area much in need of further study.

In order to look at the influence of marital status on use of health services the same procedure as described above, division of unmarried utilization rates by those of the married, has been employed. In this case a ratio greater than 1.00 means that these services are being used at a higher rate by unmarried as compared to married persons, while greater use by the married will result in a ratio of less than 1.00. While the general direction of marital status effects on morbidity was the same for both sexes, this is not true of comparable effects on medical care. Unmarried/married ratios of hospital discharge rates by age and sex are presented in Table 6. These ratios are based on rates calculated from hospital discharges reported to the U.S. National Center for Health Statistics in 1970 [33]. In all but two of 15 possible comparisons, male ratios are larger than female ratios, indicating that unmarried men use more hospital services relative to their married counterparts than do un-

married women. There is, furthermore, an absolute reversal between the two sexes. Two-thirds of the ratios presented for men are greater than 1.00, relecting higher utilization by *unmarried* as compared to married men, while two-thirds of the female ratios are less than 1.00, indicating higher utilization by *married* than by unmarried women. These data on hospitalization by marital status are consistent with information from at least one additional source [15]. Physician visits by marital status follow the same pattern (based on calculations by the author from HIS data [55]).

The data reported in this section of the paper may be summarized very briefly. By *all* criteria of health status, unmarried men are less favorably situated than married men. They have higher mortality rates, report more morbidity, and make more use of physicians and hospitals.

TABLE 6 Ratios Produced by Dividing Hospital Discharge Rates of the Unmarried by Those of the Married, United States, 1970*

Unmarried Category (Ratio)	Age				Average Ratio
	15–24	25–44	45–64	65 +	
Female	0.56	0.91	0.92	0.93	0.83
Separated: Male	1.61	1.52	1.11	0.86	1.28
Female	1.04	1.12	0.84	0.71	0.93
Divorced: Male	0.91	1.27	1.06	0.69	0.98
Female	1.24	1.18	0.92	0.60	0.99
Widowed: Male	—	1.19	1.28	1.31	1.26
Female	—	0.93	1.03	1.21	1.06

*Rates and ratios calculated by the author from: U.S. Bureau of the Census, Census of Population: 1970, Vol. 1, Characteristics of the Population—Part 1. United States Summary—Section 2. U.S. Government Printing Office, Washington, D.C. 1973, Table 203; and U.S. Department of Health, Education, and Welfare, *Utilization of Short-Stay Hospitals, Summary of Non-medical Statistics, United States*, 1970. Vital and Health Statistics, Series 13, No. 14, 1973, Table 17.

The picture with respect to women is less consistent, however. While unmarried women also experience less favorable mortality rates than married women, the difference is considerably narrower than among men. In the data presented in this paper, unmarried women report *more* morbidity than women who are married, but make *less* use of hospital services. Finally, although the protection against mortality afforded by marriage is clearly more substantial for men than for women, there is no consistent evidence in these data for a parallel effect on *morbidity*. The reader is again reminded that generalizations concerning patterns of morbidity and medical care are based on scattered evidence, and should be regarded with appropriate caution.

Issues of Method

In evaluating the data that have been presented one of the first questions that arises concerns their validity. That is, how accurately do they represent the true character of sex differences in mortality, morbidity, and medical care. Two issues of methodology that bear particularly on the question of validity are, first the selection of health indices and, secondly, the procedures that are employed for collection of data.

Selection of Health Indices

As indicated earlier, mortality data are based on information recorded at the time of death, and coded using a system of classification common to all developed countries. Experts in mortality statistics agree, however, as to the existence of differences in recording procedures both between countries and even among physicians within the same country [8, 45]. "What goes on the death certificate will be influenced by the health habits of the population, the stage of illness at which medical care is sought, the system of medical care and the training of its personnel, and even the legal structure" [8, p. 51]. The opportunity for the sex of the deceased to affect recording procedures clearly exists, although the author is unaware of any data bearing directly on this point. There is some evidence, however, that the patient's sex is a factor both in the diagnosis of disease and in its treatment [6, 45, 56–64] and, consequently, might also be expected to influence the assignment of cause of death, Insofar as this influence is present, reported sex differences in mortality from specific causes will imperfectly reflect the true nature of these differences.

If mortality data may be affected by individuals' health behavior and by local systems of medical care, how much more this will be true of data purporting to measure morbidity. Almost all of the information available to us concerning the distribution of disease in populations is based not on clinically observable disease, but on the *behavior* of individuals, either as afflicted persons or as representatives of the health care system. Insofar as this behavior varies with the sex of the subject independently of the actual presence or absence of disease, then the data used to measure sex differences in disease will be measuring these behavioral differences instead. This problem is illustrated by the health indices employed in the British General Household Survey and the U.S. Health Interview Survey.

Both of these national surveys define chronic as well as acute illness on the basis of activity restriction, either restriction of the individual's *usual* activity or restriction of activity "compared with most people of your own age." The HIS also accepts medical attention as a criteria for the presence of acute illness. Sex differences in willingness, or ability, to restrict activities are commonly assumed to exist [65–68], although there is little concrete data to support this assumption. Ample evidence of sex differences in medical attention has been presented earlier in this paper. However, even if it is accepted that sexual status does influence morbidity reports based on behavioral indices, the direction of this influence is far from clear. In a study carried out by the U.S. National Center for Health Statistics [69] in which interview reports of chronic illness were matched with medical records, the *total* amount of overreporting of illness was found to be slightly higher among females than among males. However, among persons over 65, the "accuracy and completeness of reporting" was substantially greater among women than among men.

These brief comments have done little more than call attention to the fact that sexual status *may* independently influence reports of death and disease. More detailed description and analysis of this influence must wait upon further investigation.

Procedures of Data Collection

The procedures that are employed in data collection are of particular concern in the evaluation of health survey data, although "interviewer bias" may be present in any situation where information is obtained through personal interaction (e.g. between physician and patient). Biases in health survey data arising out of the relationship between interviewer and respondent have been documented by the U.S. National Center for Health Statistics [70]. However, little consideration has been given to bias specifically caused by the respective sexual status of these two parties to the health survey.

Employment as an interviewer for the HIS is limited to women because, "the typical respondent, a housewife, is generally thought to be more willing to reveal health information to another woman than to a man" [71, p. 4]. Furthermore, HIS procedures allow interviewers to obtain information from a "related adult" if the intended respondent is not at home and, indeed, 80% of HIS respondents are women. Consequently, the bulk of HIS information concerning *male* illness and use of health services is obtained by *women* from *women*! Proxy interviews generally understate the morbidity of the absent person, but this may be only one of many effects of these data collection procedures on the value of HIS data for comparing sex differences in health status.

Interviewers for the GHS are apparently also predominantly female. However, GHS procedures are much

more strict with respect to the acceptance of proxy interviews, and
only 9% of GHS interviews were
completed by proxy. The fact that a
higher proportion of health information referring to men was obtained
directly from male respondents may
partially account for the lower male/
female sex ratios found for most
morbidity indices reported in GHS
as compared with HIS data.

The methodological issues raised
in this section of the paper create
some uncertainty as to the exact
meaning of various indices of health
status that are commonly used. This
uncertainty also gives rise to different causal interpretations of the myr-
iad sex differences in mortality, morbidity, and medical care reported
earlier in the paper. In the next section, four major classes of interpretation will be briefly considered.

Issues of Interpretation

In the introduction to this paper,
it was pointed out that no single explanatory framework would be able
to account for the variety of processes grouped together under the
general heading of "sex differences
in illness and medical care." The
first problem that arises is to decide
what is the dependent variable to be
explained, for any particular set of
observed sex differences may be the
outcome of: (1) a real disease process; (2) behavior of the individual in
response to real or perceived illness;
(3) diagnostic and treatment practices of health care providers. In an
emprical situation, of course, all
three of these processes may be at
work simultaneously, so that selec-

tion of a particular theoretical focus
becomes partly a matter of the interests and orientation of the observer.
Depending on this theoretical focus,
one of four major explanatory frameworks may be employed to account
for observed sex differences in
health status. These differences have
been attributed to: (1) biological differences between males and females;
(2) differences in the social and/or
psychological stress levels to which
men and women are exposed; (3)
differences in the characteristic behavior patterns or life styles of men
and women; (4) institutionalized sex
roles, leading to differential treatment of men and women by representatives of the health care system.
It is seldom that all four alternatives
are explicitly considered in any
single piece of work. A single framework may be used to generate hypotheses, as, for example, in Gove's
work on mortality differentials by
marital status, or, more frequently,
bits and pieces of one or more frameworks are employed in *ad hoc* fashion to account for isolated findings.

The Biological Framework

The crucial biological differences
between males and females are genetic in origin. The female possesses
two large X chromosomes, the male
one X and a very much smaller Y.
The X chromosome carries many
genes in addition to those responsible for sex determination, giving the
female "options for variability not
open to the male" [72, p. 905]. This
genetic difference has been held responsible for sex differences in infant mortality [72] as well as for

greater male susceptibility to disease generally [73–77]. A genetic hypothesis appears to be consistent with the data on sex differences in mortality and morbidity among pre-school age children, but the divergent paths assumed by these differences in older age groups suggest that other factors come quickly into play.

In addition to genetic makeup, males and females also differ in their hormonal balance and, among women, this balance changes markedly with age. Hormonal factors have been postulated to explain both low rates of coronary heart disease among women prior to the menopause [78] and low susceptibility to certain cancers following the menopause [79]. Neither of these hypotheses has been confirmed and, indeed, Moriyama, Krueger, and Stamler state that the coronary heart disease hypothesis "finds no specific support in mortality data" [78, p. 116]. Arguing in more general terms, several recently published analyses of sex differences in mortality have concluded that the sharp increases in these differences observed in recent decades, cannot be explained by biological factors [10, 12, 13].

In the past, and today in many less developed countries, the biological process of reproduction played a major role in mortality among women of child-bearing age. While this is no longer true in the developed countries, women in this age group, and particularly married women, remain high users of health services. Furthermore, much of this excess use appears to be accounted for by disorders of the reproductive

system. To what extent these findings can be explained by biological processes, and to what extent by women's unique social roles, or even by the behavior of their medical advisors, is by no means clear.

The Stress Framework

The concept of stress, here defined as the exposure of the individual to conflicting or ambiguous expectations for his behavior, has been explored in some depth with the aim of identifying its role in the etiology of disease [80, 81]. Differences in levels of conflict and ambiguity associated with male as compared with female sex role expectations have been hypothesized, and advanced as possible explanations of certain *sex differences* in disease rates [3, 13, 82, 83]. Or, in other studies lacking an explicit comparative framework, the peculiar vulnerability of one sex has been attributed to stress generated by problems in the fulfillment of sex role expectations [84–86]. There is no consensus among the investigators whose work has been cited as to *which* sex experiences the greatest stress and, indeed, the answer to this question will undoubtedly vary depending on other dimensions of the social situation. For this reason, the stress framework is unlikely to prove fruitful as a *general* explanation for patterns of sex differences in death and disease.

Recent work [10, 13], employing a variety of arguments, has rejected the differential stress explanation for increases in male mortality during the last century, and has strongly suggested that sex differences in cigarette smoking are *the* major explanatory variable. The potentially lethal consequences of many sex-linked patterns of behavior, including cigarette smoking, are highlighted by data on sex differences in mortality from specific causes reviewed earlier in this paper. While sociologists have devoted considerable attention to the role of stress in disease, these sex-linked behavior patterns have been relatively neglected. It is to a consideration of these patterns that we turn next.

The Life Style Framework

Not ony is sex universally employed as a basis for the ascription of social status, but "all societies prescribe different attitudes and activities to men and to women" [1, p. 116]. One rarely considered dimension of these attitudes and activities is the degree to which they protect the individual against insults to his biological or psychological integrity, on the one hand, or threaten this integrity, on the other. There is some evidence for sex differences along this dimension, however [42, 87], and these differences constitute a third framework for the interpretation of variation among males and females in mortality, morbidity, and use of health services. This framework may be summarized in the form of two very general hypotheses: (1) Attitudes and activities prescribed for men in the countries of Europe and North America *both* expose them to high risk of mortality and morbidity *and* restrain them from "giving in" to illness by restricting their activities or making

use of health services; (2) Attitudes and activities prescribed for women in these same countries *both* expose them to less risk directly *and* permit or encourage them to be more responsive to perceived illness.

Focusing on the problem of sex differences in mortality, Gove [42, p. 47] has listed three behavioral factors "creating different life chances for men and women." These are:

(1) Social norms regulating appropriate behavior for men and women— it is socially more appropriate for men to smoke and drink;

(2) Life style differences, creating different risks of exposure to death and disease;

(3) Modal personality differences —men are more aggressive and willing to take risks.

Gove's concern, of course, is to explain *mortality* among men. Excess morbidity and use of health services among women have also been attributed to sex differences in characteristic behavior patterns [2, p. 59]:

(1) Women *report* more illness than men because it is culturally more acceptable for them to be ill— "the ethic of health is masculine";

(2) The sick role is relatively compatible with women's other role responsibilities and incompatible with those of men.

In all of these five statements contrasting sex-linked patterns of behavior, the attitudes and activities ascribed to men are less self-protective than those ascribed to women.

The life style framework, as outlined above, is consistent with much of the data presented earlier. Men do have higher mortality from conditions where risk-taking is an important factor, and women do make more use of both preventive and curative health services. Furthermore, these differences are most pronounced during that portion of the life cycle when sex differences in expected behavior are also likely to be most profound. However, much more work is needed to develop this framework, and particularly to find measures of the "protective" dimension of behavior that are independent of the sex differences in health status this dimension purports to explain.

The Institutionalized Sex Role Framework

Sex differences in illness, in diagnosis, and in medical treatment have been attributed to variations in the behavior and attitudes of medical practitioners toward their male and female patients [6, 46, 56–64]. Much of this literature appears to have been stimulated by feminist concern for the exploitation of women by physicians and, consequently, tends to focus on women's health problems rather than on sex differences directly.

Based on analysis of historical materials, primarily from 19th century American sources, several authors have suggested that physicians' diagnostic and treatment practices have the aim of reinforcing traditional sex role definitions, and particularly of establishing masculine control over the female sex [46, 59, 60, 62]. In the 19th century, this effort took the form of attributing a large proportion of illness in women to disorders of the reproductive system, and treating the patient accordingly. Contemporary physicians are similarly accused of arbitrarily defining women's complaints as psychosomatic [61, 64], and using mood-modifying drugs, as they earlier used gynecological surgery, to calm their unruly patients [58, 59, 88].

It is a plausible hypothesis that observed sex differences in morbidity and use of health services are influenced by physician as well as by patient behavior. Physicians prescribe drugs, recommend surgery, and hospitalize their patients—and all of these actions are directed more frequently toward women than toward men. However, there are no well designed studies in which the relative influence of physician and patient on diagnostic and treatment outcomes is directly compared, and related to variations in sex role expectations. Furthermore, the attention of investigators using the institutionalized sex roles framework has been directed toward women, as noted earlier. There has been no comparable effort to determine how sex role expectations may affect the definition and treatment of complaints presented by men, so it is difficult to evaluate the extent to which women's experience is unique. Thus, while the hypothesis of medical practitioner influence on reported sex differences in health status is both intriguing and important, it has so far received very little systematic support.

Summary and Directions for Future Research

The purpose of this paper has been to summarize current knowledge concerning sex differences in mortality, morbidity, and use of health services, and to indicate a few of the methodological and interpretive problems that are presented by these data. The limitations of this review both in scope and in breadth of focus have already been noted. In trying to cover the most important points, many interesting, but isolated, findings have not been reported. Furthermore, the data are not as international in scope as the author would have preferred.

With these limitations in mind, the principle points of the review may be briefly recapitulated. In all developed countries, male mortality rates are higher than the rates of females, but in all countries for which data are available, women report more acute illness than men and make greater use of health services. Within the framework set by this broad pattern, there are systematic variations in the direction and magnitude of sex differences by cause of death and disease, by age, and by marital status. These variations suggest that the social and psychological concomitants of gender identify play a major role in accounting for observed sex differences in health status. Several alternative interpretations of this role have been advanced, and are outlined in this review.

Between the wealth of statistical data on sex differences in disease and the limited, often causal efforts at interpretation of these data, there is a profound gap of both theory and method. This gap is due partly to the relative inaccessibility to social scientists of data frequently buried in administrative reports, and partly to a lack of sustained and self-conscious attention to these data from a sociological perspective. Consequently, although the broad pattern of sex differences is reasonably clear, there have been very few detailed analyses, either of this pattern itself or of the underlying processes by which it is generated. Currently, the most important tasks of investigators interested in sex differences in disease and medical treatment are, first, to focus on the answering of specific questions, defined so that the answers are relevant to an underlying theoretical framework, and secondly, to encourage the collection of strictly comparable morbidity and utilization data in a variety of countries, using the same health indices. While the collection of statistics and their tabulation by sex will doubtless continue, this effort needs to be supplemented and informed by more careful attention to the meaning of these statistics. The choice of specific questions to which future research attention might be directed is partly a matter of personal preference. However, certain issues appear to the author to have particular importance, and it is to these issues that the following remarks are addressed.

There is, in the first place, a clear need for further refinement and clarification of the health indices that are currently employed. In the absence of information concerning the relative contribution of biological, psychological, and social processes to reported disease rates, it is difficult to know whether research in the area of sex differences should focus primarily on illness itself, on illness behavior, or on the behavior of medical practitioners. Secondly, in order to move beyond the description of sex differences to the explanation of these differences, the focus of research should be on the study of deliberately selected variations both in sex-linked behavior patterns and in illness and utilization patterns. For example, while it is clear that marital status is associated with substantial variation in patterns of illness and illness behavior among both men and women, the basis or bases of these variations have not been determined. Further clarification of this issue requires, as a first step, isolation of the specific social and/or biological variables for which martial status is an index and, secondly, examination of the consequences of differences in these underlying variables for mortality, morbidity, and use of health services.

Variation by marital status is only one of several types of variation in the overall pattern of sex differences that are highlighted by this review. Understanding of the overall pattern will be most rapidly advanced by research that is focused on specific variations, selected either on a theoretical basis, in order to test the value of one or more interpretive frameworks, or because they present a particular empirical problem that demands solution.

References

1. Linton R. *The Study of Man.* Appleton Century, New York, 1936.
2. Nathanson C. A. Illness and the feminine role: a theoretical review. *Soc. Sci. of Med.* **9**, 57, 1975.
3. Gove W. R. and Tudor J. Adult sex roles and mental illness. *Am. J. Sociol.* **78**, 812, 1973.
4. Philips D. L. and Segal B. E. Sexual status and psychiatric symptoms. *Am. sociol. Rev.* **34**, 58, 1969.
5. Broverman I. K. *et al.* Sex roles stereotypes and clinical judgements of mental health. *J. Consulting clin. Psychol.* **34**, 1, 1970.
6. Cheek F. E. A serendipitous finding: sex roles and schizophrenia. *J. abn. soc. Psychol.* **69**, 392, 1964.
7. Dohrenwend B. P. and Dohrenwend B. S. *Social Status and Psychological Disorder: A Causal Inquiry.* Wiley, New York, 1969.
8. Spiegelman M. and Erhardt C. L. International comparisons of mortality and longevity. In *Mortality and Morbidity in the United States*, pp. 39–64 (edited by Erhardt C. L. and Berlin J. E.). Harvard University Press, Cambridge, 1974.
9. Fuchs V. R. *Who Shall Live? Health, Economics, and Social Choice.* Basic Books, New York, 1975.
10. Retherford R. D. *The Changing Sex Differential in Mortality.* International Population and Urban Research, University of California, Berkeley. Studies in Population and Urban Demography No. 1. Greenwood Press, Westport, Conn., 1975.
11. Madigan F. C. Are sex mortality differentials biologically caused? *Milbank meml Fund Q.* **21**, 202, 1957.
12. Enterline P. E. Causes of death responsible for recent increase in sex mortality differentials in the United States. *Milbank meml Fund Q.* **38**, 313, 1961.
13. Preston S. H. An international comparison of excessive adult mortality. *Population Studies* **24**, 5, 1970.
14. Fairfield L. Health of professional women. *The Medical Woman's Journal* **34**, 95, 1927.
15. Avnet H. H. *Physician Service Patterns*

and Illness Rates. Group Health Insurance, Inc., 1967.

16. Anderson O. W. and Andersen R. Patterns of use of health services. In *Handbook of Medical Sociology*, pp. 386–406 (edited by Freeman H. E. *et al.*). Prentice-Hall, Englewood Cliffs, New Jersey, 1972.

17. Cole P. Morbidity in the United States. In *Mortality and Morbidity in the United States*, pp. 65–104 (edited by Erhardt C. L. and Berlin J. E.). Harvard University Press, Cambridge, 1974.

18. Verbrugge L. M. Morbidity and mortality in the United States: a riddle of the sexes. Unpublished paper. Department of Social Relations and Center for Metropolitan Planning and Research, Johns Hopkins University, Baltimore, 1975.

19. Office of Population Censuses and Surveys, Social Survey Division. *The General Household Survey, Introductory Report.* H.M.S.O., London, 1973.

20. U.S. Department of Health, Education, and Welfare. *Current Estimates from the Health Interview Survey, United States, 1971.* Vital and Health Statistics, Series 10, No. 79.

21. White K. L. *et al.* Ecologic results. In *International Comparisons of Medical Care*, pp. 31–44 (edited by Rabin D. L.). *Milbank meml Fund Q.* **50**, 1, 1972.

22. Shuval J. T. *et al. Social Functions of Medical Practice.* Jossey-Bass, San Francisco, 1970.

23. Nyman K. and Kalimo E. National sickness insurance and the use of physicians' services in Finland. *Soc. Sci. & Med.* **7**, 541, 1973.

24. Densen P. M. *et al.* Concerning high and low utilizers of services on a medical care plan and the persistance of utilization levels over a three-year period. *Milbank meml Fund Q.* **37**, 217, 1959.

25. Kessel N. and Shepard M. The health and attitudes of people who seldom consult a doctor. *Medical Care* **3**, 6, 1965.

26. Solon J. A. Patterns of medical care: sociocultural variations among a hospital's outpatients. *Am. J. publ. Hlth* **55**, 884, 1966.

27. Andersen R. and Anderson O. W. *A Decade of Health Services.* University of Chicago Press, Chicago, 1967.

28. U.S. Public Health Services. *Population Characteristics and Participation in the Poliomyelitis Vaccination Program.* PHS No. 723, U.S. Government Printing Office, Washington, D.C., 1969.

29. Foster A. *et al.* Use of health services in relation to the physical home environment of an Indian population. *Publ. Hlth Repts* **88**, 715, 1973.

30. Suchman E. Social patterns of illness and medical care. *J. Hlth hum. Behav.* **6**, 2, 1965.

31. Feldman J. J. *The Dissemination of Health Information.* Aldine, Chicago, 1966.

32. Lerner M. *Hospital Use by Diagnosis.* Research Series No. 19. Center for Health Administration Studies, University of Chicago, Chicago, 1961.

33. U.S. Department of Health, Education, and Welfare. *Inpatient Utilization of Short-Stay Hospitals by Diagnosis, United States, 1968.* Vital and Health Statistics, Series 13, No. 12, 1973.

34. Statistics Canada. *Hospital Morbidity.* Ottawa, 1971.

35. Boucher L. Canadian women: their vital and health statistics. Health Division, Statistics Canada, Ottawa, 1975.

36. U.S. Department of Health, Education, and Welfare. *Surgical Operations in Short-Stay Hospitals, United States, 1968.* Vital and Health Statistics, Series, 13, No. 11, 1973.

37. U.S. Department of Health, Education, and Welfare. *Average Length of*

Stay in Short-Stay Hospitals: Demographic Factors, United States, 1968. Vital and Health Statistics, Series 13, No. 13, 1973.

38. Feldstein P. J. Research on the demand for health services. *Milbank meml Fund Q.* **44,** 128, 1966.

39. Dunnell K. and Cartwright A. *Medicine Takers, Prescribers, and Hoarders.* Routledge & Kegan Paul, London, 1972.

40. Levine J. The Nature and Extent of Psychotropic Drug Usage in the United States. Washington: Statement before the Subcommittee on Monopoly of the Selected Committee on Small Business: 9, 1969.

41. U.S. Department of Health, Education, and Welfare. *Prescribed and Nonprescribed Medicines. Type and Use of Medicines, United States, July 1964–June 1965.* Vital and Health Statistics, Series 10, No. 39, 1967.

42. Gove W. R. Sex, marital status, and mortality. *Am. J. Sociol.* **79,** 45, 1973.

43. World Health Organization. II. Special Subject. Morbidity statistics: hospital in-patients, 1964. *World Health Statistics Rept* **21,** 1968.

44. World Health Organization. II. Special Subject. Morbidity statistics: hospital in-patients, 1968. *World Health Statistics Rept* **24,** 1971.

45. World Health Organization. II. Special subject: children at school age and their mortality and hospital morbidity throughout the world. *World Health Statistics Rept.* **28,** 1975.

46. Smith-Rosenberg C. and Rosenberg C. The female animal: medical and biological views of woman and her role in nineteenth century America. *J. Am. History* **60,** 332, 1973.

47. U.S. Department of Health, Education, and Welfare. *Limitation of Activity Due to Chronic Conditions, United States, 1969 and 1970.* Vital and Health Statistics, Series 10, No. 80, 1973.

48. Passman M. J. Hospital utilization by Blue Cross members in 1964 according to selected demographic and enrollment characteristics. *Inquiry* **3,** 82, 1966.

49. Berkman P. L. Spouseless motherhood, psychological stress, and physical morbidity. *J. Hlth soc. Behav.* **10,** 323, 1969.

50. Rivkin M. O. Contextual effect of families on female responses to illness. Unpublished Ph.D. dissertation. Johns Hopkins University, Baltimore, 1972.

51. Ortmeyer C. E. Variations in mortality, morbidity, and health care by marital status. In *Mortality and Morbidity in the United States,* pp. 159–188 (edited by Erhardt C. L. and Berlin J. E.). Harvard University Press, Cambridge, 1974.

52. Renee K. S. Health and marital experience in an urban population. *J. Marriage and the Family* **33,** 337, 1971.

53. Gove W. R. The relationship between sex roles, marital status, and mental illness. *Social Forces* **51,** 34, 1972.

54. Durkheim E. *Suicide.* The Free Press, Glencoe, Illinois, 1951.

55. U.S. Department of Health, Education, and Welfare. *Physician Visits, Volume and Interval Since Last Visit—United States, 1971.* Vital and Health Statistics, Series 10, No. 97, 1975.

56. Gross H. S. *et al.* The effect of race and sex on the variation of diagnosis and disposition in a psychiatric emergency room. *J. nerv. ment. Dis.* **148,** 638, 1969.

57. Singer B. S. and Osborn R. W. Social class and sex differences in admission patterns in the mentally retarded. *Am. J. ment. Deficiency* **75,** 160, 1970.

58. Cooperstock R. Sex differences in the use of mood-modifying drugs: an explanatory model. *J. Hlth soc. Behav.* **12,** 238, 1971.

59. Barker-Benfield B. The spermatic economy: a nineteenth century view of sexuality. *Feminist Studies* **1,** 45, 1972.

60. Smith-Rosenberg C. The hysterical woman: sex roles and role conflict in nineteenth century America. *Soc. Res.* **39,** 652, 1972.

61. Lennane K. J. and Lennane R. J. Alleged psychogenic disorders in women—a possible manifestation of sexual prejudice. *New Engl. J. Med.* **288,** 288, 1973.

62. Wood A. D. The fashionable diseases: women's complaints and their treatment in nineteenth century America. *J. interdisciplinary History* **4,** 25, 1973.

63. Ehrenreich B. and English D. *Complaints and Disorders: The Sexual Politics of Sickness.* Glass Mountain Pamphlet No. 2. The Feminist Press, Old Westbury, New York, 1973.

64. Ehrenreich B. Gender and objectivity in medicine. *Int. J. Hlth Serv.* **4,** 617, 1974.

65. Barker R. G. *et al. Adjustment to Physical Handicap and Illness.* Social Science Research Council, New York, 1953.

66. Mechanic D. Perception of parental responses to illness: a research note. *J. Hlth hum. Behav.* **6,** 253, 1965.

67. Glaser W. A. *Social Settings and Medical Organization.* Atherton Press, New York, 1970.

68. Parsons T. and Fox R. Illness, therapy, and the modern urban American family. *J. soc. Issues* **8,** 31, 1952.

69. U.S. Department of Health, Education, and Welfare. *Net Differences in Interview Data on Chronic Conditions and Information Derived From Medical Records.* Vital and Health Statistics, Series 2, No. 57, 1973.

70. U.S. Department of Health, Education, and Welfare. *The Influence of Interviewer and Respondent Psychological and Behavioral Variables on the Reporting in Household Interviews.* Vital and Health Statistics, Series 2, No. 26, 1968.

71. U.S. Department of Health, Education, and Welfare. *Quality Control and Measurement of Nonsampling Error in the Health Interview Survey.* Vital and Health Statistics, Series 2, No. 54, 1973.

72. Naeye R. L. *et al.* Neonatal mortality, the male disadvantage. *Pediatrics* **48,** 902, 1971.

73. Hamburg D. A. and Lunde D. T. Sex hormones in the development of sex differences in human behavior. In *The Development of Sex Differences*, pp. 1–24 (edited by Maccoby E. E.). Stanford University Press, Stanford, California, 1966.

74. Davidson, R. G. The Lyon hypothesis. *J. Pediatrics* **65,** 765, 1964.

75. Washburn T., Medearis D. and Childs B. Sex differences in susceptibility to infection. *Pediatrics* **35,** 57, 1965.

76. Childs B. Genetic origin of some sex differences among human beings. *Pediatrics* **35,** 798, 1965.

77. Michaels R. H. and Rogers K. D. A sex difference in immunologic responsiveness. *Pediatrics* **47,** 120, 1971.

78. Moriyama I. M., Kruegar D. E. and Stamler J. *Cardiovascular Diseases in the United States.* Harvard University Press, Cambridge, 1971.

79. Lilienfeld A. M., Levin M. L. and Kessler I. I. *Cancer in the United States.* Harvard University Press, Cambridge, 1972.

80. Cassell J. Physical illness in response to stress. In *Social Stress*, pp. 189–209 (edited by Levine S. and Scotch N. A.). Aldine, Chicago, 1970.

81. Dodge D. L. and Martin W. T. *Social Stress and Chronic Illness.* University of Notre Dame Press, Notre Dame, 1970.

82. Hinkle L. E., Jr. and Wolff H. G.

Health and the social environment: experimental investigations. In *Explorations in Social Psychiatry*, pp. 105–137 (edited by Leighton A. H. *et al.*). Basic Books, New York, 1957.

83. Nathanson C. A. and Rhyne M. B. Social and cultural factors associated with asthmatic symptoms in children. *Soc. Sci. & Med.* **4**, 293, 1970.

84. Scotch N. A. Sociocultural factors in the epidemiology of Zulu hypertension. *Am. J. publ. Hlth* **53**, 1206, 1963.

85. Wardwell W. I., Bahnson C. B. and Caron H. S. Social and psychological factors in coronary heart disease. *J. Hlth hum. Behav.* **4**, 154, 1963.

86. Wardwell W. I., Hyman M. and Bahnson C. B. Stress and coronary heart disease in three field studies. *J. chron. Dis.* **17**, 73, 1964.

87. Suchman E. A. Accidents and deviance. *J. Hlth soc. Behav.* **11**, 4, 1970.

88. Fidell L. and Prather J. Mood-modifying drug use in middle class women. Paper presented at the Western Psychological Association Meeting, Sacramento, California, 25 April 1975.

4   MEDICAL CARE AND MORTALITY: RACIAL DIFFERENCES IN PREVENTABLE DEATHS

Steffie Woolhandler, David U. Himmelstein, Ralph Silber, Michael Bader, Martha Harnly, and Alice A. Jones

Introduction

Black Americans continue to suffer markedly higher rates of death and disease than whites, undoubtedly due to class and racial oppression rather than genetic factors. However, it remains uncertain whether health services contribute to, have little effect on, or ameliorate inequalities in health. Many studies have documented racial and class disparities in health care (1, 2), lending support to the view that unequal care is in part responsible for the disparities in health. However, some have argued that the contribution of health care to health is minimal, and point out that little research convincingly relates the differences in the process of care to health outcomes (3–5). This view implies that inequalities in health care are a comparatively unimportant aspect of racial and class inequalities in U.S. society, and are unlikely to be important causes of disparities in health. Finally, over the past 20 years the availability of medical services for minorities and the poor has improved, and some have suggested that only relatively minor inequalities remain (6). If this were the case then health care might be expected to attenuate inequalities caused by oppression in other aspects of life.

The effects of health care are likely to be most pronounced in those categories of illness for which effective preventive or curative measures are available. The Working Group on

SOURCE: *International Journal of Health Services* 15, no. 1 (1985): 1–11. © 1985, Baywood Publishing Co., Inc.

Preventable and Manageable Diseases, a panel of medical experts chaired by Dr. David Rutstein, has developed lists of conditions in which the consistent application of existing knowledge would be expected to prevent death and/or disability (7). For some highly preventable conditions, they suggest that a single death should prompt an investigation into possible failures in medical care, as has been done in some locales in response to maternal deaths. They also propose that rates of death and disability due to a wider range of preventable and manageable conditions may reflect the contribution of medical care to health status as a community level and serve as a means to measure the overall quality of medical care. The working group's concept of medical intervention is broad, and the lists include conditions preventable by community education and public health measures, as well as those for which effective individual therapy is available.

We have employed the methodology proposed by Rutstein *et al.* to examine racial differences in causes of death in Alameda County, California where previous studies of large random samples of the population have documented consistent racial differences in health care (8–14). If inequalities in health services are in part responsible for excess black mortality, then blacks would be expected to suffer particularly high rates of medically preventable deaths. Conversely, if medical services principally ameliorate the health effects of broader social inequalities, rates of preventable death for blacks and

whites might be similar, and excess mortality among blacks would be accounted for predominantly by nonpreventable causes. Finally, if health services have little influence on health inequalities, black/white differences should be similar for both preventable and non-preventable causes of death.

Materials and Methods

Alameda County, California is an urban and suburban area on the eastern shore of the San Francisco Bay with a racially and economically diverse population. We obtained a list of all deaths of county residents for the year 1978 from the Alameda County Health Care Services Agency. Deaths were tabulated by race, sex, age, and cause of death coded according to the International Classification of Diseases (ICDA), eighth revision. Population estimates for 1978 were made by linear interpolation of 1970 and 1980 census figures.

The Working Group on Preventable and Manageable Conditions developed three lists of conditions, classified according to ICDA-8 codes, to serve as indices of the quality of medical care. Their List A is comprised of conditions the occurrence of a single case of which suggests inadequate preventive or therapeutic medical care. Conditions included in List B are considered indicative of poor quality of care if optimal rates (which are not specified) are exceeded. The working group recognized that the efficacy of medical interventions in the prevention and management of many conditions remains uncertain and requires further study. Examples of such conditions including alcoholism, homicides, and mental disorders are given in List C. The Lists have recently been updated for use with ICDA-9.

We defined a death as due to a preventable or manageable cause if it resulted from a condition included in Working Group Lists A or B. Conditions in which the working group specified that some proportion of cases was preventable or manageable were included if we judged that proportion to be greater than 50 percent, based upon review of the relevant medical literature. The working group specified only examples of conditions which might comprise List C. We therefore expanded the list to include all diagnoses primarily associated with drug and alcohol abuse, mental disorders, accidents, suicides, homicides and other external causes of death. Because the role of public health and medical intervention is especially uncertain in deaths due to causes in List C, we analyzed such deaths separately. All modifications were specified prior to data analysis. Deaths due to causes not included in any of the three lists were defined as "non-preventable."

Statistical Methods

The Mantel Haenszel chi square statistic was used to analyze differences in death rates for stratified samples (15). Fisher's exact test was used to analyze differences in death rates when expected numbers were small. Age-adjusted death rates for all ages combined and for those un-

der 65 were computed by the direct method and standardized to a population with an age distribution intermediate between those of the black and white populations of Alameda County. Differences in the proportion of all deaths which were due to preventable and manageable causes were analyzed by dividing the difference in standardized rates by its standard error and assuming that this ratio (approximately) follows a normal distribution (16). Potential years of life lost before the age of 65 were computed according to the method used in Morbidity and Mortality Weekly Reports (17).

Results

There were 7,143 deaths among the 958,830 blacks and whites of Alameda County in 1978, a crude death rate of 745 per 100,000 population. Age-specific and age-adjusted rates of death due to all causes are shown in Table 1 and Figure 1. Among blacks under 65 years of age, men have total death rates 65 percent higher and women 48 percent higher than the corresponding white groups ($p < .01$ for each sex). The black/white differentials for all ages combined are smaller but remain highly significant ($p < .01$ for each sex).

There were 1,726 deaths due to causes included in Working Group Lists A or B, a crude rate of 180 per 100,000 population. Nine-hundred and thirty-one deaths (97 per 100,000 population) were attributed to causes included in List C. Table 2 presents age-adjusted mortality rates

TABLE 1   Total Death Rates by Age, Sex, and Race

Age (years)	Deaths per 100,000 Population			
	White Males	*Black Males*	*White Females*	*Black Females*
0–1	1074	2035	998	1896
1–14	37	45	34	29
15–24	167	191	55	69
25–34	188	354	88	95
35–44	226	600	158	306
45–54	733	1414	435	863
55–64	1689	2347	1059	1294
65–74	3904	3863	2271	2664
75–84	9090	8276	5561	3014
85 +	18038	13226	13010	8555
0–64*	372	614	234	344
All Ages*	825	1006	697	749

*$p < .01$ for difference between blacks and whites of each sex.

for each of the three working group lists. For each list, rates for blacks under 65 years of age were significantly ($p<.05$) higher for each sex, with the exception of List C, for which females of both races had similar rates. When all ages are considered, there is a nonsignificant trend toward higher black rates for List A; findings for Lists B and C remain unchanged.

The age-specific and age-adjusted rates of death due to preventable and manageable causes, defined as

FIGURE 1   Total Death Rates by Age and Race

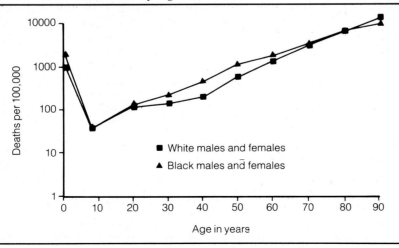

TABLE 2 Rates of Deaths from Causes Included in Working Group Lists A, B, and C by Race and Sex

Working Group List and Age Strata Analyzed	Death Rate per 100,000 Population			
	White Males	Black Males	White Females	Black Females
List A[a]				
all ages	136	156	66	82
0–64 years*	65	106	46	64
List B[b]				
all ages*	59	96	52	81
0–64 years*	29	68	17	41
List C[c]				
all ages**	116	170	61	63
0–64 years**	103	162	48	53

[a]Single cases considered evidence of failure of prevention.
[b]Elevated rates considered evidence of failure of prevention.
[c]Socio-medical conditions demanding further study to define indices of failures of prevention.
*$p < .05$ for difference between blacks and whites of each sex.
**$p < .05$ for difference between black males and white males.

conditions included in Lists A or B are shown in Table 3 and Figure 2. The overall rate for blacks compared to whites was 26 percent higher for males and 36 percent higher for females ($p < .01$ for each sex). The difference was most striking among people less than 65 years of age for

TABLE 3 Rates of Death Due to Preventable and Manageable Conditions (Working Group Lists A + B) by Age, Sex, and Race

Age (years)	Deaths per 100,000 Population			
	White Males	Black Males	White Females	Black Females
0–1	1074	2035	998	1896
1–14	7	12	4	8
15–24	17	38	12	40
25–34	31	104	16	11
35–44	40	122	24	53
45–54	147	347	94	168
55–64	435	546	257	341
65–74	1014	1054	431	560
75–84	1899	1586	672	957
85 +	3232	645	905	737
0–64*	94	174	64	105
All Ages*	195	251	118	164

*$p < .01$ for difference between blacks and whites of each sex.

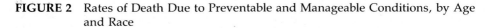

FIGURE 2   Rates of Death Due to Preventable and Manageable Conditions, by Age and Race

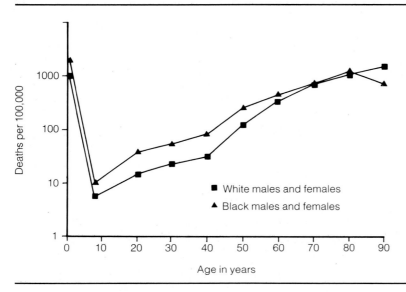

whom black death rates exceeded white death rates by 85 percent for males and 64 percent for females ($p<.01$ for each sex).

Preventable and manageable conditions accounted for a higher proportion of total deaths among blacks than whites in the younger age groups, while the proportions were similar among the elderly of both races. Causes included in Lists A or B accounted for 43 percent of all deaths among blacks younger than 35 and 33 percent among whites younger than 35 ($p<.01$), while among those less than 65 years old the figures were 28 percent of black deaths and 25 percent of white deaths ($p = .08$). Figure 3 depicts the ratio of black to white death rates due to all causes as compared to this ratio for death rates due to preventable and manageable conditions.

To examine the contribution of potentially preventable deaths to the higher death rates from all causes among blacks as compared to whites, we calculated the proportion of the excess total death rates among blacks less than 65 years of age that could be explained by the excess rates of death due to causes in Lists A or B. This amounted to 33 percent for males and 37 percent for females. When deaths due to causes in List C are included as "preventable," the excess "preventable" deaths among blacks accounted for 57 percent and 43 percent of the excess total death rates for black men and women respectively as compared to whites. Deaths from preventable and manageable conditions (Lists A and B) accounted for 4,147 years of life lost up to the age of 65 per 100,000 blacks less than 65 years old, while the comparable

FIGURE 3 Ratio of Black Death Rates to White Death Rates: All Causes, and Preventable and Manageable Conditions

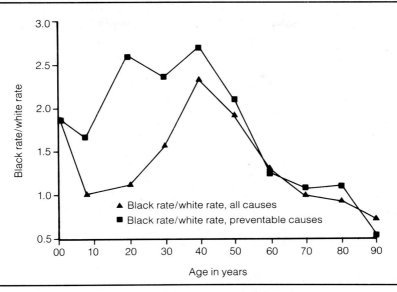

figure for whites was 1,899 per 100,000. This amounted to 44 percent of total years of life lost up to the age of 65 among blacks and 32 percent among whites ($p < .01$).

Eleven percent of deaths due to causes in Lists A or B were in infants. Since differentials in infant mortality rates are well recognized, we explored whether the Rutstein Methodology provides additional information by repeating our analyses with infants excluded. Significant ($p < .05$) black/white differences persisted in rates of total deaths, deaths due to preventable and manageable conditions, and the proportion of total deaths accounted for by preventable and manageable conditions. The calculated years of life lost up to age 65 per 100,000 population due to causes included in Lists A or B was diminished by more than 50 percent to 2,011 for blacks and 768

for whites. However the racial difference in years of life lost remained highly significant ($p < .01$) when infant deaths were excluded, and the black/white ratio actually increased from 2.2 to 2.6.

Subgroup analysis of specific preventable and manageable conditions revealed significant ($p < .05$) excess black rates of infant mortality, neoplasm of the thoracic organs, hypertension and its complications, and acute pulmonary infection in young persons. Higher black rates that did not achieve statistical significance were observed for cervical cancer, laryngeal cancer, cor pulmonale, diabetes with mention of acidosis or coma, and peptic ulcer. The only category for which white rates significantly exceeded those of blacks was chronic obstructive lung disease. Among conditions included in List C, black excesses were noted for

TABLE 4   Causes of Death for Which Blacks and Whites Experienced Differing Rates but Not Included in Lists A, B, or C

ICDA-8 Code	Causes of Death
Causes for which black death rates exceeded white death rates	
38.9	Bacteremia, unspecified organism
150	Neoplasm of the esophagus
151	Neoplasm of the stomach
199	Neoplasm, site unspecified
250	Diabetes mellitus
286.9	Other coagulation defect
343.9	Cerebral palsy, not otherwise specified
425.9	Cardiomyopathy, not otherwise specified
438.2	Cerebral edema, excludes hypertensive encephalopathy
493	Exogenous asthma
514	Hypostatic pneumonia
573.9	Liver disease, not otherwise specified
Causes for which white death rates exceeded black death rates	
410–414	Ischemic heart disease[a]
486	Pneumonia[a]
188–189	Malignant urinary tract neoplasm
200–209	Malignant neoplasm of lymphatic and hematopoietic tissue

[a]Excess white death rates observed in older age groups only.

homicides, accidental poisonings, and mental disorders, while whites experienced higher death rates from suicides and motor vehicle accidents.

Significant ($p < .05$) black/white differences in death rates were observed for several causes tabulated as "non-preventable" which are listed in Table 4. Several categories for which blacks experienced higher rates appear to represent inadequate diagnoses or inadequately specified diagnoses (e.g., "neoplasm, site unspecified").

Discussion

In Alameda County, blacks had higher rates of total deaths and deaths amenable to prevention than whites. In young people, potentially avoidable deaths constituted a significantly greater proportion of total deaths among blacks than among whites. Among those over age 75, total death rates were higher for whites than for blacks. This finding, based on a small number of elderly blacks in our sample, is in accord with other studies whose authors have suggested that blacks in the United States who survive the rigors of social privation in early life may be a particularly hardy group (18).

Excess rates of death for blacks as compared to whites were found for all three of the Working Group Lists and for a large number of conditions. No single cause of death was responsible for a major proportion of the observed differences. The differences persisted when conditions well known to be in excess among blacks, such as hypertension and infant mortality, were excluded from analysis.

Reliance on vital statistics is both a strength and weakness of the Rutstein Methodology. While death certificates are widely available, they do not allow analysis of non-fatal conditions, and the recorded cause of death may be inaccurate (19, 20). Such inaccuracies may introduce bias if physicians systematically overdiagnose preventable conditions in blacks or underdiagnose them in whites. However, we found that blacks had higher death rates from many poorly specified diagnoses which were tabulated as "non-preventable," suggesting that more accurate diagnosis might strengthen our findings. In addition, the large number of poorly specified causes of death among blacks may itself be indicative of poor quality care. Finally, the consistent racial differences we observed in the ratio of preventable to non-preventable deaths suggests that the methodology does not merely divide causes of death into arbitrary or random categories.

The Rutstein Methodology has been employed by others to examine the importance of potentially avoidable illness as a cause of hospitalization, and of temporal or geographic variation in mortality and morbidity (12, 21–25). However, these studies have not examined social inequalities in detail, and have generally employed only subsets of conditions from the Working Group Lists. Of particular interest is a study of mortality rates in England and Wales which found wide geographic variation in the rates for 14 diseases selected for Working Group List A (24). The authors speculate that the observed variability might reflect the performance of local health services.

Implications

Racial inequalities in health closely parallel social and medical care inequalities in Alameda County. Unfortunately detailed data on social class is unavailable (26) and it is difficult to differentiate the health effects of class and racial oppression. In Alameda County in 1979, median household income for whites was $20,438 and $12,202 for blacks, figures which understate actual differences in purchasing power (e.g., rents are as much as 30 percent higher in a segregated black neighborhood). Racial inequalities in health care in the county have been extensively documented in several studies including some based on large random samples of the population. Blacks are less likely to have private health insurance; a greater proportion have never been to a physician for a checkup; blacks are four times as likely as whites to rely on public sector care; more than twice as many blacks as whites have received no immunizations; fewer black women receive Pap smears; and a smaller proportion of black than white hypertensive patients are under treatment (8–14). Among patients admitted to hospitals, blacks are more often admitted through an emergency room, are more frequently transferred from private to public hospital emergency rooms, and have a higher proportion of "Rutstein events" as a cause of hospitalization (12, 27).

Our findings suggest that these disparities in the quality of health care are an important contributor to unequal death rates. While blacks suffered high death rates from many illnesses, the black/white differential was significantly greater for preventable causes than for the non-preventable group. This pattern of mortality is not consistent with the hypothesis that medical care plays little role in, or alleviates health inequalities. If health services are irrelevant to health status, then black/white ratios for preventable and non-preventable causes of death should be approximately equal; if health care ameliorates health inequalities due to broader social factors, medically non-preventable deaths should account for most of the black excess.

These theoretical positions have important practical implications. Cost control has come to dominate health policy discussion, as health care benefits have become an important cost of production for corporations, and medical programs consume an increasing proportion of government social expenditures. Cutbacks in services are more palatable to the powerful health and hospitals industry than more fundamental approaches to cost containment such as the elimination of profit making in health care. In this climate the contention that health care inequalities are insignificant or unimportant has gained wide currency, and is an important ideological foundation for attacks on health services for minorities, the poor, and the working class as a whole.

The elimination of inequalities in health will doubtless require broad social and political change. However, our findings suggest that the universal availability of existing public health and medical measures could significantly improve the health and longevity of blacks in the United States and other oppressed groups.

References

1. Rudov, M. H., Santangelo, N. *Health Status of Minorities and Low Income Groups.* Health Resources Administration, Washington, D.C., 1979; DHEW publication no. (HRA) 79-627.
2. National Institute of Medicine Committee for a Study of the Healthcare of Racial/Ethnic Minorities and Handicapped Persons. *Health Care in a Context of Civil Rights.* National Academy Press, Washington, D.C., 1981.
3. Powles, J. On the limitations of modern medicine. *Science, Medicine, and Man* 1: 1–30, 1973.
4. McKeown, T. *The Role of Medicine.* Nuffield Provincial Hospitals Trust, London, 1976.
5. Illich, I. *Medical Nemesis.* Bantam Books, New York, 1977.
6. Aday, L. A., Andersen, R., and Fleming, G. V. *Health Care in the U.S.: Equitable for Whom?* Sage, Beverly Hills, 1980.
7. Rutstein, D. D., Berenberg, W., Chalmers, T.C., et al. Measuring the quality of medical care: a clinical method. *New England Journal of Medicine* 294: 582–588, 1976.
8. Human Population Laboratory Reports. State of California Department of Public Health, Berkeley, 1974.

9. Human Population Laboratory. Health and ways of living study (working paper). State of California Department of Public Health, Berkeley, 1982.

10. *Health Systems Plan for Alameda and Contra Costa Counties 1980–85*. Alameda-Contra Costa Health Systems Agency, Oakland, 1980.

11. Borhani, N. O., *Alameda Blood Pressure Study*. State of California Department of Public Health, Berkeley, 1968.

12. Anonymous. *Primary Care Notebook: Volume 4*. Alameda County Hospitals Project, Oakland, 1978.

13. Breslow, L., and Klein, B. Health and race in California. *American Journal of Public Health* 61: 763–775, 1971.

14. Report of the Community Investigating Team on Infant Mortality. Coalition to Fight Infant Mortality, Oakland, 1980.

15. Mantel, N., and Haenszel, W. Statistical aspects of the analysis of data from retrospective studies of disease. *Journal National Cancer Institute* 22: 719–748, 1959.

16. Armitage, P. *Statistical Methods in Medical Research*. John Wiley and Sons, New York, p. 387, 1977.

17. Anonymous. Introduction to Table V, premature deaths, monthly mortality, and monthly physician contacts—U.S. *Morbidity and Mortality Weekly Reports* 31: 109–110, 1982.

18. Manton, K. G., Poss, S. S., and Wing. S. The black/white mortality crossover: investigation from the perspective of the components of aging. *The Gerontologist* 19: 291–300, 1979.

19. Gittelsohn, A., and Royston, P. M. *Annotated Bibliography of Cause-of-death Validation Studies: 1958–1980*. National Center for Health Statistics, Hyattsville, Maryland, 1982; DHHS Publication no. (PHS) 82-1363. (Data evaluation and methods research; series 2, no. 89).

20. Gittelsohn, A., and Senning, J. Studies on the reliability of vital and health records: 1. comparison of cause of death and hospital record diagnoses. *American Journal of Public Health* 69: 680–689, 1979.

21. Epidemiology and Biostatistics Unit Detroit Department of Health. *1979 Data Book*. City of Detroit Dept. of Health, Detroit, 1980.

22. Anonymous. *Evaluating Health System Performance in Vermont Communities Using an Index of Avoidable Deaths and Disease*. Cooperative Health Information Center of Vermont, South Burlington, 1978.

23. McEnvoy, L. *The use of sentinel health events in a mortality surveillance system*. Missouri Center for Health Statistics, 1980.

24. Charlton, J. R. H., Hartley, R. M., Silver, R., and Holland, W. W. Geographic variation in mortality from conditions amenable to medical intervention in England and Wales. *Lancet* i: 691–696, 1983.

25. Kisch, A., de Sola, S. F. *Algorithms for Health Planners: Vol. 5, Preventable Death and Disease*. Rand Corporation, Santa Monica, 1977.

26. Terris, M. Desegregating health statistics. *American Journal of Public Health* 63: 477–480, 1973.

27. Himmelstein, D. U., Woolhandler, S., Harnly, M., et al. Patient transfers: medical practice as social triage. *American Journal of Public Health* 74: 494–497, 1984.

5   THE HEALTH OF THE MEXICAN ORIGIN POPULATION

Ronald Angel

The Changing Focus of Research

Early ethnographic studies of the health care beliefs and practices of the Mexican origin population focused primarily on folk practices in isolated rural communities and provided a picture in which folk medicine played an important role (Saunders, 1954, 1958; Rubel, 1966; Madsen, 1964; Clark, 1959). The ethnographers documented a system of diagnosis and treatment which was intimately interconnected with daily life and served as a reflection of the fundamental social relations between community members. In isolated rural communities the health care practices of the Mexican origin propulation of the Southwest were informed by very different traditions, including the folk medical lore of medieval Spain, local Indian folklore, Anglo folk medical practices, and finally, modern scientific medicine (Saunders, 1958).

The medical care practices documented in the earliest ethnographic studies were, even then, undergoing rapid transition as the influence of modern medicine was becoming more pervasive. The pace of that change has increased in recent years, and the importance of folk medicine has decreased proportionately. Traditional health care providers such as *curanderos* (folk healers) and *parteras* (midwives), though they still exist (Kay, 1978), have been losing ground to scientific medical practitioners. The advent of Medicare and Medicaid and the introduction of public health clinics have brought modern medicine to even the most isolated individuals. Nevertheless, popular medical knowledge and customs have been kept alive and are still employed today in conjunction with modern medicine by members of the Mexican origin community (Velimirovic, 1978).

These early ethnographic studies were extremely useful in illustrating how the folk medical practices of the Mexican origin population represented a complex theory of disease causation and treatment. They were, however, based upon small local samples which, for the most part, consisted of individuals in the lower social classes. More recent epidemiological research has begun to take into account the fact that the Mexican origin population has become predominantly urban and is made up of individuals in all social classes. As is the case for non-Hispanics, the health of Mexican origin individuals depends upon their social class and the health risks they are exposed to. Affluent individuals of Mexican origin experience the disease patterns typical of other middle-class Americans while poorer and less assimi-

SOURCE: Reprinted from *The Mexican American Experience: An Interdisciplinary Anthology* edited by Rudolfo O. de la Garza, et al. Copyright © 1985 by the University of Texas Press. By permission of the author and the publisher.

lated individuals are exposed to the health risks and suffer from the diseases found more often among the lower classes.

It is difficult, therefore, to characterize the general health level of the Mexican origin population as either better or worse than that of other groups. The patterns of morbidity are simply too complex and the impact of social class too important to speak of the health of this population as a whole. Nevertheless, since a large proportion of the Mexican origin population is poor, health problems which are associated with poverty are particularly important in the study of the health of this group. It is necessary, therefore, to examine the prevalence of specific conditions for different socioeconomic strata within the Mexican origin population and to explore how they are related to culture, education, occupation, family structure, and medical care to determine what factors affect the health of particular segments of the Mexican origin population. Such a detailed understanding would allow us to identify health risk factors which might be eliminated and to provide medical care in such a way as to make it accessible to the neediest segments of the Mexican origin population.

Data Sources

Studies of physical health are based upon three types of data: (1) mortality data; (2) physiological measurements and diagnoses; and (3) self-reports of health status. There are different problems associated with the collection and interpreta-

tion of each of these types of data and with inferences made from them. Mortality data is perhaps the most objective, since death is an unambiguous event. However, the gathering of mortality data and its completeness for Hispanic subgroups can be troublesome. For example, there is evidence indicating a substantial underreporting of infant deaths among the Mexican origin population of Texas (Palloni, 1978; Powell-Griner and Streck, 1982).

A population's mortality experience is usually expressed as a rate, that is, as the number of deaths occurring during a particular period, usually a year, for a specified number of people alive at the beginning of the year (the population at risk), for example 10,000. Mortality rates are usually age-adjusted since mortality is very different at various ages. It is high among infants, low for children and young adults and then increases with age. A major problem in the computation of mortality rates is that the numerator and denominator come from different sources. The numerator, or the number of deaths occurring per year, is collected from death certificates. The denominator, or the population at risk, is usually from census figures. Underregistration of deaths or undercounts of the population at risk can lead to erroneous death rates. This problem is not simply academic, since in both 1960 and 1970 there was a large undercount of young black males. The extent of underenumeration for the Mexican origin population is unknown.

Another problem with mortality is that it gives us information on the end stage of serious illness and tells us less about the prevalence of illness in various groups. An increasing number of the diseases of industrial civilization, such as diabetes, heart disease, and cancer are chronic, and individuals can live with them for some time given proper medical care. The probability of death from any particular cause is influenced by such factors as the availability of medical care and the life-style associated with one's social class. Mortality data, then, while it provides us with information on a group's general quality of life, gives us limited information of the prevalence of morbidity in various groups.

Diagnosed illnesses and physiological measures, such as blood pressure, blood glucose levels, and serum cholesterol, are objective assessments of important aspects of physical health but are unfortunately difficult and expensive to collect. While physiological measures can be gathered from representative population samples, rates of diagnosed illness are influenced by factors which determine whether one seeks medical care. Lower social class, for example, is associated with an increased incidence of diabetes and obesity, but may also reduce the probability that an individual seeks medical treatment for these conditions.

These problems as well as the relative economy and ease of collection of survey data lead to a great reliance on various forms of self-reported health in most health services research comparing the Mexican origin population to non-Hispanics (Andersen et al., 1981). Unfortunately, this sort of data is the least objective and most troublesome when comparing culturally distinct groups. Typically, in a study of this sort the respondent is asked whether his or her health is excellent, good, fair, or poor, or whether during a particular period his or her health has caused a great deal of worry or concern, or whether he or she has experienced pain. One commonly used self-reported health status measure consists of the number of days during some period the respondent had been kept in bed or away from his or her usual activities as the result of injury or illness. Another commonly used health status measure consists of lists of symptoms which the respondent is asked whether he or she has experienced. Other questions attempt to assess a person's physical ability to function normally. There are numerous variations on these questions but the main feature of them all is that they are self-reports and, therefore, subject to biases which may result from inaccurate memory and from social class and cultural factors that influence the perception and reporting of symptoms.

Major problems in epidemiological or health services research using these sorts of questions for the Mexican origin population result from inaccuracies in the translation of survey instruments; from differential response rates to different types of surveys, that is, mail, telephone, or personal interview; and as a result of bias stemming from the impact of culture on the understanding of and response to survey questions.

Unfortunately, the determination

of the extent of bias in self-reports is difficult since we rarely have information on actual health status against which to compare self-reports. Recent investigations of this problem with scales designed to assess feelings of depression find little evidence of systematic bias associated with Mexican ethnicity (e.g., Vernon, Roberts, and Lee, 1982). Unfortunately, this research is based on a small sample, very few of whom took the interview in Spanish. Additionally, it deals only with mental health, and the findings cannot be assumed to apply to self-reported physical health.

Angel and Cleary (1984) found that language of interview, which is a rough indicator of level of assimilation, is an important predictor of reported health within the Mexican origin population. This research suggests that self-reports of physical health status may have different meanings for those whose main language is Spanish than for those who are fluent in English. Language of interview may tap residual Mexican cultural influences on health, especially since those who are not fluent in English are likely to be recent immigrants (de la Garza and Brischetto, 1982). This research also provides evidence that health may consist of different dimensions, each of which may be related to ethnicity in a different way. Spanish-speaking Mexican origin individuals, for example, report generally lower overall health levels than non-Hispanics, but do not report the worry or concern about health or the number of physical symptoms which are associated with poorer general health for non-Hispanics. This may reflect reference group factors. If, for example, most of the people in one's immediate reference group have backaches from working in the fields, such a symptom may not seem worth mentioning. There is also evidence that members of this group are more likely than others to give socially approved answers to survey questions (Ross and Mirowski, 1983). Clearly, such a tendency would lead to biased responses if certain conditions or illnesses were not reported because they are considered to be socially unacceptable. Because of these and other methodological problems, then, the seriousness of bias in self-reports of health for the Mexican origin population remains open, especially for less assimilated individuals who are not fluent in English.

It is impossible to know, therefore, the extent to which differences in self-reported health reflect inadequate translation of the survey instrument or other cultural factors and the extent to which they reflect actual differences in health. In addition to these, a number of issue problems plague health survey research. The identification of the Mexican origin population, for example identification by Spanish surname or self-identification, is a major problem for health services research as it is for all research dealing with this group. With some of the methodological limitations in mind, then, let us turn to some of the differences between the Mexican origin population and non-Hispanics in mortality, morbidity, and physiological measures.

Mortality, Morbidity, and Physiological Measures

Though comparative morbidity and mortality data for the Mexican origin population is limited, there is evidence that they have higher death rates from cirrhosis of the liver, tuberculosis, diabetes, infectious and parasitic diseases, circulatory diseases, and accidents than non-Hispanics (Quesada and Heller, 1977; Aranda, 1971). Foreign-born women of Spanish surname in California have experienced an excess mortality from lung cancer beginning at age 45 when compared to Anglos. On the other hand, foreign-born males and native-born Mexican Americans of both sexes experienced lower cancer mortality rates (Menck et al., 1975). In Houston, Texas, in 1950 Mexican Americans experienced cancer death rates higher than those of blacks or Anglos. By 1960, however, only Mexican American women had elevated cancer mortality rates, while Mexican American men had the lowest rates for males (Roberts, 1977). These patterns differ for specific types of cancer. While Mexican origin individuals in Los Angeles in the early 1970s were at higher risk of cancer of the stomach, gallbladder, liver, and cervix than Anglos, they had lower rates of cancer of the mouth, colon, rectum, larynx, lung, bladder, prostate, testes, and breast (Menck et al., 1975). The reasons for these patterns are difficult to discern. Mexican origin individuals smoke less than Anglos, and this may account for their lower lung and mouth cancer rates. The relatively high rate of cervical cancer

among Mexican origin women, particularly those born in Mexico, may be the result of early and prolonged fertility. At the same time this may protect them from breast cancer, since breast feeding appears to protect females from breast cancer. Clearly, a great deal more research must be conducted before we understand the factors which increase or decrease the risk of cancer for the Mexican origin population.

In Colorado, at least until the 1960s, the Mexican origin population had higher age-adjusted death rates than non-Hispanics at each age level below the age of 76 (Moustafa and Weiss, 1968). In addition, even with what appears to be serious underreporting of infant deaths (e.g., Palloni, 1978; Powell-Griner and Streck, 1982) the Mexican origin population suffers a substantially higher infant mortality rate than the non-Hispanic population in Texas. In Houston, Texas, in both 1950 and 1960 the Mexican origin population had overall mortality rates higher than those of non-Hispanic whites (Roberts and Askew, 1972). On the other hand, in recent years the Mexican origin population in New Mexico has experienced lower death rates from lung cancer and from chronic obstructive pulmonary disease like chronic bronchitis and emphysema than the Anglo population (Samet et al., 1982).

While overall mortality rates for the Mexican origin population have been generally higher than those for Anglos, they have, for the most part, been lower than those for blacks (Roberts and Askew, 1972). In addition, for several years differentials in mortality have been declining for all three groups. Nevertheless, though mortality rates appear to be converging, both minority groups suffer excess infant mortality and mortality from certain causes, such as diabetes.

Mexican origin individuals suffer more obesity than non-Hispanics; experience more hyperglycemia, an indication of diabetes; and have higher serum triglyceride concentrations, which is a minor coronary heart disease risk factor. Mexicans are less informed than non-Hispanic about behaviors associated with the prevention of coronary heart disease. Despite these higher risk factor, however, coronary heart disease mortality among the Mexican origin population is showing the same decrease as it has for non-Hispanics (Hazuda et al., 1983).

One intriguing explanation for elevated rates of diabetes among the Mexican origin population is the possibility of a genetic tendency toward diabetes among this group deriving from the fact that the Mexican origin population is a combination of European and Indian ancestry. American Indians have extremely high rates of diabetes, and there is evidence that this may be genetically determined. The Mexican origin population has rates of hyperglycemia intermediate between those of non-Hispanics and the Pima Indians of Arizona, which would be compatible with a genetic mixing hypothesis (Stern et al., 1981).

One must be cautious in accepting this genetic explanation, however, since social class factors alone may account for both the greater prevalence of overweight and of diabetes. In the developed nations obesity is more prevalent among the poor and is a precursor of diabetes as well as a coronary heart disease risk factor itself. The fact that Mexican origin individuals are overrepresented in the lower classes where their tendency to overweight is increased may account for their higher rates of diabetes. Unfortunately, the studies which have been reported so far do not contain sufficient socioeconomic variation to determine the relative importance of genetic and socioeconomic factors. This research, however, promises to answer many important questions concerning relative health levels within the Mexican origin population.

Samet et al. (1982) found lower rates of chronic bronchitis, emphysema, and asthma among the Mexican origin population of New Mexico. In this study, as in many others, fewer Mexican origin individuals than non-Hispanics reported that they smoke. This seems to account for their lower rates of bronchitis and emphysema but not for their lower rates of asthma; Mexican origin rates of asthma are lower than those of non-Hispanics even after smoking is taken into account. These findings suggest the importance of environmental factors in chronic lung disease. New Mexico is an environmentally clean state, and this fact, combined with the lower rates of smoking by the Mexican origin population, may account for their lower rates of serious lung disease. This is one area in which comparisons with Puerto Ricans would be useful, since they live in a much more polluted environment and their asthma rates are higher than those of non-Hispanics (Rios, 1982).

In summary then, the majority of objective evidence which exists suggests that social class is a major determinant of the health levels of Mexican origin individuals. An individual's health depends upon a complex interaction of genetics, environment, and culture. The assessment of the relative importance of each of these factors is a challenge to a new generation of researchers.

Medical Care

As mentioned earlier, interest in the medical care utilization of the Mexican origin population has shifted from a concern with the influence of folk medicine to a desire to understand how social structural factors and medical care delivery system factors influence utilization.

As a consequence, in recent years, increasing attention has been paid to the impact of such variables as income, education, occupation, social isolation, the ownership of health insurance, the availability of services, and satisfaction with medical care (Andersen et al., 1981; Chesney et al., 1982). While ethnic culture, especially in terms of the degree of acculturation and language ability, continues to draw attention (Angel and Cleary, 1984; Chesney et at., 1982; Quesada, 1976; Quesada and Heller, 1977), health services research concerning the Mexican origin population is increasingly informed by an appreciation of the interaction between culture and social class. Since the ascriptive characteristic of Mexican ethnicity increases the probability of lower-class membership, and thereby increases one's health risks and lowers one's ability to purchase adequate medical

TABLE 1   Comparisons between Anglos, Blacks, and the Mexican Origin Populations

			Mexican Origin	
	Non-Hispanic	Black	English Interview	Spanish Interview
Median family income	$13,410	$8,907	$8,887	$6,853
Median age	38	36	29	37
Mean years of education	12.2	10.9	10.3	5.4
Mean family size	3.5	3.9	4.4	5.4
Percent below poverty	11.7	33.5	35.8	67.2
Percent with private health insurance	87.2	70.4	61.8	39.0
Average number of physician visits per year	3.7	4.5	4.6	2.1
(Unweighted N)	(2,941)	(607)	(276)	(201)

Note: These statistics are weighted to reflect actual population proportions. This table is from Angel and Cleary (1984).

care, Mexican ethnicity has a significant indirect effect on health and medical care utilization in addition to any direct effect it may have.

In spite of the gains of recent years, certain segments of the Mexican origin population continue to suffer serious socioeconomic disadvantage and to receive inadequate medical care. Table 1, for example, presents data collected in 1975 and 1976 from a sample of Mexican Americans in the Southwest (Andersen et al., 1981). These results are for adults between 18 and 64 and, for the Mexican origin sample, are presented separately for those who took the interview in Spanish and for those who took the interview in English. As one can see, Mexican Americans who took the interview in Spanish have large families and are severely handicapped in terms of income, education, and health insurance. In addition, while those Mexican Americans who took the interview in English reported an average number of visits to the doctor during the previous year similar to that of Anglos, those who took the interview in Spanish reported a much lower average number of visits.

This table illustrates the importance of examining differences within the Mexican origin population based upon level of acculturation. Studies which do not differentiate between individuals who are fluent in English and those who are not find little difference between the average number of physician visits per year between Anglos and Mexican origin individuals (e.g., Roberts and Lee, 1980). If, in our present sample, instead of dividing the Mex-

ican origin group into those who took the interview in Spanish and those who took it in English we were to base our estimate on the combined sample of Mexican Americans, it would appear that there is no substantial difference between them and Anglos. Such a statistic would obscure a serious unmet need for medical services among the least assimilated Mexican origin individuals. Though language of interview is frequently used as an approximation of level of acculturation (e.g., Angel and Cleary, 1984) behavioral scientists have recently been developing more refined scales of acculturation (Olmedo, Martinez, and Martinez, 1978; Montgomery and Orozco, 1984). It would be useful to employ such scales in health surveys to examine the effect of this important variable on health and on access to medical care.

The data, then, indicate that the disadvantages suffered by the Mexican origin population are disproportionately borne by those least fluent in English. This group is particularly disadvantaged in its ability to deal with the medical care establishment because of a general lack of Spanish-speaking doctors and other health professionals. Addressing the health care needs of Mexican origin individuals who speak only Spanish requires increasing the number of Spanish-speaking health care providers (Quesada and Heller, 1977). The absence of a sufficient number of Mexican origin health professionals not only reduces utilization of services by members of this group, but also has a negative impact on the quality of their interaction with health care providers (Quesada, 1976). When patients and doctor are separated by a gulf which results from different cultures and languages, it is unlikely that either party will be satisfied. The doctor will see the patient as uncooperative, and the patient will see the doctor as insensitive to his or her needs.

Occupation and Health

One major set of factors affecting the health of the Mexican origin population is occupational health hazards. There is very little information on the health consequences of work for the Hispanic population in general, but we might safely assume that if they are overrepresented in hazardous occupations their health will be disproportionately harmed. The occupational distribution of members of the Mexican origin population is, therefore, an important determinant of the health risks they face. A disproportionate percentage of the Hispanic population are employed in industries with the highest risks of illness, injury, and fatality. These were construction, mining, transportation, public utilities, agriculture, and manufacturing. However, there is a tremendous diversity in occupational concentration depending upon specific Hispanic ethnicity. While 54 percent of Cubans were employed in white-collar occupations in 1980, the job category with the lowest health risks, only 39 percent of Puerto Ricans, and 29 percent of Mexicans were in white-collar positions. On the other hand, while less than 1 percent of Cubans

were farm workers in 1980, 6 percent of Mexicans were farm workers (Dicker and Dicker, 1980). The effects of pesticides and inadequate medical care on the health of agricultural workers are a topic about which we know very little.

While broad industry classifications tell us something about the occupational health risks faced by the Mexican origin population, we need much more detailed information concerning the specific job hazards faced by individuals in this group. Within any particular industrial category, such as manufacturing, jobs differ greatly in terms of health risks. Certain manufacturing occupations expose workers to more dangerous processes and materials than others. If Mexican origin workers are disproportionately concentrated in the most hazardous occupations, they may suffer specific health problems.

Another area about which very little is known is the causes and consequences of work-related disability. A great deal of evidence indicates that health problems which interfere with one's ability to work have serious consequences for the worker and his or her family. The inability to work up to one's potential decreases earnings and total family income and greatly increases a family's dependence on welfare (Angel, 1984).

As with occupational health risks, the Hispanic population differs greatly in the proportion of adult males who report a work-limiting health condition (Angel, 1984). Table 2 presents data on the percentage of males of the various national origins

TABLE 2 Characteristics of Disabled Males, Aged 20 to 64

	Anglo		Mexican		Puerto Rican		Central/ South American	
	Disabled	Nondisabled	Disabled	Nondisabled	Disabled	Nondisabled	Disabled	Nondisabled
Personal characteristics								
Percent disabled	12.5		12.6		17.3		8.9	
Age	46.8	38.5	44.1	34.5	44.1	35.3	42.8	38.6
Education	13.0	10.7	7.4	9.8	7.6	10.3	10.7	11.5
Labor force characteristics								
Percent employed full-time	45	83	28	81	18	77	49	81
Wage rate	$3.92	$6.53	$1.99	$4.10	$1.85	$4.44	$2.84	$4.73
Individual income								
Annual earnings	$6,579	$12,697	$3,167	$8,086	$2,364	$8,317	$6,716	$9,571
Welfare:								
Percent receiving	4	1	12	1	27	4	14	2
Amount	$1,563	$1,012	$2,445	$1,740	$3,378	$1,905	$1,070	$1,869
Total income	$9,449	$13,746	$4,895	$8,623	$4,568	$8,945	$8,968	$10,115
Family characteristics								
Percent below poverty	12	4	29	14	51	12	18	8
Family earnings	$10,967	$17,668	$6,304	$11,371	$4,865	$11,433	$10,436	$13,504
Total family income	$14,865	$19,479	$8,606	$12,305	$7,910	$12,513	$13,395	$14,648
Unweighted N	2,247	15,689	273	1,891	73	357	38	367

Note: This table is an abbreviated version of one appearing in Angel (1984). The data are weighted to represent actual population proportions.

who report a disability, their work experience, and family incomes. While approximately 12.5 percent of Anglos and those of Mexican origin report a disability, 17 percent of Puerto Ricans report such a condition. On the other hand, only 9 percent of Central and South Americans (including Cubans) report a disability. This great diversity between groups is intriguing and, no doubt, accounted for by a number of factors. For example, the various groups are concentrated in different parts of the country, with Mexicans in the Southwest and Midwest, Cubans in Florida, and Puerto Ricans in the New York/New Jersey area. As mentioned earlier, they are also exposed to different occupational health risks. Those various groups may also be different in the extent to which the family deals with the disability of one of its members outside of the formal structures of government. Groups which are familistic, cohesive, and suspicious of the agencies of the larger society, as the Mexican origin population is characterized as being, may deal with disability at home.

When the disability rates presented in Table 2 are adjusted for other socioeconomic and demographic factors which might account for differences in disability, such as age, marital status, family income, and the unemployment rate and wage rate in the area of residence, it becomes clear that the Mexican origin population disability rate is far lower than one would expect (Angel, 1984). Though their overall rate of self-reported disability is similar to that of Anglos, they are exposed

to health hazards which should increase their rate considerably above that of Anglos. This study also revealed that Mexican origin individuals who are not fluent in English are most severely affected by disability. A lack of fluency in English makes it difficult for one to successfully deal with the governmental bureaucracies which formally label one disabled and thereby make one eligible for disability payments.

Clearly, then, while the Mexican origin population is exposed to the same types of health risks as other American workers, their greater concentration in the highest-risk industries exposes them to more of those hazards. As a consequence, there may be a great deal of disability among the Mexican origin population which has not been identified. This hidden disability represents an unknown amount of unmet need for social services. Again, as in other areas of health, there are large differences within the Mexican origin community depending upon occupation, education, and income.

In conclusion, then, it is increasingly clear that the health and medical care needs of the Mexican origin population are diverse and depend upon specific vulnerabilities related to social class, environmental, occupational, and life-style risk factors. Since earlier in this century the health of the Mexican origin population has improved, and their access to medical care has increased. They have shared in decreases in coronary heart disease rates and infant mortality with other Americans, and their life expectancy has increased. As a consequence, overall health differentials between Anglos and the Mexican origin population have shrunk, though they as yet have not entirely disappeared. The major health problems which remain then are, by and large, concentrated among specific subgroups, such as the poor, the least assimilated, and migrant workers. Progress in understanding the health care needs of the Mexican origin population requires understanding how Mexican ethnicity interacts with these various vulnerabilities to affect health levels and to interfere with access to needed medical care.

References

Andersen, Ronald, Sandra Zelman Lewis, Aida L. Giachello, Lu Ann Aday, and Grace Chiu. 1981. "Access to Medical Care among the Hispanic Population of the Southwestern United States," *Journal of Health and Social Behavior*, 22 (March):78–89.

Angel, Ronald. 1984. "The Costs of Disability for Hispanic Males," *Social Science Quarterly*, 65 (June):426–43.

Angel, Ronald, and Paul D. Cleary. 1984. "The Effects of Social Structure and Culture on Reported Health," *Social Science Quarterly*, 65 (September): 814–28.

Aranda, Robert G. 1971. "The Mexican American Syndrome," *American Journal of Public Health*, 64 (January):104–9.

Chesney, Alan P., Juan A. Chavira, Rogers P. Hall, and Howard E. Gary. 1982. "Barriers to Medical Care of Mexican-Americans: The Role of Social Class, Acculturation, and Social Isolation," *Medical Care*, 20 (September): 883–91.

Clark, Margaret. 1959. *Health in the Mexican American Culture* (Berkeley: University of California Press).

de la Garza, Rodolfo, and Robert R. Brischetto. 1982. *The Mexican American Electorate: A Demographic Profile*. Occasional Paper No. 1 (San Antonio: Southwest Voter Registration Education Project and University of Texas Center for Mexican American Studies).

Dicker, Lois, and Marvin Dicker, 1982. "Occupational Health Hazards Faced by Hispanic Workers: An Exploratory Discussion," *Journal of Latin Community Health*, 1 (Fall):101–7.

Hazuda, Helen P., Michael P. Stern, Sharon Parten Gaskill, Steven M. Haffner, and Lytt I. Gardner. 1983. "Ethnic Differences in Health Knowledge and Behaviors Related to the Prevention and Treatment of Coronary Heart Disease," *American Journal of Epidemiology*, 117 (June):717–28.

Kay, Margarita. 1978. "Parallel, Alternative, or Collaborative: *Curanderismo* in Tucson, Arizona," in Boris Velimirovic, ed., *Modern Medicine and Medical Anthropology in the United States-Mexico Border Population* (Washington, D.C.: Pan American Health Organization. World Health Organization, Scientific Publication No. 359): pp. 87–95.

Madsen, William. 1964. *The Mexican-Americans of South Texas* (New York: Holt, Rinehart & Winston).

Menck, H. R., B. E. Henderson, M. C. Pike, T. Mack, S. P. Martin, and J. SooHoo. 1975. "Cancer Incidence in the Mexican American," *Journal of the National Cancer Institute*, 55 (September):531–36.

Montgomery, Gary T., and Sergio Orozco. 1984. "Validation of a Measure of Acculturation for Mexican Americans," *Hispanic Journal of Behavioral Sciences*, 6 (March):53–63.

Moustafa, A. Taher, and Gertrud Weiss. 1968. *Health Status and Practice of Mexican Americans*. Mexican American Study

Project Advance Report No. 11 (Los Angeles: UCLA Graduate School of Business Administration).

Olmedo, Esteban L., Joe L. Martinez, and Sergio R. Martinez. 1978. "Measure of Acculturation for Chicano Adolescents," *Psychological Reports*, 42 (February):159–70.

Palloni, Alberto. 1978. "Application of an Indirect Technique to Study Group Differentials in Infant Mortality," in F. D. Bean and W. P. Frisbie, eds., *The Demography of Racial and Ethnic Groups* (New York: Academic Press): pp. 283–300.

Powell-Griner, Eve, and D. Streck. 1982. "A Closer Examination of Neonatal Mortality among the Texas Spanish Surname Population," *American Journal of Public Health*, 72 (September):993–99.

Quesada, Gustavo M. 1976. "Language and Communication Barriers for Health Delivery to a Minority Group," *Social Science and Medicine*, 10 (June): 323–27.

Quesada, Gustavo M., and Peter L. Heller. 1977. "Sociocultural Barriers to Medical Care among Mexican Americans in Texas: A Summary Report of Research Conducted by the Southwest Medical Sociology Ad Hoc Committee," *Medical Care*, 15 (May):93–101.

Rios, Lydia E. 1982. "Determinants of Asthma among Puerto Ricans," *Journal of Latin Community Health*, 1 (Fall): 25–40.

Roberts, Robert. 1977. "The Study of Mortality in the Mexican American Population," in Charles H. Teller, Leo F. Estrada, José Hernández, and David Alvirez, eds., *Cuantos Somos: A Demographic Study of the Mexican American Population.* (Austin: Center for Mexican American Studies, Monograph No. 2): pp. 131–55.

Roberts, Roberts E., and Cornelius Askew. 1972. "A Consideration of Mortality in Three Subcultures," *Health Services Reports* (formerly *Public Health Reports*), 87 (March):262–70.

Roberts, Robert E., and Eun Sul Lee. 1980. "Medical Care Use by Mexican-Americans." *Medical Care*, 18 (March): 266–81.

Ross, Catherine E., and John Mirowsky. 1983. "The The Worst Place and the Best Face," *Social Forces*, 62 (December):529–36.

Rubel, Arthur J. 1966. *Across the Tracks: Mexican-Americans in a Texas City* (Austin: University of Texas Press).

Samet, Jonathan M., Susan D. Schraag, Cheryl A. Howard, Charles R. Key, and Dorothy R. Pathak. 1982. "Respiratory Disease in a New Mexico Population Sample of Hispanic and Non-Hispanic Whites," *American Review of Respiratory Diseases*, 125 (February): 152–57.

Saunders, Lyle. 1954. *Cultural Differences and Medical Care: The Case of the Spanish-Speaking People of the Southwest* (New York: Russell Sage Foundation).

————. 1958. "Healing Ways in the Spanish Southwest," in E. Gartley Jaco, ed., *Patients, Physicians, and Illness* (Glencoe, Ill.: Free Press): pp. 189–206.

Stern, Michael P., Sharon Parten Gaskill, Clarence R. Allen, Jr., Virginia Garza, Jose L. Gonzales, and Reuel H. Waldrop. 1981. "Cardiovascular Risk Factors in Mexican Americans in Laredo, Texas," *American Journal of Epidemiology*, 113 (May):546–55.

Velimirovic, Boris, ed. 1978. *Modern Medicine and Medical Anthropology in the United States-Mexico Border Population* (Washington, D.C.: Pan American Health Organization, World Health Organization, Scientific Publication No. 359).

Vernon, Sally W., Robert E. Roberts, and Eun Sul Lee. 1982. "Response Tendencies, Ethnicity, and Depression Scores," *American Journal of Epidemiology*, 116 (September):482–95.

6 STRESS, COPING, AND SOCIAL SUPPORTS

Leonard I. Pearlin and Carol S. Aneshensel

Investigations into the harmful health consequences of stress have generally followed the basic paradigm illustrated in Figure 1. The problematic life circumstances that give rise to stress and tax the individual's ability to respond are of two general types: events, usually of an undesirable and relatively abrupt nature, that result in discontinuity or change requiring readjustment; and persistent or continuing problems that occur within ongoing social roles. Although typically considered discretely, these two sources of stress are interrelated. Thus, life event change may lead to stress by altering the meaning of existing role strain, intensifying strain, or creating new strains within social roles (Pearlin et al. 1981). Role strains often present themselves insidiously and become relatively fixed and ongoing in daily experiences as chronic, low-key frustrations and hardships (Pearlin and Lieberman 1979).

Included in the broad spectrum of health outcomes that have been studied as consequences of these "naturalistic" stressors are emotional distress, physical morbidity, and mortality. Stressful experience has been regarded as contributing to specific health conditions such as heart disease (e.g. Jenkins 1976) or cancer (e.g., Schmale and Iker 1971), as well as to nonspecific morbidity, including common, relately minor physical ailments such as colds, flu, or chronic pain (e.g., Aneshensel and Huba 1984) and psychological disorder. As emphasized in several recent overviews (Kasl 1984; Kessler, Price, and Wortman 1985; Thoits 1983), methodological problems plague this body of research and inhibit confidence in assertions about the etiological role of stress. These uncertainties notwithstanding, the weight of evidence indicates that stressful circumstances exert an influence on health and well-being (Bunney et al. 1982). The magnitude of the harmful impact of stress, however, has consistently been shown to be modest in size. This has served to direct attention to those factors that exacerbate, ameliorate, or otherwise mediate the impact of stress on health and well-being, specifically to the role of coping and social supports.

SOURCE: From "Coping and Social Supports: Their Functions and Applications" by Leonard I. Pearlin and Carol S. Aneshensel in *Applications of Social Science to Clinical Medicine and Health Policy*, Linda H. Aiken and David Mechanic, Editors. Copyright © 1986 by Rutgers, The State University. Reprinted with permission of Rutgers University Press.

FIGURE 1   The Basic Stress Paradigm

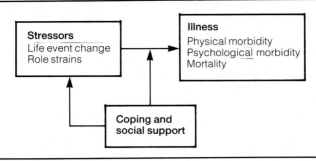

There is something beguilingly presumptive in the labels *coping* and *social supports*. The very terms imply a built-in positive consequence. They suggest that when people behave in a manner we designate as coping, or that when people have social relationships we refer to as supportive, certain desirable effects are taking place. However, this is not necessarily the case. In their study of people who had lost a spouse or child, for example, Wortman and Lehman (in press) find that would-be supporters were commonly judged by the bereaved individuals to be unhelpful. The authors speculate that would-be supporters are occasionally ineffective because the victims' loss can lead to feelings of threat, vulnerability, and helplessness on the part of the supporters. There may be, additionally, some uncertainty and anxiety over appropriate behavior, which in turn impedes empathic responses.

These findings are but a modest illustration of the broad array of mechanisms, forms, and limiting conditions that are involved in the study of coping and social supports. To immerse ourselves in these issues would quickly take us beyond the scope of this chapter. Therefore, we shall confine ourselves to an examination of the consequences or, as we refer to them, the functions of coping and social supports. Following in part from earlier conceptualizations (Pearlin and Schooler 1978), four types of functions can be distinguished: (1) *prevention* of the stressful situation; (2) *alteration* of the stressful situation; (3) *changing the meaning* of the situation; and (4) *management of the symptoms* of stress. Within the context of the stress paradigm shown in Figure 1, the functions of coping and social supports can be seen in relation to both the stressor and its effect on health. We shall describe each of these functions in turn.

Preventive Functions

Virtually nothing is known of how coping and supports protect health by preventing stressful problems from surfacing in people's lives. Yet all of us have had occasion to wonder if certain friends and acquaintances are not "snakebitten"—living under a cloud, hounded by relentless misfortune—while others appear to sail through life untouched by serious difficulties. Such difference, of course, may very well be explained by differences in the basic circumstances and life chances of people, their emotional resources, and their involuntary random exposure to hardship. But can such differences also be explained by differences in coping repertoirs and access to and use of supports? Perhaps, but we cannot be sure at this time. The reasons we cannot be certain involve the methods used to study coping and supports within the framework of the stress paradigm. Simply put, researchers typically begin to examine people's coping behavior and social supports *after* a health-threatening problem emerges. As a result, more is known of how people deal with problems than of how they avoid them.

Although we lack concrete information, it is possible to speculate about the preventive functions of coping and social supports. With regard to coping, we must recognize that there is a large class of potential health-threatening stressors whose occurrence can be forecasted far in advance of their actual appearance. We refer particularly to life-cycle transitions that can entail rather profound life change. Getting married, having children, launching them onto their own uncharted seas, entering grandparenthood, and retiring from work are such changes.

These sorts of changes are remarkably free of lasting deleterious health consequences (Pearlin 1980). One explanation is their predictability: because these life-cycle changes are foreseeable, they permit long periods of anticipatory or preparatory coping. We cannot be sure, of course, whether anticipatory preparation actually prevents problems from arising or simply helps us deal with them once they do arise. We suspect that the avoidance of problems and the readiness to deal appropriately with them are both learned beforehand.

Successfully confronting a problem at one point can help prevent the recurrence of the same problem at a later point. Menaghan's (1982) longitudinal analysis of marital problems, which are closely associated with psychological depression, provides a good example. She found that people who coped effectively with marital problems were more likely to be free of such problems four years later than those coping with the same type of problems with less effective means. Thus, efficacious coping can have a double function. Not only does it reduce stress in the short run but it actually provides a preventive barricade against the future emergence of problems in that role area. Concomitantly, of course, the less successful people are in coping with existing problems, the more likely these problems will endure into or reappear in the future.

Social supports also have preventive functions. Indeed, supports may be more important to the prevention of health-related problems than coping. The most obvious way in which such functions would be accomplished is through the "wisdom" the group imparts to its members: the ability both to anticipate problems and, once recognized, to adopt appropriate avoidance strategies. Clearly, people acquire such abilities from others. Among the norms that we absorb from our membership and reference groups are those that define what is undesirable and should be avoided, what is acceptable but should be approached warily, and what should be actively sought after. Without being aware of it, we learn a litany of dos and don'ts that will presumably shield us from risk. On the other hand, the very supports that shield may also function to increase the exposure to stress and health risks. The more extensive one's social network, for example, the more likely one is to be touched by stressors occurring to others, such as, the death of a close friend. Similarly, to the extent that a person's reference groups engage in certain patterns of behavior, such as smoking or heavy drinking, pressures to conform to group standards can have harmful health effects.

The Alteration of the Problematic Situation

If stressors cannot be prevented or avoided, the next most desirable function of coping and social supports would seem to be modification of the situation (or one's behavior within it) in a way that eliminates or

reduces its stress-producing properties. For example, if one is having problems at work, changing the problematic aspects of the work situation would be highly desirable. It is reasonable to suppose that this is a function that people would seek to maximize. With regard to coping, it is surprising that behavior serving this function does not appear particularly prominent in people's repertoires (Pearlin and Schooler 1978). One possible reason is that some problematic situations are recognized by people as intractable, as not meriting efforts to change them. Second, the source of one's stress may not always be apparent. We are capable of experiencing health-damaging stress without being certain of its origins; or, more likely, we attribute the stress to one situation while in reality it comes from another. Thus, coping may be misdirected. Third, one may decide not to act directly upon the situation because the action might trigger consequences one does not wish to face. A worker might ask his boss to eliminate dangerous job conditions but risk the possibility of being fired. Coping actions intended to alter certain aspects of a situation are also quite capable of producing unintended and unwanted alterations, thus inhibiting efforts directed at change.

Social supports, perhaps more than coping, can actively function to change situations. They do so, we believe, largely through the exercise of what is usually referred to as instrumental (in contrast to expressive) support. Instrumental supports are those that broadly involve the giving of material help, assistance, or information (House 1981). One's network, of course, serves as a nexus for such support and can be used to change certain kinds of problematic situations. If someone is unemployed, for example, relatives, friends, or neighbors, functioning as a referral system for the person, may alert him to job opportunities. Or, short of helping him find a new job, they might ease the burden by providing loans, gifts of food, or other material goods. Of course, some stressful situations can no more be changed successfully by a support group than by the individual caught up in it. Nevertheless, the resources of support groups are potentially powerful instruments in altering the stressful properties of situations.

The Alteration of Meaning

Because many situations that eventually damage psychological and physical health are resistant to change, people engage instead in actions that change the meaning of the situation. The situation remains intact, but perceptions, beliefs, and knowledge are modified in a way that reduces its threatening or harmful qualities.

A number of cognitive and perceptual devices that neutralize the meaning of potentially stressful situations have been identified (Pearlin and Schooler 1978). For example, people often trivialize problematic situations, defining them as too un-

important to be painful or threatening. Since the importance that we assign to a situation influences the threat we feel when things go wrong, diminishing a situation's importance minimizes its threat. Another perceptual process entails the relegation of difficult situations to the commonplace and normal. If we can regard a marital problem, for example, as similar to the problems that our best friends also experience, we can explain our difficulties as a normative, to-be-expected set of experiences. Misery does not simply love company; misery is in active search of company and is often assuaged by it. Many other perceptual devices that people employ vary in form but perform the same function: they endow a situation with a meaning that reduces its stress-arousing qualities.

Along with coping, social supports also contribute importantly to the perceptual management of the threatening properties of stressful circumstances. A natural product of interaction in groups is the acquisition of norms, that is, shared ways of defining situations—appraising them as good or bad, desirable or undesirable—and of prescribing or approving modes of action and reaction. Thus, although an individual's experiences might be unique, the ways the individual assesses and acts upon them may be a consequence of internalized group standards. The norms of membership and reference groups can legitimize and reinforce the perception of a situation as threatening, or they can help define the same situation as ordinary, trivial, fatalistically inexorable, or undeserving of concern, worthy only of being ignored. The objective properties of a situation often do not by themselves determine its threatening quality. Instead, people's normative aspirations, values, and ideologies shape perceptions and combine with the objective situation in giving rise to threat.

Evidence shows that support groups also mediate the stress process by helping the individual maintain a positive self-concept in the face of hardship (Pearlin et al. 1981). Here the group does not influence the perception of the situation as much as it influences the perception of the self in the situation. The support group, in effect, helps the individual maintain self-esteem and a sense of mastery by interpreting the stressful situation as one that does not reflect negatively on these prized elements of self. The maintenance of the self in difficult life situations is a crucial defense against stress.

Control of Stress Symptoms

A final function of coping and supports is seen in behaviors that control symptoms, particularly states such as anxiety and depression, keeping them within manageable bounds so that they do not overwhelm the individual. Folkman and Lazarus (1980) refer to this process as emotion-focused coping, in contrast to that which is problem focused. Much of the popular understanding of coping relates to this

function, as does the "stress management" industry that has evolved in recent years. One can turn to biofeedback or bird-watching, to meditation or massage, running or rebirth, drinking or daydreaming— indeed to virtually any activity that provides some relief either from awareness of problematic circumstances or from the tensions and other symptoms associated with them. Dealing effectively with symptoms of distress enables individuals to direct their attention to the important demands of their lives (Mechanic 1962). Based on current knowledge, it is not possible to identify techniques that are superior to others in providing relief. However, some that effectively control symptoms in the short run might very well have deleterious consequences in the long run. To take but one example, alcohol use may provide some immediate relief from symptoms of distress, but too much over too long a period can have a devastating impact on health (Aneshensel and Huba 1983; Pearlin and Radabaugh 1976).

How do social supports function for the control of symptoms? One way is by validating the individual's response to the stressor. Those confronting major life crises or persistent strains are often perplexed and frightened by their emotional and physiological arousal; open discussion of the problem and legitimization of these fears by others can be a critical factor in enabling the individual to manage distress and avoid being overwhelmed by it (Wortman and Lehman, in press). Much of what is called expressive support is provided through these kinds of exchanges. In addition, of course, social life itself is diversionary. The things that individuals do to relieve tensions are often done in groups; some stress management behaviors, in fact, require other people. Once more, then, we find that coping and social supports have striking parallel functions within the stress paradigm.

Acknowledgments

The authors' work was supported through their participation in the Consortium for Research Involving Stress Processes, founded by the W. T. Grant Foundation. Additional support came from the National Institute of Mental Health. The authors wish to thank Virginia Hansen for editorial assistance.

References

Aneshensel, C. S., and G. J. Huba. 1983. Depression, alcohol use, and smoking over one year: A four-wave longitudinal causal model. *Journal of Abnormal Psychology* 92(2):134–150.

Bunney, W., Jr., A. Shapiro, R. Adler, J. Davis, A. Herd, I. Kopin, D. Krieger, S. Matthyse, A. Stunkard, and M. Weissman. 1982. Panel report on stress and illness. In *Stress and human health*, ed. G. R. Elliott and C. Eisdorfer, pp. 255–321. New York: Springer Publishing.

Folkman, S., and R. S. Lazarus. 1980. An analysis of coping in a middle-aged community sample. *Journal of Health and Social Behavior* 21:219–239.

House, J. S. 1981. *Work stress and social support*. Reading, Mass., Addison-Wesley.

Jenkins, C. S. 1976. Recent evidence supporting psychologic and social risk factors for coronary disease. *New England Journal of Medicine* 294:987–994, 1033–1038.

Kasl, S. V. 1984. Stress and health. *Annual Review of Public Health* 5:319–341.

Kessler, R. C., R. H. Price, and C. B. Wortman. 1985. Social factors in psychopathology: Stress, social support and coping processes. *Annual Review of Psychology* 36:531–572.

Mechanic, D. 1962. *Students under stress: A study in the social psychology of adaptation*. New York: Free Press.

Menaghan, E. 1982. Measuring coping effectiveness: A panel analysis of marital problems and coping efforts. *Journal of Health and Social Behavior* 23(3):220–234.

Pearlin, L. I. 1980. The life cycle and life strains. In *Sociological theory and research*, ed. H. M. Blalock, pp. 349–360. New York: Free Press.

Pearlin, L. I., and M. A. Lieberman. 1979. Social sources of emotional distress. In *Research in community and mental health*, ed. R. Simmons, 1:217–248. Greenwich, Conn: JAI Press.

Pearlin, L. I., M. A. Lieberman, E. G. Menaghan, and J. T. Mullan. 1981. The stress process. *Journal of Health and Social Behavior* 22:337–356.

Pearlin, L. I., and C. W. Radabaugh. 1976. Economic strains and the coping function of alcohol. *American Journal of Sociology* 82:652–663.

Pearlin, L. I., and C. Schooler. 1978. The structure of coping. *Journal of Health and Social Behavior* 19:2–21.

Schmale, A. H., and H. P. Iker. 1971. Hopelessness as a predictor of cervical cancer. *Social Science and Medicine* 5: 95–100.

Thoits, P. A. 1983. Dimensions of life events that influence psychological distress: An evaluation and synthesis of the literature. In *Psychosocial stress: Trends in theory and research*, ed. H. B. Kaplan, pp. 33–103. New York: Academic Press.

Wortman, C. B., and D. R. Lehman. In press. Reactions to victims of life crises: Support attempts that fail. In *Social support: Theory, research, and application*, ed. I. B. Sarason and B. R. Sarason. The Hague: Martinus Niihof.

Section Two

Environmental and Occupational Health

It is astonishing that environmental and occupational health concerns have only recently been plummeted into the public spotlight. To be sure, miners, factory workers, railway workers, and others have long been struggling with occupational safety and health issues. Preservation-oriented environmentalists, too, have always fought for their cause. Yet these activists' efforts have only fairly recently become part of a growing national environmentalist concern, which is in part reflected in the creation of the federal Environmental Protection Administration (EPA) in 1969 and the Occupational Safety and Health Administration (OSHA) in 1970.

What is striking in terms of the late development of public interest and public policy in this area is that the stakes are so high. Each year over 115,000 workers die from work-related hazards, and 2 million suffer accidents or illness serious enough to make them miss work. Each year, 250 million tons of hazardous waste are produced in the United States, much of it winding up in public drinking water where it causes cancer and other diseases. The same corporate mentality that callously uses people's labor without regard for their health, also produces a disregard for public safety in terms of production and dumping of hazardous waste materials. Corporate profit motives are aided by government failure to enforce existing regulations, and during the Reagan administration in the 1980s, a strong antiregulation ideology severely diminished the authority of EPA, OSHA, and other regulatory agencies.

Nicholas Freudenberg provides us with an overview of "The Corporate Assault on Health," showing the interrelationships between business and government in creating and tolerating toxic hazards. He also traces the history of the production of toxic materials and demonstrates how groups have confronted hazardous wastes in their communities. Taking coal miners' black lung disease as a case study, Barbara Ellen Smith's article, "Black Lung: The Social Production of Disease," presents the central issues in occupational safety. She shows us the formative patterns in the social construction of a disease—miners and their allies work to develop public awareness of a disease that kills and maims many miners; they confront owners and officials who deny that the disease is in fact a disease; and they then take the conflict to the national political, legislative, and media stages.

7 THE CORPORATE ASSAULT ON HEALTH

Nicholas Freudenberg

Case History:
Hardeman County, Tennessee

In 1964 the Velsicol Chemical Company of Chicago bought a 242-acre farm in rural Hardeman County, Tennessee.[1] The company soon dumped 300,000 fifty-five-gallon barrels of chemical waste on the site. The bulldozer that buried the barrels occasionally burst a drum open; its contents disappeared into the soil.

In 1967 a U.S. Geological Survey report showed that the chemicals from the dump site were reaching the wells of the families that lived on a nearby road, but officials took no action. Five years later, the Tennessee Department of Public Health ordered Velsicol to close the dump.

By 1977 residents near the dump were noticing that their drinking water had a foul odor and taste. Among those who lived in the area was Nell Grantham, a licensed practical nurse, and her family. Her neighbors included her parents, her brothers and sisters, and their families. They got together and asked the state health department to analyze their water, but their request went unheeded for six months. When the local health department finally did take samples, they tested only for bacteria. Finding none, the health officer told them their water was safe.

Dissatisfied, Grantham and her relatives brought a sample to the State Water Quality Division laboratories. After making its own tests, the state

lab gave the Granthams and their neighbors some grim news: their water contained twelve chemicals including five known carcinogens—benzene, chlordane, heptachlor, endrin, and dioxin. The lab conducted more tests, the results of which were then confirmed by the U.S. Environmental Protection Agency (EPA). EPA officials gave the residents a series of recommendations, including not to drink their water and not to cook with it. They were then told not to bathe in it. Later still they were told that fruits and vegetables should not be grown on their property, or animals raised there: one resident's hog was killed and sent to the state lab, which found it to be highly contaminated with chemicals. After several months of having water shipped in by National Guard tankers, the residents were connected to the public water system of a nearby town. But before long residents challenged the quality of that water as well, for it too was found to contain chemicals.

Media coverage of the problem forced Velsicol to admit publicly that its abandoned dump might be the cause of the problem. The company agreed to pay for the new hot water heaters, dishwashers, and washing machines that residents had to buy to

SOURCE: *Not in Our Backyards!* Community Action for Health and the Environment. Copyright © 1984 by Nicholas Freudenberg. Reprinted by permission of Monthly Review Foundation.

replace their contaminated appliances. Some residents complained that Velsicol did not live up to this agreement.

Meanwhile, the residents experienced a host of health problems. Skin rashes became common. A child was born with a serious birth defect. Following that birth, none of the couples in the area of the dump were able to conceive a child for more than four years. An environmental health survey by scientists from the University of Cincinnati Medical Center found evidence of liver damage in some of those exposed to the water, and attributed it to the contamination.[2]

While residents were frightened by the ill effects they were suffering, they were even more alarmed about what might happen in the future. As Nell Grantham put it to a journalist, "Who knows? In twenty years my kids may have cancer. I may never have grandchildren. I may not even live to see my kids grown. That's something we don't know. That's something no one knows. But when you've been drinking contaminated water with chemicals that you know can cause cancer, that makes it look worse. My kids are my biggest concern. What kind of life are they gonna have?"[3]

A group of eighty people living close to the dump have filed a $2.5 billion class action suit against Velsicol. Before that, a few residents settled out of court, receiving from $12,000 to $15,000 each from the chemical company. In 1986, Velsicol was found guilty, and the plaintiffs were awarded $12.7 million.

On another level, Grantham became a leader of a new statewide coalition, Tennesseans Against Chemical Hazards (TEACH). Composed of eleven community groups across the state, TEACH does public education and legislative lobbying, and supports community organizing against polluters. It is also working for a state tax on chemical companies to be used to clean up abandoned dump sites.

All across the country the air we breathe, the water we drink, the food we eat, the land on which we build our houses and schools, and the highways we travel are being contaminated by a constantly expanding brew of health-damaging substances. As a result, all across the country concerned citizens are joining together to fight the corporations, government agencies, utility companies, and agribusiness interests that are poisoning our families and communities.

How has this corporate and governmental assault on human health come to dominate the lives of so many people in the United States? Why have the residents of Love Canal, New York, Three Mile Island, Pennsylvania, Times Beach, Missouri, and thousands of other communities been forced to organize to protect themselves?

The roots of the current epidemic of environmental disasters go back to changes in U.S. industry during and after World War II. Scientific advances in organic chemistry, biochemistry, and other basic sciences provided the foundation for technological innovations. The war speeded the application of these new technologies to industrial production, and the most spectacular advances were in the petrochemical industry, which produces everything from plastics to pesticides. Between 1940 and 1980 the production of synthetic organic chemicals increased from less than 10 billion pounds a year to more than 350 billion.[4] Each year, one thousand new compounds are added to the esti-mated seventy thousand chemicals already in use by 1980.[5]

The growth of the petrochemical industry has been both a cause and an effect of other industrial develop-ment. The burgeoning automobile industry created a steady market for petroleum products. When many families became able to afford cars, developers were able to build new suburbs, new highways, and new industrial parks, all requiring a myr-iad of the new substances turned out by industry.

The petrochemical industry also revolutionized agriculture. During the past decades chemical fertilizers, pesticides, and preservatives have become an essential aspect of U.S. food production. There are now ap-proximately 40,000 pesticide prod-ucts on the market.[6] Between 1942 and 1967 chemical fertilizer use in the United States expanded ten-fold.[7]

World War II served as the mid-wife to the nuclear industry. Mas-sive government funding spurred the research necessary to build the atomic bombs eventually dropped on Hiroshima and Nagasaki, and the military has since continued to pro-duce ever growing stockpiles of nu-clear weapons. In the 1950s tax dol-lars also helped to build the nuclear power industry. By 1978 seventy nu-clear power plants were generating 12.5 percent of the nation's electrical power.[8] Although economic prob-lems and a militant antinuclear movement now threaten the nuclear power industry's growth, dangerous waste products will remain in exis-tence for generations to come.

The petrochemical industry, agri-

business, military production, and the nuclear power industry all devel-oped into major economic forces in the years after World War II. Their environmental impact is now added to that of more traditional manufac-turing and extractive activities.

As the costs and risks of nuclear power increase and the price of oil goes up, coal has again become an important source of energy. Between 1975 and 1981, the amount of coal burned by utility companies in-creased by 50 percent.[9] Coal mining affects miners most directly. Be-tween 1978 and 1980, 40,000 miners were killed or injured in accidents in underground coal mines alone.[10] Between 1970 and 1977 more than 400,000 miners or their widows were awarded compensation for black lung disease, a chronic condition caused by exposure to coal dust. Such exposure slowly damages its victims' ability to breathe, eventually killing them.[11]

Mining coal also affects the health of people in the communities near the mines. Coal dust can cause lung disease in children living near strip mines,[12] and mine fires increase air pollution, contributing to respiratory disease in nearby areas.[13] Many Ap-palachian communities have been unable to use their drinking water because it is contaminated by coal dust.[14] And coal mining can lead to explosions, flooding, and landslides. In 1973, in Buffalo Creek, West Vir-ginia, a pile of coal waste collapsed after water had built up behind it. One hundred and twenty-five peo-ple were killed when the valley be-hind the waste site was flooded with water and coal debris.[15]

Lead mining can cause lead poisoning, a condition associated with learning problems and brain damage. In Kellog, Idaho, a 1974 government study found that 40 percent of the children living near a lead smelting plant had dangerously high levels of lead in their blood.[16] Smelters melt down raw ore after it is mined in order to extract the purified metals (in this case lead), and in the process discharge lead into the air. The study identified the Bunker Hill Company of Kellog as the source of the country's worst mass exposure of children to lead. Several years later, in 1979, tests showed that airborne lead levels in the Silver King Elementary School, just below the smelter's stacks, registered ten times the federal safety levels.[17] Two families whose nine children had high blood lead levels in 1974 had their children tested by neurologists. When the doctors found all nine had nerve or brain impairment, the parents filed a $20 million lawsuit against the Bunker Hill Company. More recently, in 1983, lead emissions from a smelter in Dallas, Texas, led the director of the Dallas Housing Authority to recommend the relocation of four hundred families living in nearby public housing. Lead levels in a neighboring day care center had reached ninety-two times the federal standard.[18]

Uranium mining is also hazardous. Uranium miners, many of whom are Navajo Indians, are ten times more likely than other people to die of lung cancer. Dr. Victor Archer, a physician at the National Institute for Occupational Safety and Health (NIOSH), has estimated that one thousand of the six thousand miners who worked in one uranium

mining area in the western Rocky Mountains will die of lung cancer.[19]

After raw uranium ore is removed from a mine, it is ground into a sand at a mill so that the uranium can be extracted. Each ton of ore yields no more than four pounds of quality uranium, or "yellowcake." The radioactive waste that remains, known as uranium tailings, is dumped near the mines and mills, and is often used as landfill. This radioactivity contaminates the environment, putting whole communities at risk. People living near a uranium mine in Colorado found high levels of radioactivity in their drinking water.[20] The Pine Indian Reservation in South Dakota is downwind from deposits of uranium tailings from abandoned mines. Researchers suspect that high rates of miscarriage, certain kinds of birth defects, and cancers are related to the exposure to radiation through the water and air.[21] An EPA study found that people living within half a mile of uranium tailings are twice as likely to die of lung cancer as is the rest of the population.[22] Other problems associated with low-level radiation include premature death and leukemia.[23] Most experts agree that there is no safe level of exposure to radiation.[24]

Another mining hazard is beryllium disease, an often fatal condition that affects beryllium miners and their families.[25] Used in fluorescent lights and atomic weapons, beryllium is mined in Pennsylvania. Still another hazard comes from phosphate mining, which has contaminated drinking water supplies in southwest Florida.[26] Finally, the extraction of iron, copper, and other metals leads to both environmental degradation and lung disease among miners.

Mining and processing ores create one set of environmental threats to health; subsequent stages of energy production are no less damaging. Fuel combustion by electric utilities contributes significantly to air pollution by producing particulates and sulfur and nitrous oxides. Each of these increases the risk of respiratory and heart diseases.[27] A study by the Brookhaven National Laboratory and Carnegie-Mellon University, for instance, estimated that each year twenty-one thousand people living east of the Mississippi River may die prematurely as a result of pollutants from coal- and oil-burning plants.[28] Burning coal is a particularly important source of air pollution. It is a major cause of "acid rain," a phenomenon that is killing fish and other animals in hundreds of lakes in the northeastern United States and Canada. Recently, new evidence suggests that acid rain can contaminate drinking water supplies, leading to human illness.[29] Coal combustion also releases carbon dioxide into the atmosphere, possibly causing long-term modification of the climate.[30]

Many of the new coal-based synthetic fuels pose similar hazards. Although synfuel processing removes many of coal's impurities, the wastes are then dumped, polluting the air and water with dangerous metals.[31]

Three Mile Island, Chernobyl, and the antinuclear movement put safety issues in nuclear power plants on the front pages of newspapers across the country. But the nuclear power industry's safety record since the Three Mile Island accident in 1978 is hardly reassuring. In 1980 the sixty-nine licensed and operable atomic reactors in the United States reported 3,804 mishaps, including spills, leaks, and equipment malfunctions.[32] The Nuclear Regulatory Commission's (NRC) first national survey, in 1981, found fifteen of fifty plants "below average" in management control, maintenance, radiation and fire protection, and overall compliance with operating regulations.[33]

While a power plant meltdown is the most serious danger, the daily release of small amounts of radioactivity into the air and water creates a continuing risk. The most persistent problem, however, is the disposal of high-level radioactive waste. Each year a single nuclear power plant generates about thirty metric tons of such waste,[34] some components of which can cause harmful health effects for up to 250,000 years.[35] Yet no permanent safe disposal site for this waste has been found. Instead, it is shipped around the country by truck, train, and barge. The Oak Ridge National Laboratory estimated that the nuclear industry will have to transport over 75,000 truckloads of used and dangerous nuclear fuel over the next twenty-five years.[36] The consequences of an accident could be disastrous.

Electricity generated by nuclear or coal-based plants is transmitted to the consumer. When electrical energy travels through extra-high-voltage power lines, it causes a variety of problems. Farmers whose animals graze under high-voltage power lines report that their cows have difficulty feeding their calves.[37] Laboratory experiments have demonstrated that mice exposed to electromagnetic fields similar to those produced by power lines lose weight and experience increased rates of infant mortality.[38] One study by researchers at the University of Colorado Medical Center found that children with cancer were more likely to live in homes close to high voltage electrical lines than were healthy children.[39]

Manufacturing chemicals, plastics, and other products poison industrial workers and pollute the air and water for everyone else. Because workers experience the most direct exposure, their toll is highest. According to NIOSH, each year 100,000 workers die from occupational illnesses, including lung cancer, heart disease, and respiratory conditions, and each year there are 400,000 new cases of work-related diseases.[40] Nine out of every ten U.S. industrial workers are inadequately protected against exposure to toxic chemicals.[41]

But toxics do not stop at the factory gate. Through smoke stacks and drainage pipes, from storage tanks, and even carried by strong winds, dangerous substances escape from the workplace into the community, where they can contaminate the air, the water, and the soil. Industrial production accounts for about 30 percent of particulate air pollution, and adds sulfur dioxide, nitrogen oxide, hydrocarbons, and carbon monoxide to the air.[42] Although scientists debate the precise impact of air pollution on health, there is solid evidence linking industrial pollutants to such health problems as chronic bronchitis, asthma, emphysema, and other respiratory illnesses, as well as to heart disease and cancer.[43] Residents of communities with many chemical factories, such as Elizabeth, New Jersey, frequently complain of pollution-related eye, ear, nose, and throat irritation.[44] Foul odors from factory emissions, while not necessarily health-damaging, can certainly make life unpleasant.

In testimony before the House Subcommittee on Health and the Environment in 1977, Dr. Carl Shy, former director of research on air pollution for the federal government, estimated that failure to meet legal air quality standards may mean that an additional 3 percent of the population (or 7 million people) will suffer more severe asthma, an additional 10 to 15 percent of the exposed adult population will face a higher risk of chronic bronchitis and emphysema, and 100 percent of exposed children will face an increased risk of disturbed lung function.[45]

Epidemiological studies have found higher than average cancer rates in heavily industrialized areas. The industrial areas of California's Contra Costa County, for example —the home of five oil refineries and thirty-seven chemical plants—have a death rate from lung cancer for white males that is 40 percent above that of the rest of the county.[46] The death rates for blacks of both sexes and for white females are also elevated in these same areas. Since blacks and white women have generally been excluded from work in the chemical industry, these figures suggest that air pollution as well as workplace exposure is an important factor. In New Orleans, another center of petrochemical production, white males have a death rate from lung and bronchial cancer that is 40 percent above the national rate for this group.[47]

Industrial production can also contribute to water pollution. Some manufacturers store raw materials in containers that leak into the groundwater. For example, in the city of San Jose, in California's "Silicon Valley," just south of San Francisco, mothers became alarmed at what seemed to be a large number of miscarriages and birth defects.[48] Tests revealed high levels of trichloroethylene (a substance suspected of causing cancer) and the toxic trichloroethane in the drinking water. State health department investigators discovered that several nearby manufacturers of silicon chips were storing these chemicals in underground tanks and that these were leaking. In 1983 an EPA official testified before the Toxic Substances Subcommittee of the Senate Committee on Environment and Public Works that between 75,000 and 100,000 storage tanks were leaking 11 million gallons of gasoline a year. He went on to say that one gallon a day leaking into an underground water source was enough to pollute the drinking water of a community of fifty thousand people.[49]

After a product has been mined or manufactured, it must be transported to its sellers and users. The growth of the petrochemical industry has led to a corresponding increase in the shipment of toxic chemicals and other hazardous materials. Every second, more than 125 tons of hazardous chemicals move onto the nation's highways, railways, and waterways.[50] Over four hundred thousand trucks regularly transport hazardous materials;[51] at least 4 billion tons are shipped each year. Moreover, the number of shipments of raw materials, finished products, and wastes is expected to double in the next decade.[52]

The U.S. Department of Transportation classifies 1,600 materials "hazardous." They range from poisons and explosives to gasoline and ammonia. In 1978 there were 18,000 accidents involving the rail, highway, or water transport of these substances, eight times the number in 1971. Injuries to drivers and passersby from these incidents increased by 400 percent in the same period.[53] In Waverly, Tennessee, in 1978, the explosion of a tank car carrying propane gas killed fifteen people and leveled the downtown section of the city.[54] In the same year a railroad accident that led to a spill of the toxic chemical phosphorous trichloride in Somerville, Massachusetts, forced the evacuation of thirteen thousand people and sent 200 to the hospital.[55] In Montebello, California, in 1981, thousands of people became nauseated and dizzy when a truck leaked ethyl mercaptan, a foul-smelling toxic substance, for twenty-five miles along a freeway.[56] And in 1982 a train derailed near Livingston, Louisiana, spilling more than 1 million pounds of such toxic chemicals as vinyl chloride, toluene, phosphoric acid, and tetraethyl lead. The ensuing explosion set off a fire that burned for two weeks, forcing authorities to evacuate 2,700 people.[57] When residents were allowed to return home two weeks later, the health department warned them not to eat vegetables from their gardens or food that had been left on shelves or even in refrigerators.

After a product has been delivered to its consumers, it can endanger health in new ways. Asbestos, a substance used for insulation and fireproofing, has become a pervasive hazard not only to its producers but also to its users. Exposure to flaking asbestos can permanently damage lungs, and it is now known that even brief exposure can lead to cancer.[58] Hundreds of thousands of schools and other buildings around the country have used asbestos tiles or insulation and 14,000 of the nation's 110,000 schools have an asbestos problem, posing a cancer risk to 4 million students and school employees.[59] Since as much as twenty years can elapse between exposure and the first sign of cancer, millions of Americans are condemned to decades of fear and uncertainty.

Another substance used for insulation, polychlorinated biphenyls, or PCBs, can cause cancer and skin disease. Exposure to PCBs has also led to birth defects in laboratory animals. In 1981 an electrical transformer in a state office building in Binghamton, New York, exploded during a fire, showering the eighteen-story building with PCBs and their by-products, including the deadly poison dioxin. The building had to be abandoned. A cleanup would cost more than $20 million —for a structure that cost only $13 million to build.[60] Several people who worked in the building suffered liver damage as a result of PCB exposure. In 1983 there were 1.8 million capacitors and 100,000 trans-

formers containing PCBs in the United States. According to Dr. Arnold Schecter, a professor of preventive medicine at the Upstate Medical Center in Binghamton, "PCB transformers are public health time bombs, medical time bombs, waiting to go off."[61]

Some of the products used to control termites have forced owners to abandon their homes. After an exterminator sprayed aldrin, a banned cancer-causing pesticide, in a Long Island house, the New York State Department of Environmental Conservation advised the family to vacate the premises within two days.[62] When laboratory tests confirmed high levels of the persistent chemical, the owner demolished his house and buried the rubble in a landfill. A subsequent investigation by state authorities found widespread use of aldrin, as well as heptachlor and chlordane, two other carcinogens used in termite control.

The forced evacuation of more than 800 families from their homes at Love Canal in Niagara Falls, New York, in 1980 alerted the public to the growing problems caused by the improper disposal of chemical waste. In 1981 more than 50,000 companies in the United States produced 165 million tons of hazardous waste, enough to fill 7,500 Love Canals.[63] The chemical industry was responsible for more than 70 percent of these. Exposure to toxic waste can lead to eye, ear, nose, throat, and skin irritations, breathing problems, kidney and liver damage, miscarriages, birth defects, and cancer.[64] People come into contact with toxic chemicals most commonly by drinking water contaminated by improperly sealed dump sites. The case of Hardeman County is only one of many such situations. Direct exposure to such waste is also common. For example, children playing near a chemical dump site in Hammond, Indiana, developed skin rashes,[65] and seepage of waste into the basements of the homes at Love Canal led to dangerous levels of chemicals inside the houses.[66] A report issued by the Congressional Office of Technology Assessment in 1983 estimates that to adequately protect public health, it will cost as much as $40 billion to clean up the fifteen thousand sites where toxic waste is known to have been dumped without controls.[67] A 1982 EPA study concludes that more than 90 percent of the eighty thousand sites where toxic chemicals are stored in pits, ponds, or lagoons threaten to contaminate the ground water.[68]

The conditions at hazardous waste disposal facilities vary widely. The best operators bury containers of chemicals in claylined pits with carefully planned drainage systems, and then carefully monitor the runoff. But William Sanjour, chief of EPA's hazardous waste implementation branch, notes that all landfills, even those with an "impermeable" clay cap, eventually leak. "So," he told the *New York Times*, "the federal government cannot come out with any set of regulations that protects human health and the environment and allows existing landfills to continue to function."[69] Many corporations ignore federal and state regulations altogether, simply paying a carter to dump their wastes in an abandoned lot, an empty warehouse, or a wooded area.

In the last five years, more and more communities built near toxic dump sites have experienced serious health problems. Although investigators have not always been able to identify the specific cause of illness, the anecdotal evidence leaves many scientists alarmed. Dr. Samuel Epstein, professor of environmental medicine at the University of Illinois School of Public Health, has called improper disposal of hazardous wastes "America's number one environmental problem."[70] A few reports from affected areas illustrate the dimensions of the problem.

In Woburn, Massachusetts, chemical companies, tanneries, and a glue-making factory dumped their wastes into empty lots for more than a century, contaminating a sixty-acre area with arsenic, lead, and chromium. Federal officials have listed Woburn as one of the ten worst hazardous sites in the country.[71] This city of thirty-five thousand people has one of the highest cancer rates in Massachusetts. Between 1969 and 1978 its rate of childhood leukemia was more than double the national average and the rate of kidney cancer was also unusually high.[72]

In Farmington, New Jersey, a small community near Atlantic City, residents complained of skin rashes and a large number of cancer deaths. For years a nearby landfill had been used by corporations such as DuPont, Union Carbide, and Procter and Gamble to dispose of toxic chemical wastes.[73] Tests of Farmington's drinking water in 1981 showed staggering concentrations of dangerous chemicals. Levels of benzene, a cause of leukemia and of aplastic anemia, were 11,000 times higher than "safe" levels. Another chemical, dichloroethane, which causes kidney and liver damage, was detected in concentrations 136,000 times greater than the EPA safety level. Other dangerous substances found in the water included arsenic, vinyl chloride, lead, mercury, cadmium, and chloroform. Farmington's inhabitants now drink bottled water. Even worse, the dump that ruined their water threatens to contaminate Atlantic City's water supply. State health officials have closed many of the wells that supply water to the resort's forty thousand year-round residents and to the millions of tourists, and are still searching for alternative sources.[74]

Recently, waste disposal firms have found new and ingenious methods to expose people to toxics. In 1982 officials from the New York City Department of Environmental Protection found illegally high levels of sulfur, benzene, and the lead in fuel tanks in residential apartment buildings.[75] According to state investigators and industry spokespersons, fuel retailers and wholesalers sometimes mix "cocktails" of toxic waste and heating oil in order to boost profits or undercut competitors.

As big business has taken over food and forestry production, agriculture has also contributed to poor health, primarily by its increased use of petrochemical products. In the last two decades, for example, the production of synthetic organic pesticides in the United States has doubled.[76] The use of herbicides, which rid land of unwanted vegetation, has grown even more dramatically. In 1977 250 million acres of land were sprayed with herbicides, as compared with 71 million acres in 1962.[77] In 1982 alone, herbicide sales increased by 20 percent.[78]

More than twenty years ago, Rachel Carson's *Silent Spring* alerted the public to the potential dangers of pesticides. In a "fable for tomorrow," she described a community where

mysterious maladies swept the flocks of chickens; the cattle and sheep sickened and died. The farmers spoke of much illness among their families. In the town the doctors had become more and more puzzled by new kinds of sickness appearing among their patients. . . . Even the streams were now lifeless. Anglers no longer visited them, for all the fish had died.[79]

Two decades later, more and more communities experience the reality of Carson's grim prophecy.

As we would expect, those who make pesticides and those who use them on the job—farm workers, forestry workers, and those who spray rights-of-way for the utilities and railroads—suffer the most serious consequences,[80] and each year 45,000 people (mostly workers) are poisoned.[81] Their symptoms include nausea, skin rashes, neurological disorders, and respiratory problems. Exposure to insecticides (pesticides used to kill insects) such as dieldrin, kepone, endrin, lindane, mirex, heptachlor, and toxaphere can cause cancer in humans or animals.[82] Studies have also linked certain pesticides with sterility.[83]

Those who live near land used for forestry or farming are also exposed. Communities in the Pacific Northwest, for example, have reported a high incidence of miscarriage and birth defects after herbicides were sprayed on commercial and government-owned forests.[84] In Scottsdale, Arizona, an upper-middle-class community bordered by farmland, crop dusters fly over the cotton fields, spraying them with pesticides. In 1978, 343 residents complained to the Arizona Pesticides Control Board that the drifting spray had made them sick.[85]

As substances sprayed on crops or forests drain into underground waterways, rivers, or streams, drinking water is contaminated. Pesticides have been found in drinking water throughout the country. In rural Suffolk County on Long Island, for instance, the pesticide Temik, used to control potato bugs, was found in several wells in 1979. A year later public outrage forced Union Carbide, the manufacturer of Temik, to install water filters in 1,700 homes whose water was contaminated,[86] and EPA banned its sale in Suffolk County. A preliminary study by the Suffolk County Health Department in 1982 showed that pregnant women living in homes with Temik-contaminated water had two times more miscarriages than did women whose water was less contaminated.[87] In 1983 Cornell University scientists predicted that Suffolk's water might remain polluted with Temik for more than 100 years.[88]

In California's agricultural Fresno County, fruit growers killed worms that attacked the roots of trees and vines with the pesticide DBCP until it was banned in 1977 after workers making the product became sterile. But five years later, 12,000 people in Fresno County and as many as fifty thousand in the San Joaquin Valley were still drinking water with unsafe

levels of DBCP, which had contaminated public water supplies.[89] People living in areas where the water was contaminated with DBCP had higher rates of stomach cancer than did the rest of the population.[90]

Pesticides also enter our bodies on the food we eat. Almost all commercially grown fruits and vegetables are sprayed at some state of their production. An incident in Hawaii in 1982 illustrates one way that such contamination occurs. After the state health department found that milk on the island of Oahu contained from three to six times the accepted level of heptachlor, a carcinogenic pesticide that causes liver and kidney damage, it recalled all milk products from grocery shelves and school cafeterias.[91] Investigators discovered that dairy cattle had been fed with pineapple leaves sprayed with heptachlor. A 1980 EPA study estimated that 93 percent of the population has in their bodies some levels of dieldrin, a carcinogenic pesticide that was banned in 1976.[92] Pesticides are also found in meat and dairy products. According to the Food and Drug Administration, between 500 and 600 toxic chemicals may be present in this country's meat supply.[93]

Food can also become contaminated by other substances. In 1973 in Michigan, 1,000 to 2,000 pounds of PBBs, a flame-retardant, were accidentally substituted for a feed additive for farm animals. PBBs are known to damage the nervous system, the liver, and the immune system. As a result of the accident, 30,000 cattle and 1.5 million chickens had to be destroyed.[94] Five years after the incident a research team from

Mt. Sinai Hospital in New York City estimated that 97 percent of Michigan residents had some level of PBBs in their bodies.[95]

The U.S. military uses many of the same chemicals and production processes as does private industry, and its impact on the environment requires close scrutiny by environmentalists. Like other industries, the military threatens its own workers most directly. At a press conference in Sacramento, California, in 1982, a former army medic testified that he had been ordered to report false data to cover up the fact that soldiers at atomic tests in the 1950s were exposed to dangerously high levels of radiation.[96] A 1982 study by the U.S. Centers for Disease Control found that the 3,027 men who took part in one of the Nevada tests had leukemia death rates three times higher than the population at large.[97] Since the end of the Vietnam war, U.S. veterans have complained of rashes, birth defects in their children, and nervous conditions that they attribute to their exposure to Agent Orange, a herbicide that was used to defoliate jungle areas during the war. While U.S. scientists are only now beginning to study the long-term health effects of Agent Orange, Vietnamese researchers reported at a 1983 international conference in Ho Chi Minh City that they had found an increase in abnormalities in children of women whose husbands had been exposed to wartime use of the herbicide.[98]

Once again, however, the dangers of military programs do not stop at the barracks gate. In 1957 a fire at the Rocky Flats nuclear weapons plant in Colorado sent a radioactive cloud across nearby Denver. Years later Dow Chemical Company, which operated the plant for the government, found high levels of carcinogenic radioactive materials at two elementary schools within twelve miles of the Rocky Flats plant.[99]

In New Brighton, a suburb of Minneapolis, the Twin Cities Army Ammunition Plant has contaminated the 23,500 residents' supply of ground water with the carcinogen trichloroethylene.[100] Unfortunately, most environmental regulations exempt military programs; government secrecy further limits our knowledge of the magnitude of the problem. In the name of national security, the defense establishment has become nearly immune to public scrutiny and criticism, which makes corrective action doubly difficult.

Causes of the Current Crisis

These examples from across the United States indicate that every community in the country faces an actual or potential threat to its health. From pesticide spraying to uranium mining, from toxic dump sites to industrial air pollution, from nuclear power plants to the national network of highways and railways used to transport toxic chemicals, Americans are experiencing a chemical and radioactive assault on their health. New technologies that could have been used to feed, clothe, house, and transport people are instead destroying the environment that sustains human life and damaging the health of present and future generations. Why is this enormous misappropriation of our nation's resources allowed to take place?

The answer requires a closer look at our economic and political system. In the economic sphere, the pursuit of profit is the force that drives a capitalist system. Capitalists invest money in those industries that will return the highest rate of profit. They design production processes that will minimize their costs and maximize their returns.

In *The Closing Circle*, environmental scientist Barry Commoner describes how natural organic products such as soap and cotton were replaced after World War II with unnatural synthetic ones such as detergents and plastics.[101] In almost every case the new technology damaged the environment more than the old one, but in each case the new production process was also more profitable. In fact, the very qualities that made the new products profitable also made them destructive to the environment. Many plastic goods, for example, are used once and then disposed of, guaranteeing both a steady market for new products and growing piles of nondegradable, often toxic, garbage.

The automobile industry provides another example of choosing profits over a cleaner environment. The average 1968 passenger car emitted more than twice the nitrogen oxide exhaust as the 1946 car. And cars in 1971 spewed out nearly twice as much lead per mile as models made in the postwar years. The major reason that automakers preferred powerful gas-guzzling cars was profit. In the late 1960s it cost General Motors only $300 more to make a Cadillac Coupe de Ville than the smaller Chevrolet Caprice. But consumers paid $3,800 more for the Caddy—

the difference went into GMs coffers.[102]

Agribusiness's hunger for profits has led it to aggressively market products that can in the long run ruin farmland. For example, pesticides and fertilizers are like heroin: the more they are used, the more they are needed. Pesticides kill not only the pest but also its predators. As birds, larger insects, or frogs that eat the pest are killed off, the pest reproduces more rapidly. More pesticides are required to maintain production. Species-specific control agents are available, but broad-spectrum pesticides—those that kill many species—are marketed more widely because they are more profitable. Similarly, as soil becomes depleted by a single crop, such as wheat or corn, that only chemical fertilizers can sustain, increasing amounts of fertilizer are needed to maintain the same level of productivity. The farmers' costs go up and fertilizer runoff pollutes the water, but agribusinesses make healthy profits.

A desire for a fast return on investment also leads to more rapid extraction of natural resources from the earth, even though a slower pace would cause less damage to both the environment and human health.

Corporate insistence on dividends for its shareholders, combined with lax regulation, leads to inadequate expenditures on pollution control. As a result, toxic wastes are often disposed of in cheaper, more dangerous, ways rather than safer, more expensive, ones. According to one chemical industry spokesman, an illegal   waste   disposal   company charges $1 a barrel to haul away and dump toxic wastes, while safe, legal disposal can cost as much as $45 a barrel.[103] Not surprisingly, most of the major chemical companies have been caught using illicit disposal firms. The continual spills and breakdowns at nuclear power plants further illustrate industry's reluctance to spend money on safety.

Since government control of pollution is weak, the corporations do not have to pay for the consequences of environmental contamination. The real costs are borne by the taxpayers, consumers, and workers who pay higher taxes for cleanup efforts, travel further or move to find clean air or water, and face devastating medical bills. To use the dramatic example of Love Canal, Hooker Chemical spent $1.7 million to dispose of its waste in an abandoned canal that the company then sold to the Niagara Falls school board. Nearly twenty-five years later, when the Love Canal residents finally forced the state and federal governments to clean up the site, New York State taxpayers alone paid out more than $61 million to remedy the situation.[104]

Manufacturers introduce hundreds of new pesticides and other chemical products into the market each year. But the rapid journey from laboratory to marketplace means that there is no time for realistic evaluation of the environmental or health impact of a new product. The disasters caused by such toxins as PCBs, dioxin, PVCs, asbestos, and formaldehyde could have been avoided by proper testing, but a company that tested its products thoroughly would have had to sacrifice first crack at the market, thus violating its obligations to its shareholders to bring in steady profits.

In sum, the U.S. economy creates incentives for environmental degradation. It encourages capitalists to find the cheapest, quickest way to make profits, no matter what the environmental cost. When laws allow corporations to pass the costs of pollution on to the public rather than their shareholders, these corporations are further encouraged to pollute. Further, industry uses its power and wealth to ensure that government regulations will not seriously interfere with making a profit.

The causes of the corporate assault on health are political as well as economic. The corporations that dominate the U.S. economy also shape our political system. Not only do they insist on their right to make a profit as they see fit, but they also want the power to construct a society that they can continue to control without undue public interference.

In the United States, citizens do not have the right to control what goes on in their communities. Decisions about where to build or move factories, where to dump toxic waste, or what technologies to invest in are made by corporate boards and the managers they hire. When community residents or workers contest these decisions, they must file expensive lawsuits, lobby distant legislators, or pressure reluctant bureaucrats, all in an arena in which corporations help to set the rules and choose the players.

To maintain its power, industry also seeks to define the nation's political agenda. Its advertising, its advocates in Congress and the White

House, and its academic supporters insist that only continued economic growth controlled by industry can ensure (or return) prosperity. The only legitimate question for these people is how to encourage such growth. Those who challenge continued corporate hegemony meet stiff resistance. Workers who refuse to sacrifice their health to increased profits face environmental blackmail—the threat of losing their jobs. Those who question the benefits of nuclear power or pesticides are labeled as extremists, impractical romantics, or communists.

But the continuing toll that industry's growth has taken on the health of the people of the United States has led increasing numbers of them to question a political and economic system that puts profit before human need. Across the country, community groups are fighting for a deeper concept of democracy, one that gives people a voice in making decisions about their neighborhoods, their communities, and their workplaces, and one that gives them the information necessary to make these judgments. At the root of this new movement lies the belief that people have the right to air, water, food, and land that will not sicken them, and the determination to create a society that guarantees this right.

References

1. The case history is based on the following sources: "Together We Can Do It: Fighting Toxic Hazards in Tennessee: Interview with Nell Grantham," *Southern Exposure* 9, no. 3 (Fall 1981): 42–47, and author interview with Nell Grantham, September 1981.
2. C. S. Clark et al., "An Environmental Health Survey of Drinking Water Contamination by Leachate from a Pesticide Waste Dump in Hardeman County, Tennessee," *Archives of Environmental Health* 37 (1982): 9–18.
3. "Together We Can Do It," p. 45.
4. Debra Lee Davis and B. H. Mayer, "Cancer and Industrial Chemical Production," *Science* 206 (1979): 1356–57.
5. Milton Weinstein, "Cost-Effective Priorities for Cancer Prevention," *Science* 221 (1983): 17–23.
6. Council on Environmental Quality, *Environmental Quality: 10th Annual Report* (Washington, DC: Council on Environmental Quality, 1979).
7. Frances Moore Lappé and Joseph Collins, *Food First* (Boston: Houghton Mifflin, 1977), p. 175.
8. Charles Komanoff and Eric van Loon, "'Too Cheap to Meter' or 'Too Costly to Build'?" *Nucleus* (Union of Concerned Scientists) 4 (1982): 3–7.
9. *New York Times*, 16 May 1982, sect. 3, p. 1.
10. *New York Times*, 2 August 1982, p. D8.
11. W. Keith Morgan et al., "Respiratory Disability in Coal Miners," *Journal of the American Medical Association* 243 (1980): 2401–4.
12. Appalachia—Science in the Public Interest, *Citizen's Blasting Handbook*, 1978, p. 30.
13. Highlander Research and Education Center (HREC), *We're Tired of Being Guinea Pigs!* (New Market, Tenn.: Highlander Center, 1980), p. 3.
14. Ibid.
15. Kai Erikson, *Everything in Its Path* (New York: Simon & Schuster, 1976).
16. Philip Landrigan et al., "Epidemic Lead Absorption Near an Ore Smelter: The Role of Particulate Lead,"

New England Journal of Medicine 292 (1975): 123–29.

17. *Washington Post,* 7 October 1979.
18. *New York Times,* 25 April 1983, p. A10.
19. Leslie J. Freeman, *Nuclear Witnesses* (New York: W. W. Norton, 1981), p. 144.
20. *Los Angeles Times,* 17 September 1979.
21. WARN, "Pine Ridge Reservation Health Study."
22. Cited during "Four Corners: A National Sacrifice Area?" WNET-TV, 14 November 1983.
23. J. C. Marx, "Low-Level Radiation: Just How Bad Is It?" *Science* 204 (1979): 160–64.
24. General Accounting Office, *Problems in Assessing the Cancer Risks of Low-Level Ionizing Radiation Exposure,* Comptroller General's Report to Congress, EMD 81–1, 1981.
25. Rachel Scott, *Muscle and Blood* (New York: E. P. Dutton, 1974), pp. 10–11.
26. *New York Times,* 9 February 1982, p. A14.
27. Advisory Committee to the Office of the Secretary, Department of Health, Education, and Welfare ("Rall Committee"), "Health and Environmental Effects of Increased Coal Utilization," *Federal Register* 43 (16 January 1978): 2229–40
28. S. C. Morris et al., *Data Book for Quantification of Health Effects from Coal Energy Systems,* Brookhaven National Laboratory Regional Energy Studies Program, Contract EV 76–C-07-0016 (Upton, N.Y.: U.S. Department of Energy, 7 May 1979).
29. *New York Times,* 29 June 1983, pp. A1, A12.
30. U.S. Environmental Protection Agency, *Acid Rain,* vol. 1 (Washington, D.C.: EPA, April 1980).
31. H. M. Braunstein et al., *Environmental Health and Control Aspects of Coal Conversion,* vols. 1 and 2 (Oak Ridge National Laboratories, prepared for Energy and Development Administration, April 1977).
32. *New York Times,* 28 July 1981, p. B4.
33. *New York Times,* 13 September 1981, p. 48.
34. Nuclear Information and Resource Center (NICR), *Nuclear Waste: Where It Comes From* (Washington, D.C.: Nuclear Information and Resource Center, 1981).
35. Anna Gyorgy, *No Nukes* (Boston: South End Press, 1979) p. 50.
36. NIRC, *Nuclear Waste: Where It Comes From.*
37. HREC, *We're Tired of Being Guinea Pigs!,* p. 10.
38. Andrew Marino and Robert Becker, "Hazard at a Distance: Effects of Exposure to the Electric and Magnetic Fields of High Voltage Transmission Lines," *Medical Research Engineering* 12 (1977): 6–9.
39. Nancy Wertheimer and Ed Leeper, "Electrical Wiring Configurations and Childhood Cancer," *American Journal of Epidemiology* 109 (1979): 273–84.
40. National Institute for Occupational Safety and Health (NIOSH), *President's Report on Occupational Safety and Health* (Washington, D.C.: Department of Health, Education, and Welfare, 1972).
41. NIOSH, *National Occupational Hazard Survey,* vol. 3 (Washington, D.C.: U.S. Government Printing Office, 1977).
42. Council on Environmental Quality, *Environmental Quality—11th Annual Report* (Washington, D.C.: Council on Environmental Quality, 1980).
43. Lester B. Lave and Eugene Seskin. *Air Pollution and Human Health* (Baltimore: Johns Hopkins University Press, 1977).
44. *New York Times,* 1 August 1980, pp. 27–28.

45. Carl M. Shy, "Testimony before Subcommittee on Health and Environment," U.S. House of Representatives, Clean Air Act Amendments of 1977, Part 1, 8–11 March 1977, pp. 244–62.

46. *New York Times*, 28 March 1982, p. 26.

47. *New York Times*, 5 April 1982, p. B6.

48. *New York Times*, 20 May 1982, p. A22.

49. Reported in *New York Times*, 30 November 1983, p. A1.

50. U.S. Congress, Senate, Committee on Commerce, Science, and Transportation, *Hazardous Materials Transportation's Regulatory Program* (Washington, D.C.: U.S. Government Printing Office, 1979).

51. National Transportation Safety Board, *Safety Effectiveness Evaluation-Federal and State Enforcement Efforts in Hazardous Material Transportation by Truck*, NTSB–SEE–81–2 (Washington, D.C.: U.S. Government Printing Office, 1981), p.6.

52. Ibid.

53. U.S. General Accounting Office, *Program for Ensuring the Safe Transportation of Hazardous Materials Need Improvement* (Washington, D.C.: U.S. Congress, 1980).

54. U.S. Congress, *Hazardous Materials Transportation*.

55. *In These Times*, 16–29 July 1980, pp. 7–8.

56. *New York Times*, 20 November 1981, p. A14.

57. *New York Times*, 13 October 1982, p. A13.

58. H. A. Anderson et al., "Household Contact Asbestos Neoplastic Risk," *Annals of the New York Academy of Medicine* 276 (1976): 311–23.

59. *New York Times*, 10 February 1983, p. D4; 1 July 1983, p. A6.

60. *New York Times*, 23 May 1982, p. B2.

61. Quoted in *New York Times*, 1 September 1983, p. A15.

62. *New York Times*, 22 April 1983, p. B2.

63. *New York Times*, 31 August 1983, pp. A1, A18.

64. "Health Effects of Construction through a Landfill," *City Health Information* (New York City Department of Health) 1/19 (1982): 1–3; Clark et al., "Environmental Health Survey of Drinking Water Contamination"; Thomas Maugh, "Just How Hazardous Are Dumps?" *Science* 215 (1982): 490–93; *New York Times*, 8 July 1982, p. B4; 2 January 1982, pp. 1, 7; 28 December 1981, p. A16; William Lowrance, ed., *Assessment of Health Effects at Chemical Disposal Sites*, Proceedings of a Symposium held in New York City on June 1–2, 1981, by the Life Sciences and Public Policy Program of the Rockefeller University, pp. 3–22.

65. *New York Times*, 29 June 1981, p. A12.

66. Michael Brown, *Laying Waste* (New York: Pantheon Books, 1980), pp. 28–59.

67. Reported in *New York Times*, 17 March 1983, p. B14.

68. Reported in *New York Times*, 29 December 1982, p. A8.

69. *New York Times*, 2 January 1982, p. 7.

70. Quoted in *New York Times*, 13 March 1983, p. F2.

71. Reported in *New York Times*, 28 December 1981, p. A16.

72. Ibid.

73. *New York Times*, 4 November 1981, pp. B1, B2.

74. Ibid

75. *New York Times*, 8 April 1983, p. B3.

76. *New York Times*, 25 May 1982, pp. C1, C7.

77. Ibid

78. *New York Times*, 19 May 1983, p. D2.

79. Rachel Carson, *Silent Spring* (Boston: Houghton Mifflin, 1962), p. 14.

80. H. P. Chase et al., "Pesticides and U.S. Farm Labor Families," *Rocky*

Mountain Medical Journal 70 (1973): 27–31; Ephraim Kahn, "Pesticide-Related Illness in California Farm Workers," *Journal of Occupational Medicine* 18 (1976): 693–96; U.S. Department of Health, Education, and Welfare, *Report of the Secretary's Commission on Pesticides and Their Relationship to Environmental Health* (Washington, D.C.: U.S. Government Printing Office, 1969).

81. HREC; *We're Tired of Being Guinea Pigs!*, p. 25.
82. Samuel Epstein, *The Politics of Cancer* (Garden City, N.Y.: Anchor Books, 1979), pp. 245–47.
83. T. H. Milvey and D. Wharton, "Epidemiological Assessment of Occupationally Related, Chemically Induced Sperm Count Suppression," *Journal of Occupational Medicine* 22 (1980): 77–82.
84. U.S. Environmental Protection Agency, *Report of Assessment of a Field Investigation of Six-Year Spontaneous Abortion Rates in Three Oregon Areas in Relation to Forest 2, 4, 5–T Spray Practices*, Epidemiologic Studies Program, 28 February 1979.
85. *Los Angeles Times*, 30 July 1979.
86. *Suffolk Times* (Greenport, N.Y.), 3 June 1982, p. 7.
87. *New York Times*, 1 August 1982, pp. LI–1, 4.
88. Reported in *New York Times*, 4 December 1983, p. 65.
89. *Oakland Tribune*, 4 July 1982.
90. *San Francisco Chronicle*, 9 July 1982.
91. R. Jeffrey Smith, "Hawaiian Milk Contamination Creates Alarm," *Science* 217 (1982): 137–40.
92. *Los Angeles Times*, 1 September 1980.
93. Reported in *New York Times*, 15 March 1983, pp. A1, D24.
94. Ellen Grzech, "PBB," in *Who's Poisoning America*, Ralph Nader, Ronald Brownstein, and John Richard, editors (San Francisco: Sierra Club, 1981), pp. 60–84.
95. Mary Wolff et al., "Human Tissue Burdens of Halogenated Aromatic Chemicals in Michigan," *Journal of the American Medical Association* 247 (1982): 2112–16.
96. *New York Times*, 8 February 1982, p. A14.
97. Reported in *New York Times*, 7 April 1983, p. A18.
98. *New York Times*, 18 March 1983, p. A30.
99. *New York Times*, 9 September 1981, p. A12.
100. *New York Times*, 26 December 1982, p. 22.
101. Commoner, *Closing Circle*, pp. 151–52.
102. Richard Kazis and Richard Grossman, *Fear at Work: Job Blackmail, Labor, and the Environment* (New York: Pilgrim Press, 1982), p. 204.
103. Cited in Larry George, "Love Canal and the Politics of Corporate Terrorism," *Socialist Review* 66 (1982): 27.
104. *Philadelphia Inquirer*, 23 September 1979; *New York Times*, 7 September 1981.

8 BLACK LUNG: THE SOCIAL PRODUCTION OF DISEASE

Barbara Ellen Smith

The recognition that certain forms of ill health are socially produced and therefore possibly preventable is one of the most important sources of progressive political vitality in the United States today. During the past decade, sporadic protest has erupted over hazardous situations in isolated workplaces and communities, from the controversy over toxic waste disposal in the Love Canal area to the protest against use of dioxin-contaminated herbicides in the Pacific Northwest. In some instances, more prolonged and widespread struggles have developed, such as the movement for black lung compensation and the current mobilization against nuclear power. These phenomena are admittedly quite diverse in their social bases, ideologies, and political goals. However, to varying degrees, all have involved the politicization of health hazards and illness, and thereby have drawn into the arena of political controversy one of the most elite professional domains in the United States —scientific medicine.

These controversies characteristically have originated in the bitter suspicions of lay people who fear that certain of their health problems are caused by industrial practices and products, but who have no scientifically credible proof to substantiate their concern. In some cases, scientists have scornfully dismissed as "housewife data" lay efforts to document these health problems (1). Indeed, health advocates' demands for compensatory or preventive action have often encountered their most formidable ideological opposition from the ranks of the medical establishment, who come armed with the seemingly unassailable authority of "science" and characteristically argue that no action is justified until further evidence is collected. Especially in contexts like that of the petrochemical industry, where workers and sometimes residential communities are exposed to manifold hazards about which little is known and whose effects may not be manifested for decades, health advocates can be forced into a no-win situation: they must prove their case with data that do not exist, using a model of disease causation that is ill suited to multiple and/or synergistic hazards, and which a growing chorus of critics argue is structurally incapable of explaining the major health problems of our place and time, such as heart disease and stress (2).

This article examines one health struggle, the black lung movement, during which the scientific authority of the medical establishment was itself questioned in the course of an intense political controversy over the definition of disease. The movement arose in southern West Virginia in 1968 and had as its initial goal the

SOURCE: *International Journal of Health Services* 11, no. 3 (1981): 343-59. ©*1981, Baywood Publishing Co., Inc.*

extension of workers' compensation coverage to victims of "black lung," a generic term for the ensemble of respiratory diseases that miners contract in the workplace. To elucidate the medical politics of this struggle, this article looks at three aspects of the history of black lung. The first section explores the major changes in medical perceptions of black lung and presents evidence suggesting that these shifting perceptions have been occasioned by social and economic factors ordinarily considered extrinsic to science. This section also points out the ideological and political functions of the medical definitions of this disease. The second part focuses on the history of black lung itself and argues that the respiratory disease burden is intimately related to the political economy of the workplace, the site of disease production. The final section describes the recent battle over black lung compensation, focusing on the strikingly different definitions of disease that miners and the medical establishment elaborated.

Medical Constructions of Black Lung

The history of science is popularly conceived as a continuum of concepts and paradigms evolving through time toward an ever more comprehensive and accurate understanding of a "given" external reality. However, there is a growing tradition of literature that challenges this positivist approach by classifying the scientific knowledge of any society as part of its historically specific belief systems, and viewing scientific concepts as both a consequence of and an influence upon the overall structure of social relations. Efforts to pursue this approach with regard to medical science have been especially fruitful and abundant. Scholarship has focused primarily on the ways in which medical practice has tended to reflect and uphold socially structured inequality (especially that based on class, sex, and race). Some analysts have also begun to investigate the exceedingly complex correspondence between the structures, forces, and dynamics that medical knowledge invests in the human body and the dynamics of social relations in the "body politic." (3)

The case of black lung provides an exceptionally clear example of the ways in which factors external to science have shaped and changed medical knowledge. In the United States, medical perceptions of black lung fall into three periods, bounded by major shifts in the political economy of the coal industry. Observations of miners' unusual respiratory disease burden and speculation as to its workplace origins characterized the first medical construction of black lung. This viewpoint originated in the anthracite coalfields of Pennsylvania during a period when medical knowledge and practice, health care delivery arrangements, and industrial relations between miners and operators were all in a state of flux. A completely different concept of black lung emerged in a later period from the expanding bituminous coalfields, where tight corporate control over the health care system, a stark class structure, and other factors were relevant to the medical outlook. A third concept of black lung developed gradually after World War II in the context of a highly unionized, increasingly capital-intensive industry with a union-controlled health plan for miners and their families.

The first written documents concerning miners' unusual respiratory trouble originated from the anthracite region of eastern Pennsylvania; here were located the first large-scale coal mining operations in the United States, dominated by the affiliates of nine railroads. During the 1860s and 1870s, a few physicians acquainted with this region began to publish articles remarking on miners' respiratory difficulties and speculating that they were related to the inhalation of dusts and gases in the workplace. These articles are remarkable for their detailed accounts of unhealthy working conditions and their inclusion of statements by miners themselves on their workplace health (4).

This period prior to the hegemony of scientific medicine was characterized by a relative eclecticism and fluidity in medical knowledge, practice, and health care delivery arrangements. Some medical historians argue that the uncertain financial, professional, and social status of physicians lent more equality and negotiability to the doctor-patient relationship than is customary today (5). In the anthracite coalfields, miners were beginning to finance their health and welfare needs through mutual benefit associations that gave financial assistance in cases of sickness, disability and death (6). This brief period of relative fluidity in the health care system was soon eclipsed, however, by the simultaneous eradication of the benefit associations and the growth of the company doctor system. The most significant episode in this process was the strike of 1874-1875, which led to the famous Molly Maguire murder trials and resulted in the disintegration of the major anthracite trade union, the Miners' and Laborers' Benevolent Association. The powerful Philadelphia and Reading Railroad, whose affiliate Coal and Iron Company was the largest anthracite coal producer, subsequently attempted to replace the union's health and welfare functions with a Beneficial Fund financed by miners and controlled by the company. During the last two decades of the nineteenth century, as mining corporations gradually extended their control over health care delivery through the company doctor system, physicians in the anthracite fields grew silent on the subject of miners' occupational lung disease. The anthracite industry subsequently entered a period of decline from which it never recovered; the center of U.S. coal production shifted to the bituminous fields, where physicians elaborated a completely different concept of black lung.

The bituminous industry of southern Appalachia achieved national economic importance around the turn of the century and by the end of World War I was rapidly becoming the heart of the U.S. coal production. In the coal camps of this rural and mountainous region, physicians did not simply ignore the existence of black lung, as many have suggested; rather, they viewed miners' diseased state as normal and non-disabling, and therefore unworthy of scientific investigation. The sources of this perception may be found partly in the political economy of the coal industry, which left a peculiarly repressive stamp on the structure of health care delivery in Appalachia (7).

In the southern bituminous industry, coal operators initially assumed a direct role in establishing, maintaining, and controlling many social and political institutions, such as the public schools, churches, and the police. Their activities derived in part from practical necessity: companies often had to import much of their labor force into this sparsely populated area, and in order to keep these workers had to provide housing, food, and a minimum of public services. However, the operators' role was neither benign nor merely practical. The profits to be made from housing, food, and to a lesser extent medical care were often quite significant to companies attempting to survive in the highly competitive, unstable business environment of bituminous coal. Moreover, totalitarian control of coal communities, including issuance of a separate currency (scrip), domination of the police, and even control of the physical access to the towns, enabled these companies to forestall what they perceived as one of the most pernicious threats to their economic status—unionization.

Health care did not escape the logic of this competitive environ-ment and direct domination of the work force. The company doctor was the only source of medical care in almost all rural Appalachian coal camps. Under this system, the coal company controlled the employment of a doctor, but miners were required as a condition of employment to pay for his services. The company doctors' accountability to the coal operators is one of the most obvious and fundamental reasons for the medical concepts of miners' occupational health developed during this period. Work-related accidents and later diseases spelled economic liability for the coal operators under the workers' compensation system. Any agitation for preventive action would have represented an even greater nuisance. There was instead a uniform tendency to ascribe accidents and diseases to the fault of the miner—his carelessness and personal habits, such as alcoholism. Thus, one physician in 1919, after reciting a litany of occupational safety and health hazards, including dust, gob piles, electricity, poisonous gases, and contaminated water supplies, managed to conclude: "Housing conditions, and hurtful forms of recreation, especially alcoholism, undoubtedly cause the major amount of sickness. The mine itself is not an unhealthful place to work." (8)

The medical ideology surrounding black lung was more complex than this outright denial of occupational causation. Physicians dubbed the widespread breathlessness, expectoration of sputum, and prolonged coughing fits "miners' asthma." These symptoms of lung disease were *constituted as a norm*; as such, they were to be expected and by definition were nondisabling. For example, in 1935, one physician in Pennsylvania wrote (9):

> As far as most of the men in this region are concerned, so called "miners' asthma" is considered an *ordinary* condition that needs cause no worry and therefore the profession has not troubled itself about its finer pathological and associated clinical manifestations (emphasis added).

A miner who complained of disability due to respiratory trouble was diagnosed as a case of "malingering," "compensationitis," or "fear of the mines." The social control aspects of this ideology are obvious: if disease was natural, inevitable, and nondisabling, then prevention was unnecessary. Moreover, exhibiting disability from a respiratory disease was a medically stigmatized sign of psychological weakness or duplicity. (10).

Although the company doctor system provides one explanation for this medical concept, it may also be related to class interactions in the coalfields and to some of the basic precepts of scientific medicine. It may be speculated that the company doctor's social as well as medical perspective on the coal miner and his family was influenced by the relative status of each within the coal camp environment (11). The monoeconomy of the Appalachian coalfields produced a rather simple and vivid class structure, in which physicians, lawyers, and a few other professionals formed an island in a working-class sea. On the one hand,

the superiority of the doctors' status relative to the working class was everywhere apparent—in their standard of living, language, etc. On the other hand, these physicians were in a distinctly inferior position by the standards of the medical profession as a whole, and moreover were denied numerous amenities available in more cosmopolitan surroundings. Their degraded social and physical environment was embodied in and no doubt in many cases attributed to coal miners themselves—their ramshackle houses, coarse language, "lack of culture," and so on. What was "normal" for miners, including even a chronic respiratory condition, was by no means normal for the company doctor (12).

The outlook of scientific medicine, which around the turn of the century was gaining hegemony over other forms of medical theory and practice, is also relevant to the company doctors' conceptualization of black lung. With the rise of scientific medicine, production of medical knowledge gradually became the province of research scientists, divorced from the human patient by their location in the laboratory. Building on the precepts of cell theory and the discovery of bacteria, their efforts focused on the isolation of specific aberrations in cell function, and their correlation with discrete disease agents. The "germ theory" of disease causation, which essentially holds that each disease is caused by a specific bacterium or agent, became the basis of scientific medicine. This theory confounded the microscopic *agent* of disease with the *cause* of disease; it thus implicitly denied a role to social and economic factors in disease causation and displaced the social medicine of an earlier period.

At the level of medical practice, diagnosis became a process of identifying separate disease entities, with confirmation of the diagnosis sought in the laboratory; the patients' own testimony as to his/her condition was relegated to a decidedly secondary status. Indeed, scientific medicine involved what Jewson (5) termed the "disappearance of the sick-man" from the medical world view. The patient increasingly appeared almost incidentally as the medium for disease, eclipsed by the focus on identifying discrete pathologies. In the absence of a verifiable clinical entity, the patient was by definition (health is the absence of disease) pronounced healthy. His/her protestations of feeling ill became a matter for the psychiatrist (13).

These features of the scientific medical outlook dovetailed with previously mentioned factors to produce the company doctors' conceptualization of black lung. To the extent that any company doctor seriously attempted to diagnose a miner's respiratory condition, the effort was informed by the search for previously established clinical entities, especially silicosis and tuberculosis. Up until very recently, silica was considered the only dust seriously harmful to the respiratory system. Moreover, silicosis possesses characteristics that scientific medicine is most conducive to recognizing as a legitimate clinical entity: it is associated with one specific agent; it pro-

duces gross pathological change in lung tissue, apparent upon autopsy; and it reveals itself relatively clearly in a characteristic pattern on an X-ray. Most coal miners were not exposed to silica in significant quantity, and their X-rays did not exhibit the classic silicotic pattern. To the extent that their X-rays revealed the pathological changes now associated with coal workers' pneumoconiosis, these too were considered normal— for coal miners (14). Moreover, as a group, miners seemed to experience a low mortality rate from tuberculosis, considered the prime public health problem of this period. Hence developed the perversely ironic "coal dust is good for you" theory: "It is in the highest degree possible that coal-dust possesses the property of hindering the development of tuberculosis, and of arresting its progress." (15)

The company doctor system did not go unchallenged by coal miners; unrest over its compulsory character occasionally led to strikes and generated the demand for a health care plan organized on the opposite basis—union control and industry financing. Following a protracted strike and federalization of the mines in 1946, miners finally won a contract establishing such a system, the Welfare and Retirement Fund. Financed by a royalty assessed on each ton of mined coal, the Fund provided pensions, hospitalization, and medical care for the miners and their families. Although officially directed by a tripartite board composed of representatives from industry, the union, and the public, in reality the Fund was controlled by the United Mine Workers. At the time of its creation, progressives in the health care field almost unanimously viewed the Fund as an innovative leap forward in health care delivery. Contradictions embedded in coal's postwar industrial relations subsequently compromised this vision and constricted the Fund's activities. Nevertheless, in its first decade and heyday, the Fund transformed the structure and quality of health care in the Appalachian coalfields (16).

The establishment of the Fund made possible the beginning of a third period in the medical conceptualization of miners' respiratory disease. Progressive physicians, many organized in prepaid group practice financed through the Fund, undertook clinical research on the respiratory problems of their coal miner patients. The Fund also employed in its central office a physician whose primary responsibility was to educate the medical profession about coal miners' dust disease. These physicians were largely responsible for the trickle of literature on coal workers' pneumoconiosis that began to appear in U.S. medical journals during the early 1950s; of the articles they did not write, most depended on data from Fund-affiliated hospitals and clinics. All argued essentially that "authoritative opinion to the contrary notwithstanding," coal miners suffer from a "disabling, progressive, killing disease which is related to exposure to coal dust." (17)

Despite these efforts, medical recognition of coal workers' pneumoconiosis did not evolve in an orderly, linear fashion, advanced by the in-

quiring gaze of these scientists. They remained a minority within the medical establishment, and coal miners in most states continued to be denied workers' compensation for occupational lung disease. The recognition that black lung was rampant among U.S. coal miners did not evolve of its own accord within the boundaries of medical science. It was forced on the medical community by the decidedly political intervention of miners themselves.

Black Lung and the Transformation of the Workplace

Since the changing medical concepts of black lung reveal more about the development of the coal industry and health care delivery systems than the nature and extent of respiratory disease among coal miners, observers may well wonder what the history of black lung actually entails. It is extremely difficult to reconstruct satisfactorily. Epidemiological data on miners' lung disease are simply nonexistent, except for the very recent period. The early commentaries cited previously suggest that pervasive respiratory problems accompanied the growth of the anthracite and bituminous coal industries, a conclusion corroborated by nonmedical sources (18); however, acceptance of "miners' asthma" and a dearth of medical literature swiftly followed. Between 1918 and 1940, a few scattered studies, primarily by the U.S. Public Health Service, uncovered "extraordinary" excess mortality from influenza and pneumonia among anthracite and bituminous coal miners; their susceptibility was likely due to the work-related destruction of their respiratory systems. However, all U.S. Public Health Service research on miners' occupational respiratory disease focused on silicosis; the resulting data were mixed, but the invariable conclusion was that bituminous miners were not exposed to silica in significant quantity and were not seriously disabled by work-related lung disease (19).

Although the lack of statistics precludes documentation of the extent of black lung, it is possible to trace the changing causes of disease by analyzing the site of disease production—the workplace. By "workplace" is meant not only the physical characteristics of the site of coal production but also the social relations that shape and are part of the workplace. The interaction between miners and operators under historically given circumstances has shaped the timing and character of technological innovation, the nature of the work process, the pace of work, and other factors relevant to the production of occupational disease. The history of black lung is thus internally related to the history of the workplace, as a physical site and a social relationship.

This history may be divided into two major periods, distinguished by their different technologies, work organizations, industrial relations, and sources of respiratory disease: handloading and mechanized mining. During the initial handloading era, which persisted until the 1930s, of utmost importance to the production of coal and disease was the highly competitive and labor-intensive

character of the industry. Fragmented into thousands of competing companies, bituminous coal suffered from chronic bouts of overproduction, excess capacity, low profit margins, and fluctuating prices. Because labor represented approximately 70 percent of the cost of production, a prime tactic in the competitive struggle was to cut the cost of labor, principally by lowering the piece rate. In addition, the craft nature of the labor process rendered companies relatively powerless to control productivity and output, except by manipulating the miners' wages (20).

These economic dynamics had important implications for the workplace as a site of disease production. The instability of the industry frequently resulted in irregular work and a lowering of the piece rate, both of which forced miners to work faster and/or longer hours in an attempt to maintain their standard of living. The impact on health and safety conditions was almost invariably negative, as miners necessarily reduced nonproductive, safety-oriented tasks, such as roof timbering, to a minimum (21). Working longer hours in mines where "towards quitting time [the air] becomes so foul that the miners' lamps will no longer burn" (22) no doubt increased the respiratory disease risk. Moreover, a financially mandated speedup encouraged miners to re-enter their work areas as soon as possible after blasting the coal loose from the face, an operation that generated clouds of dust and powder smoke (23).

Respiratory hazards often were especially grave in non-gassy mines, where ventilation tended to be poorest. The prospect of losing their entire capital investment in one explosion encouraged mine owners to install better ventilation systems in mines where methane gas was liberated; the non-gassy mines, however, tended to "kill the men by inches." (4, p. 244) Writing around the turn of the century, one mine inspector described in detail the ventilation problem and its implications for miners' health (22, pp. 449-450):

> . . . adequate ventilation is not applied in such [non-gassy] mines, because they can be wrought without going to the expense of providing costly and elaborate furnaces or fans, air-courses, stoppings, and brattice. From four to six cents a ton are thus saved in mining the coal that should be applied in ventilating, but saved at the expense of the workmen's health. . . . Constant labor in a badly-aired mine breaks down the constitution and clouds the intellect. The lungs become clogged up from inhaling coal dust, and from breathing noxious air; the body and limbs become stiff and sore, the mind loses the power of vigorous thought. After six years' labor in a badly ventilated mine—that is, a mine where a man with a good constitution may from habit be able to work everyday for several years—the lungs begin to change to a bluish color. After twelve years they are black, and after twenty years they are densely black, not a vestige of natural color remaining, and are little better than carbon itself. The miner dies at thirty-five, of coalminers' consumption.

During the 1930s, the introduction of mechanical loading equipment dramatically altered the workplace, while the organizing successes of the United Mine Workers transformed relations between miners and operators. Although mechanical cutting devices were introduced into underground coal mines as early as 1876, their adoption was gradual and associated with only a partial reorganization of the craft work process. The classic changes produced by mechanization and Taylorization, such as elevated productivity, loss of job control, de-skilling, and an increased division of labor, appeared slowly in bituminous coal during the first three decades of the twentieth century. However, the widespread introduction of loading machines in the 1930s broke the craft organization of work once and for all. More technological innovation swiftly followed, with the introduction of continuous mining technology after World War II. This technology did not increase the already specialized division of labor as much as it replaced several tasks (and miners) with one central production worker—the continuous miner operator.

Virtually all sources agree that the mechanization of underground mining greatly increased dust levels and magnified the existing problems with respiratory disease (24). Miners were quick to rename the Joy loaders "man killers" and to protest the unemployment, physical hardships placed on older miners, and health and safety problems that attended their introduction. For example, at the 1934 UMWA convention, miners debated at length a resolution demanding the removal of these machines from the mines; the few delegates who spoke against it were nearly shouted down by the tumultuous convention. One miner argued (25, p. 192):

> I heard one of the brothers say that they don't hire miners over forty years of age in their locality. I want to tell you brothers that there is no miner that can work in the mines under those conveyors [loading machines] and reach the age of forty. Those conveyors are man killers and I believe this convention should do its utmost to find some way whereby those conveyors will be abolished. . . . The young men after they work in the mine six or eight hours daily become sick, either getting asthma or some other sickness due to the dust of the conveyors and they can no longer perform their duty.

Another miner, during debate over continuous mining machinery at a UMWA convention 22 years later, echoed those comments (26):

> . . . [T]hey are putting coal moles [continuous miners] in our mines, and I hope they don't put them in anybody else's mines. We had one man die from the effects of that procedure. We had to give them a 15-minute shift. We have had any number who have had to get off because of health. It seems that someone forgot the miners who have [to operate] the moles. . . . He stands up there and inhales the fumes and the oil and the steam that is created by the heat from the mole. He doesn't get sufficient oxygen. . . .

It would be mistaken to conclude that because mechanization was associated with increased dust levels, machines themselves were the cause of this problem. Here again, the economic and political circumstances of

technological innovation were critical in determining its impact on the workplace. The large coal operators introduced continuous mining technology in the midst of a desperate competitive struggle with oil and natural gas, which by the 1950s had usurped coal's traditional markets in home heating and the railroads. By making coal a capital-intensive industry and vastly increasing labor productivity, the large operators hoped to force the small, labor-intensive producers into bankruptcy and win a respectable share of the growing utility market. Of crucial importance to the pace, nature, and success of this mechanization strategy was the role of the union. Headed by the authoritarian but charismatic John L. Lewis, the United Mine Workers not only accepted but aggressively promoted mechanization, believing that it would lead to institutional security, high wages, and economic prosperity (27). Although there was widespread rank-and-file discontent with mechanization, the very process replaced labor with machinery, rendering miners redundant and their protest ineffective. Despite scattered strikes and other expressions of unrest, miners were unable to modify the policy of their union or exert significant control over the impacts of mechanization on their workplace and communities.

The result was not simply increased respirable dust in the workplace, but social and economic disaster in the coalfields. In the space of 20 years, between 1950 and 1969, the work force shrank by 70 percent. For the unemployed, the monoeconomy of the Appalachian coalfields left no alternative but migration. Coal-dependent communities became ghost towns, as some counties lost half their population in the space of 10 years. Those who managed to keep their jobs in large mines confronted increased dust, noise, high-voltage electricity, and other hazards. Supervision intensified, as the operators attempted to recoup their investments in machinery by pushing productivity higher and higher (28).

The black lung controversy that erupted in 1968 was very much a product of and a challenge to this history. The movement represented an effort by miners and their families to reclaim the political and economic potency denied them for almost 20 years. Black lung disease in a sense became a metaphor for the exploitative social relations that had always characterized the coalfields, but worsened during two decades of high unemployment, social dislocation, and rank-and-file weakness vis-à-vis the coal industry. The goal of black lung compensation represented, in part, a demand for retribution from the industry for the devastating human effects of its economic transformation.

The Battle Is Joined

By 1968, when the black lung movement arose, the union's overt cooperation with the large operators had outworn its usefulness to the industry and outlived its tolerability for the rank and file. The major producers had thoroughly mechanized

their mines, reduced intraindustry competition from small companies, and held their own against external competition from alternative fuels. Capital was flowing into the industry not only through the enormously increased productivity of its workers, which tripled between 1950 and 1969, but also in the form of investment by the oil industry. Electric utilities seemed to offer unlimited market potential. Threatening the rosy forecasts, however, were an increasingly rambunctious work force and a projected manpower shortage. An enormous turnover was beginning in the work force, as the miners who managed to keep their jobs during postwar mechanization were now retiring en masse, replaced by young workers with no necessary allegiance to the UMWA leadership. The economic prosperity rankled workers already beginning to question the sluggish collective bargaining advances of their union leaders and made strikes a more potent weapon (29).

The first unmistakable evidence that rank-and-file rebellion was afoot erupted in the winter of 1968-1969 with the birth of the black lung movement. Originating in southern West Virginia, the movement was based in the older generation of workers who were leaving the mines. They faced retirement with a sparse pension of $100 per month (if they could meet the Fund's increasingly arbitrary and strict eligibility requirements), without the traditional cushion of the extended family and without compensation for the respiratory disease from which so many suffered (30). Discontent focused on the demand that the West Virginia legislature pass a bill recognizing black lung as a compensable disease under the state's workers' compensation statutes. Opposing the movement were the combined forces of the coal industry and the medical establishment. A member of the latter insisted, "There is no epidemic of devastating, killing and disabling man-made plague among coal workers." (31) Another argued, "The control of coal dust is not the answer to the disabling respiratory diseases of our coal miners." (32)

Exasperated by strident opposition and legislative inaction, miners began to quit work in February 1969 in a strike that eventually brought out 40,000 workers and shut off coal production throughout the state. Their solidarity and economic muscle forced a black lung compensation bill through the legislature; although less liberal than what miners had hoped for, they declared a victory and returned to work after the governor signed the bill into law.

This was the most dramatic and widely reported phase of the black lung movement, but it marked only the beginning. Coupled with the death of 78 miners in the violent Farmington mine explosion in November 1968, the black lung movement generated a national political debate over health and safety conditions in U.S. coal mines. In December 1969, the Congress passed a Coal Mine Health and Safety Act, which detailed to an unprecedented degree mandatory work practices throughout the industry and offered compensation to miners disabled by black lung and the widows of miners who died from the disease. Large coal companies vigorously opposed certain, but not all of the act's provisions. Most notably, they fought the extremely strict respirable dust standard of 3.0 mg/m^3, scheduled to drop to 2.0 mg/m^3 after three years; this was designed to prevent black lung. The compensation program, by contrast, was to their liking: not only did it seem to promise that the turmoil over black lung would dissolve, the program also relieved them of liability for compensation by financing benefits with general tax revenues from the U.S. Treasury.

Ironically, passage of the act ensured that the issue of black lung compensation would not die but remain the focus of a continuing movement. In 1970, the Social Security Administration began administering the claims process for compensation benefits; within the program's first week of operation, 18,000 claims poured into agency offices (33). By the fall of the same year, letters of denial began to flow back into the coalfields. The bitterness and confusion that ensued derived partly from a pattern that repeated itself throughout thousands of these rural communities: several disabled miners and widows received black lung benefits, but their brothers or uncles or neighbors down the road were denied, even though by all appearances they were equally or even more disabled by lung disease. In other words, the criteria by which the Social Security Administration judged claimants' eligibility appeared completely arbitrary and violated local perceptions of who was disabled by black lung. Thus miners and their families pitted themselves against Social Security and the medical establishment in a bitter struggle over who would control the definition of disease and disability.

The Social Security Administration initially based its eligibility criteria on the orthodox medical conception of black lung, a view that reflects the rigidity and narrowness of the germ theory. According to this perspective, black lung is limited exclusively to one clinical entity—coal workers' pneumoconiosis (CWP); this is the only lung disease considered occupational in origin and therefore compensable. The agent (and cause) of CWP is, by definition (pneumoconiosis means "dust-containing lung"), the inhalation of respirable coal mine dust, which produces certain pathological changes in one organ (the lungs) and which are revealed in a characteristic pattern on an X-ray. The disease process is linear and quantitative; the stage of CWP is determined by the number and size of opacities on the lung field, as revealed through an X-ray. The first stages of disease, categorized as "simple" pneumoconiosis, are considered compatible with health, whereas advanced or "complicated" pneumoconiosis is severely disabling and sometimes fatal (34).

This conception of black lung has highly significant political and ideological functions. Most important, it minimizes and depoliticizes the problem. If the *cause* of CWP is respirable dust, then prevention is a technical matter of controlling this inanimate object, rather than a polit-

ical question involving the relations of power in the workplace. Moreover, most surveys find a 3 percent prevalence of complicated CWP; if this is the only stage of disease considered disabling, then a relatively small number of coal miners are functionally impaired by occupational lung disease and deserve compensation. Respiratory disability in miners with simple CWP is attributed to nonoccupational factors, above all the victims themselves and their cigarette smoking. Obviously, this entire train of thought functions to shift medical and political emphasis away from the workplace as a source of disease and onto the worker (35).

The entire diagnostic and claims procedure also functioned to individualize what miners and other activists considered a collective problem. On a practical level, the dominant medical concept of black lung meant that claimants with evidence of complicated CWP, even if they experienced little disability, automatically received compensation; some with lesser stages who met a complex combination of other criteria also received benefits. But thousands of miners and the widows of miners, who by all appearances were equally or more disabled by respiratory disease, were denied compensation.

In the course of their movement to achieve more liberal eligibility criteria, miners and other activists implicitly elaborated a completely different understanding of black lung and its causes. Their view was not articulated by a single spokesperson or written down in a single position paper; it was woven into the culture and ideology of the movement, and in almost all respects ran counter to the dominant medical view of black lung. Indeed, the very act of insisting collectively on the reality of their own disease experience was in itself a challenge to scientific medicine, insofar as the latter tends to individualize health problems and denigrate the patients' perceptions of their own condition.

It should be stressed that the movement's ideology did not involve a wholesale rejection of science and was not based on fundamentalist religion or other antiscientific sensibilities. Indeed, some activists made skillful use of the scientific arguments of a few physicians who, because of their research findings, lent support to the black lung cause (36). Overall, the movements' ideology was based in the collective experience of its participants. Their skepticism toward the medical establishment had historical roots in the company doctor system, which for many activists was a bitter and living memory. Their view of black lung itself was based in their own holistic experience of disease —its physical as well as psychological, social, and economic aspects. And their understanding of the causes of black lung derived from their experiences with the coal industry, as workers, as widows of men killed by the mines, and as residents of coal towns where "there are no neutrals" (37)—even scientists.

For movement participants, the medical definition of black lung as a single clinical entity principally affecting one organ of the body had

little meaning, because black lung meant a transformation in their whole way of life. As one 56-year-old miner, disabled by black lung since the age of 48, described (38):

> Black lung is a cruel disease, a humiliating disease. It's when you can't do what you like to do; that's humiliating. I had to lay down my hammer and saw, and those were the things I got the most pleasure out of. The next thing I liked to do was work in my garden; now my garden's the biggest weed patch in Logan County. There were times in 1971 when I was still working that it was difficult for me to get to the bedroom when I was feeling bad. Now, of course, that's humiliating.

Many miners' analysis of the agents and causes of black lung also contrasted with the orthodox medical view. They argued that many features of the workplace had damaged their lungs, such as working in water over their ankles or breathing the fumes from cable fires. Moreover, they asserted that although respirable dust was the agent of CWP, the cause of the whole disease experience ultimately was economic:

> Where do we get the black lung from? The coal companies! They've had plenty of time to lessen the dust so nobody would get it. It's not an elaborate thing to keep it down: spray water. They just don't put enough of it on there. They don't want to maintain enough in materials and water to do that. . . . (39)
>
> Should we all die a terrible death to keep those companies going? (40)

Thus, miners developed a belief that they were *collectively entitled* to compensation, not at all because of individualized medical diagnoses of CWP but because of the common health-destroying experience that defined them as a group: work in the mines. Implicit in this view was the idea that black lung is a destructive process that begins when a miner starts work, not something that acquires legitimacy only when a radiologist can find it on an X-ray.

A disabled coal miner reported (41):

> I worked in the cleaning plant, an outside job. I had four conveyors to bring to the storage bin. I had, I'd say, 16 holes in this galvanized pipe, two rows, that's 32 holes in all, little tiny holes, to keep down the dust. I stood many a time across from that conveyor and somebody'd be on the other side, and all you could see was their cap lamp. And that's in the cleaning plant; that's outside! That's not even at the face.
>
> In the Black Lung Association, we're asking due compensation for a man who had to work in the environment he worked in. Not that a man can't choose where he works. But he's due more than just a day's wages. He and his family ought to be compensated for the environment he worked in.

These beliefs found expression in a multitude of political demands concerning the black lung compensation program, eventually and most clearly in the demand for automatic compensation after a specified number of years' work in the mines. Federal legislation to effect this change went down to defeat in 1976. However, medical and legal eligibility requirements for compensation were so liberalized by amendments passed in 1972 and 1978 that most

miners and the widows of miners who worked a substantial period of time in the mines are now receiving black lung benefits. (42).

The black lung movement has been rightly criticized for its lack of preventive focus. Despite the clear and widely held perception that the coal companies were to blame for black lung, activists never directed their struggle at the heart of the problem, prevention in the workplace. This was partly due to the initial, erroneous view that the cost of state compensation (financed by industry) would force the companies to improve health conditions in the mines. A lasting and effective prevention campaign would have required a tighter alliance between working miners, disabled miners, and widows; a much firmer conviction that black lung is not inevitable; and, at least eventually, a political vision of how miners might improve their occupational health by asserting greater control over the workplace.

However, the black lung movement suggests that even within the confines of an after-the-fact struggle for compensation, important and intensely political issues may be at stake. This article has explored the history of black lung on many levels—as a medical construct, a product of the workplace, a disease experience, and a political battle. The evidence presented suggests that miners' experientially based view of black lung and challenge to the medical establishment have historical justification. Medical science's understanding of black lung has not derived from observation unencumbered by a social and economic context, but has been profoundly shaped by that context; as a result, it has performed crucial political and ideological functions. In one era, it served to "normalize" and thereby mask the existence of disease altogether; in the more recent period, it has tended to minimize and individualize the problem.

By contrast, black lung activists succeeded in challenging the scientific medical establishment by insisting on the validity of their own definition of disease. They viewed black lung as an experience affecting the whole person in all aspects of life. Rather than focusing on a causal relationship between one discrete agent and one disease, they looked at the workplace as a total environment where the miner confronts an array of respiratory hazards. Finally, activists defined black lung as a collective problem whose ultimate cause was economic. In its entirety, the history of black lung suggests that a similar task of redefinition awaits other health advocates if they wish to challenge effectively the social production of disease.

Acknowledgments

This article was written under a research fellowship at the International Institute for Comparative Social Research in Berlin, West Germany. I wish to thank the Institute and its staff for their financial support, friendship, and intellectual stimulation. Conversations and correspondence with Norm Diamond, Gerd Göckenjan, and Meredeth Turshen were also an invaluable part of the process that led to this article.

References

1. NOVA. A plague on our children. WGBH Educational Foundation, Boston, 1979, film transcript, p. 35.
2. For a clear presentation of the overall argument, see Doyal, L. (with Pennell, I.). *The Political Economy of Health.* Pluto Press, London, 1979. See also Turshen, M. The political ecology of disease. *Review of Radical Political Economics* 9(1): 45-60, 1977. See also Eyer, J. Hypertension as a disease of modern society. *Int. J. Health Serv.* 5(4): 539-558, 1975.
3. Many analysts have pointed out this relationship on a theoretical level, but only a few have attempted to apply it in concrete investigation. See the discussion concerning the relationship between capitalist work relations and technology and the scientific model of brain function (as factory manager, telephone exchange, and, today, computer) in Rose, A. *The Conscious Brain.* Alfred A. Knopf, New York, 1974. For a more general discussion, see Figlio, K. The historiography of scientific medicine: An invitation to the human sciences. *Comparative Studies in Society and History* 19: 262-286, 1977. See also Foucault, M. *The Birth of the Clinic.* Vintage Books, New York, 1975.
4. The most comprehensive discussion I found was Sheafer, H. C. Hygiene of coal-mines in *A Treatise on Hygiene and Public Health,* edited by A. H. Buck, vol. 2, pp. 229-250. William Wood and Company, New York, 1879. Sheafer wrote: "Any one who has seen a load of coal shot from a cart, or has watched the thick clouds of dust which sometimes envelop the huge coal-breakers of the anthracite region so completely as almost to hide them from sight, can form an idea of the injurious effect upon the

health of constant working in such an atmosphere. The wonder is not that men die of clogged-up lungs, but that they manage to exist so long in an atmosphere which seems to contain at least fifty per cent of solid matter" (p. 245). See also Carpenter, J. T. Report of the Schuylkill County Medical Society. *Transactions of the Medical Society of Pennsylvania,* fifth series, part 2, pp. 488-491, 1869.

5. Figlio (3). Jewson, N. D. The disappearance of the sick-man from medical cosmology, 1770-1870. *Sociology* 10(2): 225-244, 1976.

6. On early financing of medical care in the coalfields, see Ginger, R. Company-sponsored welfare plans in the anthracite industry before 1900. *Bulletin of the Business Historical Society* 27(2): 112-120, 1953. See also Falk, L. A. Coal miners' prepaid medical care in the United States— and some British relationships, 1792-1964. *Med. Care* 4(1): 37-42, 1966.

7. A comprehensive survey of health care under the company doctor system was extracted from the U.S. government by the United Mine Workers of America during temporary federalization of the mines in 1946. The result was the so-called Boone report. U.S. Department of the Interior, Coal Mines Administration. *A Medical Survey of the Bituminous-Coal Industry.* Government Printing Office, Washington, D.C., 1947.

8. Hayhurst, E. R. The health hazards and mortality statistics of soft coal mining in Illinois and Ohio. *J. Ind. Hygiene* 1(7): 360, 1919.

9. Rebhorn, E. H. Anthraco silicosis. *Med. Soc. Reporter* 29(5):15, Scranton, Pennsylvania, 1935.

10. Those who persisted in their complaints of breathlessness were eventually referred to psychiatrists, ac-

cording to the testimony of miners and their families during interviews with the author. The argument that miners' symptoms of lung disease were psychological in origin may be found in Ross, W. D., et al. Emotional aspects of respiratory disorders among coal miners. *J.A.M.A.* 156(5): 484-487, 1954.

11. My thoughts on this relationship were stimulated and clarified by Figlio, K. Chlorosis and chronic disease in 19th century Britain: The social constitution of somatic illness in a capitalist society. *Int. J. Health Serv.* 8(4): 589-617, 1978.

12. This view persists today. Abundant examples may be found, especially in journalistic and sociological literature on Appalachia. Miners are alternately romanticized and reviled; in either case, they are "a breed apart."

13. See Brown, E. R. *Rockefeller Medicine Men.* University of California Press, Berkeley, 1979. On the germ theory and its implications for the doctor-patient relationship, see Jewson (5), Figlio (3), and Berliner, H. S., and Salmon, J. W. The holistic health movement and scientific medicine: The naked and the dead. *Socialist Review* 9(1): 31-52, 1979.

14. "One radiologist in southern West Virginia says until five years ago he regularly encountered chest X-rays from physicians that showed massive lung lesions labeled 'normal miner's chest.' " Aronson, B. Black lung: Tragedy of Appalachia. *New South* 26(4): 54, 1971.

15. Meiklejohn, A. History of lung disease of coal miners in Great Britain: Part II, 1875-1920. *Br. J. Ind. Med.* 9(2): 94, 1952. This view apparently originated in Britain and was picked up by physicians in the United States.

16. See Seltzer, C. Health care by the

ton. *Health PAC Bulletin* 79: 1-8, 25-33, 1977.

17. Martin, J. E., Jr. Coal miners' pneumoconiosis. *Am. J. Public Health* 44(5): 581, 1954. See also Hunter, M. B., and Levine, M. D. Clinical study of pneumoconiosis of coal workers in Ohio river valley. *J.A.M.A.* 163(1): 1-4, 1957. See also the numerous articles by Lorin Kerr in this period, especially Coal workers' pneumoconiosis. *Ind. Med. Surg.* 25(8): 355-362, 1956.

18. Nonmedical literature from all over the world suggests that coal miners have long experienced black lung. Friedrich Engels discusses miners' "black spittle" disease in *The Condition of the Working Class in England.* Alden Press, Oxford, 1971. Emile Zola's character Bonnemort in the novel *Germinal* is clearly a victim of black lung. And John Spargo, a progressive era reformer intent on the prohibition of child labor, discusses the respiratory problems of the anthracite breaker boys in *The Bitter Cry of the Children.* Macmillan Company, New York, 1906, p. 164.

19. U.S. Public Health Service. The health of workers in dusty trades, Part III. Public Health Bulletin Number 208, Government Printing Office, Washington, D.C., 1933; U.S. Public Health Service. Anthracosilicosis among hard coal miners. Public Health Bulletin Number 221, Government Printing Office, Washington, D.C., 1936; U.S. Public Health Service and Utah State Board of Health. The working environment and the health of workers in bituminous coal mines, non-ferrous metal mines, and non-ferrous metal smelters in Utah. 1940.

20. A lucid discussion of the labor process in this period may be found in Dix, K. *Work Relations in the Coal Industry: The Hand-Loading Era, 1880-1930.* Institute for Labor Studies, West Virginia University, Morgantown, West Virginia, 1977. On the economics of the industry, see Suffern, A. E. *The Coal Miners' Struggle for Industrial Status.* Macmillan Company, New York, 1926. See also Hamilton, W. H., and Wright, H. R. *The Case of Bituminous Coal.* Macmillan Company, New York, 1925.

21. One study actually found an inverse statistical relationship between employment levels and the rate of fatal accidents. See the discussion in Dix (20), pp. 101-104.

22. Roy, A. *History of Coal Miners of the U.S.* J. L. Trauger Printing Company, Columbus, Ohio, 1907, p. 119.

23. In some cases, state law or local practice dictated that coal be shot down at the end of the day, allowing the atmosphere to clear overnight. However, this was not uniform practice throughout the industry.

24. Physicians, miners, and government officials seem to agree on this point: representatives from industry in some cases demur. There is also disagreement about the magnitude of any increase in respiratory disease. See *Papers and Proceedings of the National Conference on Medicine and the Federal Coal Mine Health and Safety Act of 1969.* Washington, D.C., 1970. Debate on these questions also runs through the many volumes of testimony on the 1969 act. See U.S. Senate, Committee on Labor and Public Welfare, Subcommittee on Labor. *Coal Mine Health and Safety.* Hearings, 91st Congress, 1st Session. Government Printing Office, Washington, D.C., 1969

25. United Mine Workers of America. *Proceedings of the 33rd Consecutive Constitutional Convention.* United Mine Workers of America, Indianapolis, Indiana, 1934, vol. 1.

26. United Mine Workers of America.

Proceedings of the 42nd Consecutive Constitutional Convention. United Mine Workers of America, Washington, D.C., 1956, see pp. 306-331.

27. Lewis clearly articulated this position in his book, *The Miners' Fight for American Standards.* Bell Publishing Company, Indianapolis, Indiana, 1925.

28. This paragraph compresses an enormous social and economic transformation into a few sentences. For a detailed description of the changed industrial relations in this period, see Seltzer, C. The United Mine Workers of America and the coal operators: The political economy of coal in Appalachia. 1950-1973. Ph.D. dissertation, Columbia University, 1977.

29. See David, J. P. Earnings, health, safety, and welfare of bituminous coal miners since the encouragement of mechanization by the United Mine Workers of America. Ph.D. dissertation, West Virginia University, 1972. David demonstrates how miners fell behind workers in certain other unionized industries during this period.

30. In 1969, the U.S. Surgeon General estimated that 100,000 coal miners were afflicted with CWP. A study of 9,076 miners, conducted between 1969 and 1972, found a 31.4 percent prevalence of the disease among bituminous miners; among those who had worked 30 to 39 years in the mines, prevalence rose to over 50 percent. See Morgan, W.K.C., et al. The prevalence of coal workers' pneumoconiosis in U.S. coal miners. *Arch. Environ. Health* 27:222, 1973. Current prevalence in the work force runs around 15 percent. These data are all on CWP. Black lung, i.e. the whole disease experience that miners consider occupational in origin, is not considered a legitimate concept by scientific medicine, and its prevalence is unknown. In scientific medical terms, black lung includes CWP, bronchitis, emphysema, and possibly other unrecognized disease processes. The prevalence of this ensemble of diseases is of course higher than that of CWP alone.

31. Dr. Rowland Burns, as quoted in the Charleston (West Virginia) *Daily Mail,* January 15, 1969.

32. Dr. William Anderson, as quoted in the Charleston (West Virginia) *Gazette,* April 16, 1969.

33. U.S. House, Committe on Education and Labor. *Black Lung Benefits Program.* First Annual Report. Government Printing Office, Washington, D.C., 1971.

34. The views of W.K.C. Morgan and his associates represent the dominant position of the medical establishment on CWP. See Morgan, W.K.C. Respiratory disease in coal miners. *Am. Rev. Resp. Dis.* 113: 531-559, 1976.

35. For example: "The presence of severe shortness of breath in a coal miner with simple CWP is virtually always related to a nonoccupationally related disease, such as chronic bronchitis or emphysema, rather than to coal mining. . . . Smoking is by far the most important factor in producing respiratory symptoms and a decrease in ventilatory function." Morgan (34), pp. 540-541.

36. Several physicians took the side of miners in the black lung controversy, arguing that the degree of respiratory disability does not correlate with X-ray stages of CWP and that disability in miners with simple CWP is often occupationally related. Some explained this phenomenon by hypothesizing that the disease process is pulmonary vascular in nature, i.e. it affects the small vessels of the lungs, impairing their ability

to exchange gases with the blood-stream. See Hyatt, R. E., Kistin, A. D., and Mahan, T. K. Respiratory disease in southern West Virginia coal miners. *Am. Rev. Resp. Dis.* 89(3): 387-401, 1964. See also Rasmussen, D. L., et al. Respiratory impairment in southern West Virginia coal miners. *Am. Rev. Resp. Dis.* 98(10): 658-667, 1968.

37. This is a line from a famous song by Florence Reese. "Which Side Are You On?", inspired by the mine wars in Harlan County, Kentucky, during the 1930s.

38. Author's interview with disabled coal miner. Logan County, West Virginia, September 6, 1978.

39. Author's interview with disabled coal miner, Raleigh County, West Virginia, September 19, 1978.

40. Author's interview with working coal miner, Raleigh County, West Virginia, August 24, 1978.

41. Author's interview with disabled coal miner, Raleigh County, West Virginia, September 19, 1978.

42. By 1978, approved claims exceeded 420,000, and amendments enacted in that year are pushing the total even higher. This does not mean, however, that eligibility requirements will not be tightened in the future. Indeed, the current trend is to do so. See General Accounting Office. *Legislation Allows Black Lung Benefits To Be Awarded without Adequate Evidence of Disability.* Report to the Congress. Government Printing Office, Washington, D.C., 1980.

Section Three

Perspectives on Health and Illness

As with any discipline, there are various ways to approach data and issues. In this section, we examine some of the approaches that are commonly employed in medical sociology. Some, you will see, are compatible with others, while some are quite oppositional. Although medical sociologists do not always adhere to strictly defined perspectives as illustrated here, they often enough define themselves and others as belonging to particular schools of thought.

Obviously, not all scholars or students share the same set of beliefs or use the same methods. The point of this section is to show some of the range of perspectives that have been brought to bear on an understanding of health, disease, and illness, and to demonstrate that all social scientists do, in fact, have underlying, guiding principles, even if these principles are not always explicitly stated. These selections may also help you to identify your own point of view and to assess critically works you will read in this field in light of it.

Talcott Parsons applied his general theory of sociology to a large number of areas, including medical sociology. His work on the sick role was one of the earliest attempts to incorporate health and illness into a general theory of social action. Today, Parsons's concept of the sick role is often criticized for being too narrow, too pro-medical, and even politically conservative. Yet it is striking that many medical sociologists begin their articles and books with a statement concerning the sick role, even if they then go on to dispute that perspective. For this reason, it is useful to see what Parsons contributes to the study of medical sociology.

Parsons argues that illness allows people to be temporarily exempted from normal social role responsibilities, but, in exchange, the sick must accept that they cannot get well on their own, that they have a duty to get well, and that they need to seek professional help to do so. In his theory, doctors are viewed as objective and largely altruistic scientists who are universally committed to helping their patients. For Parsons, illness is a form of social deviance, and medical care is the appropriate mechanism of social control that can restore social equilibrium. In "Talcott Parsons' 'Sick Role' and Its Critiques," Candace West provides a thorough presentation of Parsons's model, followed by a critique that is shared by many more critical medical sociologists.

At the core of *Perspectives in Medical Sociology* is the notion that biomedical knowledge alone is insufficient to explain health and illness and to understand the ways in which people and institutions deal with health and illness. This core belief is central to newer approaches to medical sociology, yet few writers have produced a comprehensive critique of the *medical model*. Elliot Mishler's "Critical Perspectives on the Biomedical Model" provides us with a solid beginning for a critique of the medical model. You will note that he addresses many of the same concerns that are talked about in Parsons's perspective, though Mishler's approach to understanding these concerns is different. Mishler argues against Parsonsian notions such as the concept of disease as *deviation from the norm,* proffering instead the view that norms are culturally defined and quite variant across a single culture. Mishler tackles the biomedical *assumption of generic diseases,* which holds that disease processes and symptoms are similar in different eras and cultures. Here, too, he finds evidence for cultural constructions of health and illness. Mishler also criticizes the assumption that *medicine is a value-free profession* that stands above the structure and values of the society around it.

The critique of the medical model has led many sociologists to develop a *social construction of illness* perspective, which posits that health matters are like other social problems in that they may exist for a long time before they are perceived as problems. For example, incest, child abuse, and spouse abuse have long been present in family life. Yet only with the growth of modern social movements, especially the women's liberation movement, have these problems been brought to public attention. The definition of something as a problem involves the social conflict between those who would gain and those who would lose from such a perception. In some cases, the gains and losses involve people or groups of people, such as professional groupings (e.g. psychiatry, alcoholism counselors). At other times, they involve overarching social institutions. For instance, in the case of family violence and incest, the losses accrue to the conservative and traditional patriarchal family structure that has produced and condoned such actions.

To cite another example, we now regard lead poisoning as an important health hazard, yet it required radical action from health activists and black and Puerto Rican community activists only two decades ago to bring this problem to public attention. In this case, the losers included large landlords faced with the cost of lead paint removal and paint manufacturers faced with revisions of their production process. This phenomenon of social movements bringing attention to health hazards should be familiar to you from the preceding section, "Environmental and Occupational Health."

Another social perspective on health and illness is represented by Marxist analyses of the health care system, which have been a strong component of recent scholarship. Of particular concern to Marxist analysis is the division of society into social classes, and the various ways in which class conflict occurs. Marxists also emphasize the importance of the *state* (the totality of the structure of political power) in preserving social inequality. Howard Waitzkin's contribution, "Social Structures of Medical Oppression," provides a brief introduction to some core concepts of Marxism and then applies them to an analysis of health institutions, professions, workers, and drug and supply companies. He then examines the role of the state in the health care system, especially in providing public support for the private health sector. Waitzkin also discusses how *ideology* (a belief system) concerning health and illness often mirrors and perpetuates social inequalities.

One more social perspective on disease can be found in epidemiology. While many health practitioners concern themselves mainly with individual cases, the epidemiologist is interested in the distribution of morbidity and mortality in the population. We explored a number of areas of social epidemiology in the opening section of the book. Here we are concerned with the *theoretical perspective* through which classic epidemiology studies health. Abraham Lilienfeld, in "The Epidemiologic Approach to Disease," offers a glimpse into both observational and experimental methods of epidemiology and shows how the larger-scale ecological approach (large-scale aggregate level) can be interpolated to an individual approach. Compared to the medical model, epidemiology appears to be more socially oriented. Yet the array of social factors utilized by epidemiology is limited and doesn't always offer as complete a social context as needed.

A number of modern sociologists have adopted a *medicalization* viewpoint, which is very much akin to the constructivist perspective discussed earlier in this section. Writers in this tradition believe that a large number of social problems, which are not primarily or solely medical, have come under the medical gaze. In particular, many life processes, which are ordinary and routine, have been defined and treated as deviations from a norm of health. In "Women and Medicalization: A New Perspective," Catherine Kohler Riessman offers this point of view with reference to women's experience of childbirth, reproductive control, premenstrual syndrome, weight, and mental health. She points to the many problems with medicalization, such as the production of individual-level solutions (e.g. changing personal habits) rather than social solutions (e.g. changing health and social service systems) to vexing problems. Rather than simply "blaming" physicians and health institutions for this medicalization phenomenon, however, Riessman notes how women unwittingly aid and abet this problem.

9 TALCOTT PARSONS' "SICK ROLE" AND ITS CRITIQUES

Candace West

The Doctor-Patient Relationship

Parsons's (1951) original analytic interest in health care was in medical practice as a subsystem of the larger structure of social action in Western society. Given his focus on the organization of social systems, he approached the physician-patient relationship as an institutionalized role set, consisting of standardized behavioral expectations for patient and practitioner.

Those standardized behavioral expectations were seen to revolve around the patient's need for help from the physician. As Parsons put it: "The patient has a need for technical services because he doesn't— nor do his lay associates, family members, etc.— 'know' what is the matter or what to do about it, nor does he control the necessary facilities. The physician is the technical expert who by special training and experience, and by an institutionally validated status, is qualified to 'help' the patient in a situation institutionally defined as legitimate in a relative sense but as needing help" (1951:439). "Help," in this paradigm, means restoration to a nonpathological state. Central to the framework is the idea that illness can be seen as a form of deviance; that is, a form of disturbance of the healthy functioning of the total organism within the social system. Institutionalization of the patient-practitioner relationship is thus warranted to ensure maintenance of society (to which illness poses a major threat).

An Asymmetrical Relationship

Because it is the physician, within Western cultures, who is charged with the legal responsibility for restoring the patient to normality, "The practitioner must have control over the interaction with the patient, ensuring that the patient will comply with the prescribed regimen. If patient compliance is not ensured, then the ability of the practitioner to return the patient to a normal functioning state is undermined" (Wolinsky, 1980:163). The essential *asymmetry* of the physician-patient relationship is, for Parsons, the key to the therapeutic practice of medicine. He equates the practitioner's interactional control over patients with the ability to treat them.

Physicians' control or power over patients derives from three sources. First, patients are in a position of situational dependency vis-à-vis their doctors, in that they recognize their need for health care and their inability to provide it for themselves. Second, physicians are in a position of situational authority vis-à-vis patients, since only doctors possess the

---

SOURCE: From *Routine Complications* by Candace West, © 1984 by Candace West. Reprinted by permission of Indiana University Press.

specialized knowledge and technical qualifications required to provide medical services. Third, physicians' professional prestige provides them an additional edge in their interactions with patients. The technical skills they acquire through medical training and their societal certification as licensed healers afford physicians what Wolinsky describes as "a nonpareil social position in modern society. Therefore, in almost any social situation, the practitioner commands more respect and more prestige than does the patient. As a result, in everyday and *especially* health related interaction, the practitioner commands and receives deference from others, allowing the practitioner to dominate interpersonal encounters" (1980:164). Within the Parsonian framework, then, the doctor-patient relationship is *predicated* on institutionalized inequality between those who heal and those who must come to them for treatment.

Modifications of the Model

Originally formulated in 1951, expanded in 1952 (Parsons and Fox), and reiterated in 1975, Parsons's model of the physician-patient relationship remains the classic approach to social interaction between doctors and patients. Nonetheless, critics of this model have been many (see Bloom and Wilson, 1979, and Wolinsky, 1980:166–185, for excellent overviews of these).

Illness and the Sick Role

Some have suggested that Parsons neglected the roles of other actors in the health-care process (such as members of the patient's family, or the ever-increasing staff of personnel involved in medical services). The physician-patient relationship, notes Bloom (1963), is only one component in a larger sociocultural matrix of health care consumers and providers.

Freidson (1961; 1970a; 1970b; 1975) goes even further, avowing that patients' lay associates in fact comprise a distinct referral system, with dynamics of its own. For example: "What medicine comes to define as an illness is in part a function of the way its experience is limited by the characteristics of the laymen who happen to enter the consulting room. . . . Not a representative sample of the population. . . . The grounds for selection are not the profession's conceptions of illness, and the organization of the process is in important ways independent of the organization of the profession" (Freidson 1970b:279). Thus, Freidson maintains that the relationship between doctor and patient cannot be fully understood without analyzing lay constructions of illness, independently of practitioners' definitions of it.

Considerable research supports the view that patients' "pathways to the doctor" are rife with ambiguity and conflicting perspectives (Zola, 1973). For example, cultural differences between patients figure centrally in differing attitudes toward physical symptoms and differential responses to pain (Zborowski, 1958; Croog, 1961; Zola, 1963; 1966; Stoeckle et al., 1963; 1964; Becker, 1979). Varying interpretations of the meaning of symptoms are also found among patients of different ages, sexes, levels of education, and socioeconomic statuses (Feldman, 1966; Hetherington and Hopkins, 1969; Banks and Keller, 1971; Gutt-macher and Elinson, 1971; and Mechanic, 1972). A review of these findings leads Becker (1979) to conclude: "Perhaps Parsons' (1951:436) original formulation of the [patient's] 'sick role' is meaningful only in terms of particular sociocultural influences on the role's behavioral expectations" (p.261).

The Role of the Physician

Parsons's (1951) characterization of the physician's role has also stimulated considerable controversy, particularly among researchers with interests in medicine as a profession. For example, Freidson (1970b) questions the extent to which values comprising the physician's presumed "collectivity orientation" (achievement, universalism, functional specificity, and affective neutrality) are evidenced in clinical practice: "Parsons does not specify performance at all, but broad institutional norms connected with professions as officially organized occupations. . . . They are quite distinct, analytically and empirically, from the actual norms of individual professionals" (p.160). In practice, Freidson observes, the norms and attitudes governing medical work foster a personal and restricted sense of responsibility. Drawing on the classic investigation of students at the University of Kansas Medical School by Becker et al. (1961), Freidson argues

that the organization of medical work necessitates a particularistic (rather than collectivistic) orientation to action and concrete experience. Physicians' particularistic orientation can be seen not only in the ways they handle professional self-regulation (in matters of unethical or incompetent behavior), but also in their dealings with patients. Hence, Freidson contends that medical sociology should address itself to the ways in which medical work is organized in health-care settings rather than to characteristics of health care personnel (e.g., their training, sensitivity, or devotion).

Although Freidson (1961; 1970a; 1970b; 1975) is credited with the most comprehensive challenge to Parsons (Anderson and Helm, 1979: 260; Bloom and Wilson, 1979:285–288), others have made substantial contributions to a new approach (e.g., Becker et al., 1961; Bucher and Stelling, 1969; Davis, 1964; Hughes, 1971; Roth, 1963b; Strauss, 1970; Glaser and Strauss, 1965; Scheff, 1963). Underlying all these works are a perspective emphasizing the clash of perspectives between doctor and patient, and the three basic premises of symbolic interactionism:

1. Human beings act toward things on the basis of the meanings that things have for them.
2. Meaning derives from social interaction.
3. Meanings are modified by their interpretations, used by persons in actual situations. (Blumer, 1969:2)

Within this theoretical framework, such matters as health and illness are seen as the products of negotiated interactions between health-care consumers and providers (see Anderson and Helm, 1979, for a helpful overview of this approach). Thus, the empirical studies derived from this view have focused on the social construction of meanings in medical contexts (e.g., Ball, 1967; Becker et al., 1961; Conrad and Kern, 1981; Daniels, 1973; Danziger, 1980; 1981; Emerson, 1970; Freidson, 1961).

Such studies frequently employ particular instances of language use to illuminate the ways in which medical realities are created and sustained. For example, Danziger's (1980) analysis of physicians' terminology in obstetric visits displayed the channeling of "possible prenatals" into bona fide pregnant women. Despite suggestive clinical evidence (e.g., positive pregnancy tests), doctors in her study were loathe to categorize women as "prenatals" until their full medical work-ups were completed. Emerson's (1970) investigation of gynecological encounters found medical providers using definite articles rather than pronoun adjectives when alluding to patients' body parts. Directives with sexual connotations were shunned, and euphemistic references substituted for them wherever possible.

However, here, as in Parson's (1951) formulations, talk between physicians and patients is utilized as a resource rather than as an object of investigation: Meanings *derive* from social interaction, but meanings themselves are the proper subjects of study. Hence, works such as Emerson's (1970) invoke various as-pects of medical talk in explaining how medical realities are sustained (pp. 80–85), but the principles organizing talk itself remain unaddressed (see Frankel, 1983:25, n. 9).

The Need for Asymmetry in Therapeutic Relations

Other critics have questioned the characterization of patients' passivity implied by Parsons's (1951) discussion of their situational dependency.[1] For example, Szasz and Hollender (1956) contend that the severity of physiological symptoms is likely to influence the extent to which patients are dependent on their doctors. Thus, the traumatized, comatose, or otherwise unconscious patient is literally helpless to participate in his or her own care; under these circumstances it would of course be nonsensical to speak of a patient's "active" role in the health-care process. However, less extreme symptoms (such as those which are likely to accompany mumps or flu) are unlikely to totally incapacitate patients. So, Szasz and Hollender argue, patients seeking medical treatment for less incapacitating problems are perfectly capable of playing a larger role in their own health care; they may be looking for guidance from and cooperating with physicians, rather than being totally dominated by them. Finally, they contend that ongoing treatment of chronic but nonincapacitating conditions (e.g., allergies or diabetes mellitus) requires *mutual* participation by patients and physicians. Under these circumstances, patients usually carry out prescribed regimens (such as insulin injections) themselves with periodic visits to their physicians (see also Danziger, 1981, on pregnancy care).

Wolinsky (1980) adds an important point to Szasz and Hollender's typology of patient responsibility, noting that the "mutual participation" model also seems applicable to cases in which preventive medicine is the issue. Routine physical examinations, for example, are likely to involve patients as well as doctors in the development and implementation of strategies for continued good health. However, Wolinsky warns that this pseudo-egalitarian form of the physician-patient relationship requires considerable sophistication on the part of patients, "limiting the applicability of the mode to mature, informed adults. As such, the mutual participation model of the patient-practitioner relationship is analogous to the relationship of one adult to another with one adult having the specialized knowledge needed by the other" (1980:174). In summary, Wolinsky contends that Szasz and Hollender's modifications amount to a "recalibration" of the Parsonian model—subdividing the child-parent character of the original into "infant-parent, adolescent-parent, and adult-adult" life stages (p. 174). We are left then, with a relationship between physician and patient which is still fundamentally asymmetrical.

In fact, Parson's response to his critics (1975) re-emphasizes the *necessity* for institutionalized asymmetry in physicians' relationships with patients. While it is true, he acknowledges, that instances of self-treatment and successful folk remedies

can be found, "these marginal cases . . . cannot legitimately be used as a model for the institutionalization of these types of functions" (p. 277). To illustrate this point, Parsons draws an analogy between the physician-patient relationship and the professor-student relationship. In the latter, he contends, teachers are in the position of certified social control agents who are allocated the legal responsibility for eradicating ignorance and incompetence. Students may, of course, learn some things on their own; they may be self-taught in particular matters. Nonetheless, it is the professor rather than the student who is entrusted with the responsibility for imparting and evaluating the knowledge and competence required of cultural members. The societal certification of this responsibility (e.g., through professors' academic credentials and training, through accreditation procedures for institutions of higher learning, and through prerequisites of certain educational degrees for particular jobs) institutionalizes the essential asymmetry of the professor-student relationship. As in the case of practitioner-patient relations, the therapeutic character of the interaction requires an asymmetrical distribution of power and authority if, as Wolinsky quips, the ignorant are to be "healed" (p. 172).

In contrast to this situation, Parsons (1975) notes three types of social relationships which are predicated on an equal distribution of power. The first is that of a free market system, in which, he argues, continued participation is contingent on continued economic interest. The second is that of a voluntary or democratic organization, in which, he suggests, all members are officially declared to be equals even though elected leadership positions may rotate among members. The third and most interesting example Parsons chooses to characterize symmetrical social relationships is that of a communications network.

By "communication," Parsons —like many other organizational theorists—means an exchange of information. Here, parties to communication processes are assumed to have equal access to the symbolic meaning of information they transmit in order to communicate at all.

Herein lies a curious paradox. If, as Parsons argues, communication is predicated on *symmetrical* relations, and if, as he also contends, the practitioner-patient relationship is *essentially* asymmetrical, then communication between physicians and patients is theoretically impossible. Exchange is prohibited when parties to communication processes do not have equal access to the symbolic meaning of information they transmit.

Notes

1. To be sure, Freidson (1961) might also be read as questioning the bases for patients' passivity. In suggesting that the physician-patient relationship entails a clash of perspectives (between the professional's world of medicine and the patient's lay referral system), he does imply that medical encounters constitute occasions for negotiated conflict. However, Freidson does not debate the "technical specificity" of the physician's

role (Bloom and Wilson. 1979:288). Moreover, he agrees that physicians' authority over patients is largely conferred by institutional means: *"What distinguishes the professional from all other consulting experts is his capacity to solve some of these problems of authority by formal institutionalized means. His solution minimizes the role of persuasive evidence in his interaction with his clientele"* (Freidson, 1970a: 110; italics in original).

References

Anderson, W. Timothy, and David T. Helm
1979 "The physician-patient encounter: A process of reality negotiation." Pp. 259–271, in E. G. Jaco (ed.), *Patients, Physicians and Illness*. 3rd edition. New York: The Free Press.

Ball, Donald W.
1967 "An abortion clinic ethnography." *Social Problems* 14:293–301.

Banks, Franklin R., and Martin D. Keller
1971 "Symptom experience and health action." *Medical Care* 9:498–502.

Becker, Howard S., Blanche Geer, Everett C. Hughes, and Anselm L. Strauss
1961 *Boys in White: Student Culture in Medical School*. Chicago: University of Chicago Press.

Becker, Marshall H.
1979 "Psychosocial aspects of health-related behavior." Pp. 253–274, in Howard E. Freeman, Sol Levine, and Leo G. Reeder (eds.), *Handbook of Medical Sociology*, 3rd edition. Englewood Cliffs, New Jersey: Prentice-Hall.

Bloom, Samuel W.
1963 *The Doctor and His Patient: A Sociological Interpretation*. New York: The Free Press.

Bloom, Samuel W., and Robert N. Wilson
1979 "Patient-practitioner relation-

ships." Pp. 275–296, in Howard E. Freeman, Sol Levine, and Leo G. Reeder (eds.), *Handbook of Medical Sociology*, 3rd edition. Englewood Cliffs, New Jersey: Prentice Hall.

Bucher, Rue, and Joan Stelling
1969 "Characteristics of professional organizations." *Journal of Health and Social Behavior* 10:3–15.

Conrad, Peter, and Rochelle Kern (eds.)
1981 *The Sociology of Health and Illness.* New York: St. Martin's Press.

Croog, Sydney H.
1961 "Ethnic origins, educational level, and responses to a health questionnaire," *Human Organization* 20:65–69.

Daniels, Arlene Kaplan
1973 "The philosophy of combat psychiatry." Pp. 132–140, in E. Rubington and M. S. Weinberg (eds.), *Deviance: The Interactionist Perspective.* New York: Macmillan.

Danziger, Sandra Klein
1980 "The medical model in doctor-patient interaction: The case of pregnancy care." Pp. 263–304, in J. Roth (ed.), *Research in the Sociology of Health Care.* Greenwich, Connecticut: JAI Press

Davis, Fred
1964 "Deviance disavowal: The management of strained interaction by the visibly physically handicapped." Pp. 119–137 in H. Becker (ed.), *The Other Side.* New York: The Free Press

Emerson, Joan P.
1970 "Behavior in private places: Sustaining definitions of reality in gynecological examinations." Pp. 74–97, in H. P. Dreitzel (ed.). *Recent Sociology No. 2.* New York: Macmillan.

Feldman, Jacob J.
1966 *The Dissemination of Health Information: A Case Study in Adult Learning.* Chicago: Aldine.

Frankel, Richard M.
1983 "The laying on of hands: Aspects of the organization of gaze, touch, and talk in a medical encounter." Pp. 19–54, in S. Fisher and A. D. Todd (eds.), *The Social Organization of Doctor-Patient Communication.* Washington, D.C.: Center for Applied Linguistics.

Freidson, Eliot
1961 *Patients' Views of Medical Practice—A Study of Subscribers to a Prepaid Medical Plan in the Bronx.* New York: Russell Sage Foundation.

Freidson, Eliot
1970a *Professional Dominance: The Social Structure of Medical Care.* New York: Atherton Press.

Freidson, Eliot
1970b *Profession of Medicine: A Study of the Sociology of Applied Knowledge.* New York: Harper & Row.

Freidson, Eliot
1975 *Doctoring Together: A Study of Professional Social Control.* New York: Elsevier.

Glaser, Barney G., and Anselm Strauss
1965 "Temporal aspects of dying as a nonscheduled status passage." *American Journal of Sociology* 71:45–69.

Guttmacher, Sally, and Jack Elinson
1971 "Ethno-religious variation in perceptions of illness." *Social Science and Medicine* 5:117–125.

Hetherington, Robert W., and Carl E. Hopkins
1969 "Symptom sensitivity: Its social and cultural correlates." *Health Services Research* 4:63–70.

Hughes, Everett C.
1971 *The Sociological Eye: Selected Papers on Work, Self and the Study of Society.* Chicago: Aldine

Korsch, Barbara M., and Vida Francis Negrete
1972 "Doctor-patient communication." *Scientific American* 227:66–74.

Mechanic, David
1972 "Social psychological factors affecting the presentation of bodily complaints." *New England Journal of Medicine* 286:1132–1139.

Parsons, Talcott
1951 *The Social System*. New York: The Free Press.

Parsons, Talcott
1975 "The sick role and the role of the physician reconsidered." *Millbank Memorial Fund Quarterly* 53:257–277.

Parsons, Talcott, and Renee Fox
1952 "Illness, therapy and the modern urban American family." *Journal of Social Issues* 8:31–44.

Pendleton, David
1983 "Doctor-patient communication: A review." Pp. 5–53, in D. Pendleton and John Hasler (eds.), *Doctor-Patient Communication*. London: Academic Press.

Scheff, Thomas J.
1963 "Negotiating reality: Notes on power in the assessment of responsibility," *Social Problems* 16:3–17.

Stoeckle, John D., Irving Kenneth Zola, and Gerald E. Davidson
1963 "On going to see the doctor: The contributions of the patient to the decision to seek medical aid: A selected review." *Journal of Chronic Diseases* 16:975–989.

Stoeckle, John D., Irving Kenneth Zola, and Gerald E. Davidson
1964 "The quantity and significance of psychological distress in medical patients—some preliminary observations about the decision to seek medical aid." *Journal of Chronic Diseases* 17:959–970.

Strauss, Anselm L.
1970 *Where Medicine Fails*. Chicago: Aldine.

Szasz, Thomas, and Marc Hollender
1956 "A contribution to the philosophy of medicine: The basic models of the doctor-patient relationship." *Journal of the American Medical Association* 97:585–588.

Waitzkin, Howard
1983 *The Second Sickness: Contradictions of Capitalist Health Care*. New York: The Free Press.

Wilson, Robert N.
1970 *The Sociology of Health: An Introduction*. New York: Random House.

Wolinsky, Frederic D.
1980 *The Sociology of Health: Principles, Professions and Issues*. Boston: Little, Brown and Company.

Zborowski, Mark
1958 "Cultural components in responses to pain." *Journal of Social Issues* 8:16–30.

Zola, Irving Kenneth
1963 "Problems of communication, diagnosis, and patient care: The interplay of patient, physician and clinic organization." *Journal of Medical Education* 38:829–838.

Zola, Irving Kenneth
1966 "Culture and symptoms: An analysis of patients presenting complaints." *American Sociological Review* 31:615–630.

Zola, Irving Kenneth
1973 "Pathways to the doctor—from person to patient." *Social Science and Medicine* 7:667–689.

10 CRITICAL PERSPECTIVES ON THE BIOMEDICAL MODEL

Elliot G. Mishler

We provide here a reexamination of four key presuppositions that have shaped modern scientific medicine. These "silent assumptions" are the essential features of the biomedical model. The dominance of this model in medical theory and practice is universally recognized. Its assumptions are so deeply interwoven with ways of thinking and working in medicine that health professionals tend to forget that it is a conceptual model, a way of thinking about the world. That is, the biomedical model is treated as *the* representation or picture of reality rather than understood as *a* representation. Like other conceptual models, the biomedical model defines, classifies, and specifies relationships among events in particular ways. For example, the presupposition that there are specific disease entities, each associated with a specific biological process, is related to the further idea that etiology is biologically specific. An alternative model defines illness as a disturbance in social relationships; questions of etiology are then framed with reference to social rather than biological processes.

The question might be raised as to why an alternative perspective is useful. Essentially, we shall argue that the biomedical model strips away social contexts of meaning. Illness is then viewed as an autonomous entity, defined by standard universal criteria, isolated from the lives and experiences of patients and physicians.[1] Although symptoms and illnesses occur in people who live within sociocultural frameworks of belief and action, these contexts tend to be ignored in the biomedical approach. Problems are defined, diagnosed, and treated by physicians and other health professionals from a specialized point of view grounded in the biosciences. Further, the aims and standards of medical practice are guided by social norms and cultural values; they are shaped by political and economic interests. Health care is provided in specific settings and institutions with complex relations to other institutions in the society. These various contexts of medicine are also excluded from consideration in the biomedical model.

Modern medicine is based on and dominated by concepts, methods, and principles of the biological sciences. As Engel notes, "The dominant model of disease today is biomedical, with molecular biology its basic scientific discipline. It assumes disease to be fully accounted for by deviations from the norm of measurable biological (somatic) variables."[2]

SOURCE: *Social Contexts of Health, Illness, and Patient Care,* Elliot G. Mishler, Lorna Amara Singham, Stuart T. Hauser, Ramsay Liem, Samuel D. Osherson and Nancy E. Waxler, Editors (Cambridge: Cambridge University Press, 1981), pp. 1–23. Reprinted with the permission of Cambridge University Press. Copyright © 1981 Cambridge University Press.

We shall examine several critical assumptions and focus particularly on limitations of the biomedical model as the comprehensive and exclusive basis for either the science or practice of medicine.

In the following sections, we examine four assumptions of the biomedical model: (1) the definition of disease as deviation from normal biological functioning; (2) the doctrine of specific etiology; (3) the conception of generic diseases, that is, the universality of a disease taxonomy; and (4) the scientific neutrality of medicine.

The Definition of Disease

We begin with a central and basic assumption of the biomedical model, noted in the previous quotation from Engel, that disease is "to be fully accounted for by deviations from the norm of measurable biological (somatic) variables." Cohen offers a similar definition: ". . . disease indicates deviations from the normal—these are its symptoms and signs."[3] For modern adherents of the biomedical model, these definitions are unlikely to stir dispute. However, there have been other conceptions, for example, the classical Platonic model of health as harmony among the body's structures or processes and disease as a state of discord and dissolution of harmony, or the Galenian conception of disease as a disturbance of function.[4]

That such broader definitions are neither obsolete, nor of historical and esoteric interest only, is indicated by the definition of health proposed by the World Health Organi-

zation as a ". . . state of complete physical, mental, and social well-being and not merely the absence of disease or infirmity."[5] Engel quotes Romano's slightly more restricted definition of health as a useful starting point for a "unified" theory of disease: "Health, in a positive sense, consists in the capacity of the organism to maintain a balance in which it may be reasonably free of undue pain, discomfort, disability or limitation of action." Engel defines disease in contrast to health as ". . . failures or disturbances in the growth, development, functions, and adjustments of the organism as a whole or any of its systems."[6]

There is no way to define a biological "norm" or "deviations" without reference to specific populations and their sociocultural characteristics. Redlich poses the issue succinctly: "normal for what?" and "normal for whom?"[7] That is, assertions about the normality of levels of biological functioning, or about the normal structure of an organ, must be based on the relationship between the observed instance and the distribution in a specified population of these structures and functions. Further, implicit to any specified norm is a set of presupposed standard conditions with regard to when, how, and on whom measurements are taken.

Another problem is that the meaning or normality is ambiguous in both ordinary language and medical usage. Does normal refer to an ideal standard or to the average value of a population characteristic? The dictionary includes both meanings. The adjective is defined as an "established norm, rule, principle; type, standard, regular form; performing proper functions; regular; natural; analogical," and its noun form as an "archetypal state to which individuals may conform; ordinary or usual condition, degree, quantity, or the like, average, mean."[8]

It is obvious that the average value of a variable for some specified population may not correspond to an ideal standard. Specific characteristics of populations and their life situations are critical to understanding and interpreting the significance of average values and of "deviations" from universal or ideal standards of health. For example, personality crises of adolescents in Western societies are generally viewed as "normal" to this developmental stage. Similarly, the various bodily and mental changes that accompany aging are seen as "normal."

Ryle provides an instructive example that underscores the significance of this distinction between ideal standards and average population values as indicators of "normality." In a detailed clinical and epidemiological study of the size of thyroid glands among adolescents in populations living on different diets, he found considerable variability among the groups. He argues that the presence of "visible glands" in a population where they are common cannot be interpreted as a true clinical sign or precursor of goiter in later life, as it usually would be in Western clinical practice. He suggests that this "symptom" may represent normal adaptation rather than deviation from a universal standard of healthy thyroid function. "It

might therefore be argued that clinical hyperplasia more usually represents a pronounced degree of adaptation—or physiological enlargement—rather than an early state of disease or that it is a true example of a borderline condition which may either revert to "normality" or advance to "disease."[9]

Ryle recommends greater attention to and emphasis on the range of "normal variability." He points out ". . . that the normal, in biological usage, is something other than a mean or fixed standard can scarcely be disputed. In man, as in all animals, variation is so constantly at work that no rigid pattern—whether anatomical, physiological, psychological, or immunological—is possible."[10] He concludes that, given the natural range of variability of structure and function of "every organ and tissue" in the species as a whole and any population studied, the "normal" in biology and medicine might better be expressed in terms of variability than as a hypothetical mean or standard value.

On the way to this conclusion, Ryle makes an argument that resonates with our point of view. "The development of aetiological science must now be based more and more upon sociomedical investigation—upon the examination, that is to say, of societies or populations in relation to their own environments, their work and upbringing, their food and special hazards. The examination of individuals in the later stages of illness and in the remote and unnatural surroundings of the hospital ward can illuminate pathology and advance treatment, but they can make little contribution to studies in causation and prevention."[11]

Our examination of the concept of normality, which is an essential element in the biomedical model of disease, is a first step in our critique of this model as a guide to theory and practice in medicine. It is obvious that broad notions of health as "harmony" or "adjustment" cannot be specified without reference to sociocultural contexts. It is important to underline the general point that, even within a more limited definition of disease as "deviations from the norm of measurable biological (somatic) variables," the biomedical model is insufficient by itself to the critical task of defining normality and deviations therefrom. Normality is a standard of judgment, whether defined as an ideal or as a computed average. The development and application of this standard requires knowledge of the distribution of relevant signs and behaviors within and between populations that are specified by their particular patterns of sociocultural characteristics and life circumstances. The latter are core topics of the social and behavioral sciences, and for these reasons are as integral to the study of health and illness as the biological sciences.

The Doctrine of Specific Etiology

There is a more specific assumption within the biomedical model which Dubos refers to as the "doctrine of specific etiology."[12]

Although this doctrine does not follow as a logically necessary consequence of the general assumption of illness as deviation from normal functioning, the doctrine has been the way in which this assumption has been specified and applied in modern medical theory and practice. Engel describes the general view in medicine that explanation of an illness is more complete and more adequate to the degree that description has moved through several stages, from an initial taxonomy based on distinct symptoms through a clustering of symptoms into syndromes, and ". . . finally to disease with specific pathogenesis and pathology."[13] The extent and adequacy with which this movement is carried through to its end, in research on a specific disease, is taken as the index of how "advanced" is our understanding of the disease. Thus, Engel points out, the scientific characterization of diabetes mellitus is considered more advanced than that of schizophrenia, because the former has ". . . progressed from the behavioral framework of symptoms to that of biochemical abnormalities."[14]

This approach is the signature of modern Western medicine. It developed out of the pioneering work of Pasteur and Koch in the nineteenth century, which demonstrated conclusively that specific diseases could be produced by introduction into the body of specific virulent microorganisms. The impact of this work was pervasive and powerful, both on the profession and on the general public. So much so, that Dubos comments, "Because the decrease in death rates appeared obvious to everyone after 1900, scientific medicine and the germ theory in particular have been given all the credit for the improvement of the general health of the people . . .," despite the fact that "In truth the mortality of many other infections had begun to recede in Western Europe and North America long before the introduction of specific methods of therapy, indeed before the demonstration of the germ theory of disease."[15]

The doctrine of specific etiology spread rapidly from infectious diseases to other diseases that could be produced by physiological lesions or reflected deficiencies in growth or metabolic processes. Yet, as Dubos again comments, although the doctrine of specific etiology ". . . and the theoretical and practical achievements to which it has led constitute the bulk of modern medicine . . . few are the cases in which it has provided a complete account of the causation of disease."[16]

Although it represents the dominant perspective within medicine, the doctrine has not been without its critics. Engel, for example, proposes an alternative model, which he calls a "unified concept of health and disease."[17] He argues that explanation of illness should be approached from a "naturalistic" rather than an "institutional" perspective. The former would direct attention to necessary and sufficient conditions rather than to isolable and singular etiological factors, would recognize multiple and interactive processes, and would take into account the possible adaptive functions of bodily responses. Within such an approach, there would be a legitimate and important place for the influence of psychological and sociocultural factors on the origin and course of illness, factors that are excluded in the search for a specific etiological agent.

In a penetrating essay on the problem of etiology, Dubos poses a critical question: Why is disease rare, although infectious agents are omnipresent? He points to ". . . one of the most neglected aspects of the germ theory of disease, namely the fact that infection rarely produces fatal disease under natural circumstances. . . . Much infection in the Western world at the present time is from parasites ubiquitous in the environment and occurring normally in a very large percentage of healthy individuals which cause pathological disorders only when natural resistance to then has been undermined by the stresses and strains of life."[18] Whether or not such pathogens remain dormant or initiate an infective process is a function of many factors, which also play a significant role in the course of the infection; these include metabolic states, nutrition, and the susceptibility of tissues to infection. Dubos concludes: "Infection is the rule, and disease the exception."[19]

Dubos' analysis of the doctrine of specific etiology, and the simple cause-effect model with which it is associated, reveals serious inadequacies in this key assumption of the biomedical model. In addition to its limitations for the explanation or control of disease, there are problems with this assumption as a guide to clinical practice. These become apparent when we examine clinical situations where physicians are engaged in the tasks of diagnosing and treating patients.

From his analyses of psychological

and psychiatric problems in general medical practice, Balint[20] observed that patients initially report a variety of vague and unfocused complaints and problems. Balint calls this the "unorganized" phase of an illness. The physician and patient together proceed to "negotiate" an illness. That is, they try to reach agreement on a specific illness that the patient "has" which may then be treated. This conception of medical work suggests that only one specific subset of symptoms may be selected as significant out of the variety of presenting complaints and signs. The physician attends to and selects a subset of symptoms that will allow him or her to match the patient's problem to a particular symptom cluster or syndrome representing a specific disease. Thus, the patient's illness is "diagnosed." Balint is proposing that the diagnosed disease is not simply "out there" in the patient, but is the result of negotiation between physician and patient. This is a view of clinical history taking and diagnosis as active processes through which a disease is constructed, rather than found.

Our aim in this section has been twofold. We wished to raise some questions about the adequacy of the doctrine of specific etiology and, at the same time, suggest how an alternative perspective might be useful and relevant. Dubos and Engel argue that the doctrine, and the underlying model of disease and disease causation that it reflects, is an oversimplification of complex biological processes. Nonetheless, physicians search for specific diseases and specific pathogenic agents. From

Balint's analysis and supporting clinical observations, we have drawn the implication that how these clinical tasks are accomplished depends on a process of negotiation between physician and patient. In our perspective, diseases are found, diagnosed, and treated within the interactive context of medical practice. Together, theoretical critique and empirical observations suggest the importance of studying clinical practice and factors that influence it.

The Assumption of Generic Diseases

A third assumption of the biomedical model is that each disease has specific and distinguishing features that are universal to the human species. That is, disease symptoms and processes are expected to be the same in different historical periods and in different cultures and societies. This assumption usually takes a more specific form, namely, that diseases found in modern Western society provide a standard taxonomy much as the natural elements are represented by the standard table of atomic weights. This assumption of generic diseases is clearly a corollary of the assumptions discussed previously, that diseases may be defined as deviations from normal biological functioning and that each has a specific etiology. Nonetheless, there are specific properties and implications of this third assumption that merit separate attention.

A good vantage point for critical analysis is provided through work in cultural anthropology, particularly research in ethnomedicine. Students of ethnomedicine are interested in cultural variations in both formal and informal, or "folk," medical theories and practices. In the past, such cross-cultural studies tended to include invidious comparisons between the "scientific" medicine of advanced Western societies and the "primitive" folk medicine of less advanced societies; recent work is more descriptive and less evaluative in tone. One mark of this change is that modern Western medicine is now viewed as one alternative approach among others and, in this way, is placed more firmly in historical and cross-cultural perspective. One commentator states this view directly: "As a physician, one is trained to identify and treat disease, and as a consequence of assimilating much technical information, one often comes to view disease as an abstracted 'object' or condition. This is to say that disease is given a biomedical reality insofar as its chemical and physiological attributes are emphasized. . . . It is easy to lose sight of the fact that biomedicine and science in general are relatively recent developments in the evolution of man. Disease is and has been ubiquitous in human groups. The antiquity and universality of disease means that human groups have always had to develop theories about and treatment rationales for disease. . . . From this general frame of reference, biomedicine, the prevailing orientation of the contemporary physician, is but another view of disease."[21]

At this juncture, it is important to clarify and emphasize the point that we are not questioning the validity of observations made by bioscientists of biological processes, functions, and structures. Biological events at various levels of complexity and organization are observable, measurable, and orderly. Modern theories in the biosciences are powerful explanatory systems. However, there is a critical difference between a description of a biological process and clinical definitions of signs and symptoms of illness, even though the latter are couched in the vocabulary of the biosciences. This difference reflects the fact that medicine is not simply a bioscience, but an applied bioscience. Although this distinction is obvious, it is often obscured within medicine itself. The result is that the specific features and consequences of medicine as practice, as an applied science, are not fully recognized or given adequate attention.

One important issue for analysis that follows from recognition of this difference between medicine and the basic biosciences is the distinction between symptoms and illness. The presence of measurable "deviations from normal biological functioning" is only one of the conditions for illness, certainly not a necessary and sufficient condition and sometimes neither necessary nor sufficient. Proposing a broader and more naturalistic conception of illness, Engel points to the relativity of the two terms, health and disease, and to the lack of a sharp dividing line between them. On the one hand, "A person may satisfy all the criteria of health at any point in time simply because the adaptive capacity of a defective system, be it biomedical, physiological, or psychological, has not been exceeded."[22] On the other hand, patients may present with subjective complaints although no "objective" basis for them can be found. In these latter instances, "Regardless of the nature and severity of a patient's complaint, the failure to discover an abnormality on physical or laboratory examination means to many physicians that there is 'nothing wrong.' . . . The common slang is that the patient has 'no pathology,' and it carries the double implication that he is not sick and often also that he is not worthy of help or that he is 'fooling' the physician."[23] In developing his argument that many normal, naturally occurring phenomena of everyday life, such as the experience of grief, meet the usual criteria of disease, Engel notes, "The term 'pathological' is a relative one and is set by medical, scientific and even social convention. Conventions change, so that what may be considered as illness or disease at one time or by one person may not be so considered at another time by another person. . . . The heuristic value of differentiating between normal and pathological should not blind us to the fact that this is a relative matter based on ever-changing criteria."[24]

Medical sociologists and anthropologists, in their investigations of illness and medical care, have paid particular attention to this distinction between symptoms and illness. Within their sociomedical perspective, illness is viewed as one type of social deviance. One prominent theme in this work is that persons who display certain behaviors that

are defined as deviant from their group's sociocultural norms come to be "labeled" as sick. (Other types of deviant behavior may lead to their being labeled as delinquent, or immature, or as heretics). An individual who is socially categorized or labeled as "sick" may then be processed into a special social role, the role of patient.

Physicians are of critical importance in this process, and the practice of medicine may be viewed within this sociological perspective, as a system of rules for making symptoms into illnesses, and for transforming persons into patients. The patient role, in turn, may have consequences that are independent of the biological components of the illness. When an individual comes to behave as a patient, certain symptoms that might otherwise remit "naturally" may come instead to be "locked in" as appropriate to this new role; thus, additional symptoms may be generated. For example, many of the behaviors of hospitalized chronic schizophrenics had at one time been viewed as characteristics of their illness. Later research indicated that their behavior was in large part a function of conditions in large custodial mental hospitals. The term "hospitalitis" appeared to be a more accurate explanation of their behavior than schizophrenia.[25] Waxler[26] summarizes findings on levels of improvement in patients released from mental hospitals which suggest that psychiatric symptoms and social adjustment problems persist longer if an individual continues to be considered as a patient.

One last point on the distinction

between symptoms and illness deserves mention. We have been discussing this issue as if it were necessary for measurable "deviations from a norm of biological functioning" to be present in order for a person to be labeled as sick. We have also been emphasizing the role of physicians and other health professionals in the labeling process. As Engel notes, people without "objective" biological signs of disease may be viewed by physicians as having "no pathology"; they may be referred to as hypochondriacs or, more invidiously, called "crocks." A further implication of the argument we have been developing is that such people would be considered legitimate cases of illness if they and others in their social world treated them as sick. That is, given the distinction proposed between symptoms and illness, it is clear that a person may be asymptomatic in biological terms but ill in social terms. For example, individuals who have "recovered" medically from tuberculosis, a coronary attack, or an acute schizophrenic episode may continue to behave as though they were sick and continue to be treated as such by others.

In addition to the distinction between symptoms and illness, another question may be raised about the biomedical assumption of generic diseases. This is whether the taxonomy of disease constructed by Western medicine in particular social, cultural, and historical circumstances can be mapped on to the distributions of biological, behavioral, psychological, and social signs and symptoms found in other cultures. That is, would such a mapping be appropriate to and effective for the understanding and control of disease in these cultures?

This is not an easily resolvable question, and there is a lack of relevant comparative studies that address it. Even critics of the biomedical model are reluctant to adopt the position that our modern taxonomy of disease may be culture bound. Murphy, for example, reports evidence from her studies of Eskimos in the Bering Sea and the Yoruba in Africa that the patterns and frequencies of mental illness in these cultures are similar to those found in Western cultures, and further, that explicit criteria for insanity exist in these cultures. She concludes: "Rather than being simply violations of the social norms of particular groups, as labeling theory suggests, symptoms of mental illness are manifestations of a type of affliction shared by all mankind."[27] Similarly, Eisenberg, although arguing for the view that ". . . human disease inevitably and always reflects the outcome of the process of interaction between human biology and human social organization, a process in which culture occupies a central position," nevertheless concludes: "Close examination of the evidence demonstrates that, though improper care can retard recovery, psychiatric illness exists before the name assigned to it and independently of theories about its genesis."[28]

One approach is to apply standard diagnostic procedures and criteria to patients in different cultures. This has been attempted in a complex study conducted by the World Health Organization in nine cultures.[29] Psychiatrists from these different cultures were trained to follow a standard procedure for diagnosis of schizophrenia. Diagnostic information was then evaluated through the application of two different systematic statistical procedures in order to locate a group of patients with common yet distinctive symptoms. This latter group was defined as the concordant group of schizophrenics. Of the sample of 811 patients diagnosed as schizophrenics by trained psychiatrists in clinical settings in each culture, only 306 or 37 percent were found to be concordant on all criteria. This study does not deal with the issue we have raised about the cross-cultural validity of the diagnostic system of Western psychiatry. However, its findings are important in showing that even when standard procedures are applied, a considerable amount of unexplained variance remains in the diagnosis of a specific disease.

An important implication of our discussion must now be addressed. These questions about the assumption of generic diseases are of a somewhat different order than those raised earlier in our analyses of the biological definition of disease and the doctrine of specific etiologies. Those analyses, while critical of the biomedical model, stayed within the boundaries of the problems of health and illness as they have been defined by physicians. For example, although we used Ryle's work on "visible" thyroid glands to question the definition of disease as deviation from normality, his work does not directly challenge the disease model of modern medicine. Rather, his aim

was to correct for one of the deficiencies of the model, namely, its reliance on average values as standards for normality, by emphasizing the range of "normal" variability. Similarly with Dubos' distinction between infection and disease and his elucidation of the complex processes through which one may, or may not, be transformed into the other. Here, too, his criticism was aimed at deficiencies of modern medicine, particularly at the oversimplified model of causation that has gained prominence. But, within his critique, one may detect a continued loyalty (albeit somewhat strained) to the biological disease model.

In raising questions about the assumption of generic diseases, we have stepped outside the boundaries of medicine. The biomedical model equates illness with biological signs and symptoms. We have argued that this is *a* conceptual model and not simply *the* representation of reality. Like any conceptual model, it defines the relevance and significance of certain aspects of reality. Within the framework of the biosciences, the biomedical model takes a class of human problems and reconstructs them as "illnesses."

The alternative perspective that we develop draws on the social and behavioral sciences. It is not less "scientific" than the biomedical approach, but provides a different construction of these problems. Health and illness are defined as social rather than biological categories. This, of course, does not mean that biological processes are either irrelevant or trivial. However, there is a shift in perspective, which locates biological processes within a social context. Illnesses are made by people, we have argued, in the strict sense that giving the label of illness to certain behaviors or symptoms is an active interpretive process. This process of interpretation, through which illnesses are constructed, is guided and regulated by social rules and norms, which are central topics of inquiry in the social sciences.

Thus, in addressing the problem of generic diseases, our perspective shifts away from the study of illness as an attribute of patients. Instead, we focus on the problem of how illnesses are defined and how patients are made, particularly through the work of physicians and other health professionals. We view medicine as a subculture, with its own institutionalized beliefs, values, and practices. It may be studied and analyzed in the same way as other cultures and social institutions.

The Scientific Neutrality of Medicine

Physicians tend to see themselves as bioscientists. Their self-image as practitioners reflects a view of medicine as a discipline that has adopted not only the rationality of the scientific method but the concomitant values of the scientist, namely, objectivity and neutrality. Practitioners, of course, are aware of the distinction between the pure research scientist in pursuit of general truth and definitive knowledge and the applied physician-scientist with practical aims, such as the alleviation of pain and suffering and the prevention and cure of disease. Nonetheless, physicians tend to see the scientists as an idealized role model for themselves. Although the scientific values of rationality, objectivity, and neutrality may be difficult to achieve in practice, nevertheless they retain their force as the basis for assessing the quality of clinical work. Further, these values are used to justify the particular ways in which clinical work is done.

This "storybook image of medicine," to paraphrase the analogous idealization of science itself,[30] has a number of consequences for relationships between medicine and the larger society. Of some importance is the implication that the work of physicians as practitioners is guided primarily by "objective" scientific rules and criteria and, therefore, is relatively unaffected by wider social, cultural, and political forces. The view is often phrased normatively; that is, medicine ought to be independent of and protected from these forces, because they would undermine or distort its essential features as a science.

In contrast to this, our own view is that medicine, far from being independent of a larger society, is deeply embedded within it, has been given a legitimate mandate to carry out certain tasks and perform certain functions, and has complex relationships with other social institutions. Specifically, medicine is a special type of social institution dominated by physicians as a particular profession.

Within this perspective, the principal social function of medicine is the regulation and control of one type of deviance, namely, sickness. In carrying out this function, physicians have been granted by society the right to define criteria of sickness, to determine appropriate modes of treatment and management, and to engage in practices consistent with these definitions and determinations. This is true in all societies, but specific organizational forms and practices vary as a function of relationships between medicine and other social institutions. In the village culture of the New Guinea Highlands, for example, where medical and religious practices are closely intertwined, and where "an illness has meaning for a community, not just for an individual," treatment is directed to the solution of a variety of social conflicts, ". . . social and political competition, intra-familial disputes, quarrels, conflicts, and crimes."[31] In a similar vein, Waxler reports that in the village culture of Sri Lanka, illness and the treatment rituals it evokes serve to reintegrate families and reestablish their social boundaries during periods of stress.[32]

Special note must be taken in this connection of the organization of physicians as an autonomous profession. Friedson[33] argues that its status as a profession depended on establishing a monopoly over the exercise of its work. The profession's claim for autonomy, that is, for self-regulation and control, rests in large part on the prior claim that there is a corpus of technical and esoteric knowledge that only those who are properly initiated and trained will be able to understand and apply.

Friedson proposes that a sharper distinction be made between ". . . the body of scientific knowledge possessed by the profession [and] the knowledge used in applying knowledge to work situations. . . . 'pure' medical knowledge is transmuted, even debased in the course of application. Indeed, in the course of application knowledge cannot remain pure but must instead become socially organized as practice. . . . Insofar as it generically involves the practical application of knowledge to human affairs, it involves moral commitments and moral consequences neither justified by nor derived from the esoteric expertise which is supposed to distinguish the profession from other occupations. Medicine is not merely neutral, like theoretical physics . . . As a moral enterprise it is an instrument of social control which should be scrutinized as such without confusing the 'objectivity' of its applications."[34]

In discussing the assumption of the scientific neutrality of medicine, we have focused on medicine as a social institution, on its relationships to other institutions, and its functions for the larger society. It is worth noting here, as we did at the end of the previous section, that the issues addressed differ from those raised earlier in our discussions of the definition and etiology of illness. Within our overall approach, this is the broadest perspective that can be applied to the examination of problems in the health field. We are asking questions about how medicine functions within the larger society. Such an examination is necessarily comparative and takes into account historical, political, and economic factors.

Notes

1. A critique of context-stripping methods in the social and behavioral sciences may be found in Mishler, E.G. "Meaning in context: is there any other kind?" *Harvard Educational Review,* 1979, 49(1):1–19.
2. Engel, G. L. "The need for a new medical model: a challenge for biomedicine," *Science,* April 8, 1977, *196:*129–36, p. 130.
3. Cohen, R. "The evolution of the concept of disease," in Lush, B. (Ed.). *Concepts of Medicine.* New York: Pergamon Press, 1961, p. 169.
4. For a discussion of historical concepts of disease, see Reise, W. *The Conception of Disease.* New York: Philosophical Library, 1953. Essays on philosophical problems of medical concepts of health and disease are in Engelhardt, H. T., Jr., and Spicker, S. F. (Eds.). *Evaluation and Explanation in the Biomedical Medical Sciences.*
5. Quoted in Redlich, F. C. "The concept of health in psychiatry," in Leighton, A. H., Clausen, J. N., and Wilson, R. N. (Eds.). *Explorations in Social Psychiatry,* London: Tavistock Publications, 1957, p. 140.
6. Engel, G. L. "A unified concept of health and disease," in Ingle, D. J. (Ed.), *Life and Disease.* New York: Basic Books, 1963, p. 339.
7. Redlich, "The concept of health in psychiatry," p. 155.
8. *Webster's New International Dictionary of the English Language* 2nd ed. Unabridged. Springfield, MA: G. & C. Merriam, 1956.
9. Ryle, J. "The meaning of normal." in Lush, *Concepts of Medicine,* p. 146.
10. Ibid., p. 137.
11. Ibid. p. 144.
12. Dubos, R. *Mirage of Health.* New York: Anchor Books, 1961.
13. Engel, "The need for a new medical model." p. 131.
14. Ibid., p. 131.
15. Dubos, *Mirage of Health,* p. 129.
16. Ibid., p. 91.
17. Engel, G. L. *Psychological Development in Health and Disease.* Philadelphia: W. B. Saunders, 1962; See also Engel, "A unified concept of health and disease."
18. Dubos, R. J. "Infection into disease," In Ingle (Ed.), *Life and Disease,* pp. 100–101.
19. Ibid., p. 108.
20. Balint, M. *The Doctor, His Patient and the Illness.* New York: International University Press, 1957.
21. Fabrega, H., Jr. "Toward a theory of human disease," *Journal of Nervous and Mental Disease,* 1976, 162(5): 299–312, p. 299.
22. Engel, *Psychological Development in Health and Disease,* p. 250.
23. Ibid., p. 252.
24. Ibid., p. 254.
25. For a review of some of this work and a report of research on the effects of changes in the social milieu of mental hospitals, see Wing, J. K., and Brown, G. W. *Institutionalism and Schizophrenia.* Cambridge: Cambridge University Press, 1970. In his *The Making of Blind Men,* New York: Russell Sage, 1969, Robert Scott describes how a homogeneous "character type" may develop in a naturally diverse population through the practice of treatment agencies.
26. Waxler, N. E. "Culture and mental illness," *Journal of Nervous and Mental Disease,* 1974, 159(6):379–95.
27. Murphy, J. M. "Psychiatric labeling in cross-cultural perspective," *Science,* March 12, 1976, *191:*1019–28, p. 1027.
28. Eisenberg, L. "Psychiatry and society: a sociobiologic synthesis," *New*

England Journal of Medicine, April 21, 1977, 296(16):903–10, pp. 905 and 903.

29. WHO. *Report of the International Pilot Study of Schizophrenia, Vol. 1.* Geneva: World Health Organization. 1973.
30. For an analysis and critique of the "storybook image of science," see Mitroff, I. I. *The Subjective Side of Science.* New York: American Elsevier, 1974.
31. Glick, L. B. "Medicine as an ethnographic category: the Gimi of the New Guinea Highlands," *Ethnology*, 1967, 6(1):31–56, pp. 53 and 52.
32. Waxler, N. E. "Is mental illness cured in traditional societies? A theoretical analysis," *Culture, Medicine and Psychiatry*, 1977, I:233–53.
33. Friedson, E. *Profession of Medicine: A Study of the Sociology of Applied Knowledge.* New York: Dodd, Mead, 1970.
34. Ibid., p. 346.

11 SOCIAL STRUCTURES OF MEDICAL OPPRESSION: A MARXIST VIEW

Howard Waitzkin

Class Structure

The Marxist definition of social class emphasizes the relations of capitalist economic production. Although a brief summary perhaps oversimplifies, Marxist analysis notes that one group of people, the capitalist class, own or control the means of production: the machines, factories, land, and raw materials necessary to make products for the market. The working class, who do not own or control the means of production, must sell their labor for a wage. But the value of the product that workers produce is always greater than their wage. Workers must give up their product to the capitalist; by losing control of their own productive process, workers become alienated from their labor. Surplus value, the difference between the wage paid to workers and the value of the product they create, is the objective basis of the capitalist's profit. Surplus value also is a structural source of exploitation; it motivates the capitalist to keep wages low, to change the work process (by automation and new technologies, close supervision, lengthened work day or overtime, speedups, and dangerous working conditions), and to resist workers' organized attempts to gain higher wages or more control in the workplace (1). The contradiction between profit and safety, as noted earlier, emerges in large part from the economic relations of class structure.

Although they acknowledge the historical changes that have occurred

---

since Marx's time, contemporary Marxist studies have reaffirmed the presence of highly stratified class structures in advanced capitalist societies and Third World nations. Another topic of great interest is the persistence or reappearance of class structure, usually based on expertise and professionalism, in countries where socialist revolutions have taken place. These theoretical and empirical analyses show that relations of economic production remain a primary basis of class structure.

The health system mirrors the class structure of the broader society (2). The "corporate class" includes the major owners and controllers of wealth. They comprise 1 percent of the population and own 80 percent of all corporate stocks and state and local government bonds. The "working class," at the opposite end of the scale, makes up 49 percent of the population. It is composed of man-

ual laborers, service workers, and farm workers. Between these polar classes are the "upper middle class" (professionals like doctors, lawyers, and so forth, comprising 14 percent of the population, and middle-level business executives, 6 percent of the population), and the "lower middle class" (shopkeepers, self-employed people, craftsmen, artisans, comprising 7 percent of the population, and clerical and sales workers, 23 percent of the population). Although these definitions provide summary descriptions of a very complex social reality, they are useful in analyzing manifestations of class structure in the health system.

Control over Health Institutions

Navarro has documented the pervasive control that members of the corporate and upper middle classes exert within the policy-making

TABLE 1   Social Class Composition of the United States Labor Force and Boards of Health Institutions, 1975

| | Class[a] (Percent) | | | |
	Corporate	Upper Middle	Lower Middle	Working
U.S. labor force	1	20	30	49
Board members				
Foundations	70	30	—	—
Private medical teaching institutions	45	55	—	—
State medical teaching institutions	20	70	10	—
Voluntary hospitals	5	80	10	5

SOURCE: V. Navarro, *Medicine under Capitalism* (New York: Prodist, 1976), p. 155. Reprinted by permission of the author.
[a]See text for definitions.

bodies of North American health institutions (Table 1) (3). These classes predominate on the governing boards of private foundations concerned with health care, private and state medical teaching institutions, and local voluntary hospitals. Only on the boards of state teaching institutions and voluntary hospitals do members of the lower middle class or working class gain any appreciable representation; even there, the participation from these classes falls far below their proportion in the general population. Community-based research has documented corporate dominance of health institutions in many parts of the United States. Navarro has argued, based partly on these observations, that control over health institutions reflects the same patterns of class dominance that have arisen in other areas of North American economic and political life.

Stratification within Health Institutions

As members of the upper middle class, physicians occupy the highest stratum among workers in health institutions. Composing 7 percent of the health labor force, physicians receive a median net income (approximately $61,200 in 1977) that places them in the upper 5 percent of the income distribution of the United States. Under physicians and professional administrators are members of the lower middle class: nurses, physical and occupational therapists, and technicians. They make up 29 percent of the health labor force, are mostly women, and earn about

$12,000. At the bottom of institutional hierarchies are clerical workers, aides, orderlies, and kitchen and janitorial personnel, who are the working class of the health system. They have an income of about $8,100 per year, represent 54 percent of the health labor force, and are 84 percent female and 30 percent black (4). Several studies have analyzed the forces of racism, sexism, elitism, and professionalism that divide health workers from one another and prevent them from realizing common interests. These patterns affect physicians, nurses, and technical and service workers who comprise the fastest growing segment of the health labor force (5).

Occupational Mobility

Class mobility into professional positions is quite limited. Investigations of physicians' class backgrounds in both Britain and the United States have shown a consistently small representation of the lower middle and working classes among medical students and practicing doctors (6). In the United States, historical documentation is available to trace changes in class mobility during the twentieth century. As Ziem has found, despite some improvements for other disadvantaged groups like blacks and women, recruitment of working-class medical students has been very limited since shortly after publication of The *Flexner Report*. In 1920, 12 percent of medical students came from working-class families, and this percentage has stayed almost exactly the same until the present time.

In summary, class structure in the health system parallels the class structure of the entire society. Members of the corporate and upper middle classes predominate in the discussion-making bodies of North American health institutions. Within those institutions, workers are highly stratified. Mobility into the medical profession by individuals from working-class or lower-middle-class families remains limited. As I consider later, strategies for changing the health-care system must take into account the broader class structure of the society.

Monopoly Capital

During the past century, economic capital has become more concentrated in a smaller number of companies, the monopolies. Monopoly capital has emerged in essentially all advanced capitalist nations, where the process of monopolization has reinforced private corporate profit. Monopoly capital also has become a prominent feature of most capitalist health systems. Contributing to the problems of medical maldistribution and rising costs of care, monopoly capital manifests itself in several ways.

Medical Centers

Since about 1910, a continuing growth of medical centers has occurred, usually in affiliation with universities. Capital is highly concentrated in these medical centers, which are heavily oriented to advanced technology. Practitioners have received training where technology is available and specialization

is highly valued. Partly as a result, health workers are often reluctant to practice in areas without easy access to medical centers. The nearly unrestricted growth of medical centers has heightened the maldistribution of health workers and facilities throughout the United States and within regions.

Emphasis on science and technology led to an industrialized economic base for modern medicine and a greater use of hospitals. A technologic imperative emerged, motivating the application of high technology to many health problems. The *Flexner Report* played a crucial part in the development of capital-intensive medical centers that increasingly relied on expensive machines and equipment, relative to human labor. The medical schools that remained open after the report's impact were those capable of attracting and maintaining a large enough capital base to support extensive laboratory facilities. Medical traditions that received disfavor and eventual disenfranchisement generally were not oriented to advanced scientific methods and did not require concentrated capital or technology (7).

Finance Capital

Monopoly capital also has been apparent in the position of banks, trusts, and insurance companies, the largest profit-making corporations under capitalism. For example, in the late 1970s, the annual flow of doctors through private insurance companies was more than $45 billion, about half of the total insurance sold. Among commercial insurance companies, capital is highly concentrated; about 60 percent of the health-insurance industry is controlled by the 10 largest insurers. Metropolitan Life and Prudential each control more than $30 billion in assets, more than those of General Motors, Standard Oil of New Jersey, or International Telephone and Telegraph (8).

Finance capital figures prominently in health reform proposals (9); most plans for national health insurance would permit a continuing role for the insurance industry. Moreover, corporate investment in health maintenance organizations has increased, partly because of the assumption that national health insurance, when enacted, will assure the profitability of these ventures.

The "Medical-industrial Complex"

The "military-industrial complex" has provided a model for industrial penetration into the health system, popularized by the term "medical-industrial complex." Investigations by the Health Policy Advisory Center and others have emphasized that the exploitation of illness for private profit is a primary feature of the health systems in advanced capitalist societies. Many reports have criticized the pharmaceutical and medical equipment industries for advertising and marketing practices, price and patent collusion, and promotion of drugs before their safety is tested (10).

These industries have played a prominent role in developing and promoting expensive therapeutic innovations in cardiovascular disease (coronary care units and coronary artery bypass surgery) radiologic studies in hypertension and head trauma, fetal monitoring, computerized tomographic scanning, and so forth. The medical profession has tended to adopt technologically advanced diagnostic and treatment modalities without controlled trials demonstrating their effectiveness. Industrial growth in the health system comprises a rapidly expanding sector of the overall economy of the United States; this trend is likely to continue for some time to come.

The State

Because the state encompasses the major institutions of political power, its strategic importance is obvious. The state comprises the interconnected public institutions that act to preserve the capitalist economic system and the interests of the capitalist class. This definition includes the executive, legislative, and judicial branches of government; the military; and the criminal justice system —all of which hold varying degrees of coercive power. It also encompasses relatively noncoercive institutions within the educational, public welfare, and health-care systems. Through such noncoercive institutions, the state offers services or conveys ideologic messages that legitimate the capitalist system. Especially in periods of economic crisis, the state can use these same institutions to provide public subsidization of private enterprise.

The Private-Public Contradiction

The health system has two subsectors. The "private sector" is based in private practice and companies that manufacture medical products or control finance capital. The "public sector," as part of the state, operates through direct public expenditures and employs health workers in public institutions. Examples of institutions in the public sector are the Public Health Service, Indian Health Service, the Veterans Administration hospitals, county and municipal hospitals, public mental hospitals, and the Medicare and Medicaid systems. Despite the distinction between public and private sectors, the state frequently can channel public money or other capital into the private sector; this tendency creates a potential for abuse that I will discuss shortly.

Nations vary greatly in the private-public duality. In the United States, a dominant private sector coexists with a large public sector. The public sector is even larger in Great Britain and Scandinavia. In Cuba and China, the private sector essentially has been eliminated.

The private sector, as mentioned in the last chapter, tends to drain public resources and health workers' time, to the benefit of private profit and to the detriment of patients using the public sector. This framework has helped explain some of the problems that have arisen in such countries as Great Britain and Chile, where private sectors persisted after the enactment of national health services. In these countries, practitioners have faced financial incentives to increase the scope of private practice, which they often have conducted within public hospitals or clinics. In the United States, the expansion of public payment programs such as Medicare and Medicaid has

led to increased public subsidization of private practice and private hospitals as well as abuses of these programs by individual practitioners (11). This subsidization has heightened the problem of escalating costs for medical care.

Similar problems have undermined other public health programs (12). These programs frequently have obtained finances through regressive taxation, placing low-income taxpayers at a relative disadvantage. Likewise, the deficiencies of the Blue Cross and Blue Shield insurance plans have derived largely from the failure of public regulatory agencies to control payments to practitioners and hospitals in the private sector. If enacted, national health insurance also would use public funds to reinforce and strengthen the private sector by assuring payment for hospitals and individual physicians and possibly by permitting a continued role for commercial insurance companies.

Throughout the United States the problems of the private-public contradiction tend to worsen medical maldistribution. Private hospitals often transfer uninsured and low-income patients to public municipal or county hospitals. This process of "dumping" patients from the private to the public sector has created major financial burdens for public hospitals. Since the early 1970s, public hospitals in most large cities also have faced cutbacks, closure, or conversion to private ownership and control. The conversion of public hospitals to private control often has involved medical schools, which in many cases have assumed administrative and professional responsibility for these hospitals. Some medical schools have encountered financial difficulties in these arrangements; most schools, however, have benefited by public payment for low-income patients. In general, the public sector is weakened by the diverting of funds and professional resources to privately controlled facilities. Preliminary studies have shown that low-income patients face greater problems of access when public hospitals and clinics convert to private control, even when this conversion involves assumption of responsibility by medical schools (13).

General Functions of the State within the Health System

The state's functions in the health system have increased in scope and complexity. In the first place, through the health system, the state acts to legitimate the capitalist economic system based in private enterprise (14). The history of public health and welfare programs shows that state expenditures usually rise during periods of social protest and decrease as unrest becomes less widespread. In the early 1970s public opinion surveys uncovered a profound level of dissatisfaction with government and particularly with the role of business interests in government policies. Citizens who thought something was deeply wrong with their country and who expressed disenchantment with government became a national majority (15). Under such circumstances, the state's predictable response has been to expand health and other welfare programs. These incremental re-

forms, at least in part, reduce the legitimacy crisis of the capitalist system by restoring confidence that the system can meet people's basic needs. The cycles of political attention devoted to national health insurance in the United States appear to parallel cycles of popular discontent. Cutbacks in public health services to low-income patients in the early 1980s have followed the decline of social protest by low-income groups.

The second major function of the state in the health system is to protect and reinforce the private sector more directly. As previously noted, most plans for national health insurance would permit a prominent role and continued profits for the private insurance industry, particularly in the administration of payments, record keeping, and data collection. Corporate participation in new health initiatives sponsored by the state—including health maintenance organizations, preventive screening programs, computerized components of professional standards review organizations, algorithm and protocol development for paraprofessional training, and audiovisual aids for patient education programs—is providing major sources of expanded profit (16).

A third and subtler function of the state is the reinforcement of dominant frameworks in scientific and clinical medicine that are consistent with the capitalist economic system and the suppression of alternative frameworks that might threaten the system. The United States government has provided generous funding for research on the pathophysiology and treatment of specific disease entities. As critics even within government have recognized, the disease-centered approach has reduced the level of analysis to the individual organism and, often inappropriately, has stimulated the search for unifactorial rather than multifactorial causation. During the last decade, analyses emphasizing the importance of individual "lifestyle" as a cause of disease have received prominent attention from state agencies in the United States and Canada (17). Clearly, individual differences in personal habits do affect health in all societies. On the other hand, the life-style argument, perhaps even more than the earlier emphasis on specific cause, obscures important sources of illness and disability in the capitalist work process and industrial environment; it also puts the burden of the health squarely on the individual, rather than seeking collective solutions to health problems.

Limits and Mechanisms of State Intervention

Although the state's activity in the health system is increasing in all capitalist societies, state intervention faces certain structural limits. Simply summarized, these limits restrict state intervention to policies and programs that will not conflict in fundamental ways with capitalist economic processes based on private profit or with the concrete interests of the capitalist class during specific historical periods.

"Negative selection mechanisms" are forms of state intervention that exclude innovations or activities that challenge the capitalist system (18). For example, agencies of the state may enact occupational health legislation and enforcement regulations. However, such reforms will not reach a level strict enough to interfere with profitability in specific industries. Nor will state takeover of industries responsible for occupational or environmental diseases occur to any major degree.

Negative selection also applies to the potential nationalization of the health system as a whole. In most capitalist societies, the state generally has opposed structural changes that infringe on private medical practice, private control of most hospitals, and the profitability of the pharmaceutical, medical equipment, insurance, and other industries operating in the health system. Therefore, the state's attempts to control health-care costs have been inconsistent and largely unsuccessful. While excluding nationalization through negative selection, the state sponsors incremental reforms that control excesses in each of these spheres, thus maintaining the legitimacy of the whole. As an example of negative selection, congressional deliberations in the United States systematically exclude serious consideration of a national health service (as opposed to national health insurance) that might question the appropriateness of private medical practice or the nationalization of hospitals. Another example is governmental regulation of the drug and insurance industries; aside from its erratic effects, state regulation rules out public ownership of these industries.

The state also can use "positive selection mechanisms" that promote and sponsor policies strengthening the private enterprise system and the interests of capital. As discussed earlier, positive selection has involved sponsorship of biomedical research that assumes unifactorial etiology or, more recently, the "life style" analysis. Most importantly, state agencies tend to favor financial reforms, like health insurance, that would assure the stability of the private sector in the health system. The state's positive selection of financial reforms contrasts sharply with the exclusion of organizational reforms that potentially might change the broader political and economic structure of the present system.

Medical Ideology

Ideology is an interlocking set of ideas and doctrines that form the distinctive perspective of a social group. The events of history, in the Marxist perspective, emerge mainly from economic forces; this economic determinacy gives causal primacy to the sphere of production and class conflict. Ideology, however, helps sustain and reproduce the social relations of projection and, especially, patterns of domination. Institutions of civil society, such as the educational system, family, mass media and organized religion, promulgate ideas and beliefs that support the established order (19).

Along with other institutions, medicine fosters an ideology that helps maintain and reproduce class structure and social domination. Medicine's ideologic features do not diminish the efforts of individuals who use currently accepted methods in their clinical work and research; nevertheless, medical ideology has major ramifications beyond medicine itself. Studies of medical ideology have identified several key components:

Disturbances of Biological Homeostasis Are Equivalent to Breakdowns of Machines

Modern medical science views the human organism mechanistically (20). The health professional's advanced training permits the recognition of specific causes and treatments for physical disorders. The mechanistic view of the human body deflects attention from multifactorial origin, especially causes of disease that derive from the environment, work processes, or social stress; it also reinforces a general ideology that attaches positive evaluation to industrial technology under specialized control. This ideologic component helps justify costly and complex medical approaches that depend on advanced technology, as opposed to mundane but potentially more effective practices.

Disease Is a Problem of the Individual Human Being

The unifactorial model of disease contains reductionist assumptions, because it focuses on disruptions in individual biology rather than on the illness-generating conditions of society. A similar reductionist approach has emphasized sources of illness in life-style. In both cases, the responsibility for disease and cure rests at the individual rather than at the collective level. This orientation deflects attention from class structure and relations of production, even in their implications for health and illness.

Science Permits the Rational Control of Human Beings

The natural sciences have led to a greater control over nature. Similarly, it is often assumed that modern medicine, by correcting defects of individuals, can enhance their controllability. The quest for a reliable work force has been one motivation for the support of modern medicine by capitalist economic interests. Physicians' certification of illness historically has expanded or contracted to meet industry's needs for labor. Thus, medicine is seen as contributing to the rational governance of society, and managerial principles increasingly are applied to the organization of the health system (21).

Many Spheres of Life Are Appropriate for Medical Management

This ideologic assumption has led to an expansion of medicine's social control function; many behaviors that do not adhere to society's norms become appropriate for management by health professionals. "Medicalization," as discussed earlier, creates ambiguities of caring and humanism. The medical management of behavioral difficulties, such as hyperactivity and aggression, often coincides with attempts to find specific biologic lesions associated with these behaviors. Histori-

cally, medicine's social control function has expanded in periods of intense social protest or rapid social change (22).

Medical Science Is Both Esoteric and Excellent

According to this ideologic principle, medical science involves a body of advanced knowledge and standards of excellence in both research and practice. Because scientific knowledge is esoteric, a group of professionals tend to hold elite positions. Lacking this knowledge, ordinary people are dependent on professionals for interpretation of medical data. The health system therefore reproduces patterns of domination by expert decision makers in the workplace, government, and many other areas of social life. The ideology of excellence helps justify these patterns, although the quality of much medical research and practice is far from excellent; this paradox has been characterized as "the excellence deception" in medicine (23). Ironically, a similar ideology of excellence has justified the emergence of new class hierarchies based on expertise in some countries, such as the Soviet Union, that have undergone socialist revolutions. Other countries, such as the People's Republic of China, have cyclically tried to overcome these ideologic assumptions and to develop a less esoteric "people's medicine."

In the mass media, medical ideology appears in public statements by professional leaders and state and corporate officials whose organizations regulate or sponsor medical activities. More importantly, health professionals also express ideologic messages in their face-to-face interaction with patients.

Notes

1. For classic discussions, see K. Marx, *A Contribution to the Critique of Political Economy* (New York: International, 1971 [1859]), pp. 27–63 and K. Marx, *Capital*, Vol. 1 (Moscow: Progress Publishers, 1963 [1890]), Parts III–IV.
2. The data that follow are adapted from U.S. Bureau of the Census, *Statistical Abstract of the United States: 1980*, 101st ed. (Washington, D.C.: The Bureau, 1980), pp. 413, 424; R. Miliband, *The State in Capitalist Society* (New York: Basic Books, 1969), especially pp. 1–67; V. Navarro, *Medicine under Capitalism* (New York: Prodist, 1976), pp. 135–230. Although the definitions and categories of social class presented here are useful in analyzing the health system, they remain a source of contention in Marxist and non-Marxist circles. See, for example, N. Poulantzas, *Political Power and Social Class* (London: New Left Books, 1973) and N. Poulantzas, *Classes in Contemptorary Capitalism* (London: New Left Books, 1975).
3. Navarro, *Medicine under Capitalism*, p. 155.
4. Ibid., pp. 139–141; U.S. Bureau of the Census, *Statistical Abstract*, p. 113.
5. H. Waitzkin and B. Waterman, *The Exploitation of Illness in Capitalist Society* (Indianapolis: Bobbs-Merrill, 1974), pp. 65–75; K. Cannings and W. Lazonick, "The Development of the Nursing Labor Force in the United States," *Int. J. Health Serv.* 5 (1975): 185–216; Boston Nurses Group, *The False Promise: Professionalism in Nursing* (Somerville, Mass.: New England Free Press, 1978); B. Ehrenreich and J. Ehrenreich, "Hospital Workers: A Case Study of the New Working Class," *Monthly Rev.* 24 (January 1973): 12–27; G. Stevenson, "Social Relations of Production and Consumption in the Human Service Occupations," *Monthly Rev.* 28 (July-August 1976): 78–87; J. B. McKinlay, "The Changing Political and Economic Context of the Patient-Physician Encounter," in *The Doctor-Patient Relationship in the Changing Health Scene*, edited by E. B. Gallagher. DHEW Publication No. [NIH] 78–183 (Washington: Government Printing Office, 1978).
6. G. Ziem, "Medical Education Since Flexner," *Health/PAC Bull.* 76 (1977): 8–14, 23; M. A. Simpson, *Medical Education: A Critical Approach* (London: Butterworths, 1972); J. Robson, "The NHS Company, Inc.? The Social Consequences of the Professional Dominance in the National Health Service," *Int. J. Health Serv.* 3 (1973): 413–426.
7. Waitzkin and Waterman, *Exploitation of Illness*; S. Kelman, "Towards a Political Economy of Health Care," *Inquiry* 8 (1971): 30–38.
8. Navarro, *Medicine under Capitalism*, p. 150; Health Insurance Institute, *Source Book of Health Insurance Data* (Washington: The Institute, 1979), pp. 12–13.
9. T. Bodenheimer, "Health Care in the United States: Who Pays?" *Int. J. Health Serv.* 3 (1973): 427–434; L. Lander, *National Health Insurance* (New York: Health Policy Advisory Center, 1975); J. W. Salmon, "Health Maintenance Organization Strategy: A Corporate Takeover of Health Services," *Int. J. Health Serv.* 5 (1975): 609–624.
10. B. Ehrenreich and J. Ehrenreich

(eds.), *The American Health Empire*
(New York: Vintage, 1970); D.
Kotelchuck (ed.), *Prognosis Negative*
(New York: Vintage, 1976); Con-
cerned Rush Students, "Turning
Prescriptions into Profits," *Sci. for
the People* 8 (November–December
1976): 6–9, and 9 (January–Febru-
ary 1977): 30–32; W. Karner, "Zur
Strategie der pharmazeutischen In-
dustrie," *Fortschr. Wissenschaft (Vi-
enna)* 3/4 (1976): 8–30; R. Lichtman,
"The Political Economy of Medical
Care," in *The Social Organization of
Health*, edited by H. P. Dreitzel
(New York: Macmillan, 1971); M.
Silverman, *The Drugging of the
Americas* (Berkeley: University of
California Press, 1976); S. Lall,
"Medicines and Multinationals,"
Monthly Rev. 28 (March 1977): 19–30;
L. Rodberg and G. Stevenson, "The
Health Care Industry in Advanced
Capitalism," *Rev. Rad. Pol. Econ.* 8
(Spring 1977): 104–115.

11. Waitzkin and Waterman, *Exploitation
of Illness*, pp. 8–16; Robson, "NHS
Company, Inc.?"; H. Waitzkin and
H. Modell, "Medicine, Socialism,
and Totalitarianism: Lessons from
Chile," *N. Engl. J. Med.* 291 (1974):
171–177; H. Modell and H. Waitzkin, "Medicine and Socialism in
Chile," *Berkeley J. Sociol.* 19 (1974):
1–35.

12. T. Bodenheimer, "Health Care in the
United States: Who Pays?"; Lander,
National Health Insurance; S. Law,
Blue Cross: What Went Wrong (New
Haven: Yale University Press, 1976),
pp. 31–58, 145–160.

13. E. Blake and T. Bodenheimer, *Closing the Doors to the Poor* (San Francisco: Health Policy Advisory Center, 1975); M. I. Roemer and J. A.
Mera, "'Patient Dumping' and
Other Voluntary Agency Contributions to Public Agency Problems,"
Med. Care 11 (1973): 30–39.

14. Discussions of health services include V. Navarro, "Social Class, Political Power, and the State and Their
Implications in Medicine," *Soc. Sci.
Med.* 10 (1976): 437–457; M. Renaud, "On the Structural Constraints to State Intervention in
Health," *Int. J. Health Serv.* 5 (1975):
559–571. For a sociohistorical analysis of public welfare, see F. F. Piven
and R. A. Cloward, *Regulating the
Poor* (New York: Vintage, 1971).

15. See, for example, Committee on
Government Operations, United
States Senate, *Confidence and Concern:
Citizens View American Government: A
Survey of Public Attitudes* (Washing-
ton: Government Printing Office,
1973).

16. Waitzkin and Waterman, *Exploitation
of Illness*, pp. 89–107; Lander, *National Health Insurance*; J. W. Salmon,
"Monopoly Capital and Its Reorganization of the Health Sector," *Rev.
Rad. Pol. Econ.* 8 (Spring 1977): 125–
133.

17. I. Illich, *Medical Nemesis* (New York:
Pantheon, 1976); V. R. Fuchs, *Who
Shall Live? Health, Economics, and Social Choice* (New York: Basic Books,
1974); M. Lalonde, *A New Perspective
on the Health Of Canadians* (Ottawa:
Information Canada, 1974). For critiques, see V. Navarro, "The Industrialization of Fetishism or the Fetishism of Industrialization: A Critique of Ivan Illich," *Soc. Sci. Med.* 9
(1975): 351–363; H. Waitzkin, "Recent Studies in Medical Sociology:
The New Reductionism," *Contemp.
Sociol.* 5 (1976): 401–405.

18. For more extensive discussion of
these themes, see Offe, "Advanced
Capitalism and the Welfare State,"
Politics Soc. 2 (1972): 479–488; Navarro, "Social Class, Political Power,
and the State."

19. Classic analyses of these issues
in Marxism include, Marx, *A*

Contribution to the Critique of Political Economy, pp. 19–23; F. Engels, *The Origin of the Family, Private Property and the State* (New York: International, 1972 [1891]), pp. 94–146. Major reinterpretations are A. Gramsci, *Selections from the Prison Notebooks* (New York: International, 1971), pp. 12–14, 257–264, 364–377; L. Althusser, *Lenin and Philosophy and Other Essays* (New York: Monthly Review Press, 1971), pp. 127–186.

20. H. Berliner, "Emerging Ideologies in Medicine," *Rev. Rad. Pol. Econ.* 8 (Spring 1977): 116–124; A. Gorz, "Technical Intelligence and the Capitalist Division of Labor," *Telos* 12 (Summer 1972): 27–41.

21. E. R. Brown, *Rockefeller Medicine Men: Medicine and Capitalism in the Progressive Era* (Berkeley: University of California Press, 1979), pp. 112–134; B. Ehrenreich and J. Ehrenreich, "Health Care and Social Control," *Soc. Policy* 5 (May-June 1974): 26–40. For analysis of these patterns' impact on women, see B. Ehrenreich and D. English, *Complaints and Disorders: The Sexual Politics of Sickness* (Old Westbury, N.Y.: Feminist Press, 1973); B. Ehrenreich and D. English, *For Her Own Good* (New York: Anchor/Doubleday, 1978), pp. 141–181.

22. Waitzkin and Waterman, *Exploitation of Illness*, pp. 36–65; I. K. Zola, "Medicine as an Institution of Social Control," *Sociol. Rev.* 20 (1972): 487–504; I. K. Zola, "In the Name of Health and Illness: On Some Socio-Political Consequences of Medical Influence," *Soc. Sci. Med.* 9 (1975): 83–87; J. B. McKinlay, "On the Professional Regulation of Change," *Sociol. Rev. (Monogr.)* 20 (1973): 61–84; R. C. Fox, "The Medicalization and Demedicalization of American Society," *Daedalus* 106 (1977): 9–22; P. Conrad, "The Discovery of Hyperkinesis: Notes on the Medicalization of Deviant Behavior," *Soc. Problems* 23 (1975): 12–21.

23. G. Markowitz and D. Rosner, "Doctors in Crisis: A Study of the Use of Medical Educational Reform to Establish Modern Professional Elitism in Medicine," *Am. Q.* 25 (1973): 83–107; H. R. Holman, "The 'Excellence' Deception in Medicine," *Hosp. Pract.* 11 (April 1976): 11–21.

12 THE EPIDEMIOLOGIC APPROACH TO DISEASE

Abraham Lilienfeld

Epidemiology is concerned with the patterns of disease occurrence in human populations and of the factors that influence these patterns. The epidemiologist is primarily interested in the occurrence of disease by time, place, and persons. He tries to determine whether there has been an increase or decrease of the disease over the years; whether one geographical area has a higher frequency of the disease than another; and whether the characteristics of persons with a particular disease or condition distinguish them from those without it.

The personal characteristics with

SOURCE: From *Foundations of Epidemiology*, 2nd edition, by Abraham Lilienfeld. Copyright © 1976, 1980 by Oxford University Press, Inc. Reprinted by permission.

which the epidemiologist is concerned are the following:

1. Demographic characteristics such as age, sex, color, ethnic group.
2. Biological characteristics such as blood levels of antibodies, chemicals, enzymes; cellular constituents of the blood; measurements of physiological function of different organ systems of the body.
3. Social and economic factors such as socioeconomic status, educational background, occupation, nativity.
4. Personal habits such as tobacco and drug use, diet, physical exercise.
5. Genetic characteristics such as blood groups.

These areas of endeavor are well described by Hirsch's definition of historical and geographical pathology as a

> science which . . . will give, firstly, a picture of the occurrence, the distribution and the types of the diseases of mankind, in distinct epochs of time and at various points of the earth's surface; and secondly, will render an account of the relations of these diseases to the external conditions surrounding the individual and determining his manner of life. (12, 14)

This statement has commonly served as a base for defining epidemiology as "the study of the distribution of a disease or a physiological condition in human populations and of the factors that influence this distribution" (16). A more inclusive description was given by Wade Hampton Frost, one of the architects of modern epidemiology, who noted that "epidemiology is essentially an inductive science, concerned not merely with describing the distribution of disease, but equally or more with fitting it into a consistent philosophy" (12). Thus, epidemiology can be regarded as a sequence of reasoning concerned with biological inferences derived from observations of disease occurrence and related phenomena in human population groups. To this we can add that epidemiology is an integrative, eclectic discipline deriving concepts and methods from other disciplines, such as statistics, sociology, and biology, for the study of disease in populations.

A. General Purposes of Epidemiologic Studies

The information obtained from an epidemiologic study can be utilized in several ways:

1. To elucidate the etiology of a specific disease or group of diseases by combining epidemiologic data with information from other disciplines such as genetics, biochemistry, and microbiology.
2. To evaluate the consistency of epidemiologic data with etiological hypotheses developed either clinically (at the bedside) or experimentally (in the laboratory).
3. To provide the basis for developing and evaluating preventive procedures and public health practices.

Examples of each of these three general purposes will be presented.

Etiological Studies of Disease

A simple example of the use of epidemiologic data to determine etiological factors would be the investigation of an outbreak of food poisoning to determine which food was contaminated with the microorganism or chemical responsible for the epidemic. Another example would be the study of a disease that occurs with higher frequency among workers in occupations exposing them to particular chemicals, as illustrated by the study of arsenic and cancer by Mabuchi (18). In this study, lists were obtained of all men who had been employed in a pesticide plant. The workers were divided into those who had been predominantly exposed to arsenical compounds and those whose major exposure was to nonarsenical chemicals. Approximately 87 percent of 1,050 male and 67 percent of 343 female employees were traced to determine their mortality experience. The observed numbers of deaths from specific causes were then compared with those expected based on the death rates of the community in which the plant was located. A significantly larger number of deaths from lung cancer was found to have occurred in the group exposed to arsenic than would have been expected; further, this relationship between lung cancer and exposure to arsenic indicated a dose-response effect, i.e., the longer an employee was exposed to arsenical compounds, the greater was his or her chance of dying from lung cancer. The investigators concluded that a causal relationship existed between exposure to arsenical compounds and lung cancer.

Only occasionally do investigators find that the increased exposure of individuals to certain agents results in a decreased frequency of disease.

A classical example of this kind of relationship is that between the presence of fluorides in the water supply and dental caries. The investigation of this relationship is worth recounting, as it illustrates in concise form how a sequence of studies can be conducted to develop a preventive measure for a disease.

By the late 1930s, it had been recognized that mottled enamel of teeth was due to the use of a water supply with a high fluoride concentration (5, 7, 8). Earlier, a practicing dentist had formed a clinical impression that persons with mottled teeth had less caries than usual (2, 21, 22). This led the Public Health Service to conduct surveys of children 12–14 years of age in thirteen cities in four states where the fluoride concentration in the water supply varied considerably (6). The results indicated that dental caries decreased with increasing content of fluoride in the water, thus suggesting that the addition of fluorides to the water supply should decrease the frequency of dental caries (Fig. 1). This could best be demonstrated by a comparative experiment, where fluorides were added to the water supply of one community and the water supply remained untouched in a comparable community where the fluoride concentration was naturally low. The dental caries experience of school children in these communities could then be determined by periodic examinations over a number of years, and compared. Several such studies were initiated, including one comparing Kingston and Newburgh, New York (Table 1) (1). In the town with fluorides in the water supply,

FIGURE 1   Relationship between the Amount of Dental Caries in Permanent Teeth and Fluoride Content in the Public Water Supply

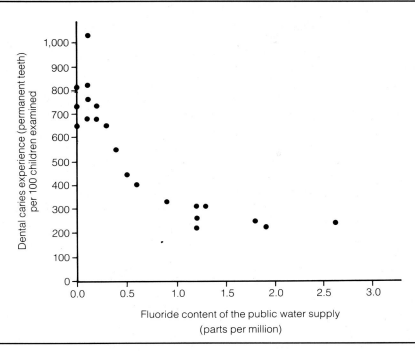

SOURCE: Dean, Arnold, and Elvove (6).

the index of dental caries (DMF) was found to be lower than in the one without fluorides. In this instance, a clinical impression led to both an epidemiologic survey and a comparative experiment, both of which demonstrated the relationship between a population characteristic, fluoride consumption, and a disease, dental caries.

Consistency with Etiological Hypotheses

The investigator attempts to determine whether an etiological hypothesis developed clinically, experimentally, or from other epidemiologic studies is consistent with the epidemiologic characteristics of the disease in a human population group(s). Many studies of the relationship between oral contraceptive use and various forms of cardiovascular disease illustrate this approach. Over a period of years, epidemiologic studies had shown a relationship between oral contraceptive use and both venous thromboembolism and thrombotic stroke (4, 27). Soon after these studies started to appear, the first of a series of case reports associated oral contraceptive use with myocardial infarction (3). This stimulated several investigators to conduct epidemiologic studies of this issue

TABLE 1 DMF* Teeth per 100 Children, Ages 6–16, Based on Clinical and Roentgenographic Examinations—Newburgh† and Kingston, New York, 1954–1955

Age‡	Number of Children with Permanent Teeth		Number of DMF Teeth		DMF Teeth per 100 Children with Permanent Teeth§		Percent Difference K–N
	Newburgh	Kingston	Newburgh	Kingston	Newburgh	Kingston	
6–9 ‖	708	913	672	2,134	98.4	233.7	—57.9
10–12	521	640	1,711	4,471	328.1	698.6	—53.0
13–14	263	441	1,579	5,161	610.1	1,170.3	—47.9
15–16	109	119	1,063	1,962	975.2	1,648.7	—40.9

* DMF includes permanent teeth decayed, missing (lost subsequent to eruption), or filled.
† Sodium fluoride was added to Newburgh's water supply beginning May 2, 1945.
‡ Age at last birthday at time of examination.
§ Adjusted to age distribution of children examined in Kingston who had permanent teeth in the 1954–1955 examination.
‖ Newburgh children of this age group were exposed to fluoridated water from the time of birth.

SOURCE: Ast and Schlesinger (1).

(19, 20). The statistically significant results of one recent study by Mann, Inman, and Thorogood for women aged 40–44 who died from myocardial infarction are presented in Table 2 (20).

Basis for Preventive and Public Health Services

Perhaps the simplest example of this objective is the epidemiologic evaluation of vaccines in controlled trials in human populations, such as the national study that was conducted to establish the effectiveness of the Salk vaccine in the prevention of poliomyelitis (11). In addition to controlled trials and the other types of epidemiologic studies already mentioned, information on the population distribution of a disease in itself provides the basis for developing certain aspects of community disease control programs. Knowledge of specific etiological factors is not essential for this purpose. For example, epidemiologic data on those persons with a higher frequency of a disease or a higher risk of developing one are useful to the physician or public health administrator in indicating those segments of the population where his activities should be focused.

The familial aggregation of diabetes mellitus illustrates this point. In a study of diabetic patients admitted

TABLE 2   Oral Contraceptive Practice among Women Aged 40–44 Years Who Died from Myocardial Infarction (MI), and Controls

Oral Contraceptive Practice	Patients with Myocardial Infarction		Controls	
	No.	Percent	No.	Percent
Never used	78	73.6	86	84.3
Current users (used during month before death or during same calendar period for controls)	18	17.0 ⎫ 28 (26.4%)	7	6.9 ⎫ 16 (15.7%)
Ex-users (used only more than one month before death or during same calendar period for controls)	10	9.4 ⎭	9	8.8 ⎭
Total	106	100.0	102	100.0
Not known	2		8	
Comparison between users and women not currently using oral contraceptives		$\chi^2 = 4.35$; P < 0.05		

SOURCE: Mann et al. (20).

TABLE 3   Frequency of Diabetes among Siblings and Parents of Diabetic Patients Admitted to the Mayo Clinic

| | | Siblings | | |
| | | | Diabetes | |
Diabetes Status of Parents	Number Families	Total	Number	Percent
Both diabetic	22	100	16	16.0
One diabetic	370	1,620	185	11.4
Neither diabetic	1,589	6,664	311	4.7
Total families	1,981	8,384	512	6.1

SOURCE: Steinberg and Wilder (26). Reprinted by permission of The University of Chicago Press. Copyright © 1952, The American Society of Human Genetics, Waverly Press, Inc.

to the Mayo Clinic, Steinberg and Wilder obtained a history of the presence or absence of diabetes among their parents and siblings (Table 3) (26). Whether one hypothesizes a genetic etiological mechanism or environmental factors common to family members as an explanation for the observed familial aggregation, the higher-than-usual frequency of the disease in certain families suggests to the physician that the examination of parents and siblings of known diabetic patients will provide for the early detection of diabetes in a high-risk group of the population.

B. Content of Epidemiologic Activities

Epidemiologists engage in four broad areas of study, each involving different methods: observations, "natural experiments," experimental epidemiology, and theoretical model construction.

Observational Epidemiology

This refers to the observation and analysis of the occurrence of disease in human population groups and to the inferences that can be derived about etiological factors that influence this occurrence. Appropriate methods for selecting specific groups in the population and for analyzing information obtained from them have been developed. Much of what the epidemiologist does falls into this category. The studies of arsenic-exposed employees, dental caries, oral contraceptives, and familial aggregation of diabetes already cited are examples of observational investigations.

"Natural Experiments"

Occasionally, the investigator is fortunate enough to observe the occurrence of a disease under natural conditions so closely approximating a planned, controlled experiment that is categorized as a "natural experiment." Any inferences about etiological factors derived from such situations are considerably stronger than if they had been derived soley from an observational study. The studies by Doll, Hill, and Peto in England of the relationship between tobacco use and lung cancer illustrate this approach (9, 10, 23). In 1951, these investigators ascertained the smoking habits of British male physicians, aged thirty-five and over, and followed them to determine their mortality from different causes, in particular, lung cancer. Initially, this study indicated that physicians who smoked cigarettes had a mortality rate from lung cancer that was about ten times that of nonsmoking physicians (9). Questionnaires were sent to these physicians again to determine their cigarette smoking habits in 1956, 1966 and 1971 (10, 23). The findings of these surveys in terms of the ratio of number of cigarettes smoked by the male physicians to the numbers smoked by all British men in the same age group is shown in Figure 2. There was about a 50 percent decline in

cigarette smoking among these male physicians. During this same period of time, the investigators continued to obtain information on the mortality experience of the physicians, comparing it with the mortality among all British men (10, 23). Figure 3 presents the trend of the physicians' mortality experience from lung cancer and from all other cancer as a percentage of national mortality. There was approximately a 40 percent decline in mortality from lung cancer with essentially no change in all other cancer deaths.

Experimental Epidemiology

In planned experiments, the investigator has control over the population groups he or she is studying (either human or animal) by deciding which groups are exposed to a

FIGURE 2   Trend in Ratio of Numbers of Cigarettes Smoked by Male Physicians to Numbers Smoked by British Men of Same Ages, by Age Groups, 1951–1971

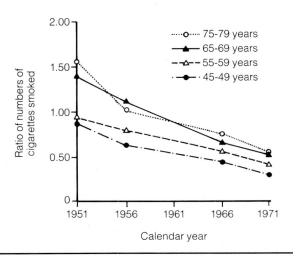

SOURCE: Doll and Peto (10).

FIGURE 3   Trend in Mortality of Male Doctors as Percent of National Mortality of
Same Ages for Lung Cancer and All Other Cancer, 1951–1971

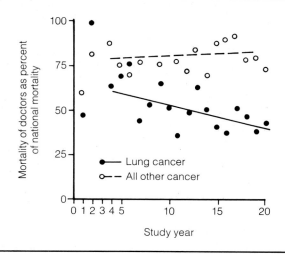

SOURCE: Doll and Peto (10).

possible etiological factor or preventive measure. The Newburgh-Kingston dental caries study, for instance, was a planned, controlled experiment. An important feature of many experiments is that the investigator can randomly allocate subjects to experimental and control groups.

Theoretical Epidemiology

This involves the development of mathematical/statistical models to explain different aspects of the occurrence of a variety of diseases. With some infectious diseases, models have been generated to elucidate the reasons for outbreaks of disease, that is, epidemics. Computer usage has broadened the scope of such model building to include the simulation of epidemics. For example, the Reed-Frost model was developed to explain the relationship of various biological and social factors to the occurrence of epidemics. Other models have been devised to interpret the age distribution of cancer.

Development and Evaluation of Study Methods

As the scope of epidemiology has been broadened to include new and/or different types of diseases, epidemiologists have had to develop new methods of study. In some cases these methods have been adapted from other disciplines, such as sociology, statistics, biology and demography. However, the appropriateness of such new methods for particular epidemiologic situations is not necessarily always apparent. Therefore, these methods need to be evaluated for different epidemiologic circumstances to determine their utility.

One often hears the statement that there are "two epidemiologies," one for infectious diseases and the other for noninfectious diseases. This is a misconception. In general, the methods used and the inferences derived are the same for both disease groups; this will be illustrated throughout our discussions. The reader should note that epidemiology is essentially a *comparative* discipline. It is mainly concerned with studying diseases and related phenomena at different time periods, in different places and among different types of people (i.e., "time, place, and persons") and then comparing them. This approach is used for all categories of disease, infectious and noninfectious alike (17).

C. The Sequence of Epidemiologic Reasoning

Epidemiology was defined at the beginning of this chapter in terms of a reasoning process. The observational study, one of the major tools of epidemiology, affords an excellent view of the reasoning process by which one achieves the objective of elucidating etiological factors of a disease. Basically, the epidemiologist uses a two-stage sequence of reasoning:

1. The determination of a statistical association between a characteristic and a disease.

2. The derivation of biological inferences from such a pattern of statistical associations.

The methods used to determine the statistical associations fall into one of two broadly defined categories:

a) Associations based on group characteristics.

b) Associations based on individual characteristics.

Although there is a certain degree of overlap between these two groups, their distinction has proved to be extremely useful.

In studying *group* characteristics, the epidemiologist concentrates on the comparison of the mortality and/or morbidity experience from a given disease in different population groups in the hope that any observed differences can be related to differences in the local environment, in personal living habits, or even in the genetic composition of these groups. In these studies, information on the characteristics of the individual members of the population groups is not usually obtained. Generally, existing mortality and morbidity statistics are utilized. For example, let us assume that Community A has a higher mortality rate from cancer of the liver than Community B. Furthermore, Community A is engaged primarily in mining, while Community B is engaged in agriculture. The comparison would suggest that mining may be of etiological importance in liver cancer. Usually, the results of such studies provide *clues* to etiological hypotheses and serve as a basis for more detailed investigations. Such an observed relationship, generally termed an "ecological correlation," may suffer from an "ecological fallacy," that is, the two communities differ in many other factors, and one or more of those may be the underlying reason for the differences in their observed mortality or morbidity experience (13, 24, 25).

After an association has been established in either a study of group characteristics, or when a lead has been developed from either clinical studies of patients, experimental work, or other sources, the investigator will attempt to determine whether this association is also present within *individuals*. He will seek answers to such questions as:

1. Do persons with the disease have the characteristic more frequently than those without the disease?

2. Do persons with the characteristic develop the disease more frequently than those who do not have the characteristic?

Such associations are established by cross-sectional, retrospective, and prospective studies.

These two general methods of determining statistical associations—those between groups and those within individuals—must be distinguished, since a relationship derived from a study of individuals is less likely to result from an ecological fallacy and is, therefore, more likely to be biologically significant than one derived from a study of group characteristics. Conversely, an association derived from studies of groups has a greater likelihood of being the result of a third common factor.

References

1. Ast, D.B., and Schlesinger, E.R. 1956. "The conclusion of a ten-year study of water fluoridation." *Amer. J. Pub. Health* 46:265–271.

2. Black, G.V., and McKay, F.S. 1916. "Mottled teeth: An endemic developmental imperfection of the teeth, heretofore unknown in the literature of dentistry." *Dent. Cosmos* 58:129–156.

3. Boyce, J., Fawcett, J.W., and Neal, E.W.P. 1963, "Coronary thrombosis and conovid." *Lancet* 1:111.

4. Collaborative Group for the Study of Stroke in Young Women. 1973. "Oral contraception and increased risk of cerebral ischemia or thrombosis." *N. Engl. J. Med.* 288:871–878.

5. Dean, H.T. 1938. "Endemic fluorosis and its relation to dental caries." *Publ. Health Reps.* 54:1143–1452.

6. _____, Arnold, F.A., Jr., and Elvove, E. 1942. "Domestic water and dental caries. V. Additional studies of the relation of fluoride domestic waters to dental caries experience in 4,425 white children, aged 12 to 14 years, of 13 cities in 4 states." *Pub. Health Reps.* 57:1155–1179.

7. _____, and Elvove, E. 1936. "Some epidemiological aspects of chronic endemic dental fluorosis." *Amer. J. Pub. Health* 26:567–575.

8. _____, Jay, P., Arnold, F.A., Jr., McClure, F.J., and Elvove, E. 1939. "Domestic water and dental caries, including certain epidemiological aspects of oral L. acidophilus." *Pub. Health Reps.* 54:862–888.

9. Doll, R., and Hill, A.B. 1950. "Smoking and carcinoma of the lung: Preliminary report." *Brit. Med. J.* 2: 739–748.

10. _____, and Peto, R. 1976. "Mortality in relation to smoking: 20

years' observations on male British doctors." *Brit. Med. J.* 2:1525–1536.

11. Francis, T., Jr., Korns, R.F., Voight, R.B., Boisen, M., Hemphill, F.M., Napier, J.A., and Tolchinsky, E. 1955. "An evaluation of the 1954 poliomyelitis vaccine trials: Summary report." *Amer. J. Pub. Health* 45:1–63.

12. Frost, W.H., 1941. "Epidemiology." In *Papers of Wade Hampton Frost, M.D.* K.E. Maxcy, ed., New York: The Commonwealth Fund, pp. 493–542.

13. Goodman, L.A. 1953. "Ecological regressions and behavior of individuals." *Amer. Soc. Rev.* 18:663–664.

14. Hirsch, A. 1883. *Handbook of Geographical and Historical Pathology, Vol. I.* London: New Sydenham Society.

15. Levy, B.S., McIntire, W., Damsky, L., Lashbrook, R., Hawk, J., Jacobsen, G.S., and Newton, B. 1975. "The Middleton outbreak: 125 cases of foodborne salmonellosis resulting from cross-contaminated food items served at a picnic and a smorgasbord." *Amer. J. Epid.* 101:502–511.

16. Lilienfeld, D.E. 1978. "Definitions of epidemiology." *Amer. J. Epidemiol.* 107:87–90.

17. Lilienfeld, A.M. 1973. "Epidemiology of infectious and non-infectious disease: Some comparisons." *Amer. J. Epid.* 97:135–147.

18. Mabuchi, K. 1978. Occupational exposure to arsenic and cancer: A study in pesticide workers. Dr. P.H. Dissertation, Baltimore, Md.: The Johns Hopkins University.

19. Mann, J.I., Doll, R., Thorogood, M., Vessey, M.P., and Waters, W.E. 1976. "Risk factors for myocardial infarction in young women." *Brit. J. Prev. and Soc. Med.* 30:94–100.

20. ———, Inman, W.H., and Thorogood, M. 1976. "Oral contraceptive use in older women and fatal myocardial infarction." *Brit. Med. J.* 2:445–447.

21. McKay, F.S. 1925. "Mottled enamel: A fundamental problem in dentistry." *Dent. Cosmos* 67:847–860.

22. ———, and Black, G.V. 1916. "An investigation of mottled teeth." *Dent. Cosmos* 58:477–484.

23. Report of the Royal College of Physicians. 1971, *Smoking and Health Now.* London: Pitman Medical and Scientific Publishing Co.

24. Robinson, W.S. 1950. "Ecological correlations and the behavior of individuals." *Amer. Soc. Rev.* 15:351–357.

25. Selvin, H.C. 1958. "Durkeim's suicide and problems of empirical research." *Amer. J. Soc.* 63:607–619.

26. Steinberg, A.G., and Wilder, R.M. 1952. "A study of the genetics of diabetes mellitus." *Amer. J. Human Genet.* 4:113–135.

27. Vessey, M.P., and Mann, J.I. 1978, "Female sex hormones and thrombosis. Epidemiological aspects." *Brit. Med. Bull.* 34:1577-162.

13   WOMEN AND MEDICALIZATION: A NEW PERSPECTIVE

Catherine Kohler Riessman

Illness expands by means of two hypotheses. The first is that every form of social deviation can be considered an illness. Thus, if criminal behavior can be considered an illness, then criminals are not to be condemned or punished but to be understood (as a doctor understands), treated, cured. The second is that every illness can be considered psychologically. Illness is interpreted as, basically, a psychological event, and people are encouraged to believe that they get sick because they (unconsciously) want to, and that they can cure themselves by the mobilization of will; that they can choose not to die of the disease. These two hypotheses are complementary. As the first seems to relieve guilt, the second reinstates it. Psychological theories of illness are a powerful means of placing the blame on the ill. Patients who are instructed that they have, unwittingly, caused their disease are also made to feel that they have deserved it.

—Susan Sontag, 1979

It is widely acknowledged that illness has become a cultural metaphor for a vast array of human problems. The medical model is used from birth to death in the social construction of reality. Historically, as a larger number of critical events and human problems have come under the "clinical gaze" (Foucault, 1973), our experience of them has been

transformed. For women in particular, this process has had far-reaching consequences.

Feminist health writers have emphasized that women have been the main targets in the expansion of medicine. These scholars have analyzed how previous religious justifications for patriarchy were transformed into scientific ones (Ehrenreich and English, 1979). They have described how women's traditional skills for managing birth and caring for the sick were expropriated by psychomedical experts at the end of the nineteenth century (Ehrenreich and English, 1973). Feminist writers have described the multiple ways in which women's health in the contemporary period is being jeopardized by a male-controlled, technology-dominated medical-care system (Dreifus, 1978; Frankfort, 1972; Ruzek, 1978; Seaman, 1972). These critics have been important voices in changing women's consciousness about their health. They have identified the sexual politics embedded in conceptions of sickness and beliefs about appropriate care. In addition, they have provided the analytic basis for a social movement that has as its primary goal the reclaiming of

SOURCE: *Social Policy* 14: 3-18 published by Social Policy Corporation, New York, New York 10036. Copyright 1983 by Social Policy Corporation.

knowledge about and control over women's bodies.

However, in their analyses, feminists have not always emphasized the ways in which women have simultaneously gained and lost with the medicalization of their life problems. Nor have the scholars always noted the fact that women actively participated in the construction of the new medical definitions, nor discussed the reasons that led to their participation. Women were not simply passive victims of medical ascendancy. To cast them solely in a passive role is to perpetuate the very kinds of assumptions about women that feminists have been trying to challenge.

This paper will extend the feminist critique by emphasizing some neglected dimensions of medicalization and women's lives. I will argue that both physicians and women have contributed to the redefining of women's experience into medical categories. More precisely, I will suggest that physicians seek to medicalize experience because of their specific beliefs and economic interests. These ideological and material motives are related to the development of the profession and the specific market conditions it faces in any given period. Women collaborate in the medicalization process because of their own needs and motives, which in turn grow out of the class-specific nature of their subordination. In addition, other groups bring economic interests to which both physicians and women are responsive. Thus a consensus develops that a particular human problem will be understood in clinical terms. This

consensus is tenuous because it is fraught with contradictions for women, since, as stated before, they stand both to gain and lose from this redefinition.

I will explore this thesis by examining five conditions that pertain to women. An examination of childbirth and reproductive control will ground the analysis historically. Premenstrual syndrome and weight will be considered in order to illustrate present-day manifestations of medicalization. Finally, I will present some beginning thoughts on the ways the analysis might be applied to mental health.

At the outset I want to state that this represents my early thinking about an interactional model that can explain the medicalization of women's lives. It is not a final analysis of the problem, but rather represents work in progress. I invite responses from readers to the ideas I have developed thus far.

The Medicalization Framework

The term medicalization refers to two interrelated processes. First, certain behaviors or conditions are given medical meaning—that is, defined in terms of health and illness. Second, medical practice becomes a vehicle for eliminating or controlling problematic experiences that are defined as deviant, for the purpose of securing adherence to social norms. Medicalization can occur on various levels: conceptually, when a medical vocabulary is used to define a problem; institutionally, when physicians legitimate a program or a problem; or on the level of doctor-patient interaction, when actual diagnosis and treatment of a problem occurs (Conrad and Schneider, 1980a).

Historically, there has been an expansion of the spheres of deviance that have come under medical social control (Freidson, 1970; Zola, 1972; Ehrenreich and Ehrenreich, 1978). Various human conditions such as alcoholism, opiate addiction, and homosexuality—which at one time were categorized as "bad"—have more recently been classified as "sick" (Conrad and Schneider, 1980). Currently, more and more of human experience is coming under medical scrutiny, resulting in what Illich has called the "the medicalization of life." For example, it is now considered appropriate to consult physicians about sexuality, fertility, childhood behavior, and old-age memory problems. It is important to note that the medical profession's jurisdiction over these and other human conditions extends considerably beyond its demonstrated capacity to "cure" them (Freidson, 1970).

There is disagreement about what causes medicalization. Some have assumed that the expansion of medical jurisdiction is the outcome of "medical imperialism"—an effort on the part of the profession to increase its power (Illich, 1976). Others have argued that an increasingly complex technical and bureaucratic society has led to a reluctant reliance on scientific experts (Zola, 1972; 1975). Other scholars have stressed the ways in which the medical establishment, in its thrust to professionalize, organized to create and then control markets (Larson, 1977). In order for the occupational strategy of this

emerging professional class to succeed, it was necessary to control the meaning of things, including interpretations of symptoms and beliefs about health care. Stated differently, professional dominance could be achieved only if people could be convinced of the medical nature of their problems and the appropriateness of medical treatment for them. Thus physicians, as part of an occupational strategy, created conditions under which their advice seemed appropriate (Starr, 1982).

In spite of the disagreement about what motivates medicalization, there is a consensus that it has mixed effects. Greater humanitarianism, tolerance, and other benefits associated with "progress" may be more likely with medical definitions than with criminal ones. Yet medical labeling also has negative social consequences. Far from reducing stigma, the label of illness may create deviance. For example, the career of a psychiatric patient begins with a diagnosis of schizophrenia. As a result, family and friends perceive and interpret the patient's behavior in light of the illness, even after the acute symptoms subside (Mills, 1962). Another consequence of medicalization is that the shroud of medical language mystifies human problems, and thus removes them from public debate (Conrad and Schneider, 1980). A deskilling of the populace takes place when experts manage human experiences. The application of medical definitions makes it more likely that medical remedies will be applied, thereby increasing the risk of iatrogenic disease. In addition, both the meaning and interpretation of an experience is transformed when it is seen as a disease or syndrome (Freidson, 1970). For example, the meaning of murder is significantly altered when the label of "sociopathic personality" is used to account for the behavior. In this way, moral issues tend not to be faced and may not even be raised (Zola, 1975). Finally and most important, awareness of the social causes of disease is diminished with medicalization. As Stark and Flitcraft state:

> Medicine attracts public resources out of proportion to its capacity for health enhancement, because it often categorizes problems fundamentally social in origin as biological or personal deficits, and in so doing smothers the impulse for social change which could offer the only serious resolution.

Medicalization is a particularly critical concept because it emphasizes the fact that medicine is a social enterprise, not merely a scientific one. A biological basis is neither necessary nor sufficient for an experience to be defined in terms of illness. Rather, illness is constructed through human action—that is, illness is not inherent in any behavior or condition, but conferred by others. Thus, medical diagnosis becomes an interpretive process through which illnesses are constructed (Mishler, 1981).

Not only is illness a social construction, but so is science itself. Although medicalization theorists have tended to stop short of a critique of science, there are at least three ways in which scientific ideology plays a role in the medicalization process.

First and most obviously, the production of scientific knowledge is a historically determined social activity, rather than what it is commonly assumed to be—the abstract, value-free pursuit of truth. Certain problems are selected for study, others are not. Certain phenomena are embraced by scientific theory, others are not. Social agenda are embedded in these choices. Thus, for example, sexist beliefs about the biological roots for gender roles formed the basis for endocrinology research in the 1920s (Hall, 1980), as did racist beliefs about the genetic basis for intelligence in the 1970s (Herrnstein, 1971). To the extent that clinical practice is rooted in science, these social agenda are incorporated by physicians in their ways of thinking about the problems of their patients. Second, in the scientific mentality, complex, dynamic, and organic processes are reduced to narrow cause-and-effect relationships. Clinical science locates the problem of disease in the individual body (Crawford, 1980). As a consequence, physicians use a particular framework in both seeing and solving human problems (Bell, forthcoming). Social and emotional aspects of illness that do not fit a physiological model are likely to be ignored, and uncertainty is excluded (Plough, 1981). Third, the assumption is that medical practice is based on scientific knowledge. In other words, science legitimates the power of physicians over definitions of illness and the form of treatment. Yet historical and contemporary evidence reveals that the assertion of therapeutic efficacy has frequently been sufficient to justify medical intervention, even when evidence was shaky (Reverby, 1981; Banta and Thacker, 1979). In sum, scientific "facts" themselves are socially constructed. Clinical practice is founded as much on ideas and beliefs as it is on hard, objective evidence. These ideological components drive the process of medicalization.

The social nature of medicine is clarified further when we note that deviance is implicit in medical definitions. Parsons made this point long ago, but failed to emphasize the negative consequences of this fact. As Hubbard states, "Medical norms don't describe what is, but rather what should be." Thus, physicians create and reinforce social norms when they define behaviors or conditions as pathological, such as hyperactivity in children or childlessness in women. A particular social order is preserved when children behave in certain ways and when women have babies.

Finally, the medicalization framework emphasizes that the power of physicians to define illness and monopolize the provision of treatment is the outcome of a political process. It highlights the ways in which medicine's constructions of reality are related to the structure of power at any given historical period. The political dimension inherent in medicalization is underscored when we note that structurally dependent populations—like children, old people, racial minorities, and women —are subject disproportionately to medical labeling. For example, children's behavior is medicalized under the rubric of juvenile delinquency and hyperkenesis (Conrad and Schneider, 1980). Old people's mental functioning is labeled organic brain syndrome or senility. Racial minorities, when they come in contact with psychiatrists, are more likely than whites to be given more severe diagnoses for comparable symptoms and to receive more coercive forms of medical social control, such as psychiatric hospitalization (Gross et al., 1969). Women, as I will argue, are more likely than men to have problematic experiences defined and treated medically. In each of these examples, it is important to note that the particular group's economic and social powerlessness legitimates its "protection" by medical authorities. Of course, physicians act on behalf of the larger society, thus further reinforcing existing power relations.

Although medicalization theory has emphasized power, it has tended to minimize the significance of class. Historically, as I will suggest, the medicalization of certain problems was rooted in specific class interests. Physicians and women from the dominant class joined together—albeit out of very different motives—to redefine certain human events into medical categories. Women from other class groups at times embraced and at other times resisted these class-based definitions of experience.

In sum, the medicalization framework provides useful analytic categories for examining the medicalization of women's problems as a function of (1) the interests and beliefs of physicians; (2) the class-specific needs of women; and (3) the "fit" between these, resulting in a consensus that redefines a human experience as a medical problem. As stated before, I will use this framework to explore five areas that are especially germane to women's experience: childbirth, reproductive control, premenstrual syndrome, weight, and psychological distress. Clearly, because of space considerations, it is impossible to discuss each example in depth. Instead, I hope to provide a fresh look at each problem and lay out the issues as I perceive them at this point.

Childbirth

Today, pregnancy and birth are considered medical events. This was not always the case. Moreover, there is nothing inherent in either condition that necessitates routine medical scrutiny. In fact, birth is an uncomplicated process in roughly 90 percent of cases (Wertz and Wertz, 1979). In order to understand the medicalization of childbirth, it must be analyzed as the outcome of a complex sociopolitical process in which both physicians and women participated.

In mid-nineteenth-century America, virtually anyone could be a doctor. As a result, there was an oversupply of healers—a series of competing sects with varying levels of training. These included "regular" college-trained physicians, physicians trained by apprenticeship, homeopaths, botanic physicians, male accoucheurs, midwives, and other healers (Drachman, 1979). The "regular" physicians—white, upperclass males—struggled to achieve professional dominance as bound-

aries between professional and lay control shifted. It is important to emphasize that this group sought control over the healing enterprise at a time when they were not more effective than their competitors in curing disease. As Larson (1977) has noted, the diffusion of knowledge about scientific discoveries in microbiology that revolutionized medical care occurred only after medicine successfully gained control over the healing market. Thus, in the absence of superior skill, it was necessary to convert public perceptions. In order to gain "cultural authority" (Starr, 1982) over definitions of health and disease and over the provision of health services, "regular" doctors had to transform general human skills into their exclusive craft. Social historians of medicine have documented the political activities that succeeded in guaranteeing a closed shop for "regular" doctors in late nineteenth- and early twentieth-century America (Reverby and Rosner, 1979; Walsh, 1977).

A central arena for the struggle over professional dominance was childbirth. In colonial America, this event was handled predominantly by female midwives who, assisted by a network of female relatives and friends, provided emotional support and practical assistance to the pregnant woman both during the actual birth and in the weeks that followed. Over a period of more than a century, "social childbirth" was replaced (Wertz and Wertz, 1979). The site of care shifted from the home to the hospital. The personnel who gave care changed from female midwives to male physicians. The techniques changed from noninterventionist approaches to approaches relying on technology and drugs. As a consequence, the meaning of childbirth for women was transformed from a human experience to a medical-technical problem.

A crucial historical juncture in the medicalization of childbirth occurred in the second decade of the twentieth century. In 1910, about 50 percent of all reported births were attended by midwives. The medical profession and the laity generally believed that the midwife—essentially a domestic worker—was an adequate birth attendant. Nature was thought to control the process of birth. As a result, there was little to be done in case of difficulty. The teaching of obstetrics in medical schools was minimal, and direct experience with birth by medical students was rare (Kobrin, 1966).

Beginning around 1910, a contest began between the emerging specialty of obstetrics, the general practitioner, and the midwife. Although seemingly about issues of science and efficacy, this struggle was also about class and race. Obstetricians were from the dominant class, whereas midwives were mostly immigrant and black women. Struggling to differentiate themselves from general practitioners, obstetricians fought to upgrade the image of their field. They searched for a respectable science to legitimate their work. They argued that normal pregnancy and parturition were an exception rather than the rule. Because they believed that birth was a pathological process, obstetricians often used surgical interventions as well as in-

struments, such as high forceps previous to sufficient dilation. These approaches, used routinely and often unnecessarily, frequently had deleterious effects on both mother and child. Over a period of several decades, obstetricians were successful in persuading both their physician colleagues and the general public of the "fallacy of normal pregnancy," and therefore of the need for a "science" of obstetrical practice. Their political activities, coupled with changing demographic trends, resulted in the demise of midwifery (Kobrin, 1966).

It is important to note that the medical management of childbirth did not result in greater safety for women, at least in the short run. The evidence suggests that both maternal and infant mortality rates actually rose during the period between 1915 and 1930 when midwives' attendance at birth abruptly declined (Wertz and Wertz, 1979). In the long run, there has been a steady decline in death rates, which has coincided with modern childbirth practice. However, it is not clear how much of this decline is due to improved environmental circumstances and nutrition and how much to medical care.

In light of these facts, what motivated women to go along with the medicalization of childbirth? Because childbirth is an event that occurs without complications in most cases, it is tempting to emphasize the many losses that accompanied its medicalization. In modern birth, the woman is removed from familiar surroundings, from kin and social support, and subjected to a series of technical procedures—many of which are dehumanizing and others of which carry significant health risks (Shaw, 1974; Rothman, 1982). A woman's experience of birth is alienated because the social relations and instrumentation of the medical setting remove her control over the experience (Young, forthcoming). Because of these negative consequences of modern birth, there is a tendency to romanticize the midwife and pretechnological childbirth and fail to consider the contradictory nature of the process.

Women participated in the medicalization of childbirth for a complex set of reasons. First, nineteenth-century women wanted freedom from the pain, exhaustion, and lingering incapacity of childbirth. Pregnancy every other year was the norm for married women, and this took a significant toll on the reproductive organs. Contraception was not a viable alternative, for reasons I will discuss shortly. For working-class women, the problems of maternity were intensified by harsh working and housing conditions. The letters of early twentieth-century women vividly portray the exhaustion of motherhood (Davies, 1978). Albeit for different reasons, women from different class groups experienced birth as a terrifying ordeal (Dye, 1980).

In the early decades of the twentieth century, relief from the pain of childbirth was promised with "twilight sleep," a combination of morphine and scopolamine, which European physicians had begun to use. Historical analysis of the twilight sleep movement in the United States reveals that it was women who demanded it, frequently pitting themselves against the medical profession who both resented lay interference and feared the dangers of the drug (Leavitt, 1980). These women—middle- and upper-class reformers with a progressive ideology—wanted to alter the oppressive circumstances of women's lives. Thus, the demand for anesthesia in childbirth was part of a larger social movement. Pregnancy was no longer seen as a condition to be endured with fatalism and passivity (Smith-Rosenberg and Rosenberg, 1973). As Miller argues, people believed that civilization had increased the subjective experience of pain in childbirth, and that anesthesia would once again make childbirth natural. The upper class experienced greater pain than working-class women, who were thought to be more like primitive peoples. People believed that upper-class women had been particularly warped by civilization. (The corset also may have distorted their internal organs.) In other words, pain had accompanied the progress of civilization. If freed from painful and exhausting labor, women could (the reformers felt) more fully participate in democratic society (Miller, 1979).

Second, because of declining fertility in upper- and middle-class women at the end of the nineteenth century, the meaning of birth was particularly significant to them. Because childbirth was a less frequent event, concern about fetal death was greater. In addition, women were fearful because it was common to have known someone who had died in childbirth (Dye, 1980). Thus, well-to-do women wanted to be attended by doctors not only because they were of higher social status compared to midwives but also because they possessed the instruments and surgical techniques that might be beneficial in cases of prolonged labor, toxemia, fetal distress, and other abnormal conditions. Of course, physicians used these fears to gain control over the entire market, including routine births.

Thus, the demise of midwifery and the resultant medicalization of childbirth were consequences of forces within the women's community as well as from outside it. Furthermore, it was a class-specific process. Well-to-do women wanted to reduce the control that biology had over their lives. They wanted freedom from pain. Most important, these women wanted control over the birthing process—the right to decide what kind of labor and delivery they would have. The contradiction was that the method these women demanded—going to sleep—put them out of control (Leavitt, 1980).

Obstetricians also wanted control. They believed that birth was a pathological process and that "scientific birth" would result in greater safety for women. In addition, it was in the interest of physicians to capture the childbirth market, because this event provided a gateway to the family, and hence the entire healing market (Wertz and Wertz, 1979). Physicians were particularly anxious to attend the births of well-to-do women, because the social status of these women lent legitimacy and respectability to the shift from midwifery to obstetrics (Drachman, 1979). In

order to control childbirth, physicians needed drugs and technology to appear indispensable (Miller, 1979). Therefore, they went along with twilight sleep, at least for a time. The irony for women was that this approach to the pain of childbirth served to distance women from their bodies and redefine birth as an event requiring hospitalization and physician attendance (Leavitt, 1980).

Currently, medicalization of childbirth is taking new forms. First, there is a trend toward more cesarean births. Although some of these are necessary for maternal health as well as infant survival, evidence suggests that many cesareans are unnecessary (O'Driscoll and Foley, 1983). In view of medicalization, it is important to point out that the potential need for a cesarean places childbirth squarely and exclusively in the hands of the physician. Vaginal delivery, by contrast, can be the province of nonphysician experts, such as nurse midwives.

Second, there is a trend to make the birth experience more humane, for both mother and baby. Hospitals are developing "birthing rooms" and other alternatives to the usual delivery room atmosphere of steel tables, stirrups, and bright lights. After birth, maternal-infant contact is permitted so as to foster "bonding." Pediatricians believe that a critical period exists for the development of an optimal relationship between mother and newborn (Klaus and Kennell, 1976).* Thus, pediatricians are join-

---

*The ideological assumptions and methodological flaws of this research tradition have been well described by Arney (1980).

ing obstetricians in medicalizing the childbirth experience. By defining what should be (and therefore what is) deviant, pediatricians create social norms for parenting.

The contradiction is that the recent changes in the hospital environment of birth have both helped and hurt women. Birthing rooms and early contact between mother and newborn are a welcome change from previous oppressive obstetrical and pediatric practices (which poor women still face because these reforms are more characteristic of elite hospitals than of public ones). Yet the contemporary feminist critique of childbirth practice has been cut short by these reforms. As in many reform movements, larger issues are silenced. Challenges to the medical domination of pregnancy and demands for genuine demedicalization have been co-opted by an exclusive focus on the birth environment. Even when "natural" childbirth occurs in birthing rooms, birth is still defined medically, is still under the control of physicians, and still occurs in hospitals (Rothman, 1981).

Moreover, the social meaning of parenting changes when scientific rationales such as "bonding" and "attachment" are used to justify mothers being near their babies after giving birth (Arney, 1980). In addition, sex roles are reinforced when it is mothers and not fathers who need to be "bonded" to their infants.

Reproductive Freedom

Abortion

Today, abortion is treated as a medical event. Yet in previous historical periods, it was defined in non-medical terms. Physicians brought specific professional and class interests to the abortion issue in the nineteenth century. To realize their interests, they needed to alter public beliefs about the meaning of unwanted pregnancy. Well-to-do women formed an alliance with doctors in this redefinition process because of their own needs.

As Mohr documents, abortion before quickening (the perception of fetal movement) was widely practiced in the mid-nineteenth century and was not seen as morally or legally wrong. Information on potions, purgatives, and quasi-surgical techniques was available in home medical manuals. As auto-abortive instruments came on the market, women became skillful in performing their own abortions, and they shared information with one another. In addition, midwives, herbal healers, and other "irregular" doctors established lucrative practices in the treatment of "obstructed menses." It is estimated that by 1878 one in five pregnancies was intentionally aborted. The growing frequency of abortion was particularly evident in the middle and upper classes (Mohr, 1978).

"Regular" physicians were central figures in redefining abortion as a social problem. The practice of abortion was leading to a declining birth rate, especially among the middle and upper classes who feared that this could lead to "race suicide" (Smith-Rosenberg and Rosenberg, 1973). One physician warned that abortion was being used "to avoid the labor of caring for and rearing children" (Silver as quoted in Mohr, 1978). In other words, women were shirking the responsibilities of their seemingly biologically determined role.

Mohr (1978) argues that physicians led the moral crusade against abortion not so much out of these antifeminist feelings, but primarily in order to restrict the practice of medicine. They wanted to get rid of competitors ("irregulars" and "doctresses") and gain a monopoly over the practice of medicine. By altering public opinion and persuading legislators, they succeeded in establishing their code of ethics (which specifically excluded abortion) as the basis for professional practice. These actions limited the scope of medicine's competitors, especially women doctors whose practices were devoted to the care of female complaints. By the late 1870s, antiabortion statutes were on the books. Professional dominance was further strengthened in the 1880s when physicians became more organized. They used the scientific paradigm to force more and more folk practitioners from the field.

It is interesting to note the social relations at work in the nineteenth-century abortion struggle. First, the "regulars"—upper- and middle-class men—had natural allies in the state legislators, who were also men from prosperous families. Second, patriarchal class interests in general and nativism in particular provided the racist and sexist ideology for the anti-abortion movement. Physicians, legislators, and other well-to-do men wanted their women to reproduce the species, or, more specifically, the dominant class of the species. These groups, fearing the increasing num-

bers of the foreign-born, were concerned that the upper classes would be out-bred. Finally, the conflict between the "regular" doctors and their competitors was not only about issues of science and professional control but also about the issues of class and patriarchy. The "irregular" doctors were, in general, not from families of the dominant class. In addition, these practitioners were more likely to be female. Thus social characteristics provided the rationale for exclusion, further reinforcing patriarchal class relations.

Women's participation in the anti-abortion crusade of the 1870s also was class-specific. Feminists of the period—well-to-do women—came out against abortion, arguing instead for voluntary motherhood. These early feminists recommended periodic or permanent abstinence as methods of birth control because they did not approve of contraceptive devices (Gordon, 1976).

It is obvious that women lost significant freedoms when abortion was defined as a medical procedure and ruled illegal. Yet, from the perspective of the sexual politics of late nineteenth-century America, it is significant that women favored abstinence over abortion. Abstinence was a more radical response to the power relations in the patriarchal family than a pro-abortion stance would have been.

Well-to-do women of the late nineteenth century had a level of hostility toward sex, both because it brought unwanted and dangerous pregnancy and because it was a legally prescribed wifely duty. Even more important, Gordon argues that these women resented the particular kind of sexual encounter that was characteristic of American Victorian society: intercourse dominated by the husband's needs and neglecting what might bring pleasure to a woman. Men's style of lovemaking repelled women. They felt that men were oversexed and violent. Furthermore, because men visited prostitutes, marital sex for women not infrequently resulted in venereal disease. Under these conditions, a woman's right to refuse was central to her independence and personal integrity.

In sum, the termination of an unwanted pregnancy underwent a series of changing definitions: it went from a human problem to a topic of medical concern to a crime. With the 1973 Supreme Court decision, it was remedicalized, but this time with the support of the medical profession. Physicians no longer needed this issue to advance their sovereignty.

Contraception

In the twentieth century, well-to-do women joined physicians again in the medicalization of reproduction with the issue of contraception. These women struggled to define a "new sense of womanhood" that did not require sexual passivity, maternity, domesticity, and the absence of ambition. In order to achieve these goals, feminists overcame their scruples against artificial contraception. Importantly, women ultimately won the battle of reproductive freedom. Technology to limit family size was developed in response to the social demand for it (Gordon, 1976).

But as women gained from this newly won independence, they also lost. Birth control technology is not without problems, both in its female centricity and its risk. Furthermore, as Gordon argues, the professionalization and medicalization of birth control stripped it of its political content. As a result of its definition as a health issue, contraception became somewhat separate from the larger social movement that gave rise to the demand for birth control in the first place. Finally, the battle over medicalization was lost again when birth control methods went in the direction of high technology. The pill, the IUD, and injectable contraceptives are forever in the hands of medicine, because access to these drugs and devices is legally controlled. In contrast, the low-technology barrier methods—the condom, cervical cap, or diaphragm—require little medical intervention or control.

These historical examples underscore the fact that women's experience was a site for the initial medicalization effort. Medicine "staked claims" for childbirth, abortion, and birth control and secured them as "medical turf" by altering public beliefs and persuading the state of the legitimacy of their claim. (For further elaboration of the metaphor of prospecting applied to medicine, see Conrad and Schneider, 1980.) Physicians used science as the rationale for professional dominance. As I have suggested, women's participation in the redefinition of each experience was the result of complex historical and class-specific motives, and they not only gained but lost with the medicalization of each area.

Medicalization of Women's Lives

Because women's health was a site for professional monopolization in the past, it is not surprising that medicine has continued to focus on women in the effort toward medicalization. A plethora of female conditions has come to be either reconceptualized as illnesses or, if they escape medical labeling, understood in ways that connote deviation from some ideal biological standard. Because they are seen as biological events, medical solutions are applied. For example, "sexual dysfunctions" are defined in terms of health and illness, and an industry of sex clinics and counselors offers treatment. Pregnancy care has been broadened to include fetal as well as maternal health, which has resulted in diagnostic procedures aimed at the fetus as well as experimental treatments, such as fetal surgery (Hubbard, 1982). Fertility is seen as a medical issue, and the production of the "custom-made child" (Holmes et al., 1981) has become the focus of a reproductive engineering industry. Menopause is understood and treated medically, with far-reaching consequences for women's health and self-esteem. Aging has spawned a new specialty—gerontology—for which women are the primary market. Teen-age pregnancy and wife battering are being conceptualized increasingly in psychiatric terms. The medicalization of women's lives can be examined by way of two other examples—premenstrual syndrome and weight.

Premenstrual Syndrome

Premenstrual syndrome (PMS) has found a place among the medical maladies of our culture. Although PMS lacks a firm definition and a base of rigorous scientific research (Parlee, 1973; Friedman et al., 1980), specific premenstrual signs and symptoms have come under medical scrutiny. These include physical manifestations such as edema (resulting in weight gain and bloatedness), breast swelling and tenderness, backache, and acne. Mood changes also may occur, including increased tension and irritability, depression and lethargy. As evidence of medicalization, both medical and lay health journals are dealing with the topic with greater frequency, and a self-help guide written by a physician has appeared (Reid and Yen, 1981; Gonzales, 1981; Burd, 1982; Harrison, 1982). Significantly, the diagnosis of PMS was used successfully by the defense in several recent legal cases (Newsweek, 1982).

What are the interests and beliefs that physicians currently bring to this new disease construction? Clearly, it is more risky to analyze motives for the medicalization of contemporary problems than it is for those of the past (such as childbirth and abortion), where the historical record can provide supporting evidence. Nevertheless, market conditions exist that suggest some reasons as to why the medical profession might be prospecting for new turf at this time. First, there is a declining birth rate. With fewer babies to be delivered, gynecologists must develop other areas in order to guarantee a successful practice. Second, there are more gynecologists per capita than ever before. As a result of federal programs in the 1960s, medical schools expanded and more physicians graduated. Consequently, the supply of obstetrician/gynecologists in the United States increased from 15,984 in 1966 to 25,215 in 1979 (Theodore and Sutler, 1966; Wunderman, 1980)—an increase of 64 percent. Finally, there are more women in the population in their thirties, as a result of the postwar baby boom. Given these conditions—lower demand, increased supply, and a pool of appropriately aged women—it is not unreasonable to hypothesize that gynecologists would actively seek out new "disease" entities to which they could apply their skills. Premenstrual syndrome, as well as endometriosis, may represent new disease constructions that are a response to these conditions.

In addition, physicians hold beliefs about women that are likely to influence the disease construction of PMS, especially when they are joined with economic interests. In medical education, physicians are trained to think about women in ways that are anything but neutral and value-free (Howell, 1974). Medical textbooks describe women's sexuality in terms that vary from most women's experience and that reinforce male opinions of sexual pleasure (Scully and Bart, 1981). Physicians are taught psychiatric theories about the development of gender identity that reinforce existing power relations between the sexes. No doubt these beliefs also influence

physicians' understanding of menstruation, although the particular ways that sexist ideology is embedded in current scientific thought about the premenstrual period needs further study.

Other communities also influence the clinical scrutiny of menstruation. The drug industry is actively looking for new markets. Corporations shape physicians' perceptions through drug advertising, personal contacts, and free samples of their products. Research has shown that physicians' behavior is remarkably sensitive to the "educational" efforts of the pharmaceutical houses (Christensen and Bush, 1981). In addition to the drug industry, other parties that can affect physicians' perceptions include the legal profession (which has found the diagnosis of PMS useful in adjudicating clients) and the insurance industry (which will have to contend with this new diagnostic category in their reimbursement policies). As Bell has demonstrated in her case study of DES, these communities are functionally interdependent. They interact in complex ways with one another and with physicians in the creation of new technologies and disease entities.

From the perspective of women, the medicalization of the premenstrual experience is filled with contradictions. On the positive side, physicians' recognition of women's experience with menstruation is important, for it legitimates an important aspect of women's lives. Women have often observed that their moods varied over the course of their menstrual cycle and shared their observations with one another, but until recently they were discounted by the medical establishment. Doctors responded either by dismissing women's premenstrual complaints or by ascribing them to unresolved problems with their femininity. The clinical construction of PMS acknowledges the cyclic nature of women's lives and opens up the possibility that attention will be paid to other phases of the menstrual cycle. For example, some suggest that a "Menstrual Joy Questionnaire" be created, using the model of the "Menstrual Distress Questionnaire" (Moos, 1963), in order to document the pleasurable feelings, increased energy, and creativity that are experienced during the cycle (Delaney at al., 1976).

Women in certain economic groups are currently seeking out physicians regarding problems with menstruation just as an earlier, similar class group sought physicians for care during pregnancy. These women are actively participating in the construction of the new medical syndrome of PMS just as they were in creating the "new childbirth." Of course, feminists are ambivalent about the new diagnostic category of PMS, for reasons I will discuss shortly. In light of this, it is interesting to note that the contemporary feminist movement is responsible for a new consciousness that, in some ways, encourages women to be assertive regarding discomfort in menstruation, just as a previous social movement encouraged women to seek relief from pain in childbirth. This is not to deny that physicians do not also have an interest in creating a

market and exploiting women for economic gain. But for the small group of women who have premenstrual problems that severely interfere with functioning, relief is possible with medical treatment (Dalton, 1977). It is also possible that scientific research can supply knowledge that might be used in nutritional, exercise, and other treatment approaches.*

On the negative side, the medicalization of menstruation has disturbing implications for women's lives. Most obviously, it reinforces the idea that women are controlled by biology in general and their reproductive systems in particular. This has been used to legitimate the exclusion of women from positions of power because of supposed emotional instability and irrationality due to "raging hormonal imbalances" (Romey, 1973). It has also been used to suggest that women are violent as a result of their biology, because of the apparent correlation between PMS and crimes committed by women. Thus, medical scrutiny of the premenstrual period serves to emphasize cyclic phenomena in women when, in fact, hormonal blood levels are episodic in both men and women (Hoffman, 1982). In addition, medical scrutiny also reinforces scientific assumptions about the existence of universal norms, or a "natural" menstrual history. This has been refuted by anthropological evidence, which demonstrates considerable cross-cultural variation in

---

*See Michelle Harrison (1982) for a model of such an approach.

all aspects of menstrual cycling (Hubbard, 1981). Further, labeling hormonal changes as a syndrome implies a pathological condition—something to be controlled—rather than suggesting that mood shifts and bodily changes are a normal part of everyone's life. Thus, there is a danger that medical treatments will be applied routinely to women, as estrogen replacement therapy has been for menopause. In other words, insufficiently tested, ineffective, or dangerous pharmaceutical remedies and surgical interventions may be used to treat premenstrual problems. Finally, medical labeling may create cultural beliefs and attitudes about the premenstrual period. It may create suffering in women who were previously asymptomatic. It may encourage them to perceive fluctuating bodily and emotional states differently, simply because a medical explanation for them exists. Support for this hypothesis was found in an experimental study conducted prior to the development of the diagnostic category of PMS. Women who were told they were premenstrual reported more severe physical symptoms than women who believed they were simply between periods (Ruble, 1977).

Most important, the medicalization of PMS deflects attention from social etiology. Rather than looking at the circumstances of women's lives that may make them irritable, depressed, or angry, their strong feelings can be dismissed ("You'll feel better when you get your period") The contradiction lies in the fact that the label of PMS allows women to be angry and say what's on their minds at a certain time each month, while at the same time it invalidates the content of their protest.

The Medical Beauty Business: Getting Thin

Like menstruation, women's physical appearance has come under the lens of the medical establishment. Cosmetic surgeons treat everything from facial wrinkles to breast size. The medical beauty business has concentrated with special intensity on the bodily changes associated with women's aging. Another subject of medical scrutiny is weight. "Obesity" is now a medical condition.

Although weight is not exclusively a women's issue, it is an excellent example of the medicalization of women's experience for a number of reasons. It highlights the relationship between the social norms for femininity and medical social control. By medicalizing weight, medical science participates in programming aesthetics for women's bodies. This has far-reaching consequences for self-esteem, as women are evaluated on the basis of personal appearance more than men (Millman, 1980). Weight is also a good example of medicalization because it illustrates in a most graphic form how power relations are maintained through medical social control, how women internalize their oppression by desiring to be thin and turning to doctors for help.

As background, let me review briefly some basic information about weight—its causes, consequences for health, and the efficacy of weight reduction programs. First, adult weight is the outcome of the interplay of a complex combination of factors, including heredity, body type, childhood eating patterns, and metabolism. Although amount of food intake is clearly relevant, its causal significance appears to lie in its interaction with these other factors (Mann, 1974). Also, it appears that obesity is more prevalent in lower socioeconomic groups. This is true for both children and adults (Goldblatt et al, 1972).

Second, it is far from clear that obesity has a strong, consistently negative effect on health status. Although associated with a variety of chronic conditions, its causal significance has not been established (Mann, 1974). With respect to specific health conditions, weight is positively related to cerebrovascular disease (Heyden et al., 1971). However, its contribution to coronary heart disease is, according to Mann, "small or nonexistent." The relationship between obesity and high blood pressure is also tenuous (Miall et al., 1968). Whatever relationships do exist between weight and the chronic disease of industrial life may, in fact, be due to an antecedent variable: physical inactivity (Mann, 1974).

Third, although it is widely believed that weight reduction is a useful treatment for a variety of chronic diseases, medical evidence does not entirely support this conclusion. Although probably beneficial for control of diabetes, Mann concludes after reviewing extensive research that weight reduction is an "improbable adjunct to therapy" for diseases such as hypertension and coronary heart disease.

Finally, therapies for weight control are far from efficacious and, in some cases, are dangerous. Dietary treatment rarely works, and recidivism rates are high (Mann, 1974). Drug treatments have also failed to demonstrate efficacy and have a definite potential for dependence (FDA, 1972). Surgical treatments, such as ileal bypass surgery, have been called hazardous by some medical evaluators (Mann, 1974). More successful are self-help groups and behavior modification approaches to weight loss (Stunkard, 1970). In general, however, the pattern for most individuals is a cycle of weight loss followed by weight gain, which is repeated over and over. The cyclical process further undermines the metabolic system's ability to regulate body weight (Beller, 1977).

In light of these facts, it is not surprising that physicians now consider obesity "a relatively incurable disorder" (Mann, 1974). Hence the medicalization of weight is a clear example of the extension of medicine into an area where it lacks the demonstrated capacity to cure (Freidson, 1970).

Weight was not always considered a medical problem, or even a liability. Renoir and other nineteenth-century artists idealized women with round, soft, voluptuous bodies. Physicians of the nineteenth century did not define excess weight as something to be treated. Even in the twentieth century, popular cultural heroines such as Mae West and Marilyn Monroe had ample bodies.

My research suggests that it was not until the late 1960s and the 1970s that medicine began to deal with the topic of weight with such intensity.

It was in the interest of physicians to define weight as a medical problem for a number of reasons. Its apparent association with chronic disease legitimated its clinical scrutiny. More important, a market for weight control opened up as the sedentary life and associated weight gain came to characterize postindustrial society. In addition, particular medical specialties had specific reasons for going into the weight business. Surgeons, for example, facing conditions of oversupply, needed to create markets for their services. The development of surgical approaches to obesity was a logical outcome. Other specialties also needed to generate demand, as the care of infectious diseases took less and less of physicians' time. Here was a potential pool of patients who were concerned about weight and who were so desperate that they were willing to try anything to bring it under control.

Nevertheless, physicians did not act in a vacuum. The medicalization of weight graphically illustrates how medical definitions, cultural ideology, and corporate interests work hand in hand.

Although the struggle to dominate the body may be endemic to patriarchal culture, Chernin argues that the preoccupation with women's slenderness has been particularly intense in the last 20 years. This "tyranny of slenderness" coincided with the feminist movement. A contra-dictory cultural process was taking place: on the one hand was the emergence of a women's movement that emphasized release of power, freeing of potential, and shaking off restraints; and on the other hand was the emergence of the self-help diet groups that emphasized keeping watch over appetites, controlling impulses, and restraining hunger. Women confronted two opposing mandates, one calling for self-control and the other for release (Crawford, forthcoming). Thus, an ideology of slenderness emerged during a historical period when women were growing in their sense of themselves as autonomous, independent beings. Chernin argues that this reflects a fear of women's power. The covert advice to women is not to grow too large or too powerful for the culture. Medical control of weight became a tool for implementing this ideology.

In my research on the clinical construction of obesity, I found a relationship between the extent of the medical literature on the topic and the growth of the women's movement. Reviewing the number of citations in *Index Medicus* by year, I found obesity to be an insignificant topic in 1960, warranting only slightly more than a page of entries. By 1981, more than seven pages were devoted to citations on the topic. Interestingly, articles referring to surgical remedies for obesity were insignificant in 1970 (only 8), rose to a high in 1976 (of 73), and declined thereafter.

In their research on cultural "ideals" of feminine beauty, Garner and his colleagues also found a shift in norms that coincided with the growth of the women's movement. They studied the weights of *Playboy* magazine centerfolds and contestants and winners of the Miss America Pageant from 1959 through 1978. They found that in both contexts the women selected as exemplars of feminine beauty were significantly thinner than the norm for comparable women in the population. More important, they found that when age and height were controlled, weight declined over the 20-year period they studied. Ideal body shape became progressively thinner in spite of the fact that the average weight of women in the general population grew slightly during the same period (Garner et al., 1980).

In addition to cultural ideals and medical definitions, once again other communities shape beliefs about weight. Several industries profit from the cultural preoccupation with women's size. Pharmaceutical companies market anorectic drugs, including amphetamines and other appetite suppressants. The food industry markets low-calorie foods and artificial sweeteners; in advertising, it depicts attractiveness in terms of weight. The fashion industry simultaneously creates and reflects images of the cultural ideal —the thin woman. The beauty business provides places to realize this ideal—the health spa and figure salon.

In this context, it is not surprising that some women have gone along with the medicalization of weight. They believe it is in their interest to be thin. Yet at the same time that they have internalized this dominant value, women have also resisted it—they gain weight. This contradiction further drives the process of medicalization. Thus, economically advantaged women become the major market for a series of weight control industries. The data uniformly show that, compared to men, women are more likely to have ileal bypass surgery, to receive prescriptions for weight-related drugs, to undertake "scientifically based" diets, and to read the physician-authored diet books on the market. Women are also the primary participants in self-help groups such as Weight Watchers, TOPS (Take Off Pounds Sensibly), and Overeaters Anonymous (Millman, 1980).*

These women want to be thin. Some think of themselves primarily in terms of their size. They develop an identity as a "fat person"; everything else becomes secondary. They feel intense psychological pain when their weight is high (Millman, 1980). They are responsive to cultural messages that suggest that they can be in control of how they look in part because of the powerlessness they

---

*Fox has stated that these approaches that rely on mutual aid, as opposed to professional intervention, are examples of the "demedicalization" of a human problem in contemporary society. However, as Conrad and Schneider note, deprofessionalization is not the same thing as demedicalization. More specifically, many of the self-help groups oriented toward weight loss share medicine's disease orientation to the problem of weight. Because many of these peer approaches to behavior change do not challenge medicine's assumptions, they do not "demedicalize" human problems, but rather medicalize under lay auspices.

feel in other areas of their lives. Yet, paradoxically, the feeling of being out of control ultimately takes over, as women discover they cannot really be successful in controlling weight through diet. Women may generalize this sense of lack of control to the rest of their lives. In despair, they collaborate willingly with surgeons and drug-oriented physicians who offer external solutions, further reinforcing their feelings of powerlessness.

Ironically, medical science has given women some tools for understanding the psychological determinants of eating. Psychiatric thought has provided insight into the meaning that food has in their lives and the conflicts that lead them to overeat. However, with the exception of therapies and diet groups with a feminist perspective, psychological approaches rarely question the cultural ideal of slenderness. Nor do they help women see that the internalization of this value reflects alienation from the natural self and the feminine nature of their bodies (Chernin, 1981).

It is clear that the medicalization of physical appearance has had many negative effects on women. Medical science, in collaboration with a series of industries, participates in creating social norms for physical appearance in the guise of supposedly neutral, objective, scientific standards for "ideal" body weight. These standards are based on white, middle-class norms and neglect the diversity of women's bodies. Further, these standards do not take into account the fact that certain cultural groups value women with substantial bodies (Millman, 1980). Further damage results when a woman feels personally to blame when her body fails to measure up to the ideal. In sum, medical scrutiny of weight can create a "spoiled identity" (Goffman, 1964; Courtot, 1982) for fat women. In addition, it may prompt a lifelong pattern—a seesaw of weight gain and weight loss—that has deleterious health consequences.

In light of the class and racial bias in medical norms for weight, it is significant that resistance has tended to come from poor and working-class women, as well as from women of color. While listening respectfully to physicians' admonitions about their weight, some of these women persist in their own beliefs about appropriate body size for themselves. As a result, they are likely to be labeled noncompliant by their doctors.

Most important, by treating weight as a medical problem, medicine diverts attention away from the social causes of poor nutrition and an obsession with thinness. Obesity is correlated with poverty. In poor communities, food preparation has been commercialized in particular ways that undermine health. Poor neighborhoods are focal markets for fast-food chains, because there is a need for high caloric, relatively inexpensive convenience meals. Nutritional status has been compromised further by junk food; especially problematic for weight is the high sugar and salt content. Thus, the food industry has played a major role in generating poor eating habits and, as a result, disease (McKinlay, 1981). In this context, the medicalization of weight is a classic case of blaming the victim.

Furthermore, by individualizing the problem of weight, crucial questions are never asked. Why is it that women are more likely than men to be defined as overweight? Why is anorexia almost exclusively a women's health issue? What is the connection between nutritional malaise and the problems of women in this culture? Does the source of the problem lie in women's roles? Or is the problem with the norms that define appropriate appearance for men compared with women? Why should women be thin anyway? So they can take up less space?*

Medicalization and Psychiatry

In addition to weight, women's psychological problems are also a central focus for the drug and medical industries. Women receive more prescriptions for valium and other psychotropic drugs than do men (Cooperstock and Parnell, 1982; Koumjian, 1981). They receive more outpatient psychotherapy (NIMH, 1981). These facts need to be analyzed in terms of the diverse interests of the various medical industries, as well as the diverse needs of women from different class groups that bring them into contact with psychiatry. In the context of this article, I can only introduce some of the issues related to this topic.

Middle-class women have been influenced in major ways by psychiat-

ric thought. Psychiatrists as well as other mental-health professionals view emotional pain as a symptom of an illness. Middle-class women have tended to internalize these sentiments, whereas working-class women have been more likely to resist them.

In the late fifties and early sixties, many middle-class women went into psychotherapy with a series of concerns about their lives—"the problem with no name," in the words of Betty Friedan. But in therapy, these women came to understand their feelings as depression. They learned to examine their early childhood for the origins of their problems. They learned to examine the ways in which they continued self-defeating behaviors in their present-day lives. Paradoxically, many highly educated women found support in psychoanalytic therapy for their private despair at being expected to find fulfillment in marriage and suburban living. The process of introspection helped individual women to voice their concerns and to act to improve their lives. At the same time, these women were subjected to an ideology of femininity that made it difficult for them to realize their ambitions outside of traditional marriage. They needed the emerging contemporary women's movement to redefine their experience in structural terms.

But there is a contradiction in this, in that presenting complaints to psychotherapists is more progressive than keeping problems behind closed doors; but then issues are depoliticized (Stark, 1982). There is an ever-present danger that feminist

---

*For thoughtful discussions of these questions, see Chernin, 1981; Crawford, (forthcoming); and Schwartz et al., 1980.

content will be diminished with medicalization. This can occur not only with psychological problems but with physical ones as well.

For example, Stark and Flitcraft found that when battered women came in contact with hospitals, their problems were exacerbated by physicians and nurses. A purely medical definition of the situation prevailed, replacing any alternative understanding of the problem. Social workers further colluded by seeing the problem as part of a larger issue of the "multiproblem family." Note also how feminist content is further undermined with the term "family violence."

The Fit between Women's Interests and Physicians' Interests

These examples illustrate a general point about medical social control: there are times when the interests of women from the middle and upper classes are served by the therapeutic professions, whose political and economic interests are in turn served by transforming these women's complaints into illnesses. In other words, both historically and currently, there has tended to be a "fit" between medicine's interest in expanding its jurisdiction and the need of women to have their experience acknowledged. I have emphasized that this "fit" has been tension-filled and fraught with contradictions for women, who have both gained and lost with each intrusion medicine has made into their lives.

While necessary, the particular interests of women and physicians do not alone explain the expansion of

the clinical domain. Other communities also influence what occurs in the doctor's office. In the context of a capitalist economy and a technologically dominated medical-care system, large profits accompany each redefinition of human experience into medical terms, since more drugs, tests, procedures, equipment, and insurance coverage are needed. As mentioned before, specific medical industries have played a direct role in influencing both physicians' and women's perceptions of reproductive control, premenstrual syndrome, and weight. Yet it is important to emphasize that corporations, in their effort to maximize profits, work *through* both physicians and women.

Implicit in my analysis is the assumption that women's experience has been medicalized more than men's.* Yet it could be argued instead that medicine has encroached into men's lives in a different but equal fashion. For example, medicine has focused on childhood hyperactivity and the adult addictions —problems more common in males

---

*Conrad and Schneider correctly identify children as another "population at risk" for medicalization. As they describe it, medical jurisdiction has expanded to cover more and more issues of childhood (normal child development, learning disabilities, child abuse, et cetera). It would be interesting to relate this expansion to the internal politics and economic issues faced by pediatrics and its subspecialties. The field needed new turf as childhood infectious diseases could be prevented or controlled. Further, the 1960s and 1970s saw a declining birth rate and an increase in the supply of pediatricians. A logical strategy for the field was to focus on "behavioral pediatrics."

than females (Conrad and Schneider, 1980). Occupational medicine has tended to focus on male jobs. In particular, "stress management" programs are targeting male executives. However, while not to diminish these examples, I believe that women's lives have undergone a more total transformation as a result of medical scrutiny. Medicalization has resulted in the construction of medical meanings of *normal* functions in women—experiences the typical woman goes through, such as menstruation, reproduction, childbirth, and menopause. By contrast, routine experiences that are uniquely male remain largely unstudied by medical science and, consequently, are rarely treated by physicians as potentially pathological. For example, male hormonal cycles and the male climacteric remain largely unresearched. Less is known about the male reproductive system than about that of the female. Male contraceptive technology lags far behind what is available for women. Baldness in men has not yet been defined as a medical condition needing treatment, even though an industry exists to remedy the problem of hair loss. Men's psychological lives have not been subjected to psychiatric scrutiny nearly to the degree that women's emotions have been studied. As a result, male violence, need for power, and overrationality are not defined as pathological conditions. Perhaps only impotence has been subject to the same degree of medical scrutiny as women's problems.

Why has women's experience been such a central focus for medicalization? In addition to the complex motives that women bring to each particular health issue, physicians focus on women as a primary market for expansion for a number of reasons. First, there is a good match between women's biology and medicine's biomedical orientation. External markers of biological processes exist in women (menstruation, birth, lactation, and so forth), whereas they are more hidden in men. Given modern medicine's biomedical orientation, these external signs make women easy targets of medical encroachment. A different medical paradigm (one that viewed health as the consequence of harmony between the person and the environment, for example) might have had less basis for focusing on women.

Second, women's social roles make them readily available to medical scrutiny. Women are more likely to come in contact with medical providers because they care for children and are the "kin keepers" of the family (Rossi, 1980). In concrete terms, women are more likely to accompany sick children and aged relatives to the doctor.

Third, women have greater exposure to medical labeling because of their pattern of dealing with their own symptoms, as well as medicine's response to that pattern. Women make more visits to physicians than men, although it is not clear whether this is due to the medicalization of their biological functions, "real" illness, behavior when ill, or cultural expectations (Nathanson, 1977). When they visit the doctor for any serious illness, they are more likely than men to be checked for reproductive implications of the illness. They are more subject to regular checks of their reproductive systems, in the form of yearly PAP smears or gynecological exams. Importantly, whenever they visit the doctor there is evidence that they receive more total and extensive services—in the form of lab tests, procedures, drug prescriptions, and return appointments—than do men with the same complaints and sociodemographic risk factors (Verbrugge and Steiner, 1981). Thus, a cycle of greater medical scrutiny of women's experience is begun with each visit to the doctor.

Finally, women's structural subordination to men has made them particularly vulnerable to the expansion of the clinical domain. In general, male physicians treat female patients. Social relations in the doctor's office replicate patriarchal relations in the larger culture, and this all proceeds under the guise of science. (Patriarchal control is most evident when physicians socialize young women regarding appropriate sexual behavior, perhaps withholding contraceptive advice, or lecturing them about the dangers of promiscuity.) For all these reasons, it is not surprising that women are more subject to medical definitions of their experience than men are. In these ways, dominant social interests and patriarchal institutions are reinforced.

As a result, women are especially appropriate markets for the expansion of medicine. They are suitable biologically, socially, and psychologically. The message that women are expected to be dependent on male physicians to manage their lives is reinforced by the pharmaceutical industry in drug advertisements and by the media in general. Yet it is far too simple to portray the encroachment of medicine as a conspiracy—by male doctors and the "medical industrial complex"—to subordinate women further. Although some have argued that medicine is the scientific equivalent of earlier customs like marriage laws and kinship rituals that controlled women by controlling their sexuality, such an analysis is incomplete. As I have stressed, medicalization is more than what doctors do, although it may be through doctors that the interests of other groups are often realized. Nor does a conspiracy theory explain why, for the most part, women from certain class groups have been willing collaborators in the medicalization process. Rather than dismissing these women as "duped," I have suggested some of the complex motives that have caused certain classes of women to participate with physicians in the redefinition of particular experiences.

In addition, a conspiracy theory does not explain why medicalization has been more virulent in some historical periods and in some medical specialties than in others. For example, gynecologists initially trivialized menopausal discomfort, only to reclaim it later for treatment. At the same time that gynecologists were unwilling to acknowledge the legitimacy of women's complaints, the developing specialty of psychiatry moved in with the psychogenic account. I have argued that these shifts and interprofessional rivalries over turf are explained by internal issues facing each specialty at particular points in history. Thus, an analysis of the market conditions faced by physicians in general, and certain specialties in particular, is necessary to explain the varying response of medicine to women's problems.

Further research is needed to capture more fully the historical aspect of these shifts in medical perception. Such an analysis needs to focus in depth on specific events in women's experience and trace their medicalization in historical and class context: the issues brought in turn by groups of women, by the particular medical specialties, by the pharmaceutical industry, and by the "fit" between these that resulted in a redefinition. A conspiracy theory fails to capture the nuances of this complex process.

Conclusion

The medicalization of human problems is a contradictory reality for women. It is part of the problem and of the solution. It has grown out of and in turn has created a series of paradoxes. As women have tried to free themselves from the control that biological processes have had over their lives, they simultaneously have strengthened the control of a biomedical view of their experience. As women visit doctors and get symptom relief, the social causes of their problems are ignored. As doctors acknowledge women's experience and treat their problems medically, problems are stripped of their political content and popular move-

ments are taken over. Because of these contradictions, women in different class positions have sought and resisted medical control.

I have argued that the transformation of such human experiences as childbirth, reproduction, premenstrual problems, weight, and psychological distress into medical events has been the outcome of a reciprocal process involving both physicians and women. Medicine, as it developed as a profession, was repeatedly redefined. The interest of physicians in expanding jurisdiction into new areas coincided with the interest of certain class groups in having their experience in those areas understood in new terms. In other words, physicians created demand in order to generate new markets for their services. They also responded to a market that a class of women created.

This analysis suggests that women have played and may continue to play a major role in stabilizing medicine in American society. Historically, establishing childbirth, abortion, and birth control as medical events were critical junctures on the road to professional dominance. New areas of medical domain are needed because old ones have become saturated. Thus, expansion is occurring in such areas as menstruation, physical appearance, emotional distress, fertility, sexuality, and aging. Furthermore, we can expect the medicalization of women's experience to increase as the supply of physicians increases. In fact, the federal government estimates that the supply of obstetrician/gynecologists will increase from the 1970 figure of 9.3 per 100,000 population to 13.6 per 100,000 in 1990 (DHEW, 1974).

As Conrad and Schneider note, the potential for medicalization increases as science discovers the subtle physiological correlates of human behavior. A wealth of knowledge is developing about women's physiology. As more becomes known, the issue will be how to acknowledge the complex biochemical components that are related to menstruation, pregnancy, weight, and the like without allowing these conditions to be distorted by scientific understanding. The issue will be to gain understanding of our biology, without submitting to control in the guise of medical "expertise." The answer is not to "suffer our fate" and return exclusively to self-care, as Illich recommends, thereby turning our backs on discoveries and treatments that may ease pain and suffering. To "demedicalize" is not to deny the biological components of experience but rather to alter the *ownership, production,* and *use* of scientific knowledge.

Ultimately, however, demedicalization may involve profound questions about the nature of science itself. The very structure of science—its system of beliefs, assumptions, methods, and the description of "reality" it offers—is problematic for understanding women's experience. As scholars have argued, and as my analysis has illustrated, science is neither objective, neutral, nor value-free. Furthermore, feminist scientists have stressed that there is an intrinsic masculine bias in Western scientific thought: an emphasis on power and control, a separation between knower and known, a distinction between objectivity and subjectivity, and an emphasis on reason rather than feeling (Fee, 1982; Hubbard, 1979; Arditti, 1980; Keller, 1978). Particularly significant for women's health is the emphasis on domination over nature that characterizes the entire scientific enterprise, especially in light of the fact that nature is seen as female (Merchant, 1980). As Keller has eloquently stated, the quest is for a different science, undistorted by masculinist bias and characterized instead by "a conversation with nature," rather than domination over nature (McClintock, as quoted in Keller, 1982).

In sum, women's health is faced by a series of challenges. We need to expose the "truth claims" (Bittner, 1968) of medical entrepreneurs who will seek to turn new areas of experience into medical events, and instead introduce a healthy skepticism about professional claims. We need to develop alternatives to the masculinist biomedical view and place women's health and problems in the larger context of their lives. Specifically, it is not at all clear what form pregnancy, menstruation, weight, sexuality, aging, or other problems would take in a society "that allowed women to normally and routinely express anger, drive, and ambition, a society in which women felt more empowered" (Harrison, 1982). We need to reconceptualize our whole way of thinking about biology and explore how "natural" phenomena are, in fact, an outgrowth of the social circumstances of women's lives (Hubbard, 1981).

In the meantime, because we will continue to need health care, the challenge will be to alter the terms under which care is provided. In the short term, we need to work for specific reforms and gain what we can while, at the same time, acknowledging the limitation of reform. As I have argued, reform is not what we want in the long run. For certain problems in our lives, real demedicalization is necessary; experiences such as routine childbirth, menopause, or weight in excess of cultural norms should not be defined in medical terms, and medical-technical treatments should not be seen as appropriate solutions to these problems. For other conditions where medicine may be of assistance, the challenge will be to differentiate the beneficial treatments from those that are harmful and useless. The real challenge is to use existing medical knowledge selectively and to extend knowledge with new paradigms so as to improve the quality of our lives.

References

R. Arditti, "Feminism and Science," in R. Arditti, P. Brennan, and S. Cavrak (eds.), *Science and Liberation* (Boston, Mass: South End Press, 1980), pp. 350-368.

W.R. Amey, "Maternal-Infant Bonding: The Politics of Falling in Love with Your Child," *Feminist Studies*, vol. 6, (1980), pp. 547-570.

D. Banta and S.B. Thacker, "Policies toward Medical Technology: The Case of Electronic Fetal Monitoring," *American Journal of Public Health*, vol. 69 (1979), pp. 931-935.

S.E. Bell, "A New Model of Medical Technology Development: A Case Study of DES," in J. Roth and S. Ruzek (eds.), *Research in the Sociology of Health Care*, vol. 4 (Greenwich, Conn.: JAI Press, forthcoming).

A.S. Beller, *Fat and Thin: A Natural History of Obesity* (New York: Farrar, Straus and Giroux, 1977).

E. Bittner, "The Structure of Psychiatric Influence," *Mental Hygiene*, vol. 52 (1968), pp. 423-430.

R. Burd, "Dealing with Premenstrual Syndrome," *Medical Self-Care*, vol. 17 (1982), pp. 46-49.

Characteristics of Admission to Selected Mental Health Facilities, National Institute of Mental Health, Series CN, no.2 (Washington, D.C.: U.S. Printing Office, 1981).

K. Chernin, *The Obsession: Reflections on the Tyranny of Slenderness* (New York: Harper & Row, 1981).

D.B. Christensen and P.J. Bush, "Drug Prescribing: Patterns, Problems and Proposals," *Social Science and Medicine*, vol. 15A (1981), pp. 343-355.

P. Conrad and J.W. Schneider, *Deviance and Medicalization: From Badness to Sickness* (St. Louis, Mo.: C.V. Mosby, 1980).

——"Looking at Levels of Medicalization: A Comment on Strong's Critique of the Theses of Medical Imperialism," *Social Science and Medicine*, vol. 14A (1980a), pp. 75-79.

R. Cooperstock, and P. Parnele, "Research on Psychotropic Drug Use: A Review of Findings and Methods," *Social Science and Medicine*, vol. 16 (1982), pp. 1179-1196.

M. Courtot, "A Spoiled Identity," *Sinister Wisdom*, vol. 20 (1982), pp. 10-15.

R. Crawford, "A Cultural Account of 'Health': Self-Control, Release and the Social Body," in J.B. McKinlay (ed.), *Issues in the Political Economy of Health Care* (New York: Methuen, forthcoming).

R. Crawford, "Healthism and the Medicalization of Everyday Life," *International Journal of Health Services*, vol. 10 (1980), pp. 365-389.

K. Dalton, *The Premenstrual Syndrome and Progesterone Therapy* (Chicago, Ill.: Year Book Medical Publishers, 1977).

M.L. Davies, *Maternity: Letters from Working Women* (New York: Norton, 1978).

M. Delaney, J. Lupton, and E. Toth, *The Curse* (New York: E.P. Dutton, 1976).

V.G. Drachman, "The Loomis Trial: Social Mores and Obstetrics in the Mid-Nineteenth Century," in S. Reverby and D. Rosner (eds.), *Health Case in America: Essays in Social History* (Philadelphia, Pa.: Temple University Press, 1979) pp. 67-83.

C. Dreifus, (ed.), *Seizing Our Bodies: The Politics of Women's Health* (New York: Vintage, 1978).

N.S. Dye, "History of Childbirth in America," *Signs*, vol. 97 (1980), pp. 97-108.

B. Ehrenreich and J. Ehrenreich, "Medicine and Social Control," in J. Ehrenreich (ed.), *The Cultural Crisis of Modern Medicine* (New York: Monthly Review Press, 1978).

B. Ehrenreich and D. English, *Complaints and Disorders: The Sexual Politics of Sickness* (Old Westbury, N.Y.: Feminist Press, 1973).

——*For Her Own Good: 150 Years of the Experts' Advice to Women* (Garden City, N.Y.: Anchor, 1979).

FDA Drug Bulletin, Food and Drug Administration (Rockville, Md.: 1972).

E. Fee, "A Feminist Critique of Scientific Objectivity," *Science for the People*, vol. 14 (1982), pp. 5-32.

M. Foucault, *The Birth of the Clinic: An Archeology of Medical Perception* (New York: Pantheon, 1973).

R. Fox, "The Medicalization and Demedicalization of American Society," *Daedalus*, vol. 106 (1977), pp. 9-22.

E. Frankfort, *Vaginal Politics* (New York: Quadrangle Books, 1972).

E. Freidson, *Profession of Medicine* (New York: Dodd, Mead, 1970).

B. Friedan, *The Feminine Mystique* (New York: Dell, 1963).

R.C. Friedman, S.W. Hurt, M.S. Aronoff, and J. Clarkin, "Behavior and the Menstrual Cycle," *Signs*, vol. 5 (1980), pp. 719-738.

D.M. Garner, P.E. Garfinkel, D. Schwartz, and M. Thompson, "Cultural Expectations of Thinness in Women," *Psychological Reports*, vol. 47 (1980), pp. 483-491.

E. Goffman, *Stigma: Notes on the Management of Spoiled Identity* (Englewood Cliffs, N.J.: Prentice Hall, 1964).

P.B. Goldblatt, M.E. Moore, and A.J. Stunkard, "Social Factors in Obesity," *Journal of American Medical Association*, vol. 192, (1972), pp. 1039-1044.

E.R. Gonzales, "Premenstrual Syndrome: Ancient Woe Deserving of Modern Scrutiny," *Journal of American Medical Association*, vol. 245 (1981), pp. 1393-1396.

L. Gordon, *Woman's Body, Woman's Right: A Social History of Birth Control in America* (New York: Penguin, 1976).

H.S. Gross, M.R. Herbert, G.L. Knatterud, and L. Donner, "The Effect of Race and Sex on the Variation of Diagnosis and Disposition in a Psychiatric

Emergency Room," *Journal of Nervous and Mental Disease*, vol. 148 (1969), pp. 638-643.

D.L. Hall, "Biology, Sex Hormones and Sexism in the 1920's" in C.C. Gould and M.W. Wartofsky (eds.), *Women and Philosophy: Toward a Theory of Liberation* (New York: G.P. Putnam's, 1976).

J. Hanmer and P. Allen, "Reproductive Engineering: The Final Solution?" *Feminist Issues*, vol. 2 (1982), pp. 53-74.

M. Harrison, *Self-Help for Premenstrual Syndrome* (Cambridge, Mass.: Matrix Press, 1982).

R. Herrnstein, "IQ," *Atlantic Monthly*, vol. 228 (1971), pp. 43-64.

S. Heyden, C.G. Hames, A. Bartel, et. al., "Weight and Weight History in Relation to Cerebrovascular and Ischemic Heart Disease," *Archives of Internal Medicine*, vol. 128 (1971), pp. 956-960.

J.C. Hoffman, "Biorhythms in Human Reproduction: The Not-So-Steady States," *Signs*, vol. 7, (1982), pp. 829-844.

H. Holmes, B. Haskins, and M. Gross (eds.), *The Custom-Made Child? Women-Centered Perspectives* (New York: Humana, 1981).

M.C. Howell, "What Medical Schools Teach about Women," *New England Journal of Medicine*, vol. 291 (1974), pp. 304-307.

R. Hubbard, "Have Only Men Evolved?" in R. Hubbard, M.S. Henifin, and B. Fried (eds.), *Women Look at Biology Looking at Women* (Cambridge, Mass.: Schenkman, 1979).

——"The Politics of Women's Biology" (Lecture given at Hampshire College, October 1981).

——"Legal and Policy Implications of Recent Advances in Prenatal Diagnosis and Fetal Therapy," *Women's Rights*

Law Reporter, Rutgers, vol. 7 (1982), pp. 201-218.

——"Women and Biology" (Lecture at annual conference, New England Women's Studies, Keene State College, Keene, N. H., 1983).

I. Illich, *Medical Nemesis: The Expropriation of Health* (New York: Pantheon, 1976).

E.F. Keller, "Gender and Science," *Psychoanalysis and Contemporary Science*, vol. 1 (1978), pp. 409-433.

——"Feminism and Science," *Signs*, vol. 7 (1982), pp. 589-602.

M.H. Klaus and J.H. Kennell, *Maternal-Infant Bonding: The Impact of Early Separation or Loss on Family Development* (St. Louis, Mo.: C.V. Mosby, 1976).

F.E. Kobrin, "The American Midwife Controversy: A Crisis of Professionalization," *Bulletin of the History of Medicine*, vol. 40 (1966), pp. 350-363.

K. Koumjian, "The Use of Valium as a Force of Social Control," *Social Science and Medicine*, vol. 15E (1981), pp. 245-249.

M.S. Larson, *The Rise of Professionalism: A Sociological Analysis* (Berkeley: University of California Press, 1977).

J.W. Leavitt, "Birthing and Anesthesia: The Debate over Twilight Sleep," *Signs*, vol. 6 (1980), pp. 147-164.

G. Mann, "The Influence of Obesity on Health: Part I," *New England Journal of Medicine*, vol. 291, no. 4 (1974), pp. 178-185.

——"The Influence of Obesity on Health: Part II," *New England Journal of Medicine*, vol. 291, no. 5 (1974), pp. 226-232.

J. McKinlay, "A Case for Refocussing Upstream: The Political Economy of Illness," in P. Conrad and R. Kern (eds.), *The Sociology of Health and Illness*

(New York: St. Martin's Press, 1981), pp. 613-633.

C. Merchant, *The Death of Nature: Women, Ecology and the Scientific Revolution* (New York: Harper and Row, 1980).

W.E. Miall, R.A. Bell, and H.G. Lovell, "Relation between Change in Blood Pressure and Weight" *British Journal of Preventive Social Medicine*, vol. 22 (1986), pp. 73-80.

L.G. Miller, "Pain, Parturition, and the Profession: Twilight Sleep in America," in S. Reverby and D. Rosner (eds.), in *Health Care in America: Essays in Social History* (Philadelphia, Pa.: Temple University Press, 1979), pp. 19-37.

M. Millman, *Such a Pretty Face: Being Fat in America* (New York: Berkley Books, 1980).

E. Mills, *Living with Mental Illness: A Study of East London* (London: Routledge and Kegan Paul, 1962).

E.G. Mishler, "The Social Construction of Illness" in E.G. Mishler, et. al., *Social Contexts of Health, Illness,and Patient Care* (Cambridge: Cambridge University Press, 1981), pp. 141-168.

J.C. Mohr, *Abortion in America: The Origins and Evolution of National Policy, 1800-1900* (New York: Oxford University Press, 1978).

R.H. Moos, "The Development of a Menstrual Distress Questionnaire" *Psychosomatic Medicine*, vol. 30 (1963), pp. 853-867.

C. Nathanson, "Illness and the Feminine Role: A Theoretical Review," *Social Science and Medicine*, vol. 9 (1975), pp. 57-62.

Newsweek, "Not Guilty Because of PMS?" (Nov. 8, 1982), p. 111.

K. O'Driscoll and M. Foley "Correlation of Decrease in Perinatal Mortality and Increase in Caesarean Section Rates," *Obstetrics and Gynecology*, vol. 61 (1983), pp. 1-5.

M.B. Parlee, "The Premenstrual Syndrome," *Psychological Bulletin*, vol. 80 (1973), pp. 454-465.

T. Parsons, "Definitions of Illness and Health in Light of American Values and Social Structure," in E.G. Jaco (ed.), *Patients, Physicians and Illness*, 2nd ed. (New York: Free Press, 1951).

A.L. Plough, "Medical Technology and the Crisis of Experience: The Cost of Clinical Legitimation," *Social Science and Medicine*, vol. 15F (1981), pp. 89-101.

R.L. Reid and S.S.C. Yen, "Premenstrual Syndrome," *American Journal of Obstetrics and Gynecology*, vol. 139 (1981), pp. 85-104.

S. Reverby, "Stealing the Golden Eggs: Earnest Amory Codman and the Science and Management of Medicine," *Bulletin of the History of Medicine*, vol. 55 (1981), pp. 156-171.

S. Reverby, and D. Rosner (eds.), *Health Care in America: Essays in Social History* (Philadelphia, Pa.: Temple University Press, 1979).

E.R. Romey, "Sex Hormones and Executive Ability," *Annals of the New York Academy of Science*, vol. 308 (1973), pp. 237-245.

S. Rose and H. Rose, "The Myth of the Neutrality of Science," in R. Arditti, P. Brennan, and S. Cavrak (eds.), op.cit, pp. 16-32.

A. Rossi, "Life Span Theories and Women's Lives," *Signs*, vol. 6 (1980), pp. 4-32.

B.K. Rothman, "Awake and Aware, or False Consciousness: The Cooptation of Childbirth Reform in America," in S. Romalis (ed.), *Childbirth: Alternatives to Medical Control* (Austin, Tex.:

University of Texas Press, 1981), pp. 150-180.

—*In Labor: Women and Power in the Birthplace* (New York: Norton, 1982).

D. Ruble, "Premenstrual Symptoms: A Reinterpretation," *Science*, vol. 197 (1977), pp. 291-292.

S.B. Ruzek, *The Women's Health Movement: Feminist Alternatives to Medical Control* (New York: Praeger, 1978).

D.M. Schwartz, M.G. Thompson, and C.L. Johnson, "Anorexia Nervosa and Bulimia: The Socio-cultural Context," *International Journal of Eating Disorders*, vol. 1 (1980), pp. 20-36.

D. Scully and P. Bart, "A Funny Thing Happened on the Way to the Orifice: Women in Gynecology Textbooks," in P. Conrad and R. Kern (eds.), *The Sociology of Health in Illness: Critical Perspectives* (New York: St. Martin's Press, 1981).

B. Seaman, *Free and Female* (New York: Coward, McCann, and Geoghegan, 1972).

N.S. Shaw, *Forced Labor: Maternity Care in the United States* (New York: Pergamon Press, 1974).

C. Smith-Rosenberg and C. Rosenberg, "The Female Animal: Medical and Biological Views of Woman and Her Role in Nineteenth-Century America," *Journal of American History*, vol. 60 (1973), pp. 332-355.

S. Sontag, *Illness As Metaphor* (New York: Vintage, 1979).

E. Stark, "What Is Medicine?" *Radical Science Journal*, vol. 12 (1982), pp. 46-89.

E. Stark and A. Flitcraft, "Medical Therapy As Repression: The Case of Battered Women," *Health and Medicine*, vol. 1 (1982), pp. 29-32.

P. Starr, *The Social Transformation of American Medicine* (New York: Basic Books, 1982).

A. Stunkard, H. Levine, and S. Fox, "The Management of Obesity," *Archives of Internal Medicine*, vol. 125 (1976), pp. 1067-1072.

C.N. Theodore and G.E. Sutter, *Distribution of Physicians in the U.S.*, Department of Survey Research, Management Services Division, American Medical Association, 1966

U.S. Department of Health, Education, and Welfare, *The Supply of Health Manpower: 1970 Profiles and Projections to 1990*, DHEW Publications No. (HRA) 75-38, (1974).

L.M. Verbrugge and R.P. Steiner, "Physician Treatment of Men and Women Patients: Sex Bias or Appropriate Care?" *Medical Care*, vol. 19 (1981), pp. 609-632.

M.R. Walsh, *Doctors Wanted: No Women Need Apply* (New Haven, Conn.: Yale University Press, 1977).

R.W. Wertz and D.C. Wertz, *Lying In: A History of Childbirth in America* (New York: Free Press, 1979).

L.E. Wurdman, *Physician Distribution and Medical Licensure in the U.S., 1979*, Center for Health Services Research and Development, American Medical Association (1980).

I.M. Young, "The Pregnant Body: Subjectivity and Alienation," *Journal of Medicine and Philosophy*, vol. 9 (forthcoming).

R.M. Young, "Science is Social Relations," *Radical Science Journal*, vol. 5 (1977), pp. 65-131.

I.K. Zola, "Medicine As an Institution of Social Control," *Sociological Review*, vol. 20 (1972), pp. 487-504.

—"In the Name of Health and Illness: On Some Socio-political Consequences of Medical Influence," *Social Science and Medicine*, vol. 9 (1975), pp. 83-87.

Becoming Patients and Experiencing Illness

Modern medical sociology has reframed how we look at the definition of health problems. In particular, the discussion in the previous section of the critique of the medical model and of social constructivism illustrates this point. While *disease* is the physiological condition that a medical professional would observe, *illness* is the way that a person experiences that physiological condition. The same disease or condition is often experienced differently by different people. For example, the existence of pneumonia may lead one person to lie in bed and demand attention, yet lead another person to stay out of bed and to try to continue routine living. The same form of cancer may engender denial by one person, while another may experience it with active dread. Pain is perceived differently according to people's social class and ethnic cultural backgrounds.

Further, not all disease is experienced as illness, nor is all illness the result of a particular disease. Some people manage to avoid active symptoms, or to attribute them to other sources. Certain people tend to experience symptoms that are not traceable to a known cause, and some spend much time fearing they will catch any number of diseases. A large number of visits to doctors are for very minor symptoms and for psychological attention.

In many cases, popular concepts of health differ from medical concepts, due to the gulf in both knowledge and perspective between consumers and providers. Understanding this divergence in viewpoint is of central concern to medical sociologists, since it underlies many conflicts that occur in the health care system. As citizens become more educated, conscious, and active in health matters, these conflicts often increase.

Differences in perception mean that people also differ in the ways that they choose to deal with their health problems. Race, class, sex, ethnic, and national differences lead to differing degrees of self-treatment and to diverse help-seeking. Irving Kenneth Zola's article, "Pathways to the Doctor—From

Person to Patient," illuminates many of these issues through a study of patient help-seeking in three clinics. Zola finds major differences between Italian Catholics, Irish Catholics, and Anglo-Saxon Protestants in the experience of illness and the ways that complaints were presented to doctors. Zola provides more evidence that much help-seeking behavior is not primarily a result of physiological problems or disease as defined by the medical model. Instead, it is triggered by five major types of occurrences: interpersonal crises, perceived interference with social or personal relations, sanctioning on the part of another family member, perceived interference with work or physical activity, and temporalizing (time-bound perceptions of symptoms).

These and many other dimensions of *illness behavior* have led sociologists to pay closer attention to patient perspectives on health, illness, and medical care. Health professionals, too, have begun to alter their perspectives on such issues. A growing number of doctors and hospitals pay particular attention to specific aspects of illness behavior rather than focusing exclusively on disease. This new outlook on the part of medical providers can have many benefits for patients, such as being put more at ease and having questions answered more fully, but as David Armstrong's article, "The Patient's View," shows, attention to the patient's view also benefits doctors. Writing in a theoretical and historical vein about doctors' changing conceptions of the body, disease, and patient involvement, Armstrong argues that medical acceptance of the patient's view often means co-optation (taking over and subverting) of the patient's active role in defining illness and negotiating about treatment. For example, doctors can achieve higher levels of adherence to doctor's orders (i.e., patient compliance) by paying attention to patient perspectives.

Ray Fitzpatrick, in "Lay Concepts of Illness," offers a cross-cultural outlook, largely anthropological, which introduces us to the importance of cultural contexts that influence the lay experience of illness. Of particular interest is his discussion of the Western medical perspective that emphasizes a mind-body dualism, in sharp contrast to the more integrated concept of mind in body in many other cultures.

Gareth Williams's contribution, "The Genesis of Chronic Illness: Narrative Reconstruction," gives us detailed glimpses into the ways in which three people reconstruct how they believe they "got" rheumatoid arthritis. Williams's respondents employ broader viewpoints than the biomedical model. One imputes a political and economic causality; another locates etiology in a nest of social relationships and psychological makeup; another uses a mystical explanation. Each of these people produces a coherent self-analysis for their own narrative, thus providing a way to repair the rupture that chronic disease causes in their relationship with the world. This selection is valuable not only because it provides examples of individual illness experience, but also because it demonstrates the usefulness of narrative methods of research, that is, reconstructing how people tell stories and give accounts of their life experience.

14   PATHWAYS TO THE DOCTOR— FROM PERSON TO PATIENT*

Irving Kenneth Zola

The problem on which we wish to dwell is one about which we think we know a great deal but that, in reality, we know so little—how and why an individual seeks professional medical aid. The immediate and obvious answer is that a person goes to a doctor when he is sick. Yet, this term "sick", is much clearer to those who use it, namely the health practitioners and the researchers, than it is to those upon whom we apply it —the patients. Two examples may illustrate this point. Listen carefully to the words of a respondent in Koos' study of the Health of Regionville as she wrestled with a definition of this concept.

I wish I really knew what you meant about being sick. Sometimes I felt so bad I could curl up and die, but had to go on because the kids had to be taken care of and besides, we didn't have the money to spend for the doctor. How could I be sick? How do you know when you're sick, anyway? Some people can go to bed most anytime with anything, but but most of us can't be sick, even when we need to be[1].

Even when there is agreement as to what constitutes "sickness," there may be a difference of opinion as to what constitutes appropriate action, as in the following incident:

A rather elderly woman arrived at the Medical Clinic of the Massachusetts General Hospital three days after an appointment. A somewhat exasperated nurse turned to her and said, "Mrs. Smith, your appointment was three days ago. Why weren't you here then?" To this Mrs. Smith responded, "How could I? Then I was sick."

Examples such as these are not unusual occurrences. And yet they cause little change in some basic working assumptions of the purveyors of medical care as well as the myriad investigators who are studying its delivery. It is to three of these assumptions we now turn: (1) the importance and frequency of episodes of illness in an individual's life; (2) the representativeness of those episodes of illness which come to professional attention; and (3) the process by which an individual decides that a series of bodily discomforts he labels symptoms become worthy of professional attention. Together these assumptions create an interesting if misleading picture of illness. Rarely do we try to

*The data collection for the first study on which this paper is based was supported by the Departments of Medicine and Psychiatry of the Massachusetts General Hospital. All subsequent data-collection as well as the final writing and analysis was supported by the National Institute of General Medical Sciences, Grant No. 11367. For her many substantive and editorial suggestions I wish to thank Dr. Leonora K. Zola.

SOURCE: Reprinted with permission from *Social Science and Medicine* 7: 677–689, Copyright © 1973, Pergamon Journals, Ltd.

understand how or why a patient goes to the doctor, for the decision itself is thought to be an obvious one. We postulate a time when the patient is asymptomatic or unaware that he has symptoms, then suddenly some clear objective symptoms appear, then perhaps he goes through a period of self-treatment and when either this treatment is unsuccessful or the symptoms in some way become too difficult to take, he decides to go to some health practitioner (usually, we hope, a physician).

The first assumption, thus, deals with the idea that individuals at most times during their life are really asymptomatic. The extensive data pouring in from periodic health examination has gradually begun to question this notion. For, examinations of even supposedly healthy people, from business executives to union members to college professors, consistently reveal that at the time of their annual check-up, there was scarcely an individual who did not possess some symptom, some clinical entity worthy of treatment [2]. More general surveys have yielded similar findings [3]. Such data begins to give us a rather uncomfortable sense in which we may to some degree be sick every day of our lives. If we should even think of such a picture, however, the easiest way to dismiss this notion is that the majority of these everyday conditions are so minor as to be unworthy of medical treatment. This leads to our second assumption; namely, the degree of representativeness, both as to seriousness and frequency, of those episodes which do get to a doctor. Here too we are presented with puzzling facts. For if we look at investigations of either serious physical or mental disorder, there seem to be at least one, and in many cases several, people out of treatment for every person in treatment [4]. If, on the other hand, we look at a doctor's practice, we find that the vast bulk is concerned with quite minor disorders [5]. Furthermore, if we use symptom-check-lists or health calendars, we find that for these self-same minor disorders, there is little that distinguishes them medically from those that are ignored, tolerated, or self-medicated [6].

With these confusions in mind, we can now turn to the third assumption. On the basis that symptoms were perceived to be an infrequent and thus somewhat dramatic event in one's life, the general assumption was that in the face of such symptoms, a rational individual after an appropriate amount of caution, would seek aid. When he does not or delays overlong, we begin to question his rationality. The innumerable studies of delay in cancer bear witness.

If we examine these studies we find that the reason for delay are a list of faults—the patient has no time, no money, no one to care for children, or take over other duties, is guilty, ashamed, fearful, anxious, embarrassed, or emotionally disturbed, dislikes physicians, nurses, hospitals, or needles, has had bad medical, familial or personal experiences, or is of lower education, socioeconomic status, or an ethnic or racial minority [7]. As the researchers might put it, there is something about these people or in their backgrounds which has disturbed their rationality, for otherwise, they would "naturally" seek aid. And yet there is a curious methodological fact about these studies for all these investigations were done on *patients*, people who *had* ultimately decided to go to a physician. What happened? Were they no longer fearful? Did they get free time, more money, outside help? Did they resolve their guilt, shame, anxiety, distrust? No, this does not seem to have been the case. If anything the investigators seem to allude to the fact that the patients finally could not stand it any longer. Yet given the abundant data on the ability to tolerate pain [8] and a wide variety of other conditions, this notion of "not being able to stand it" simply does not ring true clinically.

We can now restate a more realistic empirical picture of illness episodes. Virtually every day of our lives we are subject to a vast array of bodily discomforts. Only an infinitesimal amount of these get to a physician. Neither the mere presence nor the obviousness of symptoms, neither their medical seriousness nor objective discomfort seems to differentiate those episodes which do and do not get professional treatment. In short, what then does convert a person to a patient? This then became a significant question and the search for an answer began.

At this point we had only the hunch that "something critical" must ordinarily happen to make an individual seek help. Given the voluminous literature on delay in seeking medical aid for almost every conceivable disorder and treatment, we might well say that that statistical norm for any population is to delay (perhaps infinitely for many). The implementing of this hunch is owed primarily to the intersection of two disciplines—anthropology and psychiatry. The first question to be faced was how and where to study this "something." Both prospective and retrospective studies were rejected. The former because as Professor H. M. Murphy noted there is often an enormous discrepancy between the declared intention and the actual act. The retrospective approach was rejected for two reasons —the almost notoriously poor recall that individuals have for past medical experiences and the distortions in recall introduced by the extensive "memory manipulation" which occurs as a result of the medical interview. Our resolution to this dilemma was a way of studying the patient when he was *in the process* of seeking medical aid. This process was somewhat artificially created by (1) interviewing patients while they waited to see their physician; (2) confining our sample to new patients to the Out-Patient Clinics of the Massachusetts General Hospital who were seeking aid for their particular problem for the first time. Thus, we had a group of people who were definitely committed to seeing a doctor (i.e. waiting) but who had not yet been subject to the biases and distortions that might occur through the medical interview (though some patients had been referred, we included only those on whom no definitive diagnosis had been made). This then was where we decided to study our problem.

In what to look for we were influenced by certain trends in general psychiatry away from defining mental illness solely in terms or symptoms possessed by a single isolated individual and instead conceptualising it as a more general kind of disturbance in interpersonal behaviour and social living. (The resemblance that this bears to early classical notions of health and illness is quite striking. For then illness was conceived to be the disturbance between ego and his environment and not the physical symptom which happens to show up in ego) [9]. On the empirical level we were influenced by the work of Clausen and his colleagues at the National Institute of Mental Health on the first admission to the hospital for male schizophrenics. Most striking about their material was the lack of any increase in the objective seriousness of the patient's disorder as a factor in this hospitalisation. If anything, there was a kind of normalisation in his family, an accommodation to the patient's symptoms. The hospitalization occurred not when the patient became sicker, but when the accommodation of the family, of the surrounding social context, broke down [10]. A translation of these findings could be made to physical illness. For, given all the data on delay, it seemed very likely that people have their symptoms for a long period of time before ever seeking medical aid. Thus one could hypothesize that there is an accommodation both physical, personal, and social to the symptoms and it is when this accommodation breaks down that the person seeks, or is forced to seek

medical aid. Thus the "illness" for which one seeks help may only in part be a physical relief from symptoms. The research question on the decision to seek medical aid thus turned from the traditional focus on "why the delay" to the more general issue of "why come *now*". This way of asking this question is in itself not new. Physicians have often done it, but interestingly enough, they have asked it not in regard to general physical illness but rather when they can find nothing wrong. It is *then* that they feel that the patient may want or have been prompted to seek help for other than physical reasons.

The final issue which is essential to understanding the study concerns the nature of the sample. Here in particular there was an intersection of anthropology and psychiatry. Time and again anthropologists had called attention to the problem of designating certain behaviours as abnormal in one cultural situation but would be considered quite normal and even ignored in another. Usually, when they explained this phenomenon they did so in terms of value-orientations; namely that there was something about the fit or lack of fit of the particular problem (symptom or sign), into a larger cultural pattern which helped explain why it was or was not abnormal [11]. Why could not the same process be operating in regard to physical symptoms? Perhaps many of the unexplained epidemiological differences between groups may also be due to the fact that in one group the particular physical sign is considered normal and in the second group not. For given the enormous tolerance we have for many physical conditions, given that our morbidity statistics are based primarily on treated disorders, many of these differences may reflect differences in attention and not differences in prevalence or incidence. While anthropologists have reported their findings mostly in comparisons of non-literate groups with a more "modern" society, we decided to translate their idea of a culture into a contemporary format. We thus speculated that ethnic groups, particularly in an area such as Boston, Massachusetts, might well function as cultural reference groups and thus be an urban transmitter and perpetuator of value-orientations. The specific ethnic groups we studied were determined by a demographic study at the Massachusetts General Hospital, from which we were able to determine the three most populous ethnic groups, Italian, Irish Catholic and Anglo-Saxon Protestant.

To summarize the methodological introduction, in our first study, the sample consisted of patients completely new to the out-patient clinics who were seeking medical aid for the first time for this particular problem, who were between the ages of 18 and 50, able to converse in English, of either Anglo-Saxon Protestant, Irish Catholic or Italian Catholic background. The data-collection took place at the three clinics to which these groups were most frequently sent—the Eye Clinic, the Ear, Nose and Throat Clinic, and the Medical Clinic, which were, incidentally three of the largest clinics in the hospital. The interviewing took place during the waiting time before

they saw their physicians with the general focus of the questioning being: Why did you seek medical aid now? In addition to many such open-ended questions, we had other information derived from the medical record, demographic interviews, attitude scales and check lists. We also had each examining physician fill out a medical rating sheet on each patient. In all we saw over two hundred patients, fairly evenly divided between male and female [12].

We first examined the presenting complaints of the patients to see if there were differing conceptions of what is symptomatic [13]. Our first finding dealt with the location of their troubles. The Irish tended to place the locus of symptoms in the eye, the ear, the nose or the throat —a sense organ while the Italians showed no particular clustering. The same result obtained when we asked what was the most important part of the body. Here too the Irish tended to place their symptoms in the eyes, ears, nose and throat with the Italians not favouring any specific location. We noted, however, that this was not merely a reflection of epidemiological differences; for Italians who did have eye, ear, nose and throat problems did not necessarily locate their chief complaint in either the eye, ear, nose or throat. We thus began to wonder if this focussing was telling us something other than a specific location. And so we turned our attention to more qualitative aspects of symptoms, such as the presence of pain. Here we noted that the Italians much more often felt that pain constituted a major part of their problem, whereas the

Irish felt equally strongly that it did not. However, we had our first clue that "something else" was going on. The Irish did not merely say they had no pain, but rather utilized a kind of denial with such statements as, "No, I wouldn't call it a pain, rather a discomfort"; or "No, a slight headache, but nothing that lasts". Further analysis of our data then led us to create a typology in which we tried to grasp the essence of a patient's complaint. One type seemed to reflect a rather specific organic dysfunctioning (difficulty in seeing, inappropriate functioning, discharge, or movement etc.) while the second type represented a more global malfunctioning (aches and pains, appearance, energy level etc.). Looked at in this way, we found that significantly more Irish seemed to describe their problem in terms of a rather specific dysfunction whereas the Italians described their complaints in a more diffuse way. Thus, the Irish seemed to convey a concern with something specific, something that has gone wrong, or been impaired; whereas the Italian is concerned with or conveyed a more global malfunctioning emphasizing the more diffuse nature of their complaints.

We now had differentiated two ways of communicating about one's bodily complaints—a kind of restricting versus generalizing tendency and we thus sought evidence to either refute or substantiate it. Two "tests" suggested themselves. The first consisted of three sets of tabulations: (1) the total number of symptoms a patient had; (2) the total number of different types of mal-

functions from which he suffered (the typology mentioned above actually consisted of nine codifiable categories); and (3) the total number of different parts of the body in which a patient located complaints. Each we regarded as a measure of "generalizing" one's complaints. As we predicted the Italians had significantly more complaints of greater variety, and in more places than did the Irish. Our second "test" consisted of several questions dealing with the effect of their symptoms on their interpersonal behaviour. Here we reasoned that the Irish would be much more likely to restrict the effect of their symptoms to physical functioning. And so it was, with the Italians claiming that the symptoms interfered with their general mode of living and the Irish just as vehemently denying any such interference. Here again, the Irish presented a "no with a difference" in such statements as "No, there may have been times that I become uncomfortable physically and afraid to show it socially. If I felt that way I even tried to be a little more sociable."

Perhaps the best way to convey how differently these two groups communicated their symptoms is by a composite picture. The two series of responses were given by an Italian and an Irish patient of similar age and sex, with a disorder of approximately the same duration and seriousness and with the same primary and, if present, secondary diagnosis.

The crux of the study is, however, the decision to see a doctor. One of our basic claims was that the decision to seek medical aid was based on a break in the accommodation to the symptoms, that in the vast majority of situations, an individual did not seek aid at his physically sickest point. We do not mean by this that symptoms were unimportant. What we mean is that they function as a sort of constant and that when the decision to seek medical aid was made the physical symptoms alone were not sufficient to prompt this seeking. Typical of the amount of debilitation people can tolerate as well as the considerable seriousness and still the decision to seek medical attention made on extra-physical grounds is the case of Mary O'Rourke.

Mary O'Rourke is 49, married and is a licensed practical nurse. Her symptom was a simple one, "The sight is no good in this eye . . . can't see print at all, no matter how big." This she claimed was due to being hit on the side of the head by a baseball 4 months ago, but she just couldn't get around to a doctor before this. Why did she decide now, did her vision become worse? "Well . . . about a month ago I was taking care of his (a client's) mother . . . he mentioned that my eyelid was drooping . . . it was the first time he ever did . . . if he hadn't pointed it out I wouldn't have gone then." "Why did you pay attention to his advice?" "Well it takes away from my appearance . . . bad enough to feel this way without having to look that way . . . the same day I told my husband to call". Diagnosis—Chorioretinitis O.S. (permanent partial blindness) "lesion present much longer than present symptoms." Incidentally, no "drooping" was noticeable to either the interviewer or the examining physician.

Case after case could be presented to make this point but even more striking is that there is a "method underlying this madness". In our data we were able to discern several distinct nonphysiological patterns of triggers to the decision to seek medical aid. We have called them as follows: (1) the occurrence of an interpersonal crisis; (2) the *perceived* interference with social or personal relations; (3) sanctioning; (4) the *perceived* interference with vocational or physical activity; and (5) a kind of temporalizing of symptomatology. Moreover, these five patterns were clustered in such a way that we could characterize each ethnic group in our sample as favouring particular decision-making patterns in the seeking of medical aid.

The first two patterns, the presence of an interpersonal crisis, and the perceived interference with social or personal relations were more frequent among the Italians. The former, that of a crisis, does not mean that the symptoms have led to a crisis or even vice-versa, but that the crisis called attention to the symptoms, caused the patient to dwell on them and finally to do something about them. Two examples will illustrate this.

Jennie Bella was 40, single, and had a hearing difficulty for many years. She said that the symptoms have not gotten worse nor do they bother her a great deal (Diagnosis: Nonsupporative Otitis Media) and, furthermore, she admitted being petrified of doctors. "I don't like to come . . . I don't like doctors. I never did . . . I have to be unconscious to go . . . ." She can nevertheless not pinpoint any reason for

TABLE 1

Diagnosis	Question of Interviewer	Irish Patient	Italian Patient
1. Presbyopia and hyperopia	What seems to be the trouble?	I can't see to thread a needle or read a paper.	I have a constant headache and my eyes seem to get all red and burny.
	Anything else?	No, I can't recall any.	No, just that it lasts all day long and I even wake up with it sometimes.
2. Myopia	What seems to be the trouble?	I can't see across the street.	My eyes seem very burny, especially the right eye. . . . Two or three months ago I woke up with my eye swollen. I bathed it and it did go away but there was still the burny sensation.
	Anything else?	I had been experiencing headaches but it may be that I'm in early menopause.	Yes, there always seems to be a red spot beneath this eye . . . .
	Anything else?	No.	Well, my eyes feel very heavy . . . at night they bother me most.

These cases have been chosen precisely because they are relatively minor disorders. So straightforward are they that one should expect very little difference between patients who are their "owners." And yet not only does the Italian patient consistently present more troubles than the Irish but while the Irish patient focussed on a specific malfunctioning as the main concern, the Italian did not even mention this aspect of the problem but focussed on more "painful" and diffuse qualities of his condition.

coming at this time other than a general feeling that it should be taken care of. But when she was questioned about her family's concern, she blurted out, "I'm very nervous with my mother, up to this year I've been quiet, a stay-at-home . . . Now I've decided to go out and have some fun. My mother is very strict and very religious. She doesn't like the idea of my going out with a lot of men. She don't think I should go out with one for awhile and then stop. She says I'm not a nice girl, that I shouldn't go with a man unless I plan to marry . . . she doesn't like my keeping late hours or coming home late. She always suspects the worst of me . . . This year it's just been miserable . . . I can't talk to her . . . she makes me very upset and its been getting worse . . . .The other day . . . last week we (in lowered tones) had *the* argument". Miss Bella called for an appointment the next morning.

Carol Conte was a 45-year-old, single, bookkeeper. For a number of years she had been both the sole support and nurse for her mother. Within the past year, her mother died and shortly thereafter her relatives began insisting that she move in with them, quit her job, work in their variety store and nurse their mother. With Carol's vacation approaching, they have stepped up their efforts to persuade her to at least try this arrangement. Although she has long had a number of minor aches and pains, her chief complaint was a small cyst on her eyelid (Diagnosis: Fibroma). She related her fear that it *might* be growing or could lead to something more serious and thus she felt she had better look into it now (the second day of her vacation) "before it was too late". "Too late" for what was revealed only in a somewhat mumbled response to the question of

what she expected or would like the doctor to do. From a list of possible outcomes to her examination, she responded, "Maybe a 'hospital' (isation) . . . .'Rest' would be all right . . ." (and then in a barely audible tone, in fact turning her head away as if she were speaking to no one at all) "just so they (the family) would stop bothering me." Responding to her physical concern, the examining physician acceded to her request for the removal of the fibroma, referred her for surgery and thus removed her from the situation for the duration of her vacation.

In such cases, it appeared that regardless of the reality and seriousness of the symptoms, they provide but the rationale for an escape, the calling-card or ticket to a potential source of help—the doctor.

The second pattern—the perceived interference with social or personal relations—is illustrated by the following two Italian patients.

John Pell is 18 and in his senior year of high school. For almost a year he's had headaches over his left eye and pain in and around his right, artificial, eye. The symptoms seem to be most prominent in the early evening. He claimed, however, little general difficulty or interference until he was asked whether the symptoms affected how he got along. To this he replied, "That's what worries me . . . I like to go out and meet people and now I've been avoiding people". Since he has had this problem for a year, he was probed as to why it bothered him more at this particular time. "The last few days of school it bothered me so that I tried to avoid everybody (this incidentally was his characteristic pattern *whenever* his eyes bothered him) . . . and I want to go out with . . . and my Senior Prom coming up, and I get the pains at 7 or 7:30 how can I stay out . . . then I saw the nurse." To be specific, he was walking down the corridor and saw the announcement of the upcoming Prom. He noticed the starting time of 8 p.m. and went immediately to the school nurse who in turn referred him to the Massachusetts Eye and Ear Infirmary.

Harry Gallo is 41, married, and a "trainee" at a car dealer's. "For a very long time my trouble is I can't drink . . . tea, coffee, booze . . . eat ice cream, fried foods. What happens is I get pains if I do it."' (Diagnosis: peptic ulcer). He becomes very dramatic when talking about how the symptoms affected him. "It shot my social life all to pieces . . . we all want to socialize . . . and it's a tough thing. I want to go with people, but I can't. Wherever we go they want to eat or there's food and I get hungry . . . and if I eat there, I get sick." Of course, he has gone off his "diet" and has gotten sick. Most of the time he watches himself and drinks Maalox. He saw a doctor once 2 years ago and has been considering going again but, "I kept putting it off . . . because I got lazy . . . there were so many things. I've just been starting a new job and I didn't want to start taking off and not working, but this last attack was *too much*!" He then told how day after day the "boys at work" have been urging him to stop off with them for a few quick ones. He knew he shouldn't but he so wanted to fit in and so "It was with the boys and the other salesmen . . . I drank beer . . . I knew I was going to have more than one . . . and . . . *it* happened on the way home . . . ". Storming into his home, he asked his wife to make an appointment at the hospital, stating almost exasperatingly, "if you can't drink beer with friends, what the hell . . . ".

In these cases, the symptoms were relatively chronic. At the time of the decision there may have been an acute episode, but this was not the first such time the symptoms had reached such a "state" but rather it was the perception of them on this occasion as interfering with the social and interpersonal relations that was the trigger or final straw.

The third pattern, sanctioning, was the overwhelming favorite of the Irish. It is, however, not as well illustrated by dramatic examples, for it consists simply of one individual taking the primary responsibility for the decision to seek aid for someone else. For many weeks it looked as if one were seeing the submissive half of a dominant-submissive relationship. But within a period of 6 months, a husband and wife appeared at the clinics and each one assumed the role of sanctioning for the other.

Mr. and Mrs. O'Brien were both suffering from Myopia, both claimed difficulty in seeing, both had had their trouble for some period of time. The wife described her visit as follows: "Oh, as far as the symptoms were concerned, I'd be apt to let it go, but not my husband. He worries a lot, he wants things to be just so. Finally when my brother was better he (the husband) said to me: "Your worries about your brother are over so why can't you take care of your eyes now?" And so she did. Her husband, coming in several months later, followed the same pattern. He also considered himself somewhat resistant to being doctored. "I'm not in the habit of talking about aches and pains. My wife perhaps would say 'Go to the doctor,' but me, I'd like to see if things will work themselves out." How did he get here? It turns out that he was on vacation and he'd been meaning to take care of it, "Well I tend to let things go but not my wife, so on the first day of my vacation my wife said, 'Why don't you come, why don't you take care of it now?' So I did."

Thus in these cases both claimed a resistance to seeing a doctor, both claimed the other is more likely to take care of such problems, and yet both served as the pushing force to the other. Interestingly enough, the dramatic aspect of such cases was not shown in those who followed the general pattern, which was often fairly straightforward, but in those cases which did not. Two examples illustrate this. One was a woman with a thyroid condition, swelling on the side of the neck, who when asked why she came at this time blurted out almost in a shout, "Why did I come now? I've been walking around the house like this for several weeks now and nobody said anything so I *had to come myself*". Or the almost plaintive complaint of a veteran, kind of grumbling when asked why he came now, begrudged the fact that he had to make a decision himself with the statement, "Hmm, in the Navy they just take you to the doctor, you don't have to go yourself". It is not that these people are in any sense stoic, for it seemed that they were quite verbal and open about complaining but just that they did not want to take the responsibility on themselves.

There is a secondary pattern of the Irish, which turns out to be also the major pattern of the Anglo-Saxon group [14]. It was almost straight

out of the Protestant ethic namely a perceived interference with work or physical functioning. The word "perceived" is to be emphasized because the nature of the circumstances range from a single woman, 35 years old, who for the first time noted that the material which she was typing appeared blurred and thus felt that she had better take care of it, to a man with Multiple Sclerosis who despite falling down and losing his balance in many places, did nothing about it until he fell at work. Then he perceived that it might have some effect on his work and his ability to continue. The secondary Anglo-Saxon pattern is worth commenting on, for at first glance it appears to be one of the most rational modes of decision-making. It is one that most readers of this paper may well have used, namely the setting of external time criteria. "If it isn't better in 3 days, or 1 week, or 7 hours, or 6 months, then I'll take care of it". A variant on this theme involves the setting of a different kind of temporal standard —the recurrence of the phenomenon. A 19-year-old college sophomore reported the following:

> Well, it was this way. I went into this classroom and sat in the back of the room and when the professor started to write on the blackboard I noticed that the words were somewhat blurry. But I didn't think too much about it. A couple of weeks later, when I went back into that same classroom, I noted that it was blurry again. Well, once was bad, but twice that was too much.

Now given that his diagnosis was Myopia and that it was unconnected with any other disease, we know medically that his Myopia did not vary from one circumstance to another. This imposition of "a first time, second time that's too much" was of his doing and unrelated to any medical or physical reality.

By now the role that symptoms played in the decision to seek medical aid should be clearer. For our patients the symptoms were "really" there, but their perception differed considerably. There *is* a sense in which they sought help because they could not stand it any longer. But what they could not stand was more likely to be a situation or a perceived implication of a symptom rather than any worsening of the symptom *per se*.

I now would like to note some of the implications of this work. When speaking of implications, I ask your indulgence, for I refer not merely to what leads in a direct line from the data but some of the different thoughts and directions in which it leads me. What for example are the consequences for our very conception of etiology—conceptions based on assumptions about the representativeness of whom and what we study. We have claimed in this paper that the reason people get into medical treatment may well be related to some select social-psychological circumstances. If this is true, it makes all the more meaningful our earlier point about many unexplained epidemiological differences, for they may be due more to the differential occurrence of these social-psychological factors, factors of selectivity and attention which get people and their episodes into medical statistics rather than to any true

difference in the prevalence and incidence of a particular problem or disorder [15]. Our findings may also have implications for what one studies, particularly to the importance of stress in the etiology of so many complaints and disorders. For it may well be that the stress noted in these people's lives, at least those which they were able to verbalize, is the stress which brought them into the hospital or into seeking treatment (as was one of our main triggers) and not really a factor in the etiology or the exacerbation of the disorder.

Our work also has implications for treatment. So often we hear the terms "unmotivated, unreachable and resistance" applied to difficult cases. Yet we fail to realise that these terms may equally apply to us, the caretakers and health professionals who may not understand what the patient is saying or if we do, do not want to hear it. An example of this was seen in the way physicians in this study handled those patients for whose problem no organic basis could be found [16]. For despite the fact that there were no objective differences in the prevalence of emotional problems between our ethnic groups, the Italians were consistently diagnosed as having some psychological difficulty such as tension headaches, functional problems, personality disorder, etc.; whereas the Irish and Anglo-Saxon were consistently given what one might call a neutral diagnosis something that was either a Latinized term for their symptoms or simply the words "nothing found on tests" or "nothing wrong". Our explanation is somewhat as follows, namely that this situation is one of the most difficult for a physician and one in which he nevertheless feels he should make a differential diagnosis. Faced with this dilemma he focussed inordinately on *how* the Italians presented themselves—somewhat voluble, with many more symptoms, and somewhat dramatic social circumstances surrounding their decision to seek help. This labelling of the Italians is particularly interesting since as we mentioned above the Irish and Anglo-Saxons had similar psychological and social problems but presented them in a much more emotionally neutral and bland manner. There are no doubt other factors operating such as the greater social distance between the Italians and the medical staff, but that would constitute another paper.

One final remark as to treatment, again and again we found that where the physician paid little attention to the specific trigger which forced or which the individual used as an excuse to seek medical aid, there was the greatest likelihood of that patient eventually breaking off treatment. Another way of putting this is that without attention to this phenomenon the physician would have no opportunity to practice his healing art. Moreover, this problem of triggers etc. brooked no speciality nor particular type of disorder. So that being a specialist and only seeing certain kinds of problems did not exempt the physician from having to deal with this issue.

Such data alone supports those who urge more training in social and psychological sophistication for *any* physician who has contact with pa-

tients. With chronic illness making up the bulk of today's health problems it is obvious that the physicians cannot treat the etiological agent of disease and that the effect of specific therapies is rather limited. Nevertheless the physician may more intelligently intervene in the patient's efforts to cope with his disorder if he has the knowledge and awareness of the patient's views of health, sickness, his expectations and his reasons for seeking help.

This report has several different goals. To the social scientist we have tried to convey the somewhat amazing persistence of certain cultural characteristics which we in our cultural blindness have felt should have died and disappeared. The reason for their survival is that such behaviours may well be general modes of handling anxiety, sort of culturally prescribed defense mechanisms and probably transmitted from generation to generation in the way that much learning takes place, almost on an unconscious level. If this be true, then they constitute a group of behaviours which are much less likely to be changed as one wishes or attempts to become more American. Hopefully, the present research has also demonstrated the fruitfulness of an approach which does not take the definition of abnormality for granted. Despite its limitations our data seems sufficiently striking to invite further reason for re-examining our traditional and often rigid conceptions of health and illness, of normality and abnormality, of conformity and deviance. As we have contended in the early pages of this essay, symptoms or physical aberrations are so widespread that perhaps relatively few, and a biased selection at best come to the attention of official treatment agencies. We have thus tried to present evidence showing that the very labelling and definition of a bodily state as a symptom as well as the decision to do something about it is in itself part of a social process. If there is a selection and definitional process then focussing solely on reasons for deviation (the study of etiology) and the reasons for not seeking treatment (the study of delay) and ignoring what constitutes a deviation in the eyes of an individual and his reasons for action may obscure important aspects of our understanding and eventually our philosophy of the treatment and control of illness.

Finally, this is not meant to be an essay on the importance of sociological factors in disease, but rather the presentation of an approach to the study of health and illness. Rather than being a narrow and limited concept, health and illness are on the contrary empirically quite elastic. In short, it is not merely that health and illness has sociological aspects, for it has many aspects, but really that there is a sense in which health and illness *are* social phenomena. The implication of this perspective has perhaps been much better put by the Leightons (though quoted out of context):

> From this broad perspective there is no point in asking whether over the span of his adult life a particular individual should or should not be considered a medical case—everyone is a medical case. The significant question

becomes how severe a case, what kind of case [17].

I myself would add—how does one become a case and since of the many eligible, so few are chosen, what does it mean to be a case. In an era where every day produces new medical discoveries, such questions are all too easily ignored. The cure for all men's ills seems right over the next hill. Yet as Dubos has cogently reminded us [18], this vision is only a mirage and the sooner we realise it the better.

References

1. Koos, Earl L. *The Health of Regionville*, Columbia University Press, New York, 1954.
2. General summaries: Meigs, J. Wistar. Occupational medicine. *New Eng. J. Med.* **264**, 861, 1961; Siegel, Gordon S. *Periodic Health Examinations—Abstracts from the Literature*, Public Health Service Publication, No. 1010, U.S. Government Printing Office, Washington D.C., 1963.
3. See for example: Commission on Chronic Illness, *Chronic Illness in a Large City*, Harvard University Press, Cambridge, 1957; Pearse, Innes H. and Crocker, Lucy H. *The Peckham Experiment*, Allen & Unwin, London, 1954; *Biologists in Search of Material*, Interim Reports of the Work of the Pioneer Health Center, Faber & Faber, London, 1938.
4. Commission on Chronic Illness, *op. cit.*; Pearse and Crocker, *op. cit.*
5. Clute, Y. T. *The General Practitioner*, University of Toronto Press, Toronto, 1963, as well as many of the articles cited in Stoeckle, John D., Zola, Irving K. and Davidson, Gerald E. The quantity and significance

of psychological distress in medical patients. *J. Chron. Dis.* **17,** 959, 1964.

6. Unpublished data of the author and also Kosa, John, Alpert, Joel, Pickering, M. Ruth and Haggerty, Robert J. Crisis and family life: a re-examination of concepts. *The Wisconsin Sociologist* **4,** 11, 1965; Kosa, John, Alpert, Joel and Haggerty, Robert J. On the reliability of family health information. *Soc. Sci. & Med.* **1,** 165, 1967; Alpert, Joel, Kosa, John and Haggerty, Robert J. A month of illness and health care among low-income families. *Publ. Hlth Rep.* **82,** 705, 1967.

7. Blackwell, Barbara. The literature of delay in seeking medical care for chronic illnesses. *Hlth Educ. Monographs* No. 16, pp. 3–32, 1963; Kutner, Bernard, Makover, Henry B. and Oppenheim, Abraham. Delay in the diagnosis and treatment of cancer. *J. Chron. Dis.* **7,** 95, 1958; Kutner, Bernard and Gordon, Gerald. Seeking aid for cancer. *J. Hlth Hum. Behav.* **2,** 171, 1961.

8. Chapman, William P. and Jones, Chester M. Variations in cutaneous and visceral pain sensitivity in normal subjects. *J. Clin. Invest.* **23,** 81, 1944; Hardy, James D., Wolff, Harold G. and Goodell, Helen. *Pain Sensations and Reactions,* Williams & Wilkins, Baltimore, 1952; Melzack, Ronald. The perception of pain. *Scient. Am.* **204,** 41, 1961; Olin, Harry S. and Hackett, Thomas P. The denial of chest pain in 32 patients with acute myocardial infection. *J. Am. med. Ass.* **190,** 977, 1964.

9. Galdston, Iago. (editor) Salerno and the atom. In *Medicine in a Changing Society,* pp. 111–161. International Universities Press, New York, 1956.

10. Clausen, John A. and Radke Yarrow, Marian. The impact of mental illness on the family. *J. Soc. Iss.* **11,** 1, 1955.

11. Opler, Marvin K. *Culture, Psychiatry and Human Values,* Charles C. Thomas, Springfield, Illinois, 1956; Opler, Marvin K. (editor) *Culture and Mental Health,* MacMillan, New York, 1959.

12. All differences reported here are statistically significant. Given that there are no tabular presentations in this essay it may be helpful to remember that for the most part we are not stating that all or necessarily a majority of a particular group acted in the way depicted but that at very least, the response was significantly more peculiar to this group than to any other. Moreover, all the reported differences were sustained even when the diagnosed disorder for which they sought aid was held constant. For details on some of the statistical procedures as well as some of the methodological controls, see Zola, Irving K. Culture and symptoms, *op. cit.*

13. The findings re. symptoms are primarily a contrast between the Irish and the Italians. This is done because (1) there is a sense in which ethnicity in Boston is a much more "real" phenomenon to the Irish and the Italians than to our Anglo-Saxon Protestant, (2) these two groups are more purely "ethnic" and constitute a fairer comparison being of similar generation, education, and socioeconomic status, and (3) the differences are frankly much more dramatic and clearly drawn. If you wish to picture where the Anglo-Saxons might be in these comparisons, think of them as mid-way between the Irish and Italian responses, if anything, a little closer to the Irish. Some further discussion of this issue is found both in Zola, Irving K.,

Culture and symptom and Illness behavior . . ., *op. cit.*

14. As we have argued elsewhere (Zola, Irving K. Illness behavior . . ., *op. cit.*) this and the following pattern are also characteristic of more middle-class and more highly educated groups.

15. Mechanic, David and Volkart, Edmund H. Illness behavior and medical diagnosis. *J. Hlth Hum. Behav.* **1,** 86, 1960.

16. Detailed in Zola, Irving K. Problems of communication . . .*op. cit.*

17. Leighton, Dorothea C., Harding, John S., Macklin, David B., MacMillam, Allister H. and Leighton, Alexander H. *The Character of Danger*, pp. 135–136. Basic Books, New York, 1963.

18. Dubos, Rene. *Mirage of Health*, Anchor, Garden City, New York 1961; Dubos, Rene. *Man Adapting*, Yale, New Haven, Conn., 1965.

15   THE PATIENT'S VIEW

David Armstrong

In 1935, in the 10th edition of his teaching manual *Clinical Methods*, Sir Robert Hutchison provided details of how to go about "case-taking' [1]. "The 'taking' of any case", he pointed out, "consists of two parts: I. The interrogation of the patient. II. The physical examination". He further subdivided the former into the general and the special interrogation, prefaced with some advice on the purpose and techniques of interrogation.

The purpose of the interrogation was "to elicit information regarding (the patient's) present illness and the state of his previous health and that of his family". Although the interrogation was directed by the doctor, the patient was to be "allowed as far as possible, to tell his story in his own words". Leading questions, which might force an opinion on the patient, were strictly forbidden as was asking the same question twice (which only made the doctor look foolish).

The general interrogation itself involved establishing the patient's name, age, occupation, whether single or married and exact postal address before the two crucial questions, "Of what does he compain?" and "How long have the symptoms been present?" were asked. The answers to these were supplemented by a 'family history' on the state of health and cause of death of family members, a 'personal history'— 'what together may be grouped together as the patients environment or surroundings or habits'—and the patient's 'previous history', which was to be enquired after indirectly except for syphilis.

It is, of course, quite possible that by 1935 this particular approach to 'case-taking' had become quite dated but, in as much as the preceding editions of the book (first published

SOURCE: Reprinted with permission from *Social Science and Medicine* 18: 737–744, Copyright © 1984, Pergamon Journals, Ltd.

in 1897) covered similar ground, it is probably fair to say that these techniques elicited what might be described as a patient's view in the earlier decades of this century. In countless meetings between doctors and patients up and down the country, patients were constantly invited to report on their complaint, its longevity and its immediate context.

Some 40 years later, in 1975, the 16th edition of Hutchison's *Clinical Methods* was published under new editors [2]. 'Case-taking' was not mentioned, except in the chapter title, and in its place the student was advised on how to 'take a history'. At the same time it was never suggested that history-taking was other than a constant feature of clinical practice. "History-taking is still an art", it was explained, and it was "*a special form of the art of communication. It is necessarily a two-way business*". Indeed it was even suggested that history-taking might be improved by "active participation in sensitivity groups as pioneered by, (the GP-psychoanalyst), Balint".

In 1975, as in 1935, the patient was invited to speak while the doctor learned; but it is clear that between these two dates the form of the invitation had changed. Did the reformulated exhortation to speak have an effect on the words that were spoken? Did the newer methods more accurately establish the patient's view? Such questions are undoubtedly important for a concerned social science or an enlightened medical practice but they are misplaced. What changed between 1935 and 1975 was not simply the form of the incitement to speech but the very structure of perception: it was not what the patient said but what the doctor heard which established the reality (and accuracy) of the patient's view.

The Clinical Gaze

In his seminal work, *The Birth of the Clinic*, Michel Foucault identifies a major shift in medical perception, or what he calls the medical gaze, as occurring at the end of the 18th century [3]. In its old form "clinical reading implied an external, deciphering subject, which . . . ordered and defined kinships". This medical gaze had been directed upon the two-dimensional areas of tissues and symptoms. In its new form, however, the gaze had to map the three-dimensional volume of the human body because disease was seen to have a specific anatomical location: "Disease is no longer a bundle of characters disseminated here and there over the surface of the body . . .; it is a set of forms and accidents . . . bound together in a sequence according to a geography that can be followed step by step. It is no longer a pathological species inserting itself into the body . . . it is the body itself that has become ill" [4].

It was at this point that the now familiar techniques of clinical examination were embedded into medical practice. The clinician had to map the volume of the body by use of ear, touch and sight so as to localise and identify the pathological lesion which was inserted therein. Under the old medicine "signs and symptoms are and say the same thing . . . every symptom was a potential sign and the sign was simply a read symptom" [5]. In the new perception sign and symptom were separated: the symptom might well remain silent, the truth of the disease was contained only in what the doctor found, in the form of the sign. Symptoms, what the patient said, could provide a guide or a hint or a suspicion of which organ or system might be involved but were only preliminaries; the core task of medicine became not the elucidation of what the patient said but what the doctor saw in the depths of the body.

The teaching manuals which were published early in the 20th century reflected the dominance of signs in medical diagnosis. Stevens' *Medical Diagnosis* of 1910 offered 3 pages out of 1500 to the 'interrogation of the patient' [6]. Cabot's *Physical Diagnosis*, from its first edition in 1905 until its 12th in 1938, ignored even a token statement on interrogating the patient, concentrating entirely on the physical examination [7]. Emerson's *Physical Diagnosis* of 1928 could only manage a one page outline of advice on the lay-out of the consultation room as a preliminary to the details of the examination [8].

In the various texts which offered advice on interrogating the patient the format was almost identical. The patient's age, sex, occupation, address and marital status were noted before asking about the main complaint and its duration. This was followed by questions on the patient's previous medical history, family medical history and the so-called 'personal history' which tended to be restricted to health hazards of the occupation, past residence abroad and 'habits' such as consumption of tea, alcohol and tobacco. It is clear that the patient—construed as a 'whole person' [9]—was virtually absent from the advice on how to conduct clinical practice; indeed as the body of the patient was seen as co-terminous with the space of the illness [10] it was impossible to conceptualise the patient and lesion as separable. In effect as the lesion could not communicate in words, the patient's identity in the interrogation was provided by the ability to speak for the otherwise silent pathology. The lesion spoke through the patient, though it only finally yield its secret in the physical examination.

To provoke the lesion to speech, through the patient, was not an easy task. Indeed Keith, in his *Clinical Case-Taking* of 1918, while offering a schema for case-taking, pointed out that it was exceedingly difficult to reduce the skill of interrogatory method to print [11]. Perhaps the commonest advice was that the patient should be allowed to tell his story in his own words when it came to identifying the main complaint. Yet this did not signify the existence of a patient identity or measuring system independent of the lesion; the patient's own words were only required because they might express in purest form the communication of the pathological lesion itself. Such was the importance of these words that it was recommended that they were written down verbatim: "notes," advised Gibson and Collier in 1927, "should be made during this recitation" [12].

The patient's 'own words', however, were not necessarily free from background distortion; as Horder and Gow observed "this does not mean that the observer is to set down words or phrases which are meaningless or equivocal" [13]. Indeed an additional question was justified if the patient "tends to stray into irrelevant matters" [14]. If the 'patient' was the intermediary who stood between the disease and the medical gaze then the doctor, of necessity, had to look behind the words the patient spoke. Some common words such as the patient's ready-made diagnosis were never to be taken at face value [15]; others were only thought to be accessible by being 'dug up' from the patient's unconscious [16]; others were to be postponed "if the history is completely disjointed or the patient be well set for a three hour monologue" [17].

The patient as an idiosyncratic person was not entirely absent from this dialogue between doctor and disease. The doctor could recognise in patients different abilities to enunciate the lesion's truth: as Bourne noted in 1931 "The human being is a recording instrument of uncertain and variable power" [18]. Thus the doctor had to assess the competence of the patient to speak for the pathology. "As the patient describes his complaint," Gibson and Collier explained, "his mentality will become clearer, whether he is intelligent or dull, accurate or given to exaggeration, if his memory is good, or if there is evidence of mental aberration" [19]. Noble Chamberlain suggested that the interrogator should be alert to these possibilities and formulate specific questions for each patient's intelligence [20] while

Hutchison went so far as to advocate leading questions for patients "stupid either by nature or as the result of symptoms" [21].

The general proscription of leading questions in these texts gives a further indication of the limited identity accorded the patient. Hutchison only allowed them for stupid patients, to trap malingerers and to elicit subjective symptoms ("the morbid sensations experienced by a patient as the result of the disease of some organ or system") when the doctor felt he was engaging the pathology in dialogue [22]. In other circumstances leading questions were dangerous because of the 'suggestibility of many patients' [23]. If they were used, Horder and Gow argued, then a record of their use should be kept and the patient's reply appropriately qualified [24]. In effect patients had no independent views or autonomy, they spoke on behalf of the pathology and, without precautions, simply reflected back the leading question.

At the beginning of this century the patient's view was, in essence, the unformed words of the disease. The interrogation was concerned with "the characteristics and 'life history' of the symptom. . . . To get a clear picture of the symptom so that it stands out as if it had a personality is the ideal to be sought for" [25]. Beyond the disease, the patient only had existence as a good, bad or indifferent historian.

An Inchoate Patient

In the 12th edition of his *Physical Diagnosis*, published in 1938, Cabot made two additions: he introduced a new first chapter on history-taking ("a subject too often omitted from books on diagnosis") where before there had been none, and his chapter on the examination of the diseases of the nervous system for the first time included a two page discussion of the neuroses and the psychoses [26]. Similarly the 8th edition of Elmer and Rose's *Physical Diagnosis* (revised by Walker) of 1940 added a chapter on history taking and a few pages on psychiatric examination despite their total lack in the 1938 edition [27].

There had been a hint in Bourne's *An Introduction to Medical History and Case-Taking* of 1931 that the history was beginning to change its alignment in the cognitive map of medicine [28]. He noted, for example, that "history-taking receives scant attention in other detailed books on physical examination." In addition, he offered a discussion of the relative importance of history and physical examination and concluded that their importance in diagnosis or prognosis varied greatly with different diseases. Although his advice on history-taking followed familiar lines his attempt to compare history and examination represented a fundamental challenge to the old cognitive ordering of medicine. This challenge was furthered in Noble Chamberlain's text of 1938 which offered the observation that "structural changes may exist without functional derangement and vice-versa." In other words the lesion might be unmarked by the sign so that the patient's words were not merely preliminaries but a primary access route to the lesion—hence his statement on 'the importance of history-taking' [29].

This new analysis of disease and its indicators was characterised by a reassessment both of the patient's view and of the importance of psychiatric illness. In 1940, Elmer and Rose had extended their list of patient questions by elaborating on the old 'personal history' [30]. In the new schema, personal history—which had been more concerned with the patient's physical environment and habits—was replaced by a marital history ("domestic relationship, whether happy or unhappy, compatible or incompatible and the reasons for unpleasant relations, if they exist"), an occupational history and a social history, which enquired after such personal experiences as worries, adjustments and disappointments.

While Noble Chamberlain did not significantly alter his history-taking plan until the 6th edition of his book in 1957 when 'The home life' was introduced ("Is the patient happy and contented or are there sources of friction or worry?"), the 1938 edition did suggest a new goal for the history [31]. Whereas Horder and Gow in 1928 had "in the main . . . followed the well-proven principle of endeavouring to determine first the site of a lesion and then its probable nature" [32], some 10 years later Noble Chamberlain was suggesting that at the end of the history the physician should have "a mental picture not only of the patient's presenting symptoms, but of the manner in which these developed and the type of background of personal and family life upon which they have been grafted. Too often we are rightly accused of studying the disease rather than the patient".

In similar fashion, the 12th edition of Hutchison's *Clinical Methods* of 1949 extended the interrogation of the patient [33]. In this case the patient's personal history was replaced by a social history "which includes the patient's mental attitudes to his life and work. . . . One should endeavour to visualise the life of one's patient, sharing his emotions and viewing step by step his daily habits. . . . Sometimes one should inquire into a patient's business affairs, his ambitions, anxieties, quarrels . . . his domestic relationships, his psychological make-up, his interests, his hobbies, his hopes, his fears. . . ."

The second element in the reconstruction of the patient's view was the changes which were occurring within the field of psychological medicine. During the 1920s and 1930s the medical gaze had been focusing on 'the mind of everyone' [34]. In the 19th century when rationality had seemed all-important psychiatry was concerned with those patients, few in number, who were insane. During the 20th century the central problem of mental functioning had become 'coping' and medicine had discovered the generalised prevalence of the neuroses—particularly anxiety and depression. By the 1930s many doctor were well aware of the ubiquity of the neuroses and the need for a general mental hygiene. In consequence patient anxieties and personalities together with notions of psycho-somatic unity began to become important features of much clinical practice. These concerns made themselves felt in the gradual inclusion in manuals on clinical methods of sections on psychiatric examination. Noble Chamberlain, for example, first included a section on 'the diagnosis of the neuroses' in his chapter on the examination of the nervous system in 1938 though it was somewhat rudimentary [35]. He outlined the symptoms of the neuroses (hypochondria, neurasthenia, anxiety neuroses, compulsion neuroses and hysteria) but devoted most attention to the appropriate physical signs; in hysterics he noted, the earlobes were ill-formed and were fused to the skin near the mastoid process instead of hanging freely.

By about 1950 the old medical gaze seemed to be in a state of transition [36]. An important component of disease still existed within the human body and this, as of old, demanded interrogation through the patient. But there was now a second stand to medical perception which identified a part of illness as existing in the shifting social spaces between bodies, and clinical method required techniques to map and monitor this space. The patient's view was no longer a vicarious gaze to the silent pathology within the body but the precise technique by which the new space of disease could be established: illness was being transformed from what was visible to what was heard.

The patient's view was not, in this sense, a discovery or the product of some humanistic enlightenment. It was a technique demanded by medicine to illuminate the dark spaces of the mind and social relationships. Whereas the pathological lesion could be seen if it was given a neutral field, the illness of social spaces required the incitement of a patient's view. At first the patient's view was a fragile flower which had to be gently cultivated: as Hutchison noted in his 1949 edition "one may defeat one's own ends by wounding the sentiments or conscience of the patient long before the physical examination starts" [37]. Later it was to move to the centre of the medical gaze.

Patient Surveys

In 1954 Earl Koos published a book entitled *The Health of Regionsville: What the People Thought and Did about It* which was hailed as "the first systematic explanation of what people think and why they behave as they do in regards to health" [38]. Koos and his colleagues interviewed more than 500 families over a 4 year period in an American town which they gave the name Regionsville. Respondents received some 16 interviews, each one with a different focus. For their views on illness patients were provided with a checklist of 17 'readily recognisable symptoms' and asked which they thought should be brought to the attention of the doctor. Those who reported no disabling illness in the previous 12 months were also asked whether they had experienced any of the symptoms from the list. In addition respondents were provided with a series of questions on some suggested disadvantages of a national health insurance programme (such as 'People would take advantage of the doctor's time' or 'Medical care would be impersonal') and asked whether they disagreed or not.

Most of the Regionsville inter-views were concerned with use of services and the sub-title of the book 'what the people thought and did about it' perhaps overstates the extent to which people's thoughts were elicited. Nevertheless the analysis of 'what the people thought' marked the beginning of an increasing interest in the patient's view by medical sociology during the ensuing decades which almost exactly paralleled the growth of the requirement for an "extended history" in medicine. Whether medicine or the human sciences had priority in this new 'discovery' of the patient's view is unimportant. The fact that investigation of the patient's view was conducted in parallel by two or more distinct disciplines simply shows the irrelevance of traditional disciplinary boundaries for structures of perception. After the War the 'medical gaze' was no longer an analytic framework employed almost exclusively by medicine but embraced a series of disciplines, many new, which, by way of comprehensive health care delivery, the health care team and socio-medical research sought to analyze a new configuration of disease and illness with a variety of refined techniques.

Under the old structure of perception illness had been located to a specific point inside the body of an individual patient; in the new regime illness became distributed in the gap between bodies, in the interstices of the social, in the space which was to become known as the community. The extended medical gaze therefore required the mapping of this social space just as a century and more earlier the medical gaze had mapped the three-dimensional depths of the human body by the techniques of physical examination so as to locate the pathological lesion.

There had been rudimentary attempts in the the inter-war years to map morbidity in the community, such as the Pioneer Health Centre at Peckham, but it was not until the war-time Social Survey, which involved asking a random population sample about prevalence of symptoms, that more refined techniques were developed [39]. In the immediate post-war years, surveys within a range of medical specialties—paediatrics, general practice, psychiatry, geriatrics, social medicine—become relatively commonplace. Surveys such as those by Koos in 1954, Wadsworth *et al.* in 1971, Dunnell and Cartwright in 1972, Banks *et al.* in 1975 and Hannay in 1979 represent some of the social scientists' contributions to the mapping of symptom prevalence and the patient's view in the community [40].

A concomitant of the spread of morbidity surveys in the post-war years was the redefinition of the patient. Under the old regime the patient was no more and no less than the body which enclosed the lesion. The surveys on the other hand embraced everyone, and found that almost all experienced 'physical' symptoms or that most were mentally ill. The concept of the 'clinical iceberg' which described those under health care as only the tip of an enormous mass of morbidity in the community was first advanced in 1963 and was confirmed and reconfirmed in subsequent studies [41].

The conceptual and methodological correlation between the patient's views and the lesion began to fragment as a new referrent, the social, made its appearance.

Social Framework

The survey destroyed the old distinction between ill and healthy bodies by generating a new form of patienthood, namely the person 'at risk' (as well as a commensurate discourse on medicalisation which attempted a critical analysis of this process [42]). But if the survey could not measure the diseased body through identification of the lesion then it required other concepts of health and illness. Koos in his survey of 1954 had made an initial attempt to obtain a measure of illness through the use of the social body as a referrent. Other attempts followed. In 1960 Mechanic and Volkart studied the propensity to visit the doctor by providing 614 college students with a checklist of symptoms and asking them whether they would take them to the university health service ('certainly, probably, not very likely or very likely') if they had them [43]. In the same year Apple's description of 'how laymen define illness' involved giving 60 respondents eight descriptions of people with health problems and asking 'Are these people sick?', 'What might the illness be?' and 'What should be done about it?' By varying the degree of ambiguity and time of onset of the problem Apple was able to show the significance of various aspects of an illness for promoting patient action [44].

Similarly in 1961 Baumann invited 201 patients (and 262 medical students, acting as controls) to answer the question 'What do you think most people mean when they say they are in very good physical condition?' The replies were subjected to content analysis' to establish three elements: general feeling of well-being, absence of general or specific symptoms of illness and what a fit person would be able to do [45].

While at one level these studies attempted to obtain a new definition of health through patient views, in terms of the new configuration of illness it had already been decided. Illness was constituted by those experiences judged serious enough to warrant seeking formal medical advice. Illness was not defined by a lesion so much as by a certain behaviour pattern.

A further element in the new regime were the analytic frameworks which were deployed to interrogate illness. In his study, Koos established a checklist to determine differences between respondents: some people said they would report a loss of appetite or persistent headaches to the doctor while others would not. Yet although individual responses were noted—to the extent of providing some case-histories in the text—the analytic frame used to make sense of the data was social class. Supposed individual differences were not individual but had a meaning only within a particular social context which presumably informed them. In effect, Koos did not hear individual respondents in his interviews—no more than the old doctor saw different pathologies in a dozen patients with gastric ulcer. Social class was accessed through the patient's view and conversely the patient's view was a product of social class. Whereas before, illness had been located in the solid three-dimensional space of the human body, in the post-war years it began to be realigned in a multi-dimensional conceptual space whose axes were the psycho-social determinants of attitudes, beliefs and behaviour and which could only be monitored by constant elicitation of the patient's view.

If disease was increasingly located within a social space it was matched by the growth of psycho-social models of causation. Social class became seen as a major determinant of ill-health and of patient behaviour. Stress, despite the paucity of empirical support, became the great hope of a socio-medical gaze (as did its 'antidote' of social support) from the 1950s onwards [46]. And not only did psycho-social factors play a direct aetiological role but via a discourse on labelling and stigma from the early 1960s the illness state was held to arise at times without any physical mediation [47].

Under the old regime treatment success was evaluated by the disappearance of signs. In the new, the patient's attitudes were important. In 1947, for example, Dukes carried out the first survey of patients with permanent colostomy to see how they coped [48]. His object was to examine patient response in the light of the operative technique as otherwise, he noted, there was no other means of establishing which was the best technique. Some 5 years later however two papers had appeared which, though conducting similar surveys, had different objectives [49]. As Sutherland noted: "In the recent past, interest has extended from the colostomy to the problem of living created by it and the methods by which the patient solves those problems" [50]. In effect the patient's view, from being a measure of effectiveness, was moving to be a problem in its own right.

In similar fashion some of the earlier sociology surveys were concerned with patient satisfaction as measures of medical effectiveness. Freidson, in 1961, in his *Patient's Views of Medical Practice* contended that "performance of staff could not be understood very clearly without reference to the expectations of patients" [51] while Cartwright in her large survey of patient attitudes to hospital care of 1964 observed that "the successful application of medical knowledge depends on what patients think and feel about doctors, nurses and hospitals" [52].

The reconstruction of patient's views, from being a measure of medical effectiveness, to become the location of a major problem in its own right—through the notions of 'coping' and 'adjustment'—began to take effect from the late 1960s, though its beginnings can be identified in the extension of psychological medicine in the immediate post-war years. The 'open door' policy of the 1950s marked the symbolic end of the segregation of the insane and their final eclipse by the more generalised problem of the neuroses. Large American community studies of psychiatric morbidity such as the

Midtown Manhattan and Sterling County studies identified upwards of 60% of the population as being mentally ill—with the remainder having many transient psychological disturbances [53]. Further research found that between 30 and 90% of so-called 'organic' complaints had a psychiatric component [54].

Psychiatric examination, as has been noted above, gradually found its way into the clinical method texts. At first it was simply an extension of the neurological examination to embrace a perfunctory psychiatric overview as in Noble Chamberlain's inter-war treatment [55]. By the 5th edition of his text in 1952 he offered a more sophisticated analysis: "Something more is required to establish this diagnosis (of the neuroses). It is necessary to assess the patients personality, a task which comes more easily with age". By 1967 the formal schema for conducting history taking and clinical examination—for all patients—included a section of taking the psychiatric history and, in 1974, the introductory chapter titled 'The foundations of our art', which provided a potted history of the diagnostic process, was amended with a new paragraph on Freud and Jung.

A New Map

In the 7th edition of his teaching manual published in 1961 Noble Chamberlain added a new section and diagram in an attempt to show the complex relationship between signs and symptoms. For some diseases in different stages of their development he acknowledged that symptoms could be more important than signs. This reassessment of the significance of symptoms had been growing since the war. In the foreword for Seward's *Bedside Diagnosis* of 1949 Cohen poured derision on the student who diagnosed by structural resemblances [56]. Instead, Cohen claimed that disease was "a disturbance of function which may or may not be accomplished by structural changes", the traditional mind-body dichotomy was 'largely artificial' and both psychosomatic disturbance and somatopsychic dysfunction were real phenomena.

Perhaps one of the most successful attempts at a new integrated medicine was that of Balint in the mid-1950s [57]. He reconstructed the field of medicine by arguing that the traditional search for a localised pathological lesion was only a part —and often a small part—of clinical practice. The role of the doctor, he suggested, was to organise unorganised illness: the doctor had to reorganise the patient's problems, symptoms and worries so as to make sense of them. This might require symptoms being linked with pathological lesions in the classical triangulation method but it also required the construction of a dense web of interconnections between feelings, symptoms and social context such that the lesion was reduced to a single nodal point within a network of more abstact relationships.

This reconstruction had various implications for the patient's view. First, it established a series of different needs which required expression. Thus for example, in her study of patients and their GPs published in 1967 Cartwright could think of the effectiveness of general practice in terms of meeting patient's clinical, social and emotional needs [58]. Second, the patient's view was not only a part of the diagnostic process but also part of the therapeutic. At the very least, patient talk helped adjustment through the organisation of problems while, as a form of psychotherapy, it acted as a more formal treatment regime.

In this new theoretical context the patient's view in the consultation underwent further changes. In the inter-war years the patient's view on anything, including the possible diagnosis, not directly related to the lesion was excluded; thirty years later it had changed. "Patience is necessary", suggested Noble Chamberlain in 1967, "when the patient tries to make his own diagnosis. This may be irritating but not unreasonable as it stems from a natural desire to find a cause for the illness which perhaps can be avoided in future . . ." [59]. A decade later it was not simply tolerance which was required as it was possible, suggested Kleinman and his colleagues, that the patient's views—which were so coherent as to form 'lay theories' —could be valuable diagnostic and therapeutic tools [60]. A flurry of work in the early 1980s on patient's 'lay theories' and of their importance for a penetrating medical gaze, was further evidence of the elevation of the patient's view from an irrelevance to a theory [6]. The patient's view had been elicited in the interrogation; in the post-war years a less threatening term, 'history-taking', became more common while in many recent texts the even more secular 'medical interview' has been employed. "Clinicians are likely to consider the term 'medical interview' as synonymous with which is called history-taking" wrote Enelow and Swisher in 1972 [62]. "The medical interview is much broader than that."

The medical gaze had engaged with a new problem: the patient's view itself. The patient's words were therefore more robust and the dangers of leading questions were minimised; by and large they should not be used but "the student may observe an experienced clinician will sometimes disregard this rule" [63]. Whereas before, the patient's words which did not signify the lesion were dismissed as irrelevant or suspected of representing malingering, the new advice was that it was "important to realise that apparent evasiveness on the part of the patient is almost never deliberate" [64]. The doctor's first task was "to listen and to observe, not only to obtain information about the current problem but also to understand the patient as a person" [65].

It rapidly became apparent however that the patient's view was not constituted simply by the words themselves as words were merely signifiers. The 'view' lay behind the words and further refinement of technique was necessary to make it accessible. At first, in the 1960s and 1970s, it was through non-verbal communication: "the eyes sometimes convey more information than words; the clenched fist may demonstrate latent tension, and touch may be equally important" [66]. By the late 1970s the gaze beyond that which was spoken, began to focus with more intensity on the subjectivity behind the words.

Pain had been the archetypal symptom, the direct record of a lesion based on 'stimulation of sensory nerve endings'; some reassessment of this view had occurred in the early 1960s with the increasing importance ascribed 'central processing' in the perception of pain [67], and by the late 1970s McLeod suggested that pain was a 'purely subjective complaint' and that, moreover, "Its subjective nature is such that it is only through personal experience of pain that a doctor can have insight into the meaning of the descriptions given by patients" [68]. This reliance on self-experience to grasp the meaning of symptoms was also found in a book published in 1977 of sociologists' accounts of their own illnesses [69]. The authors criticised previous sociological studies of illness as being "too formal, objectified, detached and scientifically rigorous . . . each illness experience and encounter with organised care is unique"; the only means of transcending the interpretation of meanings, of achieving authenticity, was to observe not the illness of others but the illness of self. The patient's view, caught in a dense web of subjectivity, was becoming a reflection, another manifestation even, of the self-view.

It was therefore no longer possible to distinguish separate realms of experience for doctor and patient. The meeting between doctor and patient was not between an enquiring gaze and a passive object but an interaction between two subjects. In many ways the notion of a doctor-patient relationship failed to capture the essentially contingent and precarious scenario contained within the term doctor-patient interaction [70]. The patient's view and the doctor's view were shadows of each other. On the medical side Browne and Freeling likened the interaction to a game (drawing on transactional analysis) [71] while, in the same year, from the sociological side, Wadsworth and his colleagues set out "to investigate the rules, routines and procedures that doctors and patients use to organise consultations" [72]. Perhaps McLeod, in his *Clinical Examination* of 1976 spoke for both sides when he wrote: "In addition to the patient's response to his problem the interactions between the patient and the doctor have also to be considered. This relationship is very complex as a result of the interplay between different personalities in potentially unstable situations" [73]. The claim of Locker, in his 1981 study of patients' interpretation of symptoms, that "illness is a social phenomenon constituted by the meanings actors will employ to make sense of observed or experienced events" could be applied to either patient or doctor [74].

The doctor's opening question "What is your complaint?" was replaced by "Now please tell me your trouble" [75]. Illness, which had been constituted by the lesion deep in the body, was transformed into idiosyncratic meanings of the patient's (and doctor's) biographical space.

Codes of Perception

What then is the patient's view? When is it that the patient says? The problem is one of perception, of the difference between hearing and saying. The patient's view cannot described or isolated simply as what is said, fundamentally the patient's view is bound up with what is heard. In this sense the patient's view is an artefact of socio-medical perception.

In his discussion of the massive changes which occurred in medicine at the end of the 18th century, Foucault argues that it was neither the conception of disease nor the signs which indicated its presence which were changed first; both field and gaze were bound together by *codes of knowledge* [76]. Thus the developments of the late 18th century were not the product of enlightenment, of better methods, of finer perceptions: "new objections were to present themselves to the medical gaze in the sense that, and at the same time as, the knowing subject reorganises himself, changes himself, and begins to function in a new way".

In similar fashion the relationship between the patient's view (in its various forms, both verbal and non-verbal) and its interrogation constitute a field and a gaze, and the two are bound together by a new code of knowledge. This paper has emphasised the role of the gaze in constituting a field, but the field, in the form of what the patient says, nevertheless confirms and consolidates of gaze. A medical interrogation, for example, which probes for patient feelings and relationships cannot function if the space it examines is constituted by specific physical items of patient morbidity [77]. In this sense field and gaze are mutually self-supporting.

This paper has examined aspects of the medico-social analysis of a common space which establishes for these sciences the reality of the patient's view. It is still possible however that there are in modern society alternative structures of perception which might apprehend a different reality. Insofar as the social sciences are concerned, this paper has suggested that claims for an analysis of the patient's position which transcend medical understanding are unfounded. So what of other less formalised techniques of hearing? Can lay cultures, the social network, the popular novel hear what sociomedical perception cannot grasp? Is there a form of experience and expression which escapes the confines of medicalised illness? In part this is an empirical question; but it also raises the question of whether patienthood can exist in spaces other than those traversed by medical perception.

At each historical point medical analysis has an object and an effect: the object is the patient's view (in its contemporary form) and the effect is the 'person' who holds those views. When the doctor searched for pathological lesions, the view was the symptom and the patient was both receptacle for pathology and unreliable translator; when the doctor acknowledged the importance of the emotions in his search for illness,

the view was both the symptom and the feeling, and the patient was an emotional and somewhat less than perfect setting for pathology; when the doctor enquired of patient meanings, the view became the lay theory and the patient a subjective being.

This does not mean that the discourse which is the vehicle for this new perception necessarily has immediate or real effects on clinical practice. Despite the widespread endorsement of an extended patient's view in the literature reviewed above, most clinical practice today—particularly hospital-based —probably relies on an older scheme of interpretation. There are of course tensions between a perception and a practice, some due to a cohort effect as older clinicians (and processibly older patients too) reject the new methods, others due to a more fundamental conflict between levels of theory and of experience. Nevertheless the 'conditions of possibility' for an extended patient's view, whatever its empirical support, have begun to occur over the last few decades and this of itself (besides its ramifications into patient representation, community politics, patient's rights, and so on) signifies a change in the status of patienthood.

References

1. Hutchison R. and Rainy H. *Clinical Methods*, 10th Edition. Cassel, London, 1935.
2. Mason S. and Swash M. *Hutchison's Clinical Methods*, 17th Edition. Bailliere Tindall, London, 1975.

3. Foucault M. *The Birth of the Clinic: An Archeology of Medical Perception*. Tavistock, London, 1963.
4. *Ibid.*, p. 136.
5. *Ibid.*, pp. 93 and 159.
6. Stevens W. M. *Medical Diagnosis*. H. K. Lewis, London, 1910.
7. Cabot R. C. *Physical Diagnosis*. Bailliere Tindall, London, 1905.
8. Emerson C. P. *Physical Diagnosis*. Lippincott, Philadelphia, 1928.
9. The notion of the 'whole patient' is, of course, a modern view though the expression makes one of its earliest appearances in the medical literature of the 1930s when the transitions discussed in this paper commence. Brackenbury H. *Patient and Doctor*. Hodder & Stoughton, London, 1935.
10. Foucault M. *op. cit.*, p. 3.
11. Keith R. D. *Clinical Case-Taking: An Introduction to Elementary Clinical Medicine*. H. K. Lewis, London, 1918.
12. Gibson A. G. and Collier W. T. *The Methods of Clinical Diagnosis*. Edward Arnold, London, 1927.
13. Horder T. and Gow A. E. *The Essentials of Medical Diagnosis*, Cassel, London, 1928.
14. Gibson A. G. and Collier W. T. *op. cit.*
15. Horder T. and Gow A. E. *op. cit.*
16. Bourne G. *An Introduction to Medical History and Case-Taking*, Livingstone, Edinburgh, 1931.
17. Simpson S. L. *Medical Diagnosis: Some Clinical Aspects*. H. K. Lewis, London, 1937.
18. Bourne G. *op. cit.*
19. Gibson A. G. and Collier W. T. *op. cit.*
20. Noble Chamberlain E. *Symptoms and Signs in Clinical Medicine*, 2nd Edition. Wright, Bristol, 1938.
21. Hutchison R. and Rainy H. *op. cit.*
22. *Ibid.*
23. Simpson S. L. *op. cit.*
24. Horder T. and Gow A. E. *op. cit.*
25. Stern N. S. *Clinical Diagnosis: Physical and Differential*. Macmillan, New York, 1933.
26. Cabot R. C. *op. cit.*, 12th Edition, 1938.
27. Elmer W. P. and Rose W. D. *Physical Diagnosis*, 8th Edition, revised by Walker H. Henry Kimpton, London, 1940.
28. Bourne G. *op. cit.* This new analysis of the history and symptoms is also reflected in their frequent inclusion in the book titles during the 1930s. See Bourne G. *op. cit.*; Noble Chamberlain E. *op. cit.*; McDowall R. J. S. *The Science of Signs and Symptoms*. Heinemann, London, 1931. Symptoms were also being analyzed physiologically within the new 'clinical science' movement at this time: Lewis T. The Harveian Oration on clinical science. *Br. Med. J.* **2**, 720, 1933.
29. Noble Chamberlain E. *op. cit.*
30. Elmer W. P. and Rose W. D. *op. cit.*
31. Noble Chamberlain E. *op. cit.*
32. Horder T. and Gow A. E. *op. cit.*
33. Hutchison R. and Hunter D. *op. cit.*, 12th Edition, 1949.
34. This argument is developed further in Armstrong D. *Political Anatomy of the Body: Medical Knowledge in Britain in the 20th Century*, Chap. 3. Cambridge University Press, Cambridge, 1983.
35. Noble Chamberlain E. *op. cit.*
36. Armstrong D. *op. cit.*; see also Arney W. R. and Bergen B. *Medicine and the Management of Living*. Chicago University Press. In press; they date the revolution from about 1950.
37. Hutchison R. and Hunter D. *op. cit.*
38. Koos E. L. *The Health of Regionsville: What the People Thought and Did about It*. Hafner, New York, 1954. As a 'classic' it was reprinted in 1967.
39. Pearse I. H. and Crocker L. H. *The Peckham Experiment*. Allen & Unwin, London, 1943; Box K. and Thomas

G. The war-time social survey. *J. R. Statist. Soc.* **107,** 151, 1944.

40. Koos E. L. *op. cit.;* Wadsworth M. *et al. Health and Sickness: The Choice of Treatment.* Tavistock, London, 1971; Dunnell K. and Cartwright A. *Medicine Takers, Prescribers and Hoarders.* Routledge & Kegan Paul, London, 1972; Banks M. *et al.* Factors influencing demand for primary medical care in women aged 20–44. *Int. J. Epid.* **4,** 189–95; Hannay D. *The Symptom Iceberg.* Routledge & Kegan Paul, London, 1979.

41. Last J. M. The iceberg: completing the clinical picture in general practice. *Lancet* **2,** 28, 1963.

42. See, e.g., Zola I. K. Medicine as an institution of social control. *Sociol. Rev.* **10,** 487–504, 1972.

43. Mechanic D. and Volkart E. H. Illness behaviour and medical diagnosis. *J. Hlth Hum. Behav.* **1,** 86, 1960.

44. Apple D. How laymen define illness *J. Hlth Hum. Behav.* **1,** 219, 1960.

45. Baumann B. Diversities in conception of health and physical fitness. *J. Hlth Hum. Behav.* **2,** 39, 1961.

46. See, e.g. Selye H. *The Stress of Life,* McGraw-Hill, New York, 1956; Jarvis I. L. *Physiological Stress.* Wiley, New York, 1958.

47. See, e.g. Goffman E. *Stigma.* Penguin, London, 1961; Szasz T. S. *The Myth of Mental Illness.* Palladin, St Albans, 1962.

48. Dukes C. E. The management of permanent colostomy. *Lancet* **2,** 12, 1947.

49. Ewing M. R. Colostomy: the patient's point of view. *Post-grad. Med. J.* **26,** 584, 1950; Sutherland A. M. The psychological impact of cancer and cancer surgery. *Cancer* **5,** 857, 1952.

50. Sutherland A. M. *op. cit.*

51. Freidson E. *Patients' Views of Medical Practice.* Russell Sage, New York, 1961.

52. Cartwright A. *Human Relations and Hospital Care.* Routledge & Kegan Paul, London, 1964.

53. Srole L. *et al. Mental Health in the Metropolis.* McGraw-Hill, New York, 1962; Leighton D. C. *et al. The Character of Danger.* Free Press, New York, 1963.

54. Tredgold R. F. The integration of psychiatric teaching in the curriculum. *Lancet* **1,** 1345, 1962.

55. Noble Chamberlain E. *op. cit.*

56. Cohen H. Foreword to Seward C. *Bedside Diagnosis.* Churchill Livingstone, London, 1949.

57. Balint M. *The Doctor, His Patient and the Illness.* Pitman, London, 1956.

58. Cartwright A. *Patients and Their Doctors.* Routledge & Kegan Paul, London, 1967.

59. Noble Chamberlain E. *op. cit.,* 8th Edition, 1967.

60. Kleinman A. *et al.* Culture, illness and cure. *Annls Intern. Med.* **88,** 251–259, 1978.

61. See, e.g. Helman C. Feed a cold, starve a fever, folk models of infection in an English suburban community. *Cult. Med. Psychiat.* **2,** 107–137, 1978; Blumhagen D. Hyper-tension: a folk illness with a medical name. *Cult. Med. Psychiat.* **4,** 197–227, 1980.

62. Enelow A. J. and Swisher S. N. *Interviewing and Patient Care.* Oxford University Press, Oxford, 1972.

63. Noble Chamberlain E. *op. cit.,* 8th Edition, 1967.

64. Bomford R. *et al. Hutchison's Clinical Methods,* 16th Edition. Bailliere Tindall, London, 1975.

65. McLeod J. (Ed.) *Clinical Examination,* 4th Edition. Churchill Livingstone, London, 1976.

66. Bomford R. *et al. op. cit.* There is also, of course, the contemporary psychological literature on non-verbal communication. See, e.g. Shefler A. E. The significance of posture in communication systems. *Psychiatry*

27, 316–331, 1964; Argyle M. *Social Interaction*. Methuen, London, 1969.

67. This analysis of the importance of the context of pain (e.g. Beecher H. K. *Measurement of Subjective Responses*. Oxford University Press, Oxford, 1959) eventually led to the celebrated gate-control theory of 1965; Melzack R. and Wall P. D. Pain mechanicisms: a new theory. *Science* **150,** 971, 1965.
68. McLeod J. (Ed.) *op. cit.*
69. Davis A. and Horobin G. (Eds) *Medical Encounters*. Croom Helm, New York, 1977.
70. On the one hand new words are often used to describe new objects; on the other hand sometimes the words remain the same but their earlier meaning is forgotten. An example of the latter is the word 'consultation' which increasingly excludes those parts of the doctor-patient meeting such as the physical examination which do not bear directly on mutual communication. Compare *The Future General Practitioner*, Royal College of General Practitioners, 1972, with Pendleton D. and Hasler J. (Eds) *Doctor-Patient Communication*. Academic Press, New York, 1983. There is, in addition, an older and completely different use of the term which refers to the process of GP to specialist referral: Abercrombie G.F. The art of consultation. *J. Coll. Gen. Pract.* **1,** 5, 1959.
71. Browne K. and Freeling P. *The Doctor-Patient Relationship*, 2nd Edition. Churchill Livingstone, London, 1976.
72. Wadsworth M. and Robinson D. (Eds) *Studies in Everyday Medical Life*. Martin Robertson, New York, 1976.
73. McLeod J. (Ed.) *op. cit.*
74. Locker D. *Symptoms and Illness: The Cognitive Organisation of Disorder*. Tavistock, London, 1981.
75. McLeod J. (Ed.) *op. cit.*
76. Foucault M. *op. cit.*, p. 90.
77. It is not uncommon, for example, to find patients perplexed by questions of an 'intimate' nature when they believed their problem to be a 'physical' one.

16 LAY CONCEPTS OF ILLNESS

Ray Fitzpatrick

The elementary but important principle of this chapter is that human illness occurs, of necessity, within a particular culture that fundamentally shapes and influences the way the illness is experienced. This chapter examines the concepts and beliefs about illness that form one important part of such cultural influences. Illness beliefs shape the responses to symptoms by the sufferer and his or her social network. If health care is sought, the definitions that the lay person brings to bear on his or her illness constrain the kinds of help sought and the perceptions of benefits gained from treatment. This chapter explores the evidence that has recently accumulated about lay concepts of illness

SOURCE: *The Experience of Illness*, Ray Fitzpatrick, et al., Editors (London: Tavistock Publications, 1984), pp. 11–31.

and then discusses their significance for providers of health care.

The Anthropological Investigation of Beliefs

Anthropologists in particular have drawn attention to the ways in which cultural beliefs profoundly influence experience and behavior. They have documented enormous differences in culture from one society to another and, by analysing beliefs that seem very strange and exotic to modern western readers, they make possible a more critical awareness of one's own more familiar and taken for granted beliefs. Illness is one realm of life in which anthropology has vividly demonstrated cultural variation between societies, often documenting beliefs that appear on the surface to be most bizarre and irrational. One of the best-known examples of strange beliefs held in relation to illness is the widespread explanation of illness in terms of witchcraft.

Evans-Pritchard (1937) examined the beliefs of a simple agricultural society in the Sudan—the Azande —amongst whom beliefs about witchcraft were prevalent. For a wide variety of misfortunes, from crop failures to personal accidents and illnesses, the Azande would sometimes seek a more basic reason for their occurrence, in addition to more immediate causes such as a pest or a physical hazard. On these occasions a Zande might suspect the possibility that a neighbour had acted as a witch and brought the pest or hazard by despatching the soul or spirit of his witchcraft. To

test the hypothesis a number of different kinds of oracle were available which, if consulted by means of appropriate rituals, were believed capable of identifying the source of the witchcraft. If the oracle confirmed that someone had acted as a witch by causing an illness, that individual could be confronted with the charge and requested to withdraw their influence. If necessary, vengeance could be obtained from the guilty party by practising magic in retaliation.

Lest these ideas seem too remote and exotic to be of any relevance to understanding more western communities, Snow (1974) describes similar beliefs amongst working-class blacks who have grown up in the rural southern regions of the United States. He argues that their explanations of illness fall into three general categories: natural and environmental hazards, punishments from God, and spirits and witchcraft. Similar ideas have been described (Fabrega 1974) in Latin American peasant communities who may explain illnesses as due to the 'evil eye' (*mal ojo*) of an enemy.

For present purposes several important lessons emerge from anthropological investigations of such exotic belief systems. Clearly they demonstrate the survival of forms of explanation of illness that differ completely from interpretations found in western science. More importantly such beliefs can be seen to form a coherent pattern of ideas in terms of which illness is explained. Ideas, which on the surface seem bizarre, can be seen to make sense when considered more carefully. Evans-

Pritchard showed that Azande beliefs about witchcraft and oracles formed a closed, coherent set of ideas that made good sense of reality. Thus if a particular consultation with an oracle produced contradictory or unconvincing results, the individual was not led to question the entire system of beliefs. Instead the particular poison or ritual procedures employed were thought to be at fault. Hypotheses of witchcraft put to the oracles tended to be confined to immediate social networks, amongst whose members enmities and rivalries were more likely to exist, which would confirm the sense of the oracle's decision.

More generally the system of beliefs provided a coherent philosophy of misfortune. The immediate cause of a serious accident would be interpreted in the same way by a Zande and western observer—a branch falling from a tree. However the more fundamental explanation of why the event occurred at a particular moment and to a particular man standing beneath the tree would be found in terms of quite different underlying processes at work in the two observers.

Zande beliefs form a coherent mode of making sense of misfortunes such as illness. Of course in western societies the dominant mode of explanation of illness is quite different and in its most organized form—the science of medicine—is based upon a highly complex and integrated set of concepts of disease aetiology and organic mechanisms in the functioning of the body. Nevertheless there is substantial evidence that this mode of interpreting illness is not uniformly shared by members of western societies and takes different forms in different social groups. The task of this chapter is to review the form and content of lay concepts in western communities, and to examine the extent to which there are substantial differences in lay compared with medical professional concepts and the significance for health care of such differences.

The Cultural Shaping of Illness

First of all it needs to be appreciated that culture, understood here as a connected pattern of language and beliefs, enters into the very nature of illness. An important conceptual distinction is frequently made in this context between disease and illness. Eisenberg discusses the distinction thus: 'patients suffer "illnesses"; physicians diagnose and treat "disease" . . . illnesses are experiences of disvalued changes in states of being and in social function: diseases are abnormalities in the structure and function of body organs and systems' (Eisenberg 1977: 11). Illness therefore here refers to all the *experiential* aspects of bodily disorder which are 'shaped by cultural factors governing perception, labelling, explanation of the discomforting experience' (Kleinman, Eisenberg, and Good 1978: 252).

A useful paradigm for thinking about the influence of cultural and social context upon bodily experience is provided in experiments by the social psychologist Schacter (1975). Subjects were injected with epinephrine which stimulated the sympathetic nervous system, resulting in symptoms such as increased perspiration. Some were then informed of the likely effects of the procedure; others were misinformed or given no information. Subjects were then left in a room with another individual, who, unknown to the subjects, was acting as an assistant to the experiment. These assistants were instructed to act in a variety of moods such as with anger or humorously. Schacter then investigated the subjects' definitions of their own feelings. He found that those who had not been appropriately informed of the physiological implications of their injection were considerably influenced by the mood or example to which they had been exposed; interpreting for example their arousal as anger more often if they had previously been in the company of the assistant instructed to display anger. A control group injected with saline which did not generally stimulate physiological arousal were less influenced by their social context. Schacter developed a theory in which the nature and quality of emotions is determined in an interaction between physical state and cognitive perceptions which are in turn influenced by social context. His demonstration also offers a model for thinking about disease and illness: the cognitive meaning assigned to abnormal bodily states is socially and culturally shaped and in turn constitutes the experience for the sufferer.

The example of depressive disorders can be used to develop the point. In many non-western cultures, for example in China and the Middle East (Fitzpatrick 1983; Katon, Kleinman, and Rosen 1982), depression and other neurotic disorders are presented with a greater concentration of physical symptoms than are found in western psychiatric clinics. Often patients from such societies, although displaying depressed affect, may report few symptoms relating to internal mood states, concentrating rather on various physical symptoms. Kleinman (1980) found in his clinics for Chinese psychiatric patients in Taiwan that the majority that he diagnosed as suffering from depression presented physical symptoms as their main complaint. He points out that the languages of Taiwan are rich in terminology relating to the body but have few terms corresponding to the wide variety of western internal psychological states.

White (1982) examined the notion of cultural differences in concepts of illness by means of a sample of students in Hawaii, half of whom were Hong Kong Chinese, the other half Caucasian American. The students were given a list of psychosocial problems such as 'difficulty sleeping', 'feeling anxious and tense', 'headaches' and 'feeling lonely'. They were asked to give in as much detail as possible the likely causes of each problem. Coders classified the students' explanations. For both somatic problems such as 'headache' and psychosomatic problems such as 'appetite loss' the American students were more likely to give explanations in terms of internal emotional status. For psychological problems such as 'sadness' and for somatic problems, the Chinese students were more likely to cite external pressures such as the family or the demands of academic studies. Thus the two cultures offered different conceptual emphases in the causes of problems: American culture focusing upon internal feeling states, Chinese culture emphasizing external situational causation.

The Content of Western Lay Beliefs

In recent years investigators have begun to consider the form and content of beliefs about illness of modern western communities. The most striking result of such studies is the variety and importance of ideas about the causes of illness. Blaxter (1983) interviewed a sample of working-class, middle-aged women in Scotland about their ideas of health and illness. The women were free to discuss whichever disorders they wished in unstructured interviews focused upon the health of their families. The sample discussed 587 examples of episodes of disease and the issue of cause was mentioned in 74 per cent of examples. Blaxter then classified the causes cited by the women. Infection was by far the most common category of cause invoked. Next most frequent was heredity, followed by environmental hazards, secondary effects of other diseases, stress, childbearing and the menopause, and trauma and surgery. Less common as a category of cause was the notion of a self-inflicted disorder through neglect or behavioural choices. Blaxter observes that the search for causal patterns in their health histories was ex-

tremely important to the women and she refers to a 'positive strain towards accounting for their present bodily state . . . by connecting together the relevant health events' (Blaxter 1983: 67).

A similarly designed study by Pill and Stott (1982) allows some comparison with another region of Great Britain—South Wales. The authors report interviews conducted with women aged 30–35 years who were selected from a social background of skilled manual workers. In these interviews infection or germs were again the most commonly cited cause of illness, after which, in decreasing order of frequency, were cited life-style, heredity, and stress. Approximately half the women in this sample employed concepts of cause that involved behavioural choice and some degree of individual responsibility for illness. These women were more likely to be home owners and to have had more education, and their feeling of control in their lives may account for the greater sense of responsibility compared with Blaxter's respondents.

Although the methods of investigation in the two studies were not identical, some common themes emerged which can be put into a comparative perspective. Chrisman (1977) provides a framework from a review of cross-cultural evidence of folk ideas about illness in which he identifies different modes of thought about the causes of illness. He calls such modes of thought 'logics' and identifies four basic kinds:

1. A logic of degeneration in which illness follows the running down of the body.

2. A mechanical logic in which illness is the outcome of blockages or damage to bodily structures.

3. A logic of balance in which illness follows from disruption of harmony between parts or between the individual and the environment.

4. A logic of invasion which includes germ theory and other material intrusions responsible for illness.

These logics may be viewed as dominant themes or metaphors which permeate beliefs about illness and vary in importance from one culture to another. Thus the logic of balance is fundamental to traditional Latin American beliefs about the implication of 'hot' and 'cold' factors in illness and is also important in classical Indian ideas of the balance between 'humours' determining health. As shall be seen in the work of Herzlich (1973) such thinking may also be involved in western folk beliefs in illness as an outcome of relations between man and an 'unnatural' environment.

Ideas of degeneration were not frequently cited in the studies by Blaxter or Pill and Stott as causes of specific diseases, although disorders such as rheumatism were sometimes seen as a natural part of ageing. Clearly in modern Britain the logic of invasion is an important mode of thinking about illness and must partly be seen as the cultural result of the impact of microbiological developments in western science in the last part of the nineteenth century. The theme of heredity, frequently expressed in both Blaxter's and Pill and Stott's samples, is less easily traced back to earlier modes of medical thought and, as Blaxter observes (1983: 63), there appears to be a greater readiness to invoke genetic causation in lay culture than in medical science. Patterns of shared illness in families offer a powerful source of ideas of inheritance. However it is unclear how universal such interpretations are. A review (Janzen and Prins 1981) of traditional African systems of explaining illness makes little mention of heredity as a form of cause.

Probably one of the most characteristically western modes of interpreting illness can be found in the variety of related concepts such as 'stress', 'worry', and 'tension'. Yet it has often been argued (Eisenberg 1977; Engel 1977) that the dominant approach to health and illness in modern western society is one which seeks the explanation of disease in reductionist physical principles and operates with a mind-body dualism, that is a perspective in which the two realms are distinct and separate. Engel terms this approach the 'biomedical model':

> The dominant model of disease today is biomedical, with molecular biology its basic scientific discipline. It assumes disease to be fully accounted for by deviations from the norm of measurable (somatic) variables. It leaves no room within its framework for the social, psychological and behavioural dimensions of illness. (Engel 1977: 196)

It is therefore at this point that there may exist some of the sharpest differences between popular, lay ideas and those enshrined in the culture of medical science.

The Structure of Lay Beliefs

One of the most striking qualities of lay concepts of illness is their very complexity. Both Blaxter and Pill and Stott were impressed by the complex, multifactorial approach that their respondents frequently employed in explaining illness. This quality becomes most apparent when some systematic effort is invested in obtaining a number of respondents' ideas about one particular disease. Blumhagen (1980), as an example of such research, investigated the views about their disorder of 103 patients attending a clinic for hypertension in the United States. The members of the sample cited an average of thirteen separate items each in their view of what constituted the causes, pathophysiology and prognosis of hypertension. Blumhagen lists ten different kinds of causal factors that were commonly cited, ranging from chronic external stress to heredity, salt, water, and food generally. Thus Blumhagen argues that the folk concept of hypertension is complex, involving a large number of elements and numerous connections between elements. It is interesting that in this study too stress plays a major part in beliefs about causation. Half the sample cited chronic external stress as implicated in hypertension, either in terms of 'the build up of normal stresses of life' or 'job stresses' in particular. Specific acute stresses were also seen by more than half the sample as involved in hypertension. In fact psychosocial factors were so central to the patients' understanding of the disorder that Blumhagen sees 'Hyper-Tension' in the sense of 'excessive tenseness' as being the essence of the idea of the disorder for many patients by contrast with the professional medical model of hypertension as a systemic circulatory problem.

Although such research suggests a good deal of complexity in the patterns of ideas about illness reported by lay individuals, it may be misleading to talk of such ideas, as some writers have (for example Pill and Stott 1982: 45) as lay *theories*. The term 'theory' implies a high degree of consistency, order, stability, and rationality, properties that may not be essential to lay concepts. Blumhagen, for example, reports that some respondents gave unrelated, parallel models of hypertension at different stages in their interview. When confronted with the differences, the patients did not feel that the inconsistencies between different parts of their explanations were problematic. In relation to the illogicalities and inconsistencies that are a part of lay belief systems in every culture, Kleinman points out that 'laymen are not concerned with their theoretical rigor so much as the treatment options they give rise to' (Kleinman 1980: 93). In other words lay concepts are pragmatic, and are rarely publicly produced for critical scrutiny.

For the same reason, in so far as lay ideas are seldom formalized and normally only emerge as an element of decision-making about actual illness episodes, they are expressed extremely tentatively. Thus Pill and Stott describe their respondents as 'unsure of themselves and less articulate when discussing aetiological topics' (Pill and Stott 1982: 46). The tone of interviews became more hesitant and statements were more uncomfortable about expressing and organizing ideas which normally remain tacit background resources to be drawn upon when coping with their own or other people's illnesses. Stoeckle and Barsky argue for the importance to doctors of eliciting patients' concepts in their consultations but acknowledge that 'On initial contact patients may be reluctant to divulge their ideas for fear these will be regarded as unsophisticated, foolish or so irrational that they themselves will be met with amusement, disrespect or even reproach' (Stoeckle and Barsky 1981: 225).

Another way in which such ideas differ from theoretical knowledge is that they are *syncretic* in origin, that is, deriving from a variety of originally disparate and distinct sources. Ideas are selectively drawn upon from a variety of different traditions and adjusted according to the current concerns of the individual. This is most easily shown in the interpretations people make of illness in a society such as Sri Lanka in which a number of separate medical systems survive with quite independent traditions such as Ayurvedic practice, western scientific medicine, and folk, spiritist healing. AmaraSingham (1980) describes a family in Sri Lanka attempting to make sense of the onset of mental illness in their daughter and to obtain practical help. They turn from one kind of healer to another and although they are offered explanations and treatments that are theoretically incompatible with each other, they nevertheless selectively retrieve elements from each that help to make sense of the alarming experience. The study shows how active, constructive, and selective is the process of making sense of illness, in which ideas from a variety of sources are drawn upon and reworked. It is the syncretic nature of lay ideas about illness which explains why it is frequently observed (e.g. Blaxter 1983: 67) how difficult it is to disentangle the sources (whether the media, social networks, or doctors) that people draw upon in their ideas.

One particular way in which lay ideas differ from formal forms of thought is the flexible manner in which ideas respond to experience. Anthropologists and other social scientists normally portray the culture of a society, of which beliefs are an element, as a stable and relatively enduring means by which the society copes with its environment. In terms of general, fundamental themes, cultural beliefs about illness are quite stable. Nevertheless there is a danger of what might be termed *reifying* lay explanations of illness and viewing them as fixed frameworks in terms of which health and illness are experienced. This is the risk attached to any approach to explaining human action which focuses on beliefs and ideas: the very investigation of the beliefs may make them appear more solid and inflexible than in reality they are. One way in which this point can be illustrated is by looking at the impact that incurring an illness may have on beliefs about the nature of the particular disorder. Linn, Linn, and Stein (1982) asked two groups of patients in an American hospital about their beliefs about the causes of cancer. One group were end-stage cancer patients; the other patients suffered from other chronic diseases such as diabetes. Although both groups cited smoking and work as causes of cancer, the cancer sufferers were much more likely to cite what the researchers term 'God's will' or inheritance compared to the other patients who attributed more importance to other environmental factors such as diet. More importantly, the cancer patients were less firm in their convictions about causes than the other group. The authors suggest that the non-cancer sufferers may respond in terms of stereotypes of risk factors to which the media have drawn attention. For persons afflicted with a life threatening disease, the need to make sense of personal misfortune is immense. Publicly available ideas about causes provide only partial sense of why the individual and not others also at risk have been afflicted. Cultural beliefs about causes may therefore be a less salient part of the experience and more transcendental explanations come to the fore.

Beliefs As a 'System'

Some anthropologists take seriously the term 'system' when they talk of a community's belief system with regard to health and illness. Essentially they argue that the beliefs about illness identified in a community should be analyzed in terms of a system in the sense that beliefs are held to be interconnected and struc-tured elements of a whole, rather than a random set of items that a group of people happen to believe in common. An example of the application of this approach to the experience of illness is the work of Helman (1978) who as a general practitioner and anthropologist has examined patterns of ideas about infectious illness in a north London community. Helman argues that a folk classificatory system, with origins quite distinct from medical science, can be detected behind a variety of ideas about illnesses which are commonly viewed as departures from normal body temperature. Patients distinguish the subjectively hot illnesses which are fevers from the cold illnesses which are classified as chills or colds. From a knowledge of which category a set of symptoms indicates, it is possible to read off a set of causes, typical kinds of course, appropriate treatment and also the degree of individual blame attached to the sufferer in contracting the illness. Colds and chills are viewed as the product of the individual's relations with the natural environment and lower temperatures in the environment can, through dampness, cold winds and draughts, penetrate particularly vulnerable surfaces of the body such as the head and the feet. Transitions from hot to cold such as 'going into a cold room after a hot bath' can leave an individual particularly vulnerable. Treatment involves restoring temperature equilibrium by hot drinks or a warm bed. The individual may often be to blame for incurring the illness by irresponsible actions such as going out with wet hair. Fevers are due to invisible entities—'germs' or 'bugs'—transmitted from individual to individual. One important treatment is fluid which 'flushes out' germs. The individual is less personally responsible for fevers as they are unavoidably transmitted through social relationships. Helman points out that germs are spoken of in similar ways, and have a similarly hypothetical nature to the spirits thought responsible for illness in many simple agricultural societies.

Helman suggests that this system of beliefs is, at present, unstable: in particular, younger patients tend to view both colds and fevers as due to germs and viruses and less as a result of their own responsible actions. These changes in beliefs are partly due to changes in medicine, especially the growth in availability of antibiotics.

The derivation of such a *system* of beliefs by anthropological techniques involved interpretive methods of detecting patterns and themes behind a number of respondents' expressed views. It may well be that no individual could explicate all of the distinctions and principles that the observer would claim to exist in a community's beliefs. This is an important point because in clinical practice, or where a researcher discusses the views of a single respondent, it may be difficult to identify patterns of the kind that Helman has examined. The elements of an individual's views about illness may be more limited, tentative, inconsistent and less elaborately worked out. Young (1981) warns of the dangers of a 'Rational Man' assumption in this field if one too enthusiastically looks for cognitive patterns behind statements. Results may be the peculiar product of the exchange between researcher and respondent rather than reflecting ideas that are important to the respondent in actual episodes of illness.

Images and Associations in Concepts of Illness

So far lay concepts of illness have been discussed as if they paralleled scientific medicine in concentrating upon the symptoms, causes, and therapies of illness entities. Certainly studies such as those of Blaxter, Blumhagen, and Helman suggest that such focuses are important. However a different approach suggests that illness concepts, in addition to naming an alternative set of entities and causes to those of medicine, also operate as condensed symbols that refer to a wider variety of experiences contained in a culture. Lay concepts of illness do not merely name entities in the body but are powerful images associated with other realms of life. Good (1977) offers an analysis in these terms of a commonly reported complaint in traditional Iranian communities that he translates as 'heart distress'. It is particularly common in working-class women and frequently presented to the doctor. It is viewed as a disturbance in the heart caused by emotional distress. Traditional Iranians believe the heart to be the source of heat and vitality and the driving force of the body in contrast to western emphasis on its role in the circulation of blood. At the same time the heart is used linguistically to express emotions. Thus physical sensations of the heart and emotional feelings are intimately connected in traditional thinking. The complaint of 'heart distress' conveys a wider series of associations in Iranian society. Firstly the contraceptive pill is thought by many Iranian women to cause 'heart distress' and is also associated with ageing and infertility. Other associations link the contraceptive pill with menstrual flow and ritual pollution. Good argues that 'heart distress' is therefore a powerful idiom to express many female concerns with sexuality and fertility. Another set of associations link heart distress with on the one hand grief and melancholy from the loss of relatives and on the other hand with the anxiety of interpersonal problems and poverty of working-class life. One respondent explained to Good: 'We are poor, we don't have any money, we all have heart problems' (Good 1977: 47).

Thus Good argues that 'heart distress' in Iranian culture is not a neatly defined category referring to a specific disorder and may convey any of a variety of symptoms, illnesses, or problems. 'Heart distress is an image which draws together a network of symbols, situations, motives, feelings and stresses which are rooted in the structural setting in which the people of Maragheh live' (Good 1977: 48). Western-trained doctors are likely to misunderstand patients presenting with heart distress, examining the heart and offering reassurance that there is nothing wrong.

The importance of research by an-

thropologists such as Good is that we are reminded that lay concepts of illness may have powerful symbolic significance which cannot conveniently be expressed in so many words by the patient or informant but which form an essential element of the meaning of illness experience. They also suggest that we too narrowly limit the search for meaning if we only look for references to bodily symptoms or causes in lay ideas of illness.

Herzlich argued that there was a need for a modern anthropology of the facts of health and illness' (Herzlich 1973: 6) that would identify the images and symbols that are the counterparts in modern society to those investigated by anthropologists such as Good. She interviewed a sample of professional and middle-class French subjects about their ideas on health and illness. One of the dominant themes that emerged was the influence of 'the way of life' upon illness. Mainly respondents connected urban life-styles and illness. To some extent individual differences in reserves of health were thought to influence resistance to the impact of one's way of life, but the latter was paramount. City life was associated with a variety of other concepts: 'unhealthy', 'constraining', 'abnormal', 'chemical', 'unnatural', and 'hurried pace of life'. The toxic influences of city life were linked to an intermediate state between health and illness—a feeling of physical and mental fatigue —which rendered the individual vulnerable to illness. The unnatural and unhealthy features of urban life contrasted with the natural, the rural and past ways of life in which man was more in harmony with his environment. Herzlich's respondents viewed the unnatural as the product of modern, technological society.

The contrasts drawn between, for example, the natural and the unnatural were seldom given precise meaning and, as Good also argues, gain sense from condensing powerful associations within the culture of the respondent. Herzlich points out (1973: 26) that they are images daily reproduced by the media and require little effort or original thought when applied by individuals to their own lives. Nevertheless they provide an important vocabulary in terms of which illness is explained and one which has only superficially been replaced by the language of physiology or bodily processes. Herzlich's respondents do present particular health problems in terms of localized symptoms involving particular organs, especially when presenting to doctors, but they look for patterns and interpretations in terms of a wider set of themes.

Patients' ideas of particular illnesses can be considered in the same way to uncover their multiple associations. For example nervous tension is a frequent theme in Herzlich's study. 'Nerves' have played an important role in pre-modern medical theories of disease long before the development of neurological models of the structure and function of nervous tissues. Thus the nerves played a central explanatory role in the theories of disease of the influential Edinburgh medical school in the eighteenth century (Lawrence

1979). Since then the meaning of the concept has undergone many transformations from the development of psychoanalytic theory as well as from changes in physiological science. Thus lay ideas might be expected to reflect many of these developments. 'Nerves' are one of the categories of illness reported by Blaxter's sample of women. It is a common form of illness presentation in British general practice (Stimson and Webb 1975: 62), and one of the most common ways in which patients currently taking psychotropic drugs define their problem (Helman 1981: 524). Descriptions of nerves suggest combinations of emotional states such as agitation with such physical symptoms as a 'tight stomach'. Nerves may also cause other health problems. One-third of a sample of sufferers of rheumatoid arthritis explained their disorder in these terms (Markson 1971: 164). This damaging property of nerves clearly parallels eighteenth-century medical ideas as well as contemporary psychosomatic research. On the other hand nerves especially as a diagnosis from a doctor may be interpreted as a dismissive term, especially where it is diagnosed from only superficial acquaintance with the patient (Blaxter 1983: 64). Here the term has associations with failure to cope with normal demands in life, resulting in trivial symptoms. The images and associations of lay concepts are not easily delineated and the context of their use is most likely to give greater specificity to the intended meaning. It is quite clear that they are above all flexible and capable of a range of referents.

References

AmaraSingham, L. R. (1980) Movement among Healers in Sri Lanka. *Culture, Medicine and Psychiatry* 4 (1): 71–92.

Blaxter, M. (1983) The Causes of Disease: Women Talking. *Social Science and Medicine* 17 (2): 59–69.

Blumhagen, D. W. (1980) Hypertension: A Folk Illness with a Medical Name. *Culture, Medicine and Psychiatry* 4 (3): 197–227.

Chrisman, N. (1977) The Health Seeking Process: An Approach to the Natural History of Illness. *Culture, Medicine and Psychiatry* 1 (4): 351–77.

Eisenberg, L. (1977) Disease and Illness: Distinctions between Professional and Popular Ideas of Sickness. *Culture, Medicine and Psychiatry* 1 (1): 9–23.

Engel, G. I. (1977) The Need for a New Medical Model: A Challenge for Biomedicine. *Science* 196 (4286): 129–36.

Evans-Pritchard, E. (1937) *Witchcraft, Oracles and Magic among the Azande.* Oxford: Clarendon Press.

Fabrega, H. (1974) *Disease and Social Behavior.* Cambridge, Massachusetts: MIT Press.

Fitzpatrick, R. M. (1983) Cultural Aspects of Psychiatry. In M. Weller (ed) *The Scientific Basis of Psychiatry.* London: Balliere Tindall.

Good, B. J. (1977) The Heart of What's the Matter. *Culture, Medicine and Psychiatry* 1 (1): 25–58.

Helman, C. G. (1978) 'Feed a Cold, Starve a Fever'—Folk Models of Infection in an English Suburban Community. *Culture, Medicine and Psychiatry* 2 (2): 107–37.

Herzlich, C. (1973) *Health and Illness.* London: Academic Press.

Janzen, J. M. and Prins, G. (eds) (1981) *Causality and Classification in African Medicine and Health. Special Issue: Social Science and Medicine* 158 (3).

Katon, W., Kleinman, A. M., and Rosen, G. (1982) Depression and Somatization: A Review. *American Journal of Medicine* 72: 127–35.

Kleinman, A. M. (1980) *Patients and Healers in the Context of Culture.* Berkeley: University of California Press.

Kleinman, M., Eisenberg, L., and Good, B. J. (1978) Culture, Illness and Care. *Annals of Internal Medicine* 88: 251–58.

Lawrence, C. (1979) The Nervous System and Society in the Scottish Enlightenment. In B. Barnes and S. Shapin (eds) *Natural Order.* London: Sage.

Linn, M. W., Linn, B. S., and Stein, S. R. (1982) Beliefs and Causes of Cancer in Cancer Patients. *Social Science and Medicine* 16 (7): 835–40.

Markson, E. W. (1971) Patient Semiology of a Chronic Disease. *Social Science and Medicine* 5 (4): 159–67.

Pill, R. and Stott, N. C. H. (1982) Concepts of Illness Causation and Responsibility: Some Preliminary Data from a Sample of Working Class Mothers. *Social Science and Medicine* 16 (1): 43–52.

Schacter, S. (1975) Cognition and Peripheralist–Centralist Controversies in Motivation and Emotion. In M. S. Gazzaniga and C. Blakemore (eds) *Handbook of Psychobiology.* London: Academic Press.

Snow, L. F. (1974) Folk Medical Beliefs and Their Implications for Care of Patients. *Annals of Internal Medicine* 81: 82–96.

Stimson, G. V. and Webb, B. (1975) *Going to See the Doctor: The Consultation Process in General Practice.* London: Routledge & Kegan Paul.

Stoeckle, J. D. and Barsky, A. J. (1981) Attributions: Uses of Social Science Knowledge in the 'Doctoring' of Primary Care. In L. Eisenberg and A. M. Kleinman (eds) *The Relevance of Social Science for Medicine.* Dordrecht, Holland: Reidel.

White, G. M. (1982) The Role of Cultural Explanations in 'Somatization' and 'Psychologization'. *Social Science and Medicine* 16 (16): 1519–530.

Young, A. (1981) When Rational Men Fall Sick: An Inquiry into Some Assumptions Made by Medical Anthropologists. *Culture, Medicine and Psychiatry* 5 (4): 317–35.

17 THE GENESIS OF CHRONIC ILLNESS: NARRATIVE RE-CONSTRUCTION

Gareth Williams

Introduction

We are seated in the living-room of a modern, urban council house somewhere in the north-west of England. Bill, the fifty-eight year-old man with whom I have been talking for almost an hour, leans forward. Then, in a strained voice and with a look of exasperated incomprehension on his face, he says: 'and your mind's going all the time, you're reflecting . . . "how the *hell* have I come to this?" . . . because it isn't me' (B13.6).

Bill has rheumatoid arthritis (RA), which was first diagnosed eight years ago following two years of intermittent pain and swelling in his joints; a serious heart attack has added to his difficulties. We have never met before. His words indicate the way in which a chronic illness such as RA may assault an individual's sense of identity, and they testify to the limitations of medical science in delivering a satisfactory explanation for the physical and social breakdown to which such an illness can lead.

In the *Collected Reports* on the rheumatic diseases published by the Arthritis and Rheumatism Council, and with a beguiling acknowledgement of the popular image of the scientist as Great Detective, the experts admit their limitations and pronounce RA to be 'one of the major medical mysteries of our time'.[1] What is striking about Bill's interrogative, however, is that it points to a concern with something more than the cause of his arthritis, and what I would like to do in this paper is to examine the nature of his question, and those of two others, and to consider the significance of the answers they provide. That is to say, I want to elucidate the styles of thought and modes of 'cognitive organization'[2] employed by three people

SOURCE: *Sociology of Health and Illness* 6, no. 2 (1984): 176–200. Copyright © Basil Blackwell Ltd, 1984. Reprinted with permission.

suffering from RA in making sense of the arrival of chronic illness in their lives. I will not be claiming that these three cases are 'representative' in any statistical sense, but I *do* suggest that they symbolise, portray, and represent something important about the experience of illness. They are powerful, if idiosyncratic, illustrations of typical processes found in more or less elaborate form throughout my study group.

The fieldwork on which this study is based consisted of semistructured, tape-recorded interviews with thirty people who had been first diagnosed as suffering from RA at least five years ago prior to my contact with them. The rationale guiding selection of people at this point in their illness was that in pursuing a general interest in what might be called the structured self-image of the chronically sick person it seemed sensible to talk to those who were 'seasoned professionals' rather than novices in the difficult business of living with a chronic illness. Four members of my study-group were in-patients on rheumatology wards and the rest were out-patient attenders at rheumatology clinics at two hospitals in north-west England. The in-patients were interviewed at a relatively tranquil side-room off the busy ward while the out-patients were first approached in the clinic and subsequently interviewed in their own homes. Of the 30 respondents, 19 were women and 11 were men, so my group had proportionately more men than one would expect to find in the general population.[3] Their ages ranged from 26 to 68 years at time of interview; thir-

teen being between 26 and 49, eleven between 50 and 64, and six were 65 years of age or over. Twenty-two were married, the rest being a mixture of single, widowed, and divorced or separated.

The interview covered a variety of themes relating to the experience of living with arthritis, and the data were elicited according to a simple checklist of topics. The duration of the interview as a whole and the sequencing of particular topics were influenced more by contingent features of the interview process than by any well-considered plans of my own. Where I had to compete with an obstreperous budgerigar[4] or a boisterous young child, the interviews would likely be short and fragmented. On better days, with a minimum of interruption and an eager and lucid respondent, the interview could last for three or even four hours.

Although my central concepts— *narrative reconstruction* and *genesis*— are, I believe, novel,[5] the issues they are designed to address—how and why people come to see their illness as originating in a certain way, and how people account for the disruption disablement has wrought in their lives—have been the subject of innumerable investigations. Sociological and anthropological research into illness behaviour and health beliefs and psychological research into processes of attribution have all, in one way or another, attended to related issues; but there is so much of it! I cannot possibly indicate all my debts, but perhaps the body of work which has had most influence on this paper is that which examines lay beliefs or folk theories about the causes of specific diseases or illness in general.[6] Although much interesting material has been collected in this line, it has tended to rest content with treating people's beliefs as simply that: beliefs about the aetiology of illness. However, it seems to me that if, in some fundamental way, an individual is a social and historical agent with a biographical identity (in the fullest sense) and if the prime sociological importance of chronic illness is the 'biological disruption'[7] to which it gives rise, then an individual's account of the origin of that illness in terms of putative causes can perhaps most profitably be read as an attempt to establish points of reference between body, self, and society and to reconstruct a sense of order from the fragmentation produced by chronic illness.

In this paper, therefore, I use my three cases to illustrate the way in which people's beliefs about the cause of their illness needs to be understood as part of the larger interpretive process which I have chosen to call narrative reconstruction. Before looking at the specifics of my analysis, however, I would like to clarify the theoretical concepts which inform it.

Theoretical Prologue

The concept of 'narrative' does not hold an established theoretical place in any sociological school or tradition. In general speech it is often used, in noun form, as a synonym for 'story', 'account', or 'chronicle'. When used as an adjective, as in 'narrative history', it typically refers to the process of relating a continuous account of some set of events or processes. When A.J.P. Taylor, for example, refers to himself as a 'narrative historian', as he often does, he implies both a concern with telling a good story and also a preference for a common-sense, empirical reading of historical events, unencumbered by any theoretical baggage be it marxist, structuralist, or psychoanalytic.

As I see it the term has two aspects: the routine and the reconstructed. In its routine form, it refers to the observations, comments, and asides, the practical consciousness which provides essential accompaniment to the happenings of our daily lives and helps to render them intelligible. In this sense narrative is a process of continuous accounting whereby the mundane incidents and events of daily life are given some kind of plausible order. If 'biography' connotes the indeterminate, reciprocal relationships between individuals and their settings or milieux and between those milieux and the history and society of which they are a part[8] then narrative may be seen as the cognitive correlate of this, commenting upon and affirming the multiform reality of biographical experience as it relates to both self and society.

In his fictional, philosophical chronicle, *The Man without Qualities*, Robert Musil, speaking through his central character Ulrich, suggests that narrative order is: '. . . the simple order that consists in one's being able to say: "When that had happened, then this happened"'.

Musil/Ulrich goes on to argue:

In their basic relation to themselves most people are narrators. They do not like the lyrical, or at best they like it only for moments at a time. And even if a little 'because' and 'in order that' may get knotted into the thread of life, still they abhor all cogitation that reaches out beyond that. What they like is the orderly sequence of facts because it has the look of a necessity, and by means of the impression that their life has a 'course' they manage to feel somehow sheltered in the midst of chaos.[9]

The trouble is that sometimes the 'orderly sequence of facts' gets broken up. It cannot be sustained against the chaos and, for a time at least, the life-course is lost. The routine narrative expressing the concerns of the practical consciousness as it attends to the mundane details of daily life is pitched into disarray: a death in the family, serious illness, an unexpected redundancy and so forth. From such a situation narrative may have to be given some radical surgery and reconstructed so as to account for present disruptions. Narrative reconstruction, therefore, represents the workings of the discursive consciousness.[10]

In my interviews, the reason for the conversation and the excuse for the occasion was the fact of the person being ill. In this context, the aetiology of the affliction and the narrative history of the illness held a key place in the dialogue. I remarked earlier on the many studies examining lay theories about illness. In one such study comparing the beliefs of cancer and non-cancer patients with regard to the aetiology of that disease, the authors suggest:

The person without cancer can afford to be more dogmatic about cancers and likely to think in stereotypes. The closer he comes to dealing with the disease, the less clear-cut and more complex the explanations may become.[11]

The reason for such complexity, it seems to me, is that the explanations advanced by afflicted individuals have both causal and purposive or functional components. They represent not only explanations for the onset of a given disease, but also acts of interpretation, narrative reconstructions of profound discontinuities in the social processes of their daily lives. The illness is part of their story and as with any story, to borrow from George Orwell, the closer one gets to the scene of events the vaguer it becomes.[12] In some ways narrative reconstruction may be seen to involve a process of remembrance akin to R.G. Collingwood's notion of historical thinking where:

Every present has a past of its own, and any imaginative reconstruction of the past aims at reconstructing the past of this present, the present in which the act of imagination is going on, as here and now perceived.[13]

In confronting the experience of chronic illness, then, like any unusual or disturbing experience, Musil's narrative thread—'when that had happened, then this happened'—becomes *questionable*. The individual's narrative has to be reconstructed both in order to understand the illness in terms of past social experience and to reaffirm the impression that life has a course and the self has a purpose or *telos*. It is from this viewpoint that I have read the 'causes' to which my respondents refer both as delineations of putative, efficient connexions between the 'dependent variable' (arthritis) and various 'independent variables', and also as narratively reconstructed reference points in an unfolding historical relationship between body, self, and society. These reference points may be seen as constituents in the *genesis* of a misfortune within a narrative which imaginatively reconstructs the past so that it has meaning or purpose for the present.[14] In this way narrative reconstruction becomes a framework for teleological explanation.

Given the teleological form of narrative reconstruction, I employ the concept of 'genesis' not for stylistic or rhetorical purposes, but in order to liberate myself from the semantic straitjacket imposed by the term 'cause' as it has been generally understood since Hume,[15] and so as to establish a connexion with the Greek tradition of reflection on the origins of things which attained its apogee in Aristotle's doctrine of the four causes.[16] Robert Nisbet has remarked that the modern consciousness has been, inevitably, so influenced by Roman, Christian and sceptical thought about causality that it is difficult for us nowadays to tune-in to the Aristotelian schema. Nisbet argues:

> To Aristotle—and to the Greeks generally, I believe—something different is involved, something that is somewhat less 'cause' in our inherited sense of the word than it is a point of reference in a self-contained, developmental process.[17]

In Aristotelian philosophy different levels of causality are conceived within an overall process of becoming which includes an account of ends as well as beginnings and purposes alongside 'causes' (in the modern sense). In this regard the 'causes' to which my respondents refer are seen, in part, as points of reference within the process of becoming ill, and the genesis, or mode of formation, of the illness constitutes, in a sense, the dominant theme of the account. It is an analytic construct through which the respondent can be seen to situate a variety of causal connexions as reference points within a narrative reconstruction of the changing relationships between the self and the world; a world within which the biographical *telos* has been disrupted. In this way Humean 'constant conjunctions' are absorbed into an Aristotelian teleology.

The three case studies in this paper illustrate the way in which distinctive narrative forms are reconstructed to answer the question of genesis as it arises in different lives. The first two reformulate my abstract question: 'Why do you think you got arthritis?' into substantive questions more suitable for interrogating the genesis-of-illness experience. Bill, as we saw at the start, wants to know 'how the *hell* have I come to be like this? . . . because it isn't me'. In the same vein, Gill wonders: 'Where have I got to? There's nothing left of me.' The third case is rather different. Betty exemplifies a situation in which both 'causal' analysis and narrative reconstruction may be transcended when the *telos* of life is gently enshrouded within a powerful theodicy. She does not need to reformulate my question because: 'people say: "Why you?" Well, why not me? Better me who knows the Lord'.

Bill: Narrative Reconstruction as Political Criticism

A significant portion of Bill's working life had been disrupted. In fact, he had had a tough time. He had worked as a skilled machine operator in a paperworks and, shortly before the first appearance of symptoms, was promoted to the position of 'charge hand' which entailed his supervising three floors in the factory. It was shortly after assuming his expanded responsibilities as a 'working gaffer' that things began to go wrong:

> I was a working gaffer . . . but, you know, they were mostly long hours and the end result, in 1972, was every time I had a session like, my feet began to swell and my hands began to swell. I couldn't hold a pen, I had difficulty getting between machines and difficulty getting hold of small things.

At this time he also had a massive heart attack and was off work for five months. A series of blood tests were done by his heart specialist who then referred him to a rheumatologist, and within the space of a couple of weeks, he was hospitalized. At the time this unpleasant sequence of events was ambiguous and confusing, but over ten years Bill had become clearer about it:

> I didn't associate it with anything to do with the works at the time, but I think it was chemically induced. I

worked with a lot of chemicals, acetone and what have you. We washed our hands in it, we had cuts, and we absorbed it. Now, I'll tell you this because it seems to be related. The men that I worked with who are much older than me—there was a crew of sixteen and two survived, myself and the gaffer that was then—and they all complained of the same thing, you know, their hands started to puff up. It seems very odd.

Yes, very odd indeed. If I were simply interested in identifying his central aetiological motif no more need be said because the rest of the discussion was essentially a reiteration of this connexion. However, in order to understand the strength of his attachment to this belief, in the face of highly plausible alternatives, it is necessary to examine how his view of life has called forth this essential connexion between work and illness.

An important point about narratives, whether they be routine or reconstructed, is that they are necessarily co-authored.[18] The interview, of course, is itself a particularly clear case of co-authorship, but, more generally, narratives are bounded by and constructed in relationship with various individual people and organizations. With regard to illness, any narrative built around it needs to take account of the medical world within which the official definition of that illness has been specified. Bill described how, following the diagnosis of 'rheumatoid arthritis' resulting from clinical and laboratory investigations, the doctors disclaimed any interest in his hypothesis about workplace toxicity and pursued alternative hunches:

I was assured by them (the doctors) that this is what it was, it was arthritis. Now, it just got worse, a steady deterioration, and I put it down that it was from the works. But with different people questioning me at the hospital, delving into the background, my mother had arthritis, and my little sister, Ruth, she died long before the war, 1936/7, and she had not arthritis, just rheumatism and that naturally did for her.

From a clinical perspective and, indeed, from a common-sense appreciation of 'inheritance', there appeared to be a strong case for accepting an explanation in terms of genetic transmission. Certainly, in rheumatological circles, genetic and viral hypotheses are those receiving most serious and sustained attention. Why was he not content with this?

Bill had spent many years in the military services, and had served eighteen years with the paratroopers completing 211 successful jumps. Had he suffered any joint trouble during this time?

No, none whatever. This is why I couldn't associate it. All that time during the war we had a minimum of clothing on, we never went under shelter, we kipped in holes, slept on the deck—great stuff! You know, no problems.

What he appeared to be suggesting by reference to his life in the services was two separate but related things. Firstly, given that he had 'no trouble' during a hard life in the services, he could not realistically entertain any idea of inherited weakness. On more than one occasion he said that *because* of his harsh experiences he 'couldn't associate anything with it' (his arthritis). If there had been some inner predisposition surely it would have become manifest sooner? The second theme was that the absence of symptoms while he was in the services made it unlikely that those activities *themselves* were responsible for creating physical vulnerability. It all happened so much later and with such suddenness.

Bill was never entirely clear about his state of health while in the services. At a later point in the interview he mentioned that he *had* had some symptoms at that time, and that parachuting with 60 lb packs was a 'probable factor' but, in clarification, he remarked that many of his mates in the services had symptoms of a similar kind and that it was put down to 'fatigue'. Whilst conceding that the tough life with the paratroopers must have had some effect on his body, he could not square those experiences with the debilitating development of RA: 'To see myself as that, and now, from 1956, I can't accept it, it's not on'.

The references to the services, like the account of the workplace, make it clear that, for Bill, the body is defined by its relationship to the world of social action not in isolation from it. The medical model, employing a reduced range of clinically ascertainable factors, has no sensible meaning in the light of his pragmatic perspective. He was never dogmatic in his beliefs, but his pragmatism would not allow him to accept the validity of the medical model which appeared to rest upon an image of biological arbitrariness and caprice:

I was trying more or less self-analysis —where have I got it from? How has it come? And you talk to different people over all ages and you find that they are at a loss. They don't know, they don't know, nobody knows. And who do we ask? We ask the doctor (who says): "It's just one of them things (. . .) and there's nothing to be done about it."

At this point there is no indication of the basis for Bill's refusal of medical rationality. All we have is a statement of preference for one explanation, workplace toxics, over others. A little later we returned to the workplace and to the experiences of his fellow workers as he remembered them:

But thinking back to the way the other blokes were who are now gone, so we can't ask them, and what I remember of them, they more or less came to it in the same manner . . . I wasn't in there with them all the time, I was travelling between floors so I was coming out of it and getting fresh air and washing more frequently than they did. So this is something to do with it.

Bill had mentioned the 'odd' coincidence of similar symptoms at the start of the interview, but his thinking had clearly gone beyond a simple observed correlation. Not only, it seems, was there evidence of definite patterns of symptomatology amongst the workers, but also a differential severity which he explained by reference to the amount of time spent in contact with toxic substances. In the language of classical epidemiology Bill is invoking, unwittingly, the 'dose-response criterion', according to which the investigato

considers: 'whether the risk of disease increases commensurately with degree of exposure'[19] and then examines this in relation to characteristics of both host and environment.

It seemed then, that, notwithstanding the doctors' declared disinterest in Bill's hypothesis, there was *something* happening at the factory:

They just complained, and I noticed their hands were getting puffy, and that was one of the things, this seemed to be a common factor for everybody. Their hands started to puff and their shoes busted. And there was one guy, Joe (. . .), he was a very tall man, walked fairly rapidly, and he became slower and slower. And he said: "That's it, I'm out, it's this . . . ." He said straight: "It's killing me, I'm getting out", and it fetched him straight down. And that's where it's stuck, in the back of my mind. If Joe . . . remembering the way Joe was, a good walker, he could nip up and down steps, seeing him just shuffling till he couldn't even get from the lodge to the workshop without coming through the lift, he just couldn't make the steps. Well I got that way till I couldn't make the steps, just couldn't make the steps.

This graphic description of the destruction of men by their work adds little to the facts of the matter. What it does is to shift the quality of the discussion away from a simple description of illness associations to an intimation of the sense of revolt which existed amongst the workers in their consciousness of the situation.

Bill recognized the pressure to accept the doctors' analysis as legitimate, but in the light of his practical knowledge he felt that their analysis was inadequate:

> But putting it out of my mind, and having spoken to the specialists, they say: "No way". So you take their word for it. But it seems a bit . . . thinking in my mind when I go to bed . . . . I can't go to sleep straight away, I have to wait until I get settled and your mind's going all the time, you're reflecting "How the *hell* have I come to be like this?", you know, because it isn't me.

Bill has gone some way towards answering the question. He has identified a causal agent which seemed to explain his arthritis as well as symptoms in others, and he has described the milieu in which the causal nexus was situated. He has also portrayed a critical consciousness and a feeling of revolt amongst the workers which helps to explain his own unswerving attachment to his explanation when faced with a plausible clinical alternative. But is this observation of work experiences also part of a far more pervasive image of the world?

At another point in the interview, echoing his observation of the workers whose shoes 'busted', Bill told me of the experience of his wife who 'busted her back' while working with the local authority school meals service. How did this happen?

> Well, it was ridiculous because there were no men working there, and they had to go into a stock-room and the "veg man" had stacked spud bags which are 56lb five high. And it came to a particular day where they had to get one off the top, and she (his wife) was on her own, and she stood on a chair to get one off, and as it came down—up to that point she was a very strong woman—it just pushed her over and she went right down on the table. But she didn't realise at the time just how badly hurt she was. It was a couple of days after, she just couldn't move, she was almost paralysed.

This episode, as well as providing an analogue with his own experience, has also led to shared involvement in a long struggle with medical and governmental bureaucracy:

> She has a pension from [her employers], but the [invalidity] allowance which was taken from me has been stopped for her, and they didn't even have to give it back. It's the usual "cock-up" at the DHSS (Department of Health and Social Security).

Whilst Bill did not cite his wife's experience as an explicit parallel, these details of his biography, it seems to me, provide the basis for analogical reasoning and are central to an understanding of the explanation he elaborates for his own affliction. Taking these details into account, the narrative reconstruction of his personal experience has expanded into a more general political criticism exposing the illusions and false consciousness purveyed by various representatives of officialdom. Within this act of interpretation, the model of causation which informs his perception of his own illness and his wife's accident is one where the origins of misfortune are seen as direct, immediate, and within the bounds of human agency, but where the sick/injured person is not culpable in the slightest degree. In both episodes the workplace is defined not in terms of neutral tasks and accidental events, but as the locus of exploitative social relations in which workers are the victims of injustice and neglect.

The increasingly political tenor of his discussion of work and illness became even clearer in a section of the interview where Bill discussed issues surrounding his wife's claim for compensation. She was refused compensation, he told me, firstly because there was no witness to her accident, and secondly because the DHSS medical advisor had diagnosed 'osteoporosis' (a chronic deterioration in bone strength) antedating her accident. Bill's response to this was unequivocal:

> I think that "osteoporosis" is a cop-out. Nobody examined her or tested her, nobody took any samples from inside her bones. And this would be the only way, decalcification of the bones, because she's on calcium tablets now. But this only came up to my way of thinking because it was a cop-out, so they wouldn't have to pay a great deal of compensation. You know, so what the people at DHSS said was that everybody has this, *you* have it, I'm a liar but you've got it. They will say so without even examining you.

When issues of diagnosis are removed from the quiet location of the doctor's clinic and situated within the context of a struggle for compensation, the neutrality of the medical task and the objective validity of its procedures are thrown into doubtful relief. Bill recognised that technology and science are ideological, and that medicine can support political bureaucracy in preventing the establishment of social justice.

The tenacity of Bill's attachment to a workplace toxics explanation for the aetiology of his own arthritis takes on clearer significance in the light of these other experiences which, together, form a narrative reconstruction of the genesis of illness which carries a highly political image of the social world. Both illness, and the response of professionals to it, suggest a world of power inequality. There was much more in Bill's account that drew upon images of injustice in society. His experience of getting beaten-up by the police was introduced into the interview and recounted at some length and, as a whole, the world was presented as a place where ordinary people are exploited, conned, and manipulated by a range of social 'powers' be they doctors, bureaucrats, or the police. However, it is important not to jump the gun. So far, all I have shown is that Bill locates the onset of his arthritis within the workplace, and that other features of his account suggest mistrust and scepticisim with regard to the interests and intentions of people in positions of power. What we have to do now is to look further to see if this radical populist image of society *directly* influences his ideas with regard to the genesis of his own illness.

Following the excursions into the subjects of his wife's accident and the incident with the police, we returned to his own illness and disablement, and Bill related more scenes from his working life:

> 'cause there you had extremes of heat, in the tapes section, we were doing computer tapes. There was a special

section, and that was quite hot up there. Your entry and exit was through the fire door, and there was no air intake, no fresh air from the outside because it had to be a particular temperature. And even the chemist down there realised that they're like ovens. It's totally enclosed, it's double thick glass, and they always had the damn things shut till we opened them. We said, "Get us a vent in here or we're not running". And he got one in—that's the chairman who is now dead—he got us an intake. But it was too late for them lads. They had been in it all the time and they were much older than me, and I think their age was against them. They had minimum resistance.

Not only, then, was there a sense of revolt amongst individual workers such as Joe, but a collective refusal by a number of workers to continue what they were doing until certain health and safety measures were instigated. It was not clear how long it was from the workers' recognition of detrimental effects to management compliance, but it was certainly too long for some of them. In this way, Bill's particular arthritic symptoms and their origin became absorbed into a public issue, the issue of health and safety at work, and the original question about the causes of his arthritis was transformed into an examination of the power struggle between workers and management.

By situating the cause of his own misfortune in this context and juxtaposing it with the experience of his wife and friends, Bill's narrative reconstruction articulated a nascent political criticism of the way of life in modern society in which the genesis of his own misfortunes and those of

others could be understood as the product of malevolent social forces. Bill himself, of course, did not make such extravagant claims on behalf of his own thinking and, with an almost apologetic appreciation of the limitations of biographical evidence, he said:

> I'm just going off the way the other fellows were, that it became too much for them, and they probably had arthritis at one time, of one type or another. Because none of them walked with a proper gait apart from myself at that time.

Nonetheless, if his narrative reconstruction is read as a sort of historically rooted political criticism his original identification of workplace toxics as the cause of his arthritis can be seen as part of a more complex attempt to define the dynamics of the relationship between illness, the individual and society. This society is seen as the locus of exploitation, bureaucratic silence and multiple frauds upon the laity, where personal troubles are also public issues requiring political intervention.

Bill's analysis did not stop at the workplace. In a final statement he located the issue of illness in the workplace in the context of societal power:

> All those other lads, all their dependents got was two and a half years pay. Probably any investigation that the company made into it had been hushed up a bit 'cause the man I worked for at that time, Sir John Smith, and he became a Lord and is now deceased, and Lord Green and Lord Black were into the company and therefore had very powerful knowledge, and they shut it up if they

were giving toxics out and killing men you see. 'Cause nothing's happened since . . . nothing's happened since.

The precise extent of the damage incurred by the workers was never made entirely clear (although it is clear enough). Apparently, the company accepted liability and paid compensation, but Bill argued that the full scale of damage and responsibility was hidden within a strategy of non-decision and silence, ultimately controlled by powerful members of the ruling class who wanted to protect their economic and political interests.

The fact that Bill should have talked of all these things is not necessarily surprising. What is important is that these observations constitute essential reference points in a narrative reconstruction within which the genesis of illness and other misfortunes can be defined and rendered sensible. Within this reconstruction Bill encompassed what had happened to his body, the nature of his social roles, the quality of his immediate milieu, and the structure of power in society. In doing so, he linked his own demise with that of others, transcended the particulars of his own illness, and redefined his personal trouble as a public issue.

Gill: Narrative Reconstruction as Social Psychology

In Bill's long and detailed reconstruction, both discrete causes and biographical genesis were located essentially outside himself. Although his account encompassed social relations, it left out any reference to his

identity or self; there was no sense of personal responsibility or even of any socio-psychological involvement in the development of his affliction. Social relations, however, are also the place in which a sense of identity is developed and constrained, nurtured and broken. In this regard the genesis of an illness may be seen in terms of the body's relationship to the self and the self's relationship to the world.

Gill was a middle-aged school teacher living in a wealthy and conservative suburb. She had had RA for approximately five years, and the onset of the disease took place in a twelve-month period which included a number of tragic events. In my interview with her we spent less time discussing the cause of her affliction than had been the case with Bill. Nevertheless, her ideas were interesting and they represent an illuminating form of narrative reconstruction. As with Bill, I simply asked her why she thought she had got arthritis:

> Well, if you live in your own body for a long time, you're a fool if you don't take note of what is happening to it. I think that you can make naive diagnoses which are quite wrong. But I think that at the back of your head, certainly at the back of my head, I have feelings that this is so and that is so, and I'm quite certain that it was stress that precipitated this.

Now, there is nothing unusual about the identification of 'stress' as an important aetiological factor. Indeed, in my study group stress was one of the most popular factors, particularly amongst women and, as Allan

Young has indicated, the 'discourse on stress' is firmly entrenched in modern thinking on illness and disease.[20] However, more often than not the content of 'stress' is left unspecified and, indeed, part of its attractiveness is that it can be used to designate anything from excessive noise to bereavement. Gill, however, felt it necessary to specify exactly what she meant by stress, and having suggested that it precipitated her arthritis she went on:

> Not simply the stress of events that happened but the stress perhaps of suppressing myself while I was a mother and wife; not "women's libby" but there comes a time in your life when you think, you know, "where have I got to? There's nothing left of me".

Gill did not conceptualize stress in terms of external stressors, exogenous agents which impinge upon the body in some arbitrary fashion, rather she saw her illness as the bodily expression of a suppression of herself. However, while it was not simply a question of external stressors, neither was it a question of internal psychological pathology because she saw the stress of events and the suppression of herself as merely components in the social process of being a wife and a mother. It is within this process that the genesis of bodily breakdown finds its meaning. The causal efficacy of certain events could only be understood within a purposive account of the social process of womanhood in which her personal *telos* and a sense of identity had become lost.

However, as Gill has implied, within this overall social process there were specific events that were deemed to have a causal import and which are needed to explain why arthritis supervened at this precise moment in her life-course:

> And then on top of that feeling of . . . not really discontent, but rather confusion about identity . . . to have various physical things happen like, you know, my daughter . . . I'm quite certain that the last straw was my husband's illness. So, I'm sure it was stress induced. I think that while my head kept going my body stopped.

The various 'physical things' that happened to Gill were a number of life-events that followed in sequence in a twelve-month period. Her daughter went away from home in distressing circumstances (which she asked me not to reproduce), her husband became seriously ill, she suffered a rapid onset of RA (from ambulant to bedridden within 36 hours), her sick husband died, her youngest son was killed in a motorcycle accident, and finally, as a consequence, she lost her long-standing belief in God. Thus, within the social process of womanhood, which was itself stressful, aspects of that womanhood which gave meaning and definition to it—her relationships with her husband and daughter—were damaged. Her arthritis developed in the wake of these events only to be followed by the tragic losses of her husband and her youngest son and the obliteration of the cosmological framework that might have helped her come to terms with these losses: 'I feel very lost now that I've lost God. I do. I feel that terribly.' It was after the death of her son that she lost God, and she was left with: 'A big black hole. Nothing.' The symbolically reconstituted past revealed in her narrative reconstruction is one of almost total loss: the disappearance of her daughter, the loss of her physical competence, the death of her husband, the destruction of her youngest son, and, not surprisingly perhaps, the death of God. Now, one of the crucial criteria required for the ascertainment of a causal relationship is a clear time-order separating independent and dependent factors. In this regard, the loss of her husband, her son, and God can have no effective relationship to the onset of her arthritis, but they nevertheless lie within the same crucial matrix of social relationships within which her arthritis has arisen, and they thus form an essential component of her narrative reconstruction. They represent critical ruptures which have formed her present ideas about the causal role of other factors antedating the onset of her arthritis.

At this point, Gill has located the cause of her arthritis within a web of stressful events and processes: a genesis arising out of particular features of a woman's relationships in the modern world. It is a recognition of the distorting and constraining tendencies in these relationships that leads her to the question: 'Where have I got to? There's nothing left of me,' and to develop her narrative reconstruction around this theme of loss of self and confusion about personal identity. Gill is a good example of what

Alasdair Macintyre has in mind when he suggests:

> When someone complains—as do some of those who attempt to commit suicide—that his or her life is meaningless, he or she is often and perhaps characteristically complaining that the narrative of their life has become unintelligible to them, that it lacks any point, any movement towards a climax or *telos*.[21]

Gill did not commit suicide; her mind did not admit the problems and kept going, but her body indicated the necessity of rebellion by breaking down. Because her sense of ontological security was so firmly located within the context of conventional social relationships, the disturbance in those relationships led to an intimation of pointlessness, the development of illness, and the obliteration of all metaphysical referent.

What we have so far then is Gill's essentially sociological explanation of why she developed arthritis. But, in the years between onset of the illness and our meeting, Gill had regular contact with the medical profession and its mode of rationality. To forget this is to create an artificial abstraction. The medical model has often been disparaged by sociologists for, on the one hand, reducing the problems of the sick individual to a set of biophysical parameters and, on the other, reifying the concept of disease to a thing-in-itself.[22] In opposition to this, Mike Bury has argued that the medical model is often a useful symbolic resource which can be employed by individuals to mitigate the feelings of guilt and responsibility which often inform their response to illness, and to help them maintain some sense of integrity and autonomy in the context of meaninglessness. Whilst Gill developed a sophisticated socio-psychological model to explain her illness, she also understood that, in terms of the way illness became manifest, a general and popularized version of the medical model had a pleasing commonsense plausibility:

> I had quite forgotten until you mentioned the word virus . . . I said myself that I thought stress had precipitated this, but I would not preclude the fact that it might have been a kind of virus, because in the early stages I did feel as if I had bad "flu" . . . Do you remember when you get like that?

And, of course, I did remember. In this instance, the medical model provided us with a shared concept and a common understanding. The sociological model of 'womanhood', on the other hand, was not something which I could possibly have encompassed within my social experience. But the problem with the influenza analogy is that it merely describes a sensation from which a viral aetiology may be inferred. It does not provide an adequate account of the genesis of her illness because it fails to locate it within a context of the changing relationship between herself and the social world.

Although Gill was not racked by feelings of guilt about her illness and did not feel personally responsible, she did have a sense of involvement in what had happened:

> It's the old Adam, we've all got to be ill. No . . . well, I don't know, certainly things like osteoarthrosis, you're bound to get worn out parts, like cars . . . . Mind you, I sometimes wonder whether arthritis is self-inflicted . . . not consciously. You know, your own body says, "right, shut-up, sit down, and do nothing". I feel very strongly about myself that this happened to me, that one part of my head said, "if you won't put the brakes on, I will". Because I had had many years of very hard physical work, you know — washing and ironing and cooking and shopping and carting kids around and carrying babies and feeding babies and putting babies to bed and cleaning up their sick. It all sounds again so very self-pitying, but it's fact. Bringing up five children is hard work. That, and with the stress on top, I'm sure that I just cut out, I just blew a fuse.

In this passage from my interview with Gill, the final one relevant to the subject under consideration, the relationship of womanhood, and specifically motherhood, to illness was reaffirmed and described in the bold style of someone confident of their position. But some new elements have been introduced which elaborate that original relationship. Gill brought into play two metaphors, one religious and one mechanical, to suggest the inevitability of illness in society. The image of the Fall from Grace was introduced to account for the ubiquity of illness in human life and then, hesitatingly, wary perhaps of the fatalism in a religiosity she has lost, she rejected this in favour of the idea of an obsolescence built into the body-machine where certain kinds of mechanical degeneration are a necessary consequence of the structure and functioning of the component parts. Whilst both these images fit nicely into the teleological framework of an Aristotelian world-view, they do not explain the particular manifestation of illness in *her* life at this moment in time. Thus, following this metaphorical addendum, Gill returned to the central motif of her narrative reconstruction. Given the necessity, mechanical or metaphysical, of *some* kind of illness, the genesis of her arthritis was seen to reside in the social processes of stress and hardship which are the result of the role of women in the modern social structure. The notion of arthritis being self-inflicted implies not simply an individual flaw in a psyche brutalized by contingent events, but more the constraints placed upon the self within a social flow of essential activity.

Much of the work that has considered 'lay beliefs' about the causes of particular diseases or illness in general have drawn a line between those beliefs which refer to the source of illness as outside the individual and those which see it as coming from within the individual.[23] Gill's account indicates the inadequacy of such an analytic bifurcation. In a crude sense, she located the source of her arthritis outside herself in a variety of events and processes, but the events she cites are precisely those which speak of the complex relationship between her personal *telos* and her social roles in modern society. What she was attempting to express, it seems to me, was that illness arises out of our relationship to the social world

when personal identity and the social processes within which that identity is defined come into conflict. When the social self is forced to continue its everyday work and where personal revolt is impossible, the body may instigate its own rebellion. This is what Gill means when she refers to her arthritis being self-inflicted but not consciously.

In her illuminating account Gill managed to describe the relative autonomy of the body, the self, and the social world while indicating the way in which they interrelate. If her narrative is read as a simple description of cause and effect processes, it could be easily categorized as a belief model invoking social stress/life events plus (possible) virus, but this would be to violate it. As a narrative reconstruction, Gill's account can be read an an attempt to portray the genesis of illness within a socio-psychological interpretation of the relationships between personal identity and social roles in modern society, given the inevitability of some kind of illness and the ever-present possibility of viral attack. The complexity of her account results less from her concern to identify the causes of her arthritis and more from her need to reaffirm *telos* and to reconstruct a narrative order in the presence of profound disruptions in the biographical processes of daily life.

Betty: The Transcendence of Causality and Narrative Reconstruction

I have indicated that the degree of narrative embellishment or complexity in the process of reconstruction is related to the amount of biographical disruption to which the individual's life has been exposed. It could be argued, however, that since the amount of biographical disruption cannot be assessed apart from the actors' accounts of their perceptions the whole argument becomes circular. There is a horrible logic to this, and it is something which I cannot properly refute within the constraints of my present methods. Nonetheless, in partial mitigation of this objection, I would suggest that it is reasonable, if not entirely valid, to infer the amount of disruption from certain brute 'facts'. Bill's own premature retirement followed by his wife's accident would certainly spell disruption for the home economy of most working-class families and, in the same vein, it would be difficult to imagine the tragic chapter of accidents experienced by Gill being accepted by anyone with equanimity. Their narrative reconstructions were attempts to account for and repair breaks in the social order. I realise that there are all sorts of methodological and epistemological objections to this but, as I write, there is little else I can say in my own defence. Instead, I rest content with presenting the experiences of Betty who, in spite of inability to hold a much-needed job, to wash and dress herself, and, because of chronic pain, to sleep in the same bed as her husband, appeared remarkably composed.

There are some situations in which the central meaning of a life is defined by some transcendent principle—whether or not we accept the validity of the principle or the authenticity of the proclaimed belief in

it. Where God is a powerful feature of an individual's cosmology His existence may be adduced not as a cause of the illness, as some other studies imply,[24] but as good reason why, in matters of illness and other misfortunes, the believer is not granted automatic exemption. Where God is the Cause or the Unmoved Mover, the individual may be liberated from the burdens of narrative reconstruction and causal analysis and left free to indulge their lyrical sensibility.

Betty was in her early sixties, married, and had worked full-time and then part-time in a shop until developing disablement made continuation impossible. She had had arthritis for about seven years. Her life was not a comfortable one, and she had worked, as she put it, 'out of necessity', in order to supplement her husband's low wage, to pay off the mortgage, and to maintain a base equilibrium in the home economy. The loss of her wage rendered the future profoundly insecure. I asked her why she thought she got arthritis:

> The Lord's so near, and, you know, people say "why you?" I mean this man next door, He's German, and of course he doesn't believe in God or anything (sic) and he says to me, "you, my dear, why he chose you?" And I said, "Look, I don't question the Lord, I don't ask (. . .), He knows why and that's good enough for me." So he says, "He's supposed to look after . . ." [and] I said, "He is looking after his own (. . .) and he does look after me", I said, I could be somewhere where I could be sadly neglected (. . .), well, I'm not. I'm getting all the best treatment that can be got, and I do thank

the Lord that I'm born in this country, I'll tell you that.

Instead of simply affirming that her arthritis originated in the mysterious workings of God's will, Betty tells a story that locates her attitude to her illness within a framework of justification that has been called forth on other occasions by non-believers. She suggests that her personal misfortune can only be approached within an understanding of the good fortune in other aspects of her life. The goddess Fortuna faces both ways. The secular search for cause and meaning or what Alasdair MacIntyre calls the 'narrative quest'[25] is redundant because the cause, meaning, and purpose of all things is preordained by God:

> I've got the wonderful thing of having the Lord in my life. I've got such richness, shall I say, such meaning. I've found the meaning of life, that's the way I look at it. My meaning is that I've found the joy in this life, and therefore for me to go through anything, it doesn't matter really, in one way, because I reckon that they are testing times . . . . You see, He never says that you won't have these things, He doesn't promise us that we won't have them, He doesn't say that. But He comes with us through these things and helps us to bear them and that's the most marvellous thing of all.

So, for Betty, biographical robustness, narrative order, and the personal *telos* were not actually contingent upon what happened to her in the profane world. In fact the idea of a separate and vulnerable 'personal' *telos* would make little sense in the context of her essential relationship

with God's purpose. MacIntyre argues that teleology and unpredictability coexist in human lives and that the intelligibility of an individual life depends upon the relationship between plans and purposes on the one hand, and constraints and frustrations on the other. The anxiety to which this might give rise did not exist for Betty because the unpredictability of say, pain and illness, are part of an ulterior teleology.

This kind of interpretation of life and its difficulties is hard to appreciate in the context of a secular society with its mechanical notions of cause and effect. In talking of 'God's purpose' as a component in people's understanding of the genesis of illness, it is important to think carefully about what exactly is entailed in the use of such expressions. When Betty talked about God and personal suffering, she did not imply that God's will was an efficient or proximate cause in the development of her arthritis, rather He is the cause of everything and, as such, makes narrative quests unnecessary. Nonetheless, from a sociological viewpoint, Betty's concept of 'God' had similarities to Gill's image of 'womanhood' and Bill's notion of 'work' in that it transcended linear frameworks of cause and effect so as to define a symbolic and practical relationship between the individual, personal misfortune, social milieu, and the life-world. However, although both Gill and Bill went beyond a linear explanation of disease by placing their experiences of illness within, respectively, a sociopsychological and political narrative reconstruction of their relationships to the social world, Betty's 'God' implied a principle of meaning that transcends the social world as such. Betty did not have to reconstruct order through narrative because God, existing 'outside' both the individual and society, encompasses within his plans what appear to us as biological caprice and senseless biographical disruption. Physical suffering was only important insofar as it signified a feature of her essential relationship to God and so her sense of identity was not unduly threatened by the body's afflictions. The body itself is nothing as was made clear when, elsewhere in the interview, Betty aired her thoughts on donating her body to medical science:

Your body is dust and that is what it goes to. I mean the spirit goes to the Lord, the part of me that's telling you all that I am and what goes to the Lord.

Although much that Betty said of her material life would suggest profound disruptions in socio-economic circumstances, there was no sense of disruption because her life was part of God's unfolding purpose. Moreover, 'God's will' does not imply self-blame where the individual is bad and illness is retribution; at least, there is no direct relationship:

You see, it's got nothing to do with Man's goodness. It's all to do with Christ, all to do with Him being born to save me, to suffer my sins and everything I've ever done. I'm made righteous and sanctified by the wonder of that cross and that to me is marvellous, that to me is the jewel of life (. . .). You see, there's a beauty about everything and you can sort of go

through it in this way, you know, talking to the Lord and entering into it. He knows all about it. So people say, why you?" Well, why not me? Better me who knows the Lord.

Because she did not see herself as the author of her own narrative there was nothing for her to reconstruct or explain. For Betty the course and end of her life were defined outside herself and history:

And I think that, yes, it's helped me to understand, and even to the [point where] it can have a mental depressive [effect] on some people, because if they haven't got the Lord in their lives, of course, it must do. You know, "why am I here? why this, that and the other?" To me there's an end to it, something the Lord has for it, and He knows best what to do. I reckon, you know, that with faith I'll go through with this to an extent and that'll be it, and God will say, "well, that's it".

The interview with Betty was a particularly difficult one to conduct because my sociological questions appeared insignificant and redundant in the face of the teleological certainty of her beliefs. When interviewing someone with such a profound sense of meaning, it seemed almost meaningless to ask whether the illness had damaged her sense of self-worth or whatever. For Betty, most people live their lives in the immediacy of personal and material interests. Their lives follow a narrative thread defined by everyday events and happenings and routines, and when major problems occur in their social world their identity is bound to be threatened and it is not surprising that they should become lost and depressed. But for her 'there is an end in it' and all analytic puzzlement and personal doubt evaporate in the glare of God's purpose.

Conclusion

In his study of the Gnau tribe of New Guinea, Gilbert Lewis describes how these people say of some illnesses that they 'just come' and how they say of the sick person that he or she is 'sick nothingly'. In this way, sickness may be defined as having no cause or function, and no intent. He goes on to contrast this situation with that of western societies where illness is seen as the result of natural processes which we can study by the scientific method. However, recognizing perhaps the bluntness of this viewpoint, Lewis adds a crucial caveat:

> Individual people in our society may not accept it (the scientific view) as fully adequate to account for illness and seek religious and moral reasons for the illnesses of particular people, or even for illness in general; or individuals may feel an obscure and yet deep emotional dissatisfaction with explanation purely in natural terms, but the general view remains.[26]

The cases I have presented show a far more eclectic search than this. It is true that Bill's account, and those of some other respondents, have the same quality of systematic observation and inference that characterizes representations of scientific procedure. Many of their belief models, at least in formal terms, bear a striking resemblance to the multifactorial models of susceptibility/ vulnerability/trigger employed in so-

phisticated medical discourse, and a large number of respondents resembled those women in Mildred Blaxter's study of lay beliefs in whom:

> Their general models of causal processes, painstakingly derived from their experience as they saw it, were often scientifically wrong in detail, but were not in principle unscientific.[27]

I have tried to show that there may be more to such 'causal' models than at first meets the eye. Although in my interviews I framed the question in terms of 'what causes arthritis?' I have shown in the cases presented that this question was explicitly translated into more substantive biographical questions. It was not just that they were 'personalizing' the question they were transforming the meaning of it.

In this light, Lewis appears to be conflating two different levels of analysis—disease and illness, fact and value, science and morality. People may well draw upon some common-sense version of science and the medical model, but when Gill asks: 'Where have I got to? There's nothing left of me', she is asking a question that breaks the bounds of traditional scientific discourse and shifts into a complex social psychology and practical morality. Furthermore, developments in science itself have rendered it increasingly distant from the language and perceptions of everyday life while, at the same time, forming part of the secularization of the western mind which has made overarching cosmologies less available and less plausible. As Comaroff and Maguire put it:

In our society biomedical science and practice may provide satisfactory explanation and resolution for a wide range of afflictions often (but not always) seeming to render more thorough-going metaphysical speculation redundant. But precisely because of its apparent wide applicability in everyday life, particularly in the wake of the decline of overarching cosmological systems, we are especially bereft when we have to face events for which no rational explanation or remedy is forthcoming.[28]

This was written in relation to childhood leukaemia where the limits of rational explanation are particularly obvious, and, to paraphrase Turgenev, death may be an old jest but it comes new to everyone.[29]

RA is not a terminal illness, and therefore lacks the existential gravity of leukaemia or typhus. Nevertheless, it assaults the taken-for-granted world and requires explanation. Bill and Gill, finding no meaning in the medical view and having no overarching theodicy or cosmology, elaborated reconstructions of their experience in such a way that illness could be given a sensible place within it. These reconstructions bridge the large gap between the clinical reductions and the lost metaphysics. Once you begin to look at causal models as narrative reconstructions of the genesis of illness experience in the historical agent, moral or religious and, indeed, political and sociological factors become central to elucidating illness experience and rendering intelligible the biographical disruption to which it has given rise.

The body is not only an object amongst other objects in the world, it is also that through which our consciousness reaches out towards and acts upon the world. This is the dual nature of the body referred to by Sartre,[30] and within this duality chronic illness is a rupture in our relationship with that world. However, consciousness is itself biographically framed, so that consciousness of the body and the interpretations of its states and responses will lead us to call upon images of the private and public lives we lead. Narrative reconstruction is an attempt to reconstitute and repair ruptures between body, self, and world by linking-up and interpreting different aspects of biography in order to realign present and past and self with society. In this context, the identification of 'causes' creates important reference points in the interface between self and society. My respondents were, perhaps, not so different from the *baladi* women in Evelyn Early's study for whom 'The dialectic between the diagnosis and the life situation is crystallized in the illness narrative, where somatic progression and social developments are both documented.'[31]

For Bill, illness developed out of a working life but where the significance of work could only be understood by elaborating an image of the kind of society in which that work was situated. His attachment to workplace toxicity as a causal factor could be understood only in terms of his image of society as a place of exploitative relationships and power inequality. In Gill's case, illness was seen to arise out of a way of life in which personal identity had been defined and constrained by essential features of womanhood. The genesis of her illness was located not solely in the person nor outside in the external world, but within the relationships constitutive of social being. For Betty, the genesis of illness was seen to reside in the transcendental realm of God's purpose. This is not to say that God was seen as an efficient cause of her illness, but rather that her illness was necessitated and justified by reference to her intrinsic relationship to a suffering God.

These accounts all speak of illness experience at one moment in time. Their pasts were the pasts of those presents in which they were interviewed, and I have no evidence for or against the proposition that their image of the past would have been substantially different in other presents. To test that would require an altogether more sophisticated piece of research. Within the constraints, what I have attempted to demonstrate is that causality needs to be understood in terms of narrative reconstruction and that both causal analysis and narrative reconstruction may be rendered redundant in the presence of an embracing theodicy. For medical sociologists such an approach suggests caution in attributing particular belief models to individuals out of relation to other aspects of their narrative, and for doctors it could alert them to reasons for the apparent resistance of some patients to clinical explanations.

Acknowledgement

A shorter version of this paper was presented at the BSA Medical Sociology Conference, University of Durham, September 1982. This elaboration owes a lot to the advice and criticism of Peter Halfpenny, and to the valuable comments of Philip Wood and the anonymous referees of this journal.

Notes

1. The Arthritis and Rheumatism Council for Research, *Reports on Rheumatic Diseases. Collected Reports 1959–1977*, London: ARC, 1978, p. 6.
2. D. Locker, *Symptoms and Illness: The Cognitive Organization of Disorder*, London: Tavistock, 1981.
3. P. H. N. Wood (ed.), *The Challenge of Arthritis and Rheumatism: A Report on Problems and Progress in Health Care for Rheumatic Disorders*, London: British League Against Rheumatism/Arthritis and Rheumatism Council, 1977.
4. A small parakeet kept in a cage as a domestic pet.
5. The term 'genesis' is used by Claudine Herzlich in her monograph: *Health and Illness: A Socio-Psychological Approach*, London: Academic Press, 1979. Although I employ a somewhat different definition, I have been much influenced by both the style and substance of that excellent book.
6. For example, J. H. Mabry, 'Lay concepts of aetiology', *J. Chron. Dis.*, vol. 17, 1964, pp. 371–86; R. G. Elder, 'Social class and lay explanations for the aetiology of arthritis', *J. Hlth. Soc. Behav.*, vol. 14, 1973, pp. 28-38; M. Linn, B. Linn, and S. Stein, 'Beliefs about causes of cancer in cancer patients', *Soc. Sci. Med.*, vol. 16, 1982, pp. 835-9; R. Pill and N. Stott, 'Concepts of illness causation and responsibility: some preliminary data from a

sample of working class mothers', *Soc. Sci. Med.*, vol. 16, 1982, pp. 43–52; M. Blaxter, 'The causes of disease: women talking', *Soc. Sci. Med.*, vol. 17, 1983, pp. 59–69.

7. M. Bury, 'Chronic illness as biographical disruption', *Sociology of Health and Illness*, vol. 4, no. 2, 1982, pp. 167–82.

8. See P. Berger and B. Berger, *Sociology: A Biographical Approach*, Harmondsworth: Penguin, 1976; C. W. Mills, *The Sociological Imagination*, Harmondsworth: Penguin, 1970; D. Bertaux (ed.), *Biography and Society: The Life History Approach in the Social Sciences*, New York: Sage, 1981.

9. R. Musil, *The Man without Qualities, Two: The Like of It Now Happens (II)*, London: Picador, 1979, p. 436.

10. The terms 'practical consciousness' and 'discursive consciousness' are borrowed from: A. Giddens, *Central Problems in Social Theory: Action, Structure and Contradiction in Social Analysis*, London: Macmillan, 1979, p. 5.

11. M. Linn et al., op. cit., p. 838.

12. G. Orwell, 'Shooting an elephant', in, *Inside the Whale and Other Essays*, Harmondsworth: Penguin, 1962, p. 93.

13. R. G. Collingwood, *The Idea of History*, Oxford: Clarendon Press, 1946, p. 247.

14. This idea of the relationship of past to present is similar to that of G. H. Mead. For a useful exposition see: D. R. Mains, N. M. Sugrue, and M. A. Katovich, 'The sociological import of G. H. Mead's theory of the past', *Am. Sociol. Rev.*, vol. 48, 1983, pp. 161–73.

15. Probably the best version of Hume's ideas on causality and related issues may be found in: David Hume, *A Treatise of Human Nature*, Oxford University Press, 1978. This includes a helpful analytic index by L. A. Selby-Bigge.

16. R. Bambrough, *The Philosophy of Aristotle*, New American Library, Mentor, 1963.

17. R. Nisbet, *Social Change and History: Aspects of the Western Theory of Development*, New York: Oxford University Press, 1969, p. 27.

18. A. MacIntyre, *After Virtue: A Study in Moral Theory*, London: Duckworth, 1981.

19. N. S. Weiss, 'Inferring causal relationships: elaboration of the criterion of "dose-response",' *Am. J. Epidem.*, vol. 113, no. 5, 1981, pp. 487–90.

20. A. Young, 'The discourse on stress and the reproduction of conventional knowledge', *Soc. Sci. Med.*, vol. 14B, 1980, pp. 133–46.

21. A. MacIntyre, op. cit., p. 202.

22. For example, M. Taussig, 'Reification and the consciousness of the patient', *Soc. Sci. Med.*, vol. 14B, 1980, op. cit., p. 202.

23. For example, R. Elder, op. cit.; R. Pill and N. Stott, op. cit.

24. M. Linn, et al., op. cit.

25. A. MacIntyre, op. cit.

26. G. Lewis, *Knowledge of Illness in Sepik Society*, London: Athlone Press, 1975, p. 197.

27. M. Blaxter, op. cit., p. 68.

28. J. Comaroff and P. Maguire, 'Ambiguity and the search for meaning: childhood leukaemia in the modern clinical context', *Soc. Sci. Med.*, vol. 15B, 1981, p. 119.

29. I. Turgenev, *Fathers and Sons*, Harmondsworth: Penguin, 1965.

30. J-P. Sartre, *Sketch for a Theory of the Emotions*, London: Methuen, 1971.

31. E. A. Early, 'The logic of well-being: therapeutic narratives in Cairo, Egypt', *Soc. Sci. Med.*, vol. 16, 1982, p. 1496.

Part II

The Health Care System

INTRODUCTION

Each year over $400 billion is spent in the United States for health purposes, amounting to almost 11 percent of the Gross National Product. This money goes to hospitals, nursing homes, doctors, health workers, drugs, dentists, medical supplies, government research and support, administration, construction, and various providers. Health spending is thus a central facet of the U.S. economy.

It may be hard to consider that such a thing as the "health care system" exists, since it is comprised of such a diversity of segments: organizational (e.g., organizations of professionals and institutions), institutional (e.g., features of facilities and the interrelations between facilities), regulatory (e.g., such government agencies as the Food and Drug Administration), and financial (e.g., insurance and manufacturing). It is often hard to trace the relationships between these segments. Those who work in one part of the health system may be unclear about the impact of their actions on the other parts of the system. Indeed, we often see *unintended consequences* of policies instead of the expected outcomes. For example, the expansion of federal reimbursements for nursing home care was partly responsible for the unintended consequence of deinstitutionalization of state mental hospital patients. Above all, members of one component of the system rarely have a worldview that takes into account the overall structure of the system.

One task of medical sociology is to provide an integrated view of the health care system. Such a view not only makes logical and necessary connections between parts of the system, but it also provides linkages between the health care system and the deeper social structure of the society at large. One example of such linkages is the relationship of reproductive health services (contraception, abortion, sterilization) with general social values and restrictions on reproduction, sexuality, and family structure.

Part II contains four sections. In the first section, "Structures," we look at the growing role of profit-making hospital chains and at a major financing policy of our times—diagnosis-related groups. These structures exert increasing control over many clinical practices. The next section, "Institutional Settings," contains material on hospitals, both historically and in the present, and on the nursing home, which is a central institution in today's health care system. In the section titled "Policies," we have selections on health policy for the elderly, preventive health policies, a comparison of Canadian and United States provision of health services, and a study of how Sweden's health care system makes connections between health status and major social factors such as unemployment and housing.

The last section, "Emerging Impacts on Health Care and Policy," studies two major recent phenomena—the impact of AIDS and the growth of medical technology—which have profoundly changed the medical care system as well as public views toward health and illness.

Section Five

Structures

The health care industry follows tendencies found throughout capitalist society for profit maximization and monopolization. To be sure, much health care is provided in the public sector, but even in that sector the same mechanisms often operate. Further, a good deal of the private sector is supported by public-sector financing through government reimbursement of Medicare and Medicaid patients. Indeed, the distinction between public and private sectors in health care is increasingly a difficult one to make.

Nevertheless, the medical landscape is populated by a growing degree of monopolization as major hospital chains expand their operations. To a large degree, these chains are filling the gap left behind by many public hospitals that closed in the period of fiscal crisis. What may have seemed astounding ten years ago—the development of chains like Humana and Hospital Corporation of America—is now taken for granted as a basic component of the health care system. This *proprietarization* (private ownership) raises a number of concerns. In particular, the poor population as well as the many uninsured people in the working class have little or no access to these private facilities. Doctors and other health professionals are very concerned that the profit-maximization practices of these chains will limit their ability to serve patients in the best possible way. Examples of the harmful practices of proprietarization include turning away acutely ill indigent cases from emergency rooms and early discharge of ill patients.

Donald Light's "Corporate Medicine for Profit" provides a look into the expanding business of for-profit hospitals. He traces their development, examines their practices, and situates the for-profit chains as a central feature of the modern health care system. Importantly, Light also shows how nonprofit hospitals are mimicking the practices of their profit-making counterparts.

The federal response to these structures and contradictions of the health care system is basically to accept it and to better the government's economic position. The Congress has not moved toward a national health insurance scheme or to a more comprehensive national health service. Nor has the federal government put much, if any effort, into keeping open public hospitals or to regulating the dangerous practice of patient transfers from private to public hospitals. The Congress and the Department of Health and Human Services instead have offered cost-cutting policies. *Diagnosis-related groups* (DRGs) have been the main mechanism for accomplishing this cost containment. DRGs are a form of *prospective payment* by which the U.S. government pays hospitals a fixed amount per Medicare patient based on his or her diagnostic category. This replaces the older system of *retrospective payment* whereby a hospital simply charged the government for whatever costs it incurred. This new system arose in part due to inflationary pressures since hospitals were able to bill Medicare and Medicaid for a virtually unlimited amount of money. Nevertheless, DRGs represent a growing governmental tendency to retrenchment of the major social programs of the 1960s. Although only Medicare patients come under DRG payment on a national level, several states have instituted this method for all hospital patients, and experts believe that insurance companies will begin adopting similar methods.

Danielle Dolenc and Charles Dougherty write about the major change in health financing in "DRGs: The Counterrevolution in Financing Health Care." The authors warn that DRGs may cut costs but that they do so by threatening to restrict access to care, by compromising the quality of care, and by impeding the development of new medical technologies. They caution that the for-profit chains will benefit by DRGs since they can organize economies of scale. Many freestanding hospitals will lose out and be merged into the chains.

18 CORPORATE MEDICINE FOR PROFIT

Donald W. Light

A new era in American health care can be said to date from 1968. In that year Thomas F. Frist and Jack C. Massey—the former a Nashville doctor and the latter the man who had made Kentucky Fried Chicken into a national chain—formed the Hospital Corporation of America (HCA) to provide Frist's private hospital, Park View, with capital for expansion. HCA soon began acquiring additional hospitals, and it is now the country's largest investor-owned hospital chain. At the time of its formation few of the nation's non-Federal, acute-care hospitals belonged to a profit-making chain. By 1983 for-profit chains controlled 13 percent of those hospitals.

The transformation brought about by the for-profit chains is more extensive than the percentage sug-

SOURCE: From *Scientific American* 255 (6): 38–45. Copyright © 1986 by Scientific American, Inc. All rights reserved.

gests. By force of example and direct competition the for-profit chains have driven many nonprofit hospitals also to combine into chains. Today about a third of the country's acute-care hospitals belong to multiunit systems. Investor-owned corporations have also established themselves in many other area of health care, ranging from primary-care clinics to specialized referral centers. It is in the guise of for-profit chains, however, that the corporate presence in health care provokes the most debate.

The juxtaposition of the commercial ethos familiar in fast-food chains with hospital care challenges traditional images of medicine as the embodiment of humane service and even charity. The investor-owned chains have elicited a number of specific criticisms as well, voiced most powerfully by figures in academic medicine such as Arnold S. Relman, professor of medicine at the Harvard Medical School and editor of the *New England Journal of Medicine*. He and others believe commercial considerations could undermine the responsibility of doctors toward their patients, conceivably leading to unnecessary tests and procedures or— given other financial incentives— to inadequate treatment. Critics of for-profit chains also suspect they drive up the cost of health care, reduce its quality, neglect teaching and research and reject those who cannot pay for treatment. As the Federal Government and private insurance companies attempt to limit spending on health care, cutting into hospital profits and forcing hospitals to reduce their own costs, many of those concerns have intensified.

Research that addresses criticisms of the for-profit chains is beginning to accumulate, notably in the form of a comprehensive study recently completed by the Institute of Medicine of the National Academy of Sciences. Considered together with the institutional and economic context from which the chains emerged, the evidence makes it possible to assess their role. Some of the charges that have been leveled at them miss the mark but others are confirmed. The failings of the for-profit hospitals are not theirs alone, however. Those hospitals are only the purest expression of a commercialism that has come to prevade American medicine. They have unabashedly exploited a system that is devoted to the best possible care at any price for most of society but is effectively blind to the needs of the rest. In doing so they have served as a sensitive diagnostic of the system's inequities and excesses.

Only the scale of the commercialism embodied in the for-profit hospital chains is new to American medicine. Although most hospitals have traditionally been "voluntary," that is, run on a nonprofit basis by local community associations or religious orders, a substantial number have been run for profit by proprietors, usually doctors. In 1928, 38.9 percent of the 4,367 nongovernment general hospitals were proprietary— a much higher percentage than today, in spite of rise of for-profit chains.

Because they tended to be quite small, however, these early proprietary hospitals had only about 16 percent of nongovernment hospital beds. Doctors often founded them because there was no voluntary hospital nearby or because they could not gain admitting privileges at larger, more prestigious hospitals. The quality of care in such private hospitals was generally poor; patients in some regions called them "buckets of blood."

By 1934 the American Medical Association's annual survey of hospitals included a new category, "corporations unrestricted as to profit," in recognition of a class of hospitals owned by stockholders rather than by individuals or partners. The category encompassed 32.4 percent of the proprietary hospitals in that year and, because the corporate hospitals tended to be larger than other proprietary hospitals, 52.3 percent of the proprietary beds. Over the next three decades some of the early corporate and other proprietary hospitals went bankrupt, some were converted into community hospitals and the rest continued to operate on the fringes of the health-care system.

The roots of today's commercialism reach deep even in the main tradition of American medicine. Between 1870 and 1910 advances in major surgery and in the control of infection led to the construction of thousands of new hospitals. Earlier hospitals had served largely as a refuge for the indigent and the dying. The new hospitals attracted paying patients and introduced principles of business management into their operations. Even charity hospitals, which traditionally did not charge for care and depended largely on philanthropy, sought paying patients as the depression of the 1890's reduced donations at the same time as high inflation increased costs.

David K. Rosner, a noted medical historian at Baruch College of the City University of New York, has found that the trustees of the charity hospitals began to woo doctors who had private practices in an effort to attract their well-to-do patients. Such individuals had previously shunned hospitals in favor of home treatment. At the same time the charity hospitals refurbished their rooms and advertised their amenities: brass bedsteads, open fireplaces, serving rooms, private-duty nurses and a good chef. In 1899 the *New York Times* quoted a young woman as saying: "One is not quite in the swim nowadays if one has not had an operation performed. . . . A hospital has nothing but pleasant associations for me, and you will never find me out of one again when I am ill." The influx of paying patients not only kept the charity hospitals solvent but also enabled them to continue caring for the poor. Before the turn of the century, as a result, the practice of supporting charity care through higher charges to paying patients was established.

In the process, however, the trustees of the charity hospitals ceded a measure of control to private physicians, who altered the hospitals' traditional mission. Most of the doctors, according to Rosner, were more concerned with making the hospital an up-to-date physicians' workshop in which to treat their paying patients than they were with providing charity. Rosner concludes that such hospitals were transformed from neighborhood institutions dedicated to treating everyone into large enterprises offering specialized, up-to-the-minute care and advertising their amenities to a citywide market of affluent patients.

Thus a tradition of running hospitals like businesses evolved early, and the incentives for commercial behavior have only grown since then. As insurance developed first for hospital bills and later for doctors' bills, the hospital industry and the medical profession insisted on reimbursement for the "usual and customary" charges, charges the doctors and hospitals themselves were to have a major say in determining. Whereas European countries legislated fee schedules or established fixed national budgets for health, in the U.S. the growing amount of private insurance and the open-ended reimbursements created a golden era, starting after World War II, during which hospital budgets and physicians' incomes increased sharply.

Soon public funds supplemented the abundance of private-insurance money available for health care. In 1965 Congress established Medicare and Medicaid to pay some of the health-care costs of the elderly and the "deserving" poor respectively. By giving the elderly and some of the poor much more purchasing power than before, the programs significantly increased the number of paying patients. The legislation establishing the programs also included special provisions encouraging proprietary hospitals to expand. It allowed for-profit hospitals to depreciate their capital investment and specified that Medicare and Medicaid payments should not only cover the cost of treatment but also reimburse proprietary hospitals for inter-est on debt and give them a generous return on equity.

By the mid-1960's, then, physicians, hospitals, private insurers and the Government had devised a system of health-care financing that was ripe for big business. The form it took—the investor-owned hospital chain—reflects a further condition: the chronic need of hospitals for capital to expand, renovate or equip their facilities. Multi-hospital corporations, unlike privately owned independent hospitals, can raise capital by issuing stock. Moreover, their ability to use packages of hospitals within the chain as collateral enhances their ability to borrow money. Multihospital systems have considerably better credit ratings than independent hospitals and can borrow at lower interest rates.

During their first years the investor-owned chains grew mainly by buying other for-profit hospitals; in the 1970's more than 80 percent of the chains' growth took this form. At first many of the acquisitions were independent proprietary hospitals, but increasingly the dominant chains bought hospitals from other chains. In the 1980's public hospitals and private voluntary hospitals also began to be numbered among the acquisitions. The managers or trustees of many such hospitals, unable to raise enough capital to renovate aging facilities, have actively sought to be acquired. The chains have also built new hospitals; new construction accounted for 20 percent of their growth in the 1970's but only 4 percent from 1980 through 1984.

The chains have staged most of their growth in areas where the market is attractive: states with increasing population, rising per capita income, rising per capita income, few regulations and liberal insurance coverage. They have also sought out regions where there is limited competition from other kinds of hospitals. The chains have found those conditions most often in the South, the Southwest and the West.

Each year from 1977 through 1984 the number of hospitals affiliated with investor-owned chains increased by an average of about 11 percent, and by 1985 the 53 investor-owned chains owned or leased more than 680 hospitals with a total of more than 100,000 beds. HCA, born of the collaboration between Frist and Massey, accounted for half of those beds. Many corporations had also undertaken to employ their financing, management and marketing skills in operating hospitals they did not own: a total of 380 institutions with more than 48,000 beds.

In the past two years the phenomenal expansion of the hospital chains has slowed and their profits have declined. About half of the beds owned by the for-profit chains are now empty in part because of the cost-cutting measures recently adopted by Medicare, Medicaid and private insurers. Hospitals are now, for example, paid a preset fee for many kinds of treatment, an arrangement that encourages them to discharge patients quickly. The oversupply of beds also reflects the overbuilding and refurbishing encouraged by various provisions of Medicare and Medicaid in the previous era of generous reimbursements. The chains are now scrambling to sell off unprofitable hospitals.

They are also trying to circumvent cost-containment measures, which so far have focused mostly on hospital payments, by diversifying into other areas of health care. Psychiatric hospitals have been a favored area; insurers have not yet placed limits on their reimbursement for psychiatric care. The demand for beds in private psychiatric hospitals, moreover, is expected to rise as government-run hospitals cut back their services or close and as the stigma of psychiatric care diminishes. Nursing homes, which have traditionally been run for profit by private owners, have proved attractive to the hospital corporations as well. The corporations have also established themselves in many other kinds of health-care service: surgicenters (for ambulatory surgery), renal-dialysis programs, primarycare clinics, alcoholism and drug-abuse centers, hospices, industrial medical centers (for sick or injured workers), health-promotion programs, PPO's (preferred-provider organizations, which organize networks of physicians willing to provide discount care) and HMO's (health-maintenance organizations, which give comprehensive care as it is needed in return for a regular prepaid fee).

The hospital corporations have expanded into other services not only in an attempt to outflank cost containment but also to enable them to sell comprehensive packages of services to cost-conscious buyers. When the hospital, pharmacy, rehabilitation center, hospice and nursing home are under the same management, the care of patients who require treatment in a variety of settings can be coordinated more easily and, in theory, more efficiently. The same coordination, of course, could serve in exploiting the patient or the insurer in order to maximize profits. Some chains are integrating their services even further: they are buying or joining forces with insurance companies, enabling them both to sell insurance policies and to care for the policyholders.

The end of the era of dramatic expansion for the profit-making chains offers an opportunity to judge their impact on the health-care system. Their profoundest effect has been an indirect one: the for-profit chains have led the way to the commercialization of the entire system. Driven by many of the identical considerations that spurred the growth of for-profit chains, in particular a need for capital, clusters of nonprofit hospitals have banded together to form nonprofit chains. Until recently the nonprofit chains outstripped the phenomenal growth of their for-profit counterparts: there are now at least four times as many nonprofit chains, with twice as many beds. Of the 10 largest hospital chains in number of beds, the top four are for-profit systems. They are followed by the Adventist Health System, a religious nonprofit chain. The remaining five include two nonprofit religious systems, a for-profit chain, the New York City Health and Hospital Corporation (a public urban conglomerate) and Kaiser Foundation Hospitals, Inc. (a nonprofit HMO that owns a large system of hospitals, mostly in California).

Nonprofit systems resemble the for-profit corporations in many respects. They start or acquire PPO's, HMO's, alcohol- and drug-rehabilitation centers and the like. They manage other hospitals, invest in real estate and buy supplies at a discount. And they have been making money. Between 1983 and 1984, for example, the surpluses of the secular nonprofit chains increased faster than the profits of the investor-owned chains.

Fundamental differences remain, of course. Instead of paying dividends to stockholders, the nonprofit chains plow their surpluses into new or improved facilities, capital reserves or charity care. Many of the religious chains have one or two money-losing inner-city hospitals that are supported by more prosperous hospitals. Furthermore, most nonprofit chains are not intent on growing indefinitely. In most cases they exist primarily to serve their member hospitals rather than to establish a comprehensive system for the country or a large region. As a result the growth of the nonprofit chains has slowed down considerably. Meanwhile the big investor-owned corporations, even though they are not adding hospitals as fast as they once were, continue to expand into other areas of health care.

In another sense the distinction between the two kinds of hospitals is dissolving. A corporate ethos originating among the investor-owned chains has spread throughout the health-care system. In the past hospital administrators usually did not even know the true costs of the operating room or the intensive-care unit. Now the for-profit chains have set an example for all hospitals by introducing sophisticated management techniques and information systems for controlling the flow of supplies, personnel, patients and dollars. They have adopted aggressive marketing techniques meant to attract well-to-do patients, such as business executives, and patients for whom insurance compensation is generous, such as psychiatric cases and those covered by workmen's-comprensation policies. Increasingly, other hospitals are following suit.

Amenities such as streamlined billing and convenient hours have also figured in the chains' marketing strategy, as has an effort to create an image of efficiency and polish. Humana, Inc., for example, is known for specifying the number of seconds allowed for a meal to travel from the kitchen to the bedside and for a nurse to arrive after a patient presses the call button. Now that almost a third of the hospital beds in the U.S. are empty because of overbuilding and efforts by insurers and the Government to cut costs, all hospitals are learning these lessons in commercialism.

The for-profit chains contend that their hospitals are run more efficiently than nonprofit hospitals and offer better value for the health dollar. Most of the 13 studies that have evaluated the claims so far do not support it. In the most prominent study J. Michael Watt, Robert A. Derzon and James S. Hahn of Lewin and Associates, Inc., a consulting firm, and investigators from Johns Hopkins University matched 80 investor-owned hospitals with non-profit hospitals having a comparable location, scale of operation and mixture of services and cases. In 1978 and 1980, the years for which the workers compiled figures, the investor-owned hospitals incurred higher costs per patient per day in every category examined but one: the cost of operating their facility. The differential was largest, ironically, in administrative overhead, for which the for-profit hospitals spent an average of 57 percent more than their nonprofit counterparts. Of that difference, 83 percent reflected spending on the corporate headquarters of the chains.

At the same time, the for-profit hospitals studied also charged significantly more than the nonprofit hospitals did: an average of 22 percent more per admission. Routine bed charges did not differ much between the two types of hospitals; the disparity results from much higher charges by the investor-owned hospitals for ancillary services such as tests and drugs. After taking into account the taxes to which for-profit hospitals are subject and the gifts and subsidies nonprofit hospitals receive, the investigators found that the net revenues of the investor-owned hospitals were 10 percent higher per bed per day—enough to make such hospitals more profitable than the nonprofit ones, in spite of higher costs.

Traditionally, of course, the system of health-care financing in the U.S. has not encouraged efficiency, because it has compensated hospitals on the basis of their costs or their billed charges. Indeed, the system effectively discouraged effi-

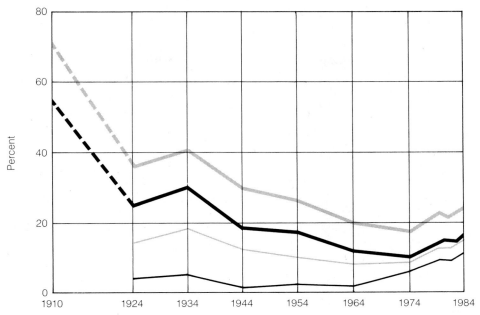

For-profit hospitals made up a large percentage of nongovernment hospitals (*gray*) and all hospitals (*black*) in the early years of this century. (The broken part of each curve represents a period for which data are scarce.) Because such proprietary hospitals were generally small, they controlled a relatively small proportion of total beds in nongovernment hospitals (thin gray line) and in all hospitals (thin black line). Most early proprietary hospitals were freestanding institutions owned by one or several doctors, and many offered substandard care. The recent increase in the number of for-profit hospitals after decades of decline reflects a new development: the emergence of chains of proprietary hospitals, owned by investors. Those hospitals are often of better quality than the older proprietary hospitals, many of which were bought and refurbished by the growing chains.

ciency: lower costs or charges led to lower reimbursements and made it difficult to justify subsequent increases. The efficient hospital in effect tightened its own financial noose. Now that cost-containment measures are putting an end to open-ended reimbursement, the for-profit corporations will need to achieve the operating efficiencies that sophisticated management should make possible.

Given the lack of incentives to cut costs, it is easy to see why the repeated charges that the chains skimp on quality have not been confirmed in half a dozen research studies that have looked into the question. The for-profit hospitals in the Watt study, for example, employed 13 percent fewer staff per adjusted patient-day than the nonprofit hospitals but paid them an average of 10 percent more in salary and benefits. Conceivably the higher pay attracts staff whose better quality offsets their proportionately smaller number. Other studies have examined such measures of quality as death rates and courses of illness,

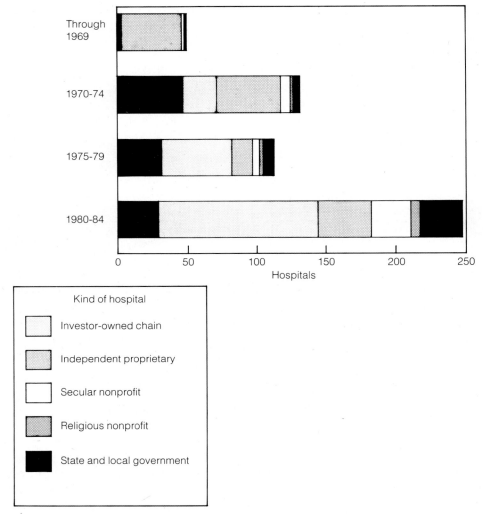

Sources of new hospitals added to investor-owned chains have varied with time. The bars combine statistics for six large for-profit chains: Hospital Corporation of America; Humana, Inc.; American Medical International, Inc.; National Medical Enterprises, Inc.; Charter Medical Corporation, and Republic Health Corporation. The chains at first grew almost entirely by buying or, in a few cases, leasing hospitals, mostly independent proprietary hospitals. More recently they have also acquired hospitals from other chains, as well as an increasing number of nonprofit and government hospitals. The chains have also grown by building new hospitals (black). Since 1984 an oversupply of hospital beds has developed and all growth has slowed. The graph is based on work done by Elizabeth W. Hoy and Bradford H. Gray of the Institute of Medicine.

malpractice liability, hospital accreditation and the proportion of board-certified specialists on the staff at investor-owned and nonprofit hospitals. Small differences emerged in individual measures, but overall the two kinds of hospitals were found to be comparable.

Because quality is an elusive attribute, meaning different things to different people, not all concerns have been dispelled. Do the for-profit chains cut corners, for example, when their hospital is the only one in town or in the county? There is no evidence that they do, but speculation continues. Another concern focuses on the bonuses an enterprising hospital might offer its staff physicians as an incentive for keeping costs down or increasing revenues. No decline in the quality of care has yet been attributed to such an arrangement, but the Institute of Medicine has declared that such bonus plans threaten doctors' obligation to act in their patients' best interests.

The many instances in which a for-profit chain has bought a small, financially troubled hospital provide another perspective on quality. In some cases the corporation has kept the hospital from going out of business, and in many more cases it has spent heavily on renovating and upgrading the facility. The generous provisions of Medicare and Medicaid regarding interest on debt, return on equity and depreciation have allowed much of the cost to be transferred to the taxpaying public. The open-ended reimbursement system has covered other costs and enabled the corporation to hire a capable staff and improve the hospital management. A study by Stephen M. Shortell of Northwestern University has shown that the corporation often gives doctors a more active role in running the hospital than they had before. Thus transformed, the hospital can attract a better medical staff, and quality probably improves.

Although any hospital exists mainly to treat patients, many hospitals traditionally have accommodated teaching and research as well. Some critics believe hospital corporations give low priority to most teaching and research and may change the character of what they do maintain. Until recently concern about the chains' attitudes toward teaching and research was largely moot, since they initially bought smaller, less distinguished hospitals, most of which had few such programs in the first place.

The chains do consider certain kinds of teaching to be good for business. In the hospitals they have taken over, many corporations have established or maintained training programs for nurses, laboratory technicians, respiratory therapists and other skilled personnel. Hospitals with good educational programs offer opportunities for advancement and hence attract higher-caliber personnel, and a better staff attracts more profitable patients.

It is also clear that the training of physicians is not by definition incompatible with corporate goals. HCA, for example, now owns or manages 34 hospitals with residency programs; 64 of HCA's hospitals have medical-school affiliations.

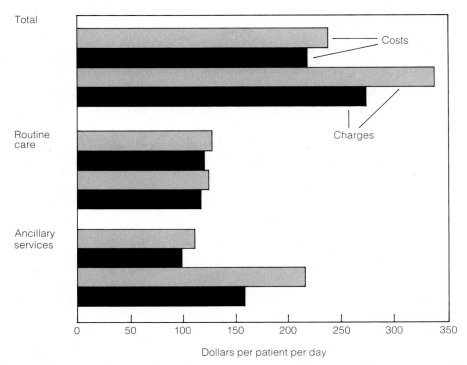

Costs and charges in hospitals belonging to investor-owned chains (white) are compared with those in nonprofit hospitals. The comparison is based on data for pairs of hospitals, one hospital nonprofit and the other investor-owned, that were comparable in their location, size, type of service and other characteristics. The average daily cost of caring for a patient was higher in the investor-owned hospitals than it was in the nonprofit facilities, and the gap remained when the cost was divided into routine costs and ancillary costs—costs for tests and drugs, for example. The disparity suggests that the investor-owned hospitals operated less efficiently. Those hospitals also charged more than the nonprofit ones did, in particular for ancillary services, enabling the for-profit hospitals to make money in spite of their lower efficiency. The comparison, done by J. Michael Watt, Robert A. Derzon and James S. Hahn of Lewin and Associates, Inc., and a group from Johns Hopkins University, is based on figures from 1978 and 1980; since then the Government and private insurance companies have introduced cost-containment measures that place a premium on efficiency. A future study might well yield a different picture.

After extensively publicized negotiations several large teaching hospitals recently became allied with other investor-owned chains. In such arrangements the university is often motivated by a lack of capital needed for renovating an aging facility and by the hope that the management and marketing skills of the corporation will render the hospital financially sound. The corporation, for its part, gains prestige, visibility and a sophisticated referral center for its other hospitals. Most observers agree it is too early to judge how corporate control will affect the character and mission of teaching hospitals.

Research as well as the training of doctors is a major function of teaching hospitals, and corporations that have taken over university hospitals have so far tended not to interfer with their research programs. In some cases the chain has provided generous financial support. On their own some of the chains have taken advantage of their extensive hospital systems for applied research. HCA, for instance, has formed a subsidiary that coordinates HCA hospitals for clinical trials of new drugs, for which the company receives grants from pharmaceutical houses. Humana supports research on new medical technologies and procedures and trains physicians in their use at certain of its hospitals, which it has designated "Centers of Excellence."

Even if its practical applications are limited, highly visible research can confer prestige and status, for which profit-making corporations are as eager as any nonprofit teaching hospital seeking star teams of investigators. Prestige was certainly one motivation for Humana's support of William C. DeVries and his research on artificial hearts at the Humana Heart Institute International in Louisville, where DeVries found the financial backing that had eluded him during his previous association with the University of Utah. Such arrangements, beneficial as they may be to individual workers, do entail ethical complexities, many observers believe. They raise the possibility of conflicts of interest when clinical research is done at an institution that stands to profit directly from the outcome.

Perhaps the sharpest criticisms of the for-profit chains concern treatment of the medically indigent—those who lack medical insurance, are ineligible for government assistance and cannot pay hospital bills on their own. Most studies have confirmed one contention: that for-profit hospital chains have acquired and built hospitals in areas that have relatively few patients who are uninsured or are covered by Medicaid, which generally reimburses hospitals and doctors at lower rates than Medicare and private insurers.

The chains have also been accused of devoting a smaller percentage of their budgets to charity care and bad debts than nonprofit hospitals do and of eliminating services that are heavily drawn on by indigent patients, such as trauma and obstetrics. The evidence bearing on these charges is somewhat contradictory, and hypotheses and anecdotes abound. An analysis done in 1981 by the Office for Civil Rights of the U.S. Department of Health and Human Services considered hospitals in for-profit chains together with freestanding proprietary hospitals and found they admitted a slightly smaller proportion of uninsured patients than nonprofit hospitals. In 1983 the American Hospital Association took unpaid charges as a measure of charity care and found no statistically significant differences between for-profit and nonprofit hospitals.

The Institute of Medicine, however, examined data on uncompensated care in five states: California, Florida, Tennessee, Texas and Virginia. Except for California, those states have relatively few public hospitals, and their Medicaid eligibility requirements are restrictive. Hence the burden of uncompensated care falls particularly heavily on voluntary and for-profit hospitals. Under those circumstances the two kinds of hospitals acquit themselves quite differently. In Florida, Texas and Virginia

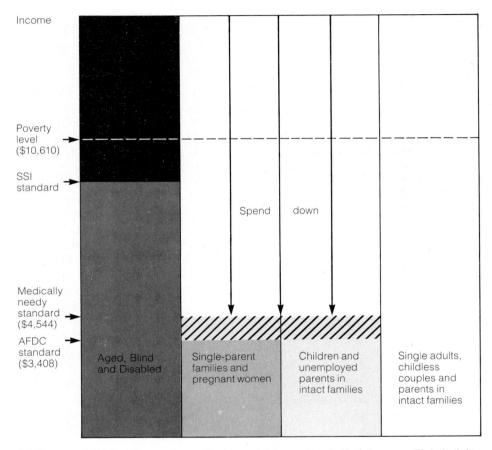

Medicare and Medicaid cover the medical costs of fewer than half of the poor. The eligibility requirements shown here are those in effect in Florida; the income levels applied to a family of four in 1984. Medicare (black) pays medical costs for the aged, blind and disabled regardless of income, and Medicaid (gray) covers single-parent families and pregnant women whose income (after certain deductions) falls at or below the income standard for the Aid to Families with Dependent Children (AFDC) program. (Each state sets its own standard, which is usually well below the poverty level.) Medicare recipients are also eligible for Medicaid if their income drops below the standard for the Supplemental Security Income (SSI) program; Medicaid then reimburses costs for services not covered by Medicare. Florida, like many other states, extends Medicaid coverage to children and unemployed parents in intact families below the AFDC standard. It also has a "spend down" provision, under which certain families can claim Medicaid benefits if medical expenses reduce their income to the "medically needy" standard or below. Many of the poor in Florida and in other states must nonetheless depend on charity care at public and private hospitals. The chart is based on one prepared by Lewin and Associates, Inc.

hospitals in private nonprofit chains spent almost twice as much on charity care as hospitals belonging to investor-owned chains. In Tennessee the non-profit hospitals spent almost three times as much.

In none of the five states did private hospitals of either kind provide as much charity care as public hospitals, and the same disparity is seen in every other state. Nationwide, for-profit and nonprofit hospitals together devote only between 3 and 5 percent of their revenues to uncompensated care. In response to cost-cutting measures and the burden of surplus hospital beds both kinds of hospitals are attempting to reduce uncompensated care still further. They limit the number of uninsured patients who are admitted by setting quotas, by eliminating or cutting down on services that attract large numbers of the uninsured and by requiring payment in advance or doing "wallet biopsies." Such practices by nonprofit hospitals have led some observers to call for an end to their tax-exempt status.

For-profit hospitals have sometimes compounded the problem by competing aggressively for paying patients, thereby depriving voluntary hospitals of the revenue needed to support uncompensated care. In Florida during the early 1980's, competition with for-profit hospitals put financial pressure on voluntary hospitals, which rejected increasing numbers of indigent patients. The burden of charity care fell more heavily than ever on the public hospitals, and because they operate on a fixed budget the burden soon threw them into financial crisis. The ensuing political crisis led to an expansion of the state's Medicaid program financed in part by an assessment on hospital revenues.

Such institutional failure exacts an appalling human cost. Private hospitals increasingly turn away indigent patients who arrive in their emergency rooms, often without first ensuring that a patient's condition is stable. A team of physicians at Cook County Hospital, a public hospital in Chicago, recently tracked 467 patients who were transferred there from the emergency rooms of for-profit and voluntary hospitals (including many nonprofit teaching hospitals). Follow-up data revealed that 24 percent of the patients were transferred in an unstable condition and 22 percent had to be admitted to an intensive-care unit on arrival. Of the nonsurgical patients who were transferred, 9.4 percent died during their hospitalization.

The investor-owned chains, through their own actions and the competition and commercialism they have spawned, draw attention to the fundamental problem: the U.S. stands as the only remaining industrialized nation, except for South Africa, that does not cover as a right of citizenship the medical expenses of anyone who becomes seriously ill. More than half of the poor are not protected by Medicaid because of restrictions on eligibility, and many more people who are not poor lack insurance because they have been laid off from their jobs or work in low-paying positions. All told, some 35 million Americans have no medical insurance for part or all of each year. Until a national solution is devised, a large part of the U.S. population will have nowhere to turn when faced with catastrophic medical bills.

By highlighting other shortcomings of the health-care system the for-profit chains are speeding its transformation. Historically the chains themselves will be seen as transitional institutions. They grew out of the generous reimbursement system sought by the medical profession, and they exploited the system deftly, teaching lessons in capital formation, management and marketing that are now expertly practiced by many of their nonprofit counterparts. In the process the chains hastened the crisis in health costs and the ensuing cost-containment measures.

Those measures in turn have led the chains to transform themselves into integrated systems offering comprehensive services and in many cases selling insurance to pay for them. In their new forms the for-profit systems will continue to grow, not only as an economic force but also as a political one. Increasingly they will have the power to shape the economic and regulatory framework of U.S. health care as well as to seek new opportunities within it.

19   DRGs: THE COUNTERREVOLUTION IN FINANCING HEALTH CARE

Danielle A. Dolenc and Charles J. Dougherty

We are in the midst of a dramatic change in health care financing. Diagnosis-Related Groups (DRGs), adopted by Congress in March 1983, are now in place in hospitals providing Medicare services around the country. Several states (Michigan, New Jersey, Ohio, Washington, Pennsylvania, and Utah) have introduced this new federal method of paying for Medicare costs into their Medicaid programs and others (Indiana, Minnesota, and North Carolina) are about to.[1] Private insurance carriers will almost certainly adopt some version of DRGs to settle their health care claims. When completed, the changeover to DRGs will be the greatest alteration in the economics of American health care since the introduction of Medicare and Medicaid in 1965. The earlier federal initiative was revolutionary in providing widespread access to quality medical care in the context of rapidly expanding technology. This is the counterrevolution. DRGs threaten to restrict access to health care, to compromise its quality, and to impede the development of new medical technologies. Furthermore, they will accelerate the takeover of American medicine by large for-profit corporations.

SOURCE: *Hastings Center Report* 15, no. 3 (June 1985): 19–29. Reprinted by permission. © The Hastings Center.

Before 1983, federal reimbursement for Medicare services was retrospective. The payment was determined by the total bill at discharge. A hospital would send the final charge for a Medicare patient to the government in much the same way that private patients send bills for reimbursement to their insurance companies. The federal government reimbursed the hospital the total charge or some reasonable percent of it. With some third party paying the bill, usually without questions asked, there was no economic incentive to contain medical costs. With the development of high-priced medical equipment and facilities, those bills grew larger and larger, accounting, in good measure, for the spiraling inflation in the health care sector of the American economy.[2]

DRGs were devised to provide incentives for cost containment. Hospitals are paid a predetermined price for their services, a price based on the average cost of treating a patient with a particular diagnosis. They can no longer charge what they want, not even what their services cost. They are reimbursed only for what the DRGs allow. Hence, hospitals must now be DRG-efficient in providing services: real costs must not exceed present DRG rates overall. And if hospitals are to generate the surplus needed for replacement of equipment, expansion of services, and salary increases, real costs must be lower than those rates more often than not.

The diagnostic groups utilized in Medicare funding were originally developed by the Yale School of Medicine to measure a hospital's case-mix, the types and ratios of illnesses a hospital typically handles. The Yale scheme listed 383 groups, but the Health Care Financing Administration has constructed 468 groups for federal use.[3] These categories of related diagnoses were designed to be medically relevant yet statistically applicable.[4] They are delimited by several parameters: length of stay as determined by primary diagnosis, secondary diagnosis, surgical procedures, and patient age (when this affects the length of stay).[5]

Patients who die or have a length of stay above or below the "trim points" for a particular diagnosis are classified as day outliers, and the costs of their care are not reimbursed by preset rates.[6] Cost outliers are those patients whose costs exceed the DRG trim points of 150 percent or $12,000, whichever is greater.[7] When New Jersey implemented a DRG system in 1980, its outlier policy was based on the assumption that a radically different length of stay within a DRG indicated unknown clinical characteristics, making DRG-based payment unfair.[8] Although an estimated 30 percent of all cases in New Jersey qualified for outlier status,[9] under Medicare the total outlier payments per hospital cannot exceed 6 percent of costs that exceed the DRG trim points.

DRG-determined rates per case are derived from the following equation: DRG weight x dollar rate $=$ prospective payment.[10] The DRG weight is an index representing resource use by particular illness. It ranges from a high of 6.8631 for

DRG 457 (extensive burns) to a low of .1842 for DRG 382 (false labor). The dollar rate is the average cost of all the hospitals' patients at discharge. Prior to 1986, this rate will be determined on the basis of regional rates plus the specific hospital's actual costs. Beginning in 1986, Medicare will calculate costs based only on which of nine geographic regions a hospital occupies and whether it is urban or rural. Cost variations due to the health characteristics of the population served by the hospital will therefore not be accounted for (after 1986) as they are in the New Jersey system.[11]

The product of DRG weight and dollar rate is the prospective payment. For example, the 1986 DRG-determined payment to an Omaha area hospital for uncomplicated asthma in a patient under 18 will be calculated as follows:

$$
\begin{array}{ll}
.4275 & \text{weight for DRG 98} \\
\times\ \$2{,}888.76 & \text{dollar rate (West North} \\
\rule{2.5cm}{0.4pt} & \text{Central, urban)} \\
\$1{,}234.94 & \text{Prospective payment}
\end{array}
$$

Should the cost of this patient's illness exceed $1,852.41 (150 percent of the prospective price), Medicare will classify the case as an outlier and pay 60 percent of costs incurred after this trim point has been reached. Note that the $617.47 difference between the DRG-determined price ($1,234.94) and the trim point ($1,852.41) is absorbed entirely by the hospital, as is 40 percent of the cost beyond that. This can entail large hospital losses. A coronary bypass outlier, for example, would cost

the hospital $5,761.78, before Medicare even began to pay 60 percent of the additional costs.

Hospitals will receive the full DRG reimbursement even if actual costs are lower than DRG projections. But this will benefit few hospitals and only then in the short run.[12] In the long run the DRG pricing system will drive costs down continually by annual recalculation of regional dollar rates. When hospitals seek to reduce costs in order to make up the difference between actual cost and DRG payment, they will be driving down the average cost of each DRG in the region. Thus (ignoring general inflation), the following year's DRG calculation will result in a lower reimbursement for all hospitals in the region, making additional efficiencies necessary and lowering the next year's reimbursement schedule accordingly. Hospital efficiency is thereby mandated but hardly rewarded. In New Jersey, hospitals fared well under the first year of DRG-based rates, but have since experienced difficulties.[13]

If this change were restricted to federal reimbursement through Medicare, most hospitals could avoid a financial crunch simply by avoiding Medicare patients or by shifting costs to patients carrying private insurance. However, prospective payment will no doubt be widely adopted for all payers in some form.[14] The Health Insurance Association of America is at the forefront of the movement toward all-payer DRGs. They cite cost-shifting as responsible for 13 percent of the private patient's bill,[15] a bill paid by health insurance companies and passed on to the consumer as higher premiums. In an all-payer DRG system, all health care institutions will feel the dramatic effects of this method of cost containment.

Surely something had to be done to contain health care costs, and DRGs and their insurance company counterparts will undoubtedly have this salutary effect. But far too little attention has been paid to the negative potential of prospective payment as a mechanism for financing health care. Although it is too early to secure firm data on the overall performance of DRGs, some trends have begun to surface. Another indicator of what the future holds is the kind of professional advice being offered publicly to hospital administrators. Finally, the present structure of DRG financing strongly suggests the likelihood of certain kinds of untoward consequences.

Reduced Access to Hospitals

Accessibility

Plainly, DRG-based financial incentives will discourage hospitals from treating outliers. When the system pays none of the costs over the preset rate until costs pass the trim points of 150 percent of $12,000 more than the DRG figure and then only 60 percent of that portion, a powerful incentive exists to avoid patients whose DRGs may be artificially low, or who may not respond to treatment within the average range. Outliers will become the pariahs of health care financing. Further, since Medicare will allow only 6 percent outlier costs per hospital, the vast majority of cases will be

paid at preset rates even if many of these are outliers, denying the hospital even the 60 percent return past trim point. Thus hospitals will try to avoid seriously ill patients, who will likely require a longer length of stay and will therefore most likely cost more than prospective payments allow.

Already some hospitals are discouraging admission of "certain types of patients to keep down the number and amount of outliers."[16] Many hospitals may have to resort to this sort of behavior for economic survival. The averaging mechanism of Medicare presumes a more or less average distribution of patients across all hospitals. But individual cases can vary widely. "In one year at one New Jersey hospital," according to Stanley Bergen and Amy Roth, "charges reportedly ranged from $1,140 to $3,900 in one DRG and from $2,933 to $8,708 in another."[17] And Bernard Pettingill and Harriet Westell write that "one study at Johns Hopkins University reported a range in cost of $57,000 for one diagnosis related group of 88 sample cases."[18]

Studies at Rush Medical Center show that DRG payments for their Medicare Patients in 1984 would end up 7 percent to 8 percent below their costs. At Yale-New Haven Hospital, where 10 percent of Medicare patients have very long lengths of stay, studies show that the hospital could lose as much as $798 on each Medicare patient treated.[19] And these wide deviations from the average cost of treating a patient with a given disease are unevenly distributed. Some hospitals—because of their locations, the demographics of nearby populations, traditional specializations and services, and a sense of institutional mission—treat sicker-than-average patients whose length of stay is routinely longer than average, and who are thereby more likely to be cost outliers.[20] Because of DRG rules, *Hospitals* magazine reports that these hospitals, "are just getting fiscally battered for it."

By way of self-defense, hospitals are being advised to establish "case-mix management" strategies,[21] a thinly veiled euphemism for attracting DRG-profitable patients and avoiding DRG-costly patients. Often this advice is disarmingly frank: "Clearly a strategy for maintaining financial solvency is to minimize the number of categories (weighted by the number of cases per year—case-mix) which offer a negative return."[22] The reality behind the jargon of "cost outlier," "case-mix management," and "categories" is that sicker-than-average human beings will be shunned by DRG-regulated hospitals.

Access to health care will be further restricted to a group already shunned by most hospitals: the medically indigent, those whose medical costs are not covered by Medicare, Medicaid, or private insurance programs and who cannot pay their own medical bills. In 1983 the Robert Wood Johnson Foundation estimated the number of adults who were both poor and uninsured at 7.5 million. Extrapolating that figure to include children yields approximately 10 million medically indigent Americans.[23] Hospitals that

continue to serve the medically indigent, usually those in the inner city and often public or teaching hospitals, have been financing this burden by shifting costs to private payers' insurance companies.[24] If 10 percent of a hospital's charges are uncollectible, that amount is typically padded into the collected bills by way of correspondingly higher prices for all the hospitals' services. This shifts the cost from nonpaying patients to paying, and represents a hidden tax on insurance premium holders. When private insurance companies adopt prospective payments, charges to them can no longer be padded with a portion of someone else's unpaid bill. Hence the main mechanism by which health care for the medically indigent has been (surreptitiously) financed will be removed.

Even those among the poor who are covered by Medicaid or who have private insurance coverage will likely find access to hospitals restricted as both state governments and private industry move to some version of DRGs. Since DRGs reflect only inpatient data, they ignore the general health of the patient on admission—unless there is a condition obvious enough to count as a secondary diagnosis. If it is reasonable to assume that the poor have a harder time finding needed primary care, have less adequate nutrition, and have less healthy lifestyles generally, then they will typically enter hospitals with a poorer overall state of health than the relatively affluent. If so, they will respond to treatment at a slower rate, have a longer length of stay and thus cost more to treat.[25] As a group, they will have an inordinately high rate of outliers. But by 1986, federal reimbursement will not reflect local conditions at all. From that time on, hospitals in neighborhoods with high rates of poverty, and by assumption poorer overall health, will have the same schedule of repayments as hospitals in the most affluent neighborhoods. This will create a strong economic incentive to avoid providing medical services to the poor, whether they are medically indigent or not.

At best, Americans have created a "two-tiered" system of health care.[26] Now, hospitals that have traditionally served the medical needs of the poor consigned to the lower tier are being advised publicly that one way to face the challenges of the new world of DRGs is by changing their mission. Even more unsettling is the prediction that there will be little resistance to this reevaluation.

> Of course, a redefinition of mission may generate a good deal of conflict for organizational members with longtime affiliations, especially if new goals diverge from their initial concept of the institution. In many cases it was the community service aspect of the enterprise that motivated them to join. On the other hand, be prepared for a few surprises. There are many who will welcome the opportunity to modify or shift from traditional directions.[27]

On this reading, many institutions traditionally serving the poor "will welcome the opportunity" to forsake them altogether.

In the current climate of federal cutbacks in social services and local taxpayers' revolts, governmental units are unlikely to step into the breach. More likely, the poor will simply be shut out. This needn't occur by literally turning persons away at hospital doors (though this crude method has already been used[28]). The poor can be excluded by closing hospital emergency rooms in their neighborhoods, thus denying them easy entry into the health care system. OB/GYN and pediatric services can also be closed or made more difficult for the poor to enter. And inner-city hospitals can move to the suburbs.

A major means of restricting access to health care is the outright closing of hospitals. If prospective payments do not reflect what a hospital spends in treating each patient in a disease category,[29] many will have no alternative to closing down. Smaller hospitals serving the poor and minorities will be the earliest casualties of DRG financing. When this occurs, the urban poor will seek access to care at the many teaching hospitals where care is inherently more costly. This will drive overall costs up, not down,[30] unless, of course, these persons are denied care at teaching hospitals as well.

Rural hospitals are also in immediate financial danger. While large urban hospitals may be able to consolidate or eliminate services to "manage case-mix," a rural hospital is often the sole local provider and must maintain a full line of service areas. St. Joseph Hospital of Del Norte, Colorado, for example, cut staff "from 105.9 to 85 and closed one floor of the hospital after three months on PPS" (prospective payment systems). Similar distress has already been reported from rural hospitals in Wisconsin and Idaho and more of the same is predicted throughout the country by a spokesman for the American Hospital Association's Section on Small and Rural Hospitals.[31] Though the strongest impact will fall on inner-city and rural hospitals, many hospitals have begun to feel the pinch of DRGs. The cost of capital to many hospitals is rising as their financial ratings are lowered, due to what *Creditweek* calls, "an increasingly onerous reimbursement environment."[32]

Chances are that the politically powerful middle class will not accept the sort of restricted access that will be forced on others. They will find some method, within or without the DRG system, to keep suburban hospitals open. But by then a great deal of damage will already have been done. Damaged most may be the aspiration to create a society in which some decent minimum level of health care is available to all, regardless of location and regardless of ability to pay.

A Threat to Quality Care

Many variables affect the quality of a hospital patient's care. They can be categorized under three general headings. The first is strictly medical: access in the hospital to appropriate tests and treatments. The second is quasi-medical: the availability of a range of support mechanisms that enhance the psychological well-being of patients. A third set of variables is nonmedical, chiefly the patient's relationship with health care providers and with the hospital itself. All three sorts of variables may be negatively affected by DRGs.

The imposition of exactly 468 categories of illnesses onto the whole spectrum of human disease and suffering is clearly arbitrary. Of course, we must often tolerate arbitrariness when policies have to be made and regulations enforced. A citizen can vote, drive, or drink at one precise age and not another, for example. But in the case of DRGs, arbitrariness is being introduced in caring for people during some of the most important moments of their lives: occasions of birth, death, suffering, anxiety, and physical disability.

DRGs threaten to turn hospital beds into procrustean beds, creating institutional inflexibility which may prevent health care professionals from responding to the infinite variations of these intimate individual occasions. Some tests that might be helpful will be omitted because of grouping and cost. Some therapies that might yield results for a particular patient will not be tried because they do not fit the DRG. And since some DRGs will inevitably be more profitable than others, there will be pressures in hospitals to favor these diagnoses.[33] The Department of Health and Human Services has in fact reported a "higher-than-expected increase in case-mix indexes." Secretary Margaret Heckler has warned that the department will scrutinize hospital records in search of "DRG creep."[34] This is not just an issue of evading government regulations. Placing a patient in a diagnostic group on the basis of a hospital's reimbursement needs is the first step in diminishing the quality of that patient's care.

Earlier discharge of hospital patients also affects the quality of medical care. The Health Care Financing Administration's data show a DRG-related decline in average length of stay from 9.5 days to 7.4 days.[35] This may indicate more efficient use of hospital services; but it may also indicate a trend toward premature discharge, several reports of which have already surfaced.[36]

A greater immediate concern centers on the fact that rehabilitation hospitals (like psychiatric, long-term care, and children's hospitals) are exempt from DRG regulation. This creates an incentive to discharge patients as early as possible from acute care hospitals and place them in rehabilitation hospitals. According to Brent England, The American Hospital Association's director of rehabilitation hospitals and programs, these hospitals and programs are now reporting that "they are seeing the sicker, more involved patients." Therapists are having to learn new skills, such as "teaching patients to ambulate when they are still attached to respirators." Edward Stein, president of the Rehabilitation Institute of Chicago, confirms that rehabilitation centers are being pressured to handle patients earlier and faster. "Since PPS," Stein says, "many patients admitted to [my] facility are not stable medically, so the rehabilitation staff has the added responsibility of resolving patients' medical problems."[37]

There are also fears that patients with certain DRGs will be discharged from hospitals prematurely only so that they can be readmitted soon afterwards under a different, more profitable DRG. Official concern about this sort of DRG scam is strong enough that in Ohio's proposed Medicaid system specific provisions have been included to guard against it.

As the DRG-fueled demand for efficiency accelerates, the patient will more and more come to be regarded as a product. The Morristown (N.J.) Hospital Authority clearly expressed this new model: "Eventually, we'll know exactly what it costs to produce an appendectomy, just like General Motors knows how much it costs to put rear tires on a car."[38] And the chief financial officer of American Medical International, the second largest for-profit hospital chain in the U.S., is equally frank about the origins of A.M.I.'s aggressive cost accounting system: "My old manufacturing and mining experience told me that process cost accounting plus standard costing would lead to (enhanced) productivity when I came to A.M.I. 13 years ago."[39] Though there was no incentive to use such methods then, "prospective payments and increased competition" are reasons enough now.

According to *Hospitals* magazine, hospitals across the country are being forced to develop "systems to obtain and project product line information and its effect on profitability." Karl Zeisler, financial vice-president for Rush-Presbyterian Hospital, a leader in developing a software system to cope with the DRGs, knows what his system must do: "It's the business of translating a manufacturing system into our kind of business."[40] In a recent bit of public managerial advice, Granada Hills Community Hospital was told that prospective payment requires that they "manage themselves on a product line basis."[41] This kind of reification of patient services will affect all hospitals. "Like other hospitals, university facilities will identify 'product lines' of greatest profit to them—that is, the care they can render competitively."[42] With presumptions like these already in place, there can be little security that hospital patients will be receiving all the strictly medical services that quality care demands. When hospitals manufacture products, let the buyer beware.

DRG incentives are causing hospitals to review all their services. As one study points out, "This, of course, may...dictate that some services traditionally offered in the hospital must now be phased out or discontinued, and, other services may now be targeted as high priority offerings." Policies will be developed "to discourage the use of supplementary ancillary services which have a minimal return."[43] The American Physical Therapists Association reports that its members are already feeling effects of the DRGs. Over half report an increase in "productivity monitoring," and 41 percent report a decrease in their budgets. According to Steve Forer, administrator at Santa Clara Valley Medical Center, the onus is now on the physical therapist "to prove that ordering more therapy, rather than less, will have a significant effect on reducing length of stay."

The patient-as-product model is likely to add to the hospital patient's psychic pressures. But quasi-medical support programs that improve the patient's psychological and emotional well-being will also be casualties of prospective payments. Already physicians estimate that 20 to 50 percent of symptoms are of psychological origin alone,[44] and the forced efficiencies of DRG financing will probably increase this percentage. At the same time, programs not directly related to shortening lengths of stay, or themselves reimbursed prospectively, will be candidates for cutback or elimination. At a Morristown, N.J., hospital, one of two art therapists in psychiatry was laid off because of prospective payment.[45] Of course, the psyche of the patient will be cared for when it makes financial sense to do so—when it helps to attract profitable patients to the hospital, for example—or when it gets unprofitable patients discharged sooner. But DRGs offer a strong incentive to avoid providing any patient support systems that are not economically justified.

Finally, the quality of care is in part a function of the relationship the patient has with health care providers and the hospital itself. The historical prevalence of trust that the health care provider, especially the doctor, is motivated by the best interest of the patient has led to the unusually favored social position of American doctors. Prospective payment financing cannot help but make patients worry that their diagnosis, treatment, and discharge are influenced by considerations other than their best medical care.

And patients may well have grounds for these worries. Hospital physicians will be placed under extraordinary new pressures. The need to translate the DRG system into real dollar expenses might well lead, for example, to the assignment of budgets for individual cases at admission. St. Joseph Hospital in Colorado supplies medical staff members with monthly physician-DRG profiles and has revamped salary and wage programs to tie the performance of employees to attainment of DRG goals. Recently the Healthcare Financial Management Association was told that a law firm had been hired to develop a system of "positive and negative incentives for physicians." The idea is to identify physicians who are "under or over the norms and reward or penalize those physicians."[46] Minnette Terlep, director of medical records at St. Joseph Medical Center in Joliet, Illinois, reports that the DRGs have prompted more stringent regulations governing physicians' completion of patients' medical records, including monetary fines for physicians not meeting the new regulations.[47] Though physicians may initially resist, management experts claim that "they will soon realize that the financially solvent hospitals with promising professional opportunities are also those with more efficient operations and professionally responsible policies."[48] Chief operating officer of Parkland Memorial Hospital in Dallas, Ray Newman, makes no overly fine point about his hospital's incentives. "Essentially," he says, "in working with department managers and physicians, 'behavior modification' is necessary."[49]

Success of such efforts may well mean the end of the role of the physician as independent patient advocate. This is bad for all patients, but potentially disastrous for those in critical care units. Surely physicians will not act against a patient's obvious best interest. However, as an article in *JAMA* points out, "in cases wherein the patient's best interests are unclear and the prognosis truly gray, decisions may now be subtly tipped in favor of discontinuing life support on the basis of financial considerations."[50] It will not take too many publicly reported cases of this kind of decision making to erode severely patient trust in physicians generally.[51]

On the other hand, doctors may insist on their traditional responsibility as patient advocates and enter into a more adversarial relationship with hospitals. Even this state of affairs, while preferable to the first, is likely to erode patient confidence in the system. The suspicion that one's physician has to battle constantly with hospital authorities in order to provide the care he or she believes is medically indicated is not likely to endear patients to hospitals and their administrators and owners.

Others working in hospitals will feel the impact of DRGs too. An informal survey of state hospital associations by *Hospitals* indicates that DRGs are responsible for the production of pink slips and refusals to fill vacancies across the country. Staff reductions and pay freezes have occurred in Hawaii, Florida, Iowa, Louisiana, Maine, Michigan, Missouri, Montana, North Dakota, Oregon, Tennessee, West Virginia, and Wyoming. Pennsylvania hospitals are adding staff DRG coordinators. DRGs have precipitated reduction in nursing hours by 5,000 at Madison Memorial Hospital in Idaho. And a recent survey of hospital employee attitudes indicates that DRGs have increased worries about job security and dissatisfaction with pay and benefits.[52] Employees under DRGs also have a greater sense that their administration does not understand their concerns and that other hospital departments are less cooperative but treated better. These changes can hardly enhance the quality of a patient's stay in a hospital.

Patients' relationships with hospitals will be further complicated by the mandatory introduction of a Peer Review Organization (formerly Professional Standards Review Organization) to review cases periodically. PROs check DRG classification, appropriateness of admission and discharge, outliers' status, and many even order hospital discharge for a patient.[53] One can hope that PROs will give physicians more muscle to resist hospital pressures for efficiency and will free them to act solely on behalf of patients' best interests. But they could just as easily do the reverse. Because PROs may be comprised of nonmedical personnel (insurance company representatives, for example),[54] they may become DRG-enforcement organizations assessing the economics but not the quality of patient care.

A Slowdown in Medical Progress

Less direct compromises in quality are also in store for those seeking care under DRGs: they follow from the difference between what will be and what might have been. Future patients may be denied a test or a treatment that might have been available but is not because there was no financial incentive for hospitals to buy it, or none to develop it in the first place.

DRG-based medical care will be less than science is capable of providing if hospitals are unable to add new programs or purchase initially expensive technology. DRG rates are set by prices charged three years earlier, plus allowance for inflation. Included is a 1 percent raise for the purchase of new medical technology, but this figure represents, at best, one fourth of current expenditures.[55] Even Stuart Altman, chairman of Medicare's Prospective Payment Assessment Commission, admits that DRGs may create a "bureaucratic maze, the end result of which will be a slowdown of technological innovation."[56]

Excessive use and redundant purchase of high technology have been a major source of explosive hospital rate increases. Sharing high technology and concentrating it in central locations (provided those locations were within reach of all patients) would be an effective and ethical cost-containing measure. But instead of encouraging this sort of cooperative planning, DRG financing threatens to eliminate any new service that is not deemed cost-effective in the short run. A point may quickly be reached when new programs and machines can be added only if existing ones are discontinued. Where would cardiac care be today if we had followed DRG-based incentives thirty years ago when bed rest was the prevailing treatment for heart trouble?

Many medical advances in the U.S. come from techniques and machinery developed initially in medical schools and their affiliated teaching hospitals. But DRGs spell hard times for these academic centers as well. University-affiliated hospitals, because they provide care to the needy and the severely ill, are in an especially precarious position. Currently, the higher costs of a teaching hospital are chalked up to its role as a provider of health care education and are paid in one lump sum by Medicare.

However, some believe that a university hospital's high costs are not entirely attributable to teaching needs, but are due in part to care required by poorer and sicker patients. If this is the case and Medicare begins to pay university institutions by DRGs only, these hospitals will lose the extra funding that ostensibly covered educational costs, but that also paid part of the legitimate expenses of caring for poor and intensively ill patients. As shown earlier, DRGs will gauge neither preexisting poor health nor the severity of illness. The discrimination of DRG payment plans against hospitals whose patients within a given DRG are more ill, is thus a threat to the health of academic medicine in the U.S.

If the university hospital is forced to choose between its roles as provider of indigent care and intensive care and as pioneer in medical technology, thus pitting the present interests of the poor and very ill against the interests of those served by a more developed medicine of the future, financial incentives will favor the latter. Even so, funding for medical research in a DRG-based health care economy will likely not match recent levels. With hospitals financially strapped and fearful of going under, there will not be the demand for new medical technologies and services. When the patient becomes a product, medicine becomes a business; and in business, where there is no demand, there is no financial incentive to supply.

Corporate Profit

Though many factors account for the dramatic growth in the for-profit sector, the difficulties hospitals face because of prospective payments will accelerate this trend.[57] In 1979 corporate hospital chains owned approximately 68,000 beds; by 1983 the number had jumped to nearly 107,000. There are just short of 7,000 hospitals in the U.S. and over 1,000 are now run for-profit by hospital chains. The five largest of these chains had combined 1983 revenues of over $10 billion and profits over $600 million.[58]

Under prospective payments, small, and even large, free-standing hospitals will be more and more inclined to seek the economic shelter and capital power of the for-profit chains, to shore up their finances. There are numerous reasons to be concerned about the prospect of the wholesale corporatization of American hospital care, a subject that has recently come in for considerable scrutiny. Here we will briefly mention a few.

First, since World War II the American public has invested handsomely in the building of hospitals when they were not-for-profit, in the education of doctors and other health care providers, and in medical research.[59] All these publicly financed assets are now being absorbed by private corporations for the benefit of stockholders. On the face of it, this seems unjust. Profits from public investments are going into private hands.

Second, absorption by corporate chains will mean a loss of local control over health care facilities. As Paul Starr points out in *The Social Transformation of American Medicine*, "Strong central management is the pattern among the for-profit chains. The majority of for-profit companies report that power to set hospital budgets, plan capital investments, appoint chief hospital administrators, and make other key decisions rests with management at corporate headquarters." Decisions to terminate or begin services and to close or open facilities will be made primarily on the basis of the chain's overall financial goals, and not the needs of the communities they serve. Having lost the ability to create rational local plans, cities and counties will have their health care agenda set for them in closed board meetings out of town, and on the basis of values they very well may not share.

As local autonomy is lost, so is the remaining pluralism of American medical care. Voluntary not-for-profit hospitals, public hospitals, religiously affiliated hospitals, and university teaching hospitals will tend more and more to fall into the proprietary chains' orbits. By way of self-defense, many nonprofit hospitals have begun to merge or to form chains of their own. The Catholic Health Association, for example, now has 44 Catholic hospital chains as members, some owning as many as twenty hospitals.[60] Still, considerable homogenization of care will result, and part of the vitality of our health care system will have been lost.

Third, increased presence of for-profit corporate medicine will make it harder yet for the poor and the very sick to find health care. Profit-making corporations cannot give their stockholders' money away unless there is more money to be made by doing so—such as a tax advantage or enhanced public relations that result in profits elsewhere.[61] Indeed, one can expect that for-profit hospital corporations will claim that care for the poor is exclusively a government responsibility. And one can predict that the major for-profit hospital corporations will develop sophisticated and efficient methods to detect and avoid potential cost outliers.

Finally, academic medicine is directly threatened by corporatization. The university of Louisville's teaching hospital is already operated by for-profit Humana, Inc.[62] St. Joseph Hospital in Omaha, the primary teaching hospital for Creighton University's Medical School, has been sold to American Medical International.[63] George Washington University is discussing a hospital sale to A.M.I. as well. And Harvard's McLean Hospital recently was saved from sale to Hospital Corporation of

America only by vocal faculty opposition. If this development continues American medical faculty may well become the research and development wing of for-profit hospital corporations and a new generation of health care professionals will be educated to the idea that medicine is just another big business whose goal is to turn a profit.

Prospective payments will likely hasten the advent of complete proprietary corporate control over the distribution of American health care by compromising the financial health of independent, not-for-profit hospitals. Even is this were the only price exacted by the DRGs, it would be too high.

The Human Price Tag

DRGs have been introduced to cut health care costs and they will probably do so. But if our concerns are valid, the human cost will be unconscionable. Access, quality of care, medical progress, and the autonomy of hospitals will all be sacrificed in the name of efficiency. At the heart of this cost-cutting counterrevolution is the assumption that health care is a commodity like any other, and therefore when regulatory adjustments force efficiencies, the unproductive elements in the economy will "shake-out" and the result will be cheaper, high quality care for all.

This simplistic assumption is rarely true in today's mixed economy even in straightforward commodity exchange. But it is certainly mistaken when applied to health care.[64] Access to decent levels of

care is more than a matter of compassion; it is a fundamental precondition for enjoying "life, liberty, and the pursuit of happiness." Thus, it is a basic American right.

The DRG approach to financing of health care inverts the natural relationship of means to ends in health care. As large institutions, hospitals have always been "big business" in a sense. But until recently the demands of efficiency were the means that served one end—the care of sick and dying persons. Now the financial pressures that prospective payment places on hospitals, and their increasingly for-profit status, will yield a new result—health care for persons when and to the extent that it makes "good business sense." If we are to avoid some of the worst of these consequences, a rethinking of the whole DRG approach is in order. This should include renewed consideration of a national system of health insurance and a serious look at how other industrial democracies finance the health care of their citizens. Short of this wider strategy, certain corrections should be immediately introduced into the DRG systems before 1986. We recommend the following:

> 1. Hospitals should be grouped by the population they serve; whether they are public or private; not-for-profit or for-profit; inner-city, suburban, or rural, whether they serve special educational and research needs and so on. Separate DRG rates should be established for each group thereby more fairly expressing the real costs of

operating different kinds of hospitals.

2. Hospitals serving a disproportionately high number of Medicaid recipients or hospitals whose average patient population earns below a certain annual income should receive special higher reimbursement rates.

3. A severity of illness index should be added to the DRG calculations so that the needs of outliers and the intensively ill can be protected.[65]

4. A federal surtax should be placed on all for-profit hospitals so that the public can begin to recoup its lost health care investments.

5. New revenue from this surtax should be pooled to assist struggling rural and inner-city hospitals, whose closure would create special hardships for local patient populations.

6. Academic health centers should receive enhanced allowances for educational programs, for research, and for the development of new medical technologies.

7. To prevent hospitals from terminating all unprofitable services, a minimal range of hospital services should be defined such that any hospital failing to provide all of these services can no longer treat Medicare or Medicaid patients.

8. Penalties should be devised to prevent hospitals from creating policies that restrict access by the poor or by potential cost outliers.

9. Penalties should be devised to prevent hospitals from prematurely discharging their patients.

10. PROs should be required to include a fixed number of community representatives who have no direct financial stake in the hospitals whose work they inspect, and who are neither physicians nor employees of insurance companies.

These adjustments cannot make a bad system good, but they might help to cut the high human price tag of DRGs until consensus can be reached about a more acceptable alternative. That new consensus must be based on different assumptions: that health care is a right, not a commodity; that hospitals provide human services, not product-lines; and that physicians and nurses are healers, not accountants.

References

1. Donald L. Zimmerman, *DRGs and the Medicaid Program*, (Washington, D.C., Intergovernmental Health Policy Project, 1984).
2. John Iglehart, "The New Era of Prospective Payment for Hospitals," *New England Journal of Medicine*, 307:20 (1982), 1288.
3. Stephen N. Keith, "Prospective Payment for Hospital Costs Using Diagnosis-Related Groups: Will Cost Inflation Be Reduced?" *Journal of the National Medical Association*, 75:6 (1983), 613.
4. Leo K. Lichtig, "Data Systems for Case Mix," *Topics in Health Care Financing* (Summer 1982), p. 14.
5. John L. Yoder and Robert A. Con-

ner, "Diagnosis-Related Groups and Management," *Topics in Health Care Financing* (Summer 1982), p. 30.

6. Robert H. Davies and George Westfall, Reimbursement under DRGs: Implementation in New Jersey," *Health Services Research*, 18:2 (Summer 1983, Part I), 237.

7 American Medical Association, *DRGs and the Prospective Payment System: A Guide for Physicians* (February 1984), p. 21.

8. Davies and Westfall, pp. 236–37.

9. Stanley S. Bergen and Amy Conford Roth, "Prospective Payment and the University Hospital," *New England Journal of Medicine*, 310:5 (1984), 316.

10. AMA, *DRGs and the Prospective Payment System*.

11. Michael J. Haley, "What is a DRG?" *Topics in Health Care Financing* (Summer 1980), pp. 56–58.

12. Haley, p. 58.

13. "With DRGs, N.J. Hospitals More in Red Than Ever," *Medical News* (March 19, 1984), p. 4. For another view see speech by J. Richard Goldstein, M.D., Commissioner New Jersey Department of Health, April 2, 1985.

14. W. Jesse and J. Suver, "Physicians and DRGs: Survival under PPS," *The Hospital Medical Staff* (April 1984). p. 3.

15. Health Insurance Association of America, *Prospective Payment—A Sound Approach to Containing Hospital Costs*, p. 4.

16. "Data Gap Complicates Product Line Analysis," *Hospitals* (September 16, 1984), p. 57. See also Allen Meadors and Nick Wilson, "Prospective Payment System for Hospital Reimbursement, Part II" *Hospital Administration Currents* 29:1 (1985), 3, for a five-step plan on how to "Avoid Outliers As Much As Possible."

17. Bergen and Roth.

18. Bernard Pettingill and Harriet Westell, "Unanswered Questions Facing DRGs," *Hospital Topics* (July/August 1984), p. 4.

19. "Medicare Prospective Payment," staff report, *Association of Academic Health Centers* (March 1984), p. 4.

20. Robert Rubin, "DRGs and the Clinical Investigator: Federal Perspective," *Clinical Research*, 32:3 (September 1984), 341.

21. "The Impact of the Medicare Prospective Payment System and DRGs on Hospital Leadership," The Hospital Research and Educational Trust, *American Hospital Association* (1983), p. 5.

22. Howard, Smith and Richard Reid, "Short and Long Run Management Strategies for DRGs," *Hospital Topics* (May/June 1984), p. 5.

23. "Special Report," The Robert Wood Johnson Foundation, Number One, (Princeton, N.J., 1983), pp. 6–7.

24. Alan Sager, "Why Urban Voluntary Hospitals Close," *Health Services Research*, 18:3 (Fall 1983), 457.

25. "With DRG Red Ink Deep, Quality of Care at Stake," *Medical News*, (March 19, 1984), p. 5.

26. See, e.g. Walter McNerney, "Two-tier System of Health Care," The Hospital Research and Educational Trust, *American Hospital Association*, 1983.

27. William Gustner and John Ruffner, "How to Respond to Prospective Payments: Strategies for Hospitals Committed to Teaching and Service to the Poor," *Hospital Forum* (January/February), p. 58. Also see "Six Texas Hospitals Refuse Care to Premature Infants," *American Medical News*, (December 28, 1984), p. 8.

28. See, e.g. Charles Dougherty, "The Right to Health Care: First Aid in the Emergency Room," *Public Law Forum*, 4:1 (1984), 101–28. For a wider perspective on hospitals, see Charles Dougherty, *Ideal, Fact, and Medicine*, (Washington, D.C.: University Press of America, 1985).

29. S.E. Berki, Marie L.F. Ashcraft, and William Newbrander, "Length of Stay Variations within ICDA-8 Diagnosis-Related Groups," *Medical Care*, 22:2 (1984), 140.

30. Donald S. Shepard, "Estimating the Effect on Hospital Closure on Area-wide Inpatient Hospital Costs: A Preliminary Model and Application," *Health Services Research*, 18:4 (Winter 1983), 535, 541.

31. "Small and Rurals See Cash Crunch Due to PPS," *Hospitals* (September 16, 1984), p. 46. Also see M.I. Vaida, "The Financial Impact of Prospective Payment on Hospitals," *Health Affairs*, (Spring 1984), pp. 112–119.

32. "Capital Costs Will Rise with Downgrading," reported in *Hospitals* (September 16, 1948), p.48.

33. James Studnicki, "Regulation by DRG: Policy or Perversion," *Hospital & Health Services Administration* (January/February 1983), pp. 107– 8. Also see "The Doctor, the Patient, & the DRG," *Hastings Center Report* (October 1983), pp. 23–25.

34. "Medicare Prospective Pricing Compromise," *Hospitals* (September 16, 1984), p. 37. See also *Hospitals'* interview with HCFA administrator Carolyn Davis, March 16, 1985, p. 96.

35. "Hospitals Reduce Costs, Length of Stay," *Hospitals*, (September 16, 1984), p. 37.

36. "Data Gap Compromises Product Line Analysis," p. 62. See also Richard Gillock and Howard Smith in "Considerations for Effectively Managing DRGs," *Hospital Topics*, March/April 1985, p. 6.

37. "PPS Has Not Encouraged Formation of Large Numbers of Rehab Hospitals," *Hospitals* (September 16, 1984), p. 72, 76. Also see Information Requirements for Evaluating the "Impacts of Medicare Prospective Payment of Post-Hospital Long-Term-Care Services: Preliminary Report" (GAO/ PEMD-85–8), February 21, 1985.

38. Pat C. Smith, "We Tightened Up, Still Lost a Bundle," *Medical News*, (March 19, 1984), p. 5.

39. Michael Nathanson, "Comprehensive Cost Accounting Systems Give Chains the Edge," *Modern Health Care*, 14:3 (1984), 122.

40. Jo Ellen Mistarz, "Cost Accounting: A Solution But a Problem," *Hospitals* (October, 1984), p. 101.

41. Barbara Danz and Judith Price, "Reviewing Hospital Operations Is the Key," *Hospital Topics*, 62:4 (July/August 1984), 10. Also see "Winners and Losers: DRGs in New Jersey Three Years After," *Healthcare Marketing Report*, (March 1984), 2:1,1.

42. Bergen and Roth.

43. Smith and Reid.

44. R.C. Simons, M.D., and Herbert Pardes, M.D., editors, *Understanding Human Behavior in Health and Illness*, 2nd edition (Baltimore: Waverly Press, 1981).

45. Sager.

46. *Hospitals* September 16, 1984) p. 58.

47. "PPS Makes Timing Key Factor in Medical Records Area," *Hospitals* (September 16, 1984), p. 67.

48. Smith and Reid, p. 38.

49. Mistarz, p. 101. Also see "Planning, Costing and Decision Making under DRG Reimbursement," *Topics in Health Care Financing* 11:3 (Spring 1985).

50. Dana Johnson, "Life, Death, and the Dollar Sign," *Journal of the American Medical Association*, 252:2 (July 13, 1984), 224.

51. Geoffrey Smith, "Roll the DRGs!" *Forbes*, Vol. 132, (September 26, 1983), 36. Also see Samuel Levey and Douglas Hesse, "Bottom-Line Health Care?" *New England Journal of Medicine* (March 7, 1985), p. 644.

52. John Baird and Linda Baird, "Pro-

spective Pay Abruptly Changes Workers' Feelings about Jobs, But Shift Isn't All Bad", *Modern Healthcare* (September 1984), p. 52.

53. John S. Thompson, "Diagnosis Related Groups and Quality Assurance," *Topics in Health Care Financing* (Summer 1982), p. 48.

54. "PROs Will Be a Variation on the PRSO Theme," *Hospitals*, 57:10 (1983), 59.

55. Gerard Anderson and Earl Steinberg, "To Buy or Not to Buy," *New England Journal of Medicine* 311:3 (1984), 1823.

56. "An Honest Broker for Fine-tuning Medicare," *Hospitals* (October 1, 1984), p. 103.

57. See e.g., Eli Ginsberg, "The Monetarization of Medical Care," *New England Journal of Medicine*, 310:18 (1984), 1162–65; Paul Starr, *The Social Transformation of American Medicine*, (New York: Basic Books, 1982), esp. pp. 430–436; and Arnold Relman, "Investor-Owned Hospitals and Health-Care Costs," *New England Journal of Medicine*, 309:6 (1983), 370–72.

58. D. Haney, "The Chain Issue; Should Hospitals Be a Business or a Social Service?" Associated Press, *Omaha World-Herald*, May 13, 1984, p. 19–A.

59. See e.g., John Arras and Andrew Jameton, "Medical Individualism and the Right to Health Care," in R. Munson, ed., *Intervention and Reflection* (Belmont, CA: Wadsworth, 1983), pp. 541–52.

60. "Profiles of Catholic Multi-Institutional Systems" published by the CHA, St. Louis, Mo., 1984.

61. See e.g., Milton Friedman, "The Social Responsibility of Business Is to Increase Its Profits," in T. Donaldson and P.H. Werhane, ed., *Ethical Issues in Business* (Englewood Cliffs, N.J.: Prentice Hall, 1979).

62. "University Hospitals for Sale," *Science* (March 2, 1984), pp. 909–11.

63. *Omaha World-Herald*, May 22, 1984, p. 1. Creighton University officials frequently cited the DRGs and the consequent end of cost shifting the financial burden of indigent care at the hospital as one of the reasons they supported the sale.

64. Eli Ginzberg, "The Grand Illusion of Competition in Health Care," *The Journal of the American Medical Association*, 249:14 (1983), 1857–59.

65. *Health Care Financing*, 1984 Annual Supplement.

Section Six

Institutional Settings

Despite the recent growth of such nonhospital institutions as hospices, freestanding clinics, and neighborhood health centers, the hospital continues to play a dominant role in the health care system. Hospitals are still the place where most people are born, suffer illness, and die. They are the location for essential work activities of many medical professionals and personnel. Hospitals are the site of major discoveries and innovations in health services. Their costs are the major component of rising overall health costs, which is why the DRG method of financing care has been so powerful. State-level regulations of the health care system usually center on control of hospital expansion and acquisition of major items. Organized lobbying groups of the hospital trade associations exert tremendous pressure on many public decisions about health care.

Charles Rosenberg's "The Rise of the Modern Hospital" is an excerpt from his important new book, *The Care of Strangers: The Rise of America's Hospital System*. This selection places the hospital as we know it today into historical context. Rosenberg complements his history of the institutional development of the hospital with his emphasis on the interwoven development of the professions of medicine and nursing. In "The Hospital as Multiple Work Sites," Anselm Strauss and his colleagues remind us that many different occupational groups (doctors, nurses, laboratory technicians, housekeeping workers) coexist in the hospital and that their interdependence is an important feature of hospital life.

In the 1970s and 1980s the nursing home has come to be a key component in the health care system. Many older patients are discharged to the nursing home following hospitalization. For them, and for many more people sent to nursing facilities from their own homes as the age structure of the country changes, nursing homes are places to live out one's life in frequently substandard conditions. For mental patients, discharged from the state mental hospitals in the era of deinstitutionalization, the nursing home has become the major institutional setting. Federal reimbursement through Medicare, Medicaid, and Social Security has played a central role in the development of the nursing home industry, which is for the most part for-profit. Charlene Harrington's contribution, "The Nursing Home Industry," provides an overview of the industry, including issues of ownership, profit, regulation, policy, quality of care, and the strong political power wielded by nursing home owner groups.

20 THE RISE OF THE MODERN HOSPITAL

Charles Rosenberg

When Thomas Jefferson was inaugurated as president in 1800, there were only two American hospitals —one in Philadelphia and the other in New York. And these novel institutions played only a minor role in the provision of medical care; the great majority of inpatient beds were provided in almshouse wards, and even these were comparatively few in number. Most Americans still lived on farms and in rural villages.

Although in this demographic sense marginal, the hospital was nevertheless a characteristic product of the society that nurtured it. The hospital could not help but reproduce fundamental social relationships and values in microcosm. Early national America was a society in which relationships of class and status prescribed demeanors and specified the responsibilities of individuals and the community. It was a society in which bureaucracy and credentials meant little—bearing and social origin much. Even in America's largest cities, traditional views of Christian stewardship shaped assumptions of a proper reciprocity between rich and poor. It was an urban world in which benevolence could still be imagined—if

not always realized—in a context of face-to-face interaction between the giver and receiver of charity.

Allied with medicine's limited technical resources, these demographic and attitudinal realities produced a medical system minimally dependent on institutional care and in which dependence and social location, not diagnosis, determined the makeup of institutional populations. Sickness in itself did not imply hospitalization—only sickness or incapacity in those without a stable home or family members to provide care.

Late eighteenth- and early nineteenth-century hospital advocates felt two kinds of motivation. One was the imperative of traditional Christian benevolence in urban communities already burdened with large numbers of "unsettled" individuals needing care. The other sort of motivation grew out of the clinical and educational goals of an elite in the medical profession. Both lay and

SOURCE: From *The Care of Strangers: The Rise of America's Hospital System*, by Charles E. Rosenberg. Copyright © 1987 by Basic Books, Inc. Reprinted by permission of Basic Books, Inc., Publishers.

medical supporters of private hospitals contended that there could be no conflict between the hospital goals of laymen and physicians, for citizens of every class would ultimately benefit from the clinical instruction that could be most effectively organized around the aggregated bodies of the poor.

But such bland assurance of a necessary consistency between the professional needs of physicians and the benevolent goals of lay trustees were not enough to banish conflict. From its earliest years, the American hospital was marked by a structured divergence of interest between those of the pious laymen who bore the moral and legal responsibility for the institution and the doctors who practiced and taught within it. Drawn largely from the same social circles, attending physicians and lay authorities shared most values and assumptions, but in regard to professional matters such as autopsies, for example, or admission policies they could and did differ. Where they did not, however, was in their assumption of stewardship and the mingled authority and responsibility that constituted it; wealth, gender, and social position implied both the right and duty to direct the lives of dependent fellow citizens.

And the hospital was—insofar as its trustees and attending physicians could manage—a reflection of such relationships and responsibilities. Patients, nurses, attendants, and to an extent the junior house officers were considered moral minors in need of direction and guidance. Trustees felt a personal responsibility for every aspect of the institution and regularly inspected its wards and interviewed patients just as they personally oversaw admissions and settled accounts.

Poverty and dependence were the operational prerequisities for hospital admission. Sickness was a necessary but insufficient condition; aside from the occasional trauma victim, even the laborer or artisan preferred to be cared for at home—if he had a home and family to provide that care. It was only to have been expected that men should have far outnumbered women among nineteenth-century hospital patients. Urban America's abundant supply of single laboring men provided the bulk of admissions.[1] If age and sex justified the father's authority in an ordinary home, so gender and class identity legitimated that authority in the hospital and implied the unquestioned deference that patients were supposed to show toward superintendent, attending physicians, and trustees.

The intimate scale of early nineteenth-century hospitals provided a context in which these more general social realities could reproduce themselves. It was expected that the superintendent would see every patient every day, that he would know all their names and be aware of their personal situations, just as he knew the cook and laundress and coachman, all of course resident in the hospital. Not surprisingly, many of these employees worked for long years at their jobs and were paid on a quarterly or semiannual basis. Like the patients they cared for, the hospital's workers bartered independence for security. This harsh quid pro quo provided nevertheless a measure of stability in a world that offered few such choices for the great majority of Americans who worked with their hands.

The hospital was part of an institutional world that minimized cash transactions, subsisting instead through a network of less tangible interactions. Physicians were paid in prestige and clinical access; trustees in deference and the opportunity for spiritual accomplishment; nurses and patients were compensated with creature comforts: food, heat, and a place to sleep. Patients offered deference and their bodies as teaching material. Few dollars changed hands, but the system worked in its limited way for those who participated in it.

In part this was possible because the antebellum hospital was not burdened by a capital-intensive technology. There was little that could be done for a patient in the hospital that could not and, in practice, was not provided equally well at home— at least if that home could provide food, warmth, and care. Just as medical treatment was not segregated in the hands of a licensed and trained corps of practitioners, so the provision of acute care was not limited to a specific institutional setting. The domain of antebellum medicine was ill defined. Domestic and irregular practice were a significant part of medical care—a vital reality even in families well able to employ trained physicians.

Boundaries between hospital and home were similarly indistinct. A limited technology as well as traditional attitudes blurred the practical

distinctions between home and hospital. In architecture as well as in terms of their social organization, America's early hospitals differed little from any large home or welfare institution. As late as the Civil War, much surgery was still done on the wards—laboratories, x-ray units, and sterile operating theaters were far in the future. The rationale for construction of early nineteenth-century surgical amphitheaters was primarily pedagogic.[2] Many antebellum hospitals did not even have specific spaces adapted to the treatment of emergencies or the evaluation of individuals for admission. A limited technology demanded little in a way of functionally differentiated space. A socially undifferentiated patient population similarly implied no need for class-distinct accommodations. Most nineteenth-century hospitals did have a few private rooms, but they were generally insignificant in terms of space or numbers of occupants. The large open ward seemed appropriate to the presumably blunted sensibilities of those sort of individuals who became hospital patients—and to the hospital's own need to minimize costs. Until the twentieth century, hospital current expense budgets were dominated by the cost of food, heat, light, and labor—costs little different from those of an orphanage, boarding school, or rich man's mansion.

Medical ideas and skills were widely disseminated in the community as well and not segregated in the profession, justifying in part the hospital's marginality and paralleling its lack of internal differentiation. Every educated gentleman was presumed to know something about medicine, every woman was something of a general practitioner. Medicine provided a striking example of a still-traditional society's more general lack of specialized roles. In terms of authority, class relations, technology, administration, and even architecture, the hospital was very much a microcosm of the community that produced it. The boundaries, in fact, between community and hospital, between medicine and its clients, remained indistinct in American cities until mid-nineteenth century—and in rural areas until much later. Even ideas of disease causation reflected, incorporated, and legitimated social values generally; this was an era in which disease was still a holistic and nonspecific phenomenon. It could be caused by poor diet, stress, alcoholism, constitutional weakness, or more frequently, some plausible combination of several such factors. Laymen could understand as well as manipulate these ideas—medicine was still practiced in the home in terms mutually understandable to medical men and their patients.

A New Kind of Hospital

All of this had changed drastically by 1920. The hospital had become a national institution, no longer a refuge for the urban poor alone. On January 1, 1923, there were 4,978 hospitals in the United States, 70 percent of them general hospitals. (In 1873, the first American hospital survey had located only 178 hospitals.)[3] By the early 1920s, few enterprising towns of any size had failed

to establish a community hospital; it had become an accepted part of medical and especially surgical care for most small town Americans as well as their urban contemporaries. Diagnosis and therapeutic capacity as well as an individual's social location had begun to determine hospital admission. Technology had provided new tools and, equally important, a new rationale for centering acute care in the hospital. Medical men and medical skills were playing an increasingly important part in the institution—gradually supplanting older norms of lay control. Bureaucracy had reshaped the institution's internal order: a trained and disciplined nursing corps, a professionalizing hospital administration, as well as an increasingly specialized medical profession had all played a role in transforming the nineteenth-century hospital.

But certain older aspects of the hospital remained tenaciously intact. One was the stigmatizing distinction between public and private sectors. Municipal or county hospital care—like its almshouse predecessor—was clearly the less desirable, less adequately founded sibling of the private sector. In some ways, however, the formal boundary between public and private remained indistinct; all hospitals were clothed with the public interest, yet not easily subjected to the control of public authority. Decentralized funding and decision making continued to characterize the hospital. The lack of formal planning did not deter long-term trends from acting themselves out in parallel ways in institution after institution and locality after locality. But collective decision making was not easily imposed on an array of institutions that jealously guarded their autonomy and often associated independence with the prestige of localities, of ethnic and religious groups. This competitiveness was, in fact, one of those trends that manifested itself in parallel fashion in city after city; planners could deplore but do little to moderate its effects.

A first generation of hospital reformers had already discovered the structural rigidities beneath the seemingly inconsistent assortment of autonomous institutions that constituted the universe of early twentieth-century American hospitals. Regional planning for the most effective use of available resources was sought after as early as the first decade of the present century. Yet, despite polite words of support, few individual institutions were willing to change their normal priorities or concede any meaningful aspect of their operational independence to some larger group. By 1910, the hospital had already begun to appear to some of its critics as a monolithic and impersonal medical factory.[4]

Many social functions were moving from the home and neighborhood to institutional sites in late nineteenth- and early twentieth-century America—but none more categorically than medical care. And in no other case was the technical rationale more compelling. From a late twentieth-century perspective, the resources of hospital medicine in the period of the First World War may seem primitive, but they were impressive to contemporaries. Antisep-

tic surgery, the x-ray, and the clinical laboratory seemed to represent a newly scientific and efficacious medicine—a medicine necessarily based in the hospital. Few practitioners could duplicate these resources in their offices or make them easily available in the homes of even their wealthiest patients. Successful physicians had come to assume, and had convinced their patients, that the hospital was the best place to undergo surgery and in fact to treat any acute ailment.

But none of these events could have taken place without changed expectations—on the part of both physicians and their patients. Each decision by a middle-class American to enter a hospital reflected the attitudes and needs of both, even if it was the physician who ultimately referred his case to a hospital bed. Although attitudinal changes are difficult to document, respectable Americans would not have begun to enter hospitals had their perceptions of the institution not changed.

Not only the hospital, but the image of medicine itself had changed radically in the last third of the nineteenth century. The establishment of the germ theory, the advances of diagnosis and therapeutics made possible by immunology and serology, and the x-ray provided a dramatic series of highly visible events that cumulatively recast traditional attitudes toward the physician. It not only raised patient expectations, but also identified medicine's new-found efficacy with the laboratory and the image of science. Few would or could have agreed on what that science might be, but such assumptions nevertheless invested medical men with a new identity, one that based its legitimacy and claims to authority on something called science.[5]

Physicians were hardly immune to the attractions of scientific medicine. A cadre of bright young men had begun in the 1880s and 1890s to orient their careers in terms of the exciting new possibilities in surgery and the specialties. Reputations would be won or lost in these areas—reputations for hospitals as well as their staff members. The stakes were high for ambitious clinicians. Technical virtuosity was being inextricably related to status for institutions as well as individuals.

By the 1920s, surgery had become the acknowledged key to hospital growth and status. Although most patients still saw physicians in their own homes or the practitioner's office, major surgical procedures had shifted to the hospital. Not surprisingly, costs rose steadily; although simple and technologically unadorned by contemporary standards, the hospital of the 1920s was a capital-intensive institution, certainly by comparison with its mid-nineteenth-century predecessors. An increasingly sophisticated technology, both medical and nonmedical, implied higher capital and operating costs and thus a ceaseless quest for reliable sources of income and endowment. Yet only a minority of proprietary hospitals could entirely dispense with the institution's traditional mission of caring for the needy. And treating the poor and lower middle class threatened unending deficits. Administrators of

nonprofit hospitals thus energetically sought to maximize private patient income. Competition in terms of elegant rooms and restaurant quality food began in the 1890s, but few institutions filled enough of these private rooms to provide a comfortable cash flow—let alone underwrite costs of treating the indigent. There were simply not enough well-to-do patients.[6]

A far greater number of Americans found themselves unable to afford private rates, yet were unwilling to enter charity wards in voluntary hospitals or their even more stigmatizing counterparts in municipal institutions. America's first generation of hospital planners had, as we have seen, grown acutely aware of this group—shut off by income or place of residence from private hospitals, consultants and specialists. The hospital had become an indispensable element in American health care, yet just as it achieved that status experts decried its failure to provide optimum care at reasonable cost.

Within the hospital itself, physicians and medical values had become increasingly important in decision making. Although there was no abrupt or categorical shift, the general trend was clear enough; even where lay authorities still controlled public or private governing boards, they deferred to doctors in a way that would hardly have been approved by their self-confidently intrusive predecessors a century earlier. The growing complexity and presumed efficacy of medicine's tools seemed to make the centrality of physicians in hospital decision making both inevitable and appropriate. More than technical judgments were relevant. Once hospitals became dependent on patient income, they became dependent as well on the doctors who could fill their private beds. Similarly, increasing scale and an ever larger and more specialized house and nursing staff also distanced laymen from the institutions they formally—and formerly—controlled.[7]

In most hospitals, the influence of attending staffs did not go uncontested, however. Like many other institutions in this period, the hospital was becoming increasingly bureaucratic, governed by a new kind of chief executive officer with the aid of a middle management of nursing superintendent, senior residents, and comptroller. Authority was negotiated as well as imposed.

No single change transformed the hospital's day-to-day workings more than the acceptance of trained nurses and nurse training schools, which brought a disciplined corps of would-be professionals into wards previously dominated by the values and attitudes of work-class patients (and attendants originally recruited from the same strata of society). In a period when few careers were open to women, trained nursing attracted a far greater variety of women, many of them rural and only a minority from the urban working class. Professional ambition and social origin set these first generations of credentialed nurses apart from the ward's accustomed occupants as much as any specific aspect of their schooling.

The status of trained nurses reflected but could not rival the growing influence of a male-dominated medical profession. In the hospital, as in the world outside its walls, female-identified occupations tended to become exclusively female and subordinate to male authority. Central to the professional identity of trained nursing was a relentless emphasis on discipline and efficiency, paralleling medicine's newly scientific self-image. This emphasis and the trained nurses who embodied and enforced it helped impose a new social order in the wards and rooms of the hospital. Nursing added an additional layer to hospital management—yet on balance enhanced rather than undermined the growing power of medicine within the hospital.[8]

The increasing prominence of technology and the physicians who employed these impressive new tools expressed itself in another and particularly tenacious way. This was the prominent role of acute care in the nonprofit hospital, and a parallel lack of interest in the chronically ill, who tended to pile up in county, municipal, and state institutions. In a good many rural areas in the 1920s, the county almshouse continued to serve as the community's repository for "chronics and incurables." Such patients were expensive and fit uncomfortably into the priority of an increasingly self-confident medical profession. Most chronic facilities, for example, found it difficult to attract housestaff; the duties were depressing and the cases "uninteresting."[9]

Surgery in particular had helped shorten voluntary hospital stays, attracted a new mix of patients and reinforced an already well-established emphasis on acute care. Diagnosis had become self-consciously scientific, determined increasingly by medical men and medical categories. By the 1920s, diagnosis had replaced dependency as the key to hospital admission (although *which* hospital one was admitted to still reflect class and ethnic factors). Socially oriented critics of the early twentieth-century hospital were already contending that the patient was in danger of being reduced to his or her diagnosis —to a biopathological phenomenon.

The hospital had been transformed not only socially and technically, but physically as well. New medical tools coupled with a new industrial and building technology had made the early twentieth-century hospital a physical artifact very different from its forerunners a century earlier. The needs of radiology and clinical pathology, of hydrotherapy and electrotherapy, and, most importantly, of antiseptic surgery demanded reorganization of the hospital's interior so as to minimize steps for its medical and nursing staff. The growth of fee-for-service practice in the hospital implied examining and consulting rooms more private than facilities previously available in ward and outpatient departments. The presumed needs and desires of valued pay patients led to the creation of more and more private and semi-private accommodations.[10] And like every other large institutional structure at the time, hospitals were being built with electric lights, dynamos, elevators, partially mechanized kitchens and laundries. Added to

the cumulative impact of a mid-century reform movement that had underlined the need for improved modes of heating and ventilation, these technological necessities were turning the early twentieth-century American hospital into a capital-intensive and internally differentiated physical entity—mirroring in a different sphere the changes in professional organization and the distribution of knowledge that were reshaping medical care more generally.

Medical knowledge, like medical practice, was gradually but inexorably being segregated in professionally accredited hands. No longer was it assumed that an educated man would understand something of medicine (or law, classics, and theology). No longer was it assumed that midwives would provide the bulk of care during childbirth and early infancy. Drugs were purchased not gathered—and even in rural areas, most Americans turned sooner to physicians than they would have several generations earlier.[11] Within the medical profession too, knowledge was gradually being segregated so that ordinary practitioners were no longer presumed to be omnicompetent (even if they might have to ignore such limitations in rural areas or choose to ignore them in cities). Practitioners as well as educated laymen assumed that the hospital was and must be the site for medicine's most advanced and specialized care.

Although laymen were certainly impressed by the scientific style and seeming efficacy of medicine, it was physicians who in fact determined the content of that medicine. The medical community shaped professional expectations and defined career patterns. And if the optimum relationship between science and its clinical applications remained unclear, the place of the hospital did not. It was central to every aspect of medicine by 1920. The hospital's wards and rooms were the place to learn clinical skills, to master a specialty, often a place to practice, and, for an increasingly influential academic minority, a place to pursue research.

If the hospital had been medicalized, the medical profession had been hospitalized in the years between 1800 and 1920. This intraprofessional development has attracted far less attention from contemporary historians than the hospital's social and economic evolution—but it is no less significant. They are in fact inseparable; the structure of medical careers and changing medical perceptions and priorities are fundamental elements of hospital history.

Hospital service had always been central to the ambitions and careers of America's medical elite. By the First World War, it had become central to the education and practice of a much larger proportion of the profession, which was itself becoming more tightly organized, uniformly trained, and systematically licensed. Since the eighteenth century, hospitals had played a key role in disseminating as well as accumulating medical knowledge, helping to communicate ideas and techniques from a metropolitan elite to a new generation of practitioners. With an ever-larger proportion of physicians serving as interns and residents, the

twentieth-century hospital became an increasingly effective tool for the diffusion of ideas and skills. By the 1920s, hospital experience had become an accepted part of medical training. With the national accreditation of hospitals and internship programs and the integration of residency and fellowship programs into board certification, the hospital had become with each passing decade more tightly integrated into the career choices and aspirations of the medical profession.[12]

With consulting and surgical practice moving increasingly into the hospital in the 1920s, interest as well as intellect united in emphasizing its importance to the practitioner. Cash transactions had become increasingly important, not only to the individual physician, but to the hospital as it sought to maximize income in the face of growing demands and rising costs. Older commitments to the provision of gratuitous care allied with institutional rivalries implied that most hospitals would not tolerate falling too far behind in their efforts to provide first-rate staff and facilities. Costs would inevitably increase.

The American hospital can be seen as having moved by the 1920s into a marketplace of discrete and impersonal cash transactions—to a style of benevolence that would have seemed inappropriate to the sort of men who managed hospitals in the first third of the nineteenth century. Efficiency, not stewardship, threatened to dominate the early twentieth-century hospital—as it did the school, state, government, and factory.

But the hospital never assumed the guise of rational and rationalized economic actor during the first three-quarters of the twentieth century. It was never managed as a factory or department store. The hospital continued into the twentieth century, as it had begun in the eighteenth, to be clothed with the public interest in a way that challenged catogorical distinctions between public and private. Private hospitals had always been assumed to serve the community at large—treating the needy, training a new generation of medical practitioners, and attracting a varied and eclectic assortment of subventions from city, county, and state authorities.[13] The late eighteenth and early nineteenth centuries had in any case never been comfortable with absolute distinctions between the public and private sphere; the idea of commonwealth subsumed collective responsibility for that community's health. It was natural for most hospital authorities to assume that they should continue to receive public funds, just as they assumed they should be free of local taxes and the constraints of tort law.

The hospital's transactions involved pain, sickness, and death, as well as the public good. An insulating sacredness surrounded the activities of the twentieth-century hospital; its "products" were, in a literal sense, beyond material accounting. The newly intensified expectations of scientific medicine were, that is, both material and transcendent. A growing number of Americans hoped and expected that this new institution could provide a refuge from the sickness and premature death that had always seemed immanent in man's corporeal body. It is not surprising that (except for a minority of proprietary, for-profit institutions) the private hospital's operations have never been entirely disciplined by the logic of profit maximization or easily bent to communally determined demands for planning and cost control. A deficit could be construed as a sign of worthiness and not culpable administrative failure.

Nor is it surprising that transactions within the hospital continued until the Second World War to be structured in part around the exchange of labor and status. The hospital was in but not of the marketplace. Nurses and house staff still exchanged labor for credentials; attending physicians bartered their ward services for prestige and admission privileges in private services. Nonprofessional workers traded a measure of autonomy and the higher wages they might have received on the commercial labor market for the security and paternalism that, presumably, characterized the hospital. Thus, even as it was being transformed into an increasingly technical and seemingly indispensable institution, the hospital remained clothed with a special and sacred quality that removed it from both normal social scrutiny and the market's discipline.

Even if the hospital could not turn itself into a income-maximizing marketplace actor, it did serve as an equity-maximizing vehicle for many of those connected with it. I use the word equity advisedly, for the hospital provided rewards in several forms. To private practitioners, it could provide income; to attending physicians, income and status; to lay trustees, it offered prestige and, in many cases, affirmation of individual or group status; to hospital suppliers, it constituted an increasingly voracious customer; to academic physicians, it provided "clinical material" for teaching and research; to nurses, workers, and attendants, it offered security; and to some, a measure of status. Even the Depression-era hospital reflected and incorporated all these, sometimes conflicting, motives as it struggled with limited budgets.

The late twentieth-century hospital already existed in embryo, waiting only the nutrients of third-party payment, government involvement, technological change, and general economic growth to stimulate a rapid and in some ways hypertrophied development. New and abundant sources of support after the Second World War only intensified well-established patterns. They provided funds on the provider's terms without fundamentally changing the provider's orientation; cost-plus contracts and outright grants are hardly ideal mechanisms for the enforcement of external control.[14]

The Past in the Present

If the hospital in Thomas Jefferson's or Andrew Jackson's America had been a microcosm of the community that nurtured it, so is the hospital of the 1980s. Although we live in a very different sort of world, the hospital remains both product and prisoner of its own history and

of the more general trends that have characterized our society. Class, ethnicity, and gender have, for example, all shaped and continue to shape medical care, and the hospital has become a specialized, bureaucratic entity of a kind that has come to dominate so many other aspects of contemporary life. National policies and priorities have come to play a significant role in affairs that had been long thought of as entirely and appropriately local. The origins of America's hospitals are hardly recognizable in their quaint forerunners in a handful of early nineteenth-century port cities.

The hospital is a necessary community institution strangely insulated from the community; it is instead a symbiotically allied group of subcommunities bound together by social location and the logic of history. This insulated character is typical of a good number of social institutions: the schools, the federal civil service, the large corporations. But there are some special aspects of the hospital that have facilitated its ability to look inward, to pursue its own vision of social good. This institutional solipsism developed in ironic if logical conjunction with the hospital's defining function of dealing with the most intimate and fundamental of human realities.

Like the U.S. Defense Department, the hospital system has grown in response to perceived social need —in comparison with which normal budgetary constraints and compromises have come to seem niggling and inappropriate. Security, like any absolute and immeasurable good, legitimates enormous demands on society's resources. Both health and defense have, moreover, become captives of high technology and worst-case justifications. In both instances, the gradient of technical feasibility becomes a moral imperative.[15] That which might be done, should be done. In both cases, cost-cutting could be equated with penny-pinching—inappropriate to the gravity of the social goals involved. Absolute ends do not lend themselves to compromise, and the bottom line is that there has been no bottom line.

In both areas, material interests obviously play a role; hospitals, doctors, and medical suppliers like defense contractors and the military have interests expressed in and through the political process. But ideas are significant as well. It is impossible to understand our defense budget without factoring in the power of ideology; it is impossible to understand the scale and style of America's health care expenditures without an understanding of the allure of scientific medicine and the promise of healing. Both the Massachusetts General Hospital and the General Dynamics Corporation operate in the market, but they are not entirely bound by its discipline; both also mock the categorical distinction between public and private that indiscriminately places each in the private domain.

This analogy can, of course, be carried too far. The hospital has, as we have emphasized, a special history incorporating and reflecting the evolution of medicine and nursing, and the parallel development of our social welfare system. The high sta-

tus of medicine has been built into the hospital, not only in the form of an undifferentiated social authority, but in the shape of particular, historically determined techniques and career choices. The ideas that rule the world-view of medicine and its system of education and research have very practical connections with the pragmatic world of medical care and medical costs.

An increasingly subdifferentiated specialization, an emphasis on laboratory research and acute care, for example, have all played an important role in the profession and thus, in the hospital. So complex and intertwined are these interrelationships that changes in any one sphere inevitably impinge on other areas. Some aspects of modern medicine seemed at first unrelated to the marketplace. One, for example, was the increasing ability of physicians to disentangle specific disease entities. This was an intellectual achievement of the first magnitude and not unrelated to the increasingly scientific and prestigious public image of the medical profession. Yet, we have seen a complex and inexorably bureaucratic reimbursement system grow up around these diagnostic entities; disease does not exist if it cannot be coded. It was equally inevitable that efforts to control medical costs should have turned on these same diagnostic categories. Thus the 1980s controversy surrounding Diagnosis Related Groups can be seen in part as a natural outcome of the intellectual and institutional history of the medical profession—and of the hospital as well.

To most contemporary Americans,

rising costs have been the key element in transforming the hospital into a highly visible social problem. And it is true that an apparent crisis in hospital finance may well be creating the conditions for fundamental changes. After all, it was not until after the Second World War that the hospital gradually emerged from the world of paternalism. Unions and a more assertive nursing profession, ever-increasing capital costs, a growing dependence on federal support, and rising insurance rates, even the need to pay house staff in dollars have moved the hospital system into the market—and exposed hospitals to the prospect of increasing external control.[16] Still clothed with the public interest and promising immeasurable equities, the hospital remains a rigid and intractable institution.

As we contemplate its contentious present and problematic future, we remain prisoners of its past. The economic and organizational problems that loom so prominently today should not make us lose sight of fundamental contradictions in the hospital's history, contradictions that have fueled two decades of critical debates.

Scientific medicine has raised expectations and costs, but has failed to confront the social consequences of its own success. We are still wedded to acute care and episodic, specialized contacts with physicians. There is a great deal of evidence that indicates widespread dissatisfaction with the quality of care as it is experienced by Americans. Changes in reimbursement mechanisms will not necessarily alter that felt reality.

Chronic and geriatric care still constitute a problem—as they always did. We cannot seem to live without high-technology medicine; we cannot seem to live amicably with it. Yet, for the great majority of Americans, divorce is unthinkable. Medical perceptions and careers still proscribe or reward behaviors that may or may not be consistent with the most humane and cost-effective provision of care. And despite much recent hand-wringing, it still remains to be seen whether physicians will be edged aside from their positions of institutional authority.

There are many equities to be maximized in the hospital, many interests to be served, but the collective interest does not always have effective advocates. The discipline of the marketplace will not necessarily speak to that interest; the most vulnerable will inevitably suffer. In any case, I see little prospect of hospitals in general becoming monolithic cost minimizers and profit maximizers. Social expectations and well-established interests are both inconsistent with such a state of things. We will support research and education, we will feel uncomfortable with a medical system that does not provide a plausible (if not exactly equal) level of care to the poor and socially isolated. Health care policy will continue to reflect the special character of our attitudes toward sickness and society.

Notes

1. Sex ratios were most disproportionate in large urban municipal and voluntary hospitals. Disparities were

not so marked in a growing number of community hospitals founded at the end of the century or at many religious and ethnic institutions. Both social and technical factors, especially antiseptic surgery, made a hospital stay in these institutions less stigmatizing.

2. And to an extent esthetic, removing the patient from the eyes and ears of ward mates.

3. This not entirely complete survey did include mental hospitals. U.S. Dept. of Commerce, Bureau of the Census, *Hospitals and Dispensaries. 1923* (Washington: Government Printing Office, 1925), p. 1; J.M. Toner, "Statistics of Regular Medical Associations and Hospitals of the United States," *TAMA* 24 (1873): 287–333. For a useful discussion of late nineteenth-century hospital growth patterns, see: Jon M. Kingsdale, "The Growth of Hospitals: An Economic History in Baltimore," (Ph.D. diss., Univ. of Michigan, 1981).

4. See the more extended discussion in chapter 13.

5. Medicine was hardly alone in clothing itself in the garb of science— this was an era in which domestic science, library science, and political science, among other disciplines and would-be disciplines, reached self-consciously for "scientific" status and academic acceptance. In the case of medicine, of course, connections with the scientific disciplines was particularly significant and increasingly relevant to care. On the other hand, medicine experienced organizational changes paralleling those undergone by other professions and occupations at the same time, suggesting that its ultimate social form and prerogatives were more than logical and necessary consequences of cognitive change alone.

6. For useful case studies illuminating the economic difficulties of hospitals in the period before 1930, see: David Rosner, *A Once Charitable Enterprise. Hospitals and Health Care in Brooklyn and New York, 1885–1915* (Cambridge, London, New York: Cambridge University Press, 1982) and (on Baltimore) Kingsdale, "The Growth of Hospitals."

7. The growing influence of professional administrators was apparent in politically colored municipal institutions as well as in their private peers. The pattern was apparent in other cultural and benevolent institutions as well where professional managers gradually came to mediate between wealthy directors and the objects of their benevolence. See, for example: Kathleen D. McCarthy, *Noblesse Oblige. Charity and Cultural Philanthropy in Chicago, 1849–1929* (Chicago: University of Chicago Press, 1982).

8. The professionalization of nursing did provide supervisory positions for women, but the great majority of such posts remained subordinate to male superintendents, medical boards, and trustees. In a small minority of women's hospitals, this was not the case and, as we have suggested, the Catholic hospitals also provided a setting in which women could exert a greater degree of real authority. They were insulated by their sex and vocation from the will of medical boards and by their orders from the unfettered control of diocesan administrators.

9. For a useful discussion, see Ernst P. Boas and Nicholas Michelson, *The Challenge of Chronic Diseases* (New York: Macmillan, 1929).

10. For a survey of the hospital's internal architectural history, centering on room and ward arrangements, see John D. Thompson and Grace

Goldin, *The Hospital: A Social and Architectural History* (New Haven and London: Yale University Press, 1975). Cf. Adrian Forty, "The Modern Hospital in France and England." In: A. King, ed., *Buildings and Society* (London: Routledge & Kegan Paul, 1980), 61–93.

11. Hospital facilities were seen by contemporary observers to be inadequate particularly in poor or isolated areas as evidenced by the interest of a number of private foundations in the 1920s and 1930s.

12. The influence of a developing specialism on the hospital and of the hospital on special practice is an extremely important part of hospital history, but one that has been on the whole neglected by historians.

13. New York, Massachusetts, Connecticut, and Pennsylvania, for example, had all found ways to support voluntary hospitals throughout the nineteenth century. For a general discussion, see Rosemary Stevens, "'A Poor Sort of Memory,': Voluntary Hospitals and Government before the Depression," *Milbank Memorial Fund Q.* 60(1982): 551–84; Stevens, "Sweet Charity: State Aid to Hospitals in Pennsylvania, 1870–1910," *Bulletin of the History of Medicine* (hereafter *BHM*) 58 (1984): 287–314, 474–95.

14. Hill-Burton did specify conditions, but they seem not to have greatly constrained institutional politics. The intra-institutional effects of externally supported research have been significant but are difficult to evaluate.

15. And the carrying out of that imperative has created economic and bureaucratic interests committed to existing procurement patterns and thus another source of rigidity in both areas.

16. The similarities between for-profit hospitals and the great majority of their not-for-profit peers are at least as significant as their differences. Both are prisoners of the same attitudes, expectations, technology, and funding realities and must pursue a good many parallel strategies.

21 THE HOSPITAL AS MULTIPLE WORK SITES

Anselm Strauss, Shizuko Fagerhaugh, Barbara Sucjek, and Carolyn L. Wiener

A useful way of conceiving of the hospital is as a large number of work sites. A walk around the different floors and sections of any fairly large or complex hospital gives one an astonishingly varied visual experience. Over here is the X-ray department—familiar to us all—with its huge mobile machines, its shielded area where the radiologist or X-ray technician pulls switches while the patient lies or stands immobile under or in front of a machine, having been carefully positioned by the technician, while other patients are lined up in a nearby area, usually in

SOURCE: *Social Organization of Medical Work*, by Anselm Strauss, Shizuko Fagerhaugh, Barbara Sucjek, and Carolyn L. Wiener. (Chicago: University of Chicago Press, 1985), pp. 5–7. © 1985 by the University of Chicago.

wheel-chairs, each waiting to be worked on. Not far away is the car-diologist's terrain, where a single patient is hooked up to a compli-cated cardiac monitoring machine, operated by another kind of techni-cian: the patient is sitting, standing, or walking on a treadmill machine, the technician is carefully operating the equipment and keeping an eye on the patient; meanwhile, a physi-cian is looking at the unwinding printout, interpreting what the pa-tient's heart is doing during his or her performance. Down in the base-ment is the central supply depart-ment; no patients are in sight, but low-salaried personnel are doing numbers of tasks related to sending supplies up to the clinical wards.

Upstairs, on the main floors of the hospital, are a variety of wards, each visually and often spatially different to the visitor's quick glance. The postoperative recovery room is heav-ily staffed with highly skilled nurses who carefully, minute by minute, monitor their relatively few and ini-tially unconscious patients, who in turn are hooked up to multiple ma-chines. Nearby is the intensive care unit (ICU) with its relatively few beds, with patients largely nonsen-tient who are relatively exposed to each other, its battery of machines for monitoring each patient's vital signs, its one-to-one ratio of nurse to patient, its floating population of easily accessible physicians, its auxil-iary specialists like respiratory tech-nicians, its frequent patient crises and quick gathering of staff for fast action. In the cancer ward, the work pace is much slower ("we take our

cues from the patient"): some pa-tients are dying, others are there for X-ray treatments or chemotherapy and are suffering from varied de-grees of physiological and psycho-logical distress—so the nurses are doing much comfort care (medical and psychological) with most pa-tients, while working on their own threatened composure and over-in-volvement with the patients.

In short, a hospital consists of var-iegated workshops—places where different kinds of work are going on, where very different resources (space, skills, ratios of labor force, equipment, drugs, supplies, and the like) are required to carry out that work, where the divisions of labor are amazingly different, though all of this is in the direct or indirect service of managing patients' ill-nesses.

Decades ago the hospital was much less differentiated. Of course, there has long been a division be-tween surgical and medical sections, though in many hospitals in devel-oping countries there often is little difference to be seen between such sections. The hospital included ser-vicing departments like X-ray and pharmacy but had nothing then like the complex array of wards that re-flect today's explosion of medical specialization or the immensely var-ied chronic illnesses found in the contemporary hospital. If one fo-cuses only on the clinical wards, however, it is easy to miss the simi-lar explosion in the number and va-riety of support and servicing de-partments like transport, physical therapy, respiratory therapy, nutrition, safety, equipment repair, bio-engineering, echotherapy, EKG, and even a full-scale clinical laboratory for doing the host of diagnostic tests ordered from the various clinical wards.

22 THE NURSING HOME INDUSTRY

Charlene Harrington

The nursing home industry is a multibillion dollar business in the United States, characterized by rapid growth in profits and large chain-owned corporations. Nursing homes were a cottage industry until the early 1960's when they began to expand with the infusion of public funds from Medicaid and Medicare. By 1980, there were 23,000 nursing homes in the U.S. serving 1.4 million residents, mostly old and disabled [1].

The industry, while private in nature, is effectively a public program defined by public policies, particularly by the Medicaid program. Demand for services is artificially generated because of a lack of public program alternatives and favorable reimbursement public policies which benefit the nursing home industry. While state and federal government regulate the industry, the effectiveness of regulatory activities in protecting the consumer is questionable, where poor quality of care is commonly found. Older persons are forced into such facilities against their will, where the facilities serve as agents of social control over those who are frail, poor, without family supports, and unwanted. While

some observers argue that the entire structure of the nursing home industry requires radical change, the politics and economics of the current situation reinforce continued expansion of the industry and the use of institutionalization as a primary modality of treatment for the frail aged.

Quality of Care

Serious questions must be raised about the appropriateness of institutional care as a treatment for many aged. In nursing homes, the residents tend to lose control of decisions about their treatment and their daily living activities. Institutionalization makes it more difficult to sustain family ties and social relationships. The morale, health status, and functional capacity of individuals placed in institutions frequently deteriorate. And many older people spend their last years in such facilities against their will. The aged have a general fear and loathing of institutional placement.

SOURCE: *Readings in the Political Economy of Aging,* Meredith Minkler and Carroll L. Estes, Editors, (Farmingdale, NY: Baywood, 1984), pp. 144–154. © 1984, Baywood Publishing Co., Inc.

The fears of institutional placement are in part related to the poor quality of care and undesirable conditions in many institutions. The quality issues have been investigated by many different groups [2, 3]. Criticism of nursing homes include a long litany of abuses: negligence leading to death and injury, unsanitary conditions, poor nutrition and inadequate amounts of food, hazards to life and safety including lack of fire protection, lack of dental care, eye care, and podiatry, lack of social services, and inadequate control of drugs and overmedication. The themes of neglect by facilities, physicians and nurses are all too common.

Nursing homes are severely short on staff, especially registered nurses, so they rely on untrained and unlicensed personnel [2–4]. Increasing the state nursing standards to a level considered adequate by professional standards would cost the public programs millions of additional dollars which they are not willing to spend during times of financial distress. These problems along with the general conditions of institutional life with its lack of privacy, impersonal atmosphere, and rigid, arbitrary schedules make basic institutional living unacceptable and undesirable except in those cases where clients are severely disabled [5].

Nursing homes play a role in caring for those aged and disabled who are least desirable in the society. Such individuals are removed from the social environment and isolated into institutions. At the same time, institutions are agents of social control over the residents, who must live according to institutional standards. The legal and ethical issues in terms of abridgement of civil rights for patients have not been well established for the aged in nursing homes. The rights to refuse drug and other treatments in nursing homes are also not established, even though such rights have been established for mental patients in mental institutions. The right to refuse institutionalization in cases where individuals have not been legally declared incompetent to make decisions and not been placed under conservatorship is also not protected.

The causes of the poor quality of care in some nursing homes are issues for debate. Some have attributed the problems to excessive profit-taking by proprietary facilities. Although research studies have not shown conclusive differences with lower quality of care in proprietary facilities than in public or nonprofit facilities, this is probably more due to inadequate research measurement than to lack of differences. Vladeck [3] and others have concluded that profit nursing homes are more associated with poor quality of care in general than nonprofits. Many other reasons are associated with poor quality of care. In some cases, fraud and abuses have led to the undesirable conditions.

The families and patients are dependent upon the facilities and find it difficult to complain about the quality of care because of fear of eviction or retaliation in situations where there are few other options of alternative facilities. In other situations, the patients have no advocates from outside the institution.

Quality of care is not assured even when facilities are charging high rates and are making profits and could thus afford to make improvements in care. On the other hand, incentives or regulations which ensure that resources will be utilized for patient care are difficult to develop.

Regulatory Activities

While nursing homes are required to meet state and federal licensing standards, the public regulatory efforts have been considered to be seriously lacking by most observers [3, 6–8]. State and federal regulations themselves are frequently too vague to be enforceable. In other situations, the public sanctions for noncompliance are ineffective, due to the complexity of preparing legal actions and length of time required to enforce such actions. In other situations, the administrative enforcement practices are inadequate due to lack of personnel and resources, weak procedures for enforcement, and the reluctance of staff to institute sanctions on the facilities. In some areas, where a shortage of available nursing home beds exists, the licensing and certification staff are reluctant to bring legal action and/or to close noncomplying facilities because there are no alternative placements for the residents.

Certainly, the nursing home industry is effective in influencing recent policies for deregulation. This has taken the form of federal program budget cuts and proposed weakening of federal certification standards. During the last two years, public protests over proposed regulatory changes to reduce standards have been effective in preventing the adoption of many of these changes. On the other hand, the federal, and in many cases, state budget cuts in licensing have reduced the licensing activities even though the regulations have been retained. Many senior advocate organizations believe that deregulation will bring about reductions in quality of care. The key question is whether the reduction in regulatory activities will have a measurable or visible effect on quality of care in nursing homes. And if so, will public policymakers, researchers, and consumer advocates be observing and evaluating such effects.

Demand for and Utilization of Nursing Home Services

Nursing home industry viability is contingent upon a high demand for services. The market for nursing homes is complex because demand is dependent upon a number of factors that are not necessarily correlated with need for services (based upon physical or psychological factors). Utilization refers to those days that services are actually delivered.

In order to maximize profits, nursing homes generally attempt to control two factors. First, nursing homes prefer to select private paying patients because they can generally obtain higher rates of payment for such patients than what is paid by Medicaid [9]. Second, nursing homes may seek those patients that have the lower level of nursing care needs to reduce their costs of delivering the services. Such a practice called "skimming" refers to selecting those patients who are the lowest cost and need the least care. The longer the waiting lists, the more likely nursing homes are able to be selective in choosing their patient population.

The demand for nursing home services as measured by waiting lists and occupancy rates continues to be high in almost all states (an average of 89 percent in 1980) [1]. The fact that nursing home occupancy rates are uniformly high regardless of the ratio of beds to the aged population in the states suggests that utilization is based upon other factors than need for services. In other words, the supply of nursing home beds stimulates demand to fill available beds because of a variety of complex factors.

Further evidence that demand and supply are artificially inflated can be shown by examining the rate of inappropriate placement. Inappropriate placement refers to those residents whose functional status is capable of functioning in a more independent manner outside of an institutional setting. The extent of inappropriate utilization is estimated to range from 5 to 75 percent depending upon the criteria used [10]. The high estimates are supported by data from the National Survey of Institutionalized Persons which showed that only 30 percent of the residents were consistently or extremely dependent in self-care activities [11]. The National Nursing Home Survey, using self-reported data from nursing homes, also showed only 39 percent of residents to be extremely dependent in self-care. [12].

Probably the primary reason for high demand for and utilization of nursing home rates, even when such services are inappropriate, is failure of the state to provide alternative services to institutional care. The majority of Medicaid dollars are spent on institutional care (nursing homes and hospitals) and professional services (physicians, dentists, drugs, glasses, and others) with only 5 percent of Medicaid dollars spent on other services [13]. States have recently been developing new community based alternatives in demonstration and waiver projects, but these still remain small in comparison to nursing home services.

Many other barriers prevent use of alternatives to institutional care. The current long term care system is incomplete, fragmented, and inadequately financed. Recently the social service programs for in-home support services have been reduced because of federal budget cuts, when such programs were not able to meet the demand before budget cuts. In other situations, the lack of information about alternative services is a factor in inappropriate placement.

In many instances, older people do not have family supports and friends that can provide assistance to keep them from being placed in institutions, even when their physical needs may not require institutional services. In other situations, the aged are unable to afford to purchase alternative services because of low incomes and high medical costs. Medicaid has restrictive eligibility policies in some states which forces the aged to become indigent to qualify for medical care. Medicare pays for very little home and hospice care, and does not pay for drugs and eyeglasses and other such services outside of institutions. Because some aged find it difficult to qualify for appropriate community based services, they are sometimes forced into institutions as their only alternative when they become eligible for Medicaid.

Nursing Home Ownership

Nursing homes have moved rapidly toward ownership by large nursing home chains. Proprietary facilities operate 75 percent of the nursing homes in the U.S. [1] and a growing number of these chains are publicly-held corporations. The nursing home industry is consolidating fast. *Forbes* reported that the ten largest chains accounted for 10 percent of the total number of beds in the country [14], and in 1983, thirty-two corporations controlled 17 percent of the beds [15]. These largest chains included Beverly Enterprises, ARA Services, National Medical Enterprises (which bought National Health Enterprises) and Cenco Inc. The top corporations are listed on the New York Stock Exchange and the American Stock Exchange.

In 1983, the chain ownership of beds increased by 30.4 percent over the previous year, but most of this growth was through acquisition of existing homes, and not new construction [15]. This trend, called hor-

izontal growth, is expected to continue to the point where five to ten nursing home corporations will own 50 percent of all the beds in the U.S. by 1990.

The chain operated corporations are able to develop sophisticated management techniques for reducing costs such as centralized planning, bulk purchasing, sharing of costly equipment, prototype construction and standardized space design [16]. Chain facilities tend to make intensive use of high margin, capital intensive services such as laboratories and supplies. And chains are generally highly leveraged with about 60 percent of their capitalization in long-term debt. The success of such activities in generating growth and profits suggests that the trends will continue toward such operations which are becoming part of larger corporations that also own hospitals and other types of health services.

Nursing home corporations are moving quickly to diversify investments. Most nursing home chains control other types of businesses such as pharmaceutical suppliers and respiratory therapy companies in what is termed vertical integration. Unicare Services, for example, a chain in Milwaukee, owned figure salons, a drugstore chain, a car wash, a restaurant chain and other businesses [3]. The latest activities of nursing homes have been to develop other long-term care businesses, because of the recent problems in building new nursing homes due to high interest rates. These activities have involved operating home health care corporations.

In California in 1983, the proprietary nursing home industry sponsored legislation that would allow
for the operation of proprietary adult
day health care centers (where only
nonprofit adult day health care programs were allowed). The expansion
into all areas of the long-term care
gives the nursing home industry
control and influence over the entire
long-term care delivery system. The
change of noninstitutional care organizations from largely nonprofit
community-based agencies to proprietary and large corporate or
chain-owned organizations will most
likely have the same negative impact
as it has for nursing homes.

Vladeck points out that the real
owners of the nursing home industry are the banks [3]. Most owners
have little equity in their facilities
with the banks holding large mort-
gages. The banks and investment corporations are promoting the move
toward consolidation of the nursing
home industry and also have promoted the growth of institutions
over that of smaller community-
based noninstitutional programs
which generally have greater financial risks.

Profits

The health care business is healthy.
The price earnings ratios in the
nursing home industry are commonly between 14 and 18 percent.
Beverly Enterprises with $450 mil-
lion in business in 1982, reported a
growth of 700 percent since 1978.
National Health Enterprises reported
900 percent growth since 1978. Beverly Enterprises added over 10,000

beds and increased its size by 25
percent in 1982 [14, 16]. Moskowitz
reported that an investment of
$10,000 at the start of 1982 in the
four top health care corporations
(including hospitals and nursing
homes) was worth $18,000 at the
end of the year [17]. An investment of $10,000 five years ago would
have been worth over $100,000 in
1983.

The investment forecasts for the
nursing home industry are strong
because of several factors. One is
what *Forbes* called "gray gold" because of the rapid growth of the
aged population from 25 to 30 million by 1990 assuring the demand
for nursing home care [14]. The demand for nursing home beds continues to be strong for a variety of
other reasons centered around lack
of other community-based program
options, discussed in the preceding
section. If demand were to continue
at its present rate, there would be a
need for 2.5 million nursing home
beds by 1985 (an increase of 90 percent between 1976 and 1985) [18].

Price increases have continued
each year for nursing homes, primarily supported by public dollars
(56 percent). Private insurance and
philanthropy pays for about 1 percent of the total care, and patients
pay for 43 percent directly out-of-
pocket. Medicaid pays for 50 percent
of the total nursing home bills while
Medicare only pays for about 2 percent and other public programs pay
for the remainder [13]. Because Medicaid pays for half of all nursing
home costs, Medicaid policies established by the states are critical in
shaping the industry.

Nursing Home Reimbursement

Medicaid reimbursement policies are a powerful device for influencing the nursing home industry [19, 20]. States have recently been focusing on controlling nursing home reimbursement costs to lower the rapid growth rates in the program, which were occurring at about 16 percent per year. Nursing home reimbursement policies are complex and usually take into account inflation, cost of services, size, hospital affiliation, nursing hours, and other factors [21–23]. Most states pay nursing homes on a prospective basis by setting ceilings on total facility costs and sometimes on specific cost centers. Other states still use a retrospective per diem payment system which generally is higher in costs [20].

While proprietary nursing home chains widely describe their profits and growth in order to attract investors, when the industry presents its cost data to states, they generally argue that higher reimbursement rates are needed. The industry has been successful in obtaining favorable reimbursement rates from state Medicaid agencies until the last two years when many states were facing budget crises and pressures to control overall program costs and reimbursement rates.

Some states such as California found that the average nursing home facility made a profit of 41 percent on net equity in 1978–79 [24]. A similar study in Texas showed an average profit on net equity of 34 percent for 1978 [25]. Since many states do not limit the amount of profits facilities can make, nursing homes are able to reduce expenditures to maximize profits.

Nursing homes have made money from their real estate and capital investments through frequent sales arrangements and also use management lease arrangements to increase revenues [2–3]. As Vladeck points out, nursing homes have used the accelerated depreciation policies under Medicare and Medicaid to pay for the capital investments plus their return on equity investments [3]. The complex mechanism used by nursing homes to increase their profits are difficult to track and to understand for those not in the financial arena. And even non-profit nursing homes operate with a growth imperative with similar pressures to maximize revenues and control costs. The differences between nonprofit and profit facilities are often blurred, and are based on management and distribution of profits rather than other corporate behavior.

Nursing Home Power and Politics

The nursing home industry is the third most powerful health association in most states, after hospitals and physicians. In terms of power, nursing home associations are highly organized, collecting large contributions for political campaigns and political lobbying activities. The associations direct major efforts toward influencing the development of administrative regulations, rates, and licensing activities, and also focus on legislators and their legislative activities. Nationally, the American Health Care Association, a proprietary trade organization, is the largest and most influential organization while the smaller American Association of Homes for the Aging represents voluntary institutions [3].

In a recent study of eight states, data showed that the industry has been particularly effective with legislative and administrative bodies [26]. Such lobbying activities have promoted weak regulation of the industry and favorable rates for the most part within certain recent limitations due to state financial constraints. Litigation has also been used as an effective tool by the nursing home industry to promote favorable public policies. The industry is able to invest substantial sums into such activities and hire talented individuals for legislative, administrative, and legal actions.

Nursing home residents and their families are seldom organized and have few recourses in influencing both public policies and the activities and quality of care in individual nursing homes. While most states have mechanisms for ombudsman programs, complaints are frequently difficult to substantiate and seldom result in corrections. In some communities, citizen groups have been organized to reform nursing homes and serve as public watchdogs for the residents in certain areas. But such groups have not developed a strong power base for effective political action. Without political contributions, citizen groups are not able to compete very effectively in most areas where they exist. Until consumers are better represented with consumer lobbyists and able to influence public policies and political de-cisions, the balance of power will remain in the hands of the nursing home industry.

One feature frequently overlooked is the political impact of the growth in large chain-owned corporations. Not only are such corporations able to build effective economies of scale and to maximize profits, the corporations are effective in using their resources to influence political decision-making at both federal and state levels. The corporations are also immune to a great extent from local political processes, unlike the small locally-owned nursing homes. Local community organizations have less influence in bringing about changes in quality, costs, or management when nursing homes are owned and operated by large corporations with management based out of the local area or even out of the state.

Even more important, professionals working with nursing homes, whether nurses, physicians, or health facility administrators, also have less influence on the policies and practices of large corporations than they do on locally owned and operated facilities. The slow erosion of power and influence by health professionals over their practice within large corporate health institutions is insidious. To reverse this trend, communities and professionals could oppose corporate management and ownership of health facilities in their communities. When given the opportunity to make decisions on certificate of need (review and approval for building or remodeling of facilities under health planning), local zoning, facility bond approvals, operating and use permits, and other approvals, individuals and groups could take steps to reverse the take-over by corporations and make decisions that promote local ownership and local control.

References

1. U.S. Department of Health and Human Services, National Center for Health Statistics, *Master Facility Inventory, 1978*, unpublished tables, U.S. Department of Health and Human Services, Washington, D.C., 1980.

2. U.S. Congress Senate Special Committee on Aging, *Nursing Home Care in the U.S.: Failure in Public Policy*, an Introductory Report and Supporting Papers N.1–7, U.S. Government Printing Office, Washington, D.C., 1974–1976.

3. B. C. Vladeck, *Unloving Care: The Nursing Home Tragedy*, Basic Books, New York, 1980.

4. U.S. General Accounting Office, *Entering A Nursing Home—Costly Implications for Medicaid and the Elderly*, U.S. Comptroller General of the United States, General Accounting Office, Washington, D.C., 1979.

5. U.S. Department of Health and Human Services, Health Care Financing Administration, *Long Term Care: Background and Future Directions*, U.S. Government Printing Office, Washington, D.C., 1981.

6. R. N. Brown, An Appraisal of the Nursing Home Enforcement Process, *Arizona Law Review*, 17:2, 1975.

7. American Bar Association, *Model Recommendations: Intermediate Sanctions for Enforcement of Quality of Care in Nursing Homes*, Commission on Legal Problems of the Elderly, Washington, D.C., 1981.

8. H. S. Ruchlin, An Analysis of Regulatory Issues and Options in Long-Term Care, in *Reform and Regulation in Long-Term Care*, V. LaPorte and J. Rubin (eds), Praeger, New York, 1979.

9. W. J. Scanlon, Theory of the Nursing Home Market, *Inquiry*, 17:2, pp. 25–41, 1980.

10. U.S. Congress Senate Special Committee on Aging, *Health Care for Older Americans: The "Alternatives" Issue*, Parts 1–7, U.S. Government Printing Office, Washington, D.C., 1977–78.

11. U.S. Department of Commerce Bureau of the Census, *1976 Survey of Institutionalized Persons: Study of Persons Receiving Long Term Care*, Current Population Reports, Special Studies, Series No. 69, U.S. Government Printing Office, Washington, D.C., 1978.

12. U.S. Department of Health and Human Services, National Center for Health Statistics, *The National Nursing Home Survey: 1977 Summary for the United States*, Publication No. (PHS) 79–1974, U.S. National Center for Health Statistics, Washington, D.C., 1979.

13. D. R. Waldo and R. M. Gibson, National Health Expenditures, 1981, *Health Care Financing Review*, 4:1, pp. 1–35, Summer 1982.

14. J. Blyskal, Gray Gold, *Forbes*, pp. 80–81, November 23, 1981.

15. S. LaViolette, Nursing Home Chains Scramble for More Private-Paying Patients, *Modern Healthcare*, pp. 130–138, May, 1983.

16. B. Keppel, Multihospital Affiliation in Hand, Beverly Aims to Double Its Size, *Modern Healthcare*, pp. 70–72, June, 1982.

17. M. Moskowitz, The Health Care Business Is Healthy, The Money Tree, *San Francisco Chronicle*, p. 50, March 28, 1983.

18. U.S. Congress, Congressional

Budget Office, *Long Term Care: Actu-arial Cost Estimates*, A CBO Technical Analysis Paper, U.S. Government Printing Office, Washington, D.C., 1977.

19. B. Spitz, *State Guide to Medicaid Cost Containment*, Intergovernmental Health Policy Project, Center for Policy Research, National Governor's Association, Washington, D.C., 1981.

20. C. Harrington and J. Swan, Medicaid Nursing Home Reimbursement Policies, Rates and Expenditures, working paper, Aging Health Policy Center, San Francisco, California, 1983.

21. C. E. Bishop, Nursing Home Cost Studies and Reimbursement Issues, *Health Care Financing Review*, 1:4, pp. 47–64, 1980.

22. R. Schlenker and P. Shaughnessy, *A Framework for Analyzing Nursing Home Cost, Case Mix and Quality In-terrelationships*, Working paper No. 7, Center for Health Services Research, University of Colorado, Health Sciences Center, 1981.

23. P. L. Grimaldi, *Medicaid Reimburse-ment of Nursing-Home Care*, American Enterprise Institute for Public Policy Research, Washington, D.C., 1982.

24. California Health Facilities Commis-sion, *Economic Criteria for Health Plan-ning Report, FY 1981-82/FY 1982-83, Volume II*, Draft Report, Health Facil-ities Commission, Sacramento, Cali-fornia, December 30, 1981.

25. C. Harrington, J. Wood, G. La Londa Berg, and M. Bogart, *Texas Case Study: Medicaid, Title XX, and SSI Programs*, Aging Health Policy Cen-ter, San Francisco, 1983.

26. C. Harrington and R. J. Newcomer, *Medicaid Programs in Eight States: A Study of Policy Changes*, Aging Health Policy Center, San Francisco, 1983.

Section Seven

Policies

We have noted previously that it is difficult to understand the health care system since it appears diffuse and varied. The same problem plagues the arena of health policy. There are a number of diverse, and often conflicting, spheres of policy-making and policy implementation. Health policies are set by various governmental units—local, state, and federal. These policies involve legislation, judicial orders, regulation, guidelines, planning, and budgeting. Some policies are limited, involving relatively specific components of the health care system (for instance revisions in Medicare reimbursement practices that we read about in the DRG article in the previous section). Other policies are quite comprehensive (for instance the incorporation of housing and jobs policies within an existing national health system in Sweden) as one of the upcoming selections discusses. Also as noted in the section introduction on Structures, outcomes are not always the same as the original intentions. There are multiple goals for the many actors in the health care system, as well as many consequences unintended by policy-makers.

Health policy falls into two large categories of health care delivery: access to services and cost containment. In the United States, health policy in the decades of the 1950s and 1960s addressed only expansion of access. This included Hill-Burton funds for hospital construction, Medicare, Medicaid, Neighborhood Health Centers, community mental health centers, and mandated health planning. In the 1970s, federal access policies provided for expanded coverage of existing efforts and support for medical schools and their students. But at the same time, cost-containment policies were also being promulgated, including federal support of health maintenance organizations, state certificate of need programs to restrict hospital expansion, and state rate-setting commissions. By the 1980s, the only access policy was federal coverage of hospice care for dying patients. Cost-containment policies, such as the DRGs already discussed, have become dominant. Severe cutbacks in Medicare and Medicaid have occurred, and *categorical grants* to specific programs and institutions (e.g., a single neighborhood health center) have been replaced with *block grants* that reduce and lump all federal health financing into a few state-level budget blocks (e.g., all alcohol, drug abuse, and mental health funding). Where societywide initiatives in health policy of earlier decades targeted basic structural inequities, current policies reinforce social stratification.

Health policies arise and are altered due to changes in the society. One of the clearest social developments, which began in the 1960s, is the "graying" of America. There are an increasing number of elderly people due to medical advances and to greater longevity stemming from nonmedical factors. At the same time, more of these elderly people live for long periods with chronic diseases, and their acute diseases are often more serious than those in younger people. Carroll Estes and Philip Lee write about these concerns in "Health Problems and Policy Issues of Old Age." The authors point out that new forms of noninstitutional care are necessary for this population, and they suggest that changes in federal reimbursement practices will have to aid these efforts. Estes and Lee also argue that it is not enough for governments and providers to focus on medical care alone—income and housing are crucial to the well-being of elderly people also.

Contemporary policies emphasize individual solutions to social problems, as compared to the more frequent programs of the 1960s. Rosemary Taylor's article, "The Politics of Prevention" takes a critical look at the ideology and politics behind preventive programs. While preventive health practices have many positive elements, a good number of prevention programs have focused on changing individuals and their habits, rather than attack the social roots of a health problem. Perhaps the best example of the failure of preventive programs to focus on societal-level solutions is the federal government's support of antismoking efforts by individuals while still granting generous subsidies to the tobacco industry. Also, in the 1980s other preventive programs have been cut back or have been incompletely implemented, since they are seen as too expensive (e.g., expanded perinatal care), too threatening to corporate profit and the ideology of the free market (e.g., factory safety and toxic waste management), and too antagonistic to conservative attitudes of family and social life (e.g., family planning and sex education).

In the first selection in this book, Victor Sidel and Ruth Sidel showed how poorly the United States compares to other Western societies on key health indicators. This poor relative ranking is more understandable when we see how other countries deal with health policy. United States policy is very far behind most other advanced industrial capitalist societies. There is a slogan, coined by health activists and now widely in use, "Health care is a right, not a privilege." This slogan is not brought to fruition in the United States, though it does more often in comparable-developed societies. Sidney Lee's article, "Health Policy, A Social Contract: A Comparison of the United States and Canada," provides a valuable comparison. Despite the fact that both countries have a fee-for-service medical system, the Canadian health care system is quite different in that it provides for universal eligibility for service, more ample benefits packages, and a far smaller number of third-party payers. As a result, Canada has a vastly lower cost of administration, as well as a more equitable delivery of services. Canada's system is aided by, and also results in, a more socially conscious medical profession.

A national health care system does not automatically solve all problems. Göran Dahlgren and Finn Diderichsen write in "Strategies for Equity in Health: Report from Sweden," that Sweden's system encountered difficulties in the 1970s, including conflicts between limited resources and growing needs. Health analysts and government officials found significant inequities in the health status of different social classes. A national discussion took place, and the goal of *equity* in health care was reaffirmed. A new policy approach was developed to diminish the gaps between classes and to better serve the needs of people for primary care (comprehensive and continuing care provided through a regularly seen doctor who is an internist, pediatrician, or family medicine doctor). Of particular importance is that the new approach involved "intersectoral" policies in which the health sector would work with other social sectors (e.g., social welfare, housing, and education) to improve working conditions, schooling, day care, housing, and nutrition.

23 HEALTH PROBLEMS AND POLICY ISSUES OF OLD AGE

Carroll L. Estes and Philip R. Lee

Social policy affecting the aged and their health is growing in importance as the number of elderly increases, the burden of illness in old age persists, and the costs of providing health care continue to rise rapidly. For most of this century, the population aged sixty-five and older has been increasing at a rate more rapid than that of the U.S. population as a whole; four-generation families are becoming a common experience in American life (U.S. Congress, Senate 1984a). From 1960 to 1980, the population aged sixty-five years and over increased from 16.7 million (9 percent) to 25.9 million (11 percent of the population)—a 55

percent increase. During the same period, the number of those aged seventy-five to eighty-four rose 65 percent while the number of those over eighty-five rose 174 percent. By the year 2000, the percentage of elderly seventy-five years and over will continue to increase more rapidly than the percentage of those aged sixty-five to seventy-four. The

SOURCE: From "Health Problems and Policy Issues of Old Age" by Carroll L. Estes and Philip R. Lee in *Applications of Social Science to Clinical Medicine and Health Policy*, Linda H. Aiken and David Mechanic, Editors. Copyright © 1986 by Rutgers, the State University. Reprinted with permission of Rutgers University Press.

former group will increase from the current 38 percent to 45 percent of the elderly population (Rice and Feldman 1983). More older people in our society are living to advanced ages. A critical question is whether they will encounter a growing burden of illness and disability as suggested by Rice and Feldman (1983), Schneider and Brody (1983), Myers and Manton (1984), and Verbrugge (1984), or whether their health will be better than that of earlier generations because of life-style and other changes as suggested by the work of Fries (1980, 1983, 1984) and Fries and Crapo (1981).

Over the past twenty years, the proportion of elderly people living below the poverty level has been substantially reduced. The aged also have more access to health care services. Yet, a host of problems remain. There are large disparities in income among the elderly; millions face a growing financial burden due to increasing out-of-pocket health care expenditures; community-based health and social services intended to supplement family care provided for the functionally dependent and chronically ill are not readily available; housing is a growing problem for the poor elderly; and many are socially isolated and live lives of quiet desperation.

Health and Well-Being of Older Persons

Declining mortality rates across the entire lifespan and changing fertility rates are the major factors contributing to the proportionate increase in the population aged

sixty-five years and older in the United States. Patterns of morbidity and mortality in the United States have changed dramatically during the twentieth century. Life expectancy at birth rose from forty-seven years in 1900 to sixty-eight years in 1950 (U.S. Department of Health and Human Services, Health Care Financing Administration 1980). This dramatic increase in longevity was the result of the sharp decline in infant mortality and the reduction in mortality from communicable diseases affecting mainly infants, children, and young adults. While life expectancy at birth increased dramatically between 1900 and 1950, life expectancy at age sixty-five increased by only two years (from 11.9 to 13.9 years). Between 1950 and 1982 life expectancy at age sixty-five increased from 13.9 to 16.8 years. There was a 3.8-year increase for women and a 1.6-year increase for men during this period (Waldo and Lazenby 1984). The overall death rate for the elderly fell 29 percent during the period 1950–1982, falling much more rapidly for women than for men (Waldo and Lazenby 1984). Most of the decline in mortality among the elderly has resulted from reductions in heart disease, cerebrovascular disease, and stroke (National Center for Health Statistics 1982, 34).

A critical question for the elderly, for health care providers, and for health-policy makers is the impact of this rapid decline in mortality on morbidity and disability among the elderly and on their need for and utilization of health and social services. The problem has been clearly defined by Rice and Feldman (1983): "Changes in levels of morbidity, in therapies and technologies, in the availability and cost of care, in social and economic conditions, will contribute to patterns and levels of utilization of medical care services, as will mortality rates and changes in the age structure of the population. Some of these factors will have to increase utilization while others may decrease it." One aspect of debate has focused on whether or not the future burden of illness in a growing elderly population suggests a greater drain on health and long-term-care resources than is predictable from projections of present patterns of utilization and expenditures (Rice and Feldman 1983; Gruenberg 1977; Manton 1982; Schneider and Brody 1983; Myers and Manton 1984; and Verbrugge 1984). Of particular import may be the burdens imposed by multiple chronic conditions—a problem that increases with advancing age and that limits activity and increases bed disability days, physician visits, and short-stay hospital care (Rice 1985). These views about the growth of morbidity and the decline of mortality contrast with those of Fries (1980, 1983, 1984), who has suggested that a compression of morbidity and a rectangularization of the mortality curve are likely to occur as life expectancy approaches the normal biological life span, which he estimates to be approximately eighty-five years.

The major causes of illness and limitation of activity among the elderly are injuries, chronic diseases, and stress related conditions, including hypertension, suicide, alcohol-ism, and drug misuse. Today, the common association between old age and physical decline in health is attributed primarily to chronic arthritis, heart disease, hearing and vision impairments, and hypertension (U.S. Congress, Senate 1983a). Alzheimer's disease, depression, and alcoholism are also major problems.

While a higher proportion of older than younger persons are afflicted by one or more chronic conditions, a majority of older persons continue to enjoy good health (U.S. Department of Health and Human Services, Health Care Financing Administration 1981). The need for assistance, however, increases with advancing age. For example, the percentage of persons extremely limited by chronic conditions is 6.2 percent among forty-five to sixty-four-year-olds, 14.4 percent for sixty-five to seventy-four-year-olds, and 33 percent for those eighty-five and older (U.S. Department of Health and Human Services, Health Care Financing Administration 1981). In the aggregate, older persons, particularly women and minorities with low incomes and lower educational levels, have a higher incidence of chronic diseases and disability (Butler and Newacheck 1981). Rural elderly also report a greater number of days per year of restricted activity (U.S. Congress, Senate 1982). In view of the lower income and educational levels of the rural elderly, this finding is not surprising.

In addition to the burden of illness and disability, income and social factors are important in determining whether an elderly person will be confined to a nursing home (Kane and Kane 1982; Butler and Newa-check 1981). It is estimated that for every nursing home resident, three people of equal functional impairment live in the community. Many functionally impaired elderly can be cared for at home largely because of services provided by family members, usually a spouse or adult offspring. Widows and widowers are five times more likely to be institutionalized than married persons; those elderly who were never married, divorced, or separated may have up to ten times the rate of institutionalization of married individuals (Butler and Newacheck 1981). Social support networks between elderly persons, relatives, and friends have been found to have a positive effect on patients' mental functioning and were a buffer between decline and risk of institutionalization (Wan and Weissert 1981). These findings emphasize the need to develop an adequate base of social support for the elderly through family, friends, and organized community services.

Income and Housing: Keys to the Health and Well-Being of the Elderly

Income

A large body of research identifies the link between income and health as measured by longevity, disability, and chronic illness (Luft 1978). Income is clearly a vital element in determining health status. Social security, the primary source of postretirement income for the majority of the elderly, thus becomes a critical element in national health policy.

Although national policies related to the prevention of impoverishment in old age date to the Social Security Act of 1935, only recently have income maintenance policies been viewed as a cornerstone of health policies for the elderly (Ball 1981). It is clear from mortality and morbidity data as well as from numerous studies of health care utilization and cost that an important link exists between health and economic well-being. Thus, assessing the economic status of older persons is an important component of health policy planning for the elderly, but this task has become complex and controversial. Multiple factors such as labor market experience, education, marital status, family-member death, chronic or acute illness onset, and Social Security and tax policies combine to create differing effects at particular points in the life cycle.

While 1982 census data indicate a decline in elderly poverty (now 14.6 percent, or 3.6 million older adults), the pervasive and unrelenting experience of poverty among elderly blacks and Hispanics, and among many elderly whites, cannot be ignored. Minorities experience two to three times the poverty rate of whites, with 35.6 percent of aged blacks and 38.2 percent of Hispanics, as compared to 12.4 percent of aged whites, living at extreme levels of poverty in 1982. Moreover, the elderly living alone have a poverty rate of 27.1 percent (U.S. Congress, Senate 1983a).

The face of poverty is not only minority, it is female. Almost half (49 percent) of the elderly white single women and 80 percent of the elderly black single women live at or near the poverty level (Women's Equity Action League 1985). Half of the aged poor are widows or women who never married, who live alone (Orshansky 1979; Leadership Council of Aging Organizations 1983). The prevalence of poverty among older women reflects earlier social and economic inequities. Labor market experience in low-wage industries, pay inequities, interrupted employment patterns and divorce are factors that will continue to adversely affect the economic well-being of future generations of retired women (O'Rand 1983).

The disparity between the worst-off elderly (those 14.7 percent with incomes less than $4,000 per year) and the best-off elderly (those 12 percent with incomes of $25,000 or more per year) corresponds to life-long conditions and opportunities. A great deal of advocacy effort and legislative policy in entitlement and discretionary programs are directed toward the poorest group, while tax policy aids the higher-income group. In between the extremes of income distribution is another equally important group known as the near poor. The aged surpass every other group at the near-poor levels. If the near poor (125 percent or 150 percent of current poverty criteria) are considered, the profile of poverty in old age rises dramatically (Lehrman 1980). For example, 21 percent of white elderly are at or below 25 percent of the 1982 poverty level ($6,465 per year), compared to 51.6 percent of black elderly and 40.9 percent of Hispanic elderly (U.S. Department of Commerce, Bureau of the Census

1983). These near-poor individuals are particularly relevant to health policy considerations because they are the least likely to be assisted by Social Security retirement programs and are the most likely to be affected by increased cost-sharing in the Medicare program and to draw on the resources of Medicaid when ill.[1]

Housing Policies

The majority of today's elderly own homes, and the market value of these homes has recently increased substantially. Over 90 percent of the total value of the housing stock owned and occupied by those over age sixty-five years is homeowner equity. However, the resource of home ownership can be quickly and unexpectedly threatened with the onset of chronic illness requiring long-term social and medical maintenance costs. Even with the combined resources of home ownership, Medicare, and supplemental private health coverage (e.g., Medigap insurance), a broad sector of middle- and low-income retired persons are inadequately protected from the potentially catastrophic costs of severe chronic disease or injury.

Retirement often reduces disposable income by one-half to one-third, making the availability of affordable housing an important consideration. Older Americans pay a larger proportion of their incomes for rent than do other age groups. Approximately 2.3 million elderly households spend over 35 percent of their incomes on housing. Forty-one percent of elderly renters with incomes below poverty level spend over 45 percent of their incomes on housing (U.S. Congress, Senate 1983a).

Experience often has borne out the essential linkages between living arrangements, adequate income, and long-term-care needs (Wan, Odell, and Lewis 1982). Yet a comprehensive policy has not been formulated, and housing remains an essential but largely ignored dimension of long-term care (Meltzer, Farrow, and Richman 1981). Overall, public policy has fostered a piecemeal approach to housing needs, which ranges from large urban public housing projects to incentives for a privately developed and publicly financed nursing home industry.

The importance of relating housing to long-term care is often realized too late, when the functional independence of an individual has been threatened and families can no longer cope. Indeed the multibillion-dollar nursing home industry has functioned as a substitute for the lack of adequate income, suitable low-cost housing, and community social supports (Scanlon, Difederico, and Stassen 1979).

Financing, Organization, and Delivery of Health and Long-Term-Care Services

Current health care financing and social service programs for the elderly involve all levels of government as well as the private sector. At the federal level, Medicare provides health insurance coverage of hospital and physician services for most individuals aged sixty-five and

over, for disabled persons under age sixty-five who meet certain criteria, and for those suffering from end-stage renal disease. There are 27 million elderly and 3 million disabled eligible beneficiaries on Medicare. Of the total Medicare expenditures for 1984 ($63.1 billion dollars), almost three-quarters was spent on hospital services (70 percent) and one-quarter on physician services (23.1 percent). Medicare expenditures were negligible in covering nursing homes (less than 1 percent) and less than 3.1 percent in covering home health care in fiscal year 1984 (U.S. Congress, Senate 1985). Medicare does not cover long-term care, out-of-institution drugs, dental care, eyeglasses, hearing aids, and other important health services for the elderly.

Because the federal government plays a dominant role in the payment for hospital and physician services for the elderly, its reimbursement policies have been important in driving costs upward. The critical policy objective of Medicare and Medicaid was to assure access to "mainstream" medical care for the elderly and the poor. To guarantee provider acceptance, Congress required that payment to hospitals would be made on the basis of their costs, determined after the care was provided. Physicians were paid on the basis of their usual, customary, and reasonable charges under Medicare and on the basis of a fixed fee scale under Medicaid. These policies held for almost twenty years, in spite of steadily rising costs that exceeded the consumer price index by a wide margin and rapidly increasing Medicare and Medicaid expenditures.

One immediate consequence of the implementation of Medicare, which had a significant impact on costs, was the dramatic increase in the use of short-stay hospital services by the elderly. There was, initially, an increase in both the rate of admission and the length of stay. After 1967 the average length of stay for the elderly began to decline, but the admission rate continued to increase (U.S. Department of Health and Human Services, Health Care Financing Administration 1980). Surgical rates also increased dramatically. In 1965 there were 6,554 operations for every 100,000 persons aged sixty-five and older; in 1975 there were 15,483 operations for every 100,000 persons aged sixty-five and older—an increase of over 100 percent (Kovar 1977). The use, outside the hospital, of prescription drugs, an item not covered by Medicare, rose even more rapidly during this period (Lee 1980).

Although the number of hospital admissions and surgical procedures per 100,000 elderly rose dramatically, the use of physicians' services outside the hospital by the elderly changed relatively little. There was an increase in the use of physicians' services by the poor elderly and a decrease by the nonpoor, with the overall average remaining close to 6.5 visits per year for 1965 through 1978 (U.S. Department of Health and Human Services, Health Care Financing Administration 1980).

The increased utilization of hospi-

tal services by the elderly and the gradually increasing number of elderly were factors affecting the rapid increase in Medicare expenditures. These factors were relatively minor, however, when compared to the impact of general inflation and the additional price increases by hospitals and physicians, and the increased complexity of care provided. Although the rise in hospital costs has been the focus of policymakers' attention, the costs of physician services have risen even more rapidly since the enactment of Medicare (Etheridge and Merrill 1984).

An issue of growing concern to both patients and policymakers has been the cost of medical care during the last year of a person's life. During 1978, 1.9 million people died in the United States; of these, 1.3 million were Medicare enrollees (Lubitz and Prihoda 1983). These 1.3 million presented only 5.2 percent of Medicare enrollees but accounted for 28.2 percent of Medicare expenditures. The Medicare program spent an average of $4,527 on enrollees in their last year of life, an amount 6.2 times the $729 spent on enrollees who did not die in 1978. For those who died, expenditures were also greater during the year prior to their death, but not as great as in the last year of life. In the last year of life, expenses increased as death approached: 30 percent of the expenditures were made during the last thirty days of life and 46 percent in the last sixty days (Lubitz and Prihoda 1983).

Although Medicare has been the most important source of payments for hospitals and physicians caring for the elderly since 1965, it is limited in scope of benefits and reimbursement policies required to meet the need of the chronically ill and disabled elderly. The cost of care, that is, the full range of services addressing the health, personal, and social needs, is borne by both the private (the elderly themselves and their families) and the public sectors, including Supplementary Security Income (SSI), Medicare, and Medicaid. The Social Services Block Grant and Older Americans Act programs, which support the non-profit voluntary agencies at the local level, are a vital part of the long-term-care picture in the community, but they garner considerably less public resources than the strictly medically defined long-term-care service.

State policy, because of the decentralization of policies relative to Medicaid and social services, has become a major factor determining the scope, structure, and availability of long-term care. The result has been a variety of approaches, in part dependent on the fiscal condition of the states. The recession of 1971–1982 and the subsequent economic recovery have affected states quite differently; as a result, the resources available for public programs at the state level varies markedly (Estes, Newcomer, and Associates 1983).

Three developments are of great importance in the organization of health and long-term-care services if the needs of the chronically ill and disabled elderly are to be met effectively: (1) the need to better link and integrate acute-care and long-term-care services in the community; (2) the need to strengthen ambula-

tory care, community-based services (e.g., adult day care, congregate meals, senior centers), and in-home services and to reduce the emphasis on inpatient care in hospitals and nursing homes; and (3) the need to recognize the benefits (as well as the limits) and potential roles of family members and other sources of social support, including the full spectrum of non-profit community agencies servicing the elderly.

There have been many positive professional and community efforts (largely demonstration projects) directed toward a more comprehensive and humane long-term-care policy. Koff (1982) envisions a long-term-care system in which institution-based and community-based services are integrated and appropriately utilized in a "continuum of care." In contrast to this ideal, there is generally no systematic link between the myriad health and social services that have emerged as alternatives to institutionalization; nor is there a systematic link between the acute and chronic care systems (Vogel and Palmer 1983).

In addition to the changes in financing and organization that are needed, the effective care of the elderly requires changes at the clinical level. Clinical care, whether provided by physicians, nurses, dentists, or other health professionals, must take account of the behavioral and social factors, as well as of the biological and medical factors that contribute to morbidity among the elderly. This biopsychosocial approach was described by Engle (1977) and has recently been applied to the elderly. From this perspective, the functional status of the elderly would be affected by the biological, social, and psychologic changes. All of these factors must be considered in patient care, and they require a more broader approach than is customary for most physicians. Physicians can no longer isolate themselves in an office-based practice or in a hospital and expect to fully meet the needs of elderly patients with multiple social as well as medical needs. Linkages with the range of services essential to the care of the disabled, chronically ill elderly will be required.

Linkage is also needed between levels of care—primary, secondary, and tertiary—as well as between acute and long-term care. One approach to the better integration of acute and long-term care could be through the expansion of health maintenance organizations (HMOs). HMOs could encompass the full spectrum of social and health (and long-term care) needs, including home care, ambulatory care (including adult day care, congregate meals), and nursing home care, on a prepaid capitation basis to control costs (Diamond and Berman 1981). Called social health maintenance organizations (SHMOs), these new types of prepaid plans not only place providers at risk and change incentives (as do HMOs), they also have the potential for redesigning both the delivery and financing of long-term care.

Another linkage model that has emerged focuses on those in greatest need of medical and social services and provides a comprehensive range of services, primarily in the home

and in the community. An example of such a model of comprehensive care for the very frail, sick, and disabled elderly is On Lok in San Francisco. Here, medical, nursing, and social services, physical, occupational, and recreational therapy, counseling, congregate meals, housing, transportation, respite care, and in-home services are provided by a single agency. For a patient population of over three hundred, all of whom were eligible for nursing home admission, it has been possible to meet the patients' needs in a humane, compassionate, and cost-effective manner. The physician and all other health professionals involved are team players, adjusting their respective roles to the patients' needs.

The emerging hospital model of acute and long-term care involves a "vertical" integration of traditional hospital inpatient services, with ambulatory care, home care, and nursing home care. Whether this approach will further fragment community-based care and whether it is the most cost-effective use of community resources remain to be seen.

These changes in health and long-term care will not be possible without substantial changes in medical, nursing, pharmacy, and dental education. Today's entering medical and nursing students particularly, as well as many of those in the other health professions, will spend an increasing part of their professional lives dealing with chronic illness and functional disability in their elderly patients. To do their jobs well, their education and training will need to place more emphasis on chronic diseases, aging, management of chronic disability, prevention and rehabilitation, and social and behavioral factors in health and disease.

Acknowledgment

The authors gratefully acknowledge the assistance of Lenore E. Gerard in the preparation of this chapter.

Note

1. Escalating health care costs and budget cuts have significantly raised the proportion of costs personally shouldered by older Americans. In 1980 the nation's elderly used 13 percent of their income for health care; by 1984 this amount had risen to 15 percent—more than before Medicare and Medicaid began in 1965. By 1988, and under 1 current law, the elderly are projected to spend 17.5 percent of their income on health care of $2,194 per elderly person (U.S. Congress, House of Representatives 1985.) Out-of-pocket health care expenses are disproportionately borne by households incomes under $5,000 (U.S. Congress, Budget Office 1983).

References

Alpha Centerpiece Report. 1984. Long-term care alternatives: Innovations in financing chronic care for the elderly. Bethesda, Md.

Ball, M. 1981. Rethinking national policy on health care for the elderly. In *The geriatric imperative*, ed. A. R. Somers and D. R. Fabian. New York: Appleton-Century-Crofts.

Belloc, N. B., and L. Breslow. 1972. Relationship of physical health status and health practices. *Preventive Medicine* 1:409–421.

Berkman, L. F. 1985. The relationship of social networks and social support to morbidity and mortality. In *Social support and health,* ed. S. Cohen and S. L. Syme. New York: Academic Press.

Berkman, L. F., and L. Breslow. 1983. *Health and ways of living.* New York: Oxford University Press.

Biles, B., C. J. Schram, and J. Atkinson. 1980. Hospital cost inflation under state rate-setting programs. *New England Journal of Medicine* 303(12):664–668.

Bovbjerg, R. R. 1984. *Medicaid in the Reagan era.* Washington, D.C.: Urban Institute.

Butler, L. H., and P. W. Newacheck. 1981. Health and social factors affecting long-term care policy. *Policy options in long-term care,* ed. J. Meltzer, F. Farrow, and H. Richman. Chicago: University of Chicago.

Butler, R. N., and M. I. Lewis. 1982. *Aging and mental health.* 3rd ed. St. Louis, Mo.: Mosby.

Cassel, J. 1976. The contribution of the social environment to host resistance. *American Journal of Epidemiology* 104(2): 107–123.

Coelen, C., and D. Sullivan. 1981. An analysis of the effects of prospective reimbursement programs on hospital expenditures. *Health Care Financing Review* 2(3):1–40.

Crystal, S. 1982. *America's old age crisis.* New York: Basic.

Diamond, L. M., and D. E. Berman. 1981. The social/health maintenance organization: A single entry, prepaid, long-term delivery system. In *Reforming the long-term care system,* ed. J. Callahan and S. S. Wallace. Lexington, Mass.: Lexington Books, D. C. Heath & Co.

Engel, G. L. The need for a new medical model: A challenge for biomedicine. *Science* 196(428):129–134.

Estes, C. L. 1979. *The aging enterprise.* San Francisco: Jossey-Bass.

Estes, C. L., R. J. Newcomer, and Associates. 1983. *Fiscal austerity and aging.* Beverly Hills, Calif.: Sage.

Etheredge, L., and J. C. Merrill. 1984. Medicare: Paying the physician. Washington, D.C.: Urga Urban Institute. Typescript.

Fisher, C. 1980. Differences by age groups in health care spending. *Health Care Financing Review* 1(4):65–90.

Fries, J. F. 1980. Aging, natural health, and the compression of morbidity. *New England Journal of Medicine* 303: 130–135.

———. 1983. The compression of morbidity. *Milbank Memorial Fund Quarterly: Health and Society* 61:397–419.

———. 1984. The compression of morbidity: Miscellaneous comments about a theme. *Gerontologist* 24(4):354–359.

Fries, J. F., and L. M. Crapo. 1981. *Vitality and aging: Implications of the rectangular curve.* San Francisco: W. H. Freeman.

Fuchs, V. R. 1984. Though much is taken: Reflections on aging, health, and medical care. *Milbank Memorial Fund Quarterly: Health and Society* 62(2):143–166.

Gibson, R. M., D. R. Waldo, and K. R. Levit. 1983. National health expenditures, 1982. *Health Care Financing Review* 5(1):1–31.

Grad, S. 1984. *Income of the population 55 and over, 1982.* U.S. Department of Health and Human Services, Social Security Administration. Washington, D.C.: Government Printing Office.

Gruenberg, E. M. 1977. The failures of success. *Milbank Memorial Fund Quarterly: Health and Society* 55(1):3–24.

Hadley, J. 1982. *More medical care, better health?* Washington, D.C.: Urban Institute.

Hambrook, A. 1984. Panel discussion on architectural issues and marketing techniques. Laventhol and Horwath First Annual Lifecare-Continuing Care Retirement Center Symposium. San Francisco, Calif.

Harrington, C., R. Newcomer, and C. L. Estes, and Associates. 1985. *Long term care of the elderly.* Beverly Hills, Calif.: Sage.

Harrington, C., and J. H. Swan. 1984. Medicaid nursing home reimbursement policies, rates, and expenditures. *Health Care Financing Review* 6(1):39–49.

———. 1985. Institutional long term care services. In *Long term care of the elderly: Public policy issues*, ed. C. Harrington, R. Newcomer, C. Estes, and Associates. Beverly Hills: Sage.

Kane, R. A., and A. L. Kane. 1982. Long-term care: A field in search of values. In *Values and long-term care.* Lexington, Mass.: Heath.

Koff, T. H. 1982. *Long-term care: An approach to serving frail elderly.* Boston: Little, Brown.

Kovar, M. G. 1977. Elderly people: The population 65 years and over. In *Health United States, 1976–1977.* National Center for Health Statistics. Washington, D.C.: Government Printing Office.

Leadership Council of Aging Organizations. 1983. The administration's 1984 budget: A critical view from an aging perspective. Washington, D.C.

Lehrman, R. 1980. Poverty statistics serve as nagging reminder. *Generations: Journal of the Western Gerontological Society* 4(1):17.

Lee, P. R. 1980. Health policy issues for the aged and challenges for the 1980's. *Generations* 4(1):38–40, 73.

Lee, P. R., C. L. Estes, L. LeRoy, and R. J. Newcomer. 1982. Health policy and the aged. In *Annual review of gerontology and geriatrics*, vol. 3, ed. C. Eisdorfer. New York: Springer Publishing.

Lee, P. R., and P. E. Franks. 1980. Health and disease in the community. In *Primary care*, ed. J. Fry. London: William Heinemann Medical Books.

Lindeman, D. A., and A. Pardini. 1983. Social services: The impact of fiscal austerity. In *Fiscal austerity and aging*, ed. C. Estes, R. J. Newcomer, and Associates. Beverly Hills: Sage.

Lubitz, J., and R. Prihoda. 1983. Use and costs of Medicare services in the last years of life. In *Health: United States and prevention profile*, pp. 71–77. U.S. Department of Health and Human Services, Public Health Service, National Center for Health Statistics. Hyattsville, Md.: Government Printing Office.

Luft, H. S. 1978. *Poverty and health: Economic causes and consequences of health problems*. Cambridge, Mass.: Ballinger.

McCoy, J. L. 1983. Overview of available data relating to board and care and care homes and residents. U.S. Department of Health and Human Services. Unpublished memo.

McKeown, T. 1976. *The role of medicine: Dream, mirage, or nemesis*. London: Nuffield Provincial Hospital Trust.

Manton, K. C. 1982. Changing concepts of morbidity and mortality in the elderly population. *Milbank Memorial Fund Quarterly: Health and Society* 60(2):183–244.

Meltzer, J., F. Farrow, and H. Richman, eds. 1981. *Policies options in long term care*. Chicago: University of Chicago Press.

Myers, G. C., and K. C. Manton. 1984. Compression of mortality: Myth or reality? *Gerontologist* 24(4):346–353.

National Center for Health Statistics. 1982. *Health, United States, 1982*. DHHS Publication No. (PHS) 83-1232. Washington, D.C.: Government Printing Office.

Newcomer, R. J., M. P. Lawton, and T. Byerts, eds. 1985. *Housing an aging society*. New York: Van Nostrand Reinhold.

New York State Office on Aging. 1983. *Medicare: Analysis and recommendations for reform*. Albany, N.Y.: State Office on Aging.

O'Rand, A. M. 1983. Women. In *Handbook of the aged in the United States*, ed. E. Palmore. Westport, Conn.: Greenwood Press.

Orshansky, H. 1979. Statement in U.S. House Select Committee on Aging, Hearing on poverty among America's aged. August 9. Washington, D.C.: Government Printing Office.

Rice, D. 1985. Personal communication.

Rice, D. P., and J. J. Feldman. 1983. Living longer in the United States: Demographic changes and health needs of the elderly. *Milbank Fund Memorial Quarterly: Health and Society* 61(3): 362–396.

Scanlon, W., E. Difederico, and M. Stassen. 1979. *Long-term care: Current experience and a framework for analysis*. Washington, D.C.: Urban Institute.

Schneider, E. L., and J. A. Brody. 1983. Aging, natural death, and the compression of morbidity: Another view. *New England Journal of Medicine* 309: 854–856.

Struyk, R. J. 1986. Future housing assistance policy for the elderly. In *Housing an aging society*, ed. R. J. Newcomer, M. P. Lawton, and T. Byerts. New York: Van Nostrand Reinhold.

Trout, J., and D. R. Mattson. 1984. A 10-year review of the Supplemental Security Income program. *Social Security Bulletin* 47(1):3–24.

U.S. Congress. Budget Office. 1983. *Changing the structure of Medicare benefits: Issue and options.* Washington, D.C.: Government Printing Office.

————. House of Representatives. Committee on Ways and Means. 1985. *Background material and data on programs within the jurisdiction of the committee.* Washington, D.C.: Government Printing Office.

————. Select Committee on Aging. 1985. *The President's 1986 budget.* Washington, D.C.: Government Printing Office.

————. Senate. Special Committee on Aging. 1982, 1983a, 1984a, 1985. *Developments in aging: 1981, 1982, 1983, 1984.* Washington, D.C.: Government Printing Office.

————. 1983b. Hearings on life care communities: Promises and problems. Washington, D.C.: Government Printing Office.

————. 1984b. *Older Americans and the federal budget: Past, present, and future.* Washington, D.C.: Government Printing Office.

U.S. Department of Commerce, Bureau of the Census. 1983. Money income and poverty status of families and persons in the United States, 1982. Washington, D.C.: Government Printing Office.

U.S. Department of Health and Human Services. Health Care Financing Administration. 1980. *10 years of short-stay hospital utilization of costs under Medicare: 1967, 1976.* Office of Research, Demonstrations, and Statistics. Washington, D.C.: Government Printing Office.

————. 1981. *Long term care: Background and future directions.* Washington, D.C.: Government Printing Office.

————. Office of the Inspector General. 1982. *Board and care homes: A study of federal and state actions to safeguard the health and safety of board and care residents.* Washington, D.C.: Government Printing Office.

————. Social Security Administration. 1984a. *Social Security Bulletin: Annual Statistical Supplement, 1980.* Washington, D.C.: Government Printing Office.

————. 1984b. Social security in review. *Social Security Bulletin* 47(2):1.

————. 1985. *Monthly benefit statistics program data: Old-age, survivors, disability, and health insurance.* Washington, D.C.: Government Printing Office.

U.S. Public Law 93-383. 1974. Housing and community development act of 1974 (as amended). Washington, D.C.: Government Printing Office.

U.S. Public Law 95-557. 1978. Congregate housing services act of 1978 (as amended). Washington, D.C.: Government Printing Office.

U.S. Public Law 97-34. 1981. Economic Recovery Tax of 1981. Washington, D.C.: Government Printing Office.

U.S. Public Law 97-35. 1981. Omnibus Reconciliation Act of 1981. Washington. D.C.: Government Printing Office.

U.S. Public Law 97-248. 1982. Tax Equity and Fiscal Responsibility Act of 1982. Washington, D.C.: Government Printing Office.

Verbrugge, L. 1984. Longer life but worsening health? Trends in health and mortality of middle aged and older persons. *Milbank Memorial Fund Quarterly: Health and Society* 62(3):475–519.

Vladeck, B. C. 1984. Medicare hospital payment by diagnosis-related groups. *Annals of Internal Medicine* 100(4):576–591.

Vogel, R. J., and H. C. Palmer, eds. 1983. *Long term care: Perspectives from research and demonstrations*. Baltimore, Md.: U.S. Health Care Financing Administration.

Waldo, D. R., and H. C. Lazenby. 1984. Demographic characteristics and health care use and expenditures by the aged in the United States, 1977–1984. *Health Care Financing Review* 6(1):1–29.

Wan, T. T. H., B. F. Odell, and D. T. Lewis. 1982. *Promoting the well-being of the elderly: A community diagnosis*. New York: Haworth Press.

Wan, T. T., and W. G. Weissert. 1981. Social support networks, patient status, and institutionalization. *Research on Aging* 3(2):240–256.

Women's Equity Action League (WEAL). 1985. Facts on Social Security. Washington, D.C.: WEAL.

Wood, J. B., and C. L. Estes, 1983. The private nonprofit sector and aging. In *Fiscal austerity and aging*, ed. C. L. Estes, R. J. Newcomer, and Associates. Beverly Hills: Sage.

———. 1985. Private, nonprofit organizations and community-based long term care. In *Long term care of the elderly: Public policy issues*, ed. C. Harrington, R. Newcomer, and C. Estes and Associates. Beverly Hills: Sage.

World Health Organization. 1948. Test of the constitution of World Health Organization. *Official Records* 2:100.

Zais, J. P., R. J. Struyk, and T. Thibodeau. 1982. *Housing assistance for older Americans*. Washington, D.C.: Urban Institute.

24 THE POLITICS OF PREVENTION

Rosemary C. R. Taylor

Prevention is the new catchword in American health care policy. What it will mean in practice in the long run, however, is the subject of an important political struggle. Increasingly, preventive strategies are being shaped by an ideology that attributes to individuals the responsibility for their own health and well-being. It is an ideology that has captured the American imagination in the last five years even though the activities it generates—jogging and exercise programs, antismoking campaigns and changes in diet—may be largely confined to the middle class. This ar-

ticle analyzes the emergence in the late seventies of the prevailing consensus about the appropriate content of a prevention policy in the United States. This policy has been constructed, in part, by a particular heterogeneous social coalition, which I shall describe. The material interests of certain historical actors do not fully explain why the assumptions about the etiology of disease

SOURCE: From *Social Policy* published by Social Policy Corporation, New York, New York 10036. Copyright 1982 by Social Policy Corporation, pp. 32-41.

that inform current preventive policy have come to constitute the dominant interpretation of social reality for Americans. Elsewhere, I explore more thoroughly the relationship between policy developments and popular beliefs (Taylor, 1981). I argue that the ideology of prevention currently adopted by the state is so widely accepted because it is congruent with changes in other cultural ideals, because it is promoted by the organization of American medical care, and because it effectively translates, for many people, their subjective experience of the relationship between their health and aspects of their everyday life. Here, I concentrate on the question of how one version of prevention has come to shape the state's health-related funding decisions and policy initiatives.

First it must be explained how any version of prevention could have assumed such importance in political debate. After all, it was not so long ago that most critics bemoaned the fact that high-technology medicine received the lion's share of resources for health care, while preventing disease was a strategy ritualistically alluded to but rarely funded to any substantial degree. To many, the roots of the new enthusiasm for prevention seem self-evident: it has been demonstrated beyond doubt that medicine is a relatively minor influence on health.

> The best estimates are that the medical system (doctors, drugs, hospitals) affects about 10 percent of the usual indices for measuring health. . . . The remaining 90 percent are determined by factors over which doctors have lit-

tle or no control, from individual lifestyle (smoking, exercise, worry), to social conditions (income, eating habits, physiological inheritance), to the physical environment (air and water quality). (Wildavsky, 1977)

If medical care has such little effect, adherents of this argument imply, we should be spending money and energy on the things that do affect our health—namely, preventive measures.

When the relationship between health and health care was questioned in this way, it fueled concern about the cost of the latter. Avoidable sickness, it was argued, was costing the nation too much and contributing to an alarming inflation rate and a shaky economy. In 1950, funding of health expenditures accounted for 4 percent of total federal expenditures. This ratio increased to 8.6 percent in 1970. 10.4 percent in 1975, and 12 percent in 1979 (Freeland and Schendler, 1981). The high cost of hospitalization—the major contributor to spiraling expenditures —has not been absorbed by insurance, and so the social cost has been increased and the poor distribution of resources exacerbated. Low-income groups have not been the only ones to protest. Large corporations turn a jaundiced eye toward medical costs, as the size of the fringe benefits they have to pay to unionized workers assumes an even greater proportion of their wage bill. Prevention, in this view, is a necessity to hold the medical cost crisis in check.

A variety of solutions has been proposed to deal with the dual problem of a health care system that is both too expensive and no longer markedly effective in promoting improvements in health levels. For rising costs, regulation of different degrees of sophistication was the favorite remedy of the late seventies. President Carter tried and failed to impose a ceiling on hospital expenditures. Other measures attempted to curtail the prerogatives of doctors. President Reagan introduced competition as the panacea of the eighties. Cutting back all social services has become a politically viable strategy and is activated in the health care system by denying Medicaid to former recipients and by closing municipal hospitals. Consumers, too, come in for their share of the blame, and it is on the question of consumer attitudes that the critics of both cost and efficacy can join forces. Consumers should become more cost-conscious, say the policy makers who are concerned about the self-indulgence of the worried well. Patients should take action themselves before they are forced to turn to ineffective health care services that may prove positively harmful to them in the long run, say the critics of modern medicine. Both propositions fall under the umbrella remedy of prevention, but there agreement ends.

While most critics agree that prevention is a good thing, they interpret the term in different ways. Disagreements are inevitable because they stem from two underlying theories about the causes of illness in contemporary society that are incompatible. For some, modern disease can be largely attributed to the stress of life and the nature of work

under capitalism (Eyer and Sterling, 1977), and to more specific environmental threats such as air pollution, carcinogenic chemicals, food additives, and industrial accidents. Prevention, then, entails far-reaching social reforms. The etiological theories that convince others focus on individual behavior. The diseases of civilization—cancer, heart disease, and stroke—are diseases of affluence, according to this view. People eat too much, drink too much, don't take exercise, and kill themselves by driving recklessly. Prevention in these terms means persuading individuals, through education or sanctions, to change their self-destructive habits.

The meaning of a prevention policy has thus been a matter of contention in the political arena. Historically, each theoretical orientation toward disease and prevention (let us call them social and individualist) has been predominant during different periods in the United States. But recently the emphasis on individual behavior has garnered more political support than efforts to tackle the social determinants of disease. Under the Reagan Administration, pressure by food manufacturers has all but killed congressional efforts to require the industry to include sodium content on food labels, the Clean Air and Clean Water Acts have been attacked, and both the Occupational Safety and Health Act/Administration (OSHA) and the Environmental Protection Agency (EPA) have been seriously weakened by cuts. Meanwhile, the office for Disease Prevention and Health Promotion, which is one of the few health-related agencies to escape the Reagan cuts this year, concentrates exclusively on life-style issues.

How can one explain the success of the individualist appeal? I shall consider three explanations, two of which are widely accepted as fact in different political circles. According to the first, scientific research has demonstrated beyond reasonable doubt that damaging life-styles are behind the modern epidemics of cancer, heart disease, and stroke. "The recognition that adult chronic disease risk factors can be easily identified in childhood, and that they are largely the result of life-style habits (i.e., cigarette smoking, poor eating habits, and lack of exercise) acquired early in life, has led many to the conclusion that the primary prevention of chronic disease must begin with children," argues an article in the *Journal of Chronic Diseases* (Williams et al. 1979). In the course of a more polemical argument, Whelan claims that "the parts of the cancer causation puzzle now assembled point directly to the harmful aspects of our individual habits, particularly cigarette smoking and dietary excesses" (Whelan, 1979). When it is acknowledged that environmental or occupational factors may be responsible for a certain percentage of deaths, pragmatism is cited as the reason to concentrate on life-styles: social reconstruction is unrealistic and expensive.

Advocates of the second explanation (for example, Salmon and Berliner, 1979) argue that particular actors—usually industry and government—stand to benefit, both ideologically and financially, from such measures as cost-sharing insurance plans that emphasize the necessity of changing personal habits. They stand to lose a great deal from analyses indicating the importance of social factors that might encourage political efforts to impose new restrictions on capital. The national emphasis on individual restraint and self-help, according to this interpretation, has been publicized, if not actually generated, by corporations under attack for the occupational and environmental hazards they promote. These corporations, says Crawford, "must seek new ways to blunt the efforts of the new health activists and to shift the burden of responsibility for health away from their doorstep" (Crawford, 1979).

Finally, Renaud has argued in a provocative paper that state intervention in the field of health care will inevitably ignore social influences on health. There are "structural constraints which preselect the issues to which the state in capitalist societies is capable of responding" (Renaud, 1975). The first and easiest option for the state will be to blame individuals for their own bad health. But one must not look to the "Machiavellian wills of some powerful individuals or groups under the control of some medical empire" (Renaud, 1975) to explain the limits to state action. It is, rather, the result of the "deeply embedded and camouflaged logic of the capitalist social order in health."

None of these explanations provide a satisfactory account of changes in health care policies concerning prevention. Research findings about the connection between life-style factors and the chronic diseases are far from conclusive. "The base of information for prevention is still imperfect," argues a recent article in *The Lancet:*

> To give a specific example, there is a well-established relation between a high incidence of coronary artery disease and a life-style which includes heavy smoking and drinking, lack of exercise, overeating, and (much more dubiously) "stress," whatever that means. But within that package, we know little of the relative importance of the various factors, and possibly no single one of them is as important as a family history of coronary artery disease (about which nothing can be done). . . . (Black, 1982)

Smoking is widely acknowledged as a significant cause of lung cancer, although adherents of the social approach argue that focusing on smokers' self-destructive behavior downplays the political and economic obstacles to antismoking campaigns such as the revenues to federal, state, and local governments from tobacco taxes. The relationship between other life-style factors and cancer causation is contested (Epstein and Swartz, 1981). Moreover, the argument that the empirical findings of science accumulate and gradually yield a body of data that persuades policy makers of the necessity for individual-focused preventive measures ignores what we know of their social construction. Much of the data now being heralded as conclusive proof of the self-destructiveness of human habits is not new. What we need to account for is the way it has been used.

Blaming corporate pressure for the individualist approach is also unsatisfactory. Theoretically this argument is based on a view of the state as a simple instrument of capital, and of ideas as the direct reflection of capital's interests. It is also not clear that costs could be controlled or that corporations would gain substantially from preventive measures of this kind. Holtzman has argued, for example, that in times like the present when unemployment is high,

> it might even be argued that with labor in plentiful supply, there is little incentive to improve the health of potential workers. As the demand for skilled labor diminishes, it may not cost too much to train a replacement for a worker who dies prematurely or who becomes disabled. Companies could even save money by premature deaths; long disability and retirement payments would be reduced. (Holtzman, 1979)

Politically such an explanation is also problematic, because it essentially dismisses many of the "preventive" alternatives in the health care field—self-help groups, holistic health advocates and practitioners—as the peddlers of reformism and the victims of co-optation. It overlooks the genuinely progressive movements of the 1960s and 1970s within health care to demystify medicine and encourage patients to rely on their own resources.

While Renaud is careful not to allocate blame for restrictive state intervention and preventive policies to specific individuals or groups, he does not cast much light on the politics of policy development. Politics, in fact, almost disappears from his account. His emphasis on the overall tendency of capitalism to turn health needs into a commodity leads him to omit the details of that process. While he does admit the possibility of the emergence of class struggle and thus partial reform—"timid efforts . . . to partially implement a new, more preventive and more community-oriented medicine" (Renaud, 1975) under particular historical conditions—it remains for others to spell out those political and economic circumstances.

I suggest that the prevailing ideology of prevention must be understood within a broader framework than perspectives stressing the autonomy of science, the exclusive influence of industry, or the logic of capitalism will allow. Policy decisions take place within a shared cognitive understanding of a problem and its causes. We need to understand how a consensus was forged at the level of national policy on the advisability of the individualist approach. To disentangle the theoretical and intuitive bases of the viewpoints espoused by legislators, physicians, and corporate managers among others, we must examine the social relations and the economic constraints that make those theories plausible to the various actors. Medicine, for example, is a system of relationships involving, at the minimum, client and physician. Preventive strategies used in practice must therefore stem to some extent from the contemporary requirements of the doctor/patient relationship (Rosenberg, 1979). Having clarified what it is about the social situations of different groups that leads them to adopt different theories about the etiology of chronic diseases, I argue that the apparent consensus about the appropriateness of individual-focused preventive measures emerges from a political struggle. Advocates for the social approach exist, but they currently have little influence on policy decisions.

Costs and Benefits: Capital and Labor

Bernard Kramer, in a 1977 *American Journal of Public Health* editorial, reflects on the reasons for the antagonism directed at antismoking campaigns (and many other attempts at public intervention on behalf of the public's health). He concludes that in a time of austerity people may have become increasingly responsive to "corporate foot-dragging with respect to public-health measures" (Kramer, 1977). I suggest that although capital in the United States may be opposed to certain preventive measures, it has seized on others with enthusiasm.

Large American corporations with a highly unionized work force are worried that their health care costs have become a significant business expense: "Second only to energy costs, their expenditures for health care are rising more rapidly than any other factor in the cost of industrial products" (Gifford and Anlyan, 1979). Physicians, according to *Forbes*, don't recognize "the depths of concern on the part of those paying the bills—and that is business" ("Physician Heal Thyself" 1977). But health care, asserts General Motors, is an expensive proposition not just for the corporations directly affected: such costs added $175 to the cost of every car and truck built by GM in 1976 (Burns, 1977). By 1980, spurred on by information from the President's Council of Physical Fitness that premature deaths cost American industry more than $25 billion and 132 million workdays of lost production annually, Xerox, Exxon, Pepsico, General Foods, and North American Rockwell developed extensive physical fitness programs for employees (Lowery, 1980).

At first glance, it would seem that industry should try anything and everything currently being marketed as "prevention." If illnesses were to be prevented, detected earlier, and treated wisely when they proved to be chronic conditions, surely less would be paid in employee health benefits, and so group health insurance premiums for companies would go down. It turns out, however, that prevention may be the new watchword in corporate benefit plans, although corporations are more interested in certain kinds of health hazards and certain kinds of sick workers than others. The bulk of corporate advertising regarding ill health and destructive life-styles has concentrated on executives and their vulnerability to heart attacks. A personnel director interviewed by *Harvard Business Review* makes clear why. "Our experience indicates that the cost of a heart attack or heart failure ranges from a minimum of three times an executive's annual salary to millions, depending on the severity of the illness and his role in the corporate structure." "Think of the cost," the article urges, "hospital and physician's fees, disability com-

pensation, work loss, life insurance, and other rehabilitation costs or replacement costs" (White, 1978).

Recent work, however, suggests that the image of the driven executive—miserable in spite of his power, money, and prestige, overstressed, and unable to relax—is largely a myth. Several studies have shown that executives actually have fewer heart attacks than blue-collar workers and that their mortality rate ranges from 30 percent to 10 percent lower than that of the general population. A survey of the working and living habits of 2,000 executives in the New York City area concludes, "The great bulk of executives—87 percent—cope well with their jobs, have better than average health habits, are not dismayed by the pressures of business" (Boroson, 1978). Why then does the myth persist that executives run a special risk from the pressures of an increasingly stressful work life, and why are companies so willing to subsidize preventive measures for a reasonably healthy group among their workers? One answer is certainly that they see executives as more valuable workers who need to be nurtured with more care. "There is no provision in the federal income-tax law," asserts one analyst advocating the benefits of a tax-deductible medical reimbursement plan, "which prevents the corporate employer from discriminating in favor of, and limiting the health and medical care benefits to, the officers, executives supervisors, and other highly paid employees" (Bartz, 1977).

There is also a second answer to the paradox. By focusing on heart disease as the real threat to workers' health and by promoting the relatively low-cost strategies required to foster preventive care in this area, companies direct attention away from those diseases that claim as many lives but that affect "less valuable" workers and are potentially more expensive to alleviate. An estimated 100,000 workers die each year, according to OSHA, and three or four times that number are disabled, as a result of occupational disease (illnesses attributable to new chemicals being introduced into industrial products and processes, as opposed to workplace accidents, which occur at a rate of 2,000 a month). But corporations rarely mention the threat of industrial accidents or cancer in their new-found zeal for prevention. In fact, they are currently engaged in disputing the figures and the measures of federal agencies like EPA, OSHA, the Consumer Product Safety Commission (CPSC), and the United States Department of Agriculture (USDA), which are promulgating regulations to protect workers and consumers from these hazards.

Recent political developments have woven a new strand in corporate ideology. The techniques employed in the ongoing battle with government regulatory agencies have definitively shaped the emerging industry-wide imagery about disease patterns and their etiology. The core of these techniques is cost-benefit analysis, which, as David Noble (1980) has documented, lies at the heart of the petrochemical industry's efforts to fight the recent health and environmental challenge to its activities. Its demand that regulating agencies pay greater attention to the economic costs of regulation and that they adopt formal quantitative procedures for estimating and comparing the costs and benefits of alternative actions has been successful. Noble reports that regulatory agencies are now "clogged with reports, studies, consultants, and procedural motions," regulators have been hamstrung by "mathematical gymnastics" and the basic policy questions have been obscured. Above all, the appeal of the chemical industry to risk-accounting methods has generated a new political rhetoric: life is inescapably risky, and the acknowledged risk of cancer from some of its products is to be put "in perspective," compared with other risks and balanced against product benefits. The net result is to trivialize concern with carcinogens in the workplace.

Unions continue to pressure management over a wide range of occupational health issues. Petrochemical workers have pressed for investigations into the high incidence of brain cancer among them; miners have fought efforts to reduce fines for mine safety violations. But in a period of economic recession, when many unions are more concerned with the threat of wide-spread lay-offs and plant closings, occupational health and safety problems must often take second place. In this context it becomes plausible for companies to focus on the vulnerability of a few executives to heart attacks, to indict unhealthy life-styles, and to place the burden of health squarely on workers and consumers.

Corporate profits, however, are affected by more than the growth of the social wage and the threat of stiffer pollution and safety standards. Perhaps the most chronic worry for many American corporations in the seventies has been productivity, which, they believe, has been adversely affected by absenteeism. In accounting for their absence from work, American workers reported that illness and injury kept them off the job twice as often as personal and civic reasons. From 1973 to 1976, illness and injury accounted for about three-fourths of all hours lost in manufacturing (Hedges, 1977). Absenteeism statistics probably do not accurately reflect social and medical reality. Employees stay away from work on occasion because it is boring. Nevertheless, many corporations are coming to agree with the president of Blue Cross in Wisconsin who worked with Kimberley-Clark to set up a health maintenance program for its salaried employees, the entire cost of which was paid by the firm. "Preventive medicine has enormous potential dividends of greater health and happiness, lower medical costs, and increased productivity," he declared, and the proposition is increasingly reflected in business publications ("Kimberley-Clark," *Paper Trade Journal*, 1977). Healthy workers, they assert, are happier, more efficient workers. Preventive programs can reduce turnover, sick leave, and workers' compensation payments, improve productivity, and prevent unionization (Fields 1978; Wright, 1978; Pritchett, 1977).

The insurance industry has concurred with and encouraged this trend, which has become even more attractive with the current recession.

"Until the recent financial squeeze, insurers of health had little to worry about other than competition between companies and regulation by government," argues an insurance publication. But now, "squeezed financially and facing a crisis of credibility, the providers of health care are no longer considered infallible, the doctor is no longer God, and we, the insurers, are on the spot" (Melcher, 1981). Efforts to restrain costs have focused on the wrong things—"the supply side of the health economics equation." The solution is to focus on the demand side, a demand generated by a growing and aging population. Insurance recognizes that higher costs won't reduce demands because "that demand is driven by mortal fear" (Maher, 1981). Prevention is the logical way to break the cycle of spiraling costs: "The next step is ours, not the government's. We must find a way to package, market, sell, and make money on wellness" (Melcher, 1981). And wellness, as Blue Cross and Blue Shield have advertised for some time, comes from helping yourself since "you, the individual, are in control of the major risk factors" for most chronic diseases.

The preventive strategies of individual companies will doubtless vary, conditioned by the status of the economy, the character of their work force, and the particular brand of risk accounting that they adopt in making their calculations. However, from the character of the programs that now exist, one can predict that they will all be inspired by a restrictive individualist version of prevention. Perhaps the most persuasive evidence for this claim comes from the proceedings of the National Conference of Health Promotion Programs in Occupational Settings sponsored by the Department of Health, Education, and Welfare in 1979. Representatives from industry, unions, insurance companies, and the scientific community discussed ideal approaches to health promotion programs in the workplace. All the "risk reduction components" dealt with factors that individuals could be motivated to change in some way. Most striking is the discussion of "stress management," the component most likely to indicate the part played by larger environmental and occupational hazards in illness. While acknowledging that "studies have suggested an association between environmental stress and disease . . . it must be recognized," continues the report,

> that it is a combination of factors within and outside the work situation that interact and contribute to disease. . . . Certain personality, cognitive, and behavior characteristics of an employee interact with characteristics of the environment and influence this association. . . . An occupationally based stress reduction program could cause people to *change their life-styles* for the sake of their health and at the same time reduce absenteeism, enhance productivity, and decrease insurance and medical costs. (McGill, 1979; emphasis added)

The concrete procedures advocated to help people change their lifestyles are assertiveness training and "coping" procedures such as the relaxation response. Changing the workplace is not at issue. This orientation was strengthened by the overturning in court of citations issued by OSHA against a chemical plant that excluded women of child-bearing potential from working the lead pigment department because exposure to lead levels might harm fetuses or affect fertility. The director of health and safety of the union involved summed up the pervasive company ideology: "Alter the worker, don't alter the workplace" ("Pigment Plant . . . ," The *New York Times*, 1980; Shabecoff, 1980).

Medical Practice and Social Decision Rules

Within the medical profession there is a vigorous debate about the meaning and scope of preventive *medicine*. The field is conventionally divided into three categories: tertiary prevention (the containment, amelioration, or cure of clinical disease), secondary prevention (the detection and diagnosis of disease, often through screening procedures), and primary prevention (the removal of the underlying cause of disease through immunization, controlling environmental factors, or modifying personal behavior) (White, 1975). Physicians would agree that historically tertiary prevention has been their proper domain. The debate is joined over the proper form of primary prevention. Results from behavior modification will be trifling, argues Leon Eisenberg, compared with "the potential from state and federal action against environmental pollution, adulteration of food and water, and occupational hazards. Much more is known than is being put to use because of the political difficulties and the economic dislocation that would be involved" (Eisenberg, 1977). By contrast, an editorial in *Preventive Medicine* asserts:

> In the past it was possible to prevent major mortality and morbidity by relatively simple governmental or public health action on water, nutrition, and housing. But the underlying causes of today's "top five" disease categories are quite different. Most of the conditions in question are linked to aspects of personal behavior. . . . It is time preventive medicine came to terms with current patterns of disease and tried to modify the personal behavior of those at particular risk rather than attempt to change the behavior of whole communities. (Holland, 1975)

The medical profession seems, at first sight, to be afflicted with the same disagreements that divide the public.

In practice, however, physicians tend to focus on treatment to the detriment of prevention of any kind. Therapeutics, as Charles Rosenberg has argued, have to be understood within the configuration of ideas and relationships that constitute medicine. A doctor's therapeutic tools condition how he understands health and disease. Modern surgery, drugs, and technology lead him to interpret disease in terms of the classical biomedical model, which claims that most diseases are caused by specific identifiable agents and that basic medical research, if adequately funded will yield the answer. Eisenberg (1977) argues that the vaccine model of prevention dominates physician understanding of today's health problems.

Physicians will evaluate preventive measures in light of the requirements of the contemporary doctor/patient relationship. "We don't know the causal mechanisms of most chronic diseases," claims one physician, "but our patients think we do and many of us pretend we do too. Everyone, including doctors, wants an explanation for the occurrence of disease, so we provide it" (Spencer, 1978). Patients may want some tangible action from their doctor while prevention, more often than not, means that the doctor does nothing. The patient seeks short-term relief rather than the long-term solutions and regimens that primary prevention dictates. Physicians too may be deprived of some of the satisfaction of their profession by preventive measures. "Doctors get their pleasure from making people feel better, and it's hard to make an asymptomatic patient feel better" (Smith, 1976), argues a candid physician. The medical profession will often advise patients to change their behavior only if that strategy does not interfere with the emotional and personal relationships both doctors and patients expect from medicine.

To be accepted, primary prevention strategies would have to be in accord with a physician's conception of scientific medical practice. Do they confirm his experience with prognosis and the natural history of certain diseases? When preventive medicine was used as a justification for the development of Health Maintenance Organizations (HMOs), the

American Medical Association (AMA) disputed it first on the grounds of cost. "The maintenance function— examinations and preventive care —will have the benefit of identifying some previously undiagnosed illness," argued John R. Kernodel, spokesman for the AMA, during hearings before the Subcommittee on Health of the Senate Labor and Public Welfare Committee in November, 1971. "But the process of examination itself may be disproportionately high, resulting in higher overall costs rather than savings. We just do not know the cost-benefit ratio" (Brown, 1976). Furthermore, said Kernodel, prevention wasn't like medicine, it was tricky stuff.

> But can HMOs discover a magic so far unrevealed to the rest of us? A magic that will somehow motivate people to drive more carefully, exercise more frequently, eat more sensibly, smoke less, and worry less? Can the HMOs discover an educational magic, so far unavailable to the Public Health Service, which will reduce the incidence of the single most common communicable disease—gonorrhea? (Brown, 1976)

True, the medical profession hadn't been able to cope with these problems, but, AMA representatives were arguing, neither had anyone else. They were primarily opposed to HMOs because they would undermine traditional modes of practice, but Kernodel's remarks reflect the belief of many physicians that perhaps trying to change individuals' behavior was a lost cause and it certainly wasn't scientific.

But prevention is an idea sup-ported by constituencies that the medical profession cannot afford to ignore. When they acknowledge its importance, physicians' discourse is increasingly shaped by the individualist version. It is an ideology that derives its power from changes not only in the character of modern medicine but also in the social situation of the medical profession.

Challenges to the authority of the latter in the last decade have not been without effect. The attack on the medical profession in the sixties differed from earlier criticism: it focused on the nature of social relationships in medicine and the scope of physicians' jurisdiction. Too many social and personal problems were being defined as merely or primarily medical problems, it was argued, granting the profession a dangerous degree of power (Illich, 1976). There are some indications that physicians do not altogether welcome the wideranging responsibility they have acquired, or at least not in all areas. Power over decisions about when they turn off life-sustaining machinery is a mixed blessing. Physicians are also frustrated by the intractable problems posed by patients suffering from alcoholism, mental illness, obesity, and drug addiction. In these circumstances the ideology of individual responsibility is seductive. Typical of its articulation is the conclusion to an article on the philosophy of preventive medicine: "This theme of 'Feeling Good,' a nationally televised weekly series on health, puts the responsibility for health where it should be, on the individual rather than on the physician" (Smith, 1976). These ideas are echoed in the editorials and the correspondence of the major medical journals over the last five years (Cimmino, 1978; Baker, 1978).

Social theories about the etiology of the chronic diseases would require physicians to step outside the traditional purview of scientific medicine and dabble in politics, or at least involve themselves with the larger social world of their patients. Acknowledging the importance of patients' life-styles, on the other hand, does not necessarily mean embroiling themselves in the dangerous, uncharted waters of behavior change. Patients will have to do most of the work themselves, but "if the patient has become aware of his personal risks and has resolved to make changes, the physician then assumes leadership in guiding the patient's own actions to improve his health" (Fowinkle, 1977). Paramedical personnel can then tend to the minimal services patients may require from the medical world, but "we need physicians to determine what should be done in the first place by paramedical personnel, we need physicians to evaluate the outcome of such services, and certainly a physician is needed initially to help determine the *content* of any health educational program" (Carter, 1976).

Confronted by the surge of public interest in holistic medicine, self-help techniques, and other preventive measures, the profession has moved to assert its authority in the field. It has not been a pioneer by any means, preferring to refine and adapt the area of curative medicine,

but it does not wish to watch a new health-related area of activity grow and develop outside the domain of medicine. So, while it will not itself leap to experiment with new techniques, it will draw under the wing of "preventive medicine" individualist innovations that garner critical public support.

Legitimacy and Politics

Under both the Carter and Reagan Administrations, prevention has become a central plank in the federal government's health care policy. As the eighties began, Health and Human Services Secretary Richard S. Schweiker left no doubt that prevention was to be defined in individualist terms: "Across the spectrum of health care policy, we will turn to the self-healing power of consumer choice and patient awareness" (Fisher, 1981).

Concern over health care costs is one major impetus for the state's embrace of the life-style approach to preventive measures. Until World War II the state was not really involved in the direct financing of health care. After the war the state's involvement deepened: first through the Hill-Burton program that provided federal money for the construction of hospitals, then through the establishment of the National Institutes of Health with biomedical research, and finally with the introduction of the Medicare and Medicaid programs in the mid-sixties. The United States spent an estimated $247 billion for health care in 1980, an amount equal to 9.4 percent of the Gross National Product, which was viewed as a serious contribution to inflation. Of that expenditure 42.2 percent came from public funds (Gibson and Waldo, 1981). In its role as provider of medical assistance to eligible old and poor people, the state is now in the business of paying for direct services. In addition, it is a large employer, with responsibility for financing a significant part of the health-insurance premiums of its 10 million employees and annuitants and their family members (Iglehart, 1981). Rising medical care costs, therefore, pose a series of problems for the state; competition and prevention have been adopted as the solutions.

Yet the implementation of cutbacks and the appeal to self-restraint have not met growing political opposition. Health care is a particularly important realm symbolically. The events of the sixties raised expectations and created a sense of entitlement to good medical care. The legitimacy of the welfare state is closely tied to developments in health care, and the notion that health means more and better services dies hard. The choice for the state between a prevention based on life-style changes versus a prevention of social reform may take second place to the choice between the status quo of high-technology curative medicine and prevention of any kind. In 1978, summarizing the state's priorities in health care, President Carter observed that "prevention is both cheaper and simpler than cure," yet he acknowledged:

We have stressed the latter and have ignored to an increasing degree the

former. In recent years we have spent 40 cents out of every health dollar on hospitalization. In effect we've made the hospital the first line of defense instead of the last. By contrast we've spent only three cents on disease prevention and control, less than half a cent on health education, and one quarter of a cent on environmental health research. (Venkateson, 1978)

The Carter Administration tried to expand both social and individualist preventive measures. Several state agencies, pressured by the environmental movement, moved to curb the power of industry to pollute the air and water and adulterate the nation's food. While capital sought to focus attention solely on heart disease, the state also emphasized the economic loss and the suffering caused by cancer. Many of the sanctions brought to bear by OSHA on industry hardly constituted severe penalties, but EPA took a tougher line with a greater degree of success. U.S. Steel, for example, whose steel mills situated in heavily industrialized areas are among the worst industrial polluters, agreed to comply with antipollution laws on a fixed schedule (Shabecoff, 1979). The government went so far as to admit liability itself in certain cases of occupational disease, notably asbestosis, where it recognized both the failure of Public Health Service doctors to warn asbestos workers of hazardous conditions in plants and the right to a safe workplace under federal law of workers on defense contracts—a move that, according to a senior corporate official in one of the nation's largest chemical companies, could encourage further suits against industry and "become a powerful monkey wrench" in dealing with occupational-health problems (Burnham, 1977).

At the same time, the agencies within the health care bureaucracy attacked destructive life-styles with a vengeance. The Office of Health Promotion focused on antismoking campaigns. In 1979, smoking was listed in HEW publications as a major, if not *the* major, risk factor in every significant cause of death in the United States, illustrating what one entrepreneur (the then Secretary of HEW Joseph Califano) with a particular theory about the relationship between individual habits and health can do. In the introduction to the Surgeon General's report, *Healthy People*, he expanded his criticism of self-indulgent behavior:

> Indeed, a wealth of scientific research reveals that the key to whether a person will be healthy or sick, live a long life or die prematurely, can be found in several simple personal habits: one's habits with regard to smoking and drinking; one's habits of diet, sleep, and exercise; whether one obeys the speed laws and wears seat belts; and a few other simple measures. (U.S. Department of Health, Education and Welfare, 1979)

President Reagan was inaugurated in 1981 and faced growing budget deficits, a deepening fiscal crisis, and an outcry on the part of capital against regulatory controls. In the area of prevention the life-style emphasis flourished, consistent with the political ideology of republicanism, which "emphasizes voluntarism, decentralization, and education to empower people to advance

their own interests" (Allegrante and Green, 1981). The state continued its attack on cancer, but through different means because its etiology was defined. "The public is growing increasingly aware of the link between cancer and their life-styles," said Schweiker. "With our help they are becoming prevention-oriented" ("Cancer Prevention Cited," *The Blue Sheet*, 1982). He lauded the National Cancer Institute's new chemo-prevention program for "focusing more on how we can interfere in the later stages of carcinogenesis [with synthetic vitamin A] to prevent cancer, instead of concentrating exclusively on substances which initiate the cancer process." Social approaches to prevention, however, were abruptly curtailed: the hazardous waste program was cut for fiscal 1982 from $141.4 million to $107.2 million; the 1983 air research budget will be 42 percent lower in actual purchasing power than in 1981; the Centers for Disease Control are being systematically stripped of their scientists and researchers, to mention but a few of the cuts ("Supplement," *The Nation's Health*, 1982).

There is nothing inevitable about the shift in health policy toward an individualist definition of prevention (and toward competition rather than regulation to control costs). A particular social coalition espouses it, albeit for somewhat different reasons. Yet even within that coalition there are tensions over the content and direction of the prevention/competition strategy. In the seventies, Califano's promotion of antismoking campaigns as Secretary of HEW finally led him to question tax subsidies for tobacco companies. As President Carter's popularity declined in the polls, his assurances to the tobacco industry increased. This issue was central in Califano's departure from the Administration. Schweiker's promise to put preventive medicine "at the very top of the department's health agenda" was greeted with a stony silence at the annual meeting of the AMA in 1981 (Reinhold, 1981). The Administration's proposals to reduce levels of coverage or change the content of the Federal Employees Health Benefits Program have led to a battle between the Office of Personnel Management, which administers the program, health insurers who provide the coverage, and several federal-employee unions (Iglehart, 1981).

Although health clubs and exercise salons are enjoying an unprecedented boom, acceptance of the individualist version of prevention is not total. A Harris poll at the beginning of 1982 found that the public seems to oppose many of the cutbacks in social preventive measures: "People are scared to death over toxic waste spills and carcinogens in drinking water, such that a 94 percent majority wants the Clean Water Act kept as it is or made tougher" ("Reagan Health Policy," *The Blue Sheet*, 1982). Union leaders in the Northeast are trying to start a national movement to resist union concessions on wages, benefits, work rules, and health and safety issues (Serrin, 1982).

The battle over prevention brings into conflict not only the interests of capital, labor, the environmental movement, the insurance companies, and the medical profession,

but those of state agencies such as EPA, the Office of Management and Budget, and the Department of Health and Human Services (DHHS). When, for example, a bill was proposed by Waxman, the House Energy and Commerce Health Subcommittee chairman, advocating the "mandatory creation" of assistant directors for prevention in NIH, it was opposed by the DHHS Assistant Secretary for Health who claimed that "NIH and its institutes have already acted, or are taking actions, to accomplish the subcommittee's goals" ("HHS Opposes," *The Blue Sheet*, 1982). One of those actions turned out to be the adoption of a revised definition of prevention research, which allowed the percentage of its activities that qualified as prevention-related to rise from 16.9 percent to 70 percent. Waxman questioned the move, arguing that:

> public health people . . . feel that what may be happening is that the prevention professionals are not being consulted or brought in to look at how prevention in a more traditional sense could be carried out at NIH, and what we have is a redefining of what could fit into the category called prevention without rethinking strategies to direct research toward it.

These kinds of conflicts produce contradictions in state policy: DHHS vigorously pursues health education while the Medicare provisions do not permit reimbursement of preventive services. Internal conflict is exacerbated because many health-related activities do not fall under the jurisdiction of the official "health" agencies. Although organized labor and environmental groups have won some important victories in the last 20 years—the formation of EPA, OSHA, and the Toxic Substances Control Act are notable examples—they have been promoted by agencies other than the Department of Health and Human Services. They are not, therefore, always included in discussions of the nation's health care policy. Especially when they fall under the jurisdiction of the Department of Labor, a conservative Administration can justify reduction of funding and minimal implementation in the name of reducing constraints on the productivity of industry. The state, as neo-Marxists emphasize, should not be conceptualized as a monolithic entity governed by a self-conscious, united group of managers. The different strands of opinion resulting from the clash between the objectives of labor and capital are reflected in the positions of different agencies within the state. Certain agencies—the Food and Drug Administration (FDA), for example—while acting within the confines of a capitalist state, will be more open to pressure from different class factions. The exact form that the conflict within the state takes will be shaped by the state's structure. What kind of access is guaranteed for representatives of labor to OSHA? What relationships are structurally possible between the scientific community and the FDA?

Conclusion

Prevention has become a battle cry to deal with a variety of issues, but its content and its underlying strat-egy are contested. It grows out of the intersection of different sets of problems and different sets of solutions that do not always neatly correspond. For capital and the state the critical problems are costs, productivity, and credibility; for the medical profession they are public hostility, new corporate interests in health care whose power parallels their own, and a state intent on controlling physicians; for the public they are a decrease in medical services, a declining economy, and the fear that everyday life is becoming less amenable to control. Sometimes some of these forces can join together under one banner to attack their respective demons: prevention is the answer to all problems.

Consensus is lacking, however, on the specific programs that should constitute a strategy of prevention. Two etiological theories dictate two very different directions: a theory that blames self-destructive habits and a theory that points to social factors. The advocates of neither theory can agree on all the practical implications of their theoretical orientation. Part of the resultant confusion is undoubtedly due to the state of medical knowledge in the field. There is no tried body of practice on which to base predictions about which techniques of behavior change will work and which will not. The debates drag on, for example, over the relative contribution of smoking and air pollution to cancer and then over what techniques will actually dissuade people from smoking, drinking, or worrying. Studies of behavior change require long time periods to yield convincing results, and critics emphasize that there is no clear cost-benefit calculation that one can make about their payoff.

But policy makers choose selectively among available research to justify the decisions they make about the strategies they choose to label preventive. Conclusive data on the etiology of chronic disease would not dramatically change the character of the contemporary debate over prevention. Corporations will continue to argue for the control of heart disease, hoping to preserve their executives and decrease the size of the social wage; the state seeks to cut back on the services it can no longer afford in favor of exhortations to its citizens to live better lives; parts of the labor movement will fight for improved safety and health at work. Self-destructive habits will probably continue to be the focus of attack at the level of national policy in the immediate future, but Renaud's predictions about the inexorable logic of capitalism and the inevitable indifference of the state to social influences on health are too absolute. The relative power of "scientific" arguments will depend on how they are translated by the medical community, and how they resonate with more intuitive popular images of health and medicine. The individualist version of prevention makes sense to Americans in a period marked by antagonism to state intervention and the celebration of individual self-reliance. But as the attack on their standard of living becomes more severe, they are likely to find less plausible the claim that health, like everything else, is simply a matter of willpower.

Acknowledgment

An earlier version of this paper was presented at the Annual Meetings of the Society for the Study of Social Problems, New York, 1980. Thanks are due to Susan Bell, Peter Dreier, Susan Eckstein, Stuart Gardner, Joel Krieger, Sara Mattes and members of the Boston Health Study Group for their comments on that draft and to Marian Hannan for her research assistance.

References

Allegrante, J.P. and Green, L.W. "Sounding Board—When Health Policy Becomes Victim Blaming." *New England Journal of Medicine* 305 (December, 1981), pp. 1528–1529.

Baker, H. "Let's Try More Prevention," correspondence. *Canadian Medical Association Journal* 118 (May, 1978), pp. 1034–1036.

Bartz, Dan. "Received Business Deduction for Personal Medical Expenses." *Supermarketing* 32 (April, 1977), p. 46.

Black, D. "The Aims of a Health Service." *Lancet* 1 (Apr. 24, 1982), pp. 952–954.

Boroson, Warren. "The Myth of the Unhealthy Executive." *Across the Board* 15 (February, 1978), pp. 10–16.

Brown, Lawrence D. "The Story of HMO." Case prepared for Executive Programs in Health Policy and Management, Harvard School of Public Health (1976).

Burnham, David. "Asbestos Workers' Illness—and Their Suit—May Change Health Standards." The *New York Times* (Dec. 20, 1977), p. 30.

Burns, John E. "Spiraling Hospital Costs and the 41st Annual IMS Clinic," editorial. *Industrial Management* 19 (May/June, 1977), editorial page.

"Cancer Prevention Cited as Alternative to Environmental Emphasis." *The Blue Sheet*, vol. 25, no. 2 (June 2, 1982), pp. 8–9.

Carter, Earl T. "Preventive Medicine," correspondence. *Minnesota Medicine* 59 (June 1976), pp. 399–401.

Cimmino, Christian V. "Preventive Medicine: Applause and Argument," correspondence. *Virginia Medical* 105 (August, 1978), p. 549.

Crawford, Robert. "Individual Responsibility and Health Politics in the 1970s," in Susan Reverby and David Rosner (eds.), *Health Care in America* (Philadelphia: Temple University Press, 1979), pp. 247–268.

Eisenberg, Leon. "The Perils of Prevention: A Cautionary Note," editorial. *New England Journal of Medicine* 297 (December, 1977), pp. 1230–1232.

Epstein, S. and Swartz, Joel B. "Fallacies of Lifestyle Cancer Theories." *Nature* 289 (Jan. 15, 1981), pp. 126–130.

Eyer, Joseph and Sterling, Peter. "Stress-Related Mortality and Social Organization." *The Review of Radical Political Economics* 9 (Spring, 1977), pp. 1–44.

Fields, Gregg. "Occupational Health Becomes a Specialty for More Physicians: Workers, Government Insist on Preventive Medicine; Companies Expect Savings." *Wall Street Journal* (Oct. 24, 1978), p. 18.

Fisher, M.J. "Competition, Prevention Keys to Reagan Health Strategy." *National Underwriter* 85 (June 26, 1981), p. 43.

Fowinkle, Eugene W. "New Directions in Preventive Medicine." *Journal of the Tennessee Medical Association* 70 (December, 1977), pp. 894–896.

Freeland, M.S. and Schendler, C.E. "National Health Expenditures: Short-Term Outlook and Long-Term Projections." *Health Care Financing Review* 2 (Winter, 1981), pp. 97–126.

Gibson, R.M. and Waldo, D.R. "National Health Expenditures, 1980." *Health Care Financing Review* 2 (September 1981), pp. 1–54.

Gifford, James F. and William G. Anlyan. "Sounding Board—The Role of the Private Sector in an Economy of Limited Health-Care Resources." *New England Journal of Medicine* 300 (April, 1979), pp. 790-793.

Hedges, Janice Neipert. "Absence from Work—Measuring the Hours Lost." *U.S. Bureau of Labor Statistics, Monthly Labor Review* 100 (October, 1977) pp. 16–23.

"HHS Opposes 'Mandatory' NIH Prevention Plan; Definition Shift Questioned." *The Blue Sheet* (Apr. 28, 1982), p. 5.

Holland, Walter W. "Prevention: The Only Cure," editorial. *Preventive Medicine* 4 (1975), pp. 387–389.

Holtzman, Neil A. "Prevention: Rhetoric and Reality." *International Journal of Health Services* 9 (1979), pp. 25–39.

Iglehart, J.K. "Health Policy Report: The Administration Responds to the Cost Spiral." *New England Journal of Medicine* 305 (November, 1981), pp. 1359–1364.

Illich, Ivan. *Medical Nemesis: The Expropriation of Health* (New York: Random House, 1976).

"Kimberly-Clark Is Spending Millions to Insure Employees' Health, Well-Being." *Paper Trade Journal* 161 (December, 1977), p. 40.

Kramer, Bernard M. "Behavioral Change and Public Attitudes towards Public Health," editorial. *American Journal of Public Health* 67 (October, 1977), pp. 911–913.

Lowery, Donald. "In Andover, an Ex-coach Fits Right In." *The Boston Globe* (Aug. 15, 1980), p. 56.

Maher, T.M. "HIAA Urges Disease Prevention Programs." *National Underwriter* 85 (Aug. 22, 1981), pp. 1, 25.

McGill, Alice M. (ed.). Proceedings of the National Conference on Health Promotion Programs in Occupational Settings. (Washington, D.C.: U.S. Department of Health, Education, and Welfare, 1979).

Melcher, G.W., Jr. "A New Challenge for Health Insurers." *National Underwriter* 85 (May 2, 1981), pp. 11, 14, 16, 17.

Noble, David. "Cost-Benefit Analysis." *Health/Pac Bulletin*, vol. 11, no. 6 (July/August, 1980), pp. 1–2, 7–12, 27–40.

Pamphlets in *Design for Life* series. Blue Cross, Blue Shield, Connecticut.

"Physician, Heal Thyself . . . Or Else!" *Forbes* (Oct. 1, 1977), pp. 40–46.

"Pigment Plant Wins Fertility-Risk Case: Government's Challenge Rejected on Policy Excluding Women from a 'Hazardous' Area." *The New York Times* (Sept. 8, 1980), p. A14.

Pritchett, S. Travis. "Can Employee Benefits Also Be Employer Benefits?" *American Society of Chartered Life Underwriters—CLU Journal* 31 (April, 1977), pp. 40–45.

"Reagan Health Policy Opposed by Most of Public." *The Blue Sheet* (June 9, 1982), pp. 13–14.

Reinhold, Robert. "Medical Leaders Growing Wary over Reagan Health-Care Plans." *The New York Times* (Feb. 16, 1981), p. A12.

Renaud, Marc. "On the Structural Constraints to State Intervention in Health." *International Journal of Health Services*, vol. 5, no. 4 (1975), pp. 559–570.

Rosenberg, Charles F. "The Therapeutic Revolution: Medicine, Meaning, and Social Change in Nineteenth-Century America," in Charles F. Rosenberg and Morris J. Vogel (eds.), *The Therapeutic Revolution, Essays in the Social History of American Medicine* (Philadelphia: University of Pennsylvania Press, 1979), pp. 3–25.

Salmon, J. Warren and Berliner, Howard S. "Can the Holistic Health Movement Turn Left?" Paper presented to the Annual Meeting of the American Public Health Association, New York, November 7, 1979.

Serrin, William. "Labor Is Resisting More Concessions." *The New York Times* (June 13, 1982), p. 29.

Shabecoff, Philip. "E.P.A. Reported Near an Accord with U.S. Steel." *The New York Times* (May 22, 1979), p. A1.

Shabecoff, Philip. "U.S. Appeals Ruling on Women in Hazardous Jobs." The New York *Times* (Sept. 9, 1980), p. B9.

Smith, John E. "The Philosophy of Preventive Medicine." *Minnesota Medicine* 59 (March, 1976), pp. 196–199.

Spencer, F.J. "The Great Preventive Life-Style Cop-Out," editorial. *Virginia Medical* 105 (April, 1978), p. 327.

"Supplement: The President's Budget Proposal." *The Nation's Health* (March, 1982).

Taylor, R.C.R. "The Transformation of Collective Demands." Paper presented to the Conference on the Crisis in the Welfare State, Trieste, Italy, June, 1981.

U.S. Department of Health, Education, and Welfare, Public Health Service. *Healthy People: The Surgeon General's Report on Health Promotion and Disease Prevention* (Washington, D.C.: USGPO, 1979).

Venkateson, M. "Preventive Health Care and Marketing: Positive Aspects," in Philip D. Cooper, William J. Kehoe, and Patrick E. Murphy (eds.), *Marketing and Preventive Health Care: Interdisciplinary and Interorganizational Perspectives* (Chicago: American Marketing Association, 1978), pp. 12–25.

Whelan, Elizabeth. "The Politics of Cancer." *Policy Review* 10 (Fall, 1979), pp. 33–46.

White, James R. and Steinbach, Gary. "Motivating Executives to Keep Physically Fit." *Harvard Business Review* 56 (March/April 1978), pp. 16, 184, 186.

White, Kerr L. "Prevention as a National Health Goal," editorial. *Preventive Medicine* 4 (1975), pp. 247–251.

Wildavsky, Aaron. "Doing Better and Feeling Worse: The Political Pathology of Health Policy." *Daedalus* (Winter, 1977), pp. 105–123.

Williams, C.L., et al. "Chronic Disease Risk Factors among Children. The 'Know Your Body' Study." *Journal of Chronic Diseases* 32 (1979), pp. 505–513.

Wright, H. Beric. "Why Keep Fit?" *Accountant* 16 (March, 1978), pp. 350–352.

25   HEALTH POLICY, A SOCIAL CONTRACT: A COMPARISON OF THE UNITED STATES AND CANADA

Sidney S. Lee

This discussion of health policy in the United States and Canada is based on many years of experience in public health and medical care administration in the United States, and nine recent years in a similar capacity in Canada. My observations are biased by my own preconceptions and experience, and my opinions are, of course, open to argument.

Any deliberation about social policy for health must take account of the society from which it springs. Looking at the United States and Canada, one perceives significant similarities as well as substantial differences. Here are two huge countries, among the largest physically in the world. Their beginnings as countries emanated from colonization by Western Europeans. Each was initially colonized in the east with expansion to the west, both spanning an entire continent of which each makes up approximately half. Each still views itself as a frontier society. Canada is larger in land mass, but the U.S. population is ten times as great as that of Canada; Canada's population of twenty-three million is about equivalent to that of California. Both are immigrant societies with much population growth due to immigration from all over the world. While the U.S. has typically viewed itself as a melting pot of these groups, Canada has more comfortably and probably more correctly seen itself as a mosaic of ethnic groups.

Both societies have, over time, seen substantial internal conflict: in Canada between the French and English as the predominant groups, and in the U.S. between North and

SOURCE: From *Journal of Public Health Policy*, September 1982, pp. 293–301. Copyright © 1982. Reprinted by permission of *The Journal of Health Policy*.

South and between black and white populations.

The U.S. broke away from English domination, declared independence in 1776, fought a bloody war, and wrote its own constitution. Canada relinquished colonial rule in 1875 and became progressively independent from England in relatively civilized fashion over time. After fifty years of internal squabbling, Canada finally achieved a new constitution in 1982, replacing the British North America Act, the last vestige of colonialism.

The central government of the U.S. was created by the people, and the states were formed afterwards. While states' rights have been an issue in many political campaigns in the U.S., there is pretty solid acceptance today of federal legislation and federal policy-setting as a vital part of American life. In contrast, Canada is a federation of provinces, with predominant powers in many spheres held by the individual provinces and much frustration of federal initiatives through coalitions of provinces.

Each country has a democratic form of government. In the U.S., the presidential system provides for a balancing of power between the executive and legislative branches, with a judicial branch maintaining the constitution as a guiding force for the country as a whole.

In the U.S. system, each legislative proposal attracts varying coalitions of adherents and opponents; party discipline is generally weak. The President may propose, but it is indeed Congress which disposes, and the Congressional process is complex and repetitive. Conference committees between the House and the Senate emerge with compromises after the initial enactment of legislation by each. Then separate legislation is introduced to provide for the funding of programs and must again be subject to compromise after initial enactment. It is easy to make bold promises, and terribly difficult to gain adoption and funding.

In contrast, in Canada's parliamentary system at both federal and provincial levels, the executive powers are held by the elected members of the parliament. Cabinet members are appointed by the leader of the party in power from among his legislative colleagues. There is thus no separation of powers. Once a policy is decided by the party in power, it will be enacted, and the government may then proceed to implement it; the budget is the government's budget so long as it is in power. Of course, governments may be formed by coalitions and may be dismissed on the loss of a vote of confidence or a major policy vote.

There are obvious advantages and disadvantages to each of these systems of government. In the U.S. it is almost always a compromise that wins out. In Canada, it is the government's program that wins. But in both of these forms of democratic government, the name of the game is the same—for every politician the watchword is "get re-elected." In the U.S. system, unfortunately, that may require more consideration of the views of special-interest groups than in the Canadian system where adherence to party discipline is of greater importance.

Another major area of difference

between these two countries is less accessible to formal analysis, but is very evident to anyone who has lived in both countries: that is the matter of perception of equity. Both countries express views about helping the poor, the handicapped, the aged or others defined as less well off or less well able to help themselves. In the U.S., however, that is the historical cornerstone of health policy. Since the early days of the republic, the U.S. has identified defined segments of the population through special legislation offering direct medical care, or alternatively, payment for medical care. We started with merchant seamen in 1796 as a nation of a few states along the Atlantic seaboard heavily dependent on merchant shipping, and the seamen were away from home almost all the time and were exposed to considerable hazard of both disease and injury; that is how the U.S. Public Health Service began. Over the years since 1796, the U.S. has added dozens of classes of beneficiaries: veterans, the blind, families of dependent children, the disabled, the aged, people with chronic kidney disease, to name but a few.

Canada did some of the same for a time, but beginning in 1947 in Saskatchewan, and then across Canada, offered hospital and diagnostic services to all, and subsequently medical care services to all. This was accomplished through two major pieces of federal legislation which provided powerful incentives to the provinces to adopt the program. By 1971, to all intents and purposes, all Canadian residents were entitled to tax-based services equivalent to the broadest coverage you can buy in the United States.

The health policies of these two nations display two very different notions of equity, different forms of social contract between government and the governed. On the one hand, in the U.S., we raise the downtrodden by offering services or dollars to buy services. On the other hand, in Canada, government says that health care is a right for everyone and finances it largely out of a highly progressive income tax: equity in Canada is for everyone, but those who earn more pay more in taxes. In the U.S. there remain 25 million people, equivalent to more than the entire population of Canada, who have no coverage from any source—those who are ineligible for Medicare, Medicaid, Blue Cross, or commercial insurance. They appear as bad debts or unpaid bills in the nation's hospitals and doctors' offices—or they do without.

Health policy, as I view it, is a form of social contract between governments and the governed. Its terms are not always as explicit as those which appear in a contract to purchase or sell goods or services. In addition to reading the lines, one must read between the lines; what is excluded may be as significant as what is included. One must, as Carl Stevens, a noted economist, has suggested, be aware of who benefits, what are the benefits, who administers, and who pays for such a contract. Here again, one sees great differences between the U.S. and Canada.

Who benefits in the American system? The beneficiary classes in the U.S. are well-defined in terms of age, social class, previous military service, disease conditions, employment status, economic status, place of residence, family structure, disabilities, etc. By so defining beneficiaries, one leaves a residue of non-beneficiaries and, of course, the range of benefits from class to class of beneficiaries varies substantially. Not everyone is entitled and not everyone gets the same benefits. American health policy requires millions and millions of decisions at various points in time, some at each point of service. To take a single example, the automobile plant worker who is entitled to some of the broadest benefits in American society as part of his union's contract with the auto manufacturer, loses his coverage when he loses his job. Unemployment compensation plus a union contribution may permit him to continue to carry some of his insurance cost at a reduced benefit level, and then if his assets are low enough and his unemployment coverage runs out, he may apply for a determination of eligibility for Medicaid, under the Medicaid eligibility rules of his state of residence. Alternatively, if he is a veteran who is certified as disabled or declares poverty, he has access to care at a Veterans Administration facility if he requires hospitalization, but probably not if he requires only out-of-hospital care. Of course, care as a veteran is only for him, not for his family. Normally, if he goes back to work he is eligible for reinstatement of his former benefits, perhaps with a waiting period for some of them.

At each step along the line, there are new eligibility requirements—new interviews, new forms to fill out, and time for processing.

Who benefits in Canada? Essentially everyone who has been a legal resident of the country for ninety days, and that is the only condition that must be satisfied. There are no restrictions as regards age, social class, military service, disease conditions, employment status, economic status, place of residence, family structure, disabilities, etc. Everyone is covered from conception to death.

What are the benefits in the U.S.? Each American has his own benefit package or none at all. The benefits available may depend on who his employer is, because most American benefits are tied to employment. Eighty-five percent of all Americans have some form of benefit for hospitalization, a lower proportion have surgical coverage, and relatively few have coverage for out-of-hospital services. The largest numbers with out-of-hospital coverage are beneficiaries of governmental programs, such as Medicare for the aged, Medicaid for the poor, and some veterans. In addition, members of Health Maintenance Organizations and those with broad-coverage insurance policies have ambulatory care benefits. Many Americans try to plug the holes in their basic range of benefits by purchasing multiple forms of insurance, and duplicating and overlapping benefits are not at all uncommon, especially where there are two wage-earners in the same household. Many services are not covered at all, others are covered only in part. There are almost always limitations in duration of coverage as well as in the modalities of care that are covered.

For Canadians, the basic benefits are quite broad indeed: hospitalization and diagnostic services and medical care in office, at home, and in hospital, and these benefits are portable across Canada. What are called basic benefits in Canada are roughly equivalent to benefits under a Blue Cross/Blue Shield major medical policy, or membership in the Kaiser plan or an equivalent Health Maintenance Organization (HMO) in the United States.

Who administers these benefits in the U.S.? A remarkable panoply of about 1500 insurance companies, both commercial (tax-paying) and nonprofit (nontax-paying); a multitude of governmental agencies, federal, state, and local; about 200 Health Maintenance Organizations of various types, each of which has its own rules and its own contractual arrangements; and the Blue Cross and Blue Shield plans. Typical insurers write hundreds of different kinds of contracts. Some government programs are sub-contracted to commercial carriers or the Blues for administration, others are directly administered by individual agencies of government or combinations of governmental agencies. For example, it is possible to be on Medicare for the aged, administered by Blue Cross under contract to the federal government, on Medicaid which is state-administered or delegated by the state to local administration, and be eligible for veterans' benefits simultaneously. Each has its own

administrative structure and eligibility requirements.

Here again, the Canadian system is vastly simpler. Ten provincial governments and two territories are each responsible for the administration of a provincial health plan. All plans are publicly administered, either directly by provincial government or by a public agency established by provincial government. There are no fiscal intermediaries. If more than one provincial agency is responsible, such as in Quebec where hospital benefits and medical care are separately administered, the bookkeeping between the agencies is carried on at provincial level, but the beneficiary is not involved and is generally unaware of the process. He or she merely presents identification and receives the service. In Quebec, for example, every individual—some 6,300,000 residents—has a plastic credit card which is presented at each encounter with a provider in the system. Standard forms are used throughout, facilitating payment and the compilation of statistics.

Who pays for all this in the U.S.? For the employed, it is usually a combination of employer-employee payments to an insurance carrier or an HMO. Some governmental programs such as Medicare or benefits for end-stage kidney disease are financed through the Social Security system. Medicaid is financed through general tax revenues at the federal level and combinations of state, county, and local funds. Most hospitals are voluntary, others are proprietary, others are directly operated by various governmental agencies at each level of government. Some receive funds from all potential sources in the system, others from a principal single tax-based source. For most Americans there is some out-of-pocket payment in addition to insurance premiums and the payment of taxes. Several thousand third-parties are involved in transferring dollars from the individual recipient of service to the individual providers of service. Each of these, in turn, attempts to limit or control its particular costs of purchasing the services provided. The insurers want to keep *their* costs down so that they can sell their policies in the marketplace. Governmental agencies want to keep *their* costs under control to avoid accusations of waste and extravagance. But there is no single place in the U.S. system where the aggregate expenditure is susceptible to control. Hundreds of piecemeal legislative and regulatory provisions have been adopted in efforts to effectuate control of a segment of expenditure. These are, in turn, administered by thousands of agencies and hundreds of thousands of people charged with controlling entry, standards of care, capital investment as well as payment for individual services. If one had deliberately set out to produce as complex and costly an administrative system as possible, the U.S. system represents an excellent model.

Who pays in Canada? Provincial governments are not only the administrators but the paymasters as well. Both federal and provincial taxes are used for this purpose.

Moderately complex formulas are involved for the allocation of federal dollars to the provinces, but there is no federal interference in provincial administration. The buck stops at the door of provincial government. It may increase benefits as it chooses but may not remove basic benefits. It may choose any mix of tax revenues to pay for the benefits. Some provinces use more progressive mixes of taxation than others. But provincial government is the payer and each province accepts that responsibility under its own legislation. Almost all provinces have some mix of out-of-pocket payments by beneficiaries as well, either by permitting providers to bill additional amounts or by requiring payment for some services such as private rooms, ambulance transportation, etc. It is possible to buy insurance to cover these out-of-pocket costs.

A word about costs. For many years I have heard rhetoric in the U.S. about how the nation can't afford health insurance for all. Canada's cost to cover everyone is actually more than one hundred U.S. dollars per capita less than the cost of the U.S. system which excludes 10% of the population. Most of the difference is accounted for by the lower cost of administering the Canadian system. Most of the excess U.S. cost is used to pay for determination of eligibility, for selling costs and commissions to insurance agents, for multiple and complex filling out of forms for reimbursement, for maintaining large and complicated billing systems, for carrying charges on accounts receivable, for multiple bureaucracies both governmental and commercial, for duplicating hospital systems, and so forth. Each year, the U.S. system chews up a larger piece of the gross national product—this year it will be about 10% of all goods and services produced. In Canada, health services have hovered between 6.9 and 7.1% of gross national product over the past decade, some years up a bit, others down a bit.

All of this is not to suggest that Canada has achieved an ideal health system. It's just damn good. It has its problems, but none of them are beyond resolution. It is subject to the same inflationary forces as obtain in the U.S.; many of the goods used are indeed purchased in the U.S. or from U.S. corporations operating in Canada. Eastern Canada heats its hospitals with oil from the same sources as the U.S. There is the same push of the technological imperative in Canadian medicine as in the U.S. Canadian medical education is essentially identical to that of the U.S. and is accredited by the same bodies.

But in addition to simpler, less costly administration of health benefits, Canada benefits from a more socially conscious, more responsible medical profession. The wide acceptance of fixed fee schedules facilitates administration and reduces the costs of that administration. Yes, the profession fights with government for more money in every province, and that's understandable and part of the rules of the game. There's much less disparity of income within the profession than in the U.S., and

this, too, is widely although not universally accepted. Most Canadian doctors could not morally accept the U.S. system. Those that do migrate to the U.S. are often horrified by the complexity of practice administration they face, even though they may be laughing all the way to the bank.

Canadian hospitals, too, are much easier to administer; they operate for the most part on prospective budgets set in negotiation with provincial governments. They scream for more money, of course, but they are very happy to see the regular bank checks that pay from 95 to 100% of their operating costs.

In implementing health policy, both the U.S. and some Canadian provinces have attempted different models for the delivery of health services, mostly on a small scale and in response to somewhat different perceptions. For example, in the U.S., efforts to respond to the needs of the poor led to neighborhood health centers, funded by the federal government but locally administered. The health center movement in Canada has had less targeted motives. In the province of Quebec, about one hundred exist, more oriented to the breadth of response by government to broadly defined need for access to social services than to health services. Thus far, these have been inadequately evaluated as to effectiveness.

In the U.S., there have been incentives provided for the formation and operation of Health Maintenance Organizations, both prepaid group practices and independent practitioner plans. In Canada, those prepaid group practices that existed have largely been destroyed by the predominant fee-for-service orientation of the provincial health insurance plans.

Fee-for-service is, in both countries, the prevailing mode of payment of physicians. For most Americans and for most Canadians, this means there is a powerful force, however moderated, toward providing more services and especially those that are most remunerative to the physician; the more one does, the more one gets. The specialist who controls the use of a technology is thereby a major beneficiary in both systems. To the extent that there is application of such technologies in an excessive fashion, and there appears to be evidence that this is the case, both systems bear substantial cost burdens that do not benefit the patient.

So here we have two different health systems reflecting very different health policies, two different social contracts between governments and the governed on a single continent. As social contracts they reflect different social philosophies, different perceptions of priorities, different cultures and different forms of government. There are advantages and disadvantages to each. There are lessons that each might learn from the other. For me, it has been an extraordinary experience to have had the opportunity to work with both.

I often wonder to what extent the U.S. government reflects the will of the people as regards health policy. Don't Americans want what Canadians have: a social contract that as-

sures everyone that an illness will not yield bankruptcy, that financial access is available to all, that the health system should respond to the needs of all? Do we Americans not want this for everyone? Must we argue about the virtues of competition or the apparent alternative of petty regulatory process designed to exclude rather than include people? Do we really need to spend 20 to 30 billion dollars a year in excess administrative costs while denying benefits to 25 million people? I would argue that present levels of national expenditure in the U.S., differently arranged, would permit us to provide for all.

For Canadians, I would raise a different array of questions. Should provincial governments and provincial medical organizations continue to erode the system? Conflict about principle is really conflict about money. Opting out and overbilling, as is permitted in some provinces, only add to the costs of administration; they do not add one single service to the health system. Other provinces should learn from the positive experience of Quebec in this regard, and from the negative experience in the U.S. Yes, doctors will have to be paid more, but the cost of purchasing their full participation is a marginal item in the whole system, and will guarantee continued equity for the people. This is a cornerstone of the Canadian initiative, a social contract which we in the United States would do well to study, understand, and perhaps even emulate.

26 STRATEGIES FOR EQUITY IN HEALTH: REPORT FROM SWEDEN

Göran Dahlgren and Finn Diderichsen

Background

During the 1970s, Sweden faced a critical development in its health sector similar to that in other Western countries. The escalating conflict between limited resources and increasing needs was fought against a background of a leveling off of the health benefits for the population. The solution to this development was similar to that of other nations: more primary care, more prevention, and more planning (1). A new health and medical services act was passed in parliament in 1982 emphasizing the responsibility of the regional political bodies, the county councils, for the planning for health and care—public and private, preventive as well as curative (2).

One of the key aspects of the health care act is *equity*—in health and in care. The overall goal of the health care services is to achieve "good health and health care on equal terms for the entire population." During 1981–84, a national expert committee published a large number of reports on what these goals imply for practical health policy concerning prevention, structure of the health system, and staff and educational planning (3).

One of the major problems focused on by this so-called HS90 study is the prevailing inequities in health between different socioeconomic groups in today's Sweden. There are several reasons why this is regarded as a major problem by national authorities:

1. A high degree of equity in welfare and consumption between social classes has traditionally been a high priority of the Social Democratic Party in Sweden.

2. Social inequities illustrate the potential benefits of preventive work among underprivileged groups.

3. One of the major arguments to keep the health sector public (vs. private) is that it is needed to ensure equity in access and outcome.

4. In periods of cost-containment, the prevailing inequities emphasize the need for a resource allocation that recognizes the differences in health care needs between segments of the population.

5. A preliminary analysis of the remedies needed to combat inequities in health shows that remedies to a very limited extent fall within the responsibility of the health care sector, but are highly dependent on improved mechanisms for intersectoral action on the national and local level.

SOURCE: *International Journal of Health Services* 16, no. 4 (1986):517–537. © 1986, Baywood Publishing Co., Inc.

Social Inequities in Health

Our present knowledge of inequities in health is based on several sources. There is, however, still the major problem that statistics produced within the health sector (e.g., causes of death, in-patient statistics, and health insurance) mostly lack data on occupation and other socioeconomic variables. The data presented here are therefore mainly the result of ad hoc studies, which are based on national census data linked with registers of medical data.

Mortality

Mortality shows moderate social differences between major occupational groups (Table 1). These groups, however, are very heterogeneous, and when we look at specific occupations and causes of death there are dramatic differences. Men in domestic work in hotels etc., seaman, miners, and commercial travelers have a very high mortality in all Scandinavian countries (4).

Perceived Ill Health

Ill health, according to the lay opinions reflected by the national survey of living conditions (5, 6), is a good deal more common among manual workers than among salaried employees (Fig. 1). When compared to the low mortality figures, a strikingly large proportion of farmers and entrepreneurs report prolonged illness and reduced working capacity.

The periodic health interviews also provide an opportunity of studying illness in certain population groups that are presumably exposed to particularly heavy risks. Table 2 shows data for the following groups: low-pay groups (full-time employees earning not more than SEK 51,000 per year in 1978), unemployed persons (job seekers), very poorly educated persons (noncompletion of compulsory schooling), foreign nationals, single persons with no family links (living alone and in touch with relatives less than once a week), and single mothers

TABLE 1 Indirect Standardized Mortality Rate (SMR) among Swedish Men Aged 25–64 Years (all causes), 1976–80

Occupational Category	25–44 Years	45–64 Years
Technical and scientific	71	85
Administrative and clerical	87	96
Commercial	90	100
Forest and agriculture	103	82
Mining and stoneworks	168	128
Transportation	110	108
Industry and construction	112	108
Service and domestic	118	112
Not economically active	204	245
All men	100	100

FIGURE 1   Percentage of Men and Women Aged 16–84 Years Suffering from Severe Chronic Illness (with severe pain and/or disability), according to ULF 1980/81

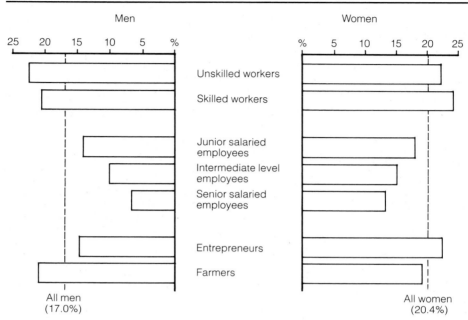

Note: The data are age standardized. (ULF is the regular survey of living conditions carried out by the National Bureau for Statistics.)

SOURCE: reference 6.

TABLE 2   Cases of Chronic Illness and Deviations from the Average (coevals of the same sex) among Risk Groups Aged 16–74 Years. ULF 1977/78[a]

	Chronically Ill		Percentage of Population
	Total	With Reduced Working Capacity	
Low pay	30 (−3)	5 (−3)	9.3
Unemployed	37 (+6)	9 (+2)	1.9
Very poorly educated	43 (+15)	18 (+17)	4.3
Foreign nationals	34 (+2)	10 (+4)	4.3
Single persons with no family contacts	50 (+9)	20 (+8)	6.1
Single mothers	32 (−4)	6 (−4)	2.2
Entire population aged 16–74 yrs	38	10	100

[a]Data from reference 5. ULF is the regular survey of living conditions carried out by the National Bureau for Statistics. Deviations from the average are shown in parentheses.

(with children living at home aged 18 years or under).

Single persons with no family contacts are very often chronically ill. Low-pay employees are afflicted with ill health less frequently than manual workers (more than 20 percent of low-pay employees are salaried workers). Those who did not complete their elementary or compulsory schooling run an extremely high risk of prolonged illness with reduced working capacity later in life. Foreign nationals also have considerable health problems in comparison with coeval Swedish citizens. This still holds true when they are compared with Swedish coevals having the same educational and occupational backgrounds.

The national survey carried out in 1968 was repeated in 1974 and 1981 on the same cohort and gives us the opportunity to follow changes in the frequency of different symptoms in the population (7). It seems that during the second half of the 1970s, health problems in the musculoskeletal system (with pain in muscles and joints) increased, while mental complaints decreased (Table 3). In both cases socioeconomic differences are rather stable.

Absence from Work Because of Illness

There is a clear correlation between income and sick leave for men and women (Fig. 2). Both the number of illnesses and the number of sick days per individual are higher among full-time employees in the lower income bracket (8). However, there is no reason to assume that income in itself is an explanation of differences in official sickness figures: the covariance found more reflects working and general living conditions.

Use of Health Care

The use of in-patient health services is, at a given out-put of services, also likely to reflect differentials in health status of various socioeconomic groups in a health system with a fairly good socioeconomic access to these services (9).

The general pattern is that the use

TABLE 3   Percentage of Swedish Population Aged 15–75 Years in Different Social Strata Suffering from Severe Pain (in muscles, joints) and Mental Complaints[a]

	1968	1974	1981
Severe pain			
Social group I	13.9	10.6	11.7
II	14.9	15.8	18.5
III	18.3	21.0	21.7
Mental complaints			
Social group I	16.4	15.0	14.4
II	17.8	16.5	14.2
III	21.2	22.3	17.8

[a]Data from reference 7. Figures are standardized for age and sex.

FIGURE 2   Number of Cases of Sickness Cash Benefit Terminated in 1982 Per Person
Insured for Sickness Cash Benefit, Distributed by the Amount of the
Daily Benefit

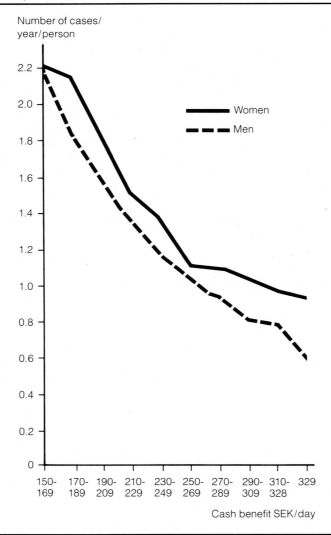

SOURCE: reference 8.

of in-patient services is higher for
unskilled and skilled workers than
for higher civil servants and salaried
employees, farmers, and entrepreneurs (Fig. 3). Focusing on certain
disease-groups, the socioeconomic
pattern of use can of course differ,
as shown in Figure 3 for admissions
in hospitals following accidents. Selective mechanisms in mental care

FIGURE 3   Admissions in Hospitals in Five Swedish Counties of Employed Men
Aged 45–64 Years

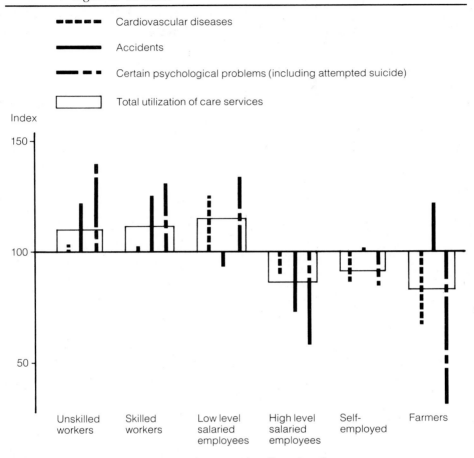

Note: Figures are age standardized: index = 100 for all employed men.

SOURCE: reference 3.

may contribute to strong differences here (1).

Equity Targets for Health

The first target in the Health-for-All Strategy for Europe as agreed upon by the member states of the World Health Organization—and thus also by Sweden—is to reduce the differences in health status between, for example, different socio-economic groups by at least 25 percent from 1985 to the year 2000.

Even though few explicit and quantified equity targets for specific diseases have as yet been formulated by the Swedish government and local health authorities, greater attention is, from a political point of view, being paid to the inequities observed and the need for formulating specific strategies to reduce them.

In the Health Policy Bill of 1985 (10) it is also explicitly stated that the greatest positive effects on public health can be achieved by means of improvements in health status of those groups that are presently exposed to the greatest health hazards and therefore have the highest morbidity and mortality. It might be of particular interest to observe that all political parties—except the Conservative Party—voted in favor of this Health Policy Bill. The Conservatives, on the other hand, claimed that the distribution of poor health within the population is mainly random and when differences between various groups occur they can primarily be explained in terms of different lifestyles, which can be controlled by each individual.

Another line of opposition—mainly voiced by the medical profession—was to explain the observed socioeconomic and class differences by stating that people with poor health often end up in the working class or are attracted to certain occupational groups. "It is the propensity for poor health which governs the social class/occupations people occupy," as stated by the Swedish Society of Medicine in its official comments on HS90 reports.

There is little doubt that we have a health-related social mobility even in Swedish society with its comprehensive insurance system, but mobility between classes is quantitatively small compared to mobility within classes. The data presented above

are, however, heavily influenced by the "healthy worker" effect: persons suffering from severe chronic illness are given early retirement pensions and thus disappear from the occupational groups as defined above in the studies or mortality, in-patient care, and sickness insurance. The differences found are thus very low estimates of the actual differences in morbidity and mortality (4).

The approach suggested in the Health Policy Bill of 1985 to reduce inequities in health is—against this background—very much in line with what is stated in the WHO Health-for-All Strategy for Europe:

The reduction of health inequalities will require first and foremost the general availability of basic prerequisites for health and the reduction of risks related to lifestyles. Most of the present differences in health status are determined by living and working conditions. The disadvantaged nations and groups are not only more exposed to environmental hazards but also to the acquisition of health-damaging habits. The prosperous ones are not only more protected from environmental threats but also more likely to benefit from health promotion. Therefore, if the present trend continues, the actual gaps will widen.

Infant mortality 100 years ago was 150 per thousand. During the 1930s, thanks to an improved nutritional standard and better education and hygiene, great reductions in infant mortality were achieved. But still there were great differences in the infant mortality rate between different socioeconomic groups. In Stockholm, for example, there was a variation in infant mortality of between

14 and 49 per thousand, depending on the socioeconomic situation of the family.

The National Board of Health in 1935 emphasized that there was no reason to accept an infant mortality for any group of society that was higher than the infant mortality rate for children born in the most wealthy families: "What one social group can buy for money society must provide for others." The efforts needed to reach this target were primarily improved hygiene and nutritional standards, as well as a health care system characterized by good access for the whole population. Against this background, the parliament approved a proposal for free mother and child health care. Today the infant mortality has fallen to below 7 per thousand and the differences between various socioeconomic groups are very small.

We have used this example to illustrate how, with a comprehensive health policy, we have managed to reach—by international standards —a very low infant mortality. The experiences gained are certainly rele-vant for the health policy of today and tomorrow.

Mortality Decreasing— Inequities Increasing?

Sweden, as well as a number of European countries, had an increasing mortality in ischemic heart disease among men during the 1970s. The trend leveled off in the second half of the decade and has, at least in major metropolitan areas, turned into a reverse trend with a rather fast decrease (Table 4).

The causes for this development are no better known in Sweden than they are for a similar development in North America. Decreasing numbers of smokers and decreasing alcohol consumption are without doubt important contributing factors in Sweden. A large number of preventive actions have been taken in traffic policies. At the same time, the economic development has been without serious signs of crisis, i.e., the level of unemployment has been constantly very low, at least in the Stockholm area.

TABLE 4   Percentage Annual Changes in Mortality 1975–84 in Stockholm County in Some Major Causes of Early Death[a]

	1975–80		1980–84	
	Men	Women	Men	Women
Ischemic heart disease (age 45–74 years)	+ 0.7	− 0.6	− 6.0	− 6.1
Traffic accidents (all ages)	− 2.1	− 4.0	− 9.8	− 11.7
Alcohol related disease (all ages)	− 0.7	+ 1.0	− 4.6	− 6.7
Suicide (all ages)	+ 1.2	− 1.6	− 1.9	− 2.7
All causes	− 1.4	− 1.6	− 4.2	− 4.0

[a]Trends are calculated as the age-standardized regression coefficient in percent.

TABLE 5   Percentage of Swedish Cities' Population (aged 15–75 years) Smoking More Than 10 Cigarettes Per Day, 1968–81[a]

Social Group	1968 Male	1968 Female	1974 Male	1974 Female	1981 Male	1981 Female
I	31.2	12.2	27.6	23.2	17.2	17.7
II	32.0	11.1	29.0	21.7	21.9	15.9
III	31.0	9.1	36.3	22.9	33.5	25.8

[a]Data from reference 7.

We know very little about changes in the social distribution of these different risk factors. However, the smoking habits are showing an interesting development from an equity point of view. The numbers of heavy smokers are decreasing among well educated men, but at the same time increasing among poorly educated men and—more pronounced—among women (Table 5). The consequences of this may very well be an increase of the already prevailing class differences in cardiovascular and other types of morbidity related to smoking. This development provides us with one of the signs about successes and failures in the anti-smoking programs of the 1970s.

Intersectoral Actions for Reduction of Inequities

The Risk Approach

There is no doubt that existing inequities in health can, first of all, be reduced by deliberate risk reduction and health promotion programs within sectors other than the health care sector. Health hazards are not randomly distributed within the population, as shown by the epidemiological data presented above on the socioeconomic and occupational distribution of morbidity and mortality. Ideally, the epidemiology of health hazards should be considered at least as important as the traditional field of epidemiology, i.e., the prevalence and distribution of diseases.

One aspect of crucial importance when describing and analyzing the prevalence and distribution of various health hazards is to recognize the *cumulative effects* of a combination of risk factors. The reason for this is the strong tendency that those at greatest risk, because of poor working environment, for example, also are those at greatest risk for many other risk factors, e.g., in housing and unemployment. In addition, there are often interrelationships between different risk factors, for example, smoking and exposure to asbestos increase the health risk more than would be suspected if these two risk factors were looked upon not as reinforcing, but as separate and isolated entities. These cumulative and reinforcing factors are in fact one of the most important aspects to consider when trying to for-

TABLE 6 Various Health Hazards, by Socioeconomic Groups, in 1977/78[a]

| | Health Hazards[b] | | | | | |
Socio-economic Categories	1	2	3	4	5	6
Menial staff	+7	+4	+18	+7	+5	+10
Unskilled workers	+2	+12	+20	+7	+3	+8
Skilled workers	−1	+7	+18	+1	0	+8
Salaried employees, junior	0	−5	−16	−3	+3	+5
Salaried employees, intermediate	−5	−5	−29	−7	−4	−2
Salaried employees, senior	−5	−11	−44	−9	−5	−3
Entrepreneurs	+1	−	+5	−6	−1	+5
Farmers	−4	−	+20	−6	0	−23
Total. 16–64 yrs	12%[c]	17%[c]	65%[c]	11%[c]	9%	37%

[a]Data from reference 5. Figures in the table are sex- and age-adjusted percentage deviations from the national average, given on the bottom line.
[b]1, unemployed at some time during the past 5 yrs; 2, unsocial working hours; 3, physical strain at work; 4, intense, monotonous work; 5, overcrowded or outmoded housing; 6, daily smoker.
[c]Percentage of employed population.

mulate a strategy for reducing health inequalities.

Table 6 shows some empirical facts regarding the distribution of various health hazards between various socioeconomic categories. These can serve as an example of how high exposure to one risk factor very often is linked with high exposure to a number of other health hazards, and vice versa. It may be noted that, for the indicators of physical and social health hazards at work, there is a clear difference between exposure of manual and salaried workers. The risk of unemployment has hitherto been particularly high among menial staff and unskilled workers. For housing conditions, the line of demarcation tends more to be located between manual workers and junior salaried workers on the one hand and farmers, entrepreneurs, and intermediate and senior salaried employees on the other. Smoking is particularly common among manual workers, junior salaried employees, and entrepreneurs.

Understandably, the distribution of risks in the occupational environment appears to be more adequately captured by the occupationally based socioeconomic classification, but certain other groups are particularly exposed to certain other health risks, as illustrated in Table 7. It may be observed that persons whose education has been very brief (nowadays comprising less than nine years' compulsory schooling) not only have intensive, monotonous jobs, but also poorer housing conditions and less healthy living habits than the average population. Single mothers have poor material living conditions coupled with a high risk of unemployment, monotonous jobs, and substandard dwelling environments; they smoke more often than any other category. Foreign

TABLE 7   Some Health Hazards Related to Certain Risk Groups[a]

Risk Groups	Health Hazards					
	1	2	3	4	5	6
Unemployed	—	—	—	—	+7	−15
Low-pay	+9	−5	+12	+3	+4	−9
Extremely poorly educated	+4	+12	+11	+11	+13	−8
Single mothers	+11	+1	+2	+5	−2	−5
Single persons with no family contacts	+5	+5	−2	−1	+4	−5
Foreign nationals	+2	+12	+6	+12	+9	+13

[a]Data from reference 5. See footnotes a and b in Table 6 for an explanation of the health hazards and the percentage deviation figures.

nationals have inferior social working and dwelling environments.

Thus one finds that the socioeconomic differences in exposure to risks are greatest in the occupational environment, but are also substantial for such risk factors as unemployment and smoking. The role of education seems crucial. Extremely poorly educated and highly educated salaried employees constitute the opposite poles of distribution in many respects.

The strategy presented in the Health Policy Bill of 1985 includes two complementary types of action programs for improved health and reduced inequities.

The Health Policy Matrix

The first type of action program focuses on a *certain disease group.* The objectives of this type of action program are expressed in terms of reduced incidence/prevalence of diseases. Two such National Health Action Programmes, for reducing cardiovascular diseases and accidents, are presented in the Health Policy Bill, and two more, for the prevention of mental illness and diseases of the skeletomuscular system, will be ready during 1986.

The second type of approach, *the risk approach*, directly focuses on the various health risks related to *various sectors such as housing, labor market, work environment etc.*

The supplementary character of these two approaches can be illustrated by means of a simple matrix in which one dimension refers to the health problem and the other indicates the sector in which the various health hazards occur (Fig. 4).

Starting with a particular health problem, e.g., injuries, cardiovascular disease, or tumors, one can describe its incidence and the underlying causal mechanisms. In this way a picture is obtained of the various social sectors within which one can identify factors and mechanisms that may be amenable to a measure of health improvement and disease prevention. A descriptive method of this kind can be termed a "health policy action program" for, say, cardiovascular disease, and can be

FIGURE 4   Health Policy Matrix: The Connection between Health Hazards and Disease Categories

	Cardiovascular diseases	Mental illness	Skeletomuscular diseases	Tumors	Injuries	Respiratory diseases
Social upbringing environment	*	**			*	*
Social work environment and unemployment	**	**				
Physical work environment		*	**	**	**	**
Social living environment		*				
Physical living environment				*	**	*
Air/water pollutants				*		*
Traffic				*	**	*
Diet	**			**		*
Alcohol and drugs	*	**		*	**	*
Tobacco	**			**		**

* some correlation   **strong correlation

Note: * indicates some degree of relationship; ** indicates a close relationship

SOURCE: reference 3.

made to include preventive measures and inputs that health and medical services themselves are authorized and able to administer, e.g., preventive medical treatment and health education. The program also provides an indication of those sectors with which health and medical services need to collaborate. This mode of description can be especially useful in locally organized collaborations between health and medical services and other social planning agencies.

One can also adopt a "sectoral" perspective, i.e., describe the various causes of ill health (health hazards) relating to a particular sector in society, e.g., the food manufacturing and farming sector, the labour market sector, the housing sector, the traffic sector, etc., according to the various ways in which public activities are subdivided. The role of the health service sector in this perspective is to provide the decision-making bodies of other sectors with relevant facts about, for example, linkages between certain health hazards and various diseases, and with whatever epidemiological evidence there is about, the geographical and socioeconomic distributions of diseases and—even more important—health hazards. The professional groups within the health sector thus improve the possibilities for the other sectors to identify the potential health impact of various development projects and programs, and consequently to formulate the health policy component for that particular sector or program. This type of health impact analysis, as an integrated part of the planning process, can provide an important foundation for decisions at both national and regional levels, and also for dialogue and cooperation at the primary care level between various sectors of society.

Our understanding of the mechanisms behind the present inequities in health in Sweden is still very limited. Thus, in the Health Policy Bill of 1985, the major emphasis is on the intersectoral action for health with very little said about how these actions may more specifically influence prevailing inequities.

The following section gives an example of how the HS90 Commission and the Health Policy Bill have discussed health-related policies within the health sector as well as in the sectors of the labor market, food, and agriculture.

Examples of Intersectoral Programs

Unemployment—A Health Hazard

There is an increasing number of research reports showing that unemployment can cause ill health and be a contributory cause of premature death, i.e., that it should also be considered a health hazard. It is pos-sible to demonstrate physiological changes among unemployed persons and persons threatened with unemployment, in the form of an increase of "stress substances" in the body and increased blood pressure. Arthritic disorders and gastritis increase, resulting in a growth of medical care contacts and drug consumption. Mental disorders and apathy occur. Suicide, attempted suicide, and cardiovascular morbidity become more prevalent. Families experience conflicts and divorce and their children get into difficulty at school.

Research into unemployment (11) and ill health has followed three principal lines of inquiry. One line of research has focused on health handicaps leading to unemployment. A second line of research focuses on the effects of unemployment in terms of decreasing economic resources and the extent to which this causes a deterioration of health. The third and major line of research today, however, is concerned with the effects of unemployment on individual health, relating mainly to noneconomic values of employment, i.e., employment as a means of identity, contact, and community participation.

Rising levels of unemployment—at a macro-level—covary with rising male mortality from cardiac infarction, stroke, malignant tumors, cirrhosis of the liver, and suicide, among other causes (12). Macro-analysis however, does not yet afford any reliable documentation on the extent to which the reported covariations can be interpreted as direct causal connections. Micro-studies focusing on specific work places and individuals must therefore be the foundation for this type of research (11, 13).

Surprisingly enough, there are only a few survey reports concerning the relationship between unemployment and drug abuse. There are, however, studies showing that persons who had alcohol problems before becoming unemployed are liable to become heavily alcoholic during unemployment.

Geographical mobility in the labor market has also proved to have an impact on health. Poorly educated persons who have difficulty in asserting themselves in the labor market are particularly hard hit. It follows that a regional policy serving to reduce the numbers of enforced migrations will also have a bearing on health (14).

A concerted health strategy focusing on equity goals in health will have to consider the effects of unemployment and thus labor policies. The negative health effects of unemployment therefore provide a further substantial argument in favor of minimizing overt unemployment, even when economic safeguards are provided for the unemployed. Furthermore, commercially unprofitable jobs can be socioeconomically viable if both direct costs (loss of output, unemployment benefit, etc.) and indirect costs (increased morbidity and mortality, a heavier load on medical services, impaired personal well-being) are taken into consideration.

From the vantage-point of health policy, it is also essential to stress the serious health risks that still persist in spite of a low general level of unemployment. The first victims of unemployment, and those whose prospects of regular employment are most limited, are frequently those persons whose health is most seriously affected by unemployment (11).

In terms of age groups, unemployment is most common among young persons. It is also high among young parents, especially if they are single parents. Unemployment is high among persons with heavy economic burdens (especially single mothers) and among those living in adverse economic circumstances— below or close to the breadline. In terms of occupational/educational background, unemployment is most common among unskilled manual workers and among persons with extremely little schooling, i.e., persons who failed to complete their compulsory education. Socially isolated persons and persons with health problems or occupational handicaps are also heavily over-represented among the unemployed.

Swedish surveys do not afford any systematic information on which groups suffer the greatest negative effects as a result of unemployment. It is possible, however, on the strength of various international surveys to specify several groups as being particularly vulnerable during unemployment. One group is persons already suffering from chronic illness. Another is single men, especially those who are middle-aged and elderly. Ethnic minorities have also been found to incur an elevated risk of ill health during unemployment. This is also very much the case with drug abusers and, above all, alcoholics. A health objective of the labor market policy should therefore be to pay special attention to the provision of employment for categories such as these, whose health is particularly at risk (11). This will mean concentrating on particular regions and occupational sectors, which in turn will probably call for a close knowledge of the labor market for the poorly educated, the single, elderly men, and immigrants (especially women), as well as intensified efforts to find suitable jobs for these particular categories.

One general requirement from a health policy viewpoint is that unemployment should be kept to a minimum. At the same time one is bound to observe that, even when unemployment is low, a large proportion of the effects of unemployment persist because they are very much related with the most disadvantaged groups in the labor market. Besides, long-term job security is called for because, according to many research reports, the very threat of unemployment is probably just as prejudicial to health as unemployment itself. Specific measures are needed on behalf of the groups liable to suffer ill health as a result of unemployment. Improved unemployment insurance would reduce the risk of the unemployment problem being medicalized through sicklisting and early disability pensions, with the attendant aggravation of adverse effects on health.

The health and medical care sector at various levels must take part in social planning, partly by reporting its experiences and knowledge con-

cerning, for example, the health impact of unemployment. In this way, the health and medical care sector can supply documentation on which labor market policy can be based. The National Board of Health and Welfare should compile overviews that can be made available in health and medical care and elsewhere. The board should endeavor to ensure that health and medical care statistics are compiled in such a way that they also shed light on the consequences of unemployment; statistics should be compiled and analyzed in such a way as to elucidate these aspects (10).

At the local level—through primary care and personnel health care—rehabilitation and retraining, instead of disability pensions, should be supported as a response to unemployment when working together with patients. This also means that personnel within primary health care should help to chart the health impact of unemployment at the local level. At the same time, especially in the problem fields of unemployment and ill health, it should be emphasized that the involvement of health and medical services *must not lead to a medicalization of social and economic problems of society. The problems of unemployment can only be solved by measures within the framework of general economic policy.*

Health Policy Aspects of Diet and Food Policy

Outright deficiency diseases due to malnutrition are uncommon in Sweden nowadays, although they can occur in particular groups. The practice of food enrichment, for example by addition of vitamins and iron, counteracts the qualitative malnutrition that can occur partly because many people, owing to a low level of physical activity, do not require a very large energy intake through their food.

The problems that do exist are concerned with inappropriate diet and excessive energy intake in relation to energy consumption. There is a connection between high fat intake—high blood fats—the development of ischemic heart disease and the consequent elevated risk of cardiac infarction. There are strong suspicions that dietary fat plays a part in bringing about certain forms of cancer, e.g., cancer of the breast. High blood pressure is connected with high amounts of sodium, e.g., cooking salt, which are administered to the body through food intake. Constipation is partly due to a diet containing insufficient fiber. It is also suspected that a low fiber diet favors the development of cancer of the large intestine.

The connection between dental caries and eating habits (e.g., heavy consumption of sugar) has been well known for a long time, and it has been established that diet information can be an effective countermeasure. Excess weight is generally due to excessive consumption, particularly of high energy nutrients such as fats and sugar. Heavy obesity is a risk factor for many types of disease such as diabetes and cardiovascular disease, and for accidental injuries. In addition, it imposes extra strain on the organs of locomotion. There

is a great deal to suggest that unsuitable eating habits can precipitate symptomatic diabetes.

For a long time now there has been widespread agreement among dieticians concerning the changes that need to be made in the eating habits of the Swedish people so that diet can be made conducive as possible to health and adverse health effects can be reduced to a minimum. These recommendations are as follows (14):

- Energy supply must be adapted to energy needs, partly through an increase in general physical activity.
- Consumption of fat must be reduced to less than 30 percent of total energy intake.
- Consumption of sugar must be reduced to about 10 percent of total energy intake.
- Intake of necessary nutrients must be increased.

In practice this means that people should:

- Increase their consumption of non-fat instead of high-fat dairy produce, and their consumption of lean meat and blood-based foods instead of fat meat and cured meat products.
- Reduce their consumption of animal fats, sugar, and sweetened products.

The health requirements for foodstuffs and diet also demand that vitamins and trace elements must be present in sufficient quantities and concentration, and that additives such as coloring agents and preservatives, as well as impurities resulting from the environmental impact of infectious substances and chemicals, must not entail any risk of injury to health. In the preparation process, foodstuffs can sometimes be depleted of their natural content of iron and vitamins, for example. This depletion may have to be offset by, for example, the addition of iron and iodized salt.

Increased popular knowledge about eating habits conducive to good health is an instrument of diet and food policy. Efforts are therefore needed in the sphere of educational policy, so that health questions (including, for example, diet questions) can be given a prominent position in preschool education, compulsory schooling, upper secondary schooling, voluntary educational activities, and higher education. This prominence must also be reflected in the training given to teachers of the subjects concerned.

Health requirements should provide the point of departure for public food and diet policy and should be taken into account when deciding on price controls, taxation, and subsidies in the food sector. New or revised methods of producing and upgrading foodstuffs are quite often introduced without sufficient investigation of their health impact. From a health viewpoint, it is essential for such methods to be carefully examined prior to upgrading and for good resources to be provided for the inspection of foodstuffs at various stages of manufacture.

In the best interests of consumers, food advertising should be nutritionally informative and moderate. There may be cause to investigate the possibility of marketing legislation being applied to food stuffs in the same way that it has been applied to tobacco.

Collective meals account for a very large proportion of popular diet, and this makes it essential, that for example, school meals should be of a high nutritional standard and should be served in such a way as to lay the foundations of a positive attitude toward good eating habits. Health and medical institutions can set a good example in this respect.

Research and development work in the diet sector is in need of reinforcement. For example, a regular system of eating habit surveys a population level is needed in order to furnish documentation on which to base, among other things, an evaluation of the effects of diet policy and food policy measures.

Questions concerning foodstuffs and diet involve several government departments and central authorities. Stronger mechanisms are therefore needed for the general planning and coordination of food and nutrition policy. Food policy is thus a sphere in which considerations of health policy should be made to play a more prominent part than they have hitherto.

In the promotion of popular health, conflicts are liable to arise between health objectives and the free will of the individual. There is an obvious conflict of this kind, for example, in the field of alcohol policy, but the same is true for other fields in which public measures to improve people's security and safety are regarded as encroachments on liberty. As long as eating habits are not generally regarded as an essential health factor or a risk area, public measures to steer consumption will be interpreted by many people as officious. Public agencies must therefore state their motives very clearly, and the measures taken must not entail unnecessary restrictions of freedom of choice. At the same time, however, it is important to specify the sources of "demands for liberty." There are many vested interests in the diet and foodstuffs sector: freedom of choice can mean quite different things to consumers and to producers.

Legislative bills and public debate in Sweden during the past few years have drawn attention to the need for a concerted food policy which, unlike the agricultural policy pursued hitherto, would put more emphasis on consumer interests, not least from a nutritional viewpoint. Agricultural policy has above all been concerned with incomes, the aim being for farmers to achieve and retain equality of income with other sectors of the population. But food consumption, that is, its impact on popular health, has been steered in a negative direction by price policy. A survey of the effects of subsidies reveals that they have helped increase the consumption of those foodstuffs for which increased consumption has not been recommended from a health point of view.

We can make comparisons between food prices and the prices of cigarettes and alcohol, which have risen a good deal less rapidly. Alcohol pricing has formed part of an alcohol policy aimed at limiting consumption. All the same, the rise in alcohol prices has been relatively moderate. Thus food, alcohol, and tobacco prices have been developed on different premises.

The general level of food prices and the prices of individual foodstuffs do a great deal to influence household eating habits. In times of austerity, many households sacrifice quality and allow price alone to guide their purchases. Those with good knowledge and good incomes can easily maintain a good standard of diet. The opposite is true for the low-income groups.

From this perspective—and combined with health education—agricultural and food policies certainly have an impact on health in general and on the socioeconomic distribution of food-related morbidity and mortality.

Intersectoral Actions for Health— The Role of the Health Care Sector

The health care sector has an important role to play in assisting other sectors with facts about morbidity, mortality, health hazards, and possibilities to promote healthy living conditions. The role of the health care sector is to assist in, and thus facilitate, the formulation and implementation of the health policy component of employment, working conditions, education, housing, etc. This active intersectoral dialogue must be combined with research focusing on the causal links between various sector policies programs and health. Considering the importance of reduced inequities to health, special attention should (according to the Health Policy Bill of 1985) be paid to research aimed at elucidating causes underlying the class differentials identified. This calls for a multidisciplinary approach and a close collaboration between, for example, medicine, social sciences, and engineering.

In addition to this intersectoral dialogue and intensified research, it is of the utmost importance that knowledge about health hazards and possible actions to improve health conditions within the population are forwarded to the public and to the individual by the health sector. Thus an important dimension of the health education provided by, for example, professional groups within the health sector is information about health hazards such as those related to the environment at work and in the traffic, unemployment, etc. Changes in these living conditions call for collective actions and political decisions. Health education should help individuals to promote and demand such changes.

References

1. Diderichsen, F. Ideologies in Swedish health sector today. The crises of the social democracy. *Int. J. Health Serv.* 12(2), 1982.
2. Regeringsproposition 1981/82:97. Hälso- och sjukvårdslag m m (Health Care Act 1982). Riksdagen, Stockholm, 1982.
3. *The Swedish Health Services in 1990s* (HS90). National Board of Health and Welfare, Stockholm, 1985.
4. Inequalities in health and health care. *Nordic School of Public Health.* Report 1985:5.
5. Social Report on Inequality in Sweden. Living Condition Report No. 27. *Official Statistics of Sweden.* National Bureau of Statistics, Stockholm, 1981.
6. Ill Health and Medical Care. Living Condition Report No. 42. *Official Statistics of Sweden.* National Bureau of Statistics, Stockholm, 1985.
7. Eriksson, R., and Aberg, R. (eds.). *Välfärd i förändring.* Prisma, Stockholm, 1984.
8. National Insurance 1982. *Official Statistics of Sweden.* National Insurance Board, Stockholm, 1984.
9. Haglund, B. Health care for whom? A statistical and cartographic study of health care utilization in the County of Uppsala. *Uppsala Dissertation from the Faculty of Medicine I.* Almquist & Wiksell International, Stockholm, 1986.
10. Regeringsproposition 1984/85:181. Om uteckligslinjer för härlso- och sjukvården m m (Health Policy Bill 1985). Riksdagen, Stockholm, 1985.
11. Janlert, U., and Dahlgren, G. *Unemployment, Health and the Labour Market—Some Aspects of Public Health Policy* (HS90). National Board of Health and Welfare, Stockholm, 1983.
12. Brenner, H. M. Importance of economic change in Swedish health and social well being, 1950–1980. Initial analysis and feasibility study (Mimeo). Baltimore, 1983.
13. *Health Policy Implication of Unemployment.* World Health Organization—Europe, Copenhagen, 1985.
14. Hälsopolitik i Samhällsplaneringen (HS90). *SOU 1984:44* (Swedish Government Official Report). Stockholm, 1984.

Emerging Impacts on Health Care and Policy

The modern health care system is continuously in flux. In the introduction to the previous section on policies, we noted one source for change—the social development of an aging population. A growing elderly population produces new challenges to the health care system, especially common chronic diseases (e.g., cardiovascular disease, lung disease) and long-term care (in hospitals, nursing homes, and at home). Until recently, health problems of aged people were the most widely discussed disease-based impact on America's medical system.

But the last few years have seen the debilitating epidemic of AIDS (acquired immunodeficiency syndrome). Identified as recently as 1981, it has begun to affect many parts of the health financing, planning, and delivery systems. In addition, AIDS has generated enormous fear and anxiety, has changed sexual behavior of people across the United States, has intensified bias and discrimination towards gay people, has led to stigmatizing of victims, and has raised difficult issues of medical ethics and social control. Like many other diseases, AIDS also holds the promise of monumental profits for drug and biotechnology firms, many of whom are racing to develop and sell palliative drugs such as AZT (which in 1988 cost $10,000 per patient per year) and to synthesize dummy receptors that might attract the AIDS virus and thus keep it from the body's natural cells. As of 1988, 35,980 cases of AIDS have been recorded, with 20,798 deaths. By 1991 an estimated 174,000 people with AIDS will be still living, and each will require from $45,000 to $130,000 for care. The secretary of the Department of Health and Human Services (DHHS) has estimated that by 1991 AIDS care and research will require annual expenditures of $10–15 billion. Indirect costs of $55 billion will also accrue, based on lost earnings and productivity of those stricken and killed by AIDS. DHHS secretary Otis Bowen has thus requested $1.145 billion for fiscal year 1989 for federal AIDS-related research and education.

In "The Social Meaning of AIDS," Peter Conrad examines the social and cultural meanings of AIDS. He focuses on the problems associated with the already marginal and stigmatized high risk groups of homosexuals and intravenous drug users, on the specific fears associated with sexually-transmitted diseases, and on the often irrational fear of contagion. The sum of these social processes leads to inhumane social treatment of victims and hinders effective control of AIDS.

Medical technology plays an increasingly central role in the direction of health care. Current innovations promise many fundamental changes in health beliefs and practices. Biotechnology synthesizes new life forms that offer great promises for disease prevention and cure, but which also have the potential for uncontrolled spread of dangerous organisms of unknown power. Organ transplants give life to many who would otherwise die, yet the mechanisms of patient selection for transplants are often open to question. Reproductive technologies such as in-vitro fertilization offer hope to boundless numbers of infertile people, but also raise the threat of eugenics and custom-created, genetically engineered babies. New medical and surgical procedures (e.g., kidney dialysis, coronary artery bypass) treat diseases previously intractable to treatment, while providers and third-party payers worry about the enormous expense. Modern diagnostic technologies (e.g., CAT scans, fetal heart monitors) allow for new glimpses into disease, but also lead to overuse in nonindicated cases.

H. David Banta and his colleagues talk about such matters as those outlined above in "Concerns about Medical Technology." The authors look at both benefits and risks of medical technology, and they include not only esoteric new technologies but also common problems such as drug side effects. Banta et al. want us to know the multitude of issues that must be taken into account when a new technology is instituted, rather than simply accept all advances because they appear to represent medical progress. Reminiscent of our earlier discussion of the medical model, this article points out that our society has a technological imperative that often favors scientific sophistication at the expense of humane interpersonal caregiving.

27   THE SOCIAL MEANING OF AIDS

Peter Conrad

Disease and illness can be examined on different levels. Disease is understood best as a biophysiological phenomenon, a process or state that affects the body. Illness, by contrast, has more to do with the social and psychological phenomena that surround the disease. The world of illness is the subjective world of meaning and interpretation; how a culture

SOURCE: From *Social Policy*, Summer 1986, 51-56. Copyright ©1986 by Social Policy Corporation. Reprinted by permission.

defines an illness and how individuals experience their disorder.

In this article I am going to examine the social and cultural meanings of Acquired Immunodeficiency Syndrome or AIDS as it is manifested in late-20th-century America and relate these meanings to the social reaction that it has engendered. When I talk about the social meaning of AIDS, I am including what Susan Sontag has termed the metaphorical aspects of illness: those meanings of diseases that are used to reflect back on some morally suspect element of society.[1] As Sontag suggests, metaphorical aspects of illness are especially prevalent with dread diseases that have great unknowns about them. We need to look at AIDS not only as a biomedical entity, but as an illness that has a socially constructed image and engages particular attitudes. The social meanings of AIDS are simultaneously alarmingly simple and bafflingly complex, but are key to understanding the social reaction to AIDS.

The Social Reaction to AIDS

Five years ago virtually no one had heard of AIDS. In the past five years, however, AIDS has become a household term and a feared intruder in the society.

The medical reality of AIDS, as we know it, remains puzzling but is becoming clearer. AIDS is a disease caused by a virus that breaks down the immune system and leaves the body unprotected against "opportunistic infections" that nearly invariably lead to death. The number of AIDS cases is growing dramatically

and AIDS is considered an epidemic in the society. Over 19,000 cases have been diagnosed, with four or five times that many people having a chronic disorder called AIDS-Related Complex (ARC) and perhaps over a million individuals having an antibody-positive response to HTLV-III, the virus believed to cause AIDS. It is estimated that 5 to 20 percent of this exposed group will contract AIDS, but no one knows who they will be.

Over 90 percent of AIDS victims come from two risk groups: homosexual or bisexual men and intravenous drug users. (Hemophiliacs and others requiring frequent blood transfusions and infants born to mothers with AIDS are also considered risk groups.) The evidence is clear that the AIDS virus is transmitted through the direct exchange of bodily fluids, semen and blood; the most common mode of transmission is anal intercourse among male homosexuals and unsterile needle-sharing among intravenous drug users. There is virtually *no* evidence that the virus can be transmitted by everyday "casual contact," including kissing or shaking hands, or exposure to food, air, water, or whatever.[2] With the exception of very specific modes of semen or blood-related transmission, it does not appear that the AIDS virus is very easy to "catch."

Yet the public reaction to AIDS has bordered on hysteria. Below are a few examples of the reactions to AIDS or AIDS victims.

- 11,000 children were kept out of school in Queens, New

York, as parents protested the decision to allow a 7-year-old girl with AIDS to attend second grade (despite no evidence of transmission by school children).

- Hospital workers in San Francisco refused to enter the room of an AIDS patient. When ordered to attend the patient, they appeared wearing masks, gowns, and goggles.

- A Baltimore policeman refused to enter the office of a patient with AIDS to investigate a death threat and donned rubber gloves to handle the evidence.

- A local school district in New Jersey tried to exclude a healthy 9-year-old boy whose sister has ARC (despite no sign of sibling transmission).

- An Amarillo, Texas, hospital fired a cafeteria worker who participated in a blood drive. This worker showed no signs of being ill nor unable to perform his duties, but his blood had registered seropositive.

- In early 1985, Delta Airlines proposed a rule (later dropped) forbidding the carrying of AIDS patients.

- In New York, undertakers refused to embalm AIDS victims, householders fired their Haitian help, and subway riders wore gloves, all from fear of contracting AIDS.

- One child, hospitalized with AIDS, had a "do not touch" sign on her bed and was isolated from all physical contact with her parents.

- The New York Times reported cases of dentists who refused to treat gay patients (not just confirmed AIDS cases).

- In Dallas, a small group of doctors and dentists formed Dallas Doctors Against AIDS and began a campaign to reinstate Texas' sodomy laws.

- In a Boston corporation, employees threatened to quit en masse if the company forced them to work with an AIDS patient.

- Dade County, Florida, voted to require the county's 80,000 food workers to carry cards certifying they are free of communicable diseases, including AIDS, despite no known cases of AIDS transmitted through food and even though public health officials opposed this policy.

- The U.S. military is beginning to screen all new recruits for AIDS anti-bodies, with the likely result of declaring those who test seropositive ineligible for service.

- Several major life insurance companies are requiring certain applicants (young, single, male, living in certain areas) to undergo an HTLV-III antibody test.

- Public health officials in Texas passed a measure allowing quarantine of certain AIDS patients. A candidate with a platform calling for the quarantining of all people with AIDS won the Democratic party's nomination for lieutenant governor in Illinois.

The list could go on. There is clearly a great fear engendered by the spectre of AIDS, a fear that has led to an overreaction to the actual problem. This is in no way to say that AIDS is not a terrible and devastating disease—it is—or to infer that it is not a serious public health concern. What we are seeing is an overblown, often irrational, and pointless reaction to AIDS that makes the disease more difficult for those who have it and diverts attention from the real public health concerns.

The Social and Cultural Meanings of AIDS

To better understand the reaction to AIDS, it is necessary to examine particular features of the disease: 1) the effect of marginal and stigmatized "risk groups"; 2) sexually-related transmission; 3) the role of contagion; and 4) the deadly nature of the disease.

The Effect of Marginal and Stigmatized "Risk Groups"

There are some illnesses that carry with them a certain moral devaluation, a stigma. Leprosy, epilepsy, mental disorder, venereal disease, and by some accounts, cancer, all reflect moral shame on the individuals who had the ill luck to contract them. Stigmatized illnesses are usually diseases that in some fashion are connected to deviant behavior: either they are deemed to produce it as with epilepsy or are produced by it, as in the case of VD.

The effect of the early connection of AIDS to homosexual conduct cannot be underestimated in examining its stigmatized image. The early designation of the disorder was Gay Related Immune Deficiency Syndrome (GRID) and was publicly proclaimed as a "gay plague." It was first thought to be caused by the use of "poppers" (amyl-nitrate) and later by promiscuity.[3] Something those fast-track gays were doing was breaking down their immune system. However, AIDS is not and never was specifically related to homosexual conditions; viruses don't know homosexuals from heterosexuals.

Within a short time, other "risk" groups were identified for what was now called AIDS—intravenous drug users, Haitians, and hemophiliacs. With the exception of hemophiliacs (who made up less than two percent of the cases), AIDS' image in the public eye was intimately connected with marginal populations. It was a disease of "those deviants," considered by some a deserved punishment for their activities. In 1983 Patrick J. Buchanan, who later became a White House staffer, wrote: "Those poor homosexuals. They have declared war on nature, and nature is exacting an awful retribution."[4] It is certain that fear of AIDS was amplified by the widespread and deeply rooted "homophobia" in American society.

Sexually-Related Transmission

The dominant vector of transmission of AIDS is through sexual activity, particularly anal intercourse of male homosexuals. Although scientifically AIDS is better seen as a "blood disease" (since contact with blood is necessary for transmission), this common form of transmission has contributed to its image as a sexually transmitted disease.

Venereal diseases are by nature also stigmatized. They are deemed to be the fault of the victims and would not occur had people behaved better. As Allen Brandt points out, venereal diseases have become a symbol of pollution and contamination: "Venereal disease, the palpable evidence of unrestrained sexuality, became a symbol for social disorder and moral decay—a metaphor of evil."[5]

AIDS, with its connection to multiple sex encounters and once-forbidden "sodomy," touches deep Puritanical concerns and revives alarms of promiscuity and "sexual permissiveness" that have become more muted in recent decades. The connection of AIDS to "sexual irresponsibility" has been made repeatedly.

Now that it appears AIDS can be transmitted through heterosexual intercourse as well, although apparently not as efficiently and rapidly, there is increasing concern among sexually active people that they may be betrayed in their most intimate moments. This connection with intimacy and sexuality amplifies our anxieties and creates fears that one sexual act may bring a lifetime of pollution and ultimately death.

The Role of Contagion

We have almost come to believe that large-scale deadly epidemics were a thing of the past. The polio panics of the early 1950s have receded far into our collective memory, and the wrath of tuberculosis, cholera, or diphtheria have become, in American society at least, artifacts of the past. Everyday models for contagion are more limited to the likes of herpes, chicken pox, and hepatitis. When we encounter AIDS, which is contagious but apparently in a very specific way, our fear of contagion erupts almost without limits. When little is known about a disease's transmission, one could expect widespread apprehensions about contagion. But a great deal is known about AIDS' transmission—it appears only to be transmitted through the exchange of bodily fluids and in *no* cases through any type of casual contact. In fact, compared to other contagious diseases it has a relatively low infectivity. Yet the fear of contagion fuels the reaction to AIDS.

Given our extant medical knowledge, what are the sources of fear? We live in a society where medicine is expected to protect us from deadly contagious diseases, if not by vaccine, then by public health intervention. And when medicine does not do this, we feel we must rely on our own devices to protect ourselves and our loved ones. Contagion, even of minor disorders, can engender irrational responses. Several months ago my 5-year-old daughter was exposed to a playmate who came down with chicken pox. A good friend of mine, who happens to be a pediatrician, did not want his 4-year-old to ride in the car with my daughter to gymnastics class, even though he knew medically that she could not yet be infectious. He just did not want to take any chances. And so it is with us, our reactions to contagion are not always rational.

With AIDS, of course, the situation is much worse. When we read in the newspapers that the AIDS virus has been found in saliva or tears, though only occasionally, we imagine in our commonsense germ-theory models of contagion that we could "catch AIDS" in this manner. Reports that no transmission has ever occurred in this fashion becomes secondary. The public attitudes seem to be that exposure to the AIDS virus condemns one to the disease.

While AIDS is contagious, so is the fear and stigma. The fear of AIDS has outstripped the actual social impact of the disease. But, more importantly for families of people who suffer from AIDS, the stigma of AIDS becomes contagious. They develop what Erving Goffman has called a courtesy stigma, a taint that has spread from the stigmatized to his or her close connections.[6] Family members of people with AIDS are shunned and isolated by former friends and colleagues, for fear that they too might bring contagion.

A Deadly Disease

AIDS is a devastating and deadly disease. It is virtually 100 percent lethal: 75 percent of people with AIDS die within two years. There are few other diseases that, like AIDS, attack and kill people who are just reach-

ing the prime of their lives. Currently, AIDS is incurable; since there are no treatments for it, to contract AIDS in the 1980s is to be served with a death warrant. Many sufferers waste away from Kaposi's sarcoma or some rare form of chronic pneumonia.

As various researchers have shown, caretakers and family alike tend to distance themselves from sufferers who are terminally ill with diseases that waste away their bodies.[7] The pain of suffering and the pollution of dying are difficult for many people to encounter directly in a society that has largely removed and isolated death from everyday life.

Taken together, these features form a cultural image of AIDS that is socially as well as medically devastating. It might even be said that AIDS is an illness with a triple stigma: it is connected to stigmatized groups (homosexuals and drug users); it is sexually transmitted; and, like cancer, it is a terminal, wasting disease. It would be difficult to imagine a scenario for a more stigmatizing disease, short of one that also makes those infected obviously visible.

The Effects of AIDS

The social meaning affects the consequences of AIDS, especially for AIDS sufferers and their families and the gay community but also for medicine and the public as well.

The greatest consequences of AIDS are of course for AIDS sufferers. They must contend with a ravaging disease and the stigmatized social response that can only make coping with it more difficult. In a time when social support is most needed, it may become least available. And in the context of the paucity of available medical treatments, those with AIDS must face the prospect of early death with little hope of survival.

People with ARC or those who test antibody-positive must live with the uncertainty of not knowing what the progression of their disorder will be. And living with this uncertainty, they must also live with the fear and stigma produced by the social meanings of AIDS. This may mean subtle disenfranchisement, overt discrimination, outright exclusion, or even total shunning. The talk of quarantine raises the anxiety of "why me?" Those symptomless seropositive individuals, who experts suggest have a 5 to 20 percent chance of developing full-blown AIDS, must live with the inner conflict of who to tell or not to tell, of how to manage their sexual and work lives, and the question of whether and how they might infect others. The social meanings of AIDS make this burden more difficult.

Families and lovers of people with AIDS, ARC, or an antibody-positive test are placed in an uncomfortable limbo status. Many live in constant fear that they might contract the AIDS virus, and thus limit their contact with the infected individual. Others wonder whether they too might be or become infectious. As mentioned earlier, families often share the AIDS stigma, as others see them as tainted, cease visiting their home, or even sever all contact with them. In one recent study of screening for AIDS among blood

donors, the researchers noted they "have interviewed people in the pilot phase of [their] notification program who have been left by their spouses or significant others after telling them about their blood test results."[8]

The gay community has been profoundly affected by AIDS. The late 1960s and 1970s were an exciting and positive period of the American gay community. Thousands of gay men and women came "out of the closet" and proclaimed in a variety of ways that "gay is good." Many laws forbidding gay sexual activity were removed from the books. Gay people developed their own community institutions and more openly experimented and practiced alternative lifestyles. Although the celebration of anonymous sex among some gay males resulted in high rates of sexually-transmitted diseases and hepatitis B, the social atmosphere in the gay community remained overwhelmingly positive. While the attitudes toward homosexuality never became totally accepting, public moral opprobrium toward gays was perceptibly reduced.[9]

And along came AIDS. With its image as a "gay disease" related to a fast-track gay male lifestyle, the fear of AIDS tapped into a reservoir of existing moral fear of homosexuals. It was a catalyst to the reemergence of a latent "homophobia" that had never really disappeared. Now there was a new reason to discriminate against gays. Thus AIDS has led to a restigmatization of homosexuality. Every avowed male homosexual is a suspected carrier of AIDS and deemed potentially dangerous. This, of course, has pushed many gay men back into the closet, living their lives with new fears and anxieties. It is clear that AIDS threatens two decades of social advances for the gay community.

Concern about AIDS has also become the overriding social and political concern of the gay community, consuming energy that previously went toward other types of social and political work. The gay community was the first to bring the AIDS problem into the public arena and to urge the media, medicine, and government to take action. Action groups in the gay community have engaged in extensive AIDS educational campaigns. This was done out of concern, but not without a fear of government surveillance and invasion of privacy. There was also apprehension that the images of "bad blood" and depictions of gays as health risks might lead to new exclusions of gays.[10]

The scourge of AIDS in the gay community has led, on the one hand, to divisions among gays (e.g., should bath houses be closed) and, on the other, to unprecedented changes in sexual behavior (e.g., witness the dramatic drop in the number of sex partners and types of sexual encounters reported in several studies and indexed by the large decrease in new cases of rectal gonorrhea).[11]

There is also a great emotional toll from the AIDS epidemic in the gay community. Nearly everyone in the community has friends or acquaintances who have died from the disease. As one gay activist recently put it, many people in the gay community were suffering a "grief-overload" as a result of the losses from AIDS.[12]

The social image of AIDS has affected medical care and scientific research as well. In general, the medical voice concerning AIDS, at least in terms of describing it to the public and outlining its perils, has on the whole been cautious and even-handed. The tenor of information has been factual and not unduly emotional. The Center for Disease Control (CDC) has again and again declared that AIDS is not transmitted by casual contact and, although it is a major epidemic and a public health threat, it is one with specific risk groups.

However, some medical scientists have placed the dangers of AIDS in a highly negative light either to raise the public's concern or to elicit private or governmental research funds. For example, "Dr. Alvin Friedman-Klein, an AIDS researcher who saw the first cases, said that AIDS will probably be the plague of the century."[13] Dr. Mathilde Krim was quoted in *The New York Post* last September as saying that "it is only a matter of time before it afflicts heterosexuals on a large scale" while presenting no evidence or data to support the claim.[14] The media, of course, picks up these assertions, often highlighting them in headlines, which reinforces the public fear.

The stigma of AIDS in a few cases has affected medical practice. There have been some reports of doctors, health workers, or hospitals who have refused to treat AIDS patients. But fortunately, these extreme examples are rare and, for the most part,

AIDS sufferers seem to have received at least adequate care from most medical facilities. But a mistrust of the ramifications of the public attitudes toward AIDS may well keep some "high risk" individuals from seeking medical diagnosis or care. The fear of being found seropositive and becoming a social pariah might well keep carriers of the AIDS virus from medical attention.

Finally, stigmatized attitudes toward a disease can constrain medical progress. As Allen Brandt points out, the negative social meanings attached to VD actually obstructed medical efforts. He noted that research funding was somewhat limited because the issue was thought to be best dealt with behaviorally. Among many VD researchers the discovery of penicillin was treated with ambivalence, since they were afraid a cure of syphilis would promote promiscuity.[15]

While medical scientists have recently gained a great deal of knowledge about AIDS, including isolating the virus, describing the modes of transmission, and developing a test for screening HTLV-III antibodies in blood (although it is imperfect for screening people[16]), the stigma AIDS presents has probably limited public funding for AIDS research and deterred some types of community research on AIDS natural history. Several commentators have noted that federal funding for research and prevention of AIDS was slow in emerging because AIDS was seen as a "gay disease." It was only when it threatened blood transfusions and blood products that public consciousness was aroused and fed-

eral support was forthcoming. Unfortunately, this increased support for research and education was "misinterpreted as an indicator that AIDS was a universal threat destined to work its way inexorably through all segments of society."[17]

One of the most striking aspects about the social reaction to AIDS is how fear and stigma have led to a resistance to information about AIDS. While at times the media has sensationalized AIDS, there has also been a great deal of information communicated concerning AIDS, its characteristics, and its modes of transmission. Yet study after study finds a small but substantial and consistent proportion of the population that exhibits profound misinformation about AIDS. An October, 1985, Harris Poll reported that 50 percent of those asked believed one could get AIDS from living in the same house with someone who had it or from "casual contact," and one-third of the respondents thought that one can catch it from "going to a party where someone with AIDS is."[18]

Another study of high school students in San Francisco found that 41.9 percent believed you could get AIDS if kissed by someone with the disease; 17.1 percent thought if you touched someone with the disease you could get AIDS; 15.3 percent believed just being around someone with AIDS can give you the disease; and 11.6 percent thought all gay men have AIDS.[19] In a study of adolescents in Ohio, fully 60 percent believed that touching or coming near a person with AIDS might transmit the disease.[20] These authors contend that low knowledge of AIDS is correlated with high perceived susceptibility.

In a survey in San Francisco, New York, and London, the researchers found that "more knowledge was significantly negatively correlated with general fear of AIDS and with anti-gay attitudes among risk groups."[21] It appears that rather than low knowledge creating fear, the social meaning of AIDS creates resistance and barriers to taking in accurate information about AIDS.

Such misinformation is also prevalent among health-care providers. In a Massachusetts study of the effect of AIDS educational programs on health-care providers, the researchers reported that before the program, "20.5 percent of providers thought AIDS could be transmitted by shaking hands and 17.2 percent thought it could be acquired simply by being in the same room with a patient."[22] Many of these beliefs seem resistant to change. In the Massachusetts study, "after the [educational] programs, 15 percent of the providers still thought AIDS could be transmitted by sneezing or coughing, and 11.3 percent thought it could be transmitted by shaking hands. [In addition] after the . . . programs, the majority (66.2 percent) still thought that gowns were always necessary and a substantial minority (46.3 percent) still considered quarantine necessary."[23] While the educational programs affected some change in knowledge about AIDS, the researchers found a strong resistance to changing knowledge and attitudes among a substantial minority of health-care providers. Such misinformation among health-care providers can only have negative effects on AIDS patients.

One of the social tragedies of the fear and stigma is that it has constrained compassion for AIDS sufferers. In our culture, we generally show caring and compassion for severely and terminally ill patients. The social meaning of AIDS mutes this compassion in families, among health-care providers, and with the public at large. It is a shame that a victim of any disease in our society must suffer the plight of Robert Doyle of Baltimore. After discovering he had pneumonia brought on by AIDS, no nursing home or hospice would take him. His family rejected him and his lover demanded that he move out of the apartment. With only months to live, he had no support, resources, or place to die. He finally rented a room in a run-down hotel, where the staff refused to enter the room and left food for him in the hallway. After a newspaper story, a stranger took him into her home, only to ask him to leave in a few days; next an elderly couple took him in, until threatening telephone calls and vandalism forced him to move again. He finally found a home with three other adults, one also an AIDS victim. Soon he was returned to the hospital where he died.[24] The fear of AIDS turned this sick and dying man into a social outcast.

Conclusion

The social meaning of AIDS has added to the victim-blaming response common to sexually and behaviorally-related diseases a powerful victim-fearing component. This has engendered an overreaction to the perils of AIDS and fueled the public fears of the disease. Some dangers and threats are, of course, very real, but the triple stigma of AIDS presents a frightening picture to the public, which leads to misguided attempts at "protection" and to resistance to contrary information. This only makes managing life more difficult for the sufferers and does not make the world "safer" from AIDS.

Since a medical cure or prevention for AIDS in the near future is unlikely, it is important that efforts be made to reduce the "hysteria" and overreaction surrounding this disease. We need to redouble our efforts to diffuse the unwarranted aspects of the fear of AIDS and to reduce its stigma. There are several strategies for attempting to accomplish this.

AIDS appears to be "out of control." If some type of medical intervention emerged that could limit the spread and/or symptoms of the disease, this sense of lack of control might be decreased and the public expectations of medicine's protective function might be somewhat restored. But given the historical examples of epilepsy and syphilis, available and efficacious medical treatments do not in themselves alter the image of a disorder. The stigma of these diseases, while perhaps reduced, are still prevalent in our society.

Activists, policymakers, and medical personnel must directly attempt to change the image of the disease.

Sometimes a disease's stigmatized image is reinforced by incorrect information. A classic example is the notion that leprosy was highly contagious and sufferers needed to be placed in isolated colonies. We know now that leprosy is not easily communicable. With epilepsy, myths developed that both emerged from and sustained the stigma including notions like epilepsy is an inherited disease or it causes crime. These myths often gained professional support and led to misguided public policies such as forbidding marriage or immigration.[25] Such incorrect information and mythology must be unmasked and not be allowed to become the basis for social policies.

Another strategy to reduce stigma is to "normalize" the illness; that is, to demonstrate that not only "deviants" get the disease. It is important to show that conventional people can suffer the disease and, to the extent possible, lead normal lives. For example, Rock Hudson's belated public disclosure of his AIDS was an important symbol. He was identified as a solid, clean-cut American man, almost an ideal. He was also a movie hero with whom many people had made some kind of vicarious relationship. To a certain extent Rock Hudson helped bring AIDS out of the closet. An important public policy strategy should be to "normalize" AIDS as much as possible—to present exemplars of people who still can live relatively normal, if difficult, lives, with positive antibodies, ARC, or even AIDS. The media has done this to a degree with children—depicted as innocent victims of the disease—but we need to bring other

AIDS sufferers back into our world and recreate our compassion for them.

We need to develop policies that focus on changing the image of AIDS and confront directly the stigma, resistance to information, and the unnecessary fears of the disease. Given the social meaning of AIDS, this won't be easy. While studies have shown us how difficult it is to change public attitudes toward illnesses,[26] images of diseases like leprosy (Hanson's disease) and, to a lesser degree, epilepsy have changed. We must develop the professional and public resolve to change the social meanings and response to AIDS and make this a high priority, along with the control, treatment, and eventual eradication of the disease. It is incumbent upon us to reduce the social as well as the physical suffering from AIDS.

Notes

1. Susan Sontag, *Illness as Metaphor* (New York: Farrar, Straus and Giroux, 1978).
2. Merle A. Sande, "The Transmission of AIDS: The Case against Casual Contagion," *New England Journal of Medicine*, vol. 314 (1986), pp. 380–82. See also, June E. Osborn, "The AIDS Epidemic: An Overview of the Science," *Issues in Science and Technology* (Winter, 1986), pp. 40–55.
3. Jacques Liebowitch, *A Strange Virus of Unknown Origin* (New York: Ballantine, 1985), pp. 3–4.
4. Cited in Matt Clark et al., "AIDS," *Newsweek* (October 12, 1984), pp. 20–24, 26–27.
5. Allen M. Brandt, *No Magic Bullet* (New York: Oxford University Press, 1985), p. 92.
6. Erving Goffman, *Stigma* (Englewood Cliffs, NJ: Prentice-Hall, 1963), pp. 30–31.
7. Sontag, 1978. See also, Anselm Strauss and Barney Glaser, *Awareness of Dying* (Chicago: Aldine, 1965).
8. Paul D. Cleary et al., "Theoretical Issues in Health Education about AIDS Risk." Unpublished paper, Department of Social Medicine and Health Policy, Harvard Medical School, 1986.
9. Peter Conrad and Joseph W. Schneider, *Deviance and Medicalization: From Badness to Sickness* (St. Louis: C. V. Mosby, 1980).
10. Ronald Bayer, "AIDS and The Gay Community: Between the Specter and the Promise of Medicine," *Social Research* (Autumn, 1985), pp. 581–606.
11. Donald E. Riesenberg, "AIDS-Prompted Behavior Changes Reported," *Journal of the American Medical Association* (January 10, 1986), pp. 171–72; Ronald Stall, "The Behavioral Epidemiology of AIDS: A Call for Anthropological Contributions," *Medical Anthropology Quarterly* (February, 1986), pp. 36–37; Jonathan Lieberson, "The Reality of AIDS," *New York Review of Books* (January 16, 1986), p. 47.
12. Christopher Collins, "Homosexuals and AIDS: An Inside View," Paper presented to the American Society of Law and Medicine conference on "AIDS: A Modern Plague?" Boston, April, 1986.
13. Lieberson, 1986, p. 45.
14. Ibid., p. 46.
15. Brandt, 1985, p. 137.
16. Carol Levine and Ronald Bayer, "Screening Blood: Public Health and Medical Uncertainty," *Hastings Center Report* (August, 1985), pp. 8–11.
17. George F. Grady, "A Practitioner's Guide to AIDS," *Massachusetts Medicine* (January/February, 1986), pp.

44–50. See also, Kenneth W. Payne and Stephen J. Risch, "The Politics of AIDS," *Science for the People* (September/October, 1984), pp. 17–24.

18. Cited in Lieberson, 1986, p. 44.
19. Ralph J. DiClemente, Jim Zorn, and Lydia Temoshok, "A Large-Scale Survey of Adolescents' Knowledge, Attitudes, and Beliefs about AIDS in San Francisco: A Needs Assessment." Paper presented at the meetings of the Society for Behavioral Medicine, March, 1986.
20. Cited in Ibid., p. 4.
21. Lydia Temoshok, David M. Sweet, and Jane Zich, "A Cross-Cultural Analysis of Reactions to the AIDS Epidemic." Paper presented at the meetings of the Society for Behavioral Medicine, March, 1986.

22. Dorothy C. Wertz et al., "Research on the Educational Programs of the AIDS Action Committee of the Fenway Community Health Center: Final Report." Submitted to the Massachusetts Department of Public Health, AIDS Research Program, 1985, p. 11.
23. Ibid., p. 12
24. Jean Seligman and Nikki Fink Greenberg, "Only Months to Live and No Place to Die," *Newsweek* (August 12, 1985), p. 26.
25. Joseph W. Schneider and Peter Conrad, *Having Epilepsy: The Experience and Control of Illness* (Philadelphia: Temple University Press, 1983), pp. 22–46.
26. Elaine Cumming and John Cumming, *Closed Ranks* (Cambridge: Harvard University Press, 1957).

28   CONCERNS ABOUT MEDICAL TECHNOLOGY

H. David Banta, Clyde J. Behney, and Jane Sisk Willems

The concerns about the effects of medical technologies parallel those in other areas of technology: How can we identify the appropriate role of the technologies in question? And how can we assure that they will be put to that most appropriate use? For medical technologies, appropriate use depends on such factors as the health benefits and risks of the technologies, their financial effects, and their effects on social systems and values (Banta et al., 1979).

Benefits of Medical Technology

In many instances knowledge about disease has made it possible to develop effective methods of control—that is, technology. In some cases, this knowledge has been the result of epidemiological research, as when John Snow recognized patterns of cholera in London, resulting from ingestion of water from the Broad Street pump, and removed the handle of the pump as a disease preventive (MacMahon, 1960, pp. 154–155). Other preventive measures, such as vaccines, have resulted in part from knowl-

From *Toward Rational Technology in Medicine* (New York: Springer Publishing Company, 1981), pp. 11–19. Reprinted with permission.

edge of the structure of microorganisms; and many diagnostic and curative technologies have resulted from biomedical research, as well as research in such areas as engineering and physics.

These successes are most clearly seen in the case of infectious diseases. Vaccines have been developed for many of them. In other cases, antibiotics have made treatment and cure possible. Bennett has listed the following lethal and dangerous infectious diseases that medical technology can now control effectively: epidemic meningitis, infantile diarrhea, epidemic typhus, trachoma, scarlet fever, cholera, yellow fever, bacterial endocarditis, typhoid fever, leprosy, syphilis, gonorrhea, lobar pneumonia, malaria, measles, rubella, whooping cough, diptheria, smallpox, tetanus, puerperal sepsis, and neonatal infection (Bennett, 1977). Figure 1 shows that in 1900 the leading causes of death were influenza and pneumonia, tuberculosis, gastritis, diseases of the heart, vascular lesions affecting the central nervous system, accidents, chronic nephritis, malignant neoplasms, diseases of early infancy, and diptheria. Although six of these remain in the top ten causes of death in 1967 statistics, their relative importance has changed, so that the chronic diseases now predominate. Mushkin (1979, p. 24) has reviewed studies of the costs and benefits of biomedical research, and finds some dramatic successes.

Many chronic diseases have also become controllable. Some examples are pellagra, rickets, scurvy, erythroblastosis fetalis, Addison's disease, juvenile diabetes, and certain types of cancer (Bennett, 1977). However, many chronic diseases do not have effective preventive and treatment measures. Large investments in biomedical research, high public expectations, and generous reimbursement systems have all helped to foster a kind of technology in these cases, which Thomas has called "halfway technology" (1974, p. 34). Such technologies are attempts to compensate for the incapacitating effects of certain diseases whose course one is unable to do much about. "It is a technology designed to make up for disease, or to postpone death." Thomas cites transplantations of hearts, kidneys, livers, and other organs, and the equally spectacular artificial organs. These measures address those diseases for which no definitive technology is available: stroke, heart attack, congestive heart failure, most forms of cancer, atherosclerosis, cirrhosis of the liver, emphysema, glomerulonephritis, pyelonephritis, osteoarthritis, asthma, multiple sclerosis, senility, schizophrenia, depression, mental retardation, muscular dystrophy, cystic fibrosis, and so forth (Bennett, 1977). It is not true that medicine has nothing to offer for these diseases. Rather, what it has to offer is often caring for the person rather than curing the disease. The result may be increased comfort or mobility, relief of pain, and reduced anxiety. These technologies often lack dramatic benefit, and they are often very expensive (Rosenthal, 1979).

From the above discussion it is clear that medical technologies have

FIGURE 1   Percent of All Deaths, by Specified Causes of Death* (U.S.A., 1900** and 1974)

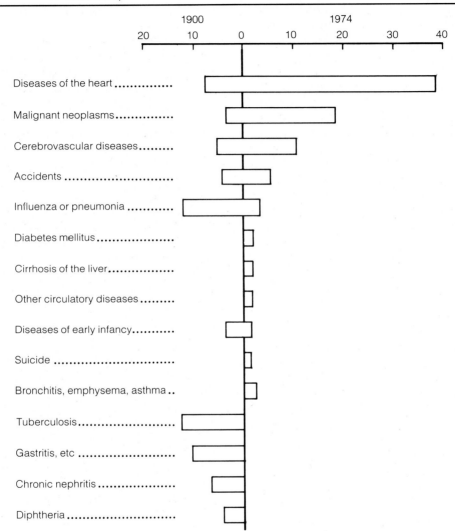

*10 leading causes of death in 1900 and 1974, with the latter arranged in descending order of importance.
**Death registration states only.

SOURCES: (1) for 1900: U.S. National Office of Vital Statistics. *Vital Statistics of the United States, 1950, Vol. 1,* Washington, D.C., 1950, table 2.26, p. 170.
(2) for 1974: U.S. Department of Health, Education, and Welfare. Public Health Service, National Center for Health Statistics. *Monthly Vital Statistics Report.* Vol. 23. no. 13. May 1975, table C, p.3.
This figure is reprinted by permission of the University of Michigan. It appeared as chart B-5, *Medical Care Chartbook*, sixth edition, 1976.

helped provide effective care to millions of people. They indisputably provide dramatic benefits in some cases and are of some benefit in many others. How much benefit is gained, and—critically—under what circumstances, however, remains relatively unknown. Concerns have been raised about the benefits of a great many modern technologies; for example, electronic fetal monitoring (Banta and Thacker, 1979), other obstetric practices (Chalmers and Richards, 1977), respiratory therapy (Barach and Segal, 1975), and oral drugs for diabetes (Knatterud et al., 1971; Chalmers, 1975).

McKeown has approached the question of the importance of medical technology historically (1976). He describes the vast improvement in health during the past three centuries, and concludes that nutrition and the physical environment have been much more important for the prevention of sickness and death than have personal health care services. Death rates in England and Wales fell from about 22 per 1000 in 1841 to about 6 per 1000 in 1971. He shows that 92 percent of the fall between 1848 and 1901, and 73 percent from 1901 to 1971, is due to reduction in the number of deaths from infectious diseases. The greatest contributor to this fall was tuberculosis, which he analyzes in depth.

Figure 2 shows annual death rates due to respiratory tuberculosis beginning in 1838. The death rate has fallen steadily, although chemotherapy for tuberculosis did not begin until 1948. Figure 3 shows the period 1921 to 1970 in more detail, and it can be seen that after 1948 there is a change in the trend in the death rate, indicating an effect of therapy.

McKeown (1976) also examines other disease conditions. After tuberculosis, the greatest causes of mortality have been bronchitis, pneumonia, and influenza. The death rate for these conditions has been little affected by the introduction of antibiotics. Based on these and other observations, McKeown draws the following conclusions (pp. 93–94):

1. Improvement in nutrition was the earliest, and, over the whole period since about 1700, the most important influence.

2. Hygienic measures were responsible for at least a fifth of the reduction of the death-rate between the mid nineteenth century and today. . . .

3. With the exception of vaccination against smallpox, whose contribution was small, the influence of immunization and therapy on the death-rate was delayed until the twentieth century, and had little effect on national mortality trends before the introduction of sulphonamides in 1935. Since that time it has not been the only, or probably the most important influence.

4. The change in reproductive practice which led to the decline of the birthrate was also very significant. . . .

He states in summary, "We have overestimated the effectiveness of

FIGURE 2   Respiratory Tuberculosis: Mean Annual Death Rates (Standardized to 1901 Population): England and Wales

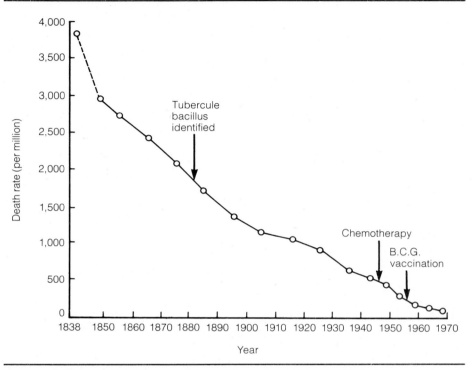

many procedures and services in current use, and indeed most have been adopted without adequate evaluation" (pp. 118–119). Note that this does not imply that technology has been unimportant in the improvement in death rates, but rather that it has been environmental and other technologies more than clinical medical technologies that have brought the impact.

Mushkin has criticized this approach as putting too much emphasis on one biomedical advance. Using a different approach, a multivariate analysis of the products of research and of mortality rates, she finds that biomedical advances accounted for 30 to 40 percent of the reduction in deaths during the period 1900 to 1975.

It should also be noted that medical care is more than just technology. Diseases occur in people, who have fears and anxieties. Therefore, much of medical practice is taken up with psychological problems and physical complaints that do not require the application of technology, but do require a concerned health care provider to provide reassurance and advice. Furthermore, there is no

FIGURE 3   Respiratory Tuberculosis: Annual Death Rates of Males: England and Wales.

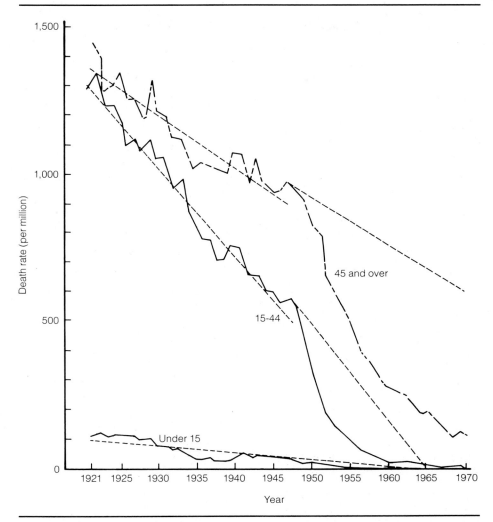

SOURCE: McKeown, T. *The Role of Medicine: Dream, Mirage or Nemesis?* London: Nuffield Provincial Hospitals Trust, 1976. Redrawn by OTA. Used by permission.

effective therapy for many chronic conditions. "Traditionally, medical care has served as much to relieve pain and anxiety and system function as it has to effect cures. Medical care is a highly personalized service with both physical and psychologic elements; these are highly related in the consumer's motivation to seek service and in the physician's ability to achieve cooperation by his advice and to change behavior to be conductive to health" (Sun Valley Forum, 1972).

Risks of Medical Technology

All technology has risks. In many cases, these are small, unquantifiable risks, and perhaps can be ignored if benefits are significant. However, the risks of many medical technologies are significant and have not been taken fully into account.

Drug risks have perhaps been more publicized than any other. It was the effect of thalidomide on the unborn child that led to the 1962 amendments to the Food, Drug, and Cosmetic Act (Dowling, 1970, p. 201). A more recent dramatic example of a side effect is the vaginal cancer now appearing in young women whose mothers were given estrogens during pregnancy (Lambert, 1978, p. 94). Although these are dramatic, the more typical risk is probably similar to that which accompanies drug treatment for hypertension: dizziness, impotence, and general tiredness (OTA, 1978, p. 49). Although not life-threatening, these side effects are annoying enough to keep many patients from taking medication faithfully.

The risks of major surgery are obvious. For example, the risks of coronary bypass surgery include a hospital mortality of about 4 percent and myocardial infarction during surgery in about 7 percent of patients (Avery et al., 1976, pp. 429–431). Morbidity from complications such as thrombophlebitis (clots in the leg veins) is common with any major surgical procedure. Estimates of deaths from tonsillectomy range as high as 300 per year in the United States (OTA, 1978a, p. 44).

In many cases the risks are not so obvious. For example, screening for breast cancer by mammography, a special X-ray examination, exposes the breast to X-rays, which themselves cause cancer. The dose from the procedure can be below one rad, which has not been proved to be associated with a measurable risk. The risk of such X-rays may be finite, but this has not been quantified (OTA, 1978a, p. 33; BEIR Report, 1972).

Since essentially all technology is associated with risk, it is necessary to consider benefit in relation to risk for any given technology.

Financial Costs of Medical Technology

Medical technology has become a policy issue primarily because of the rapidly rising expenditures on medical care. Health expenditures as a percentage of the Gross National Product have doubled from 4.5 percent in 1950 to 9.1 percent in 1978 (National Center for Health Statistics, 1980, p. 244). These changes are primarily attributable to changes in the size, complexity, and cost of the service package provided by hospital or physician, and are not due to increased utilization of services (Hanft et al., 1978). The price of a semiprivate hospital room more than tripled from 1965 to 1975, and physician fees nearly doubled over this 10-year period.

These dramatic increases have led to a search for the culprit (Altman and Blendon, 1979). The profusion of costly medical equipment is an obvious contributor to rising expenditures, and indeed Federal officials have concluded: "the long-term cumulative effect of adopting new health care technology is a major cause of the large yearly increases in national health expenditures" (Gaus and Cooper, 1978). Various attempts have been made to quantify the contribution of technology to these increases. It does appear that technology accounts for up to 50 percent of the increase in the cost of hospital care over the last decade. However, analyses have not shown clearly what type of technology is most responsible for the rising costs. "Are the increases mostly small ticket items, such as tests and procedures, or are they big ticket purchases, such as open heart surgical units and intensive care facilities. Also we cannot say what proportion of the increase was the result of technological advances or other factors, such as billing equipment" (Altman and Wallack, 1979). The work of Scitovsky and McCall (1976) documents a rise in the cost of treating a number of conditions over time, and shows that the cost rise resulted from more diagnostic and therapeutic procedures. For example, the average number of diagnostic tests for a perforated appendix rose from 5.3 in 1951 to 31.0 in 1971. This work is suggestive, but needs to be replicated and extended.

The contribution of a number of discrete technologies to rising costs has been analyzed. Although this work does not indicate which are the most important causes of the rise, it does have credibility in documenting that technology does cause

a rise in costs. For example, intensive care alone has been found to account for approximately 15 percent of 1975 hospital costs (Russell, 1979). The costs of CT scanning are more than $500 million a year (Banta, 1980). The cost of renal dialysis is nearing $1 billion a year (Rettig, 1979). The costs of diagnosis appear to be increasing rapidly, with a cost of clinical laboratory services between $15 and $20 billion a year and a cost of X-rays of about $5 billion a year (OTA, 1976).

Thus, there seems little doubt that medical technology is a significant factor in the rising cost of medical care; hence there is pressure to scrutinize its value.

Social Impacts of Medical Technology

The effects of medical technologies on health (benefits and risks) and on costs are usually the most direct and obvious implications of their use. However, some medical technologies have social implications that may be at least as important as those more direct effects. For example, who can deny that the birth control pill and other contraceptive technologies have had enormous social impact? The changes in our society's values and institutions that have occurred in whole or in part because of birth control techniques include altered sexual mores and a changing role for women in society (McConnell, 1974).

Renal dialysis is another example. Questions have been raised about: Who shall live? (Whom shall we dialyze if we can't dialyze everyone in need? How do we decide?) Who will pay? (Most renal dialysis is now covered by a special program of Medicare.) This is more than a question of finances because it raises issues of individual and social responsibility, equity, and whether there is a right to life and health (Fox and Swazey, 1974, 1979). What is the impact on the quality of life for those on dialysis three times a week for the rest of their lives?

Procedures such as amniocentesis (testing for chromosomal abnormalities and biochemical defects in the fetus) raise questions about manipulating society's gene pool, about increased abortions, about societal sex ratios, and others. The artificial heart has overpowering ethical, economic, and psychiatric implications (OTA, 1976; National Heart and Lung Institute, 1973).

The use of medical technologies can affect: (1) ethics and morals, changing or challenging our fundamental values or beliefs; (2) the legal and political system, pertaining to allocating scarce resources, defining death and life, informed consent, and so on; and (3) the economic system, going beyond issues of the cost of health care by affecting such factors as employment, productivity, and the necessity for and size of income maintenance programs. In fact, medical technologies, dealing as they do with health, which is a socially defined concept, can affect nearly every aspect of society and its institutions (Illich, 1976).

Not all or even most medical technologies have such significant social implications. The importance of this type of implication, however, lies not in how frequently it may occur, but in the degree of social upheaval that may be caused. The aggregate effect of the many new technologies of medicine is itself important. Also, these types of effects are of concern because of the subtlety of their occurrence; they are often very difficult to anticipate or to identify.

References

Altman, S. and Wallack, S. Technology on Trial—Is It the Culprit Behind Rising Health Costs? The Case For and Against. In Altman, S. and Blendon, R. (Eds.), *Medical Technology: The Culprit Behind Health Care Costs?* DHEW Publication No. (PHS) 79–3216. Hyattsville, Maryland: National Center for Health Services Research and Bureau of Health Planning, 1979.

Avery, A. et al. *Quality of Medical Care Assessment Using Outcome Measures: Eight Disease-Specific Applications.* Santa Monica, California: Rand, 1976.

Banta, D. The Diffusion of the Computed Tomography (CT) Scanner in the United States. *Int. J. Health Services* 10:251, 1980.

Banta, D. and Thacker, S. Assessing the Costs and Benefits of Electronic Fetal Monitoring. *Obstet. Gyn. Survey 34* (Suppl.):627, 1979.

Banta, D. et al., Weighing the Benefits and Costs of Medical Technologies. *Proc. IEEE 67*:1190, 1979.

Barach, A. and Segal, M. The Indiscriminate Use of IPPB. *JAMA 231*:1141, 1975.

BEIR Report. *The Effects on Populations of Exposure to Low Levels of Ionizing Radiation.* Report of the Advisory Committee on the Biological Effects of Ionizing

Radiations. Washington, D.C.: National Academy of Sciences, 1972.

Bennett, I. Technology as a Shaping Force. *Daedalus 106:*125, 1977.

Chalmers, I. and Richards, M. Intervention and Causal Inference in Obstetric Practice. In Chard, T. and Richards, M. (Eds.), *Benefits and Hazards of the New Obstetrics.* London: Heinemann Medical Books. 1977.

Chalmers, T. Settling the UGDP Controversy. *JAMA 231:*624, 1975.

Dowling, H. *Medicines for Man.* New York: Alfred A. Knopf, 1970.

Fox, R. and Swazey, J. *The Courage to Fail.* Chicago: University of Chicago Press. 1974.

Fox, R. and Swazey, J. Kidney Dialysis and Transplantation. In Fox, R., *Essays in Medical Sociology: Journeys into the Field.* New York: John Wiley & Sons, Inc., 1979.

Gaus, C. and Cooper, B. Technology and Medicare: Alternatives for Change. In Egdahl, R. and Gertman, P. (Eds.), *Technology and the Quality of Health Care.* Germantown, Maryland: Aspen Systems Corporation, 1978.

Hanft, R. et al. *Hospital Cost Containment.* New York: Prodist (for the Milbank Memorial Fund), 1978.

Illich, I. *Medical Nemesis: The Expropriation of Health.* New York: Pantheon Books, Random House, Inc., 1976.

Knatterud, G. et al. Effects of Hypoglycemic Agents on Vascular Complications in Patients with Adult-Onset Diabetes. *JAMA 217:*777, 1971.

Lambert, E. C. *Modern Medical Mistakes.* Bloomington, Indiana: Indiana University Press, 1978.

Rettig, R. The Role of Formal Analysis in Federal Policy Formulation Toward End-Stage Renal Disease. Draft Paper for the Office of Technology Assessment, Congress of the United States, Washington, D.C., 1979.

Scitovsky, A. Changes in the Use of Ancillary Services for Common Illness. In Altman, S. and Blendon, R. (Eds.), *Medical Technology: The Culprit Behind Health Care Costs?* DHEW Publication No. (PHS) 79—3216. Hyattsville, Maryland: National Center for Health Services Research and Bureau of Health Planning, 1979.

Sun Valley Forum on National Health. Medical Cure and Medical Care. Summary. *Milbank Memorial Fund Quarterly 50:*231,1972.

Thomas, K. *Religion and the Decline of Magic.* New York: Charles Scribner & Sons, 1971.

Part III

The Health Care Work Force

INTRODUCTION

Although other sections of this book look at various kinds of interactions between health providers and their clients, it is important to spend time looking at the structural makeup of the health care work force. These are the people who provide direct patient care in offices, clinics, and hospitals. If we saw patient care as the sole or primary goal in health care delivery, we might expect that members of the health work force would have a unified agenda. But professional and nonprofessional groups have different, and often conflicting, goals. These goals include the different work groups' particular needs for control of the work process, control of relations with other groups, and general advancement of the profession or group. Even when different groups do agree that patient care is central, they might have drastically different points of view, as we know from classic tales of discrepancies of patient care practices between nurses and physicians. If we understand the background and interests of the groups that make up the health work force, we can better understand their actions in the health care system.

Part III is divided into two sections. The first, "Physicians," gives us material on the historical development of the medical profession, the uncertainties facing medical students, and the role of women physicians in a changing work force. The section titled "Nonphysician Providers" offers studies of two professional groups (nurses and chiropractors) and one nonprofessional group (nursing home aides). Although there are clearly other groups in the health care work force that deserve attention, we focus on a select few due to space limitations; the lessons of group differences and conflict are applicable to other groups.

Physicians

If health and illness are so salient because of their life-and-death nature, then it is no surprise that doctors are held in such importance, since they are often the people who exercise that control over life. Yet physicians are viewed in a curiously ambivalent way by the public. They are often endowed with great power and authority, even with magical qualities. Yet at the same time, they are blamed for our personal misfortunes and for situations that may well be outside of their control. To be sure, contemporary culture questions the authority of the doctor. Doctors have faced changes in salaried versus self-employed status, in the centrality of the hospital as a location for medical practice, in the growth of for-profit hospital chains, in the control over who pays their bills, in the degree to which their medical work is monitored and regulated by state and federal governments, and in ethical and legal challenges to their practice decisions. Yet it would be incorrect to say, as some theorists do, that medical authority has eroded.

Physicians have always been a group that serves as a focus for the study of professions. Our definitions of what a profession is, notions of professional socialization, and beliefs about professional-lay relations often stem from our observation of physicians. Physicians provide a basis upon which to study how professionals codify a body of knowledge, certify a method of training, determine a model of legal licensure and control, police themselves, and define their relationship to the society at large. As many sociologists note, physicians are the profession *par excellence*, and this has strongly influenced medical sociologists who have studied medical education, diagnostic conceptualization, practice styles, and professional group behavior. Sociologists have also been interested in the political clout of physicians, ranging from legislative lobbying to cultural and ideological commentary.

Paul Starr's contribution, "The Growth of Medical Authority," takes a historical look at how organized medicine grew and how this growth went hand in hand with the growth of hospitals (a look back to Charles Rosenberg's article on the development of hospitals would be a valuable complement to the Starr piece). Starr shows the interconnection between social mobility and the struggle for cultural authority, placing this in the context of both internal professional development and larger changes in the sociocultural realm. We see here the development of the previously mentioned elements of professionalism in Starr's discussion of personal versus institutionalized authority, mechanisms of legitimation, and physicians' historical maneuverings to gain power and authority. In their professional development, physicians have achieved what sociologists call *medical dominance*, their control over other health care professionals and groups. Of special interest is Starr's notion that physicians' expansion both created a new marketplace for their services and at the same time restricted the marketplace due to the social need to regulate the medical world. An understanding of the many issues in this article can illuminate the upcoming Part IV of this book, "Relations between Patients and Providers."

The lay public may wish for scientific certainty on the part of doctors, and so may the doctors themselves. Yet science is full of uncertainties. Facing this uncertainty and coming to grips with it is an integral part of medical education. Based on her intensive field work in a medical school, Renée Fox's "Training for Uncertainty" gives us a picture of the conflicts and contradictions in medical education. She finds three forms of uncertainty in medical education: the first from incomplete mastery of medical knowledge, the second from the limits of available knowledge itself, and the third from the difficulty in distinguishing between the first and second types. Many sociologists have used Fox's uncertainty framework to study the practice of medicine following medical school. Uncertainty and contradiction continue to play an important role in the doctor's world. This has important implications for medicine as a profession since medicine cannot in fact be as certain about its knowledge and skills as it would like. The current malpractice crisis is perhaps the most significant reflection of this problem; injured and dissatisfied patients often argue that they should not be subject to any level of uncertainty about medical outcomes.

The profession of medicine has undergone a number of significant changes in the last decade or two. There has been increasing specialization and subspecialization, a shift toward more group and salaried practice, and the easier entry of women and minorities into the field. In comparing women physicians in the United States, England, and the Soviet Union, Judith Lorber's "Women Physicians in Three Countries" argues that women physicians have become a kind of "reserve army of labor" and have wound up largely at the lower end of whatever internal stratification system exists. Even in the Soviet Union, where women are a majority of all doctors, they are found in the less prestigious and less powerful sectors of medical practice. Lorber believes, however, that the stratification system alone does not completely determine the career paths of women physicians. She argues that women doctors make a choice of moving up the hierarchy or working with others in a woman-identified cooperative approach for social reform. The study of the status of women physicians provides insights into more than the system of medical stratification. As Lorber queries, if women in the very powerful profession of medicine face such enormous structural inequalities, what does this tell us for the status of women throughout the society?

29 THE GROWTH OF MEDICAL AUTHORITY

Paul Starr

The rise of the professions was the outcome of a struggle for cultural authority as well as for social mobility. It needs to be understood not only in terms of the knowledge and ambitions of the medical profession, but also in the context of broader changes in culture and society that explain why Americans became willing to acknowledge and institutionalize their dependence on the professions. The acceptance of professional authority was, in a sense, America's cultural revolution, and like other revolutions, it threw new groups to power—in this case, power over experience as much as power over work and institutions.

In a society where an established religion claims to have the final say on all aspects of human experience, the cultural authority of medicine clearly will be restricted. But this was no longer the principal barrier to medicine in the early nineteenth century. Many Americans who already had a rationalist, activist orientation to disease refused to accept physicians as authoritative. They believed that common sense and native intelligence could deal as effectively with most problems of health and illness. Moreover, the medical profession itself had little unity and

was unable to assert any collective authority over its own members, who held diverse and incompatible views.

Authority, as I've indicated, involves a surrender of private judgment, and nineteenth-century Americans were not willing to make that surrender to physicians. Authority signifies the possession of a special status or claim that compels trust, and medicine lacked that compelling claim in nineteenth-century America. The esoteric learning, knowledge of Latin, and high culture and status of traditional English physicians were more compelling grounds for belief in a hierarchically ordered society than in a democratic one. The basis of modern professionalism had to be reconstructed around the claim to technical competence, gained through standardized training and evaluation. But this standardization of the profession was blocked by internal as well as external barriers—sectarianism among medical practitioners and a general

SOURCE: From *The Social Transformation of American Medicine,* by Paul Starr. Copyright © 1982 by Paul Starr. Reprinted by permission of Basic Books, Inc., Publishers.

resistance to privileged monopolies in the society at large.

The forces that transformed medicine into an authoritative profession involved both its internal development and broader changes in social and economic life. Internally, as a result of changes in social structure as well as scientific advance, the profession gained in cohesiveness toward the end of the nineteenth century and became more effective in asserting its claims. With the growth of hospitals and specialization, doctors became more dependent on one another for referrals and access to facilities. Consequently, they were encouraged to adjust their views to those of their peers, instead of advertising themselves as members of competing medical sects. Greater cohesiveness strengthened professional authority. Professional authority also benefited from the development of diagnostic technology, which strengthened the powers of the physician in physical examination of the patient and reduced reliance on the patient's report of symptoms and superficial appearance.

At the same time, there were profound changes in Americans' way of life and forms of consciousness that made them more dependent upon professional authority and more willing to accept it as legitimate. Different ways of life make different demands upon people and endow them with different types of competence. In preindustrial America, rural and small-town communities endowed their members with a wide range of skills and self-confidence in dealing with their own needs. The division of labor was not highly developed, and there was a strong orientation toward self-reliance, grounded in religious and political ideals. Under these conditions, professional authority could make few inroads. Americans were accustomed to dealing with most problems of illness within their own family or local community, with only occasional intervention by physicians. But toward the end of the nineteenth century, as their society became more urban, Americans became more accustomed to relying on the specialized skills of strangers. Professionals became less expensive to consult as telephones and mechanized transportation reduced the cost of time and travel. Bolstered by genuine advances in science and technology, the claims of the professions to competent authority became more plausible, even when they were not yet objectively true; for science worked even greater changes on the imagination than it worked on the processes of disease. Technological change was revolutionizing daily life; it seemed entirely plausible to believe that science would do the same for healing, and eventually it did. Besides, once people began to regard science as a superior and legitimately complex way of explaining and controlling reality, they wanted physicians' interpretations of experience regardless of whether the doctors had remedies to offer.

At a time when traditional certainties were breaking down, professional authority offered a means of sorting out different conceptions of human needs and the nature and meaning of events. In the nineteenth century, many Americans, epitomized by the Populists, continued to believe in the adequacy of common sense and to resist the claims of the professions. On the other hand, there were those, like the Progressives, who believed that science provided the means of moral as well as political reform and who saw in the professions a new and more advanced basis of order. The Progressive view, always stated as a disinterested ideal, nevertheless happily coincided with the ambitions of the emerging professional class to cure and reform. The cultural triumph of Progressivism, which proved more lasting than its political victories, was inseparable from the rise in status and power of professionals in new occupations and organizational hierarchies. Yet this was no simple usurpation; the new authority of professionals reflected the instability of a new way of life and its challenge to traditional belief. The less one could believe "one's own eyes"—and the new world of science continually prompted that feeling—the more receptive one became to seeing the world through the eyes of those who claimed specialized, technical knowledge, validated by communities of their peers.[1]

The growth of medical authority also needs to be understood as a change in institutions. In the nineteenth century, before the profession consolidated its position, some doctors had great personal authority and they pronounced on all manner of problems, by no means restricted to physical illness. Indeed, in the small communities of early Ameri-

can society, where the number of educated men was relatively small, some physicians may have possessed even broader personal authority than do most of their counterparts today. What I am talking about here, on the other hand, is authority that inheres in the status of physician because it has been institutionalized in a system of standardized education and licensing. The establishment of such a system reproduces authority from one generation to the next, and transmits it from the profession as a whole to all its individual members. Before the profession's authority was institutionalized in the late nineteenth and early twentieth centuries, physicians might win personal authority by dint of their character and intimate knowledge of their patients. But once it was institutionalized, standardized programs of education and licensing conferred authority upon all who passed through them. The recognition of authority in a given doctor by laymen and colleagues became relatively unambiguous. Authority no longer depended on individual character and lay attitudes; instead, it was increasingly built into the structure of institutions.

"Built-in" dependence on professional authority increased with such developments as the rise of hospitals. I do not mean only the development of mental hospitals and procedures for involuntary commitment, though the asylum is obviously an important and radical form of institutionalized medical authority. Even the voluntary shift of seriously ill patients from their homes to general hospitals increases the dependent condition of the sick. At home, patients may quite easily choose to ignore the doctor's instructions, and many do; this is much more difficult in a hospital. For the seriously ill, clinical personnel subordinate to the doctor have, in effect, replaced the family as the physician's vicarious agent. They not only administer treatment in the doctor's absence, but also maintain surveillance, keep records, and reinforce the message that the doctor's instructions must be followed.

Other institutional changes have also made people dependent on medical authority regardless of whether they are receptive or hostile to doctors. As the various certifying and gatekeeping functions of doctors have grown, so has the dependence of people seeking benefits that require certification. Laws prohibiting laymen from obtaining certain classes of drugs without a doctor's prescription increase dependence on physicians. "The more strategic the accessories controlled by the profession," Eliot Freidson writes, "the stronger the sanctions supporting its authority."[2] In the twentieth century, health insurance has become an important mechanism for ensuring dependence on the profession. When insurance payments are made only for treatment given by physicians, the beneficiaries become dependent on doctors for reimbursable services. A doctor's authorization for drugs and prosthetics has become necessary for a host of insurance and tax benefits. In all these ways, professional authority has become institutionally routine, and compliance has ceased to be a matter of voluntary choice. What people think about doctors' judgments is still important, but it is much less important than it used to be.

In their combined effect, the mechanisms of legitimation (standardized education and licensing) and the mechanisms of dependency (hospitalization, gatekeeping, insurance) have given a definite structure to the relations of doctors and patients that transcends personalities and attitudes. This social structure is based, not purely on shared expectations about the roles of physicians and the sick, but on the institutionalized arrangements that often impose severe costs on people who wish to behave in some other way.*

---

*Role expectations are the heart of what was once the most influential schema in the sociology of medicine—that of Talcott Parsons. According to Parsons, the social structure of medical practice can be defined by the shared expectations about the "sick role" and the role of the doctor. On the one hand, the sick are exempt from normal obligations; they are not held responsible for their illness; they must try to get well; and they must seek competent help. On the other, the physician is expected to be "universalistic," "functionally specific," "affectively neutral," and "collectivity-oriented." These complementary normative rules have a functional relation to the therapeutic process and the larger society.[3]

While useful as a point of departure for understanding doctor-patient relations, Parsons' model is open to severe objections as a model of medical practice. It fails to convey the ambivalence of doctor-patient relationships and the contradictory expectations with which each party must contend.[4] It also accepts the ideological claims of the profession—for example, to be altruistic ("collectivity-oriented")—and ignores evidence of contrary rules of behavior, such as tacit agreements to ignore colleagues' mistakes.[5] Parsons' ap-

The institutional reinforcement of professional authority also regulates the relations of physicians to each other. The doctor whose personal authority in the nineteenth century rested on his imposing character and relations with patients was in a fundamentally different situation from the doctor in the twentieth century whose authority depends on holding the necessary credentials and institutional affiliations. While laymen have become more dependent on professionals, professionals have become more dependent on each other. Both changes have contributed to the collective power of the profession and helped physicians to convert their clinical authority into social and economic privilege.

From Authority to Economic Power

The conversion of authority into high income, autonomy, and other rewards of privilege required the medical profession to gain control over both the market for its services and the various organizational hierarchies that govern medical practice, financing, and policy. The achieve-

proach concentrates almost entirely upon the system of norms in purely voluntary doctor-patient relations. That such relations are not wholly voluntary both because of dependency conditions and the historical process that lies behind the professional dominance is a point Parsons simply overlooks. The distribution of power, control of markets, and so on do not enter significantly into his analysis. Parsons also neglects other relations important to medical practice, such as those among doctors and between doctors and organizations. The more important these collegial and bureaucratic relations become, the less useful Parsons' approach appears.

ment of economic power involved more than the creation of a monopoly in medical practice through the exclusion of alternative practitioners and limits on the supply of physicians. It entailed shaping the structure of hospitals, insurance, and other private institutions that impinge on medical practice and defining the limits and proper forms of public health activities and other public investment in health care. In the last half century, these organizational and political arrangements have become more important as bases of economic power than the monopolization of medical practice.

The emergence of a market for medical services was originally inseparable from the emergence of professional authority. In the isolated communities of early American society, the sick were usually cared for as part of the obligations of kinship and mutual assistance. But as larger towns and cities grew, treatment increasingly shifted from the family and lay community to paid practitioners, druggists, hospitals, and other commercial and professional sources selling their services competitively on the market. Of course, the family continues even today to play an important role in health care, but its role has become distinctly secondary. The transition from the household to the market as the dominant institution in the care of the sick—that is, the conversion of health care into a commodity—has been one of the underlying movements in the transformation of medicine. It has simultaneously involved increased specialization of labor, greater emotional distance between the sick and those responsible for their care, and a shift from women to men as the dominant figures in the management of health and illness.

What sort of commodity is medical care? Do doctors sell goods (such as drugs), advice, time, or availability? These questions had to be worked out as the market took form. To gain the trust that the practice of medicine requires, physicians had to assure the public of the reliability of their "product." A standardized product, as Magali Sarfatti Larson points out about the professions, requires a standardized producer.[6] Standardization of training and licensing became the means for realizing both the search for authority and control of the market.

Through most of the nineteenth century, the market in medical care continued to be competitive. Entry into practice was relatively easy for untrained practitioners as well as for medical school graduates; as a result, competition was intense and the economic position of physicians was often insecure. Toward the end of the century, although licensing laws began to restrict entry, many doctors felt increasingly threatened by the expansion of free dispensaries, company medical plans, and various other bureaucratically organized alternatives to independent solo practice. In the physicians' view, the competitive market represented a threat not only to their incomes, but also to their status and autonomy because it drew no sharp boundary between the educated and uneducated, blurred the lines between commerce and professionalism, and threatened to turn them into mere employees.

The contradiction between professionalism and the rule of the market is long-standing and unavoidable. Medicine and other professions have historically distinguished themselves from business and trade by claiming to be above the market and pure commercialism. In justifying the public's trust, professionals have set higher standards of conduct for themselves than the minimal rules governing the marketplace and maintained that they can be judged under those standards only by each other, not by laymen. The ideal of the market presumes the "sovereignty" of consumer choices; the ideal of a profession calls for the sovereignty of its members' independent, authoritative judgment. A professional who yields too much to the demands of clients violates an essential article of the professional code: Quacks, as Everett Hughes once defined them, are practitioners who continue to please their customers but not their colleagues. This shift from clients to colleagues in the orientation of work, which professionalism demands, represents a clear depature from the normal rule of the market.

When fully competitive, markets do not obey the organized judgment of any group of sellers. A market is a system of exchange in which goods and services are bought and sold at going prices. In the ideal case cherished by economists, each buyer and seller acts independently of every other, so that prices are set impersonally by levels of supply and demand. There are no relations of dependency in the ideal market: Any individual buyer is supposed to have a free choice of sellers, any seller a free choice of buyers, and no group of buyers or sellers is supposed to be able to force acceptance of its terms. Nor are there supposed to be any relations of authority in the market, except those necessary to provide rules of exchange and the enforcement of contracts. Whereas the household and the state both allocate resources according to decisions made by governing authorities, the distinctive feature of a market is the absence of any such authoritative direction. The absence of power is, paradoxically, the basis of order in a competitive market. Collectively, sellers might wish to keep the prices of commodities higher than their marginal cost, but so long as they act individually, they are driven to bring them down into equilibrium to secure as large as possible a share of the market for themselves.

This is not a prospect that sellers usually enjoy and, whenever the means are available, it is one they quickly subvert. Power abhors competition about as intensely as nature abhors a vacuum. Professional organization is one form resistance to the market may take. Similarly, concentrations of ownership and labor unions are other bases of market power. These cases are parallel. Just as property, manual labor, and professional competence are all means of generating income and other rewards, so they can be used by a monopolistic firm, a strong guild or union, or a powerful, licensed profession to establish market power.

This was what the medical profession set about accomplishing at the end of the nineteenth century when corporations were forming trusts and workers were attempting to organize unions—each attempting, with varying success, to control market forces rather than be controlled by them.

Doctors' increasing authority had the twin effects of stimulating and restricting the market. On the one hand, their growing cultural authority helped draw the care of the sick out of the family and lay community into the sphere of professional service. On the other, it also brought political support for the imposition of limits, like restrictive licensing laws, on the uncontrolled supply of medical services. By augmenting demand and controlling supply, greater professional authority helped physicians secure higher returns for their work.

The market power of the profession originated only in part from the state's protection. It also arose from the increasing dependence of patients on physicians. In the ideal market no buyer depends upon any seller, but patients are often dependent on their personal physicians, and they have become more so as the disparity in knowledge between them has grown. The sick cannot easily disengage themselves from relations with their doctors, nor even know when it is in their interests to do so. Consequently, once they have begun treatment, they cannot exercise that unfettered choice of sellers which characterizes free markets.

One reason that the profession

could develop market power of this kind was that it sold its services primarily to individual patients rather than organizations. Such organizations, had they been more numerous, could have exercised greater discrimination in evaluating clinical performance and might have lobbied against cartel restrictions of the physician supply. The medical profession, of course, insisted that salaried arrangements violated the integrity of the private doctor-patient relationship, and in the early decades of the twentieth century, doctors were able to use their growing market power to escape the threat of bureaucratic control and to preserve their own autonomy.

Notes

1. For an excellent account of the struggle for authority and its relation to changing social organization, see Thomas L. Haskell, *The Emergence of Professional Social Science* (Urbana, Ill.: University of Illinois Press, 1977).

2. Eliot Freidson, *Professional Dominance: The Social Structure of Medical Care* (New York: Atherton, 1970), 117.

3. For Parsons' classic statement, see *The Social System* (Glencoe, Ill.: Free Press, 1951), Chap. 10.

4. See Robert K. Merton and Elinor Barber, "Sociological Ambivalence," in *Sociological Theory, Values and Sociocultural Change*, ed. Edward A. Tiryakian (New York: Free Press, 1963), 91–120.

5. See Freidson, *Profession of Medicine*, esp. Chap. 7.

6. Magali Sarfatti Larson, *The Rise of Professionalism* (Berkeley: University of California Press, 1977), 14.

30 TRAINING FOR UNCERTAINTY

Renée C. Fox

"There are areas of experience where we know that uncertainty is the certainty."

—James B. Conant

Voluminous texts, crammed notebooks, and tightly-packed memories of students of Cornell University Medical College attest to the "enormous amount"[1] of established medical knowledge they are expected to learn. It is less commonly recognized that they also learn much about the uncertainties of medicine and how to cope with them. Because training for uncertainty in the preparation of a doctor has been largely

SOURCE: Reprinted by permission of the publishers from *The Student-Physician*, R. Merton, G. G. Reader and P. L. Kendall, editors, Cambridge, Mass.: Harvard University Press. Copyright © 1957, 1985 by the Commonwealth Fund.

overlooked, the following discussion will be focused exclusively on this aspect of medical education, but with full realization that it is counterbalanced by "all the material [students] learn that it is solid and real as a hospital building."

There is of course marked variation among students in the degree to which uncertainty is recognized or acknowledged. Some students, more inclined than others to equate knowing with pages covered and facts memorized, may think they have "really accomplished a lot . . . gained valuable knowledge," and that what they have learned is "firmly embedded and clear in their minds." Other students are more sensitive to the "vastness of medicine," and more are conscious of ignorance and superficiality in the face of all they "should know," and of all the "puzzling questions" they glimpse but cannot answer. Many students fall somewhere between these two extremes, half-aware in the course of diligent learning, that there is much they do not understand, yet not disposed "at this point to stop the lament." Discussion will be limited to the training for uncertainty that seems to apply to the largest number of students, admitting at the outset that inferences from the data must be provisional.

The Kinds of Uncertainty that the Doctor Faces

In Western society, where disease is presumed to yield to application of scientific method, the doctor is regarded as an expert, a man professionally trained in matters pertaining to sickness and health and able by his medical competence to cure our ills and keep us well. It would be good to think that he has only to make a diagnosis and to apply appropriate treatment for alleviation of ills to follow. But such a Utopian view of the physician is at variance with facts. His knowledge and skill are not always adequate, and there are many times when his most vigorous efforts to understand illness and to rectify its consequences may be of no avail. Despite unprecedented scientific advances, the life of the modern physician is still full of uncertainty.[2]

Two basic types of uncertainty may be recognized. The first results from incomplete or imperfect mastery of available knowledge. No one can have at his command all skills and all knowledge of the lore of medicine. The second depends upon limitations in current medical knowledge. There are innumerable questions to which no physician, however well trained, can as yet provide answers. A third source of uncertainty derives from the first two. This consists of difficulty in distinguishing between personal ignorance or ineptitude and the limitations of present medical knowledge. It is inevitable that every doctor must constantly cope with these forms of uncertainty and that grave consequences may result if he is not able to do so. It is for this reason that training for uncertainty in a medical curriculum and in early professional experiences is an important part of becoming a physician.

An effort will be made to identify

some experiences as well as some agency and mechanisms in medical school that prepare students for uncertainty and to designate patterns by which students may gradually come to terms with uncertainty. In the initial inquiry we shall content ourselves with a general view of the sequence through which most students pass, but in a concluding section we shall suggest some variations that might be considered in further investigation of training for uncertainty.

The Preclinical Years

Learning to Acknowledge Uncertainty

The kind of uncertainty which the student encounters has its source in his role as a student. It derives from the avoidance of "spoon-feeding," a philosophy of the preclinical years at Cornell Medical College (as at many other medical schools).

> You will from the start be given the major responsibility for learning [students are told on the first day that they enter medical school]. Most of your undergraduate courses to date have had fixed and circumscribed limits; your textbooks have been of ponderable dimensions. . . . Not so with your medical college courses. . . . We do not use the comfortable method of spoon-feeding. . . .[3] Limits are not fixed. Each field will be opened up somewhat sketchily. . . . You will begin to paint a picture on a vast canvas but only the center of the picture will be worked in any detail. The periphery will gradually blur into the lazy background. And the more you work out the peripheral pattern, the more you will realize the vastness of that

which stretches an unknown distance beyond. . . . Another common collegiate goal is to excel in competition with others. . . . [But] because an overly-competitive environment can hinder learning, student ratings are never divulged [in this medical school], except to the extent that once a year each student is privately informed as to which quarter of the class he is in.

From the first, the medical school rookie is thus confronted with the challenge of a situation only hazily defined for him. Information is not presented "in neat packets";[4] precise boundaries are not set on the amount of work expected. Under these conditions the uncertainty which the beginning student faces lies in determining how much he ought to know, exactly what he should learn, and how he ought to go about his studies.

This uncertainty, great as it is, is further accentuated for the beginner by the fact that he does not receive grades, and therefore does not have the usual concrete evidence by which to discover whether he is in fact doing well:

> In college, if you decide to work very hard in a course, the usual result is that you do very well in it, and you have the feeling that studying hard leads to good grades. You may tell yourself that you don't give a damn about grades, but nevertheless, they do give you some reassurance when you ask yourself if the work was worth it. . . . In medical school, there is no such relationship. Studying does not always lead to doing well—it is quite easy to study hard, but to study the wrong things and do poorly. And if you should do well, you never know it. . . . In my own case, I honestly

think the thing that bothers me most is not the lack of grades, but rather the feeling that even after studying some in a given course, I always end up knowing so little of what I should know about it. . . . Medicine is such an enormous proposition that one cannot help but fall short of what he feels he should get done. . . .

Thus, it would seem that avoidance of spoon-feeding by the preclinical faculty encourages the student to take responsibility in a relatively unstructured situation, perhaps providing him with a foretaste of the ambiguities he may encounter when he assumes responsibility for a patient.

From the latter parts of the comment under review it would appear that the same teaching philosophy also leads to the beginning awareness of a second type of uncertainty: by making the student conscious of how vast medicine is, the absence of spoon-feeding readies him for the fact that even as a mature physician he will not always experience the certainty that comes with knowing "all there is to know" about the medical problems with which he is faced. He begins to realize that no matter how skilled and well-informed he may gradually become, his mastery of all that is known in medicine will never be complete.

It is perhaps during the course of studying Gross Anatomy that the student experiences this type of uncertainty most intensely. Over the centuries this science has gradually traced out what one medical student describes as the "blueprint of the body." As a result of his struggle to master a "huge body of facts," he

comes to see more clearly that medicine is such an "enormous proposition" he can never hope to command it in a way both encompassing and sure:

> . . . Men have been able to study the body for thousands of years . . . to dissect the cadaver . . . and to work on it with the naked eye. They may not know everything about the biochemistry of the body, or understand it all microscopically . . . but when it comes to the gross anatomy, they know just about all there is to know. . . . This vast sea of information that we have to keep from going out the other ear is overwhelming. . . . There's a sense in which even before I came to medical school I knew that I didn't know anything. But I never *realized* it before, if you know what I mean—not to the extent that it was actually a gripping part of me. Basically, I guess what I thought before was, sure, I was ignorant *now*—but I'd be pretty smart after a while. Well, at this point it's evident to me that even after four years, I'll still be ignorant. . . . I'm now in the process of learning how much there is to learn. . . . [5]

As in this case, the student's own sense of personal inadequacy may be further reinforced by the contrast he draws between his knowledge and that which he attributes to his instructors. Believing as he does that "when it comes to the gross anatomy, they know just about all there is to know," he is made increasingly aware of how imperfect his own mastery really is.

There are other courses and situations in preclinical years which acquaint the Cornell student with uncertainties that result, not from his own inadequacies, but from the limitations in the current state of medical knowledge. For example, standing in distinction to the amassed knowledge of a discipline such as Gross Anatomy is a science like Pharmacology, which only in recent years has begun to emerge from a trial-and-error state of experimentation:

> Throughout the history of pharmacology, it would appear that the ultimate goal was to expedite the search for agents with actions on living systems and to provide explanations for these actions, to the practical end of providing drugs which might be used in the treatment of the disease of man. As a result of many searches there now exist such great numbers of drugs that the task of organizing them is a formidable one. The need for the development of generalizations and simplifying assumptions is great. It is to be hoped that laws and theories of drug action will be forthcoming, but the student should at this point appreciate that few of them, as yet, exist.[6]

The tentativeness of Pharmacology as a science, then, advances the student's recognition that not all the gaps in his knowledge indicate deficiencies on his part. In effect, Pharmacology helps teach medical students that because "there are so many voids" in medical knowledge, the practice of medicine is sometimes largely "a matter of conjuring . . . possibilities and probabilities."

> When Charles was over for dinner last week, I remarked at the time that I was coming to the conclusion that medicine was certainly no precise science, but rather, it is simply a matter of probabilities. Even these drugs today, for example, were noted as to their wide range of action. One dose will be too small to elicit a response to one individual; the same dose will be sufficient to get just the right response in another; and in yet another individual, the same dose will produce hyper-sensitive toxic results. So, there is nothing exact in this, I guess. It's a matter of conjuring the possibilities and probabilities and then drawing conclusions as to the most likely response and the proper thing to do. And Charles last week agreed that a doctor is just an artist who has learned to derive these probabilities and then prescribe a treatment.

In Pharmacology (and in the other basic medical sciences as well) it is assumed that "laws and theories will be forthcoming" so that the uncertainties which result from limited knowledge in the field will gradually yield to greater certainty. However, the "experimental point of view" pervading much of early teaching at the Cornell Medical College promotes the idea that an irreducible minimum of uncertainty is inherent in medicine, in spite of the promise of further scientific advance. The preclinical instructors presenting this point of view have as a basic premise the idea that medical knowledge thus far attained must be regarded as no more than tentative, and must be constantly subjected to further inquiry. It is their assumption that few absolutes exist:

> If you were having a great deal of trouble finding some simple sort of cell in histology and you asked him about it, Dr. A. always made a point to give you information from the experimental point of view. He would (a) point out that this cell has five different names; (b) point out that this

cell might actually be a _____ cell or a _____ cell that has undergone a transformation and that indeed, this cell might be able to change into almost anything; (c) also mention that even though the cell has five names, it may not, in fact, exist in the first place—perhaps it's just an artifact.

Or, take the way the Bacteriology Department pushes the theme of "individual differences"—how one person will contract a disease he's been exposed to, while another one won't. The person may have a chill, or not; the agent may be virulent or not; and that determines whether pneumonia will occur or not. . . . "The occurrence, progression and outcome of a disease is a function of the offense of the microorganism and the defense of the host." That's the formula they keep pounding home . . . .

. . . In the course of the demonstration of drugs affecting respiration, Dr. S. quoted Goodman and Gilman [a pharmacology textbook universally recommended and respected] as to the dramatic effect of one certain drug in respiratory failure. And then, they proceeded to show the falsity of that statement. So pharmacologists are now debunking pharmacologists? Heretofore they simply showed the drugs commonly used by many physicians had no effect. If this keeps up, we will all be first-class skeptics!

This is not to say, a student cautions, that we don't learn "a lot of established facts . . . tried and true things about which there is little or no argument." But in course after course during the preclinical years at Cornell, emphasis is also placed on the provisional nature of much that is assumed to be medically known.

The experimental point of view set forth by his teachers makes it more apparent than it might otherwise be that medicine is something less than a powerful, exact science, based on nicely invariant principles. In this way, the student is encouraged to acknowledge uncertainty, and, more than this, to tolerate it. He is made aware, not only that it is possible to act in spite of uncertainties, but that some of his teachers make such uncertainties the basis of their own experimental work.

Up to this point we have reviewed some of the courses and situations in the preclinical years at Cornell which make the beginning student aware of his own inadequacies and others which lead him to recognize limitations in current medical knowledge. The student has other experiences during the early years of medical school which present him with the problem of distinguishing between these two types of uncertainty—that is, there are times when he is unsure where his limitations leave off and the limitations of medical science begin. The difficulty is particularly evident in situations where he is called upon to make observations.

Whether he is trying to visualize an anatomical entity, studying gross or microscopic specimens in pathology, utilizing the method of percussion in physical diagnosis, or taking a personal history in psychiatry, the preclinical student is being asked to glean whatever information he can from the processes of looking, feeling, and learning.[7] In all these situations, students are often expected to see before they know how to look or what to look for. For, the ability to "see what you ought to see," "feel what you ought to feel," and "hear what you ought to hear," students assure us, is premised upon "a knowledge of what you're suppose to observe," an ordered method for making these observations, and a great deal of practice in medical ways of perceiving. ("We see only what we look for. We look for only what we know," the famous Goethe axiom goes.)

Nowhere does this kind of uncertainty become more salient for medical students during their preclinical years than in Physical Diagnosis:

Physical Diagnosis is the one course I don't feel quite right about. I still have a great deal of difficulty making observations, and I usually don't feel certain about them. . . . Dick and I had a forty-year-old woman as our patient this morning. Though I thought we were doing better than usual at the time, we nevertheless missed several important things—a murmur and an enlarged spleen. . . .

"This sort of thing happens often in a course like Physical Diagnosis," the same student continues, and "it raises a question that gives me quite a bit of concern—*Why* do I have . . . difficulty making observations?"

There are at least two reasons for which a student may "miss" an important clinical sign, or feel uncertain about its presence or absence. On the other hand, his oversight or doubt may be largely attributable to lack of knowledge or skill on his part:

One of the problems now is that we don't know the primary clinical signs of various disease processes. . . . For

example, today we suspected subacute bacterial endocarditis, but we didn't know that the spleen is usually enlarged, and as a result, we didn't feel as hard as we should have. . . .

On the other hand, missing a spleen, for example, or "not being sure you hear a murmur" is sometimes more the "fault of the field" (as one student puts it) than "your own fault." That is, given the limitations in current medical knowledge and technique, the enlargement of a spleen may be too slight, the sound of a murmur too subtle, for "even the experts to agree upon it."

The uncertainty for a student, then, lies in trying to determine how much of his own "trouble . . . hearing, feeling or seeing is personal," and how much of it "has to do with factors outside of himself." (Or, as another student phrases the problem: "How do you make the distinction between yourself and objectivity?")

Generically, the student's uncertainty in this respect is no different from that to which every responsible, self-critical doctor is often subject. But because he has not yet developed the discrimination and judgment of a skilled diagnostician, a student is usually less sure than a mature physician about where to draw the line between his own limitations and those of medical science. When in doubt, a student seems more likely than an experienced practitioner to question and "blame" himself.

His course in Gross Anatomy, it has been suggested, gives a Cornell student some awareness of his own inadequacies; Pharmacology emphasizes the limitations of current medical knowledge; and his training in observation, particularly in Physical Diagnosis, confronts him with the problem of distinguishing between his own limitations and those in the field of medicine. But in his second year his participation in autopsy both epitomizes and summarizes various other experiences which together make up the preclinical student's training for uncertainty.

Before witnessing their first autopsy, second-year students may, on occasion, sound rather complacent about the questions which death poses. For example, speculating on the causes of death, one group of Sophomores decided to their satisfaction that the cessation of life could be explained in simple physiological terms and that, armed with this knowledge, the doctor stands a good chance of "winning the fight" against death:

> We found that one very important matter could be traced back to one of two basic actions. The important matter—death. The two basic actions —the heart and respiration. For death is caused, finally, by the stopping of one of these two actions. As long as they both continue, there is life. . . . It's all a fight to keep the heart beating, the lungs breathing, and, in man, a third factor—the brain unharmed. . . . With all the multitude of actions and reactions which are found in this medical business, it seems strange and satisfying to find something that can really be narrowed down. . . .

But the conviction that death "can really be narrowed down" is not long-lasting. Only a short time later, commenting on an autopsy he had just witnessed, one of these same students referred to death with "disquietude" as something you "can't pinpoint" or easily prevent.

One of the chief consequences of the student's participation in an autopsy is that it heightens his awareness of the uncertainties that result from limited medical knowledge and of the implications these uncertainties have for the practicing doctor. This is effected in a number of ways. To begin with, the experience of being "on call" for an autopsy ("waiting around for someone to die") makes a student more conscious of the fact that, even when death is expected, it is seldom wholly predictable.

> In groups of threes, we all watch at least one autopsy—and my group is the third one in line. The first group went in for theirs this morning; this means that ours may come any time now. You can't be sure when, though, so you have to stay pretty close to home where you can be reached. . . .

In other words, although ultimate death is certain, medical science is still not far enough advanced so that the physicians can state with assurance exactly when an individual will die.

Of even greater importance, perhaps, in impressing the student with the limitations of current medical knowledge is the fact that, although the pathologist may be able to provide a satisfactory explanation of the patient's death, the student usually finds these "causes of death" less "dramatic" and specific than he expected them to be:

> While our case was unusual, it was a bit of a letdown to me, for there was

nothing dramatic to be pointed to as the cause of death. The clinician reported that the patient had lost 1,000 cc. of blood from internal bleeding in the G.I. tract. . . . Well, we saw no gaping hole there. There was no one place you could pinpoint and say: "This is where the hemorrhage took place." . . . Rather, it was a culmination of a condition relating to various factors, I suppose most causes of death are this way. But still . . . (though I'm not really sure why it should be) . . . it was somewhat disquieting to me.

A third limitation of the field is implied in lack of control over death. For example, the student observes that "the various doctors connected with the case being autopsied . . . wander in while the procedure is going on." This serves to remind him that the "body on the autopsy table" belongs to a patient whose death no physician was able to prevent.

It is not only the limits of the field which are impressed upon the student during his participation in an autopsy. This experience also serves to make him aware of the personal limitations of even the most skilled practitioners. For instance, an autopsy gives a student an opportunity to observe that "the doctors aren't always sure what caused the patient's death"; rather, as one student puts it, "they come . . . to find out what was really wrong." Furthermore, the student may be present at an autopsy in which the pathologist's findings make it apparent that the physician was mistaken in his diagnosis (when, for example, the pathologist "doesn't find any of the things in the doctors' diagnoses").

From experiences such as these the student learns that, not only he, but also his instructors have only an imperfect mastery of all there is to know in medicine.

These varied aspects of the autopsy, in other words, give it central significance in the student's training for uncertainty.

Notes

1. Unless otherwise indicated, all the quoted phrases and passages in this paper are drawn from the diaries that eleven Cornell students at various points along the medical school continuum have kept for us over the course of the past three years; from interviews with these student diarists and some of their classmates; and from close-to-verbatim student dialogue recorded by the sociologist who carried out day-by-day observations in some of the medical school situations cited in this paper.

2. It is not only the doctor, of course, who must deal with the problem of uncertainty. To some extent this problem presents itself in all forms of responsible human action. The business executive or the parent, for example, has no assurance that his decisions will have the desired results. But the doctor is particularly subject to this problem for his decisions are likely to have profound and directly observable consequences for his patients.

3. This particular sentence was taken from the "Address of Welcome to the Class of 1957" delivery by Dr. Lawrence W. Hanlon. Everything else in the paragraph quoted above is extracted from "Some Steps in the Maturation of the Medical Student," a speech delivered by Dr. Robert F. Pitts at Opening Day Exercises, September 1952.

4. Pitts, *ibid.*
5. Such a felt sense that there will always be more to learn in medicine than he can possibly make his own, is the beginning of the medical student's acceptance of limitation. It might also be said that this same realization is often one of the attitudinal first signs of a later decision on the part of a student to enter a specialized medical field. This is of some relevance to the discussion of specialization by Patricia L. Kendall and Hanan

C. Selvin, "Tendencies toward Specialization in Medical Training," in this volume.
6. Joseph A. Wells, "Historical Background and General Principles of Drug Action" in: Victor A. Drill, ed., *Pharmacology in Medicine* (New York: McGraw-Hill Book Company, 1945), p. 6.
7. The physician is called upon to use his sense of smell and of taste on occasion too, but not as frequently as those of sight, touch, and hearing.

31   WOMEN PHYSICIANS IN THREE COUNTRIES

Judith Lorber

Twentieth Century Medicine: "On the Inside Sitting Alone"[1]

The upgrading of medical education in the twentieth century produced practitioners who were more scientifically trained and clinically experienced than those of the nineteenth century, but it also restricted legal medical practice only to those holders of the MD degree and those health workers under MD authority. For the first time in Western history, lay workers were rejected by the populace, who were more and more persuaded of the efficacy of modern medicine, as practiced by MDs, through a growing series of drugs, vaccines, anesthetics, and surgical procedures. Knowledge of modern medicine was widely disseminated through public health campaigns, the routine examination of school children, and free well-baby care for poor families (Starr 1982: 180–

97). With the encouragement of the American Medical Association, muckraking propaganda against non-licensed healers and patent medicines further damned sectarianism, self-medication, lay midwifery, and folk healing (Starr 1982: 123–44; Kobrin 1966). Legal medical practice was brought under the control of one group of professionals, who now monopolized access to training, clientele, hospitals, and clinical research. To trace the position of women physicians in the twentieth century, one must look at differences in the organization of medical work, which I will do for the United States, England, and the Soviet Union.

SOURCE: From *Women Physicians: Careers, Status and Power* by Judith Lorber, pp. 21–29. Reprinted by permission from Tavistock Publications.

United States

In the United States, the twentieth century saw a shift from client-controlled practices dependent on the whims and beliefs of patients to colleague-controlled practices dependent on the good opinion and reciprocal favors of other physicians (Friedson 1960). Not only did established physicians determine who got into medical school, what they studied there, and whether they were competent to practice, but the same inner circles of physicians controlled the selection for specialty training programs, making it possible to locate novice physicians on the basis of gender, religion, race, and ethnic group into "appropriate" types of practices.

The prestigious, research-oriented, and better paying specialties were reserved for white, Protestant, upper middle-class men. Obstetrics and gynecology, a lucrative specialty until the late 1960s, was heavily male once midwifery was driven underground. General surgery and specialty surgery, which command high fees and have developed a charismatic aura, are almost exclusively male. Pediatrics, pathology, public health, anesthesiology, radiology, and dermatology accepted women, Jews, Catholics, blacks, and, after World War II, foreign medical graduates into their training programs. Industrial and occupational medicine was of such low status that, in 1918, when Harvard wanted to hire someone to teach it, the only qualified candidate was a woman physician, Alice Hamilton. Harvard hired her, but she was not allowed to march in the commence-ment academic processions, was not allowed into the faculty club, and was never promoted, in fifteen years, above assistant professor (Walsh 1977: 211–12).

Control by powerful colleague groups continued after training and, unlike medical school admissions, was unmitigated by state intervention. As gatekeepers of hospital privileges and referrals of patients, the established physicians in a community determined future physicians' career advancement. Discrimination by race and ethnic group was so widespread that Catholic, Jewish, and black doctors encouraged their respective philanthropic societies to endow hospitals, so that they would have places to train, staff appointments, and beds for their patients. Their alternatives were the municipal hospitals, with access controlled by urban political bosses (Starr 1982: 173–74).

The power of the local colleague group was enhanced by the rules of liability in malpractice suits, which were set in the late nineteenth century as the standard of care in the local community of physicians. The locality rule limited expert testimony for and against a physician to immediate colleagues. Local medical societies promised to defend their members and were able to get low malpractice insurance rates for them, while doctors who did not belong had a hard time getting any insurance at all (Starr 1982: 111–12). Thus, as Starr says, "the local medical fraternity became the arbiter of a doctor's position and fortune, and he (sic) could no longer choose to ignore it" (Starr 1982: 111).

As early as 1904, Dr Bertha Van

Hoosen felt that the women who attended the American Medical Association's annual meeting were isolated and ineffectual. She said, "A generation earlier, women doctors were on the outside standing together. Now they were on the inside sitting alone. Their influence was nil" (quoted in Walsh 1977: 213). However, with concerted pressure, their influence could still be brought to bear on at least one issue—maternal and child health.

After World War I and the victory of female suffrage, women reformers helped pass the Sheppard-Towner Act, which, in 1921, set up state and federally funded prenatal and child health centers throughout the country (Rothman 1978: 136–53). They were staffed and directed by female physicians and public health nurses, who offered preventive care, hygiene education, and low cost medical services in the best tradition of the nineteenth-century women's dispensaries. But by 1929, the American Medical Association coopted preventive care for the private physician and led the fight to deny further funding for the Sheppard-Towner clinics. The 1930 White House Conference on the Health and Protection of Children was dominated by male physicians (Costin 1983). After 1930, faced with the Depression and World War II, and handicapped by low numbers, geographical isolation, the power of the American Medical Association, and the waning of active feminism, women physicians faded into virtual invisibility (Lorber 1975).

American women physicians from the 1930s to the 1950s may have found it easier to assimilate than to build their own networks and institutions, as Jewish, Catholic, and black male physicians did, because they tended to be recruited from the upper middle classes and to attend the prestigious women's colleges that were the counterparts of the Ivy League schools of their white, Protestant, male colleagues (Lopate 1968: 31–33; Williams 1971). The women's upbringing, education, and family ties may have made them acceptable as "friendly" colleagues, as long as they did not assertively counter the open discriminatory practices that permeated medical education and practice during this period.

Also important in dampening their ambitions was the "cultural mandate"—the supposed need of the family for the mother's commitment to its concerns, a commitment that was held to outweigh any professional commitment (Bourne and Wikler 1978). As Kessler-Harris says of the women workers of the post-World War I period:

> To induce women to take jobs while simultaneously restraining their ambition to rise in them requires a series of socially accepted constraints on work roles. Unspoken social prescription —a tacit understanding about the primacy of home roles—remained the most forceful influence. This is most apparent in professional jobs where the potential for ambition was greatest.
>
> (Kessler-Harris 1982:231)

Rossiter (1982) details this process for women scientists.

In the 1960s, under the impact of the civil rights movement and the new feminist consciousness, overt discrimination in education, hiring, and promotion was outlawed, and careers for women met with more public approval. The 1960s also saw a jump in third-party reimbursements, and a consequent rise in demand for physicians' services. The women physicians of this transition period tended to act on their own to further their careers, seeking out medical institutions that were most open (or least hostile) for training and staff positions. They made the most of limited sponsorship (Lorber 1981).

The youngest cohort of women physicians in the United States are still at the beginning of their careers. They have two advantages. As junior physicians, they are least threatening as colleagues, and most likely to receive the help of established male senior physicians. They also have more senior women to turn to for mentorships and sponsorship, active women's professional organizations, and a new feminist movement for support, attitudinal change, and clientele. But if the senior women do not garner resources to distribute to the junior women doctors under their wing, and the men who still dominate the upper echelons of national and community medical institutions do not become more amenable to grooming women as their successors, these younger women, too, may find that their accomplishments do not bring them the ranks and statuses equal to those of their male peers.

Medical work in America is coming more and more under government and corporate regulation. Large-scale tax-supported medical institutions, such as teaching and research centers, overshadow the prestige and political power of the local community practitioner (Miller 1977). With primary care and specialty practice paid for by third-party insurance payments, governments and profit-oriented corporations are imposing cost-cutting regulations (Starr 1982: 420–49). Before speculating on how these developments may affect women physicians' careers in the United States, I will discuss how the organization of medicine affected women physicians' careers in England under the National Health Service and in the Soviet Union, where medicine is completely under state control. While neither medical system is likely to be replicated in the United States in the near future, some lessons might be learned from women physicians' experiences under systems of prepaid office practices and salaried clinic and hospital positions.

England

Women physicians in England, like those in the United States, were recruited from the upper middle classes, encountered similar quotas in medical schools, had relatively powerless national and provincial women's medical associations, were underrepresented in policy-making bodies, and expressed dissatisfaction with the progress of their careers (Elston 1980, 1977; Leeson and Gray 1978). Although the power of the profession was located in national and regional councils, rather than in the local community colleague group, women physicians' careers in England were similar to those of their American counterparts. They were relegated to low-paying, low-status specialties, and were offered more opportunities for work in primary care than in hospital consultantships.

The plans for the National Health Service in 1944 recommended coeducation for all English medical schools and the admission of a "reasonable" proportion of women students. Although the ceiling was set at 20 percent, the actual quota was 15 percent, the pre-World War II national average. The women who went to medical school, as in the United States, tended to be better qualified than the men because of the restrictions on their numbers.

The quotas were abolished in the late 1960s, when there was an expansion of hospitals and an increased demand for, as Elston puts it, "pairs of hands," especially in the less popular specialties and in the peripheral hospitals. As in the United States, the lower-trade positions and the less prestigious specialties tended to be staffed by women and foreign-trained physicians. Women are half of the physicians in community medicine, family planning clinics, and child health. These fields are underfinanced and of lower prestige than the surgical specialties and hospital consultantships, where women hold a tenth of the posts (Leeson and Gray 1978: 37–8).

The central planning and careful structuring of the medical labor supply under the National Health Service relegated women physicians to the less advantageous sector of what is essentially a dual labor market (Elston 1977). The higher paying sectors, with open career ladders and stable demands for workers, have been reserved for Anglo-Saxon males, while women and foreign-trained MDs are generally found in the secondary sector, which is characterized by lower pay, blocked upward mobility, and fluctuating demand for workers. While women's family commitments and interests are used as the rationale for this internal segregation, a better explanation is the demand for low-cost medical workers. Given their underrepresentation in the policy-making councils of the National Health Service and the British Medical Association, women physicians became an exploitable reserve pool of inexpensive medical labor.

Soviet Union

The status of women physicians in the Soviet Union seems to be the complete antithesis of that of American women doctors. Because men were in short supply after World War I and the revolution, women are the majority of the profession. Their numbers in medical schools went down, rather than up, in the 1960s in order to achieve parity for men students (Lapidus 1978: 188). They are salaried employees in community and work enterprise polyclinics, where their duties are preventive as well as curative. Haug notes that "they get to know the workers well, check on their health, follow up those with chronic conditions, lecture on health matters, and monitor compliance with safety and health rules" (Haug 1976: 98). In the neighborhood polyclinics, women physicians are very much part of the social scene, and their relationship with patients tends to be maternal and solicitous rather than objective and scientific (Haug 1976: 98). Soviet physicians' relations with patients are not entirely benign, as their mandate is to keep the labor force at work.

The domination of the medical profession by women indicates that it is not one of high economic priority, since the work women do in the Soviet Union is routinely paid less than the work men usually do (Swafford 1978). Not only are physicians not a powerful occupational group, but within medicine, women physicians do not dominate the positions of power. Even though three-quarters of Soviet physicians are women, they are only half the directors, deputy directors and chief physicians in clinics and hospitals (Dodge 1971: 218).

Women in general are underrepresented on the national levels of Communist Party membership and activity, the chief avenue to power in the Soviet Union. Again, their own motivations and family responsibilities (despite institutionalized child care services) are given as the reason for their low political participation. But, as Lapidus points out, ". . . within the Party itself there is considerable hesitation in promoting women to positions of real authority" (Lapidus 1978: 227).

The work and professional status of women physicians in the Soviet Union resemble that of the women doctors in England who staff the community health, family planning, and child health clinics. Similar

medical workers in the United States are public health nurses and family care nurse practitioners, and school and employee health service physicians, all of whom tend to be female. In all three countries, low-paid, low-prestige women health workers carry the bulk of primary, preventative, and routine care—the everyday, unglamorous work of medicine.

The overall situation of women physicians in all three countries is more alike than different despite the dissimilarities in the organization of medical work, which is entrepreneurial and collegial in the United States, government controlled and locally coordinated in England, and state planned in the Soviet Union. And, in all three countries, women physicians are absent, as professionals and as ordinary citizens, from the corridors of power.

Twenty-First Century Medicine: "The Peak of The Pyramid?"[2]

In the United States, physicians, including women physicians, are at the top of the pyramid of health-care workers. The crucial issue is whether the status and power of women physicians will rise commensurately with their increase in numbers, or whether, like women physicians in England and the Soviet Union, they will increasingly find themselves doing mainly primary and preventive care. These vital areas of medical work bring women doctors in competition with other women health workers, particularly nurse practitioners, who claim expertise in the same areas of health care (Lurie 1981). If nurse practitioners also offer diagnoses and treatment of routine illnesses and preventive care, and offer it at lower cost, women physicians will be hard pressed to claim superior status or payment. And yet, it is as primary care practitioners that the new women physicians are being "welcomed" into the profession (Geyman 1980; Relman 1980; Wallace 1980). A typical statement is as follows:

> The women's groups in the United States now trying to take steps to improve women's health care are the consumer, nurse midwives, and nurse practitioners. One would expect women physicians to be in the vanguard of this movement, but this is not the case. Similarly, one would hope that the care of women of the childbearing age and the care of infants and children would be delivered together. Thus, women physicians have a unique opportunity and role to play in improving the system by delivery of health care in the United States. This should be one of the top priorities for women physicians for today and tomorrow.
>
> (Wallace 1980: 211)

Would such a mandate give women physicians a powerful position in medicine? Only if family health care had top priority in funding, and women doctors were given the authority to organize and direct these services. In the United States, under entrepreneurial practice, when services become lucrative, they are taken over by male physicians (Pawluch 1983). In England, under the National Health Service, this sector of medical care is underfunded (Elston 1977). In the Soviet Union, where extensive primary and pre-

ventive care is mandated by the state, women physicians have authority over patients, but not over state medical policy (Lapidus 1978; Haug 1976).

In the United States, as medical practice becomes more bureaucratized under governmental and corporate control, women physicians will probably be overrepresented in the rank-and-file of provider institutions.[3] Rather than forming the vanguard of a consumer-oriented, open-access medical system, women physicians are likely to find themselves in competition for autonomy, status, and even jobs with nurse practitioners, nurse midwives, and physicians' assistants. They will all be doing virtually the same work, and professional status will lay in political power games (Lorber and Satow 1977). Such infighting makes the colleague group in the workplace crucial, and it is precisely here that women lose out (Olson and Miller 1983; Wolf and Fligstein 1979a, 1979b). With increasing numbers of doctors and growing competition from non MD licensed health workers, male physicians are not likely to forego the chance to point to women's family commitments or unsuitability for leadership in an effort to retain a competitive edge and administrative control of health care delivery institutions and academic medicine. Under pressure from outside, the colleague group can be expected to close ranks against competitors, and for male physicians, these competitors may very well be women physicians.

In the near future, women physicians in the United States are likely to split into two groups: those who align with other physicians in the fight to maintain professional dominance, and those who align with other women health-care workers and consumers in the fight for a health care system with a flatter hierarchy and a holistic and self-help perspective (Howell 1977; Kleiber and Light 1978; Ruzek 1978; Shapiro and Jones 1979). As with so much else about women physicians, their opportunities and dilemmas mirror the structured choices and political strategies of other women workers in their respective societies. Their elite professional position in the United States makes them an excellent test case for the chances of women in an individualistic, capitalist society, for if women in a prestigious, highly paid profession can't make it to the top, which women can? The women physicians in England and the Soviet Union are also important object lessons for women physicians, for they demonstrate that national planning and funding and state control, in the absence of a built-in structure for gender equality, end up being just as exploitative as entrepreneurial collegiality.

Notes

1. Walsh 1977:213.
2. Jones and Shapiro 1979.
3. For analyses of the current structure of the health care delivery system in the United States, and predictions of the future see Freidson 1983; Starr 1982: 235–49; Mechanic 1976.

References

Bourne, P. G. and Wikler, N. J. (1978) Commitment and the Cultural Mandate: Women in Medicine, *Social Problems* 25: 430–40.

Costin, L. B. (1983) Women and Physicians: The 1930 White House Conference on Children. *Social Work*, March–April: 108–14.

Dodge, N. (1971) Women in the Soviet Economy. In A. Theodore (ed) *The Professional Woman*. Cambridge, Mass.: Schenkman.

Elson, M. A. (1977) Women in the Medical Profession: Whose Problem? In M. Stacey, M. Reid, C. Heath and R. Dingwall (eds) *Health and the Division of Labour*. London: Croom Helm.

———— (1980) Medicine: Half Our Future Doctors? In R. Silverstone and A. Ward (eds) *The Careers of Professional Women*. London: Croom Helm.

Freidson, E. (1960) Client Control and Medical Practice. *American Journal of Sociology* 65: 374–82.

———— (1983) The Reorganization of the Profession by Regulation. *Law and Human Behavior* 7(2/3): 279–90.

Geyman, J. P. (1980) Increasing Number of Women in Family Practice: An Overdue Trend. *Journal of Family Practice* 10: 207–8.

Haug, M. R. (1976) The Erosion of Professional Authority: A Cross-Cultural Inquiry in the Case of Physicians. *Health and Society* Winter: 83–106.

Jones, H. B. and Shapiro, E. C. (1979) The Peak of the Pyramid: Women in Dentistry, Medicine, and Veterinary Medicine. *Annals of the New York Academy of Sciences* 323: 79–91.

Kleiber, N. and Light, L. (1978) *Caring for Ourselves: An Alternative Structure for Health Care*. Vancouver, Can.: University of British Columbia School of Nursing.

Kobrin, F. E. (1966) The American Midwife Controversy: A Crisis of Professionalization. *Bulletin of the History of Medicine* 40: 350–63.

Lapidus, G. W. (1978) *Women in Soviet Society*. Berkeley: University of California Press.

Leeson, J. and Gray, J. (1978) *Women and Medicine*. London: Tavistock.

Lopate, C. (1968) *Women in Medicine*. Baltimore: The Johns Hopkins Press.

Lorber, J. (1975) Women and Medical Sociology: Invisible Professionals and Ubiquitous Patients. In M. Millman and R. M. Kanter (eds) *Another Voice: Feminist Perspectives on Social Life and Social Science*. Garden City, New York: Anchor/Doubleday.

———— (1981) The Limits of Sponsorship for Women Physicians. *Journal of the American Medical Women's Association* 36: 329–38.

Lorber, J. and Satow, R. (1977) Creating a Company of Unequals: Sources of Occupational Stratification in a Ghetto Community Mental Health Center. *Sociology of Work and Occupations* 4: 281–302.

Lurie, E. (1981) Nurse Practitioners: Issues in Professional Socialization. *Journal of Health and Social Behavior* 22: 31–48.

Mechanic, D. (1976) *The Growth of Bureaucratic Medicine*. New York: Wiley.

Miller, A. E. (1977) The Changing Structure of the Medical Profession in Urban and Suburban Settings. *Social Science and Medicine* 11: 233–43.

Olson, J. and Miller, J. (1983) Gender and Interaction in the Workplace. In H. Lopata and J. H. Pleck (eds) *Research in the Interweave of Social Roles: Jobs and Families*, vol. 3, Greenwich, Conn.: JAI Press.

Pawluch, D. (1983) Transitions in Pediatrics: A Segmental Analysis. *Social Problems* 30: 449–65.

Relman, A. S. (1980) Here Come the Women. (Editorial) *New England Journal of Medicine* 302: 1252–253.

Rossiter, M. W. (1982) *Women Scientists in America: Struggles and Strategies to 1940*. Baltimore: Johns Hopkins University Press.

Rothman, S. M. (1978) *Woman's Proper Place*. New York: Basic Books.

Ruzek, S. B. (1978) *The Women's Health Movement*. New York: Praeger.

Shapiro, E. C. and Jones, A. B. (1979) Women Physicians and the Exercise of Power and Authority in Health Care. In E. Shapiro and L. M. Lowenstein (eds) *Becoming a Physician: Development of Values and Attitudes in Medicine*. Cambridge, Mass.: Ballinger.

Starr, P. (1982) *The Social Transformation of American Medicine*. New York: Basic Books.

Swafford, M. (1978) Sex Differences in Soviet Earnings. *American Sociological Review* 43: 657–73.

Wallace, H. M. (1980) Women in Medicine. *Journal of the American Medical Women's Association* 35:201–11.

Walsh, M. R. (1977) *"Doctors Wanted: No Women Need Apply" Sexual Barriers in the Medical Profession, 1835–1975*. New Haven, Conn.: Yale.

Williams, P. A. (1971) Women in Medicine: Some Themes and Variations. *Journal of Medical Education* 46: 584–91.

Wolf, W. C. and Fligstein, N. D. (1979a) Sex and Authority in the Workplace: The Causes of Sexual Inequality. *American Sociological Review* 44: 235–52.

———— (1979b) Sexual Stratification: Differences in Power in the Work Setting. *Social Forces* 58: 94–107.

Nonphysician Providers

When we study the history of Western medicine, we see many examples of physicians' advances built on the defeat of other healing professions. Witness the case of midwifery. The Flexner Report of 1920 capped an era in which doctors were influential in chasing out midwives, homeopaths, and naturopaths and in forcing osteopaths to be more like allopaths, the modern Western doctors.

Physicians' power and authority give them control over other professions. This holds not only for authority within the hospital or clinic but also for such external control as regulation and licensing of other professionals. Although *medical dominance* sometimes yielded better medical education, and medical care, early nineteenth century doctors were quite open about their fear of competition from other providers. Modern approaches to medical sociology have placed much importance on the ways in which medical dominance has operated. These more recent scholars have been very interested in the medical and social roles of other types of providers and in the different insights those providers have on disease, illness, and patient care.

Keep in mind that *de jure* (by law) control doesn't always mean *de facto* (in practice) control. Think back to the Anselm Strauss article on the hospital as a multiple work site, and you will remember that other health professionals, as well as nonprofessional workers, are quite important in patient care. In fact, they even act as checks on and competitors with doctors in carrying out certain routine tasks and functions.

Efforts of other health providers to improve their status often involve defining their own group or profession as central to fulfilling the needs of the medical practice as a whole. What we see is a generalized attempt at *professionalization* by the other health professions, an attempt that mirrors the past efforts of physicians. There are pitfalls in this occupational strategy, since the public and the state are not that eager to accept the argument that everyone is a professional and therefore deserving of special privileges. Certainly the hospitals and the financing apparatus of the health care industry are not eager to pay higher salaries and fees to other professionals. Nor do administrators wish to have additional parties with any claim to power and authority in health care settings.

Clearly there are economic and career gains to be made by the other health professions, but we must understand them in the appropriate context. For example, some nurses have risen in power and status, but often at the expense of others. The RN (registered nurse) has supplanted the LPN (licensed practical nurse). The RN with a baccalaureate degree has supplanted the RN with a certificate. The RN with a master's degree has supplanted the RN with a B.S. Most recently, the nurse practitioner has replaced the master's level nurse. This process of upgrading professional credentials, requirements, and responsibilities is part of the ongoing *restratification* of the health field.

In "A Caring Dilemma: Womanhood and Nursing in Historical Perspective," Susan Reverby traces the development of nursing, pointing to the many conflicts between female nurturing roles and medical professionalism. Reverby argues that in order to develop professionally over time, nurses were forced to professionalize their altruism, at the expense of their own autonomy. The duty to care became merely the duty to follow physicians' orders in the medical hierarchy. Recent changes in nursing ideology, as well as in the structure of health service settings, have opened the doors to greater autonomy. Ultimately, Reverby asserts, the historical conflict experienced by nurses can be resolved by adopting a political ideology that links altruism with autonomy in nursing as well as in other spheres of social life.

Unlike nurses, chiropractors have not been subject to the hierarchical control of physicians. Rather, they practice in a kind of parallel track, treating some of the same patients who might otherwise go to doctors. Years of efforts by organized medicine (mainly through the American Medical Association) have failed to weaken or destroy the chiropractic profession. In fact, chiropractic has grown in size and has won a substantial degree of power in obtaining third-party payment from federal and private sources. Walter Wardwell, in "The Future of Chiropractic," compares the path of chiropractic professionalism in New Zealand and the United States and offers several possible models for the future relations between chiropractors and physicians. The potential future for chiropractors to be "limited professionals" who coexist with physicians can be viewed as a prototype for other health providers. It is interesting to consider that the growth of other professions is linked to third-party payers' awareness that those other professionals can provide services at far lower costs than doctors. Thus the financial justification may be playing a larger role than any evaluation of skills and abilities.

Many of the actual caring functions in health institutions are performed by nonprofessionals with little or no prior training. Nursing homes, a rapidly increasing location of long-term care, employ nursing assistants (aides) to carry out most of the work. Timothy Diamond writes in "Social Policy and Everyday Life in Nursing Homes: A Critical Ethnography," about these workers, their charges, and their workplace. Methodologically, this article is an example of participant observation. By working in nursing homes as an aide, Diamond was able to obtain a deep understanding of the problems faced by his co-workers. His ethnographic approach brings us a very personal view of the working conditions of the aides, a mostly black and female work force. At the same time, Diamond shows how the nature of the institution itself leads to, indeed even demands, a dehumanization of the residents. If you think back to the article on nursing homes by Charlene Harrington in an earlier section of this book, you will remember the degrading conditions that generally characterize what is now a pivotal American health institution. This is particularly worrisome since nursing homes will play an even greater role in long-term care in the future.

32   A CARING DILEMMA: WOMANHOOD AND NURSING IN HISTORICAL PERSPECTIVE

Susan Reverby

"Do not undervalue [your] particular ability to care," students were reminded at a recent nursing school graduation.[1] Rather than merely bemoaning yet another form of late twentieth-century heartlessness, this admonition underscores the central dilemma of American nursing: The order to care in a society that refuses to value caring. This article is an analysis of the historical creation of that dilemma and its consequences for nursing. To explore the meaning of caring for nursing, it is necessary to unravel the terms of the relationship between nursing and womanhood as these bonds have been formed over the last century.

The Meaning of Caring

Many different disciplines have explored the various meanings of caring.[2] Much of this literature, however, runs the danger of universalizing caring as an element in fe-

male identity, or as a human quality, separate from the cultural and structural circumstances that create it. But as policy analyst Hilary Graham has argued, caring is not merely an identity; it is also work. As she notes, "Caring touches simultaneously on who you are and what you do."[3] Because of this duality, caring can be difficult to define and even harder to control. Graham's analysis moves beyond seeing caring as a psychological trait; but her focus is primarily on women's unpaid labor in the home. She does not fully discuss how the forms of caring are shaped by the contexts under which they are practiced. Caring is not just a subjective and material experience; it is a historically created one. Particu-

source: Copyright © 1987, American Journal of Nursing Company. Reprinted with permission from *Nursing Research*, January/February 1987, Vol. 36, no. 1, pp. 5–11.

lar circumstances, ideologies, and power relations thus create the conditions under which caring can occur, the forms it will take, the consequences it will have for those who do it.

The basis for caring also shapes its effect. Nursing was organized under the expectation that its practitioners would accept a duty to care rather than demand a right to determine how they would satisfy this duty. Nurses were expected to act out of an obligation to care, taking on caring more as an identity than as work, and expressing altruism without thought of autonomy either at the bedside or in their profession. Thus, nurses, like others who perform what is defined as "women's work" in our society, have had to contend with what appears as a dichotomy between the duty to care for others and the right to control their own activities in the name of caring. Nursing is still searching for what philosopher Joel Feinberg argued comes prior to rights, that is, being "recognized as having a claim on rights."[4] The duty to care, organized within the political and economic context of nursing's development, has made it difficult for nurses to obtain this moral and, ultimately, political standing.

Because nurses have been given the duty to care, they are caught in a secondary dilemma: forced to act as if altruism (assumed to be the basis for caring) and autonomy (assumed to be the basis for rights) are separate ways of being. Nurses are still searching for a way to forge a link between altruism and autonomy that will allow them to have what

philosopher Larry Blum and others have called "caring-with-autonomy," or what psychiatrist Jean Baker Miller labeled "a way of life that includes serving others without being subservient."[5] Nursing's historical circumstances and ideological underpinnings have made creating this way of life difficult, but not impossible, to achieve.

Caring as Duty

A historical analysis of nursing's development makes this theoretical formulation clearer. Most of the writing about American nursing's history begins in the 1870s when formal training for nursing was introduced in the United States. But nursing did not appear de novo at the end of the nineteenth century. As with most medical and health care, nursing throughout the colonial era and most of the nineteenth century took place within the family and the home. In the domestic pantheon that surrounded "middling" and upper-class American womanhood in the nineteenth century, a woman's caring for friends and relatives was an important pillar. Nursing was often taught by mother to daughter as part of female apprenticeship, or learned by a domestic servant as an additional task on her job. Embedded in the seemingly natural or ordained character of women's expression of love of others, and was thus integral to the female sense of self.[6] In a society where deeply felt religious tenets were translated into gendered virtues, domesticity advocate Catharine Beecher declared that the sick were to be "commended" to a "woman's benevolent ministries."[7]

The responsibility for nursing went beyond a mother's duty for her children, a wife's for her husband, or a daughter's for her aging parents. It attached to all the available female family members. The family's "long arm" might reach out at any time to a woman working in a distant city, in a mill, or as a maid, pulling her home to care for the sick, infirm, or newborn. No form of women's labor, paid or unpaid, protected her from this demand. "You may be called upon at any moment," Eliza W. Farrar warned in the *The Young Lady's Friend* in 1837, "to attend upon your parents, your brothers, your sisters, or your companions."[8] Nursing was to be, therefore, a woman's duty, not her job. Obligation and love, not the need of work, were to bind the nurse to her patient. Caring was to be an unpaid labor of love.

The Professed Nurse

Even as Eliza Farrar was proffering her advice, pressures both inward and outward were beginning to reshape the domestic sphere for women of the then-called "middling classes." Women's obligations and work were transformed by the expanding industrial economy and changing cultural assumptions. Parenting took on increasing importance as notions of "moral mothering" filled the domestic arena and other productive labor entered the cash nexus. Female benevolence similarly moved outward as women's charitable efforts took increasingly institutional forms. Duty began to take on new meaning as such women were advised they could fulfill their nursing responsibilities by managing competently those they hired to assist them. Bourgeois female virtue could still be demonstrated as the balance of labor, love, and supervision shifted.[9]

An expanding economy thus had differing effects on women of various classes. For those in the growing urban middle classes, excess cash made it possible to consider hiring a nurse when circumstances, desire, or exhaustion meant a female relative was no longer available for the task. Caring as labor, for these women, could be separated from love.

For older widows or spinsters from the working classes, nursing became a trade they could "profess" relatively easily in the marketplace. A widow who had nursed her husband till his demise, or a domestic servant who had cared for an employer in time of illness, entered casually into the nursing trade, hired by families or individuals unwilling, or unable, to care for their sick alone. The permeable boundaries for women between unpaid and paid labor allowed nursing to pass back and forth when necessary. For many women, nursing thus beckoned as respectable community work.

These "professed" or "natural-born" nurses, as they were known, usually came to their work, as one Boston nurse put it, "laterly" when other forms of employment were closed to them or the lack of any kind of work experience left nursing as an obvious choice. Mehitable

Pond Garside, for example, was in her fifties and had outlived two husbands—and her children could not, or would not, support her—when she came to Boston in the 1840s to nurse. Similarly Alma Frost Merrill, the daughter of a Maine wheelwright, came to Boston in 1818 at nineteen to become a domestic servant. After years as a domestic and seamstress, she declared herself a nurse.[10]

Women like Mehitable Pond Garside and Alma Frost Merrill differed markedly from the Sairy Gamp character of Dickens' novel, *Martin Chuzzlewit*. Gamp was portrayed as a merely besotted representative of lumpen-proletarian womanhood, who asserted her autonomy by daring to question medical diagnosis, to venture her own opinions (usually outrageous and wrong) at every turn, and to spread disease and superstition in the name of self-knowledge. If they were not Gamps, nurses like Garside and Merrill also were not the healers of some more recent feminist mythology that confounds nursing with midwifery, praising the caring and autonomy these women exerted, but refusing to consider their ignorance.[11] Some professed nurses learned their skills from years of experience, demonstrating the truth of the dictum that "to make a kind and sympathizing nurse, one must have waited, in sickness, upon those she loved dearly."[12] Others, however, blundered badly beyond their capabilities or knowledge. They brought to the bedside only the authority their personalities and community stature could command: Neither credentials

nor a professional identity gave weight to their efforts. Their womanhood, and the experience it gave them, defined their authority and taught them to nurse.

The Hospital Nurse

Nursing was not limited, however, to the bedside in a home. Although the United States had only 178 hospitals at the first national census in 1873, it was workers labeled "nurses" who provided the caring. As in home-based nursing, the route to hospital nursing was paved more with necessity than with intentionality. In 1875, Eliza Higgins, the matron of Boston's Lying-In Hospital, could not find an extra nurse to cover all the deliveries. In desperation, she moved the hospital laundress up to the nursing position, while a recovering patient took over the wash. Higgins' diaries of her trying years at the Lying-In suggest that such an entry into nursing was not uncommon.[13]

As Higgins' reports and memoirs of other nurses attest, hospital nursing could be the work of devoted women who learned what historian Charles Rosenberg has labeled "ad hoc professionalism," or the temporary and dangerous labor of an ambulatory patient or hospital domestic.[14] As in home-based nursing, both caring and concern were frequently demonstrated. But the nursing work and nurses were mainly characterized by the diversity of their efforts and the unevenness of their skills.

Higgins' memoirs attest to the hospital as a battleground where nurses, physicians, and hospital managers contested the realm of their authority. Nurses continually affirmed their right to control the pace and content of their work, to set their own hours, and to structure their relationships to physicians. Aware that the hospital's paternalistic attitudes and practices toward its "inmates" were attached to the nursing personnel as well, they fought to be treated as workers, "not children," as the Lying-In nurses told Eliza Higgins, and to maintain their autonomous adult status.[15]

Like home-based nursing, hospital nurses had neither formal training nor class status upon which to base their arguments. But their sense of the rights of working-class womanhood gave them authority to press their demands. The necessity to care, and their perception of its importance to patient outcome, also structured their belief that demanding the right to be relatively autonomous was possible. However, their efforts were undermined by the nature of their onerous work, the paternalism of the institutions, class differences between trustees and workers, and ultimately the lack of a defined ideology of caring. Mere resistance to those above them, or contending assertions of rights, could not become the basis for nursing authority.

The Influence of Nightingale

Much of this changed with the introduction of training for nursing in the hospital world. In the aftermath of Nightingale's triumph over the British army's medical care system

in the Crimea, similar attempts by American women during the Civil War, and the need to find respectable work for daughters of the middling classes, a model and support for nursing reform began to grow. By 1873, three nursing schools in hospitals in New York, Boston, and New Haven were opened, patterned after the Nightingale School at St. Thomas' Hospital in London.

Nightingale had envisioned nursing as an art, rather than a science, for which women needed to be trained. Her ideas linked her medical and public health notions to her class and religious beliefs. Accepting the Victorian idea of divided spheres of activity for men and women, she thought women had to be trained to nurse through a disciplined process of honing their womanly virtue. Nightingale stressed character development, the laws of health, and strict adherence to orders passed through a female hierarchy. Nursing was built on a model that relied on the concept of duty to provide its basis for authority. Unlike other feminists at the time, she spoke in the language of duty, not rights.

Furthermore, as a nineteenth-century sanitarian, Nightingale never believed in germ theory, in part because she refused to accept a theory of disease etiology that appeared to be morally neutral. Given her sanitarian beliefs, Nightingale thought medical therapeutics and "curing" were of lesser importance to patient outcome, and she willingly left this realm to the physician. Caring, the arena she did think of great importance, she assigned to the nurse. In order to care, a nurse's character, tempered by the fires of training, was to be her greatest skill. Thus, to "feminize" nursing. Nightingale sought a change in the class-defined behavior, not the gender, of the work force.[16]

To forge a good nurse out of the virtues of a good woman and to provide a political base for nursing. Nightingale sought to organize a female hierarchy in which orders passed down from the nursing superintendent to the lowly probationer. This separate female sphere was to share power in the provision of health care with the male-dominated arenas of medicine. For many women in the Victorian era, sisterhood and what Carroll Smith-Rosenberg has called "homosocial networks" served to overcome many of the limits of this separate but supposedly equal system of cultural division.[17] Sisterhood, after all, at least in its fictive forms, underlay much of the female power that grew out of women's culture in the nineteenth century. But in nursing, commonalities of the gendered experience could not become the basis of unity since hierarchial filial relations, not equal sisterhood, lay at the basis of nursing's theoretical formulation.

Service, Not Education

Thus, unwittingly, Nightingale's sanitarian ideas and her beliefs about womanhood provided some of the ideological justification for many of the dilemmas that faced American nursing by 1900. Having fought physician and trustee prejudice against the training of nurses in hospitals in the last quarter of the nineteenth century, American nursing reformers succeeded only too well as the new century began. Between 1890 and 1920, the number of nursing schools jumped from 35 to 1,775, and the number of trained nurses from 16 per 100,000 in the population to 141.[18] Administrators quickly realized that opening a "nursing school" provided their hospitals, in exchange for training, with a young, disciplined, and cheap labor force. There was often no differences between the hospital's nursing school and its nursing service. The service needs of the hospital continually overrode the educational requirements of the schools. A student might, therefore, spend weeks on a medical ward if her labor was so needed, but never see the inside of an operating room before her graduation.

Once the nurse finished her training, however, she was unlikely to be hired by a hospital because it relied on either untrained aides or nursing student labor. The majority of graduate nurses, until the end of the 1930s, had to find work in private duty in a patient's home, as the patient's employee in the hospital, in the branches of public health, or in some hospital staff positions. In the world of nursing beyond the training school, "trained" nurses still had to compete with the thousands of "professed" or "practical" nurses who continued to ply their trade in an overcrowded and unregulated marketplace. The title of nurse took on very ambiguous meanings.[19]

The term, "trained nurse," was far from a uniform designation. As nursing leader Isabel Hampton Robb lamented in 1893, "the title 'trained nurse' may mean then anything, everything, or next to nothing."[20]

The exigencies of nursing acutely ill or surgical patients required the sacrifice of coherent educational programs. Didactic, repetitive, watered-down medical lectures by physicians or older nurses were often provided for the students, usually after they finished ten to twelve hours of ward work. Training emphasized the "one right way" of doing ritualized procedures in hopes the students' adherence to specified rules would be least dangerous to patients.[21] Under these circumstances, the duty to care could be followed with a vengeance and become the martinet adherence to orders.

Furthermore, because nursing emphasized training in discipline, order, and practical skills, the abuse of student labor could be rationalized. And because the work force was almost entirely women, altruism, sacrifice, and submission were expected, encouraged, indeed, demanded. Exploitation was inevitable in a field where, until the early 1900s, there were no accepted standards for how much work an average student should do or how many patients she could successfully care for, no mechanisms through which to enforce such standards. After completing her exhaustive and depressing survey of nursing training in 1912, nursing educator M. Adelaide Nutting bluntly pointed out: "Under the present system the school has no life of its own."[22] In this kind of environment, nurses were trained. But they were not educated.

Virtue and Autonomy

It would be a mistake, however to see the nursing experience only as one of exploitation and the nursing school as a faintly concealed reformatory for the wayward girl in need of discipline. Many nursing superintendents lived the Nightingale ideals as best they could and infused them into their schools. The authoritarian model could and did retemper many women. It instilled in nurses idealism and pride in their skills, somewhat differentiated the trained nurse from the untrained, and protected and aided the sick and dying. It provided a mechanism for virtuous women to contribute to the improvement of humanity by empowering them to care.

For many of the young women entering training in the nineteenth and early twentieth centuries, nursing thus offered something quite special: both a livelihood and a virtuous state. As one nursing educator noted in 1890: "Young strong country girls are drawn into the work by the glamorer [sic] thrown about hospital work and the halo that sanctifies a Nightingale."[23] Thus, in their letters of application, aspiring nursing students expressed their desire for work, independence, and womanly virtue. As with earlier, non-trained nurses, they did not seem to separate autonomy and altruism, but rather sought its linkage through training. Flora Jones spoke for many such women when she wrote the superintendent of Boston City Hospital in 1880, declaring, "I consider myself fitted for the work by inclination and consider it a womanly occupation. It is also necessary for me to become self-supporting and provide for my future."[24] Thus, one nursing superintendent reminded a graduating class in 1904: "You have become self-controlled, unselfish, gentle, compassionate, brave, capable—in fact, you have risen from the period of irresponsible girlhood to that of womanhood."[25] For women like Flora Jones, and many of nursing's early leaders, nursing was the singular way to grow to maturity in a womanly profession that offered meaningful work, independence, and altruism.[26]

Altruism, Not Independence

For many, however, as nursing historian Dorothy Sheahan has noted, the training school, "was a place where . . . women learned to be girls."[27] The range of permissible behaviors for respectable women was often narrowed further through training. Independence was to be sacrificed on the altar of altruism. Thus, despite hopes of aspiring students and promises of training school superintendents, nursing rarely united altruism and autonomy. Duty remained the basis for caring.

Some nurses were able to create what they called "a little world of our own." But nursing had neither the financial nor the cultural power to create the separate women's institutions that provided so much of the basis for women's reform and rights efforts.[28] Under these conditions, nurses found it difficult to make the collective transition out of a woman's culture of obligation into an

activist assault on the structure and beliefs that oppressed them. Nursing remained bounded by its ideology and its material circumstances.

The Contradictions of Reform

In this context, one begins to understand the difficulties faced by the leaders of nursing reform. Believing that educational reform was central to nursing's professionalizing efforts and clinical improvements, a small group of elite reformers attempted to broaden nursing's scientific content and social outlook. In arguing for an increase in the scientific knowledge necessary in nursing, such leaders were fighting against deep-seated cultural assumptions about male and female "natural" characteristics as embodied in the doctor and the nurse. Such sentiments were articulated in the routine platitudes that graced what one nursing leader described as the "doctor homilies" that were a regular feature at nursing graduation exercises.[29]

Not surprisingly, such beliefs were professed by physicians and hospital officials whenever nursing shortages appeared, or nursing groups pushed for higher educational standards or defined nursing as more than assisting the physician. As one nursing educator wrote, with some degree of resignation after the influenza pandemic in 1920: "It is perhaps inevitable that the difficulty of securing nurses during the last year or two should have revived again the old agitation about the 'over-training' of nurses and the clamor for a cheap worker of the old servant-nurse type."[30]

First Steps toward Professionalism

The nursing leadership, made up primarily of educators and supervisors with their base within what is now the American Nurses' Association and the National League for Nursing, thus faced a series of dilemmas as they struggled to raise educational standards in the schools and criteria for entry into training, to register nurses once they finished their training, and to gain acceptance for the knowledge base and skills of the nurse. They had to exalt the womanly character, self-abnegation, and service ethic of nursing while insisting on the right of nurses to act in their own self-interest. They had to demand higher wages commensurate with their skills, yet not appear commercial. They had to simultaneously find a way to denounce the exploitation of nursing students, as they made political alliances with hospital physicians and administrators whose support they needed. While they lauded character and sacrifice, they had to find a way to measure it with educational criteria in order to formulate registration laws and set admission standards. They had to make demands and organize, without appearing "unladylike." In sum, they were forced by the social conditions and ideology surrounding nursing to attempt to professionalize altruism without demanding autonomy.

Undermined by Duty

The image of a higher claim of duty also continually undermined a direct assertion of the right to determine that duty. Whether at a bedside, or at a legislative hearing on practice laws, the duty to care became translated into the demand that nurses merely follow doctors' orders. The tradition of obligation almost made it impossible for nurses to speak about rights at all. By the turn of the century necessity and desire were pulling more young women into the labor force, and the women's movement activists were placing rights at the center of cultural discussion. In this atmosphere, nursing's call to duty was perceived by many as an increasingly antiquated language to shore up a changing economic and cultural landscape. Nursing became a type of collective female grasping for an older form of security and power in the face of rapid change. Women who might have been attracted to nursing in the 1880s as a womanly occupation that provided some form of autonomy, were, by the turn of the century, increasingly looking elsewhere for work and careers.

A Different Vision

In the face of these difficulties, the nursing leadership became increasingly defensive and turned on its own rank and file. The educators and supervisors who comprised leadership lost touch with the pressing concern of their constituencies in the daily work world of nursing and the belief systems such nurses continued to hold. Yet many nurses, well into the twentieth century, shared the nineteenth-century vision of nursing as the embodiment of womanly virtue. A nurse named

Annette Fiske, for example, although she authored two science books for nurses and had an M.A. degree in classics from Radcliffe College before she entered training, spent her professional career in the 1920s arguing against increasing educational standards. Rather, she called for a reinfusion into nursing of spirituality and service, assuming that this would result in nursing's receiving greater "love and respect and admiration."[31]

Other nurses, especially those trained in the smaller schools or reared to hold working-class ideals about respectable behavior in women, shared Fiske's views. They saw the leadership's efforts at professionalization as an attempt to push them out of nursing. Their adherence to nursing skill measured in womanly virtue was less a conservative and reactionary stance than a belief that seemed to transcend class and educational backgrounds to place itself in the individual character and work-place skills of the nurse. It grounded altruism in supposedly natural and spiritual, rather than educational and middle-class, soil. For Fiske and many other nurses, nursing was still a womanly art that required inherent character in its practitioners and training in practical skills and spiritual values in its schools. Their beliefs about nursing did not require the professionalization of altruism, nor the demand for autonomy either at the bedside or in control over the professionalization process.

Still other nurses took a more pragmatic viewpoint that built on their pride in their work-place skills and character. These nurses also saw

the necessity for concerted action, not unlike that taken by other American workers. Such nurses fought against what one 1888 nurse, who called herself Candor, characterized as the "missionary spirit . . . [of] self-immolation" that denied that nurses worked because they had to make a living.[32] These worker-nurses saw no contradiction between demanding decent wages and conditions for their labors and being of service for those in need. But the efforts of various groups of these kinds of nurses to turn to hours' legislation, trade union activity, or mutual aid associations were criticized and condemned by the nursing leadership. Their letters were often edited out of the nursing journals, and their voices silenced in public meetings as they were denounced as being commercial, or lacking in proper womanly devotion.[33]

In the face of continual criticism from nursing's professional leadership, the worker-nurses took on an increasingly angry and defensive tone. Aware that their sense of the nurse's skills came from the experiences of the work place, not book learning or degrees, they had to assert this position despite continued hostility toward such a basis of nursing authority.[34] Although the position of women like Candor helped articulate a way for nurses to begin to assert the right to care, it did not constitute a full-blown ideological counterpart to the overwhelming power of the belief in duty.

The Persistence of Dilemmas

By midcentury, the disputes between worker-nurses and the

professional leadership began to take on new forms, although the persistent divisions continued. Aware that some kind of collective bargaining was necessary to keep nurses out of the unions and in the professional associations, the ANA reluctantly agreed in 1946 to let its state units act as bargaining agents. The nursing leadership has continued to look at educational reform strategies, now primarily taking the form of legislating for the B.S. degree as the credential necessary for entry into nursing practice, and to changes in the practice laws that will allow increasingly skilled nurses the autonomy and status they deserve. Many nurses have continued to be critical of this educational strategy, to ignore the professional associations, or to leave nursing altogether.

In their various practice fields nurses still need a viable ideology and strategy that will help them adjust to the continual demands of patients and an evermore bureaucratized, cost-conscious, and rationalized work setting. For many nurses it is still, in an ideological sense, the nineteenth century. Even for those nurses who work as practitioners in the more autonomous settings of health maintenance organizations or public health offices, the legacy of nursing's heritage is still felt. Within the last two years, for example, the Massachusetts Board of Medicine tried to push through a regulation that health practitioners acknowledge their dependence on physicians by wearing a badge that identified their supervising physician and stated that they were not doctors.

Nurses have tried various way to articulate a series of rights that allow them to care. The acknowledgment of responsibilities, however, so deeply ingrained in nursing and American womanhood, as nursing school dean Claire Fagin has noted, continually drown out the nurse's assertion of rights.[35]

Nurses are continuing to struggle to obtain the right to claim rights. Nursing's educational philosophy, ideological underpinnings, and structural position have made it difficult to create the circumstances within which to gain such recognition. It is not a lack of vision that thwarts nursing, but the lack of power to give that vision substantive form.[36]

Beyond the Obligation to Care

Much has changed in nursing in the last forty years. The severing of nursing education from the hospital's nursing services has finally taken place, as the majority of nurses are now educated in colleges, not hospital-based diploma schools. Hospitals are experimenting with numerous ways to organize the nursing service to provide the nurse with more responsibility and sense of control over the nursing care process. The increasingly technical and machine-aided nature of hospital-based health care has made nurses feel more skilled.

In many ways, however, little has changed. Nursing is still divided over what counts as a nursing skill, how it is to be learned, and whether a nurse's character can be measured in educational criteria. Technical knowledge and capabilities do not easily translate into power and control. Hospitals, seeking to cut costs, have forced nurses to play "beat the clock" as they run from task to task in an increasingly fragmented setting.[37]

Nursing continues to struggle with the basis for, and the value of, caring. The fact that the first legal case on comparable worth was brought by a group of Denver nurses suggests nursing has an important and ongoing role in the political effort to have caring revalued. As in the Denver case, contemporary feminism has provided some nurses with the grounds on which to claim rights from their caring.[38]

Feminism, in its liberal form, appears to give nursing a political language that argues for equality and rights within the given order of things. It suggests a basis for caring that stresses individual discretion and values, acknowledging that the nurses' right to care should be given equal consideration with the physician's right to cure. Just as liberal political theory undermined more paternalistic formulations of government, classical liberalism's tenets applied to women have much to offer nursing. The demand for the right to care questions deeply held beliefs about gendered relations in the health care hierarchy and the structure of the hierarchy itself.

Many nurses continue to hope that with more education, explicit theories to explain the scientific basis for nursing, new skills, and a lot of assertiveness training, nursing will change. As these nurses try to shed the image of the nurse's being ordered to care, however, the admonition to care at a graduation speech has to be made. Unable to find a way to "care with autonomy" and unable to separate caring from its valuing and basis, many nurses find themselves forced to abandon the effort to care, or nursing altogether.

Altruism with Autonomy

These dilemmas for nurses suggest the constraints that surround the effectiveness of a liberal feminist political strategy to address the problems of caring and, therefore, of nursing. The individualism and autonomy of a rights framework often fail to acknowledge collective social need, to provide a way for adjudicating conflicts over rights, or to address the reasons for the devaluing of female activity.[39] Thus, nurses have often rejected liberal feminism, not just out of their oppression and "false consciousness," but because of some deep understandings of the limited promise of equality and autonomy in a health care system they see as flawed and harmful. In an often inchoate way, such nurses recognize that those who claim the autonomy of rights often run the risk of rejecting altruism and caring itself.

Several feminist psychologists have suggested that what women really want in their lives is autonomy with connectedness. Similarly, many modern moral philosophers are trying to articulate a formal moral theory that values the emotions and the importance of relationships.[40] For nursing, this will require the creation of the conditions under which it is possible to value caring and to understand that the empowerment of others does not have to require self-immolation. To achieve this, nurses will have both to create a new political understanding for the basis of caring and to find ways to gain the power to implement it. Nursing can do much to have this happen through research on the importance of caring on patient outcome, studies of patient improvements in nursing settings where the right to care is created, or implementing nursing control of caring through a bargaining agreement. But nurses cannot do this alone. The dilemma of nursing is too tied to society's broader problems of gender and class to be solved solely by the political or professional efforts to one occupational group.

Nor are nurses alone in benefiting from such an effort. If nursing can achieve the power to practice altruism with autonomy, all of us have much to gain. Nursing has always been a much conflicted metaphor in our culture, reflecting all the ambivalences we give to the meaning of womanhood.[41] Perhaps in the future it can give this metaphor and, ultimately, caring, new value in all our lives.

Notes

1. Gregory Wticher, "Last Class of Nurses Told: Don't Stop Caring," *Boston Globe*, May 13, 1985, pp. 17–18.
2. See, for examples, Larry Blum et al., "Altruism and Women's Oppression," in *Women and Philosophy*, eds. Carol Gould and Marx Wartofsy (New York: G.P. Putnam's, 1976), pp. 222–247; Nel Noddings, *Caring*. Berkeley: University of California Press, 1984; Nancy Chodorow, *The Reproduction of Mothering*. Berkeley: University of California Press, 1978; Carol Gilligan, *In a Different Voice*. Cambridge: Harvard University Press, 1982; and Janet Finch and Dulcie Groves, eds., *A Labour of Love: Women, Work and Caring*. London and Boston: Routledge, Kegan Paul, 1983.
3. Hilary Graham, "Caring: A Labour of Love," in *A Labour of Love*, eds. Finch and Groves, pp. 13–30.
4. Joel Feinberg, *Rights, Justice and the Bounds of Liberty* (Princeton: Princeton University Press, 1980), p. 141.
5. Blum et al., "Altruism and Women's Oppression," p. 223; Jean Baker Miller, *Toward a New Psychology of Women* (Boston: Beacon Press, 1976), p. 71.
6. Ibid; see also Iris Marion Young, "Is Male Gender Identity the Cause of Male Domination," in *Mothering: Essays in Feminist Theory*, ed. Joyce Trebicott (Totowa, NJ: Rowman and Allanheld, 1983), pp. 129–146.
7. Catherine Beecher, *Domestic Receipt-Book* (New York: Harper and Brothers, 1846) p. 214.
8. Eliza Farrar, *The Young Lady's Friend —By a Lady* (Boston: American Stationer's Co., 1837), p. 57.
9. Catherine Beecher, *Miss Beecher's Housekeeper and Healthkeeper*. New York: Harper and Brothers, 1876; and Sarah Josepha Hale, *The Good Housekeeper*. Boston: Otis Brothers and Co., 7th edition, 1844. See also Susan Strasser, *Never Done: A History of Housework*. New York: Pantheon, 1982.
10. Cases 2 and 18, "Admissions Committee Records," Volume I, Box 11, Home for Aged Women Collection, Schlesigner Library, Radcliffe College, Cambridge, Mass. Data on the

nurses admitted to the home were also found in "Records of Inmates, 1858–1901," "Records of Admission, 1873–1924," and "Records of Inmates, 1901–1916," all in Box 11.

11. Charles Dickens, *Martin Chuzzlewit*. New York: New American Library, 1965, original edition, London: 1865; Barbara Ehrenreich and Deirdre English, *Witches, Nurses, Midwives: A History of Women Healers*. Old Westbury: Glass Mountain Pamphlets, 1972.

12. Virginia Penny, *The Employments of Women: A Cyclopedia of Women's Work* (Boston: Walker, Wise and Co., 1863), p. 420.

13. Eliza Higgins, Boston Lying-In Hospital, *Matron's Journals, 1873–1889*, Volume I, January 9, 1875, February 22, 1875, Rare Books Room, Countway Medical Library, Harvard Medical School, Boston, Mass.

14. Charles Rosenberg, "'And Heal the Sick': The Hospital and the Patient in 19th Century America," *Journal of Social History* 10 (June 1977):445.

15. Higgins, *Matron's Journals*, Volume II, January 11, 1876, and July 1, 1876. See also a parallel discussion of male artisan behavior in front of the boss in David Montgomery, "Workers' Control of Machine Production in the 19th Century," *Labor History* 17 (Winter 1976):485–509.

16. The discussion on Florence Nightingale is based on my analysis in *Ordered to Care*, chapter 3. See also Charles E. Rosenberg, "Florence Nightingale on Contagion: The Hospital as Moral Universe," in *Healing and History*, ed. Charles E. Rosenberg. New York: Science History Publications, 1979.

17. Carroll Smith-Rosenberg. "The Female World of Love and Ritual," *Signs: Journal of Women in Culture and Society* 1 (Autumn 1975):1.

18. May Ayers Burgess, *Nurses, Patients and Pocketbooks*. New York: Committee on the Grading of Nursing, 1926, reprint edition (New York: Garland Publishing Co., 1985), pp. 36–37.

19. For further discussion of the dilemmas of private duty nursing, see Susan Reverby, "'Neither for the Drawing Room nor for the Kitchen': Private Duty Nursing, 1880–1920," in *Women and Health in America*, ed. Judith Walzer Leavitt. Madison: University of Wisconsin Press, 1984, and Susan Reverby, "'Something Besides Waiting': The Politics of Private Duty Nursing Reform in the Depression," in *Nursing History: New Perspectives, New Possibilities*, ed. Ellen Condliffe Lagemann. New York: Teachers College Press, 1982.

20. Isabel Hampton Robb, "Educational Standards for Nurses," in *Nursing of the Sick 1893* (New York: McGraw-Hill, 1949), p. 11. See also Janet Wilson James, "Isabel Hampton and the Professionalization of Nursing in the 1890s," in *The Therapeutic Revolution*, eds. Morris Vogel and Charles E. Rosenberg. Philadelphia: University of Pennsylvania Press, 1979.

21. For further discussion of the difficulties in training, see JoAnn Ashley, *Hospitals, Paternalism and the Role of the Nurse*. New York: Teachers College Press, 1976, and Reverby, *Ordered to Care*, chapter 4.

22. *Educational Status of Nursing*, Bureau of Education Bulletin Number 7, Whole Number 475 (Washington, D.C.: Government Printing Office, 1912), p. 49.

23. Julia Wells, "Do Hospitals Fit Nurses for Private Nursing," *Trained Nurse and Hospital Review* 3 (March 1890): 98.

24. Boston City Hospital (BCH) Training School Records, Box 4, Folder 4, Student 4, February 14, 1880, BCH Training School Papers, Nursing

Archives, Special Collections, Boston University, Mugar Library, Boston, Mass. The student's name has been changed to maintain confidentiality.

25. Mary Agnes Snively, "What Manner of Women Ought Nurses to Be?" *American Journal of Nursing* 4 (August 1904):838.

26. For a discussion of many of the early nursing leaders as "new women," see Susan Armeny, "'We Were the New Women': A Comparison of Nurses and Women Physicians, 1890–1915." Paper presented at the American Association for the History of Nursing Conference, University of Virginia, Charlottesville, Va., October 1984.

27. Dorothy Sheahan, "Influence of Occupational Sponsorship on the Professional Development of Nursing." Paper presented at the Rockefeller Archives Conference on the History of Nursing, Rockefeller Archives, Tarrytown, NY, May 1981, p. 12.

28. Estelle Freedman, "Separatism as Strategy: Female Institution Building and American Feminism, 1870–1930," *Feminist Studies* 5 (Fall 1979):512–529.

29. Lavinia L. Dock, *A History of Nursing*, volume 3 (New York: G.P. Putnam's, 1912), p. 136.

30. Isabel M. Stewart, "Progress in Nursing Education during 1919," *Modern Hospital* 14 (March 1920):183.

31. Annette Fiske, "How Can We Counteract the Prevailing Tendency to Commercialism in Nursing?" *Proceedings of the 17th Annual Meeting of the Massachusetts State Nurses' Association*, p. 8, Massachusetts Nurses Association Papers, Box 7, Nursing Archives.

32. Candor, "Working and Wages," Letter to the Editor, *Trained Nurse and Hospital Review* 2 (April 1888): 167–168.

33. See the discussion in Ashley, *Hospitals, Paternalism and the Role of the Nurse*, pp. 40–43, 46–48, 51, and in Barbara Melosh, *"The Physician's Hand": Work Culture and Conflict in American Nursing* (Philadelphia: Temple University Press, 1982), passim.

34. For further discussion see Susan Armeny, "Resolute Enthusiasts: The Effort to Professionalize American Nursing, 1880–1915." PhD dissertation, University of Missouri, Columbia, Mo., 1984, and Reverby, *Ordered to Care*, chapter 6.

35. Feinberg, *Rights*, pp. 130–142; Claire Fagin, "Nurses' Rights," *American Journal of Nursing* 75 (January 1975):82.

36. For a similar argument for bourgeois women, see Carroll Smith-Rosenberg, "The New Woman as Androgyne: Social Disorder and Gender Crisis," in *Disorderly Conduct* (New York: Alfred Knopf, 1985), p. 296.

37. Boston Nurses' Group, "The False Promise: Professionalism in Nursing," *Science for the People* 10 (May/June 1978):20–34; Jennifer Bingham Hull, "Hospital Nightmare: Cuts in Staff Demoralize Nurses as Care Suffers," *Wall Street Journal*, March 27, 1985.

38. Bonnie Bullough, "The Struggle for Women's Rights in Denver: A Personal Account," *Nursing Outlook* 26 (September 1978):566–567.

39. For critiques of liberal feminism see Allison M. Jagger, *Feminist Politics and Human Nature* (Totowa, NJ: Rowman and Allanheld, 1983), pp. 27–50, 173, 206; Zillah Eisenstein, *The Radical Future of Liberal Feminism*. New York and London: Longman, 1981; and Rosalind Pollack Petchesky, *Abortion and Women's Choice*

(Boston: Northeastern   University Press, 1984), pp. 1–24.
40. Miller, *Toward a New Psychology*; Jane Flax, "The Conflict between Nurturance   and   Autonomy   in Mother-Daughter Relationships and within Feminism," *Feminist Studies* 4 (June 1978):171–191; Blum et al., "Altruism and Women's Oppression."
41. Claire Fagin and Donna Diers, "Nursing as Metaphor," *New England Journal of Medicine* 309 (July 14, 1983):116–117.

33   THE FUTURE OF CHIROPRACTIC

Walter I. Wardell

What is to be done about chiropractors? Efforts by organized medicine to eliminate them have been unsuccessful. The label "quack" has not stuck. Despite the most strenuous opposition, they have attained licensure in every state in the United States and in Canada and many foreign countries. Over 23,000 chiropractors treat some 8 million Americans for a wide variety of conditions. Reimbursement for their services has been authorized by Medicare, Medicaid,   Workmen's   Compensation plans, and by many Blue Shield plans and other private insurance carries. Chiropractors received more than $30 million of Medicare funds in 1978. Over 2000 new chiropractors will be graduated this year, more than 70 per cent of them from colleges federally recognized as accredited. Chiropractors appear to be winning their struggle to survive.

Awareness of these facts is finally appearing in medical circles.[1,2] Perhaps the most important stimulus, however, has come from the antitrust suit filed in 1976 by five Illinois chiropractors against the American Medical   Association   (AMA),   the American Osteopathic Association, 10 other medical organizations, and four individuals,[3] followed by antitrust suits in several other states. The medical code of ethics has already   been   modified   to   remove restrictions on professional association with chiropractors, but the broader question of the role that chiropractors will play in the American health-care   system   must   still   be faced by makers of health policy, legislators, and the leaders of organized medicine.

An informative discussion of the worth of chiropractic therapy is contained   in   a   recent   report,   "Chiropractic in New Zealand," by an official Commission of Inquiry.[4] I agree that it is "probably the most comprehensive   and   detailed   independent examination of chiropractic ever undertaken in any country." Its principal conclusions are that

SOURCE: From *The New England Journal of Medicine*, vol. 302, pp. 688–90. Copyright © Massachusetts Medical Society, 1980. Reprinted by permission.

modern chiropractic is far from being "an unscientific cult," . . . is safe, . . . can be effective in relieving musculo-skeletal symptoms . . . In a limited number of cases where there are or-ganic and/or visceral symptoms, chiro-practic treatment may provide relief, but this is unpredictable, and in such cases the patient should be under con-current medical care if that is practica-ble . . . There must be no impediment to full professional cooperation be-tween chiropractors and medical prac-titioners . . . Chiropractors should, in the public interest, be accepted as partners in the general health care sys-tem . . . Patients should continue to have the right to consult chiropractors direct.

An impartial evaluation of chiro-practic in the United States should, and probably would, come to essen-tially the same conclusions as the New Zealand Commission. In any case, the makers of American health policy need to consider carefully the roles that chiropractors might play in the future.

One alternative seems clearly foreclosed—the route that osteopa-thy has followed. The notion that chiropractic's evolution has, a gener-ation later, been modeled after that of osteopathy is not historically ac-curate,[5] nor is such a route likely in the future. Despite their shared pre-occupation with manipulation, chi-ropractors simply do not practice like osteopaths, who prescribe drugs nearly as much as medical doctors do. Although chiropractors envy the greater prestige and comprehensive-ness of medical practice, and some claim to provide complete primary care, their hostility toward drug therapy strongly inhibits the desire

to become allopathic practitioners. This impediment is, of course, rein-forced by the vigorous opposition of organized medicine to any claims by chiropractors to practice comprehen-sive medicine.

A second possible alternative—for chiropractors to function under med-ical prescription as physical thera-pists do—is equally unlikely, al-though it is what President Carter first proposed to Congress, but later dropped, in his 1979 National Health Insurance Plan. It would not work because chiropractors already have too autonomous a professional sta-tus to be willing to subordinate themselves to medical doctors. In addition, medical doctors are not trained to know when chiropractic would be beneficial or contraindi-cated, and they have regarded chiro-practors as unfit for professional as-sociation for so long that they would generally be unwilling to send pa-tients to chiropractors.

A variant on this "solution" would be for physical therapists to become skilled spinal manipulators and offer patients all that chiropractors do—but under medical prescription. James Cyriax, M.D., himself a skilled manipulator, urges physi-cians and physical therapists to mas-ter the manipulative therapy that he calls "orthopaedic medicine," and he offers training workshops for those who wish to learn.[6] Similarly, the physical therapist Stanley Paris tells me that he offers postgraduate in-struction in "orthopaedic physical therapy"; he organized the Institute of Orthopaedic Physical Therapy on Staten Island, N.Y., and in 1974 helped establish a Section on Orthopaedics of the American Physical Therapy Association. However, if physical therapists were to follow this route, not only would the prescribing physicians have to know much more about the indications and contraindications for manipulative therapy than they do now, but physical therapists would in effect have to become chiropractors, although their current baccalaureate-level training does not qualify them to diagnose general pathology or to prescribe for it. Hence, it is not likely that the problem of chiropractic can be eliminated by a concerted effort to replace chiropractors with upgraded physical therapists.

A third option is to maintain the status quo. Chiropractors would remain a "marginal" profession independent of organized medicine, their therapy continuing to be stigmatized as a dubious value, and their ability to make differential diagnoses suspect.[7] Perhaps chiropractors could gradually elevate themselves to a profession "parallel" to medicine (a status somewhat like that of osteopaths in the recent past) through continuing to upgrade the quality of their schools and their diagnostic competence. But if this were to happen, the "separate but equal" dilemma would probably appear, just as it has with race relations. Separated groups are seldom truly equal; invidious comparisons are inevitably made. The reverse also occurs: Groups of equal status tend not to remain separate. Just as racial groups of equal standing integrate more easily, so too do professional groups that are close to equal status—thus, the recent rapproche-

ment between medicine and osteopathy. Since chiropractic, for reasons stated earlier, is not likely to follow the path of osteopathy by broadening its scope of practice and upgrading itself to the level of medicine, the attempt to maintain the status quo in professional relations between chiropractic and medicine would be more likely to keep chiropractic "marginal" rather than "parallel." Still, this is a viable option.

The final alternative, and the most promising one for many reasons, is the gradual evolution of chiropractic to a "limited" or "limited medical" profession. The most familiar examples are dentistry, podiatry, and optometry; psychology, speech therapy, and audiology occupy similar roles. These professions limit their scope of practice to a specific part of the body or its functioning, and the range of therapies they employ is also limited. Unlike chiropractic, they do not challenge orthodox medical theories of disease and therapy. Hence, they can coexist with organized medicine. However, the road can be rocky, as demonstrated by the long history of disputes between ophthalmologists and optometrists and between psychiatrists and psychologists.[8]

It is far more difficult for a marginal profession like chiropractic, which has historically subscribed to a suspect theory explaining the source of all illnesses, to achieve the satisfactory relation with medicine that the limited medical professions have. The different definitions in state laws of chiropractors' scope of practice have relatively little effect on how chiropractors actually practice or on major trends in chiropractic practice. One critical question will be to what extent chiropractors will abandon some of their central principles, a process that has indeed already begun. Policy makers should not misled by pronouncements of the chiropractic "superstraights," a very small group of doctrinaire practitioners who disavow the vast majority of chiropractors and who are in turn disavowed by them.

With most states now requiring that candidates for licensure be graduated from accredited colleges, there is increasing uniformity in chiropractors' education as well as guaranteed minimum of competence in the basic medical sciences. Furthermore, the colleges now use standard medical textbooks and university-trained instructors, most of whom are not chiropractors, for the basic sciences. Although the colleges are still weak, recent graduates are less doctrinaire, more aware of the limitations of chiropractic theory and therapy, and better able than their predecessors to identify conditions beyond their competence to treat. Therefore, they can function satisfactorily as "portals of entry" into the health-care system without being the providers of total primary care that medical doctors are (and that some chiropractors still claim to be). As a result, chiropractors have the potential for evolving into "limited" or "limited medical" practitioners even though many of them would deny it and many medical doctors would resist it.

There are several forces pushing chiropractors toward becoming limited practitioners. Chiropractic is in fact a limited therapy, not as limited as most physicians have assumed, but certainly not as broad as chiropractors originally claimed, and as chiropractors become better educated in the basic medical sciences, they better understand the limited role of spinal manipulation. They devote most of their time to treatment of musculoskeletal conditions and closely related conditions such as sciatica that manipulative therapy has been shown to help. These conditions are the ones that chiropractors are most associated with in the public view, the ones for which third-party payers are most willing to reimburse chiropractors, and the ones for which medical doctors would be most likely to refer patients to chiropractors.

If chiropractors were to become limited practitioners there would be advantages for them, organized medicine, the health-care system, and public health. Chiropractic would be "contained" to a limited role, and organized medicine could cease its active opposition to chiropractors. Medical doctors would be more likely to refer patients to chiropractors, and vice versa. There would develop a greater consensus among chiropractors as to what chiropractic is, and the public would have a clearer understanding of what chiropractors do, which should lead to an improved public opinion of this form of treatment and its practitioners. Insurance companies would more readily reimburse chiropractors for services performed. Chiropractors would attain a more secure place in the health-care system, and the health of the American public would be enhanced.

It may seem utopian to expect chiropractors to accede to such a limited role, and just as utopian to expect organized medicine even to consider it. But that is what the New Zealand Commission of Inquiry seems to be recommending for its country. In Ontario, where chiropractors are routinely reimbursed under a socialized system, hostility between medical doctors and chiropractors is minimal. There is no fundamental reason why the same situation could not prevail in the United States. The AMA has already lost its struggles to keep chiropractors unlicensed, to prevent payments to them under Medicare, Medicaid, and most other third-party payers, and to prevent the accreditation of chiropractic colleges. Organized medicine faces further assaults on its prerogatives and practices from the courts and in legislative chambers. The leaders of organized medicine and other makers of health policy need to become better informed concerning the current status of chiropractic education and practice, and should seriously consider where the limited-practice model could be the basis of

accommodation between the two groups that have been so hostile to each other for so long.

References

1. Manber MM. Chiropractors: pushing for a place on health-care team. Med World News. 1978; 19(25):57–72.
2. Relman AS. Chiropractic: recognized but unproved. N Engl J Med. 1979; 301:659–60.
3. Wilk CA, Bryden JW, Arthur PB, Lumsden SG, Pegido MD. Complaint #76C3777 filed October 12 in the United States District Court for the Northern District of Illinois, Eastern Division, 1976.
4. Chiropractic in New Zealand: report of the Commission of Inquiry. Wellington, New Zealand: PD Hasselberg, 1979.
5. Wardwell WI. Social factors in the survival of chiropractic: a comparative view. Sociol Symp. 1978; 22:6–17.
6. Cyriax J. Textbook of orthopaedic medicine. Vol. 1. 7th ed. London: Baillière Tindall, 1978.
7. Wardwell WI. A marginal professional role: the chiropractor. Soc Force. 1952; 30:339–48.
8. *Idem*. Limited and marginal practitioners. In: Freeman HE, Levine S, Reeder LG, eds. Handbook of medical sociology. 3d ed. Englewood Cliffs, N.J.: Prentice-Hall, 1979:230–50.

34   SOCIAL POLICY AND EVERYDAY LIFE IN NURSING HOMES: A CRITICAL ETHNOGRAPHY

Timothy Diamond

Introduction

This is a preliminary report on a sociological research project in which I worked as a nursing assistant (or nurses' aide) in a series of nursing homes in the United States. Here, long term care systems are being developed along the organizational model of business and nursing homes are considered an industry. This study focuses on the ongoing creation of that industry. It does so from the standpoint of the everyday life of some of the people inside, especially nursing assistants and patients. The study starts with my own situated experience and those of my co-workers, links these experiences to the social organization of nursing homes, and places these experiences and this social organization within the context of larger social and economic policies.

I began the project by attending a vocational school which trains nursing assistants. After completing the training, I worked full time in three nursing homes for a period of just under two years. The primary objective in undertaking the participant observation project was to get to know personally nursing assistants and patients over time, and to experience everyday life in different kinds of homes. This initial analysis describes some aspects of that everyday life and links them to social and political forces beyond them.

Some of the roots of this study are in medical sociology, especially that based in critical approach to health care institutions [1–6]. Gerontological research has also been informative [7–17]. Ethnographic research in health care settings has been part of the background literature as well [18–20]. Feminist literature has been conceptually essential [21–26]. Almost all nursing home workers and most nursing home residents are women. Both substantially and methodologically, the writing of Dorothy Smith has been especially instructive [24–26]. Smith suggests a method of critical ethnography, drawn from Marx and Engels' outline of the materialist method [27], in which researchers begin with actual situations of people and link these activities to more general characteristics of the society. It is a method for exploring macropolitical forces in the micropolitical moments of their everyday execution.

An Introduction to Nursing Assistant Work

The owner of our vocational school stood tall in his three-piece suit on that first night of class as he welcomed the new nursing assistant

SOURCE: Reprinted with permission from *Social Science and Medicine*, vol. 23, no. 12, pp. 1287–1295. "Social Policy and Everyday Life in Nursing Homes: A Critical Ethnography" by Timothy Diamond. Copyright © 1986, Pergamon Journals, Ltd.

trainees with a mix of medical and military imagery: "Welcome to the firing line of health care." We were recruits in an area of work that is being formalized as a new profession. While the job of nurses' aide has existed for many years, it is now being organized for nursing homes and home health care. By 1990 nursing assistants will constitute one of the largest and fastest growing occupational groups in the U.S. [28]. While their work is supervised by the more highly trained registered nurse and licensed practical nurses, nursing assistants are by far the largest group of workers in nursing homes. Although some men do the work, almost all nursing assistants are women.

In the training course, we learned that we were to become members of the health care team, a part of the noblest of professions. We learned elementary biology, and how we were never to do health care without first consulting someone in authority; and we learned not to ask questions but to do as we were told. As one of the students, a black woman from Jamaica, used to joke, "I can't figure out whether they're trying to teach us to be nurses' aides or black women."

Most of the students laughed at the joke; most were black women. The majority of the nursing assistants I met throughout the research were non-white. As a white man it was not always easy to explain to the people I met why I was studying and working this way. The director of the school turned out to be one of the last white men I was to see in this work, except for administrators

and some patients. While men may own and direct nursing homes, it is not a white man's land inside. So my place in this world was continually at issue, and I explained it in different ways to my classmates and to many of the nursing assistants and patients. I told them I was doing research, and most were supportive. It was not as easy with administrators, however. Initially, I indicated on my job applications that I was a researcher interested in studying nursing homes. The people reading the applications were, I inferred, not nearly as supportive, for not once was I offered a job. They seemed not to value research from this vantage point. Eventually, I began to emphasize my training as a nursing assistant rather than as a researcher. Using this strategy, I was soon employed. I was not alone as a man, yet as one of the very few white men, my presence was never without suspicion. It was one of the administrators who first expressed the general skepticism of my presence when he asked, "Why would a white guy want to work for these kind of wages?"

It was a shock when I finally began to work and experience the conditions to which he was referring. Deborah Saunders, (all names in this paper are fictitious) a co-worker, expressed the situation with a shriek after looking at her first pay-check: "take-home pay of $209, after two weeks of work, including a weekend. $209?", she asked with a sense of shock, "How do they expect us to live on $209?" Deborah's complaint was no idle grumbling over low pay. She was expressing, and indeed living, a contradiction present in certain emerging forms of wage labor. In some service sectors, occupied overwhelmingly by women, pay rates fall below the actual cost of subsistence [29]. This appeared to be the case for many nursing assistants with whom I worked. Many, if not most, were sole supporters of a family. At $104.50 per week, which is $3.50 per hour minus deductions (15 cents above minimum wage), they often complained about not having enough money for essentials—food, rent, utilities, transportation, and their children's needs. In short, the wage creates poverty; the newly professionalized health career workers earn less than family subsistence even with a full-time job. The feminization of poverty, in this case, seems to extend to full-time workers. Solange Ferier from Jamaica summarized it: "You know, Tim, I done this job for six years in my country. One thing I learn when I come to the States—you can't make it on just one job." Most of the nursing assistants I met work more than one job if they can, and live in hope of overtime. Even a full-time job at slightly over minimum wage is not enough. 'Minimum' wage turns out to be an abstraction; it may make sense to policy makers and economists, but it is considerably less than minimum in these people's lives. The policies that name these wages as 'minimum' are far removed from the everyday contingencies that this pittance involves.

Economic Policy and the Path of Poverty

I worked in both private and state-subsidized homes. From the conversations I had with patients in these homes I conclude that in the United States there is an economic life course involved in being a long-term patient. Meeting people in different homes disrupted my image of nursing home life as a static existence. One does not 'end up' in a nursing home; one precedes on a path that is the consequence of social policy and the embeddedness of nursing homes within the organizational model of business and industry. In the United States, care is based on ability to pay. Long-term patients tell about living through the phases of Medicare, private resources (if any), bankruptcy, and public aid. Given present economic arrangements for long-term care, a patient moves along a path: the more time in long-term care, the poorer one becomes.

There are two types of nursing homes, distinguished by the hours of 'skill' nursing compared with those of 'intermediate' care that is provided. I worked in both types. Medicare, the U.S. federal program, pays only for skilled nursing care (as is the policy of most insurance companies). Medicare enters at the beginning of an acute health crisis and pays most of the bill. Yet this is a short-term, rehabilitation-centered program: it has time, sickness, and doctor limits. This is the United States' only federal program for long-term care, but it is actually a very short-term program: one is supported only for a matter of months. It is probably more correct to say that the United States has no federal long-term program, except for Medicaid, which is funded in part by the states. Medicaid, a form of public aid, pays a nursing home for care only after a patient has become indigent. Since long-term care can mean years, indigence is frequently a part of nursing home life.

Many patients told me of their fears as those last weeks of Medicare drew near and, for example, that "damn hip wouldn't heal." Every day Grace DeLong asked me to hand her her checkbook and bank statements. At the time she had about $10,000 in life savings, having worked as a secretary all of her life. She stared at the book for long periods every day, as though to clutch those savings. She lived fearing that they would be drained from her. She had seen it happen to others. Nursing homes are expensive. Costs vary by home from $1500 to $3000 per month. Medicare lasts only a matter of months, after which patients are on their own, relying on whatever personal resources are available through insurance supplements and savings. As mentioned above, most insurance policies, like Medicare, pay only when one is classified as in need of skilled care. Joyce Horan was nervous that insurance people would visit her; she was afraid they would see she was better enough to be reclassified as only needing 'custodial' or intermediate care, be dropped from the rolls, and probably sent to a different ward or home.

Jim McCheever was not so lucky. Jim was 78 years old, had an inoperable brain tumor, and was surely dying. He lasted only six months, so in some ways he was not even a long-termer. Right to his death, Jim remained sturdy, stoic, and, for the most part, continent. Unfortunately, this worked to his disadvantage. It

was determined that he did not need skilled nursing care, and so was not eligible for Medicare. The social policy is that the government will help based only on a strict criterion of medical need. Increasingly, a patient's illness must be such that it fits into one of the predefined categories that are part of the emerging 'prospective payment' systems. Jim did not fit into any category. I knew his family well enough to learn that, because of this, it cost his 78 year-old widow over $17,000 to pay for his care during his last six months. Living through long-term care means feeling constant insecurity over having to pay to live in a home, while at the same time realizing the impossibility of doing so for long. It is a journey toward indigence. Grace DeLong, seeing it coming and clenching her checkbook, used to go on and on in her fear; her pleas were quite high-pitched and frenzied: "Get me out of here! I can't stay here! I've got to get out of here!" A passer-by or someone who had only a fleeting contact with her might interpret her clamor as senile ranting. But she was afraid of losing that $10,000. She had no one at home to care for her, and felt trapped.

There are many patients who really do need to stay in nursing homes. Some like Grace, simply have no other place to go; some are confused and unable to cope with life on their own; some are sick or weak or frail; some have run out of money. Many enter a nursing home by a combination of these forces. Some of these people may regain strength and maintain a relatively high level of physical and psychological functioning; then they are placed in intermediate wings or floors or in separate facilities. Although patients' psychic or physical states may stabilize, their economic base never does.

When resources are depleted there is Public Aid. In the abstract language of government, Medicare and Medicaid are two different 'support systems' for older people. In actuality, living through these policies, they are sequential: a person moves from one to the other and it is a movement toward becoming a pauper. Under Medicaid, the government, partly federal, partly state, pays the nursing home a per capita fee for care. It is not exactly correct to say that a patient 'receives' this public aid; it is closer to say that she or he is 'on' Medicaid. The state pays the nursing home, not the patient. What the nursing home gets currently amounts to about $1500 per month. What the patient receives out of this $1500 is about $25 per month, or less than a dollar a day. This is a severe economy, even for bedridden patients. Personal items, phone calls, cigarettes, coffee from the machine—and $25 is gone by the middle of the month. On public aid, nursing home life is the life of a pauper.

Contrary to the popular image of rest or retirement, nursing home life is not an economically stable situation. This became evident in conversations I had with people who linked the experience of private-pay and public aid in their own lives. The women and men I met at the expensive home started out in the posh two lower floors. When their money had run out they were moved to the public aid wings, there to receive noticeably inferior care. There was a certain pressure within the home that many residents complained about. The management had made it clear that they preferred more short-term Medicare patients, since these patients were worth more. One could feel a murmur of fear among the public aid patients that many would be asked to leave or go to another home. No doubt this would happen to some. I know because I met women and men in the poor homes who had started as private pay residents in other homes and had been forced to leave them. Meeting them made me understand that there is a distinct economic progression in nursing home life— the longer one stays the more impoverished one becomes, and the more unstable one's environment becomes.

Frequently, nursing homes are approached in our thinking as though they were a series of separate places: the idea is to find a good one, or a good model and eliminate the bad ones. To live in long-term care, however, may well refer to homes in a series rather than *a* home. One does not live in just 'a' home, but moves through a system—a maze of different wards, floors, and homes.

The relationship these people have to the society, than, is precarious even before one begins to consider their physical or psychological conditions. These organizational disruptions (moving from one home or ward to another) are beyond the internal workings of a particular home and something about which anyone inside, including those with authority, can do little. They are a by-product of current social policies related to long-term care. These policies themselves breed a fear that derives directly from living in the society. When Grace was screaming "I've got to get out of here!", she was screaming not just at the nursing home, but also at her society beyond it. I came to change my image of nursing home life as a static enterprise. It is not sitting in a chair 'doing nothing.' Rather than being passive, it is always a process. The policies that shape this environment inform every moment of nursing home life. Each person is situated somewhere on an overall turbulent path. Each person sits in a chair, or lies in a bed, often appearing motionless, but is moving and being moved, however silently, through the society.

The Everyday Making of Patients

Another image of passivity that I carried into the research related to preconceptions I had about patients. Having 'ended up' in a nursing home, I thought of them as recipients of someone else's acts, acted upon rather than acting. Patients are formally defined into the organization in a passive way: that is, they are named in terms of diseases, and their basic record of care—the chart—is all about what health care goods and services are rendered to them, about what is done to them, not about what they themselves do. It appears as a passive existence to outside observers, visitors who get snapshot views and carry snapshot imagery of people 'just sitting.'

Working in the local reality of everyday relations dissolved that image. From here there is another way of thinking about nursing homes that conceives of patients as actually quite active. The question might be asked, "what kind of work is involved in surviving in a nursing home?" The notion of passive runs close to making patients objects, which, at worst, leads to the ongoing presumption that "they are out of it," and even at best leads only to questions like, "What can we do for them?" Yet as one gets to know patients it becomes clear that almost all are thinking, conscious people, however fragile and intermittent that consciousness might be. This point of departure presumes patients to be present, actively aware, conscious, at some level—participants in the setting, not just acted upon, and struggling to be at the helm of their own consciousness, even with all the appearances to the contrary.

I say 'struggle' because there can develop within nursing homes an impersonal ethos in which frail, senile patients are assumed to be 'out of it.' They are inserted into an impersonal mode with pervading notions that their minds are 'gone.' Yet, getting to know people in their ongoing lives, it becomes evident that being in long-term care is not just a passive existence. It is also very active. It takes a lot of effort.

Nursing homes are medical environments. They are not short-term hospitals for these people, yet still they operate on the organizational model of a hospital. When one enters a nursing home, a chart is slid into its slot, there to record the units of health care one receives—all related to the first page of the chart, the diagnosis, or sickness category. One is a patient treated in an environment that mimics a hospital, with its spotless, sanitized floors, its PA system blaring, its white-uniformed staff, its air of emergency.

In our daily round of work, as in the schooling, the texts and the manuals, nursing assistant work was defined in a task-centered, physical way. The first assignment as the day began was usually expressed like this: "Diamond, today you have beds 206 to 230." This did not refer to the beds I had to make but to the people who occupied them. The first task was to wake the residents, get them up if at all possible, and prepare them for breakfast and medications. This was the hardest part of the day for many nursing assistants, and a source of continual sharing of jokes and complaints. It was hard because it was so hard for the residents, and something they fought against, so the first moments of the day were often spent in conflict. "Work all my life waiting for retirement," Miss Black used to grumble, "and now I can't even sleep in the mornings." I used to try to explain to her that this was a hospital—at least we followed hospital regimens here—but at 7 a.m. that made little sense to her, or to me.

After the patients were awakened, those who were able to leave their beds were transported to the day room for breakfast. Some residents could not perform all the complex tasks of eating, and had to be helped. The rush was on to finish breakfast by 8:30, so there was pressure when one had to help several people eat. The luck of the bad draw was noted in the question. "How many feeders you got today?" 'Feeder' referred to a patient who needed help eating. The one who is doing the eating becomes an object in this term, the object of feeding, and under the pressure of time, an object of scorn. Buried underneath this pressured moment, however, was the act of feeding a frail sick person—a delicate process, requiring much skill. To learn the extremely slow pace of an old person's eating, or how to vary portions and tastes, how to communicate non-verbally while feeding—these are refined skills, but unnamed, indeed suppressed, by the dictates of the organization.

After breakfast, the 'menial' tasks began that would occupy the assistants until lunch: showers or bed baths, toileting or bed pans, changing beds, taking vital signs, continually charting it all. The body was recorded. 'Vitals,' a word drawn directly from the Latin word for 'life,' was a continual activity. As the work is lodged in our current vocabulary, it is part of a medical regimen, meaning blood pressure, temperature, pulse, and respiration. Since many people had identical vital signs day in and day out for all their years of residency, this procedure seemed more like a ritual than a requirement of health care, at least to residents, who frequently mocked it, "I guess you got to make sure I'm alive again today, eh?" 'Vitals,' in the homes, meant physical life, not biography, emotions, or social milieu.

It seems hardest of all for these people to cope when their behavior is called a disease, when that link between this confused present and that known past is severed. Yet even to be placed on certain wards and floors is to be treated as mentally impaired. Meanwhile, a constant life in a total institution is a source of confusion [18] especially for older people. At the very time of their life when they are struggling to maintain their own cognitive abilities and sanity, they become enmeshed in a cultural ethos that says they are "going through their second childhood" or they are "out of their minds." Many residents express anger at this ethos, but a nursing home is not a place where anger is spoken about or permitted. Patienthood is an engulfing identity and, over time, many residents seem to become resigned in the face of its power.

Yet, sometimes the anger has a clear social and political content. Miss Black had been a math teacher. At 74, when I met her, she was confined to a wheelchair, and had lived through the economic pathway to the public aid phase. She was furious that, as a result, she had lost complete control over her social security check. It was absorbed by the institution as partial payment. She would sit in her wheelchair in the hall and yell, "Where's my social security. Get me the administrator! I want my social security checks!" Once or twice the administrators did stop by to explain to her that her

check was only part of what it cost to keep her there. That was not an adequate explanation for her. She would get frantic in her fury, trying to move beyond the logic of that answer, trying to reclaim control over the old age support to which she had contributed all her working life. When she yelled too much, the health care staff took over to calm her, sometimes through chemical means. Her anger was then charted in ways congruent with the world of patienthood: "Miss Black was acting out again today."

Although a nursing home is often a chaotic and angry place, there are within each home and within most patients pockets of creativity, of insightfulness, of competence. Patients are active participants in the setting in complex, humorous, and gracious ways. "And how are you today?", a visiting volunteer or physician or minister would ask Mary Ryan, frequently in a voice too loud. "Oh. . . fine . . ." she would respond, though very slowly. ". . . And you?" Mary was being polite, as she always was to outsiders. She was not fine, she was miserable. She complained about her restraints all day, and after the visitors were gone, she would complain about them once again. The question "And how are you today?" from a stranger had very little to do with her ongoing life. But in this snapshot visit and irrelevant question, she graciously had carried on the conversation, as we all do, with "Fine, thanks. And you?" Meanwhile, the visitors, unaccustomed to her slow, spacey manner (for they lived their lives at a much faster pace than she), and full of presumptions about the institution, walked out the door with a vaguely focused sympathy: "Poor Mary—a shame she's so out of it."

While they no doubt mean well, many of the visitors, like the above, will never be more than strangers, at least emotionally, to the patients. Some patients have friends within the nursing home, but for the most part the home, too, is a gathering of strangers, people alone with others. Some sit next to each other for months and years and do not talk to each other, often do not even know each others' names. One can look out on a room where 40 or 50 people are eating and hear little or no conversation. Residents seem alienated from one another. Ties to the world, even the local world, diminish as the overwhelming passification process of patienthood sweeps over. People curl in socially, as they are continually remade into patients.

'Curl in,' however, does not mean passivity. Life inside the home is neither rest nor passive nothingness; it is a repository of effort. It is passive only to outsiders, who with snapshot methods, create a 'them' and a 'we,' and create a passivity. In our creation of images and concepts of passivity, what the patients do while sitting there doing nothing is outside our understanding. Meanwhile patients in long-term care are actively engaged in the work of being a patient.

As a historical process, this creation of the impersonal mode of patienthood is accelerating. Soon nursing homes in the United States will be reimbursed on the basis of an abstract, quantified index, just as hospitals now are on the basis of diagnostic related groups. This index will be derived in a purely mechanical fashion, based on what is called activities of daily living, the components of which are the time it takes to feed, transport, and toilet any given patient. The patient as a subject in this process is further obliterated, becoming the acted upon, encased in a discourse of crude behaviorism.

It is also a discourse based on the isolation of individuals. A patient is not defined or diagnosed or written about in terms of social relations in or out of the home, but in terms of sickness. At the end of the evening, Claudia Moroni, age 66, used to go to visit her mother, Maria, age 88; by an odd set of circumstances, both were residents of the home, though were on different floors, separated by different medical categories. Then they were told that they could no longer visit at night. It seems that Claudia became too fond of crawling into the bed with her mother, and cuddling with her. The report of this decision appeared on their separate charts in this way: "Claudia is no longer allowed to visit her mother after 8 p.m. At night they practice lesbianism."

This was not the only time I encountered references to 'lesbianism' as a taboo in nursing homes. However, I mention this incident at the conclusion of this section not to raise the issue of homophobia, but to illustrate the separation of relational units, the isolation of individuals as individuals, that seems to be an essential part of making people into patients. Each person is defined as a separate unit, to be treated, charted, and changed. The power of the medical model is such that for some, like Claudia's mother, every act is interpreted as a manifestation of disease. Patients seem to expend considerable effort holding fast against the force of these ideas.

The Invisibility of Caring Work

In one home it was emphasized repeatedly that the two most important tasks nursing assistants had to accomplish were to make sure patients were available to take their medications and to be sure that everything we did was charted. "If It's Not Charted," read a large sign behind the nurses' station, "It Didn't Happen."

Nursing assistants are trained in and judged in terms of the performance of physical tasks, like taking blood pressures and pulses, giving bed pans, and turning, showering and feeding patients. When these tasks are accomplished, they are coded and recorded in the all-important link between that work and the outside world—the chart. Recording tasks on the chart fits them into the overall organizational scheme of things, called health care. In terms of this participation, what nursing assistants do is considered unskilled.

I found the work that nursing assistants do far more complex than a conception of 'unskilled' or 'menial' would imply. Much of what they do does not fit into the chart as it is presently constructed. This other, non-physicalist dimension of what nursing assistants and others might do might be called caring work [30, 31]. The social relations involved in holding someone as they gasp for breaths fearing that it might be their last, or cleaning someone, or laughing with them so as to keep them alive, feeding them or brushing their teeth, helping them hold on to memories of the past while they try to maintain sanity in the present—these are constant, essential and difficult parts of the work. They are unskilled and menial practices only if nursing assistants are presumed to be subordinates in a medical world. Yet this caring work is invisible in the language of business and medicine, and is written out of the charts. On the chart it is physical life that is monitored and recorded.

Formally, nursing assistants' tasks have nothing to do with talking with patients. It is, in fact, probably more efficient not to converse. In two of the homes we were explicitly not allowed to sit with patients. Should the Board of Health appear, or one of the occasional physicians drop in, this would appear as loafing. We were told to keep moving, unless we were charting, for to keep moving is to look busy. Supervisory nurses are under considerable pressure to see that all tasks get charted, and that all the patients' units of health care are properly recorded.

Yet there is work beyond this merely physical work that remains invisible and unmentioned. There is a special knowledge and skill involved in caring work. It begins with being in touch with someone else's body, and its need for constant, intimate tending. There is the mental work, much of which is only obvious when it is not done, as when someone turns up poorly dressed, or becomes incontinent when it was the nursing assistant's job to insure against it. There is much more emotional work—holding, cuddling, calming, grieving. There is a great deal of thought work—tending to one patient, thinking of another. What distinguishes this kind of work is that it involves social relations, more than simple tasks. The tasks themselves are only part of wider social relationships, though the only part that gets documented in the formal language and record keeping of the work. In the charting process (but not before), these tasks become the reality of the job, and become separated from social relations.

The lesson that nursing assistants' tasks are performed within the context of social relationships was taught to me best by Mary Gardner, a 14-year veteran of nursing assistant work. It was she who told me, in all seriousness, that "some shit don't stink." I asked her to explain a bit more what she meant. As she was teaching me how to make a bed, she made it perfectly clear: "It depends on if you like 'em pretty well; it's hard to clean somebody new, or somebody you don't like. If you like 'em, its like your baby." A bit later she made reference to a man with whom she had had to struggle every day: "But now take Floyd, that bastard, that man's shit is foul." Through her explanation it became clear that the work is not a set of menial tasks, but a set of social rela-

tions in which the tasks are embedded.

At this point in the development of nursing homes, the social relations of caring work which contextualize these patients' and nurses' aides lives are relegated to an oral tradition. They are not incorporated into the textbooks or charts or reimbursement schemes. They are erased from the formal record. Or perhaps they do not happen at all. For, in this environment, if it's not charted, it didn't happen.

The Commodification of Care

As systems of long-term care develop in advanced capitalist societies, they increasingly come to be defined in terms of business. The nursing home industry is supposed to be a business based on care. 'Care' is the basic stock-in-trade, that which is advertised, bought, and sold. There seems to be a question at this historical moment that is still worth asking, even as nursing homes proceed on what looks like an inexorable course toward corporatization. Can caring be a business? What happens when this web of social relations is placed into the contemporary terms of market discourse? How does day-to-day care for human beings get turned into a commodity?

One day, in a lecture to the workers on our ward, the administrator of one of the homes reprimanded the nursing assistants with a dictum commonly heard in staff meetings: "I hope I don't have to remind you," he said, "that a nursing home is a 24 hour a day, 365 day a year business." He took for granted that he was operating a business, and was chiding us to be more productive in those terms. Business was a taken for granted reality for him. Yet the business model is not a natural fact, but a historically specific mode of organization. The everyday work of human caring and the social relation between carer and patient is molded into the language of business: costs, beds, profit margins, cost-accountability, turnover, bottom lines. The power of this logic is such that these terms are made to seem reality itself, and dominate everyday life in the homes.

Nursing homes are major growth corporations, growing in rate of profit, and becoming increasingly private, and multinational in ownership. It is an industry, also, that is being built from a world system of labor. The abstract dictate of multinational capital to search for ways of reducing labor 'costs' creates a situation in which Third World nurses, usually trained in their own countries, are imported to work in First World nursing homes. Nursing is becoming a part of the world economy [32]. In the United States, for example, supervisory nursing is often done by Filipino nurses. These women and men are well-trained medically in their own country, although in a markedly different culture than that of the United States. In the daily life of a nursing home, this creates some chaos, both in terms of the nurses' difficulties with the colloquial language and customs of the States, and in terms of their

often bitter feeling of exploitation, since working conditions for them are not what they were told when recruited. Yet their difficulties with the cultural transition and language is of little consequence to the formal order of the organization, which requires only that they are adequately trained in the profession and science of health care. That a nursing staff can be in charge by virtue of this training, but unable to understand the social customs or slang of a patient, is not even considered a paradox in the business terms which dictate the employment of foreign nurses. By the time this 'capital-labor' relation is translated into cost effectiveness for the corporation, the day-to-day chaos it creates has become invisible.

Concrete human relations get changed when they are transformed into the documentary reality of commodities, when care is encoded in reimbursement concepts. The local reality is erased from the view of those whose contact with nursing homes is mediated by these abstract business terms. One of the key notions that facilitates this translation is cost-accountability. To make sense in the language of cost-accountability, units of service have to be coded into dollars and cents, care into units of care. One day during our clinical training we had completed all our assigned tasks and had returned to our instructor to see what our next order might be. After some reflection the R.N. instructor suggested, "Why don't you go do some psycho-social stuff?" Hearing this psuedo-scientific notion for the first time, one of the student trainees (whispering 'moron' under her breath) whipped back, "What do you mean, talk to them? What do you think we've been doing all day?" We had continually conversed with our patients while tending to them. Now we were receiving a new, distinct managerial directive and it could fit into the cost-accountability of the administrative logic, like vitals or showers. Now we could go talk to (or, rather, "do some psycho-social stuff with") the patients and it could be entered into the records as a discrete nursing task, and be separately charted and charged under the heading of hours of nursing care.

For another example, in one home, Saturday night dinner almost always consisted of one cheese sandwich and watery tomato soup. This dinner was carefully recorded and open for inspection, with one slight twist. The administrative heading that this meal comes under is nutrition, for which we have units of measurement. Each tray had a card on it with the amount of protein and carbohydrates that the food purportedly contained: we had to turn in the cards after every meal. So the records showed that each resident got x grams of protein and y grams of carbohydrates—what becomes in that frame of reference a nutritionally balanced meal. The State Board of Health inspected one day, and the rumor was that they were particularly concerned with nutrition on this visit. The inspection consisted of examining the computerized records. We passed the inspection.

In each of these examples, the re-

ality of the local, everyday life is transformed—annihilated, actually. The administrator's admonition to us that this was a business was certainly correct, more than I imagined when he spoke it. In this language people are market phenomena. It begins in defining people as bodies. The body is conceptualized and treated and recorded in a quantitative way compatible with reimbursement. Terms like beds, costs, turnovers and profit margins are taken for granted as part of nursing home life. These are economic units. The discourse of nursing home life becomes subsumed under that of nursing home management.

Generating a commodity involves transforming a good or service from its everyday meaning as a support for social relationships into an abstract meaning for private profit. Even more than hospitals, which operate with high technology, nursing homes throughout the western world depend on caring work as a means of profit. In order for commodities to be created, social relations must be redefined. In the process of transforming these social relations into formal tasks, caring work is turned into a commodity. Caring work is turned into discreet and quantifiable tasks: these then become the nuts and bolts that allow nursing homes to run as enterprises for profit. The caring relations are coded into measurable and cost-accountable tasks: talk into 'psycho-social stuff,' emotional into technical, the cheese sandwich into units of protein, quality into quantity. The cheese sandwich is disconnected from the world, or, rather, is transformed from something it may or may not be (i.e. good food) into what it must be: units of costable measurement. Measures are scattered throughout the chart, linking the ongoing daily care to business, and, in the process, remaking it.

One of the dangers of this transformation is that the local reality of patient's lives can become invisible and the caring relations remain implicit and unnamed. After these caring relations are filtered into the documentary reality [24], what emerges in their place are separate individuals ('beds') with sickness, which demand discrete units of health care, and menial workers to feed, transport and toilet them — tasks which are all measured in time units required to execute the tasks. The charts record individuals broken down into units of costable measurement; these units can then be built back up as commodities. Life inside the home can then be talked about in terms congruent with any other capitalist organization producing a product for profit. This is the logic of commodities, a logic that informs every moment in the day-to-day production of nursing home life.

Conclusion

This study is about alternatives within nursing homes, not alternatives to them. None of this discussion leads to the conclusion that nursing homes should not exist. They could, however, be radically reorganized. I presume that it is preferable that people with common needs for nursing care live in groups rather than alone, and that it is pref-

erable that a society provide nursing homes rather than insist that those people be taken care of by kin [30]. As a result of the forthcoming rise in the population of old people, dependency caretaking relations will be an increasing feature of social life [15]. In this study, just as patients and nursing assistants constitute its empirical base. I propose that they be considered a vital voice in nursing home research and political action. They know a lot about how they would like their lives to be different, and analysis of their situation can provide concrete bases for change. Their everyday life provides the counter-logic against which to evaluate the industry, profit logic in which it is encased, and a point of departure for deconstructing it.

The starting point for the counter-logic is the presupposition that patients are conscious of and active in the world in which they live, and active in its daily construction. It is not a situation of passivity. There is action, resistance, some expressed need; this is a point from which change might proceed. This is different from policy directed toward nursing home life from the outside in. It is different because in this procedure the people and their relations — not the homes — are the units of analysis. Approaching the analysis in this way is to move away from a sociology of structures, and toward one grounded in people's actual everyday situations. The discussion of the pathway to poverty offered an example of the results of this change of focus. In the lived experience of current policy, it is not a question of designing good homes and sanctioning bad ones, but of designing a policy that will stabilize the turbulent path that is now beyond most patients' control.

This is a historical period in which there is great need for an overall long-term care policy. I arrive at this conclusion from talking with many patients who were shocked and confused upon arriving in their nursing home(s). They were frightened of their future precisely because of the absence of existing social policy that would enable them to predict it. They were lost in a society that has little or no national long-term care policy.

The research objective here is to start with everyday situations and link them to social policy. I try to argue throughout the study that many social policies now do not reflect an understanding of their consequences for everyday life. In this procedure one gets to know people over time and study how their lives are shaped by policies. This necessarily involves a redefinition of who constitutes the social actors in social politics to include not only those who make policies, but also those who live them out. To include the latter is to conceptualize nursing home patients not just in terms of their sicknesses, but also as social and political beings, and to listen to their world, even its babble, for its social and political significance.

Nursing assistants and patients are not classes of people who are essentially silent and passive. They communicate ideas and emotions with specific social and political content—content which is tied directly to the conditions of the orga-

nization and, in turn, to the society. Nursing assistants wonder why after 40 hours work they still have to seek overtime just to survive; they wonder why the work they do, even if it is tending to someone during their last days, or even to their deaths, is still dismissed as menial and unskilled. Residents frequently express a desire to reclaim control over their own social security checks, and wonder why after paying into social security all their lives they are now reduced to public aid; they wonder why they have to be hungry again one hour after their Saturday night dinner; and why the staff is so convinced that they are crazy. These are questions that permeate life on a ward. They are derived from social conditions. The method of analysis I am suggesting involves seeing these people within the context of these social conditions as political participants in the ongoing production of everyday life, though at the present time caught in a set of relationships over which they have little or no control.

From the accounts of the people with whom I spoke, it became clear that living through current Medicare policies creates its own insecurities, while living through Medicaid is to face the life of a pauper. In addition, these policies give rise to economic instability and often residence not in 'a' home, but in a series of different wards, floors and homes. These policies can be reconstructed, and one way to begin is to explore how they disrupt everyday life.

I also raised issues concerning minimum wage, conceptions of nursing assistant work, the encasement of the hospital environment over time, passive versus active conceptions of patients' lives, and social relations of caring work, and the task-centered quantitative focus of current business-centered organizational models. All of these issues were drawn from everyday experiences [26].

In this method research is not teleological, that is, it does not seek the answer to the perfect nursing home. The object, rather, is to work toward empowerment for those whose lives become objectified in this context. One does not lay out a utopia and work backwards. Nor does one deconstruct commodification en masse, as a whole; it is deconstructed word by word proceeding from the everyday activity, the local reality, of the people encased by it.

Current patients and nursing assistants tell us that the lives they are living now portend what is to follow. They are in a way pioneers. How much of their knowledge gets recorded depends in large part on how effectively researchers bridge the worlds of the everyday and its larger contexts and cultivate the methods for giving them speech. When we get to know patients and nursing assistants as social and political participants, they offer a different perspective on social security, Medicaid, caring work, nursing, and old age. The issues I raise in this study grow out of just a few of the societal relations being lived out in nursing homes, there for us to learn about, or, more to the point in terms of this method, there for the women and men inside to teach.

Acknowledgements

This paper is part of a forthcoming book. The research was funded under grants from the Midwest Council for Social Research in Aging and the Retirement Research Foundation. Their support is gratefully acknowledged.

References

1. Friedson E., *Profession of Medicine*. Dodd Mead, New York, 1970.
2. Gill D. G. and Twaddle A. Medical sociology: what's in a name? *Int. Soc. Sci. J.* **29**, 3, 1977.
3. Doyal L. *The Political Economy of Health*. Pluto Press, London, 1979.
4. Stacey M. Who are the health care workers? Patients and other unpaid workers in health care. Paper given at the International Sociological Association Conference, Mexico City, 1982.
5. Davies C. Comparative occupational roles in health care. *Soc. Sci. Med.* **13**, 515–521, 1979.
6. Campbell M. Social organization of knowledge research on nursing. Paper given at International Nursing Conference: Research—A Base For the Future? University of Edinburgh, 1981.
7. Neugarten B. L. (Ed.) *Age or Need?: Public Policies for Older People*. Sage, Beverly Hills, Calif., 1982.
8. Estes C. L., Gerard L. E., Zones J. S. and Swan J. H. (Eds.) *Political Economy, Health and Aging*. Little, Brown, Boston, Mass., 1984.
9. Ingman S., MacDonald C. and Lusky R. An alternative model in geriatric care. *J. Am. Geriat. Soc.* **27**, 6, 1979.
10. Luken P. Social identity in later life: a situational approach to understanding old age stigma. *Int. J. Aging Human Dev.* In press.

11. Peterson W. A. and Quadagno J. (Eds.) *Social Bonds in Later Life: Aging and Interdependence*. Sage, Beverly Hills, Calif., 1985.

12. Kayser-Jones J. S. *Old, Alone and Neglected: Care of the Aged in Scotland and the United States*. University of California, Berkeley, Calif., 1981.

13. Gubrium J. *Living and Dying at Murray Manor*. St Martin's, New York, 1975.

14. Newton E. *This Bed My Center*. Virago, London, 1979.

15. Walker A. Care for elderly people: a conflict between women and the state. In *A Labour of Love: Women, Work, and Caring* (Edited by Finch J. and Groves D.). Routledge and Kegan Paul, Boston, Mass., 1983.

16. John R. Prerequisities of an adequate theory of aging: a critique and reconceptualization. *Mid-Am. Rev. Sociol.* **9,** 2, 1984.

17. Brents B. G. Capitalism, corporate liberalism and social policy: the origins of the Social Security Act of 1935. *Mid-Am. Rev. Sociol.* **9,** 1, 1984.

18. Goffman E. *Asylums*. Doubleday, Garden City, N.Y., 1961.

19. Emerson R. and Warren C. (Eds.) Trouble and the politics of contemporary social control institutions. *Urban Life* **12,** 243-367, 1983.

20. Glazer B. and Strauss A. *Awareness of Dying*. Aldine, Chicago, Ill., 1967.

21. Jagger A. *Feminist Politics and Human Nature*. Rowman & Allanheld, Totowa, N.J., 1983.

22. Harding S. and Hintikka M. B. (Eds.) *Dis-Covering Reality*. Reidel, Boston, Mass., 1983.

23. Dilorio J. Nomad vans and lady vanners: a critical feminist analysis of a van club. Ph.D. dissertation, The Ohio State University, Columbus, Ohio.

24. Smith D. The social construction of documentary reality. *Sociol. Inquiry* **44,** 3, 1974.

25. Smith D. A sociology for women. In *The Prism of Sex* (Edited by Sherman J. A. and Beck E. T.). The University of Wisconsin Press, Madison, Wis., 1979.

26. Smith D. *The Experienced World as Problematic: A Feminist Method*. Twelfth Annual Sorokin Lecture, University of Saskatchewan, Saskatoon, 1981.

27. Marx K. and Engels F. *The German Ideology* (Edited by Arthur C. J.). International Publishers, New York, 1947.

28. Alexander C. P. The new economy. *Time* May 30, 1983.

29. Beechey V. Women and production: a critical analysis of some sociological theories of women's work. In *Feminism and Materialism: Women and Modes of Production* (Edited by Kuhn A. and Wolpe A.). Routledge & Kegan Paul, Boston, Mass., 1978.

30. Finch J. and Groves D. (Eds) *A Labour of Love: Women, Work and Caring*. Routledge & Kegan Paul, Boston, Mass., 1983.

31. Diamond T. Caring work (review essay of Finch and Groves' *A Labour of Love*). *Contemp. Sociol.* **13,** 4, 1984.

32. Diamond T. Elements of a sociology for nursing: considerations on caregiving and capitalism. *Mid-Am. Rev. Sociol.* **9,** 1, 1984.

Part IV

Relations between Patients and Providers

INTRODUCTION

As noted in the general introduction, one of the central issues I am concerned with is the relationships and interactions between people and their health care providers. A number of selections in other sections also underscore this theme, but in this section we put special emphasis on the topic.

The study of interaction has preoccupied the recent generation of medical sociologists. By studying the ways in which care-seekers and caregivers deal with one another, we are able to learn more about the lay experience of illness (a topic covered earlier in this book) and to delve into the often unspoken and implicit assumptions of medical ideologies and conceptions. At the same time, studies of interaction show how medical practice often mirrors the biases that occur throughout our society, particularly those involving class, gender, and race. Because the doctor-patient relationship is a classic power relationship, it can provide a model for the study of the interpersonal dynamics and social biases that transpire in other forms of social encounters as well.

This part of the book contains two sections. In the first, "Interaction and Negotiation," both conceptual and field work approaches are used to examine the ways in which patients and providers interact. In the second part— "Rights, Responsibilities, and Social Control"—we look at more direct power relations and mechanisms of social control that involve illegitimate research on human beings, disclosure and withholding of medical information, and the conflicts between patients and physicians over the choice of medical procedures.

Section Eleven

Interaction and Negotiation

Although the study of doctor-patient interaction has a long tradition in medical sociology, the classic thrust was to increase the patient's compliance with the doctor's orders and, relatedly, to increase patient satisfaction. This earlier work tended to avoid qualitative observations and field work in favor of discrete quantitative measurement of variables such as level of comprehension, symptom reporting, understanding of prescriptions, and anxiety. This work also tended to focus on the microcosm of the interaction, without attention to the larger social contexts that affect it.

Recent approaches to interaction and negotiation take a more critical standpoint. They are not concerned primarily, if at all, with increasing the efficiency of the medical system. Rather, they are attempting to understand the social dynamics of medical interactions in their own right. The goal of the research is more likely to be empowerment of patients than greater efficiency for practitioners. In order to capture the complexity of the problem, recent studies of interaction and negotiation typically involve ethnographic field work where scholars immerse themselves in the field (see, for example, the article by Gerry Stimson and Barbara Webb in this section). Qualitative observations sometimes are accompanied by coding of encounters and even administration of standardized questionnaires. Researchers focus on such issues as who raises questions and who gives answers, what level of information is requested by patients and disclosed by providers, what linguistic devices are used to control the situation, what biases are introduced as a result of patients' social backgrounds, and if and how the parties reach agreement.

The differences mentioned above between these traditional and critical perspectives can be understood as a feature of the distinction between "sociology *in* medicine" and "sociology *of* medicine," which was discussed in the introduction to this book.

Eliot Freidson's "The Social Organization of Illness" starts off this section by noting how institutional settings impose their own organization on the social behavior of illness. He then explores various typologies of doctor-patient interaction, showing how they vary according to illness type, practice style, and lay perceptions. Freidson concludes that medical interaction is

509

always conflictful to some degree, and that for this reason we usually observe a *negotiation* process between the two parties. Negotiation can involve determination of symptom severity, the actual diagnosis of disease, treatment choices, and future restrictions or limitations.

In "Face-to-Face Interaction" Gerry Stimson and Barbara Webb pursue the same negotiation theme with reference to their field work. These writers caution us that we must not view interaction as solely a microlevel issue, since the actors are constrained by the overall health care system, the actors' perception of what is realistically possible, and the fact that there are some implicit agreements that people bring with them to the interaction. Given these constraints, Stimson and Webb point out, there is still considerable room for patient and doctor to attempt to set the tone of the encounter and to influence each other.

From the perspective of a physician attuned to these kinds of concerns, Rita Charon writes in "To Learn, To Recognize" about how doctors need to listen for the *stories* that patients tell, rather than to proceed with a traditional mode of questioning and diagnostic workup. Charon goes further in recommending that doctors write their own stories about medical encounters so that they can better understand both their patients and themselves. This emphasis on narrative approach to disease and illness brings us back to the earlier piece by Gareth Williams, "The Genesis of Chronic Illness," in the section "Becoming Patients and Experiencing Illness."

35   THE SOCIAL ORGANIZATION OF ILLNESS

Eliot Freidson

The Institutional Organization of Responses to Illness

Remembering that for the sociologist, medical treatment constitutes one kind of societal reaction to a type of deviance, the essential fact bearing on the organization of illness in institutions is that the staff, unlike the patient himself or his lay associates, is performing a job. For the job to be performed at all requires some administrative routine, and it requires the reduction of individual patients to administrative and treatment classes, all members in

each class to be managed by much the same set of routines. If the job is to be performed to the satisfaction of the staff, procedures that minimize interference with their routine and maximize their convenience are required.

Consequently, we find that there are standard administrative courses through which a patient is likely to travel in spite of variation in his

SOURCE: From *Profession of Medicine* by Eliot Freidson. Published by The University of Chicago Press. © 1970, 1988 by Eliot Freidson

condition from others in the same treatment category. Rosengren and DeVault[1] observed that in one lying-in hospital the staff attempted to maintain a definite spatial and temporal organization of its work irrespective of individual variations in condition. In the traditional movement from admitting office, to prep room, labor room, delivery room, and finally the lying-in room, no step was skipped even when the patient was well past the need of it; instead, she was moved through the step more rapidly than otherwise. By the same token, the staff tolerated the expression of pain by the patient only in the delivery room, where it was considered appropriate to the "illness" and where it could be managed by anesthetic: elsewhere, it was deprecated and ridiculed. And in order to maintain the "routine" tempo of work flow established by the staff, laggard women were helped along (with foreceps and other techniques) to get them to deliver on schedule. Another example of the way the staff imposes standardized organization on the course of treatment (and therefore the social course of illness) is to be found in Roth's observations of the way the staff in tuberculosis hospitals has a conception of how long it "should" take to get cured that is imposed on the clinical course of the individual's illness, organizing the progressive steps of managing the illness on the basis of the normative timetable rather than on the results of laboratory tests that may be taken to reflect the biological status of the illness "itself."[2] And I cannot fail to mention, finally, that mordant analysis by Roth of the circumstances in which tuberculosis was and was not treated as infectious.[3]

In the process whereby the treatment institution can impose its own organization on the social behavior connected with illness, two prominent characteristics facilitate staff control. First, the patient may be isolated from the lay community and those of his associates who are concerned with his welfare. Contact with the lay world is rationed where possible. While there may be medical reasons for such isolation, it is frequently a matter of administrative convenience, minimizing "bother" for the staff more than protecting the patient from disturbance. The social consequences are to isolate the patient from the sources of social leverage that supported him while in ambulatory consultation and that could sustain his resistance to the therapeutic routine in the institution. Second, and more important, is the tendency of the staff of all such institutions to carefully avoid giving the patient or his lay associates much information about the illness and what is supposed to be done for it. Virtually every study of patients in hospital points out how ignorant of condition, prognosis, and the medically prescribed regimen are both the patients and their relatives and how reluctant is the staff to give such information.[4] In Davis' words, describing staff behavior toward parents of children stricken with poliomyelitis, the parent's questions were "hedged, evaded, rechannelled, or left unanswered."[5]

As Davis noted in his analysis, the staff's reluctance to give information is often explained as a desire to avoid an emotional scene with the parents. Sometimes, as Glaser and Strauss note in the case of the dying patient, the staff withholds information in the belief, based on "clinical experience," that it will protect the patient and his family from shock and excessive grief.[6] Sometimes this reluctance to give information is explained by a genuine uncertainty, so that no really reliable information is available. However, as Davis has noted in detail, "in many illnesses . . . 'uncertainty' is to some extent feigned by the doctor for the purpose of gradually getting the patient ultimately to accept or put up with a state-of-being that initially is intolerable to him."[7] Whatever the reason, however, the net effect of the withholding of information is to minimize the possibility that the patient can exercise much control over the way he is treated. If he does not know that he is supposed to have a yellow pill every four hours, he cannot comment on the fact that it is sometimes overlooked and insist on getting it regularly. And if he does not know that his condition normally responds to a given treatment in a week, he cannot insist on a consultation after several weeks have passed without change in condition or treatment.[8]

A great deal more can be said about the institutional shaping of illness, particularly in qualification of the point I have been trying to make here. Not all treatment institutions are the same, nor are all patients or treatment staffs. For example, the rehabilitation institution studied by Roth and Eddy[9] had a particularly powerful influence on the course of illness behavior because its patients were largely supported by public funds and lacked effective advocates from the community outside. They rarely, therefore, "got well enough" to leave. This helplessness is somewhat tempered by the fact that in rehabilitation, tuberculosis, and other institutions, many patients have similar illnesses and are in a position to socialize and organize each other. When these conditions exist, the patients are able to develop a common conception of the way their illness should be managed and to generate the influence required to impose some of their own conceptions on the staff.[10] Furthermore, institutions can be dominated by a staff ideology which specifies that the patient participate in his treatment. In fact, there are a number of patterns of interaction that reflect the degree of influence and activity allowed the patient in the course of his treatment and that express the meaning of his illness to himself and to those treating him.

Patterns of Interaction in Treatment

I have already suggested that when in treatment in a client-dependent practice, interaction will be fairly free between doctor and patient, the latter initiating and controlling some part of it. Conversely, when in treatment in a colleague-dependent practice, interactions will likely be lesser in quantity and less free, the physician initiating and controlling the greater part of it. By the time the patient reaches the latter practice, which often involves institutionization, he has been rendered relatively helpless and dependent, perhaps, as Goffman suggests, already demoralized by a sense of having been stripped of some part of his normal identity.[11] In other cases he has been rendered helpless by his failure to find help on his own or by the way his physical illness has incapacitated him.

A second element that seems to be able to predict some part of the quality of the interaction between patient and physician lies in what physicians consider to be the demands of proper treatment for a given illness. This is to say, all that doctors do is not the same and does not require the same type of interaction. Following Szasz and Hollander's typology of doctor-patient relationships[12] but reversing the direction of analysis, we may note that under some circumstances—as in surgery and electroconvulsive therapy—the patient must be thoroughly immobilized and passive, wholly submissive to the activity of the physician. The work itself requires such minimal interaction: attendants, straps, anesthesia, and other forms of restraint are employed to enforce the requirement of submission. This model for interaction Szasz and Hollander call *activity-passivity*. In it, the patient is a passive object.

The second treatment situation, discussed by most writers as *the* doctor-patient relationship, is one in which the patient's consent to accept advice and to follow it is necessary. Here, the patient "is conscious and has feelings and aspirations of his own. Since he suffers . . . he seeks help and is ready and willing to 'co-operate.' When he turns to the physician, he places [him] . . . in a position of power. . . . The more powerful . . . will speak of guidance or leadership, and will expect cooperation of the other."[13] The interaction is expected to follow the model of *guidance-cooperation*, the physician initiating more of the interaction than the patient. The patient is expected to do what he is told; he assumes a less passive role than if he were anesthetized but a passive role nonetheless, submissive to medical requirements.

Finally, there is the model of *mutual participation*, found where patients are able or are required to take care of themselves—as in the case of the management of some chronic illnesses like diabetes—and therefore where initiation of interaction comes close to being equal between the two. Here, "the physician does not profess to know exactly what is best for the patient. The search for this becomes the essence of the therapeutic interaction."[14] Obviously, some forms of psychotherapy fall here.

Szasz and Hollander's scheme, however, is defective logically and empirically, for their models represent a continuum of the degree to which the *patient* assumes an *active* role in interaction in treatment without being extended to the logical point where the *physician* assumes a *passive* role. Such a defect reflects the characteristically normative stance of the medical thinker: while the existence of situations where the practitioner more or less does what the patient asks him to do may not be denied, such situations are rejected out of hand as intolerably nonprofessional, nontherapeutic, and nondignified to be conceded for mere logic and dignified by the recognition of inclusion.[15] Logic and fact do, however, require recognition, and they dictate the suggestion of two other patterns of interaction— one in which the patient guides and the physician cooperates, and one in which the patient is active and the physician passive. It is difficult to imagine an empirical instance of the latter possibility, which requires that the physician cease being a consultant, so we may label it "merely" a logical construct. For the former instance, however, we may find empirical examples in a fair number of the interactions in client-dependent practices, particularly where the practice is economically unstable and the clientele of high economic, political, and social status.[16]

As I have noted, what distinguishes Szasz and Hollander's models from those I have added is the fact that they represent patterns of relations with patients that medical practitioners *wish* to establish and maintain on various occasions for various illnesses and patients. Assuming one type of interaction pattern is necessary for the therapist's work to proceed successfully, what social circumstances are prerequisite to its existence and how are they established? When the *activity-passivity* model does not automatically exist by virtue of coma or the like, some of the physician's behavior must be devoted to soothing the patient in order to get him to submit to the straps, injections, face-masks or whatever. The basic prerequisite,

however, is *power* as such— sustained by the a priori incapacity of the patient, or by *making* the patient incapacitated. Such power is created by the fact that the individual is, let us say, unconscious and in a coma. In other instances, the exercise of power to overcome resistance when the patient is not in a coma is legitimized by the social identity imputed to the patient: he is just an infant, a cat, a retardate, a psychotic, or in some other way not fully human and responsible and so cannot be allowed to exercise his own choice to withdraw from treatment. Aside from circumstances where the patient's identity legitimizes the exercise of force, this pattern of interaction is most likely to be found where cultures diverge a great deal. There, few patients voluntarily enter medical consultation: their participation may be required by political power or may be facilitated by the incapacitating force of the disease itself.

The second pattern of interaction, *guidance-cooperation*, is essentially the one most people have in mind when they speak of the doctor-patient relationship. Obviously, its existence is contingent on a process that will bring people into interaction with the therapist in the first place, the process of seeking help that leads to the choice of utilizing one service rather than another. Here, the patient must exercise his own choice. Utilization is not merely something that facilitates establishing the relationship; it constitutes one-half of the battle in interaction: to actively choose to utilize a doctor in the first place requires that one in some degree concede his value and authority in advance[17] and that one in some degree already shares the doctor's perspective on illness and its treatment. The problem of interaction in treatment lies in the details of this acceptance, in the concrete areas in which lay and professional cultures converge. The doctor's tool for gaining acceptance is his "authority," which is not wholly binding by his incumbency in a formal legal position as expert.[18] Here, to the extent that the patient's culture is congruent with that of the professional, the authority of the latter is likely to be conceded in advance and reinforced in treatment by the fact that what the professional diagnoses and prescribes corresponds with what the patient expects and that communication between the two is relatively easy, so that confidence can be established when the professional must make new or unexpected demands on the patient. In this situation, what is problematic most of all is the physician's authority as such: it must be conceded before examination can begin and if treatment is to proceed. It is the *motive* for cooperation. Only secondarily problematic but problematic nonetheless is the capacity of the physician to make his desires for information and cooperation known and the capacity of the patient to understand the physician sufficiently to do as he is told. Essentially, then, faith and confidence on the part of the patient, and authority on the part of the physician, are the critical elements.

Finally, there is the pattern of *mutual participation*. Clearly, the interaction specified by this model requires

characteristics on the part of the patient that facilitate communication. Communication is essential in order to determine what is to be done in therapy. Cultural congruence is thus obviously one necessary condition for such free interaction. According to Szasz and Hollander, the relationship "requires a more complex psychological and social organization on the part of both participants. Accordingly, it is rarely appropriate for children, or for those persons who are mentally deficient, very poorly educated, or profoundly immature. On the other hand, the greater the intellectual, educational, and general experiential similarity between physician and patient the more appropriate and necessary this model of therapy becomes."[19] However, it is not only educational and experiential similarity but also a collaborative *status* that is required. Here the patient is not to merely accept the authority of the doctor; each must accept the other as an equal in the search for a solution to the problem. Deference on the part of either patient or physician is likely to destroy such mutual participation. Thus, status congruence is necessary to the relationship in order that the interaction of each *can* be fairly equal, and the influence of the doctor on the patient will hinge essentially not on physical power or professional authority but on his capacity to *persuade* the patient of the value of his views.[20]

These characterizations of different patterns of interaction may be used to distinguish (1) the needs of different kinds of medical work, (2) the way different kinds of illness are managed, and (3) the problems of practice that arise when the character of the lay community and particularly the lay referral system varies. (1) Veterinary medicine, pediatrics, and surgery are among those practices obviously prone to require the activity-passivity model, though the families of pets and pediatric patients are prone to interfere more than the model predicts. Internal medicine and general practice are among those prone to require the guidance-cooperation model. And verbal psychotherapy as well as rehabilitation and the treatment of the chronic diseases are all prone to need the mutual-participation model. (2) Stigmatized illnesses that spoil the identities of the sufferers are prone to be managed by the activity-passivity pattern, as are those with severe trauma, coma, and psychosis, and with patients who are extremely variant in culture or capacity: these characteristics prevent the patient *or* the physician from being socially responsive in treatment. In any single community, most "normal"—which is to say conditionally legitimate—illnesses are prone to be managed by the guidance-cooperation pattern; in those cases not clearly legitimized by lay culture (and so withholding authority from the physician), the mutual participation pattern is likely to be common and the pattern where the patient guides and the physician cooperates is possible. (3) I might note that the activity-passivity pattern of interaction in treatment is most likely to be found where lay culture diverges greatly from professional culture and where the status

of the layman is very low compared to the professional. Where these divergences are lesser, the guidance-cooperation pattern is likely to be found, whereas where both the lay culture and status of the patient are very much like that of the professional, the mutual-participation pattern is likely to be used often.

The Conflict Underlying Interaction

In discussing interaction in treatment, I have adopted here, as elsewhere, a situational approach: I have attempted to discern whether some regularities in situations exist such that, by specifying the situation, we can predict the kinds of people likely to be in it, the kinds of illness, and the kinds and amount of interaction likely to take place. This seems to me to be an eminently useful approach, but we should not lose sight of the fact that it is merely an approach specifying regularities across arrays of individuals— statistical regularities. Furthermore, those regularities are defined as *relative*, not absolute. Nevertheless, it is unwise to assume too much regularity in the interaction in treatment settings. While the patient can be more or less excluded from assuming an active role in interaction, he can rarely be wholly excluded. He can at least, as do low-status and poorly educated patients everywhere, practice evasive techniques and act stupid in order to avoid some of what is expected of him. And while the patient can be involved in mutual participation by virtue of his similarity to the therapist, he is never wholly cooperative.

Given the viewpoints of two worlds, lay and professional, in interaction, they can never be wholly synonymous. And they are always, if only latently, in conflict. Indeed, I wish to suggest that the most faithful perspective on interaction in treatment is one reflecting such conflict in standpoint, not on assuming an identity of purpose to be discovered by better education or a disposition to cooperate sometimes hidden by misunderstanding or by failure to cooperate.[21]

Hence, interaction in treatment should be seen as a kind of negotiation as well as a kind of conflict. This point is suggested in Balint's psychiatric sense that the patient is using his symptoms to establish a relationship with the physician[22] but more particularly in the sense of negotiation of separate conditions and of separate perspectives and understandings. The patient is likely to want more information than the doctor is willing to give him—more precise prognoses, for example, and more precise instructions. As Roth's study indicated, just as the doctor struggles to find ways of withholding some kinds of information, so will the patient be struggling to find ways of gaining access to, or inferring such information.[23] Similarly, just as the doctor has no alternative but to handle his cases conventionally (which is to say, soundly), so the patient will be struggling to determine whether or not he is the exception to conventional rules. And finally, professional healing being an organized practice, the therapist will be struggling to adjust or fit any single case to the convenience of

practice (and other patients), while the patient will be struggling to gain a mode of management more specifically fitted to him as an individual irrespective of the demands of the system as a whole. These conflicts in perspective and interest are built into the interaction and are likely to be present to some degree in every situation. They are at the core of interaction, and they reflect the general structural characteristics of illness and its professional treatment as a function of the relations between two distinct worlds, ordered by professional norms.

Notes

1. William R. Rosengren and Spencer DeVault, "The Sociology of Time and Space in an Obstetrical Hospital," in Eliot Freidson, ed., *The Hospital in Modern Society* (New York: The Free Press of Glencoe, 1963), pp. 266–292.
2. Julius A. Roth, *Timetables: Structuring the Passage of Time in Hospital Treatment and Other Careers* (Indianapolis: Bobbs-Merrill Co., 1963).
3. Julius A. Roth, "Ritual and Magic in the Control of Contagion," *American Sociological Review*, XXII (1957), 310–314.
4. See the detailed analysis Raymond S. Duff and August B. Hollingshead, *Sickness and Society* (New York: Harper and Row, 1968), Chapter 13.
5. Fred Davis, *Passage Through Crisis: Polio Victims and Their Families* (Indianapolis: Bobbs-Merrill Co., 1963), p. 64. For other observations on the extent to which patients are kept ignorant, see Ailon Shiloh, "Equalitarian and Hierarchal Patients," *Medical Care*, III (1965), 87–95.
6. Barney G. Glaser and Anselm L. Strauss, *Awareness of Dying* (Chicago:

Aldine Publishing Co., 1965), pp. 29ff.

7. Davis, *op. cit.*, p. 67, and see Fred Davis, "Uncertainty in Medical Prognosis, Clinical and Functional," *American Journal of Sociology*, LXVI (1960), 41–47.

8. See James K. Skipper, Jr., "Communication and the Hospitalized Patient," in James K. Skipper, Jr., and Robert C. Leonard, eds., *Social Interaction and Patient Care* (Philadelphia: J. B. Lippincott Co., 1965), pp. 75–77.

9. See Julius Roth and Elizabeth Eddy, *Rehabilitation for the Unwanted* (New York: Atherton Press, 1967).

10. For a very useful discussion of the implications of such characteristics, see Stanton Wheeler, "The Structure of Formally Organized Socialization Settings," in O. G. Brim, Jr., and Stanton Wheeler, *Socialization After Childhood* (New York: John Wiley & Sons, 1966), pp. 53–116.

11. See Erving Goffman, "The Moral Career of the Mental Patient," in his *Asylums* (New York: Anchor Books, 1961), pp. 125–161. In the context of the succeeding discussion of interaction, it is also appropriate to cite, in the same book, pp. 321–386, "The Medical Model and Mental Hospitalization."

12. See Thomas S. Szasz and Mark H. Hollander, "A Contribution to the Philosophy of Medicine," *A.M.A. Archives of Internal Medicine*, XCVII (1956), 585–592.

13. *Ibid.*, pp. 586–587.

14. *Ibid.*, p. 589.

15. This lack of concern for being logically consistent and systematic is characteristic of virtually all writing about the doctor-patient relationship by medical men. Another interesting analysis of the doctor-patient relationship explores other facets to be found in nature but restricts itself to the "pathological." See F. W. Hanley and F. Grunberg, "Reflections on the Doctor-Patient Relationship," *Canadian Medical Association Journal*, IXXXVI (1962), 1022–1024, where nine "syndromes" are constructed out of three stereotypical patients and three stereotypical physicians. So long as medical writers persist in crippling their logic by normative considerations, they cannot expect serious intellectual considerations.

16. See Eliot Freidson, *Patients' Views, of Medical Practice* (New York: Russell Sage, 1961), pp. 171–191 for historical and contemporary examples of such relationships.

17. See Theodore Caplow, *The Sociology of Work* (Minneapolis: University of Minnesota Press, 1954), p. 114.

18. See Eliot Freidson, *Professional Dominance* (New York: Dodd, Mead, 1970).

19. Szasz and Hollander, *op. cit.*, p. 387.

20. In this sense the influence of the expert rather than the authority of the professional is indicated.

21. For a more extended analysis of the conflict see Freidson, *Patients' Views, op. cit.*, pp. 171–191. And see the discussion in Carl Gersuny, "Coercion Theory and Medical Sociology," *Case Western Reserve Journal of Sociology*, II (1968), 14–20.

22. See Michael Balint, *The Doctor, His Patient and the Illness* (New York: International Universities Press, 1957), *passim.*

23. See Roth, *Timetables, op. cit.*, and Julius A. Roth, "Information and the Control of Treatment in Tuberculosis Hospitals," in Eliot Freidson, ed., *The Hospital in Modern Society, op. cit.*, pp. 293–318.

36   FACE-TO-FACE INTERACTION

Gerry Stimson and Barbara Webb

The study of the patient perspective must be undertaken within the assumption that he is as much a participant in the play as he is recipient or audience.

—*Hans O. Mauksch, 1972, p. 27*

Two themes guide our analysis of the face-to-face consultation: strategies and negotiation. Essentially both actors (although we concentrate on the patient) are concerned with the same problem. This problem is effective self-presentation. As in all interaction, the conscious and unconscious presentation of the self affects the behaviour of the other and calls forth a reaction by the other. But in the consultation there is the problem of the outcome that is desired by both actors. People do not hand over all control and decision-making to the doctor merely by becoming patients. The presentation of the self can be used as a strategy. The aim of strategies used by both patient and doctor is to attempt to control and direct the consultation along their own desired lines, to persuade the other to recognise or accept a particular perspective on, and orientation to, the problem that has been brought.

Seeing the consultation in terms of each actor trying to influence the other brings in the concept of negotiation. For, far from the outcome of the consultation being determined only by the problem that the patient brings and by the diagnosis of the doctor, the outcome is a result of the mutual interaction. An examination of the literature on the diagnostic process (Maddox, 1973) suggests

that there is so much room for variability in diagnosis, even with seemingly 'hard' information such as the results of X-ray photographs, that diagnosis is not the cut-and-dried scientific exercise that it is often made out to be. Roth (1963) discusses this problem of diagnosis and treatment in his study of the career of the patient with tuberculosis. Patients and doctors argue about the interpretation of tests, about what treatment is necessary, about the pacing of treatment and about restrictions on their behavior at different stages in the treatment. Roth sees the treatment of the tuberculosis patient not as the result of specific treatment plans and decisions made by the medical staff but as emerging from the ongoing negotiation and bargaining between the patient and the medical staff.

In the psychiatric interview, Scheff (1968) has shown how the reality of the patient's problem is negotiated by the psychiatrist. In the example of the psychiatric interview which he gives, an interview which is taken from a gramophone record for teaching psychiatrists, the psychiatrist is faced with a woman who comes to

SOURCE: From *Going to See the Doctor: The Consultation Process in General Practice*, pp. 37–50. Reprinted with permission from Routledge & Kegan Paul Ltd.

him with a problem which she at first blames on her husband. By the end of the interview the psychiatrist has the patient agreeing that the problem might lie more in herself than in her husband. In a study of doctor-patient interactions in two pediatric out-patient clinics Strong and Davis (1972) describe how parents have their own definitions of their child's problem: 'Both doctor and patient can accept or reject the other's categorisations. . . . The diagnostic outcome of the interview is therefore continually negotiated.' The doctor is shown as using various techniques to maintain his status as expert, particularly when faced by the parents' 'loss of faith' in his competence.

Negotiation is a process. That patient and doctor both use strategies to influence each other does not mean that one or other is going to be successful. But the concept of negotiation means that we see the outcome as the result of their interaction and the strategies they have each adopted, rather than as determined solely by the facts that are brought and the application of the skills that the doctor has.

The consultation does not take place in a vacuum. First, both doctor and patient may have met before and will have foreknowledge of each other. This, as we have seen, allows the patient to anticipate the consultation and rehearse strategies. Where the doctor and illness condition are well known and the patient feels certain of the encounter and able to predict its probable course, we suggest that presentation and control strategies may have less of a persua-sive content and the effort may be concentrated on reinforcing a common understanding and on following the usual pattern of activity. The most obvious example of this is the repeat prescription régime, which Marinker (1970) refers to as the 'truce', where a pattern of consultation has become routine. Yet negotiation does not cease; the inference behind the stereotyped actions is that reinforcement is necessary in order to ensure the continuation of such relations. Of course it may happen that the approach of the doctor is well known, but the patient is dissatisfied with that approach. For example, a doctor may tend to treat many conditions with his 'favourite drug' and the patient may desire some other form of treatment. Or he may be predisposed to certain actions:

> '[He is known as] Doctor Undress— he makes you strip to the waist and that's only when you've got a sore throat, and he is very partial to internals for everything you have.'

The patient may feel this behavior is inappropriate and tactics may then be used by the patient to dissuade the doctor from his usual routine. Although strategies such as these may be planned through the patient having prior expectations of the encounter and having anticipated the problematic aspects of communication, they may also develop in the course of the interaction. This emphasizes the emergent and negotiable features of the interaction.

In emphasising the negotiable aspects of the consultation, however, we do not pretend that the strategies are enacted in an open arena. There are three limits on the possibilities for action. First, there is the limitation on the interaction imposed by the organisation of medical care in this country. The patient usually sees just one doctor for primary medical care and has limited ability to change doctors. Furthermore, the patient is somewhat limited in his possibilities for action in that he perceives his knowledge, and the information available to him, to be of a different order from that of the professional. We deal with these problems more fully in the final chapters.

A second limit is in the actors' perceptions of what is possible. Thus patients may perceive that they are constrained by the amount of time available for the consultation, or they may feel constrained because the interaction takes place on the doctor's territory.

The third limitation to the strategic interaction concerns areas of implicit agreement in interaction. Order in the consultation is maintained by complicity, by agreements on the way certain aspects of the encounter are to be managed: such things as the use of jokes, the modes of address each use, the emotional flatness of the consultation and the use of reassurance and empathy. Such aspects might, in lay terms, be summed up as 'good manners.'

What is important to realise with these limitations to negotiation is *not* that the above are not all negotiable—for example, the patient can insist that the doctor devotes more time to the problem—but that they are *less* negotiable than other aspects of the consultation.

Presenting a Problem to the Doctor

In discussing the patient's prognosis in the consultation, a report from a working party of the Royal College of General Practitioners (1972) advises the doctor to ask himself certain questions:

> What must I tell this patient? How much of what I learned about him should he know? What words shall I use to convey this information? How much of what I propose to tell him will he understand? How will he react? How much of my advice will he take? What degree of pressure am I entitled to apply? (p. 17).

If we change the second from last of these questions to read, 'How much notice will he take of what I say?' then these could be exactly the questions that the patient poses to himself when seeing the doctor. For the patient considers, both prior to and during the consultation, *what to say* to the doctor. Under this heading we deal with the patient's interpretation and selection of facts and the ways in which he attempts to put these across to the doctor with the maximum effect.

In perceiving his symptoms, the patient attempts to *interpret* them, and in explaining these symptoms to himself and to the doctor, he is defining, categorising and causally linking them to other factors which he feels may be related. Thus the disorder may be presented in conjunction with another physical condition that the patient believes to be relevant. One woman explained her problem to the doctor in this way: 'I've had a lot of headaches lately—I wondered if it could be anything to do with my blood pressure?' The symptoms may be described in terms of a social context which the patient sees as significant, e.g. the woman patient who told the doctor she believed her anxiety and 'nerves' stemmed from her worries about a delinquent daughter. This interpreting is partly an attempt at self-diagnosis and partly an attempt to 'put the doctor on the right lines'. What is significant to the patient may not be so for the doctor, who may dismiss the patient's perceptions and interpretations as having little relevance and may probe for other factors that the patient has not mentioned. Strauss *et al.* (1964) give an example of this situation among patients in a psychiatric hospital who cannot understand the approach of their doctors. One patient was troubled:

> . . . by what the doctor considered important and the kinds of judgement the doctor made. What he himself considered important and talked about at length, the doctor usually dismissed as unimportant. What he thought trivial the doctor might seize upon (p. 268).

As well, therefore, as having to define or recognise a problem and putting this into words, the patient is also involved in 'figuring out' the doctor. Both parties are 'sizing each other up'. The patient may not agree with the doctor's interpretation of his symptoms, especially when this does not accord with his own preconceived ideas and the doctor has not stated his interpretation in terms sufficiently convincing to persuade the patient to accept it. One young

woman, consulting the doctor about her small child whose problem the doctor had interpreted as being unimportant and 'nothing to worry about', persistently reiterated that the symptoms in her child were both unusual and worrying:

> Yes, but it's most unusual for him to keep vomiting up his feed like this. And as I say, he's never been like this before.

In cases such as this, the patient may make further and more obvious attempts to persuade the doctor to acknowledge her own perspective on the problem:

> 'I said, "Well, what about these dizzy spells I've been having doctor?" And he just sat back and stared at me blankly . . . so to help him I said, "Could it be anything to do with my age?"'

From all the many and varied pieces of information that could be given, the patient has also to be *selective* in verbal presentation. This selection may be largely unconscious —in any communication the speaker is necessarily selective—or it may be consciously planned. The problem in selecting what to say is that of estimating what is relevant and significant and what it is necessary or expedient to verbalise.

Very often all information is not given at the onset, almost as though the patient is not sure what is relevant. During the course of the interaction, the patient may select and introduce other topics in response to the doctor's own interpretation and approach to the problem. For example, at a late stage in the presentation of her daughter's symptoms, a mother said: 'She has had a lot of injections lately.' Although this was phrased as a statement rather than a question, it was offered in a way that seemed to raise the question of whether the injections could have had anything to do with the child's present symptoms. The patient may offer various facts, suggesting or hinting at a possible causal relationship. The patient may select his information according to criteria he thinks the doctor wants or needs to hear (those aspects which he believes will have meaning for a doctor) and what he, the patient, wants to tell the doctor and thinks he should be told.

Our chosen research strategy was to interview different people at different stages in the consultation and not to follow the same people throughout. We are therefore unable to show, with any certainty, the relationship between prior anticipations and expectations and what the patient actually says and does when with the doctor. Certainly, that many people do have anticipations and expectations means that they prepare for the consultation in some way. It is probable that their presentation of themselves to the doctor is guided by this presentation. However, the actual consultation can develop along different lines from those the patient anticipated or intended, because he has limited ability to control the doctor's reactions to him. Again, despite having rehearsed beforehand what to say the patient may fail to verbalise this. The reaction of the doctor to the information the patient gives may prompt the patient into giving details which he did not expect to give, or into remembering other information. One man during a consultation disclosed after the doctor had mentioned that certain foodstuffs could cause discoloured urine, the fact that he had taken an Iron Jelloid a few days earlier. Conversely, the statements a doctor makes to the patient and his general approach may result in the patient lapsing into silence or making non-committal sounds.

The doctor too is selective in what he decides to tell the patient. The doctor may not inform the patient of the type of drug he is prescribing or of possible side effects of the treatment. Similarly, the patient may withhold from the doctor information that he feels will place him in a disadvantaged position, e.g. an admission that he has not followed instructions or that he fears a course of action proposed by the doctor. A woman told the interviewer that she was 'terrified' of her forthcoming operation:

> '. . . but don't write that down. Don't tell the doctor I said that, he'd shout at me if he heard me say that.'

An elderly woman omitted to tell her doctor certain facts about her treatment and recovery because she did not consider it expedient that he should learn of them.

> 'He said I'd been a very lucky woman not to have any more trouble, but I didn't tell him I'd been treating myself too; I'd get a friend to come in and rub my back three times a day.'

Either doctor or patient may interrupt the speech of the other, jump from one topic to another, refer back to statements previously made, or formulate the problem in a different way if either feels the other has not reacted as desired. This makes for what would appear to an observer to be the uneven nature of the exchange in the consultation; there is often a great deal of skipping and back-tracking as the problem is being defined, redefined and reformulated and some kind of solution or compromise is reached.

Yet whilst both are involved in this process, the initiative is usually taken by the doctor in pulling the various strands of conversation together, drawing out and summarising what he considers to be the significant points from the information given by the patient. After one patient had brought-up various matters in the consultation, the doctor interjected with a question which, to him, summarised her reason for being there: 'So it's just a sick note and a prescription you want, is it?' Just as the doctor defines the significant, and may ignore what he sees as irrelevant, so too, the patient is selective in the assimilation of information given by the doctor, paying attention to that which appears important to him.

We categorise the second problematic aspect of communication as *how to talk to the doctor*, which includes the ordering and emphasis of the information given to the doctor, as ways of ensuring that the mode of expression used by the patient is convincing. Patients order their descriptions of symptoms, requests for action, questions and presentation of different problems, partly as a result of the process by which they have perceived and given meaning to those symptoms and problems, partly as a method of remembering everything they have selected to tell the doctor and, equally important, as a way of structuring the encounter from their own perspective. The sequence which the patient intends to follow is not usually stated in such clear terms as those used by the young mother who said to the doctor: 'I've come about myself and the baby—first of all the baby. . . .' The anticipated order or presentation is not usually verbalised to the doctor although the patient may have an idea in his own mind about this. As one woman in a group discussion said, when asked how she talked to the doctor: 'If you've got a couple of things wrong with you, you explain—well, you think, "I'll tell him I've got this first and I'll tell him I've got that."' The way in which the consultation progresses and the more spontaneous occurrences, may of course upset the intended order of presentation by determining at what point and in what manner certain issues can be raised by the patient.

One type of ordering is where the patient, having several things to discuss with the doctor, decides to raise a 'physical' problem first. A female patient began with a two-minute discourse on the menopausal symptoms she was suffering. She then asked about her latest chest X-ray results and finally raised the matter of her daughter's illegitimate baby. Such ordering may be related to a conception of the physician dealing with physical symptoms and to the way in which the presentation of a physical complaint may be seen as an appropriate way of leading into other, more socially-oriented problems.

The patient's assessment of the seriousness of his problems may also affect the order in which they are presented. One woman was not able to voice her fear of cancer until the consultation was virtually at an end, whereas a mother consulting with her son raised her fears on the subject of his convulsions before turning to more routine problems of the family's health. Similarly, a patient's ordering of direct requests may vary according to his perception of the most appropriate time for a request to be effectively presented in the particular circumstances. A young man who had attended the surgery several times over a number of weeks with a knee injury immediately asked for a sickness certificate on entering the doctor's room, whilst an elderly male patient stated: 'I could do with a tonic as well', just as his consultation with the doctor was drawing to a close.

Giving adequate and explicit verbal expression to subjective internal states would seem to be inherently problematic for the patient, accentuated in this context by the patient's need not to exaggerate symptoms nor allow them to sound trivial. This problem of *emphasis* in presentation is well illustrated by the nineteen-year-old male patient who said in interview:

'I used to get this giddiness a lot, and when you're trying to explain it, you know it's very difficult, everything seems sort of three times as big when you're trying to put it in words to a doctor, get it across to him. I mean you don't know the proper medical terms. You either make it sound much more serious than it is, or a very minor thing that's not worth mentioning.'

If the patient feels, or is made to feel, that the problem is trivial, then the patient may also feel that he is guilty of 'wasting the doctor's time.' Emphasis in the language used by the patient is one way of attempting to validate his presence by lending weight to symptoms that could possibly be dismissed as trivial by the doctor. The problem for the patient lies in distinguishing the minor from the potentially serious. What may have appeared important when at home may seem less so once the patient is in the surgery a few hours or days later, attempting to verbalise the reasons for being there:

'You may feel really ill, but once you get into the surgery you usually begin to feel a bit better. Or whenever I ring the doctor to come up and see the children, once he comes through the door, the children are running around. It is just like when you go to the dentist—you have toothache, but once you get to the door your toothache stops.'

Although the patient's presence in the surgery denotes the elevation of the problem above the status of a 'minor matter' and worthy of the doctor's time, the patient also appreciates the doctor endorsing this. The doctor has a basis for evaluating the trivial and serious that is not available to the layman. Bloor and Horobin (1974) suggest that conflict in the contact between doctor and patient is generated by a 'double bind' expectation of the patient.

> . . . the sick person is expected to analyse his condition in terms—is it serious or non-serious, does it require medical treatment or some other alleviative action, etc.—which imply diagnostic and prognostic evaluation, but on presentation to the doctor, the sick person is expected to 'forget' his own prior assessment of the condition and defer to the doctor's.

The doctor's motives in making statements such as 'It's nothing much', or 'That's nothing serious' may be to reassure the patient there is no cause for concern. Yet an unintended consequence can be to place the patient in a position where he feels the doctor is inferring that he has consulted unnecessarily. Alternatively, the doctor may be trying to evoke this feeling in the patient. Either way the patient may then attempt to justify his presence by re-emphasising his reason for consulting. Consider the following exchange between an elderly woman and her general practitioner:

Doctor:

> 'It shakes you up a bit, a fall does. Let's have a look now.'

Examination begins.

Patient:

> 'It's the pain here, thought I'd better come down to see if I'd sprained anything.'

Pause in dialogue. Examination continues.

Patient:

> 'My daughter said, "Go to the doctor's and see what your chest is like."'

Doctor still examining.

Doctor:

> 'Did she pass her driving test?'

Discussion of daughter's driving test follows, until examination completed.

Doctor:

> 'This'll get better on its own. Nothing to worry about there but your chest may be sore for a week.'

Patient:

> 'My angina . . .'

Doctor (interrupts):

> 'No, you won't damage your heart by a fall like this.'

Patient:

> 'Oh. Just that my daughter said to go down and see about my chest.'

Emphasis may become insistence. A woman in a group discussion describing her father's illness explained:

> 'He [the doctor] sent him for three mass X-rays and my father said, "I'm still not getting any better. I'm still not at all well." "Oh," he said, "I'll send you for a deep X-ray." Only mass X-rays until my father insisted that he wasn't getting any better.'

Another aspect involved in the consideration of what to say to the doctor and how to say it, is the use of an *appropriate language* to describe symptoms. The patient in consultation with the doctor says he has brought 'a specimen' and described his complaint as 'blood-coloured acidic urine'. This illustrates the use of a 'middle-ground language' by patients, which is not entirely derived from a lay or medical culture, but is a combination of elements from both—lay knowledge about medicine, disease and treatment, previous experience of symptoms and diagnoses, and medical descriptive terms with which the patient is familiar.

The language used to describe symptoms to a doctor may differ from that used in a description of the same symptoms to friends (or interviewers). One woman amongst a group of friends stated that she was to have a minor operation: 'I'm waiting for a small repair job.' Another said of a member of her family: 'One doctor came and gave him stuff to rub in . . . he was treating him for muscular.' And a man interviewed at the surgery said he had 'a bit of blood pressure'. This is not to suggest that people necessarily use terms such as 'blood pressure' with no knowledge of their meaning (although that knowledge may be discrepant with the definitions of the medical profession) but that the terminology used to describe bodily conditions may be adapted to fit the status of the listener. A good example of this was the woman who was to have a hysterectomy and described this to the interviewer as 'having my womb removed' and later in conversation with friends when the interviewer was also present referred to it simply as 'having it all taken away'.

Influencing the Doctor

The ways in which people present themselves in the surgery may be viewed as strategies influencing the course of the consultation. We do not claim that the patient or the doctor always consciously adopt strategies to influence each other. The desire to influence may only be implicit in the presentation. The way in which the facts are presented to the doctor is an expression of a certain approach on the part of the patient, whether this approach is a request for a sickness certificate, a desire that the doctor should give his attention to symptoms that are seen to be a problem, or simply a desire that the doctor makes all the decisions. Verbal and non-verbal control strategies are attempts to put across and reinforce that approach. Likewise, the doctor attempts to influence the interaction along his own desired course. The doctor may have repeated his actions so often that they are generally performed at the level of routine and are not consciously invoked except when that routine is disrupted. For both, the strategies are part of a repertoire, to be invoked when the situation permits. The efforts made by each to influence the interaction give the consultation its bargaining quality.

In the following example from a surgery consultation, a patient is trying to persuade the doctor that her problem merits medical attention. The woman patient presents her symptoms to the doctor. He can find no explanation for them in the examination he makes or from the medical history on the patient's record card. As a position of stalemate is reached, the patient herself finally offers a proposed course of action in the light of the doctor's seeming inaction. She persists in offering the symptoms as a matter of concern and succeeds by proposing a solution of her own, in gaining the doctor's recognition that some action should be taken. The consultation began with the woman describing 'odd pains' and giddiness and complaining that she had put on weight. We begin the dialogue with her speaking whilst the doctor examines her.

Patient:

'I've taken tablets. I thought I could fight it off.'

Doctor:

'Mmm. Uh-huh.'

Patient:

'This morning I couldn't even drink my cup of tea so I knew something was wrong.'

Examination ends.

Doctor:

'Well, that's normal, there's nothing wrong there.'

Patient:

'Well, I don't know what causes it, I'm sure.'

Doctor:

'Your blood pressure's all right, there's nothing the matter there.'

Patient:

'Nothing to worry about? Oh well, there you are then.'

Doctor:

'Are you sure you've put on half a stone?'

Patient:

'Definitely.'

Pause in dialogue.

Patient:

'Is there something I could stop eating? I can't wear my clothes now.'

Doctor:

'Cut out sugar in your tea and flour products, take them only in moderation. Try that and see how you go on. It'll take some time mind.'

Patient:

(laughing): 'Oh I know that!'

Both begin to joke about eating and weight problems.

There is rarely open conflict in the negotiation in the consultation. Both parties generally recognise and retain some semblance of formality and exercise restraint to prevent the encounter from completely 'breaking down'. A patient seldom makes accusations to a general practitioner's face about what are considered to be inefficiencies and inadequacies; similarly, a doctor rarely loses his temper with a patient. If it appears that this point is being approached, one actor seems to step down and attempts to avoid the issue or heal the breach. A patient who failed to keep her hospital appointment evoked the doctor's annoyance. During the consultation he said to her: "Well I'm sorry Betty. What do you expect me to do? I've done as much as I can. . . . What's the use if you don't do anything I say?' Betty remained silent throughout, muttering her apologies just before leaving. Verbal and non-verbal control strategies are often covert and rarely obvious or explicit. On the part of the patient particularly they appear to operate beneath a façade of compliance and acquiescence. The thoughts of the patient which are not articulated during tense or difficult exchanges such as that above, may form the basis for 'stories' told about doctors when the patient is well away from the surgery.

For the doctor's part, the control he exercises can be more overt because in some respects he is expected, as a doctor, to instruct and direct; to act 'like a doctor'. This gives him certain strategic advantages when we consider the possible controlling techniques available to each actor. In one sense the doctor holds the 'trump card' because ultimately he controls access to treatment resources.

References

Bloor, M. J. and Horobin, G. W. (1974), 'Conflict and conflict resolution in doctor-patient interactions', in A. Mead and C. Cox, *Sociology of Medical Practice*, London: Collier-Macmillan.

Maddox, E. J. (1973), 'The Diagnostic Process: a sociological approach to some factors affecting outcomes with special reference to variation', Aberdeen University: Master's thesis.

Marinker, M. (1970), 'Truce', in Balint *et al.* (1970), ch. 7.

Mauksch, H. O. (1972), 'Ideology, interaction and patient care in hospitals'; paper presented at the Third International Conference on Social Science and Medicine, Elsinore, Denmark.

Roth, J. A. (1963), *Timetables: Structuring the Passage of Time in Hospital Treatment and other Careers*, Indianapolis: Bobbs-Merrill.

Royal College of General Practitioners Working Party (1972), *The Future General Practitioner*, London: Royal College of General Practitioners.

Scheff, T. J. (1968), 'Negotiating reality: notes on power in the assessment of responsibility', *Social Problems*, 16, 1, pp. 3–17.

Strauss, A., Schatzman, L., Bucher, R., Ehrlich, D. and Sabshin, M. (1964), *Psychiatric Ideologies and Institutions*, London: Collier-Macmillan.

Strong, P. M. and Davis, A. G. (1972), 'Problems and strategies in a paediatric clinic'; paper presented at the Third International Conference on Social Science and Medicine, Elsinore, Denmark.

37 TO LISTEN, TO RECOGNIZE

Rita Charon

The practice of medicine requires powerful instruments for visualizing patients' bodies. We now know that we must see clearly the lives of patients as well as their bodies. This article describes instruments for visualizing and comprehending the lives of patients. These instruments are stories and the imagination. Let me describe some of the stories we tell each other and then suggest

SOURCE: Copyright © 1986 by Alpha Omega Alpha Honor Medical Society, reprinted by permission from *The Pharos*, Volume 49, Number 4.

ways in which different kinds of stories may enrich our practice by allowing us to recognize our patients more fully.

"This is the first Presbyterian Hospital admission for this seventy-two-year-old woman with a chief complaint of shortness of breath." So begins a story that a student tells about a patient. "The patient was well until two weeks prior to admission when she noted gradually increasing dyspnea on exertion. She denies chest pains, palpitations, cough, or fever." As the attending listening to this story, I pay attention to the content and to the form of the story. I await the unfolding of the narrative according to the rules of the literary genre of the presentation. The student who offers me lab data before giving me the vital signs bewilders me. The student who mishandles the dramatic structure of the story, who does not build suspense toward climax and then deftly turn to denouement, disappoints the drama coach in me. In our work storytelling is a powerful instrument that defines our concerns and allows us to share them. Our genres also define us. By following our own literary rules, we accept each other into a circle.

We tell other kinds of stories for many different reasons. An internist tells me, "The guy with the neck from last week, it was Hodgkins." All I might have to say to a hematologist is, "85K," and he will know that our patient with idiopathic thrombocytopenic purpura is getting better on steroids. We go through our days telling stories to each other in these truncated, elliptical, tele-graphic forms, and it is through that kind of exchange that we grow in our knowledge, that we aid each other in our work, that we take care of patients. The scraps of information are legal tender among us. They satisfy our curiosity; they resolve our uncertainty; and they bind us to each other in very special ways.

It is in the stories we tell and how we tell them that we learn the basic lessons of medicine. Our genres limit us in significant ways. By telling our stories in the way that we do, we impose limits on admissible data; we insist on a particular stance toward the material. The formal medical presentation is stunning in its control, its precision, its flatness. There is for sure an intellectual playfulness about it—Why does the presenter choose those negatives to include? Is that historical fact a clue or a red herring? Listeners derive joy from following along an inventive and dense presentation. Yet, the genre prohibits certain behaviors and observations. Has a presenter ever mentioned his or her own response to the patient in question, or explained what sense the patient makes of the symptoms? The genre, in the end, is the distillation of many medical lessons, and by teaching our students how to tell this type of story, we teach them deep lessons about the realms of living that are included and excluded from patient care.

But there are other, more complex stories to hear, to tell, and to write. These are the stories that will give us great rewards. John Berger wrote in *A Fortunate Man* of a family doctor in rural England.[1] He says that patients think of the doctor as the "clerk of their records," the one who recognizes patients in fraternity. He writes eloquently about the physician who acknowledges narratives by patients, narratives that will be heard by no one else. He casts the doctor in the fairly humble role of clerk. In fact, clerking is what we all do. The doctor witnesses and documents meaningful events in his or her patients' lives. Medical charts are journals, chronicles of lives and of times. Doctors are allowed to recognize the events and the people who dwell in them, and patients come to them for that recognition. Our work is centered on telling stories and on hearing stories, and by choosing one kind of story over another, we can transform our practice of medicine.

Eudora Welty says in *One Writer's Beginnings,* an autobiography, "Long before I wrote stories, I listened for stories. Listening *for* them is something more acute than listening to them. I suppose it's an early form of participation in what goes on."[2]

When I sit in my examining room with patients, I use my writer instincts. A woman came to see me because of back pain. She was an obese middle-aged woman with multiple vague complaints. She seemed sad. When I examined her, I discovered surgical evidence of a breast reduction procedure and tiny vertical scars behind each ear. This was a woman who cared deeply about her personal appearance. She had gained fifty pounds in the past four years. My literary curiosity was aroused. There was a gap in this character's motivational history. "You're an attractive woman," I said, "and you care about your appearance. What happened four years ago to change you?"

She started to cry. Four years ago her daughter was found to have breast cancer. "I can't tell anybody about this," the patient said. "They talk, they talk, and if they know somebody has cancer, they won't pick up a cup if that person touched it." As she spoke, she picked up an imaginary coffee cup and then spat it away from herself. "They're all afraid, so it stays inside me like a secret." Had I not listened for her story, I would have made the mistake we all dread: I would have missed something.

Listening for stories is the first step in developing respect for their power. The next level in approaching stories is to write them, and to write them in genres different from the clinical presentation. When I teach second-year students how to interview patients, I ask them to write histories of present illness using the patient's narrative voice.[3] They write in the first person from the patient's point of view. Some complain about these assignments. "This isn't a creative writing class, is it?" they'll mumble. Most have never tried writing stories before. When they sit down to find the voice of the patient, they find the feelings and perspective of the patient as well. By taking on the patient's stance, they experience events as the patient might have. They discover the remarkable powers of writing, and I suggest, of empathy.

I use the writing of fiction to clarify my own feelings and understandings about patients. When I am confused or distressed about a patient, I write that patient into a short story. I give myself full license of the novelist. I start with known details, often scanty, about the patient's life. I fill in with fiction the gaps there are in fact. I find ways in which to tie together the events, complaints, and actions of the patient. I also place myself in the story, and this is a crucial element of my exercise. I describe myself from the patient's point of view. I play with the distance between myself as doctor and the patient, as well as the distance between myself as author and the patient.

What does this exercise do for me or for the patient? I am not surprised when details that I imagine about a patient turn out to be true. There is, after all, a deep spring of knowledge about our patients that is only slightly tapped in our conscious work. We know more about our patients than we think we do. This intuition is the basis for diagnosis as well as for interpersonal aspects of patient care. As scientists and as artists, and I submit that we are always both when we act as doctors, we rely on hints, guesses, and connections that are made not so much by our minds as by our imaginations.

Writing stories about my patients does something more important for me and my patients than discover things that I know about them. It gives me appropriate distance. Aesthetic distance, it turns out, is akin to clinical distance. Both writers and doctors have to find that perfect middle ground between identification and objectification. They neither merge with their subjects nor separate from them. They do not expropriate the subjects' experience as if it were theirs. Rather, they experience the events through the character. They let go of the characters and allow them to act, trying only to keep up with them. They open themselves to the weight and the meaning of the stories they receive.

Doctors struggle to find that middle ground. They overshoot into passive helpless sympathy with patients only to overshoot in the opposite direction into intellectual detachment. They look for a place to stand. Writing helps to find the foothold, for it allows the writer to partake of the context of that patient's life. It makes the patient become kindred without becoming self.

Michael Balint observed that a diagnosed disease is not simply "out there" in the patient, but is the result of negotiation between physician and patient. Clinical history taking and diagnosing are active processes through which a disease is constructed rather than found.[4]

This process points to the physician's part in defining the problem and deciding what is wrong. A patient does not approach us saying, "I have congestive heart failure." Rather, she approaches saying, "I feel tired all the time, and I have a hard time breathing if I work too hard." She may add, for clarity, "It all started when my daughter moved in with her three kids, and ever since then I just can't keep up with everything."

What is the problem? What is the

relationship between the symptoms of shortness of breath and being overwhelmed with family responsibilities? The physician chooses an avenue of questioning and excludes data that do not belong to that line of thought. We frame patients' complaints, we array them in our minds in ways that make sense to us. Perhaps the patient would have included different material in her frame. Elliot Mishler described medical encounters as conversations between the "voice of medicine" and the "voice of the lifeworld." He suggested that effective patient care rests on both languages being heard.[5] We have to be alert to the patient's frame as well as to our own.

The point, then, is that the patient's story is coauthored by doctor and patient. They share in drawing that frame; together they select the subplots and the minor characters. They agree through practice on the relevant data to be included. When a doctor-patient relationship breaks down, it is usually because this tacit agreement was not reached and one or the other participant is uncomfortable with the frame that has been drawn.

In order to hear patient's stories, we have to acknowledge the subtexts of those stories. Patients come to doctors for trivial or tragic problems. We occupy a peculiar position for them. We are the ones who diagnose and treat their physical problems, but we also stand for a level of the transcendent in their lives. We preside at scenes of human crisis—pain, loss, death, as well as joyous ones like birth and recovery. Members of few other occupations can stand on the ground that we do—clergy perhaps, police officers in a different way. Like ministers or rabbis or police officers, we are granted entrance into private, sometimes horrifying, often sad, and always significant worlds. We are the interpreters for patients' dealings with dark and troubling events. We as physicians embody patient's hopes that they will live forever, and they expect that we can intercede with the gods or the fates when their time comes.

We are the gatekeepers not only to services of subspecialists and fancy technology but also gatekeepers to the land of the living. Susan Sontag in *Illness As Metaphor* talks about the kingdom of the well and the kingdom of the sick, and says that one is born with a citizenship in both kingdoms.[6] "Illness is the nightside of life," she says, and we, because we know about that territory, are the guides for travelers in it.

Some readers will recognize my last name from Greek mythology. Charon is the boatman who ferries souls of the dead across the river Styx to Hades. During my medicine rotation when I was a third year student, a patient recognized my name. The patient was a twenty-six-year-old man with metastatic hepatocellular carcinoma. He looked at my name tag and said, "So this is it?" He died two days later of pulmonary hemorrhage. I seriously considered changing my name, until I realized that my task is to accompany people ultimately to their deaths, and that my name was most appropriate for medicine.

Because of the nature of the work we do with patients, we are in touch with deep levels of meaning in their lives. A forty-year-old woman tries to decide whether or not to have a child. Another patient tries to decide whether the time has come to place an elderly parent in a nursing home. Another has to choose his resuscitation status.

These are the conversations that we have to train ourselves to listen for. The hesitant glance, the inarticulate sigh, or, as William Carlos Williams says, "the hunted news I get from some obscure patients' eyes"[7] carry with them profound challenge about the meaning of lives and the meaning of deaths. Even if the problem at hand is a trivial one, it will cascade through these other thoughts, because we doctors are the ones who deal in that stuff, and any brush with us connotes a brush with it.

I suggested earlier that the doctor and the patient coauthor the story. What part should the doctor play in the patient's narrative? We are taught not to get personally involved in our patients' care, that we are not to allow our personal biases or values to interfere in the care of patients. We are warned not to take friends or relatives as patients. This is all true. Yet, when a doctor sits in a room with a patient, that doctor is an active presence. The personal history of that man or woman cannot help but be involved in an encounter as fragile and as powerful as the one between doctor and patient.

A physician said to me recently, "My mother died last year, and I had to place my father in a home; he has Alzheimer's. And you know, it was my patients who saw me through it. They knew what was happening, and they were the ones who supported and comforted me through the whole thing." Another physician told me of a patient who was dying of lung cancer, a young woman. The doctor got to know the patient's family quite well. This doctor had recently lost a sister in a hiking accident. She was able to sit with the sister of this dying woman, to cry with her, to share the depth of a sister's loss.

Mr. Glade is an eighty-two-year-old patient of mine with hypertension, diabetes, and mild renal insufficiency. When I first examined him, I discovered a prostatic nodule that turned out on biopsy to be prostatic cancer. He went through surgery and radiation therapy, and suffered uncomfortable and personally shameful side-effects of the treatment. I rued the day that I had found that mass.

He is a jazz musician who had been active in the thirties jazz scene in Harlem, and he would tell me about clubs to go to in New York, and releases of Bessie Smith records. He came in to see me recently. He was feeling sick, had a urinary tract infection; his diabetes was out of control. I looked behind him as he sat in the chair in my examining room, and I saw a vision of him in hospital johnny with a 40 percent face mask, Foley in place, cefoxitin dripping in. In my vision, his creatinine was 7, his BUN 93. He was not able to respond to my voice; he was slipping away.

When I snapped back to the present tense, I was distant, coolly efficient with my questions and physical exam. I resented his being sick. I know for sure that he will die soon, and that my vision is an accurate prediction of how he will die. I was feeling prematurely my anger at his leaving. I was angry that he planned to abandon me. I know that I shall miss him once he is gone. I found a way to tell him that I wanted him to get better; I treated his UTI; and he is now doing well.

Were we physicians overstepping the boundaries between professional and personal relationships? By accepting the support of patients, by reflecting on our own losses, by forming bonds with patients that then hurt us when they die, were we being naive and maudlin?

Quite the opposite. We were appropriately using human skills and responses in human settings. We were using our own personal histories in comprehending and embracing the narratives of our patients. We did more. We increased the effectiveness of our therapeutic interventions with our patients and their families by offering our own experience into the encounter.

We all know on some level that medicine has to do with personal relationships. We chose this life because it lets us know people, lets us help them. However acute may be our interest and skill in the biotechnical aspects of medicine, we chose to become doctors because we would have patients.

A remarkable thing happens after we have known a patient for a while. We allow ourselves to sit back in the chair with peace and receptivity, to not dawdle over the Aldomet and the Inderal, but to ask with true interest, "How's it going?" It becomes clear over time that people have few opportunities to be asked those kinds of questions. Because we have been clerking the records, we know about the daughter who has been in trouble with the law, about the son who is graduating with honors from Bronx Science, about the beautician course that the patient is just finishing up, hoping to open up her own shop in the neighborhood. We follow each subplot with interest, and with interest that contributes to that patient's health. It is in these subplots that we recognize the patient in his or her uniqueness and strength. Virginia Woolf says that "the body is a sheet of plain glass through which the soul looks straight and clear. . . . The creature within can only gaze through the pane—smudged or rosy."[8] We never take care of the body without peering through it to the soul.

It turns out that there is much less difference between the sick and the well than any of us imagine. The brutal and isolating aspects of medical training and practice can be transformed into the most humanizing experience if we allow ourselves to see our fellowship with our patients. Medicine lets us glimpse the nobility, the strength, the tenacity of our fellow human beings. If we can open to the journeys of our patients, we are rewarded with a stunning landscape of the human spirit.

Doctors have an important gift to offer to people in crisis. We have seen this before. We have seen people in pain; we have seen people die. We have made it our business to learn about these things, these terrible moments for people. They rely on our having been there before.

This is our offering—to recognize. We recognize symptoms, emergencies, the need for action. If we couple this with a recognition of the people in the midst of their distress, we become complete doctors.

The stories of patients fill us with joy. It is at times a black joy, to use the words of Richard Selzer,[9] a joy incomprehensible because it is rooted in tragedy and loss. Yet there is tremendous joy in sharing meaningful events with people, strangers even, and making of those events something that can transcend the accidents of life. Our presence and recognition can endow events with grace. By entering into the deep experiences that people have within our field of vision, we can first of all learn of them ourselves, and then give wisdom to others going through them. If we allow ourselves to be instruments of hope, of resourcefulness, and of acceptance, we shall have fulfilled our oaths, we shall have used our knowledge well, and we shall be rewarded in the way only a physician can: we shall have healed.

References

1. Berger, J, and Mohr, J: A Fortunate Man. New York, Pantheon Books, 1967, pp. 69, 109.
2. Welty, E: One Writer's Beginnings. Cambridge, Massachusetts, Harvard University Press, 1984, p. 14.
3. Charon, R: To render the lives of patients. Literature and Medicine 5: 39–48, 1986, in press.
4. Balint, M: The Doctor, His Patient and the Illness. New York, International University Press, 1957, p. 18.
5. Mishler, E: The Discourse of Medicine: Dialectics of Medical Interviews. Norwood, New Jersey, Ablex Publishing Corporation, 1984, p. 192.
6. Sontag, S: Illness as Metaphor. New York, Vintage Books, 1979, p. 3.
7. Williams, WC: The Autobiography of William Carlos Williams. New York, New Directions Books, 1967, p. 360.
8. Woolf, V: On being ill. In The Moment and Other Essays. London, The Hogarth Press, 1947, pp. 14–24, p. 14.
9. Selzer, R: Letters to a Young Doctor. New York, Simon & Schuster, 1982, p. 125.

Section Twelve

Rights, Responsibilities, and Social Control

The concept of medicine as an institution of social control has received much support in recent years. This is an idea that Talcott Parsons introduced, but he did not see it as problematic. Social control in the medical sphere is, in part, a result of *medicalization*, the claim of medical professionals to power and clinical authority in more and more areas of everyday life (e.g., sexuality, family relations, child rearing, crime). Social control also stems from the inequality in most medical relationships, with the patient having too little control over decision making. Social control is exacerbated by the tendency for physicians to act rather than not to act; they are more likely to find illness than not to find it, and if they are surgeons, to perform surgery rather than to recommend against surgery. In addition, social control can result from the application or withholding of medical techniques by political and economic power-holders, a situation quite common in reproductive issues such as contraception and abortion.

The articles in this section portray medical coercion and control on a variety of levels. James Jones writes about "The Tuskegee Syphilis Experiment," an experiment ended as late as 1972, which many commentators have likened to Nazi medical experimentation in concentration camps. For forty years the federal Public Health Service conducted a project in which black men with syphilis were deliberately left untreated so that researchers could view the results of the disease's natural progress. Poor Southern black men had been tricked into believing that they were getting medical attention, and the nature of the Tuskegee study was widely known in medical circles. Jones shows the clear racism that underpinned such endeavors, and he further emphasizes that the Tuskegee experiment was in some ways a logical outgrowth of a system in which medical and scientific research can transcend the bounds of normal morality in its frequently unmonitored and allegedly value-free search for knowledge.

Jeanne Guillemin takes on a less consciously malevolent topic in "Babies by Cesarean: Who Chooses, Who Controls?" Pointing to the alarming rise in cesarean sections, she argues that obstetricians have created a major change in childbirth practice, while persuading themselves and their patients of the benefits. But the many drawbacks to cesarean sections are not only medical ones. There are powerful emotional and psychological issues involving personal control and involvement in the birthing process. There are also ethical issues such as who is in control of the birthing experience. Guillemin discusses the array of contexts influencing this trend: professional authority, hospital resources, health policy, public perceptions of risk, and the resulting physician fear of malpractice. By virtue of this array of contexts, this article pulls together many concepts covered in earlier articles.

38 THE TUSKEGEE SYPHILIS EXPERIMENT

James Jones

In late July of 1972, Jean Heller of the Associated Press broke the story: for forty years the United States Public Health Service (PHS) had been conducting a study of the effects of untreated syphilis on black men in Macon County, Alabama, in and around the county seat of Tuskegee. The Tuskegee Study, as the experiment had come to be called, involved a substantial number of men: 399 who had syphilis and an additional 201 who were free of the disease chosen to serve as controls. All of the syphilitic men were in the late stage of the disease when the study began.[1]

Under examination by the press the PHS was not able to locate a formal protocol for the experiment. Later it was learned that one never existed; procedures, it seemed, had simply evolved. A variety of tests and medical examinations were performed on the men during scores of visits by PHS physicians over the years, but the basic procedures called for periodic blood testing and routine autopsies to supplement the information that was obtained through clinical examinations. The fact that only men who had late, so-called tertiary, syphilis were selected for the study indicated that the investigators were eager to learn more about the serious complications that result during the final phase of the disease.

The PHS officers were not disappointed. Published reports on the experiment consistently showed higher rates of mortality and morbidity among the syphilitics than the controls. In fact, the press reported that as of 1969 at least 28 and perhaps as many as 100 men had died as a direct result of complications caused by syphilis. Others had developed serious syphilis-related heart conditions that may have contributed to their deaths.[2]

The Tuskegee Study had nothing

SOURCE: Reprinted with permission of the Free Press, a Division of Macmillan, Inc. from *Bad Blood: The Tuskegee Syphilis Experiment* by James Jones. Copyright © 1981 by the Free Press.

to do with treatment. No new drugs were tested; neither was any effort made to establish the efficacy of old forms of treatment. It was a non-therapeutic experiment, aimed at compiling data on the effects of the spontaneous evolution of syphilis on black males. The magnitude of the risks taken with the lives of the subjects becomes clearer once a few basic facts about the disease are known.

Syphilis is a highly contagious disease caused by the *Treponema pallidum,* a delicate organism that is microscopic in size and resembles a corkscrew in shape. The disease may be acquired or congenital. In acquired syphilis, the spirochete (as the *Treponema pallidum* is also called) enters the body through the skin or mucous membrane, usually during sexual intercourse, though infection may also occur from other forms of bodily contact such as kissing. Congenital syphilis is transmitted to the fetus in the infected mother when the spirochete penetrates the placental barrier.

From the onset of infection syphilis is a generalized disease involving tissues throughout the entire body. Once they wiggle their way through the skin or mucous membrane, the spirochetes begin to multiply at a frightening rate. First they enter the lymph capillaries where they are hurried along to the nearest lymph gland. There they multiply and work their way into the bloodstream. Within days the spirochetes invade every part of the body.

Three stages mark the development of the disease: primary, secondary, and tertiary. The primary stage lasts from ten to sixty days starting from the time of infection. During this "first incubation period," the primary lesion of syphilis, the chancre, appears at the point of contact, usually on the genitals. The chancre, typically a slightly elevated, round ulcer, rarely causes personal discomfort and may be so small as to go unnoticed. If it does not become secondarily infected, the chancre will heal without treatment within a month or two, leaving a scar that persists for several months.[3]

While the chancre is healing, the second stage begins. Within six weeks to six months, a rash appears signaling the development of secondary syphilis. The rash may resemble measles, chicken pox, or any number of skin eruptions, though occasionally it is so mild as to go unnoticed. Bones and joints often become painful, and circulatory disturbances such as cardiac palpitations may develop. Fever, indigestion, headaches, or other nonspecific symptoms may accompany the rash. In some cases skin lesions develop into moist ulcers teeming with spirochetes, a condition that is especially severe when the rash appears in the mouth and causes open sores that are viciously infectious. Scalp hair may drop out in patches, creating a "moth-eaten" appearance. The greatest proliferation and most widespread distribution of spirochetes throughout the body occurs in secondary syphilis.[4]

Secondary syphilis gives way in most cases, even without treatment, to a period of latency that may last from a few weeks to thirty years. As if by magic, all symptoms of the disease seem to disappear, and the syphilitic patient does not associate with the disease's earlier symptoms the occasional skin infections, periodic chest pains, eye disorders, and vague discomforts that may follow. But the spirochetes do not vanish once the disease becomes latent. They bore into the bone marrow, lymph glands, vital organs, and central nervous systems of their victims. In some cases the disease seems to follow a policy of peaceful coexistence, and its hosts are able to enjoy full and long lives. Even so, autopsies in such cases often reveal syphilitic lesions in vital organs as contributing causes of death. For many syphilitic patients, however, the disease remains latent only two or three years. Then the delusion of a truce is shattered by the appearance of signs and symptoms that denote the tertiary stage.

It is during late syphilis, as the tertiary stage is also called, that the disease inflicts the greatest damage. Gummy or rubbery tumors (so-called gummas), the characteristic lesions of late syphilis, appear, resulting from the concentration of spirochetes in the body's tissues with destruction of vital structures. These tumors often coalesce on the skin forming large ulcers covered with a crust consisting of several layers of dried exuded matter. Their assaults on bone structure produce deterioration that resembles osteomyelitis or bone tuberculosis. The small tumors may be absorbed, leaving slightly scarred depressions, or they may cause wholesale destruction of the bone, such as the horrible mutilation that occurs when nasal

and palate bones are eaten away. The liver may also be attacked; here the result is scarring and deformity of the organ that impede circulation from the intestines.

The cardiovascular and central nervous systems are frequent and often fatal targets of late syphilis. The tumors may attack the walls of the heart or the blood vessels. When the aorta is involved, the walls become weakened, scar tissue forms over the lesion, the artery dilates, and the valves of the heart no longer open and close properly and begin to leak. The stretching of the vessel walls may produce an aneurysm, a balloonlike bulge in the aorta. If the bulge bursts, and sooner or later most do, the result is sudden death.

The results of neurosyphilis are equally devastating. Syphilis is spread to the brain through the blood vessels, and while the disease can take several forms, the best known is paresis, a general softening of the brain that produces progressive paralysis and insanity. Tabes dorsalis, another form of neurosyphilis, produces a stumbling, foot-slapping gait in its victims due to the destruction of nerve cells in the spinal cord. Syphilis can also attack the optic nerve cells in the spinal cord. Syphilis can also attack the optic nerve, causing blindness, or the eighth cranial nerve, inflicting deafness. Since nerve cells lack regenerative power, all such damage is permanent.

The germ that causes syphilis, the stages of the disease's development, and the complications that can result from untreated syphilis were all known to medical science in 1932– the year the Tuskegee Study began.

Since the effects of the disease are so serious, reporters in 1972 wondered why the men agreed to cooperate. The press quickly established that the subjects were mostly poor and illiterate, and that the PHS had offered them incentives to participate. The men received free physical examinations, free rides to and from the clinics, hot meals on examination days, free treatment for minor ailments, and a guarantee that burial stipends would be paid to their survivors. Though the latter sum was very modest (fifty dollars in 1932 with periodic increases to allow for inflation), it represented the only form of burial insurance that many of the men had.

What the health officials had told the men in 1932 was far more difficult to determine. An officer of the venereal disease branch of the Center for Disease Control in Atlanta, the agency that was in charge of the Tuskegee Study in 1972, assured reporters that the participants were told what the disease could do to them, and that they were given the opportunity to withdraw from the program any time and receive treatment. But a physician with firsthand knowledge of the experiment's early years directly contradicted this statement. Dr. J. W. Williams, who was serving his internship at Andrews Hospital at the Tuskegee Institute in 1932 and assisted in the experiment's clinical work, stated that neither the interns nor the subjects knew what the study involved. "The people who came in were not told what was being done," Dr. Williams

said. "We told them we wanted to test them. They were not told, so far as I know, what they were being treated for or what they were not being treated for." As far as he could tell, the subjects "thought they were being treated for rheumatism or bad stomachs." He did recall administering to the men what he thought were drugs to combat syphilis, and yet as he thought back on the matter, Dr. Williams conjectured that "some may have been a placebo." He was absolutely certain of one point: "We didn't tell them we were looking for syphilis. I don't think they would have known what that was."[5]

A subject in the experiment said much the same thing. Charles Pollard recalled clearly the day in 1932 when some men came by and told him that he would receive a free physical examination if he appeared the next day at a nearby one-room school. "So I went on over and they told me I had bad blood." Pollard recalled. "And that's what they've been telling me ever since. They come around from time to time and check me over and they say, 'Charlie, you've got bad blood.'"[6]

An official of the Center for Disease Control (CDC) stated that he understood the term "bad blood" was a synonym for syphilis in the black community. Pollard replied, "That could be true. But I never heard no such thing. All I knew was that they just kept saying I had the bad blood—they never mentioned syphilis to me, not even once." Moreover, he thought that he had been receiving treatment for "bad blood" from the first meeting on, for Pollard added:

"They been doctoring me off and on ever since then, and they gave me a blood tonic."[7]

The PHS's version of the Tuskegee Study came under attack from yet another quarter when Dr. Reginald G. James told his story to reporters. Between 1939 and 1941 he had been involved with public health work in Macon County—specifically the diagnosis and treatment of syphilis. Assigned to work with him was Eunice Rivers, a black nurse employed by the Public Health Service to keep track of the participants in the Tuskegee Study. "When we found one of the men from the Tuskegee Study," Dr. James recalled, "she would say, 'He's under study and not to be treated.'" These encounters left him, by his own description, "distraught and disturbed," but whenever he insisted on treating such a patient, the man never returned. "They were being advised they shouldn't take treatments or they would be dropped from the study," Dr. James stated. The penalty for being dropped, he explained, was the loss of the benefits that they had been promised for participating.[8]

Once her identity became known, Nurse Rivers excited considerable interest, but she steadfastly refused to talk with reporters. Details of her role in the experiment came to light when newsmen discovered an article about the Tuskegee Study that appeared in *Public Health Reports* in 1953. Involved with the study from its beginning, Nurse Rivers served as the liaison between the researchers and the subjects. She lived in Tuskegee and provided the continuity in personnel that was vital. For while the names and faces of the "government doctors" changed many times over the years, Nurse Rivers remained a constant. She served as a facilitator, bridging the many barriers that stemmed from the educational and cultural gap between the physicians and the subjects. Most important, the men trusted her.[9]

As the years passed the men came to understand that they were members of a social club and burial society called "Miss Rivers' Lodge." She kept track of them and made certain that they showed up to be examined whenever the "government doctors" came to town. She often called for them at their homes in a shiny station wagon with the government emblem on the front door and chauffeured them to and from the place of examination. According to the *Public Health Reports* article, these rides became "a mark of distinction for many of the men who enjoyed waving to their neighbors as they drove by." There was nothing to indicate that the members of "Miss Rivers' Lodge" knew they were participating in a deadly serious experiment.[10]

Spokesmen for the Public Health Service were quick to point out that the experiment was never kept secret, as many newspapers had incorrectly reported when the story first broke. Far from being clandestine, the Tuskegee Study had been the subject of numerous reports in medical journals and had been openly discussed in conferences at professional meetings. An official told reporters that more than a dozen articles had appeared in some of the nation's best medical journals, describing the basic procedures of the study to a combined readership of well over a hundred thousand physicians. He denied that the Public Health Service had acted alone in the experiment, calling it a cooperative project that involved the Alabama State Department of Health, the Tuskegee Institute, the Tuskegee Medical Society, and the Macon County Health Department.[11]

Apologists for the Tuskegee Study contended that it was at best problematic whether the syphilitic subjects could have been helped by the treatment that was available when the study began. In the early 1930s treatment consisted of mercury and two arsenic compounds called arsphenamine and neoarsphenamine, known also by their generic name, salvarsan. The drugs were highly toxic and often produced serious and occasionally fatal reactions in patients. The treatment was painful and usually required more than a year to complete. As one CDC officer put it, the drugs offered "more potential harm for the patient than potential benefit."[12]

PHS officials argued that these facts suggested that the experiment had not been conceived in a moral vacuum. For if the state of the medical art in the early 1930s had nothing better than dangerous and less than totally effective treatment to offer, then it followed that, in the balance, little harm was done by leaving the men untreated.[13]

Discrediting the efficacy of mercury and salvarsan helped blunt the issue of withholding treatment during the early years, but public health officials had a great deal more difficulty explaining why penicillin was denied in the 1940s. One PHS spokesman ventured that it probably was not "a one-man decision" and added philosophically, "These things seldom are." He called the denial of penicillin treatment in the 1940s "the most critical moral issue about this experiment" and admitted that from the present perspective "one cannot see any reason that they could not have been treated at that time." Another spokesman declared: "I don't know why the decision was made in 1946 not to stop the program."[14]

The thrust of these comments was to shift the responsibility for the Tuskegee Study to the physician who directed the experiment during the 1940s. Without naming anyone, an official told reporters: "Whoever was director of the VD section at that time, in 1946 or 1947, would be the most logical candidate if you had to pin it down." That statement pointed an accusing finger at Dr. John R. Heller, a retired PHS officer who had served as the director of the division of venereal disease between 1943 and 1948. When asked to comment, Dr. Heller declined to accept responsibility for the study and shocked reporters by declaring: "There was nothing in the experiment that was unethical or unscientific."[15]

The current local health officer of Macon County shared this view, telling reporters that he probably would not have given the men penicillin in the 1940s either. He explained this curious devotion to what nineteenth-century physicians would have called "therapeutic nihilism" by emphasizing that penicillin was a new and largely untested drug in the 1940s. Thus, in his opinion, the denial of penicillin was a defensible medical decision.[16]

A CDC spokesman said it was "very dubious" that the participants in the Tuskegee Study would have benefited from penicillin after 1955. In fact, treatment might have done more harm than good. The introduction of vigorous therapy after so many years might lead to allergic drug reactions, he warned. Without debating the ethics of the Tuskegee Study, the CDC spokesman pointed to a generation gap as a reason to refrain from criticizing it. "We are trying to apply 1972 medical treatment standards to those of 1932," cautioned one official. Another officer reminded the public that the study began when attitudes toward treatment and experimentation were much different. "At this point in time," the officer stated, "with our current knowledge of treatment and the disease and the revolutionary change in approach to human experimentation, I don't believe the program would be undertaken."[17]

Journalists tended to accept the argument that the denial of penicillin during the 1940s was the crucial ethical issue. Most did not question the decision to withhold earlier forms of treatment because they apparently accepted the judgment that the cure was as bad as the disease. But a few journalists and editors argued that the Tuskegee Study presented a moral problem long before the men were denied treatment with penicillin. "To say, as did an official of the Center for Disease Control, that the experiment posed 'a serious moral problem' after penicillin became available is only to address part of the situation," declared the *St. Louis Post-Dispatch*. "The fact is that in an effort to determine from autopsies what effects syphilis has on the body, the government from the moment the experiment began withheld the best available treatment for a particularly cruel disease. The immorality of the experiment was inherent in its premise."[18]

Viewed in this light, it was predictable that penicillin would not be given to the men. *Time* magazine might decry the failure to administer the drug as "almost beyond belief or human compassion," but along with many other publications it failed to recognize a crucial point. Having made the decision to withhold treatment at the outset, investigators were not likely to experience a moral crisis when a new and improved form of treatment was developed. Their failure to administer penicillin resulted from the initial decision to withhold all treatment. The only valid distinction that can be made between the two acts is that the denial of penicillin held more dire consequences for the men in the study. The *Chicago Sun Times* placed these separate actions in the proper perspective: "Whoever made the decision to withhold penicillin compounded the original immorality of the project."[19]

The human dimension dominated the public discussions of the Tuskegee Study. The scientific merits of the experiment, real or imagined, were passed over almost without comment. Not being scientists, the journalists, public officials, and concerned citizens who protested the study did not really care how long it takes syphilis to kill people or what percentages of syphilis victims are fortunate enough to live to ripe old age with the disease. From their perspective the PHS was guilty of playing fast and loose with the lives of these men to indulge scientific curiosity.[20]

Many physicians had a different view. Their letters defending the study appeared in editorial pages across the country, but their most heated counterattacks were delivered in professional journals. The most spirited example was an editorial in the *Southern Medical Journal* by Dr. R. H. Kampmeir of Vanderbilt University's School of Medicine. No admirer of the press, he blasted reporters for their "complete disregard for their abysmal ignorance," and accused them of banging out "anything on their typewriters which will make headlines." As one of the few remaining physicians with experience treating syphilis in the 1930s, Dr. Kampmeir promised to "put this 'tempest in a teapot' into proper historical perspective."[21]

Dr. Kampmeir correctly pointed out that there had been only one experiment dealing with the effects of untreated syphilis prior to the Tuskegee Study. A Norwegian investigator had reviewed the medical records of nearly two thousand untreated syphilitic patients who had been examined at an Oslo clinic between 1891 and 1910. A follow-up had been published in 1929, and that was the state of published

medical experimentation on the subject before the Tuskegee Study began. Dr. Kampmeir did not explain why the Oslo Study needed to be repeated.

The Vanderbilt physician repeated the argument that penicillin would not have benefited the men, but he broke new ground by asserting that the men themselves were responsible for the illnesses and deaths they sustained from syphilis. The PHS was not to blame, Dr. Kampmeir explained, because "in our free society, antisyphilis treatment has never been forced." He further reported that many of the men in the study had received some treatment for syphilis down through the years and insisted that others could have secured treatment had they so desired. He admitted that the untreated syphilitics suffered a higher mortality rate than the controls, observing coolly: "This is not surprising. No one has ever implied that syphilis is a benign infection." His failure to discuss the social mandate of physicians to prevent harm and to heal the sick whenever possible seemed to reduce the Hippocratic oath to a solemn obligation not to deny treatment upon demand.[22]

Journalists looked at the Tuskegee Study and reached different conclusions, raising a host of ethical issues. Not since the Nuremberg trials of Nazi scientists had the American people been confronted with a medical *cause célèbre* that captured so many headlines and sparked so much discussion. For many it was a shocking revelation of the potential for scientific abuse in their own country. "That it has happened in this country in our time makes the tragedy more poignant," wrote the editor of the *Philadelphia Inquirer*. Others thought the experiment totally "un-American" and agreed with Senator John Sparkman of Alabama, who denounced it as "absolutely appalling" and "a disgrace to the American concept of justice and humanity."

Memories of Nazi Germany haunted some people as the broader implications of the PHS's role in the experiment became apparent. A man in Tennessee reminded health officials in Atlanta that "Adolf Hitler allowed similar degradation of human dignity in inhumane medical experiments on humans living under the Third Reich," and confessed that he was "much distressed at the comparison." A New York editor had difficulty believing that "such stomach-turning callousness could happen outside the wretched quackeries spawned by Nazi Germany."[23]

The specter of Nazi Germany prompted some Americans to equate the Tuskegee Study with genocide. A civil rights leader in Atlanta, Georgia, charged that the study amounted to "nothing less than an official, premeditated policy of genocide." A student at the Tuskegee Institute agreed. To him, the experiment was "but another act of genocide by whites," an act that "again exposed the nature of whitey: a savage barbarian and a devil."[24]

Most editors stopped short of calling the Tuskegee Study genocide or charging that PHS officials were little better than Nazis. But they were certain that racism played a part in

what happened in Alabama. "How condescending and void of credibility are the claims that racial considerations had nothing to do with the fact that 600 [all] of the subjects were black," declared the *Afro-American* of Baltimore, Maryland. That PHS officials had kept straight faces while denying any racial overtones to the experiment prompted the editors of this influential black paper to charge "that there are still federal officials who feel they can do anything where black people are concerned."[25]

The *Los Angeles Times* echoed this view. In deftly chosen words, the editors qualified their accusation that PHS officials had persuaded hundreds of black men to become "human guinea pigs" by adding: "Well, perhaps not quite that [human guinea pigs] because the doctors obviously did not regard their subjects as completely human." A Pennsylvania editor stated that such an experiment "could only happen to blacks." To support this view, the *New Courier* of Pittsburgh implied that American society was so racist that scientists could abuse blacks with impunity.[26]

Other observers thought that social class was the real issue, that poor people, regardless of their race, were the ones in danger. Somehow people from the lower class always seemed to supply a disproportionate share of subjects for scientific research. Their plight, in the words of a North Carolina editor, offered "a reminder that the basic rights of Americans, particularly the poor, the illiterate and the friendless, are still subject to violation in the name of scientific research." To a journalist in Colorado, the Tuskegee Study demonstrated that "the Public Health Service sees the poor, the black, the illiterate and the defenseless in American society as a vast experimental resource for the government." And the *Washington Post* made much the same point when it observed, "There is always a lofty goal in the research work of medicine but too often in the past it has been the bodies of the poor . . . on whom the unholy testing is done."[27]

The problems of poor people in the rural South during the Great Depression troubled the editor of the *Los Angeles Times,* who charged that the men had been "trapped into the program by poverty and ignorance."[28]

Yet poverty alone could not explain why the men would cooperate with a study that gave them so little in return for the frightening risks to which it exposed them. A more complete explanation was that the men did not understand what the experiment was about or the dangers to which it exposed them. Many Americans probably agreed with the *Washington Post's* argument that experiments "on human beings are ethically sound if the guinea pigs are fully informed of the facts and danger." But despite the assurances of PHS spokesmen that informed consent had been obtained, the Tuskegee Study precipitated accusations that somehow the men had either been tricked into cooperating or were incapable of giving informed consent.[29]

An Alabama newspaper, the *Birmingham News,* was not impressed by the claim that the participants were all volunteers, stating that "the majority of them were no better than semiliterate and probably didn't know what was really going on." The real reason they had been chosen, a Colorado journalist argued, was that they were "poor, illiterate, and completely at the mercy of the 'benevolent' Public Health Service." And a North Carolina editor denounced "the practice of coercing or tricking human beings into taking part in such experiments."[30]

The ultimate lesson that many Americans saw in the Tuskegee Study was the need to protect society from scientific pursuits that ignored human values. The most eloquent expression of this view appeared in the *Atlanta Constitution.* "Sometimes, with the best of intentions, scientists and public officials and others involved in working for the benefit of us all, forget that people are people," began the editor. "They concentrate so totally on plans and programs, experiments, statistics—on abstractions—that people become objects, symbols on paper, figures in a mathematical formula, or impersonal 'subjects' in a scientific study." This was the scientific blindspot to ethical issues that was responsible for the Tuskegee Study—what the *Constitution* called "a moral astigmatism that saw these black sufferers simply as 'subjects' in a study, not as human beings." Scientific investigators had to learn that "moral judgment should always be a part of any human

endeavor," including "the dis-
passionate scientific search for
knowledge."[31]

Notes

1. *New York Times*, July 26, 1972, pp. 1,
   8.
2. Because of the high rate of geographic mobility among the men, estimates of the mortality rate were
   confusing, even in the published articles. PHS spokesmen in 1972 were
   reluctant to be pinned down on an
   exact figure. An excellent example is
   the Interview of Dr. David Sencer by
   J. Andrew Liscomb and Bobby Doctor for the U.S. Commission on Civil
   Rights, Alabama State Advisory
   Committee, September 22, 1972, unpublished manuscript, p. 9. For the
   calculations behind the figures used
   here, see *Atlanta Constitution*, September 12, 1972, p. 2A.
3. During this primary stage the infected person often remains seroneg-
   ative: A blood test will not reveal the
   disease. But chancres can be differentiated from other ulcers by a dark
   field examination, a laboratory test
   in which a microscope equipped
   with a special indirect lighting attachment can view the silvery spirochetes moving against a dark background.
4. At the secondary stage a blood test
   is an effective diagnostic tool.
5. Dr. Donald W. Prinz quoted in *Atlanta Journal*, July 27, 1972, p. 2;
   Birmingham News, July 27, 1972, p. 2.
6. *New York Times*, July 27, 1972, p. 18.
7. Dr. Ralph Henderson quoted in
   ibid.; *Tuskegee News*, July 27, 1972, p.
   1.
8. *New York Times*, July 27, 1972, p. 2.
9. Eunice Rivers, Stanley Schuman,
   Lloyd Simpson, Sidney Olansky,
   "Twenty Years of Followup Experience in a Long-Range Medical

Study," *Public Health Reports* 68
(April 1953): 391–95. (Hereafter Rivers et al.)
10. Ibid., p. 393.
11. Dr. John D. Millar quoted in *Birm-
    ingham News*, July 27, 1972, pp. 1, 4;
    Atlanta Journal, July 27, 1972, p. 2.
12. Prinz quoted in *Atlanta Journal*, July
    27, 1972, p. 2.
13. Millar quoted in *Montgomery Adver-
    tiser*, July 26, 1972, p. 1.
14. Ibid.; Prinz quoted in *Atlanta Journal*,
    July 27, 1972, p. 2.
15. Millar quoted in *Montgomery Adver-
    tiser*, July 26, 1972, p. 1; *New York
    Times*, July 28, 1972, p. 29.
16. Dr. Edward Lammons quoted in
    Tuskegee News, August 3, 1972, p.
    1.
17. Prinz quoted in *Atlanta Journal*, July
    27, 1972, p. 2; Millar quoted in *Mont-
    gomery Advertiser*, July 26, 1972, p. 1.
18. *St. Louis Dispatch*, July 30, 1972, p.
    2D.
19. *Time*, August 7, 1972, p. 54; *Chicago
    Sun Times*, July 29, 1972, p. 23.
20. Their reactions can be captured at a
    glance by citing a few of the legends
    that introduced newspaper articles
    and editorials that appeared on the
    experiment. The *Houston Chronicle*
    called it "A Violation of Human
    Dignity" (August 5, 1972, Section I,
    p. 12); *St. Louis Post-Dispatch*, "An
    Immoral Study" (July 30, 1972, p.
    2D); *Oregonian*, an "Inhuman Experi-
    ment" (Portland, Oregon, July 31,
    1972, p. 16); *Chattanooga Times*, a
    "Blot of Inhumanity" (July 28, 1972,
    p. 16); *South Bend Tribune*, a "Cruel
    Experiment" (July 29, 1972, p. 6);
    New Haven Register, "A Shocking
    Medical Experiment" (July 29, 1972,
    p. 14); and Virginia's *Richmond Times
    Dispatch* thought that "appalling"
    was the best adjective to describe an
    experiment that had used "Humans
    as Guinea Pigs" (August 6, 1972, p.
    6H). To the *Los Angeles Times* the

study represented "Official Inhumanity" (July 27, 1972, Part II, p. 6); to the *Providence Sunday Journal,* a "Horror Story" (July 30, 1972, p. 2G); and to the *News and Observer* in Raleigh, North Carolina, a "Nightmare Experiment" (July 28, 1972, p. 4). The *St. Petersburg Times* in Florida voiced cynicism, entitling its editorial "Health Service?" (July 27, 1972, p. 24), while the *Milwaukee Journal* made its point more directly by introducing its article with the legend "They Helped Men Die" (July 27, 1972, p. 15).

21. R.H. Kampmeir, "The Tuskegee Study of Untreated Syphilis," *Southern Medical Journal* 65 (1972):1247–51.

22. Ibid., p. 1250.

23. Roderick Clark Posey to Millar, July 27, 1972; Tuskegee Files, Center for Disease Control. Atlanta, Georgia. (Hereafter TF-CDC); *Daily News,* July 27, 1972, p. 63; see also *Milwaukee Journal,* July 27, 1972, p. 15; *Oregonian,* July 31, 1972, p. 16; and Jack Slater, "Condemned to Die for Science," *Ebony* 28 (November 1972), p. 180.

24. *Atlanta Journal,* July 27, 1972, p. 2; *Campus Digest,* October 6, 1972, p. 4.

25. *Afro-American,* August 12, 1972, p. 4. For extended discussions of the race issue, see Slater, "Condemned to Die," p. 191, and the three-part series by Warren Brown in *Jet* 43, "The Tuskegee Study," November 9, 1972, pp. 12–17, November 16, 1972, pp. 20–26, and, especially, November 23, 1972, pp. 26–31.

26. *Los Angeles Times,* July 27, 1972, Part II, p. 6; *New Courier* also stated, "No other minority group in this country would have been used as 'Human Guinea Pigs,' " and explained, "because those who are responsible knew that they could do this to Negroes and nothing would be done to them if it became known," August 19, 1972, p. 6

27. *Greensboro Daily News,* August 2, 1972, p. 6; *Gazette-Telegraph,* Colorado Springs, August 3, 1972, p. 8A; *Washington Post,* July 31, 1972, p. 20A. See also *Arkansas Gazette,* July 29, 1972, p. 4A.

28. *Los Angeles Times,* July 27, 1972, p. 20A.

29. *Washington Post,* July 31, 1972, p. 20A.

30. *Birmingham News,* July 28, 1972, p. 12; *Gazette-Telegraph,* August 3, 1972, p. 8A; *Greensboro Daily News,* August 2, 1972, p. 6A.

31. *Atlanta Constitution,* July 27, 1972, p. 4A.

39 BABIES BY CESAREAN: WHO CHOOSES, WHO CONTROLS?

Jeanne Guillemin

For anyone whose last child was born before 1965, having a baby in a hospital today must appear nothing less than a space-age revolution. A proliferating diagnostic technology, notably the still-debated fetal monitoring, now accompanies the process of labor. Delivery itself commands a heavy concentration of professional expertise, not only from obstetrics

SOURCE: From *The Hastings Center Report,* June 1981, pp. 15–18. Reprinted by permission. © The Hastings Center.

but also from the pediatric service that oversees newborn intensive care. But by far the most dramatic change has been the increased incidence of delivery by cesarean section, a surgical procedure that used to be extraordinary and is now an everyday occurrence. Between 1969 and 1980, the rate of cesarean deliveries in the United States increased from 5 to 18 percent, with rates in large teaching hospitals reaching 25 percent and higher.[1] Although the extent of the increase may vary with particular circumstances, the trend toward increased cesarean rates is universal, evident in all types of medical facilities, in all regions of the country, and among women at all income and educational levels.

The ethical issues posed by this decided shift to surgery are similar to those generated by any change in medical treatment. How reliable is the profession as an arbiter of innovation? How do both obstetric patients—mother and newborn—stand to benefit? Is there conflict between their medical interests? Do women choose the conditions of childbirth or do the priorities of the physician and hospital routine take precedence? Is information about safe alternatives available?

Recent uncertainties over this change in medical practice have precipitated three federally sponsored reports. The first, from the General Accounting Office, offers a broad, preliminary statement on problems in American obstetric care.[2] The second, the work of Dr. Helen Marieskind, is an encyclopedic volume commissioned by the U.S. Office of Planning and Evaluation.[3]

The third is the report of a National Institutes of Health Consensus Task Force,[4] of which I was a member; it focuses almost exclusively on the clinician's rationale for relying increasingly on the cesarean procedure.

Taken together, these reports document those major changes in professional and lay approaches to childbirth that have swelled the rate of cesarean deliveries. On the medical side, they reveal that obstetricians have effected a significant change in therapy, while persuading their patients and each other of the benefits of the innovation. Access to hospital resources has played a key role in the change, as it has in most instances of climbing surgical rates. Without the technical back-up and medical expertise that a well-equipped hospital offers, it is impossible to do major surgery such as the cesarean routinely at a tolerable level of safety.

The national climate has also been conducive to rising cesarean rates. Government health policy regarding hospital insurance in general and maternal and child health in specific has established surgical priorities for solving problems of pregnancy and childbirth. Finally, as the national birth rate declines and families become smaller, American attitudes toward fetal life, the newborn, and the child are shifting toward a protectionism based exclusively on the biological vulnerability of the young.

The complicated interplay of these four categories of influence—professional authority, hospital resources, health policy, and public opinion—has done more than increase rates of cesarean delivery. By broadening notion about the risk associated with pregnancy and promoting hospital-based means of reducing that risk, modern medicine has transformed the American way of having children. Obstetricians played a much smaller role in this transformation than the army of biomedical researchers who have successfully manipulated the timing of conception and are now intent on controlling fetal development. Laboratory break-throughs, from contraceptive pills and drugs for pregnant women with diabetes to in vitro fertilization, have brought child-bearing into the realm of rational decision making. In contrast to times when pregnancy was thought of as a mystery or an accident or some combination of both, we now expect control of reproduction and depend on medicine and medical practitioners as aids in planning.

Ironically, our heightened public consciousness of reproduction options far outstrips our scientific understanding of the stages of pregnancy, fetal growth, or the onset of labor. As is common at the frontiers of medical research, diagnostic tests are far more refined than applicable therapies are—or may ever be. Consequently, the power of medicine to deliver hard-and-fast guarantees against risks of infertility, spontaneous abortion, genetic mistakes, prematurity, and iatrogenic damage to mother and fetus cannot meet our expectations.

In this phase of misalignment between public awareness and scientific quest, between the patient's fears and the practitioner's capacities, the work of medical professionals must be aimed at reducing risks by whatever clinical means are available, despite the differences between sophisticated diagnostic techniques and neolithic therapies. Thus, prenatal diagnosis by amniocentesis, which reveals serious fetal defects, is normally followed by abortion. Similarly, the cesarean delivery, an innovation only because it is occurring more often, has become an imperfect solution for a broad range of potential mishaps.

The Role of the Obstetrician

How has the specialty of obstetrics fared as the number of physicians has increased? Very well indeed. The professional community of practitioners in Ob-Gyn has been growing faster than most other medical specialties, with the exception of internal medicine and pediatrics.[5] Between 1968 and 1978, the percentage of all medical graduates in the specialty rose from 5.4 to 6.5, which in absolute numbers meant an increase from 759 first-year residents in 1968 to 1,163 a decade later.[6] Reflecting this trend, membership in the American College of Obstetricians and Gynecologists grew from 9,655 in 1970 to 18,438 in 1979. Similarly, though the rate of change was less dramatic, those listed as obstetrician-gynecologists with the American Medical Association increased from 18,876 to 22,603 over the same time period. Obstetricians have also expanded their role in delivering newborns at the expense of the general practitioner. In 1969, obstetric specialists handled 68 percent of deliveries in the United States, general practitioners 31 percent. By 1977 specialists in Ob-Gyn performed 71 percent of all deliveries while the general practitioners' share had been reduced to 12 percent.

An increase in the numbers and activity of obstetricians would have no bearing on a rise in cesarean delivery rates if the specialty were immune to pressures to augment its surgical skills and practice. A peculiar distinction of obstetrics is its dual identity as a surgical specialty and a variation of family medicine, not unlike pediatrics in providing access to the household unit. The specialty's current popularity among residents and its growing attraction for female students undoubtedly stems from the ideological return to a primary medicine focused on the community rather than on patients in the large centralized hospital. The countervailing pressure within the profession, however, is to maximize command of hospital resources lest other specialties, such as neurosurgery and orthopedic surgery, outdistance obstetrics in their claims to the operating room, laboratory tests, bed days, revenues, and, not the least, prestige.

Unlike pediatricians who have contributed to the science of neonatology, most obstetricians have remained aloof from academic medicine and biomedical research; thus for them surgery remains a major avenue of professional expansion and reward. Along with cesarean delivery rates, total gynecological surgical procedures have increased by over 200 percent in the last decade.[7] This rise accords with an overall national upsurge in surgery; still, the risk of women for under-

going sex-specific procedures is increasing disproportionately to the general increase in surgical rates.[8]

An obstetrician's fees are also on a par with other surgeons, rather than with generalists. This is obviously so in cesarean procedures, where charges can be more than double those for uncomplicated vaginal deliveries, but it extends to other fees as well. Obstetricians currently charge about one and a half times as much for maternity care as either general or family practitioners, and their charge for a total hysterectomy is about twice that of a general surgeon.[9]

In turning to obstetricians for expertise, have women understood the predilection for the scalpel and the conservatism that is often the unfortunate mark of the specialty? Take the matter of repeat cesareans. Between 1970 and 1978, repeats accounted for 27 percent of the overall rise in cesarean delivery rates. In 1978, 98.9 percent of all pregnant women with a previous cesarean delivered operatively. This was so despite a radical change in procedure dating at least as far back as the 1960s from vertical to low transverse—which considerably reduced the possibility of scar rupture. The automatic choice of repeat cesarean also reflects major changes in medical indications for cesarean, for example fetal distress, which go well beyond cephalopelvic disproportion.

Hospital Resources and Cesarean Delivery

The impetus toward more surgery is not confined to obstetrics. Since World War II, the gradual segregation of long-term patients in chronic care facilities has converted the contemporary hospital into a virtual temple of radical therapy with special emphasis on surgery. The United States' investment in high-technology equipment (and the accompanying professionalization of staff) is the largest of any industrialized nation. Despite rising medical costs, acute care facilities are widely available. Since nearly all American women give birth in hospitals, it is no wonder that delivery is managed as a potential medical emergency.

With a nod to the natural childbirth movement, some hospitals provide the option of home birthing rooms devoid of technologic trappings. But a much better defense against closing the maternity ward is a well-equipped operating room to handle difficult cases and emergencies. The benefits are twofold. The hospital reinforces its reputation as a progressive provider. And investment in high-level resources pays off with increasing use and longer hospital stays after surgery. According to data from the National Hospital Discharge Survey for 1965 and 1978 as well as the Professional Activities Surveys for 1967 and 1974, increase in cesarean delivery rates is definitely associated with the hospital's size and teaching status. The highest rates of increase in cesarean delivery occurred in the Northeast, with its considerable concentration of hospital resources, and in the South, with its fast-growing investment in new facilities.

Offsetting the simplistic argument that the United States has more surgeons per capita and therefore performs more surgical procedures than

any other country in the world, come professional assurances that our surgery is safe, or safer than elsewhere, or safer than it was as little as a decade ago. Improvements in anesthesialogy, antibiotics, and transfusion and surgical techniques, coupled with the spread of intensive care units, make it unusual for a patient to die of surgery per se.

Longitudinal data on maternal mortality rates associated with cesarean delivery make this point quite clearly. According to the Professional Activity Survey, 113.8 maternal deaths occurred per 100,000 cesarean deliveries in 1970. In 1978, the ratio dropped to 40.9. Other studies appear to corroborate the reduction in risk of mortality, thereby offering a clue to growing medical choice for the procedure. If the problem were to weigh a high risk of maternal death against a high risk of fetal morbidity, cesarean delivery would be not an attractive option. Instead, the choice appears to be between minimal risk of mortality for the mother and high risk of infant morbidity, defined by parental concern and by advances in fetal research. Hence the turn from forceps to cesarean delivery, best exemplified by the New York City data for 1968–1977, without any increase in the proportion of low-birth-weight infants (a major risk factor) and with a substantial increase in the cesarean delivery of otherwise low-risk infants (over 2,500 grams).[10]

Still, there is reason to question both the data on maternal mortality and the physician's perception of maternal and infant morbidity. The complex organization of many hospitals disallows accurate reporting of deaths that occur after transfer to intensive care units, or after discharge and readmission. Maternal morbidity remains uninvestigated, save for the residue of emotional and physical anguish witnessed by educators in the cesarean birth movement and a few researchers in psychology. Nor is there much documented proof that cesarean delivery has reduced infant morbidity; cases of iatrogenic prematurity in elective cesareans illustrate at least one liability that has emerged from common use of this procedure.

The lack of follow-up information on mother and infant makes it impossible to get a complete picture of any patient and obscures the ultimate repercussions of medical treatment, leaving doctors to base their judgments on episodic experience. By obscuring the ultimate repercussions of medical treatment, routinized acute care falsifies the knowledge behind professional decision making and gradually widens the gap between the specialist and the believing clients. Since in this country the professional emphasis on acute care is supported by government policy, however, the consumer-patient may have no alternative but skeptical dependence.

Incentives and Disincentives in Health Policy

The haphazard provision for health insurance that characterizes more than policy offers a powerful incentive to stress the acute care approach to pregnancy and childbirth. Some policies, for example, reimburse for cesarean delivery as surgery while excluding reimbursement for vaginal delivery. Such an incentive for the choice of cesarean is debatable, yet the fact that the distinction was drawn and applied by carriers is telling.

More telling still is the national tendency for young people in their twenties to fail to carry any form of health insurance whatsoever.[11] Granting the predictably low medical needs of this segment of the population, these are the principle childbearing years for American women. Those who are above the state income line for Medicaid and without extra means for physician and hospital fees are least likely to seek out prenatal care. In circular fashion, undiagnosed maternal and fetal pathologies can lead directly to real delivery room crises that justify acute obstetric intervention.

Variability by state in Medicaid plans also impedes universal coverage for antenatal care. Two studies of Health Maintenance Organizations (HMOs) suggest that this type of prepaid plan, which deemphasizes hospital care in favor of preventive care, lowers cesarean delivery rates.[12,13] Discounting differences between the populations served by HMOs and other plans the HMOs may well systematically reduce need for acute care at the time of delivery by offering closer prenatal management of high-risk mothers, and physicians who are significantly less oriented to surgical intervention. Both suppositions need further study, but the HMO type of reimbursement is markedly different than the majority of insurance plans in its stress on preventive and non-acute medical care.

Ethical Concerns of the Task Force on Cesarean Childbirth

The ethical issues associated with cesarean birth are not specific to this procedure, but are shared with other specialized treatments. The ethical principles involved, even when confronting maternal and fetal interests, are similar to the generally established principles governing all relationships between physician and patient. These principles involve the commitment to placing the patient's interest above that of the physician, and the rights for decision making to include consideration for the mother as well as for the fetus. No separate consensus recommendation was made, since the Task Force felt these are the accepted principles for obstetrical practice today.

Draft Report of the Task Force on Cesarean Childbirth, NIH, 1980

Information from European countries with comprehensive prenatal and postnatal medical programs is even more convincing. Current rates of cesarean delivery in England, France, Norway, and The Netherlands are a fraction of those in the United States.[14] If we take prenatal, neonatal, and infant and maternal mortality figures as a gross measure of outcome, European populations, including "guest-workers" from other countries, are doing quite well without this obstetric surgery.

On the other hand, not even the most aggressive government campaign to increase effective prenatal diagnosis, such as are waged in France and The Netherlands, have kept cesarean delivery rates in Europe from climbing, along with rates for other types of intervention: forceps, inductions, and vacuum extractions. In Holland, as obstetricians there pointed out to me, the yearly 2 percent decline in home births (now at 38 percent) in favor of hospitalization is directly linked to greater reliance on obstetricians, which in turn leads to increased intervention in the delivery room. As in the United States, the ascendance of obstetrics as a specialty in Europe has undercut the professional position of generalists and midwives, while promoting the growth of regionalized high-technology centers for in-hospital maternal and infant care. Still, long-term government controls over hospital development and physician practice have made it nearly impossible to duplicate the technological resources found in this country.

Public Opinion and the Perception of Risk

The evidence of climbing rates raises an important question. Are women in industrialized countries actively choosing more births by cesarean delivery, and if so, why? One preliminary study of French mothers indicated the educated, professional women were more likely to have cesareans than less educated women.[15] This would seem to be consistent with a French government finding that educated, upper-class parents choose the specialist's services, while the generalist tends to minister to the poor and rural maternity cases.[16] In The Netherlands, low-risk, affluent women not medically designated for hospital birth will pay twice the ordinary maternity fee for hospitalization, although they tend to leave after the first day for home or a clinic.

In the United States, two groups of women are most likely to have a cesarean. One is educated and wealthy, the other is from the lowest economic ranks and relatively uneducated. Within the latter group, a high rate of cesarean delivery might be justified by the high probability of risk inevitably associated with poverty, although one would have to appreciate the diversity of indicators for surgery and the vagary of the one most frequently recorded, *dystocia* (failure to progress in labor). With more affluent and educated women in America, as with their European counterparts, one has to assume fewer medical risks and a determination to eliminate even these. The option to do so comes from financial means; the motivation to eliminate all risk has more mysterious and complex origins.

In part it arises from the growing concentration on the fetus, on the vulnerability of the infant, and on the child in the face of declining birth rate. Abortions have been legalized, but the advent of the neonatal intensive care unit makes it possible for even an aborted fetus with signs of viability to be rescued. Every large hospital in the country makes this occasional gesture toward the preciousness of life.

The pressure of malpractice suits is another factor in eliminating risk.

Obstetricians claim it heavily influences their choices in the delivery room, making therapeutic extremes necessary with or without the aid of neonatologists. The cesarean delivery for breech presentation is but one example. In lieu of manually reversing the infant's *in utero* position and risking asphyxia or other physical damage, most obstetricians routinely section for breech babies. In training younger doctors, the argument is made that there aren't enough cases of breech presentation for them to learn the manual technique; the surgical procedures then are judged safer for the fetus.

Obstetricians are prime targets for litigation and can be held liable for long-term effects of malpractice should state law permit. The concept of "wrongful life" as a basis for suit has also been introduced, making it possible for the heavily damaged survivor of a "botched birth" to gain recompense for an unwarranted and costly existence. But the most immediate pressure an obstetrician feels is likely to be parental fear of the emotional and financial burden of a damaged infant. Conversation between parent and physician becomes easy to imagine with its dual emphasis on the potential biological disaster and the fierce protection of the unborn. It is a dialogue in which, for private and professional reasons, both parties abhor the notion of an imperfect newborn.

To return to the issue of free choice, increasing cesarean delivery rates can be interpreted in diametrically opposite ways. The mother's decision to have the operation can be seen as akin to the liberated woman's pro-abortion stance ("I shall control my body") or it can be equated with the pro-life position ("Anything for the baby"). Either way one frequently hears stories of women being asked to give informed consent for an emergency cesarean without really understanding what the operation will entail. In such cases, the request is a demand; the choice cannot be considered as autonomous. In many other instances, women do have the time to reflect; if they are lucky, they go to parent education classes that will prepare them for the efficiency, as well as the impersonality, of many hospital deliveries. The trick is to take advantage of the high level of technological back-up without being forced into the hospital's surgical agenda or manipulated by the physician's concentration on delivery as a potential disaster. This is somewhat akin to espousing military preparedness while remaining at heart a pacifist; it is very difficult to avoid enlistment once the vote has been cast for professionalism.

The Raw Edge

In one of his classic essays on professions, Everett Hughes described "the raw edge" where "professional definition and practice do not utterly match wants and active demands and where the mandate of the professional establishment is questioned."[17] In women's health there are activities that bespeak much experimentation beyond the fringes of the hospital-based specialist's orientation. The home birth movement is one of these; women's health groups are another. Yet women persistently and overwhelmingly continue to believe in surgical solutions to gynecological problems. After numerous indictments of unnecessary hysterectomies, the national rate has at last diminished. Now dilation and curretage, tubal ligations, and cesareans have taken up the slack.

Perhaps the basic problem with all these procedures and especially with cesareans is that we distinguish so poorly between necessary and unnecessary procedures. Physicians define the avoidance of infant morbidity as a goal that has been achieved with cesarean delivery, but it remains unclear how forceps, vacuum extractions, and episiotomies became unnecessary means to the same end. Given the choice between short-term harm to the mother and any harm to the newborn, most parents would opt for the adult's suffering over risk to the infant, but is this choice necessary? Faddism and fashion affect medicine as they do any other service industry. In this field, more than any other, innovations should be scrupulously examined to make certain the performance lives up to the promise.

References

1. Paul Placek and Selma Taffel, "Trends in Cesarean Section Rates for the United States," 1970–78, *Public Health Reports* 95,6:540–548.
2. *Evaluating Benefits and Risks of Obstetric Practices—More Coordinated Federal and Private Efforts Needed* (Washington, D.C.: U.S. General Accounting Office, 1979).
3. Helen I. Marieskind, *An Evaluation of Cesarean Section in the United States,*

(Washington, D.C.: USDHEW, Planning and Evaluation/Health, 1979).

4. M. Rosen et al., *Consensus Development Conference on Cesarean Childbirth, Draft Report of the Task Force on Cesarean Childbirth* (Washington, D.C.: U.S. Department of Health and Human Services, 1980).

5. Carol Weisman, et al., "Male and Female Physician Career Patterns: Specialty Choices and Graduate Training," *Journal of Medical Education* 55 (1980), 813–25.

6. Information supplied by the American College of Obstetricians and Gynecologists, 1980, Chicago, Illinois.

7. Dorothy Rice and Anne S. Cugliani, "Health Status of American Women," *Women and Health* 5 (1980), 1.

8. Eugene G. McCarthy and Madelon Lubin Finkel, "Surgical Utilization in the U.S.A.," *Medical Care* 18 (1980), 883–91.

9. "Fee Survey," *Medical Economics* (October 13, 1980), pp. 214–22.

10. Rosen et al., *op. cit.*, pp. 157–230.

11. Maureen Baltay, *Profile of Health Care Coverage: The Haves and Have-Nots* (Washington, D.C.: Congressional Budget Office, 1979).

12. R.L. Williams and W.E. Hawes, "Cesarean Section, Fetal Monitoring, and Perinatal Mortality in California," *American Journal of Public Health* 69 (1979), 864–74.

13. S.I. Wilner, R.R. Monson, S.C. Schoenbaum, and R.N. Winickoff, "A Comparison of Pregnancy Outcome between a Health Maintenance Organization and Fee for Services Practices," paper presented at American Public Health Association Meetings, 1979, New York.

14. I. Chalmers, "The Epidemiology of Perinatal Practice," *Journal of Maternal and Child Health* (Nov. 1979), 435–36.

15. M. Saurel-Cubizolles, "Influence de l'activité professionnelle de la femme enceinte sur le déroulement et l'issue de la grossesse," Master's thesis in sociology, Paris: Université René Descartes, 1979.

16. C. Rumeau-Rouquette et al., *Naître en France, Enquêtes Nationales sur la grossesse et l'accouchement* (Paris: Institut National de la Santé et de la Recherche Medicale, 1979).

17. Everett C. Hughes, "The Humble and the Proud" in *The Sociological Eye: Selected Papers on Work, Self, and the Study of Society* (Chicago: Aldine, 1971), pp. 417–30.

Part V

Social Movements, Social Change, and Health

INTRODUCTION

You have probably heard on many occasions the slogan that the health status of a country is an indicator of its overall strength and well-being. Data on infant mortality, overall mortality, and disease rates are often cited to indicate a nation's place in the world. Changes in health data are often used to measure a country's progress and modernization. Given such a common approach, it is reasonable to conceive of health and illness as central components of the overall social structure of a society. Taking this idea further, it also makes sense to see health reform as part of overall social reform. Indeed, in societies where revolutionary groups have come to power, health reform is often central to their political agenda. In the ordinary fabric of political debate and elections, health reforms have become central issues.

In nations around the world, health care issues and national health plans have been inextricably tied to broader social welfare programs. Importantly, those programs have not dealt solely or primarily with the poor or with certain other powerless, needy groups. Rather, social welfare reforms and accompanying health coverage are seen as universal rights of citizenship, available to all. This is a remarkably different attitude and ideology than in American society where health services are typically seen as a commodity that reaps profit for the sellers and that is available to consumers based largely on their ability to pay.

In this part of the book, we first examine "Reform and Change within Medicine" by looking at three examples of social movements that were primarily directed at improving or altering health services. In the second section, "Reform and Change within the Larger Society," we study efforts at effecting fundamental social changes via health politics. It is important to remember that these two categories of reform and change are not mutually exclusive and are often hard to disentangle. The authors of the articles on reform and change *within* medicine in fact see their efforts as linked to larger social change, even if they are focusing on a particular medical reform at the moment.

Reform and Change
within Medicine

In the United States, health politics have been manifestations of political struggle and social conflict. We see this when we examine the efforts of organized medicine to originally oppose Medicare and Medicaid and to continually oppose national health insurance. We see this in the battles during the Reagan administration over cutbacks in federal health programs.

The introduction of Maternal and Child Health Services (1963), Community Mental Health Centers (1963 and 1965), Neighborhood Health Centers (1964), and Medicare and Medicaid (1965) were part of a national reform program, and the results of those efforts should be seen in that larger social context, not just as limited health interventions.

That social context of the 1960s was one of general social protest—the largest national insurgency since the Great Depression of the 1930s. Health concerns were very important in this period. The women's movement put much energy into organizing for abortion rights, an end to sterilization abuse, and other reproductive rights. This was also a period of unionization of hospital workers, a movement that played a key role in the repoliticization of part of the trade union movement because it linked civil rights and opposition to the Vietnam War to trade unionism. Related to the growth of radical sectors of the labor movement, there was an upsurge of occupational safety and health issues. Struggles over black lung in coal miners (which we read about earlier in Barbara Smith's article), asbestosis and mesothelioma in asbestos workers, white lung in textile mills, toxic threats in chemical plants, and shopfloor safety in factories involved union efforts as well as large social pressures to push through the Occupational Safety and Health Act (1970).

Political organizations often saw the establishment of their own health centers as a major focus for organizing efforts. Most notable were the Black Panther Party's community health clinics and a large number of women's clinics. The women's health movement went very far in providing alternative services, reforming established institutions, creating self-help groups, pushing for the empowerment of and participation by patients, and examining core social perceptions and ideologies held by laypeople and health professionals. In its many ramifications, the women's health movement has exerted tremendous positive influences on the field of medical sociology. As you will have noted, feminist perspectives have appeared in a number of other articles in this book (e.g., Catherine Kohler Riessman's "Women and Medicalization," Susan Reverby's "A Caring Dilemma," Judith Lorber's "Women Physicians in Three Countries," and Jeanne Guillemin's "Babies by Cesarean").

In "Feminist Visions of Health: An International Perspective," Sheryl Ruzek gives an overview of the issues raised by this movement in the United States and Europe. In reading through this article, you will see that the women's health movement has been active in many areas of concern. Further, you will gain an understanding of how the women's movement has wielded such tremendous influence at a time when many other social movements were having difficulties.

Susan Bell, in "Political Gynecology: Gynecological Imperialism and the Politics of Self-Help," describes a specific program in which workers in a women's clinic taught medical students to conduct more humane and informative pelvic examinations. Bell explores the problems inherent in activists' trying to work within a very traditional institution. Despite some successes, the most innovative techniques proposed by the pelvic teaching program activists were considered too threatening by the medical school staff. Further, there was an omnipresent threat of co-optation, whereby the medical school might take control of all or part of the program and weaken it in the process.

In the activist 1960s doctors in training organized house-staff unions to demand less strenuous hours, more control over the work setting, and better community access to health care. Medical students, doctors, and others in the Student Health Organization worked with poor and minority populations to establish local health centers in extremely underserved areas. Community activists also pushed for community control, which was built in to the federal regulations for these new facilities, though it was not always practiced. In some cases, doctors joined community activists in organizing against hospital expansion into communities, since such expansion often did not go hand in hand with better services to the community. You get a sense of these types of efforts in Gallagher's article on Columbia Presbyterian Hospital, "The Presbyterian Story: The People Pull the Strings for a Change." Gallagher tells the story of a successful campaign in New York City in which community residents negotiated with the hospital and the State Commissioner of Health and held public meetings and rallies. The activists won a number of medical services as well as greater participation in decision making.

40   FEMINIST VISIONS OF HEALTH: AN INTERNATIONAL PERSPECTIVE

Sheryl Ruzek

Introduction and Background

Over the past 15 years feminists in North America, Europe, and increasingly other parts of the world have directed attention to the quality and quantity of health services available to women, the social control aspects of medicine, and the need for women to assert control over their own bodies and reproductive potential. Women have organized and taken political action, and established alternative services to improve women's health and create a more caring, humane approach to providing health and medical care services.

Health Issues Concerning Women

While feminists readily agree that the health care systems of most western industrialized countries are unresponsive to the needs of both men and women, they find health care systems particularly problematic for women. In many western countries the organization of health care systems emphasizes women's reproductive roles. In the United States, women are encouraged to use obstetrician-gynaecologists (surgical specialists) as their primary-care physicians. From puberty until well past menopause, many women see no other type of physician regularly. Thus analysis of women's relationships with obstetrician-gynae-cologists in the United States has re-flected women's use pattern and perception of this experience as shared with other women. The centrality of reproductive rights in the larger contemporary feminist movement has also been a key factor in the shaping of the women's health movement, first in the United States and later in Canada and Europe.

With the resurgence of feminism in the United States in the late 1960s and early 1970s, women rebelled at the control men had over women's bodies and reproductive functions. Doctors, health policy-makers, and bio-medical researchers as well as lawmakers, predominantly male, were viewed as acting in men's rather than women's 'best interests'. Attempts to gain equal rights in education, politics, employment and the family were recognized as impossible unless women could control their reproductive capacity. Arguing for women's right to both contraception and abortion, many feminists assumed that, if women were freed from bearing and rearing unwanted children, the traditional role expectations that subordinate them might lose their strength. Women might then choose not to have children, or not to marry, or they might choose

SOURCE: From Ann Oakley and Juliet Mitchell, eds., *What Is Feminism*, pp. 184–207. Copyright © 1986 by Pantheon Books, A Division of Random House, Inc.

to experience and express their sexuality in ways which are not culturally approved.

The abortion issue was and remains controversial. It is a powerful issue for feminists, because women are socialized to value motherhood, yet at the same time motherhood oppresses women and limits life chances in the wider society. In virtually every country where there is feminist activity, reproductive control is a central issue and has proven to be a rallying point for educational programmes, alternative services, lobbying, and sometimes underground or illegal provision of abortion. Without this core of reproductive rights and reproductive health issues, there would not be an international women's health movement.

In recent years older health activists have become concerned that young women—women who came of age sexually after the legalization of abortion in most western industrialized countries—fail to understand the critical importance of the availability of abortion to women's well-being. Because they have not experienced the fear of unwanted pregnancy without the possibility of recourse to abortion as a backup to contraceptive failure or sexual risk-taking, younger women are less motivated to work to maintain abortion rights or provide access to abortion services. Abortion is not simply a neutral 'medical service', but one which is or is not available depending on historical political circumstances. Therefore, ensuring every woman's right to abortion (whether she chooses to have one or not) is a central tenet of contemporary western feminism.

Reproductive rights are not the only feminist health issue, however. The safety and efficacy of treatments and the social control aspects of medicine are also central concerns. Over the past fifteen years, women have learned that, despite physicians' claims about the safety of oral contraceptives, there is alarming evidence of serious side effects (Seaman 1980). Diethylstilbestrol (DES) was recognized as the cause of a rare form of vaginal cancer in young girls, yet continued to be prescribed as a 'morning after' pill on college campuses (Seaman and Seaman 1977). Standard hospital childbirth practices seemed organized more for the convenience of doctors than for the health and well-being of mothers and babies (Wertz and Wertz 1977; Rothman 1982; Boston Women's Health Book Collective 1976). Unnecessary hysterectomies were sometimes performed for profit or to give doctors in training surgical experience (Corea 1977; Bunker 1970; Lembcke 1956; Scully 1980). Poor women were sometimes sterilized against their will, or without their informed consent, because of personal biases of physicians and social policies reflecting race and class discrimination (Clarke 1984; Petchesky 1979). Even fairly sophisticated critics of the health care system in the United States were shocked to learn that intra-uterine devices (IUDs), touted as extremely safe and effective, were never tested by the Food and Drug Administration (FDA) or any federal regulatory body before being marketed. The brewing controversy over the efficacy of radical mastectomy as compared to less mutilating modes of treatment came to light, and women in the United States could not understand why physicians remained so attached to this disfiguring treatment compared to physicians in some European countries. Ironically, the liberalization of the abortion laws in the United States, coupled with the rise in demand, subjected women to some of the most exploitative medical experiences imaginable. In New York, for example, in 1971 a woman could pay $75 for a first-trimester abortion at a non-profit clinic or up to $1,500 for the same service if she fell prey to a profiteering referral service (Ruzek 1978).

Whilst many of these 'facts' about American medicine existed in the medical and social science literature, it was only with the advent of a social movement that this information came to be widely disseminated. The women's health movement quickly grew into a separate social movement, largely because of the pre-existing communication networks in the general feminist movement. Feminist newspapers, journals and bookstores all served key roles in letting women know about health issues and organizing them for action. Over time, there emerged publications and organizations focussing almost exclusively on health issues, first in North America and later in Europe.

Feminist Visions of Health

Feminist health activists organized to educate themselves and other women about health issues, provide alternative services, and work to influence public policies affecting women's health. These activities reflect (1) a commitment to self-determination in seeking health and health care, (2) an emphasis on the caring and sharing aspects of health rather than the deployment of technologies alone, (3) a recognition of the multiple definitions and political nature of assessments of 'quality of care', and (4) a concern that medical services be both accessible and affordable in relation to women's actual economic position. After considering these central themes I will go on to explore some strategies for implementing change in different types of health care systems.

Self-Determination in Seeking Health Care

Abortion has already been discussed as an inalienable feminist right to ensure women's self-determination in their medical care more generally. The key to this is shifting the social distribution of medical knowledge (anatomy, physiology, medical procedures, use of simple technologies, treatments) from being the exclusive property of certain health professionals to being the shared property of patients and a widening array of non-physician health providers. This shifting of knowledge includes the right of women to make crucial decisions about where and under what conditions they will give birth, to be involved in decision-making about treatment approaches even for serious diseases such as breast cancer, and to be fully informed about the risks and benefits of all diagnostic and treatment procedures.

Caring and Sharing

Sharing, caring and nurturing characterize women's roles in relation to others in the family and in women's professional health work—prototypically nursing and midwifery. These forms of caring and sharing are seen as inappropriately undervalued in the larger society. Alternative services are organized to elevate these elements of medical care to a central place in service delivery. To do this, however, requires a significant reorientation of health care providers which has been attempted in feminist self-help groups and clinics. Although it is often difficult to achieve the ideals set forth by feminists for caring and sharing, the humanistic philosophy embodied in the ideal contrasts starkly with the approach of conventional western industrialized medicine. The latter is organized around a narrow biomedical model in which professionals deliver medical technologies and lay people are passive receivers.

Feminists involved in clinics conceptualize routine health care as an ongoing process and seek to minimize distinctions between providers and receivers of care, experts and lay persons. Group discussion and care is encouraged in order to give women opportunities to share common health concerns with peers as well as experts. In group sessions, women have time to think of questions and relay important diagnostic information, information which is often lost in hurried three- to five-minute individual medical consultations—the norm in most highly industrialized medical care systems.

The advantages and disadvantages of contraceptive methods, childbirth procedures, and treatments for menopausal symptoms or routine gynaecological disorders can be explained more thoroughly in a group than individually, and groups offer social-psychological peer support simply unavailable in the one-to-one doctor-patient relationship.

Quality of Care

Disillusionment with the quality of western medical care involves both the evaluation of the efficacy and risks of many technical diagnostic and therapeutic procedures, and the social and psychological aspects of medical care. Thus, quality of health care involves integrating both 'objective' criteria of safety and efficacy and 'subjective' experiences of medical care.

Western medicine tends to focus on the efficacy of treatment in rational, objective terms such as 'reduction in mortality' or 'reduction in hospital days' and ignores the process and experience of health care. While 'outcome' criteria are appropriate measures for some health problems, they are neither as concrete nor as indicative of 'quality of care' as they seem at first glance. The quality of care and quality of life issues in human, subjective terms, are also more difficult to measure. They do not fit the bio-medical model on which the practice of contemporary medicine is built. In the bio-medical model the patient's own experience of physical, social and psychological disequilibrium receives relatively little attention and is often discounted unless it can be shown to be 'objectively measurable', or simply an obstacle to the receipt of medical care in the first place.

Thus, for example, women's complaints about side-effects of oral contraceptives and IUDs were discounted by most professionals until 'objective' scientific evidence confirmed that they pose serious hazards including death (Seaman 1980; Seaman and Seaman 1977). Women's concerns about overmedicated labour and delivery and separation from their infants after birth were at first largely ignored. Consumer groups' pressure for alternative childbirth approaches came at a time when the birth rate was dropping and hospitals had to compete vigorously to fill their beds to keep up revenues. Thus, some changes were made, but under the rubric of advances in 'scientific knowledge'. Thus more 'natural births' were defined as facilitating mother-infant 'bonding' which could be measured using quantifiable psycho-social indices (Wertz and Wertz 1977; Rothman 1982; De Vries 1985).

Physicians today face such an array of elaborate technology to provide them with 'objective' evidence that they have lost faith in their clinical judgement (Reiser 1978). Reliance on tests reduces the time practitioners feel they need to spend listening to the patient or making diagnoses. This reliance on tests also reinforces an emphasis on rare medical events and downplays the reality that most medical visits involve rather routine problems easily manageable by less highly specialized practitioners. This creates yet another layer of mystification to reinforce the power and control of physicians, and makes it even more difficult for women themselves to make decisions about their care.

For women, the potential for suffering the iatrogenic effects of medical drugs, devices, and practices is heightened by the fact that women's biological life-events—menstruation, conception, pregnancy and childbirth, lactation, and menopause—are all medically managed in industrialized societies. Over the life-cycle, women are more often exposed to medical intervention than are men and thus more at risk of suffering iatrogenic effects. In addition to the medical hazards already noted, new childbirth technologies such as electronic fetal monitoring are associated with increased maternal morbidity and mortality and infant morbidity (Banta and Thacker 1979). DES (diethylstilbestrol) given to prevent miscarriage caused vaginal cancer in some exposed females' children and is now suspected of causing sterility in exposed males, and breast cancer in the mothers who took the drug. Estrogen replacement therapy, widely used to alleviate menopausal symptoms, is suspected of increasing the risk of breast and uterine cancer (Seaman and Seaman 1977).

Cost of Care

Ideally medical care should be available to women at no cost or at a cost they can afford, given the reality of their economic status in society. The cost of medical care has been a more salient issue in the United States than in Canada or Europe where routine care, including childbirth and gynaecological examinations, are provided either by a national health service or within a near-universal health insurance coverage. In 1981 in the United States, the median income for full-time year-round women workers was $12,000. Many women are the sole support of their families. Close to six million families are maintained by women in the United States (Department of Labor 1983). Women are frequently left without any medical insurance whatsoever. When they become divorced or widowed they usually lose the right to coverage under their husbands' employer-provided policy. Women also lose coverage when they lose their own jobs which provided medical insurance. In 1984, over 33 million Americans were without any medical insurance. Eligibility for public state-paid coverage has been tightened over the past five years to the point that a woman must be nearly destitute to receive coverage (The National Citizens' Board of Inquiry into Health in America 1984).

While, theoretically, individuals may purchase individual fee-for-service health insurance coverage, a woman must pass a screening examination. Women are rejected when they have medical histories of hypertension, back problems, obesity, or cancer. In short, women with health problems who need coverage the most are least likely to be able to purchase it. In addition, premiums are costly. In 1985, an individual Blue Cross plan which pays 80% of covered charges cost $62.00 per month—nearly 6½% of the average working woman's monthly income. The Kaiser Plan, a capitation plan which provides most services for under $5.00 per visit, is more affordable at $57.65 per month, but still costs 6% of a woman's average monthly income.

The lack of insurance coverage and 20% co-payment required by plans such as Blue Cross means that American women pay a substantial proportion of their personal income for medical services.

In Canada and Europe where cost is less often a major deterrent to women's access to care, the emergence of alternative services has proceeded quite differently. In Canada, the near universal coverage for fee-for-service reimbursement allowed an organization such as the Vancouver Women's Health Collective to collect standard fees billed by volunteer physicians (Kleiber 1978). In the United Kingdom, feminists have been deterred from establishing alternative services by the example of, and need to support, the National Health Service.

It seems likely that the high cost of medical services in the United States has been a major factor accounting for the strength of the women's health movement there. When one is forced to pay a large proportion of one's income for services which are humiliating, hazardous, and ineffective, resentment is certain to exist. With the availability of a broad based social movement to interpret and channel this discontent, a separate social movement focusing on health could develop fully. Over time, certain features of this movement spread throughout other countries as part of a larger feminist movement.

Strategies for Change

Feminist health activists engage in a wide array of activities which reflect their desire to enhance women's self-determination, promote caring and sharing, improve the quality of medical care, and make medical care more accessible and affordable. They hope that such strategies will alter the quality, quantity, content, and control of medical services on the societal level, institutional level, and in face-to-face interaction with professionals. Activists view all changes at all levels as necessary and interrelated, for what a woman actually experiences in seeking health care is the result of a complex interaction of interlocking values, beliefs, practices and institutional arrangements. How well these mesh with a woman's own identity, and cultural and personal preferences is significantly affected by her race, ethnicity, age, and socioeconomic status. What 'women' want often should be delineated to specify what women in certain life circumstances want. Feminists have gradually come to see the salience of race and class, but only slowly and with some difficulty.

Many health activists believe that it is virtually impossible to create a truly humane health care system for women in a capitalist society. Yet none of the strategies used directly attack the underlying economic organization of society. For example, major efforts are directed toward removing control of obstetrics and gynaecology from male professional dominance and making professionals accountable to consumers, women. This is an example of a strategy many would regard as 'reformist' in that it is designed to persuade or force physicians, hospitals, politicians, the drug industry, and regulatory agencies that it is 'good business' to promote self-determination, freedom of choice, and appropriate definitions of quality care. The major ways in which feminists work to promote women's health include (1) creating new knowledge and educating women, (2) providing alternative services, and (3) influencing public policy.

Creating New Knowledge and Educating Women

Consciousness raising and education on women's health issues is by far the most common feminist strategy for improving women's health. Health activists believe that it is crucial for women to come together and share their personal experiences of health and illness. Unlike conventional health education programs, feminist self-help health groups promote the view that the personal is political by giving women opportunities to discover that many of their experiences are shared by other women. These groups also incorporate a political analysis, pointing out the ways in which interest groups ranging from medical specialities to drug companies cannot be relied upon to act in the best interests of women.

Over time, self-help groups have become more structured and more focused around specific topics. The length and comprehensiveness of groups vary considerably. Some are one day or less; others meet from six to eight weeks or longer. The most common topics for self-help groups include basic anatomy and physiology of women's reproductive system, routine gynaecological problems and treatments, childbirth and menopause experiences, and gynaecological surgery. Individual sessions are sometimes devoted to learning pelvic self-examination—to demystify that part of the body which many women have been taught not to look at or touch. Self-examination skills are also taught to help women to recognize early symptoms of vaginal infections, identify commonly prescribed drugs, and use home remedies for minor problems. Some self-help groups are organized for women at a particular life-cycle stage or a particular sexual orientation; others are mixed. The Black Women's Health Project sponsors over 45 self-help groups by and for black women, many of which focus on diet and exercise for control of hypertension, a condition disproportionately affecting black women in the United States.

Much of the impetus for the spread of self-help and other women's body education came from the Boston Women's Health Book Collective and from the Los Angeles Feminist Women's Health Center, each of which creates and promotes innovative knowledge about women's health by and for women. The Boston Women's Health Book Collective's highly successful *Our Bodies, Ourselves* (1976, 1984) started as mimeographed notes written by women participating in feminist discussion groups and classes. This book has sold over 2½ million copies in the United States alone. In addition there are 14 foreign language editions available—including Spanish, French, Italian, Dutch, Swedish and German. Each of these editions was written in conjunction with women in the countries in which they will be used. They are not simply 'translations' but reflect the needs, concerns and experiences of women throughout the world.

The Los Angeles Feminist Women's Health Center which launched cervical self-examination and has trained feminist health workers from many countries also continues to produce important women's health material. *A New View of a Woman's Body*, for example, includes colour photographs of women's cervixes at different stages of the menstrual cycle—an important contribution to women's self-knowledge (Federation of Feminist Women's Health Centers 1981). The Black Women's Health Project is producing health information focusing on special concerns of black women in the United States—hypertension, lupus, obesity, stress, high perinatal mortality, violence and the social and psychological effects of internalized oppression in black women (Spelman College 1984; National Black Women's Health Project 1985).

Feminist health groups in Canada and Europe also produce important educational material by and for women and offer self-help and body courses modelled after those started by the Boston and Los Angeles women. For example, Feministisches Frauen Gesundheits Zentrum, a West Berlin self-help centre, offers self-help health courses and publicizes information on hazardous drug and other medical issues. Gruppo Feminista per la Salute della Donna in Rome carries on similar activities and publishes health booklets. The most extensive description of worldwide feminist health education materials and programmes is the Women and Health Resource Guide produced jointly by the Boston Women's Health Book Collective and ISIS, the Women's International Information and Communication Service which has offices in Geneva and Rome.

Feminist educational activities differ significantly from more conventional health education in several ways. The educational material itself is highly personal, written in women's own voices and from their own experiences. Considerable attention is given to the fact that their is great diversity among women in terms of what is 'normal'. Feminist health education and self-care also emphasizes the right and responsibility of the individual woman to make decisions about her health care—and provides the basic information which helps women to do so. Women's clinics often maintain lists of local physicians and hospitals recommended by other women. Some of these attempts to evaluate services systematically in large metropolitan areas. The Vancouver Women's Health Collective, for example, carried out a detailed study of mater-

nity services in local hospitals and also started a physician evaluation service (A Woman's Place 1972). In addition to aiding individual women seeking services, surveys and pamphlets raise awareness in the community about discrepancies in what is available—an important step in organizing for improvements in services.

Alternative Services

One important debate concerns the long-term consequences of providing women's health services in alternative clinics rather than pressing mainstream health providers to improve services. Proponents of alternative services cite women's immediate need for routine gynaecological care, contraceptive counselling, abortion, and childbirth in supportive, woman-controlled settings. Some argue as well that the participatory care provided in women's clinics could serve as a model for reorganizing conventional services. For instance, in some communities in the United States the competition from women's clinics has brought down fees for abortion in local hospitals. Conversely, other health activists, while supportive of alternative services, feel that the presence of these services may simply take pressure off doctors to improve the quality of care, since women who might be most assertive and active in pressing for change have removed themselves from conventional settings. In the United Kingdom, alternative services have not been much promoted by health activists because of the danger that

such a development could undermine the National Health Service. It
is argued that the NHS provides
greater equity and access to women
from all socio-economic groups than
private medicine ever could. In addition, women in the United Kingdom
are unaccustomed to paying for
health services and may be unwilling to pay for alternative services
(Doyal 1983).

Many alternative services are popular and heavily used. The Lyon-
Martin Clinic in San Francisco which
started as a small alternative service
for lesbians expanded rapidly and
now serves over 300 women each
month. About 70 per cent of Lyon-
Martin's clients identify themselves
as lesbians (personal communication
1985). In Geneva, Dispensaires de
Femmes, the oldest feminist wom-
en's health care group in Europe,
cannot serve all the clients who wish
to receive basic gynaecological and
pediatric health care there. Priority
is given to women in the surrounding geographical area, relatives of
regular clients, and women who
have had serious problems with
the medical care system or who are
stigmatized in some way in conventional settings (Gramoni and
Chipier 1983). The Feminist Wom-
en's Health Centers (FWHC) which
started in Los Angeles have expanded into a federation of clinics in
the United States offering gynaecological and abortion services (personal communication July 1985; see
International Women and Health Resource Guide 1980 for information
on women's clinics throughout the
world).

Influencing Public Policy

Feminist health groups in the
United States, Europe and in other
countries make efforts to influence
public policy on matters affecting
women's health in ways which fit
their own health care systems. As
Erica Bates points out, consumers
have very different leverage points
in different health care systems
(Bates 1984).

Because health groups have been
in existence for over a decade in the
United States, the policy 'successes'
are quite extensive and impressive.
The National Women's Health Network is the only national membership organization in the United
States working exclusively on wom-
en's health and influencing health
policy at the local, national and international level. With a membership of over 20,000 (including several hundred organizations which
represent a constituency of half a
million people) the Network can
speak on behalf of a sizeable interest
group. With headquarters in Washington, DC, Network committees
work on reproductive health, occupational and environmental health;
alcohol, smoking, drugs; health law,
regulations and planning; health
needs of women with special needs
and backgrounds; and diseases such
as breast cancer affecting women.
Expert witnesses from the Network
have testified at numerous United
States Senate and House hearings
on birth control, drugs and devices,
contraceptive research priorities,
nurse-midwifery and hospital childbirth practices, sterilization abuse,

and abortion. The Network has also filed class action suits against companies whose products have injured women and has pressured drug companies into publishing patient information on the risks of contraceptive and menopausal estrogen drugs (Boston Women's Health Book Collective 1984).

Many other groups work on the local and regional level to influence policy. In Oakland, California, the Coalition to Fight Infant Mortality (CFIM) conducted a community investigation of the problem of infant mortality in poor and minority neighbourhoods. Their study showed 26.3 infant deaths per thousand live births in 1976 in their community, compared to 3.5 per thousand in a nearby affluent white neighbourhood. The local public hospital finally recognized the problem and made some needed changes, including hiring obstetricians with a commitment to community-based health care. Working with other groups, the CFIM got legislation passed to fund comprehensive perinatal services for low-income women (Boston Women's Health Book Collective 1984).

Other groups organize nationally around a single issue. For example, in the United States, the Committee to End Sterilization Abuse (CESA) testified first in New York and then in Washington to get federal regulations to ensure informed consent and impose a waiting period before sterilization can be performed in order to prevent coercive sterilization of poor and non-English speaking women. Initially, some feminist health groups with largely white, middle-class constituencies testified against these regulations on grounds that they wanted no state interference in a woman's right to obtain medical services. Over time, however, coalitions were formed between largely minority health activist groups and white middle-class organizations which came to recognize that at times the needs of women with fewer resources and greater vulnerabilities had to be protected by the state—even though the state can, and has, used such authority to prevent some women from exercising what are viewed by feminists as their inalienable right to control their reproduction in any way they see appropriate (Shapiro 1985). In England the campaign against the injectable contraceptive Depo-Provera involves similar issues about social control and the lack of informed consent, as well as necessary concerns about safety (Rakusen 1981).

In many countries women attempt to influence policies by direct action intended to draw attention to problems. Public demonstrations and informational campaigns are common. For example, women in Turin, Italy, occupied a hospital ward to protest at poor service and to negotiate better abortion and maternity care (International Women & Health Resource Guide 1980). Gathering data and evaluating the quality of care is another common approach. The Association of Radical Midwives in London presented an evaluation of maternity policies in the National Health Service to the Subcommittee

on Perinatal and Neonatal Mortality of the Expenditure Committee of the House of Commons (International Women & Health Resource Guide 1980).

The very existence of feminist health activity and alternative services can influence policy indirectly. Health professionals working within conventional institutions are able to study the alternative models and approaches pioneered by alternative groups and find ways to incorporate key ideas into these conventional settings. The persistence of alternative services can also provide policymakers with the awareness that not everyone is satisfied with conventional care. When the dissatisfaction is both widespread and persistent, as in the case of maternity care, studies sponsored by organizations such as the World Health Organization which document the pervasiveness of alternative approaches are potentially important levers for social change (see e.g. Houd and Oakley 1983).

Notes

The author wishes to thank Theresa Montini for research assistance and Kristin Hill and Sally Maeth for typing the manuscript. This reading draws on two papers prepared by the author for the WHO Regional Office for Europe, Health Education Unit: 'Whose Needs Do Industrialized Health Systems Meet?' Background Paper, Conference on Women & Health, Edinburgh, Scotland, May 1983, and 'Positive Approaches to Promoting Women's Health', a working paper co-authored with Jessica Hill, 1984.

Banta, H. D. and S. B. Thacker, *Costs and*

Benefits of Electronic Fetal Monitoring: A Review of the Literature (DHEW Publication No. PHS 79–3245). National Center for Health Services Research. Washington, D.C.: Government Printing Office, April 1979.

Boston Women's Health Book Collective, *Our Bodies, Ourselves—A Book by and for Women.* Second edition, revised (Simon and Schuster, New York, 1976).

Boston Women's Health Book Collective, *The New Our Bodies, Ourselves* (Simon and Schuster, New York, 1984).

Bunker, John, 'Surgical Manpower: A Comparison of Operations and Surgeons in the United States and in England and Wales', *New England Journal of Medicine* 282 (1970), 135–44.

Clarke, Adele, 'Subtle Forms of Sterilization Abuse: A Reproductive Rights Analysis' in R. Arditti, R. D. Klein and S. Minden (eds), *Test-Tube Women: What Future for Motherhood?* (Pandora Press, London, 1984).

Corea, Gena, *The Hidden Malpractice: How American Medicine Treats Women as Patients and Professionals* (William Morrow, New York, 1977).

De Vries, Raymond, *Regulating Birth. Midwives, Medicine and the Law* (Temple University Press, Philadelphia, 1985).

Doyal, Leslie, 'Women, Health and the Sexual Division of Labour: A Case Study of the Women's Health Movement in Britain', *Critical Social Policy* 7 (1983), 21–33.

Federation of Feminist Women's Health Centers, *A New View of a Woman's Body: A Fully Illustrated Guide* (Simon and Schuster, New York, 1981).

Gramoni, Rosangela and Françoise Chipier, 'The Geneva Woman's Health Clinic: Promoting Demedicalization and Self-Reliance in Health' (WHO/Euro. Health Education Unit, Copenhagen, 1983).

Houd, Susanne and Ann Oakley, 'Alternative Perinatal Services in the European Region and North America: A Pilot Survey' (WHO/Euro., Maternal and Child Health Unit, Copenhagen, 1983).

International Women & Health Resource Guide. A Joint Project of ISIS, Women's International Information and Communication Service, Geneva, Switzerland, and the Boston Women's Health Book Collective, Boston, MA, USA, 1980.

Kleiber, Nancy and Linda Light, *Caring for Ourselves: An Alternative Structure for Health Care.* Vancouver, B.C.: School of Nursing, University of British Columbia. National Health Research and Development Project No. 610–1020A of Health and Welfare, Canada, 1978.

Lembcke, P. A., 'Medical Auditing by Scientific Methods, Illustrated by Major Female Pelvic Surgery', *Journal of the American Medical Association* 162 (1956), 646–55.

National Black Women's Health Project, 450 Auburn Avenue, N.E., Suite 134, Atlanta, GA 30306.

The National Citizens' Board of Inquiry into Health in America. Health Care USA: 1984. Vol. 1, *National Report.* Washington, D.C.: The National Council on Aging, 1984.

Personal communication, June 1985. Lyon-Martin Clinic, 2480 Mission Street, Suite 214, San Francisco, CA 94110.

Personal communication, July 1985. Federation of Feminist Women's Health Centers, 330 Flume Street, Chico, CA 95928.

Petchesky, Rosalind, 'Reproduction, Ethics, and Public Policy: The Federal Sterilization Regulations', *Hastings Center Report* Vol. 5, 29–41, 9 October 1979.

Rakusen, Jill, 'Depo-Provera: The Extent of the Problem. A Case Study in the Politics of Birth Control', in Helen Roberts, ed., *Women, Health and Reproduction* (Routledge & Kegan Paul, London, 1981).

Reiser, Stanley Joel, *Medicine and the Reign of Technology* (Cambridge University Press, Cambridge, 1978).

Rothman, Barbara Katz, *In Labour: Women and Power in the Birthplace* (W. W. Norton & Company, New York, 1982).

Ruzek, Sheryl Burt, *The Women's Health Movement: Feminist Alternatives to Medical Control* (Praeger, New York, 1978).

Scully, Diana, *Men Who Control Women's Health: The Miseducation of Obstetrician-Gynecologists* (Houghton-Mifflin, Boston, 1980).

Seaman, Barbara, *The Doctors' Case against the Pill.* Revised edition (Doubleday & Company, Garden City, NY, 1980).

Seaman, Barbara and Gideon Seaman, *Women and the Crisis in Sex Hormones* (Rawson Associates, New York, 1977).

Shapiro, Thomas, *Population Control Politics. Women, Sterilization, and Reproductive Choice* (Temple University Press, Philadelphia, 1985).

Spelman College, Atlanta, Georgia. *Spelman Messenger* Vol. 100, 1, Spring 1984.

U.S. Department of Labor, Women's Bureau *Time of Change: 1983 Handbook on Women Workers.* Bulletin 298. Washington, D.C.: Government Printing Office, 1983.

Wertz, Richard W. and Dorothy C. Wertz, *Lying-in: a History of Childbirth in America* (The Free Press, New York, 1977).

A Woman's Place, A Vancouver Women's Health Booklet (Press Gang Publishers, Vancouver, 1972).

41   POLITICAL GYNECOLOGY: GYNECOLOGICAL IMPERIALISM AND THE POLITICS OF SELF-HELP

Susan Bell

Introduction

How do health activists institute change in the medical system? A problem commonly faced by them is whether to work to improve a basically sexist and oppressive medical care system or to create their own structures. Does it make sense to institute short range reforms or to struggle for long term radical change? By "improving" the health care system it may be possible to generate more humane health care but at the cost of strengthening an already oppressive system.

Change in the medical system can be instituted in a number of spheres: at the level of federal or state policy making; in private and public funding; in the area of services or scientific research; and in education. In this article is a discussion of these issues in light of the experiences of a group of feminists involved in a program to teach pelvic examinations to medical students in 1975–76 in Boston. Hence, the focus of this article is on change in the medical system at the level of physician education.

There have been numerous analyses of medicine as an institution of social control and of the particular ways in which medicine oppresses women(1): Women consume the largest proportion of health services (for themselves and their children), take more prescription drugs than men, and are admitted to hospitals more often than men. Most physicians are white men. Whether women seek private gynecological care, clinical or hospital services, most of them encounter practitioners who have learned how to perform pelvic examinations in the organized medical structure which is part and parcel of the larger racist and sexist society.(2)

Medical students traditionally learn incorrect and/or distorted information about women in textbooks and lectures.(3) They are taught to act as if the pelvic examination is as matter-of-fact as any routine examination, while at the same time learning to use unnecessary and uncomfortable examining techniques.(4) They are told to use stirrups and drapes routinely: both of these techniques are usually unnecessary and often uncomfortable for routine examinations. Traditionally they have practiced pelvic examinations on prostitutes, plastic "gynny" models, clinic "patients",† and anesthetized women. The women are often not asked for consent to furnish their bodies for teaching material.

It has been acknowledged by some educators, critics of medical education, and dissatisfied students

---

†(Footnotes appear at the end of the article.)

SOURCE: From *Science for the People*, September/October 1979, pp. 8–14. Reprinted by permission from *Science of the People*.

that this way of teaching is unsatisfactory. To remedy the situation, some educators have altered the information taught to students and the way in which they learn practical skills. One such improvement, introduced in the 1960s, has been the use of "Simulated Patients" (also called "Programmed Patients") instead of real "patients."(5) "Simulated Patients" are people who have been taught to exhibit historical, physical, and psychological manifestations of an illness when examined by students. They have been employed in a variety of settings to teach cognitive, interpersonal, and technical skills.(6) Prostitutes, friends of medical students, and community women have been recruited to serve as "Simulated Patients" to teach pelvic examinations and patient management skills to medical students. Depending on the emphasis of a program, women might be chosen because they are healthy or because they have specific ailments.

Students, physician-instructors, and "patients" benefit by the use of "Simulated Patients." Students try out practical techniques on them, thereby decreasing their own anxiety and embarrassment about examining people, and increasing their ability to discuss the examination openly in front of the "Simulated Patients." They learned to perform examinations in a realistic way and physician-instructors are able to evaluate students' performances in a standardized way. Hospital and clinic "patients" are saved from repetitive, inept examinations, and ultimately receive care from better-trained physicians.

The Pelvic Teaching Program

In mid-1975, women medical students at Harvard Medical School approached a member of the Boston Women's Health Book Collective to discuss the possibility of finding women to serve as paid "pelvic models." The women medical students were displeased with current teaching practices. They specifically wanted feminists since they thought that the use of feminists as "pelvic models" would greatly improve the learning process and would provide a counterbalance to institutionalized attitudes toward women as passive recipients of medical care. The book collective contacted women at Women's Community Health Center (WCHC) in Cambridge who agreed to a limited number of "modelling" sessions for second year Harvard medical students at local hospitals.

The members of WCHC, a self-help women's health center, saw themselves as part of the movement for radical social change, committed to the eradication of sexism, racism, capitalism, and imperialism. In practical terms, this means basic changes in the medical system as part of changing the overall structure of society: for instance, a breakdown of hierarchical relations among provider and consumer in which the provider has a monopoly over skills and information, women providing health care for women, and an end to "for-profit" medical services.(8)

Implementing a program to teach medical students was a focus of controversy in the WCHC from its inception. Some health center women saw it as a low priority issue in the sense that it would entail putting energy into professional medical education and detract from other health center programs which were directed towards implementing long-term changes. In addition, some women expressed concern that the program would serve to strengthen the medical system by teaching physicians how to "manage" their "patients" (by changing their behaviors without changing their power in doctor/patient encounters). Other members of the collective thought that teaching medical students would be a way to improve existing services for women and therefore that it would be a useful interim reform. They also thought that it would be a way to direct money from the medical schools to part of the women's health movement and a way of gaining access to the medical educational system. This controversy influenced the process of setting up the Pelvic Teaching Program (PTP) and of evaluating and changing it over time and was never completely resolved at the Women's Community Health Center.

In late 1975, the WCHC expanded this program by recruiting women who were not members of the collective. They also formalized the program by creating an ongoing group called the Pelvic Teaching Program. The PTP was a semi-autonomous program of the Women's Community Health Center. It was also the first attempt in which collective members worked along with women who were not members of the collective. This led in part to difficulties in communication and questions about power and decision-making among group members and also between the group and WCHC. For instance, to what extent could the Pelvic Teaching Program devise and implement its own structure and to what extent was it accountable to WCHC? Were WCHC members in the PTP more powerful than the others in the group? Could WCHC direct the PTP? The course of the PTP can be traced in stages, each marked by a new protocol.

The First Protocol

In the first sessions changes in standard teaching methods were relatively superficial: "pelvic models" were each paid $25 for each teaching session. In each teaching session, four or five medical students did a bimanual pelvic examination* on a consenting, knowledgeable woman, while taught by a physician-instructor. Sessions focused on attitudes and the manner in which students learned to perform a pelvic examination. They left intact the role of physician-instructor. Meanwhile, the feminists did research to find out what had been taught at Harvard and what the professors and students were interested in implementing. The feminists met to evaluate this limited program and then met with the professors and medical students to draw up a protocol. The physician-instructors and medical students were pleased by this limited program. It facilitated more efficient, comfortable teaching sessions. The feminists were dissatisfied. In a retrospective analysis they wrote that "although we gave active feedback as the exam was being performed, the physicians were the major instructors and the students looked to them to handle the tough problems and to field questions regarding pathology. We had very little control over the teaching sessions."(9) The success of these limited sessions was disquieting; the women realized that while they were ensuring more humane and better exams for women, they were also solidifying physicians' power over women by participating in training sessions in which students learned how to instill trust in themselves by making women more comfortable and informed about pelvic examinations. They saw that this accommodation to the current medical system was a way to strengthen the medical system rather than to change it. They thus proposed a new protocol, which was accepted and implemented.(10)

A Second Protocol

The second protocol included changes both in the teaching group and in the teaching sessions. The feminists created a formal group, called the Pelvic Teaching Program, and recruited community women to become members. Community women were selected using the following criteria: prior enrollment in a self-help group (this would ensure their familiarity with the concepts and practice of the self-help movement and WCHC familiarity with them); a willingness to share skills with medical students; a commitment to delineate and to critique the underlying goals of the current medical system in their teaching

sessions; and a commitment to interrupt sexist, professionalistic, or otherwise offensive behaviors during the sessions. WCHC members were included on the basis of their willingness to put energy into teaching medical students and to participate in a controversial new program.

In teaching sessions, they implemented the following: two feminist instructors from the PTP met with four or five students, at least one of whom had to be a woman. Members of the PTP instructed students; and physicians, if present at all, assumed the role of silent observers. The feminists required a written contract and were paid $50 for each session instead of $25 for each "model" to emphasize their altered status. Each session was focused on a well-woman approach to medical care, describing the wide range of normal conditions. They demonstrated how women can examine their own genitals using a plastic speculum, light, and mirror. Each teaching institution agreed to reproduce and distribute to the medical students "How to Do A Pelvic Examination," written by the feminists from WCHC.

Part of their proposal was not accepted by Harvard. This included purchase of an information packet written by feminists for each student as well as a separate second session to give information about women's health concerns in more detail to the students.

The Pelvic Teaching Program, now consisting of five WCHC members and six affiliated women, began to meet in an ongoing self-help group amongst themselves, to share criticisms, and perspectives about the program, as well as to devote energy to practical training, information, and skill sharing on a personal and political level. They used the group as a way to cope with embarrassing or offensive encounters and to devise strategies to avoid them in future sessions. They also used the group as a way to share their feelings about their dual roles as "models" and instructors.

They shared information about their program through meetings with other women, in reports to WCHC, and through the health center newsletters. At times, women in the PTP felt misunderstood or unsupported by WCHC. One of the ways in which the PTP and WCHC addressed this issue was by requesting that WCHC members who were not in the PTP observe teaching sessions to understand through first-hand observation what the instructors experienced. Within WCHC and the PTP individually, as well as in dialogues between the two, they addressed the controversial questions about the usefulness of an interim reform in physician education compared with other long term changes; they looked at power relations and communications between the PTP and WCHC.

The PTP wrote to *HealthRight*, a newsletter published by women's health activists, outlining their new protocol, and pointing out why specific changes were made. They requested that any women thinking of teaching pelvic examinations to medical students contact them. They thought that this would be a way of empowering themselves and other women, realizing how isolated they had been when their own program began. As a result of their own experiences they strongly suggested that any women who were going to teach pelvic examinations be involved in a group, so that they could share skills and support for each other.

The report in *HealthRight* generated criticism as well as excitement within the women's health community. Although some thought it was a victory to find members of the women's health movement being asked to teach medical professionals, others felt that training doctors was simply a cooptation of long-term strategies.

Up to this point, the PTP was similar to parts of other "Simulated Patients" programs. Responses to the PTP by students and physician were similar to those enumerated in accounts of "Simulated Patient" programs that I surveyed: student response was favorable, with a few exceptions. Physicians who observed sessions reported that the teaching was excellent. Generally students felt more at ease, learned technical skills more thoroughly, and were better equipped to perform examinations on patients. Some of the negative responses of the students reflect the difference in the PTP from the "Simulated Patient" programs: some were distressed by the "women's libbers" stance of the feminists.

In the Spring of 1976, the members of the PTP analyzed the program and began to assert their unique political perspective. It happened in three ways:

1. Through the political development of the group itself.
2. By means of the issues that the feminists, as part of the women's health movement, wanted to address through the PTP.
3. In the institutional response of the medical schools to the Third Protocol.

The second protocol left basic contradictions unresolved. As nonprofessionals, they taught professionals techniques that only professionals could use legally; men learned how to practice medical care for women; fragmented medical care was encouraged by the program since the feminists met only once with students, thereby offering limited and isolated information; hierarchical power relationships between provider and receiver and amongst providers were not confronted.

After their analysis of the second protocol and its implementation, the members of the PTP met as a group to write the *Position Paper* to evaluate their experiences as a group and as individuals, and to devise a new protocol that would meet their needs and serve their political purposes. The *Position Paper* outlined their self-criticism and their suggestions for questions to be raised by other women before beginning to teach pelvic examinations. They circulated this in Boston women's publications, in *HealthRight*, and in *Women and Health*, and sent out copies of it to any people who had inquired about the PTP over the past year. By this time, members of the medical profession had heard about the PTP as well, and wanted information about the program and copies of the manual written by the feminists as a sourcebook for their own programs.(11)

In discussions leading up to the formulation of the third protocol, the women in both the PTP and the WCHC addressed the ongoing issue of reform versus radical change. In their analysis of events, they concluded that as a reform within the medical system the PTP had been successful, but that it had failed to institute long term change.

In order to emphasize their self-help politics, a third protocol was devised which would make explicit the differences between their point of view and the point of view exhibited by creators of the "Simulated Patient" programs. They devised a program which would be acceptable to them and thereby, they expected, not acceptable to the medical schools. Rather than presenting a critique, they proposed a new program, thereby requiring that the medical school officials respond.

The Third Protocol

The third protocol included the following changes: first, teaching would be limited to women. The PTP as part of the self-help/women's health movement was committed to reciprocal sharing, and learning through reciprocity is not only different from, but more meaningful than, one-way learning. The PTP could only have integrity as a self-help experience if there was reciprocal sharing. This would entail being examined as well as examining. By definition, then, the teaching of pelvic examinations would be limited to women. By limiting the teaching to women, they wanted to force all the medical students to address the question: should men be providing gynecological care for women?

The feminists had also found that despite their efforts to the contrary, they had felt embarrassed and exploited by some of the male students —and they wished to avoid focusing attention on this part of the training. By teaching only women, they thought that it would be a more positive experience for themselves and rid them of sexual exploitation during the sessions.

Second, each teaching group of four or five women would include not only medical students, but also other hospital personnel and consumers, taught by two women from the PTP. By doing this, the feminists would address the issues of hierarchy and elitism among medical care providers and between providers and consumers, which encourage physicians to maintain a monopoly of skills and information. Instructors would exchange roles with others in the teaching group, emphasizing the need for a breakdown of the rigid hierarchy among physicians, nurses and other health workers as well as that between powerful physicians and passive "patients." They would also promote identification and recognition of similarities between provider and consumer rather than objectification and distance. This would help to demystify and defuse the physician's power and be a way of stimulating discussion about these issues.

Third, the new protocol called for three or four sessions with the same individuals to allow time for analysis of the politics of medical care, to share health information of special relevance to women, to discuss what a good examination should include, and to perform self-examination. This would challenge the teaching of medical care as fragmented and episodic. By placing the technical skills and information within the general context of the politics of medical care, they would stimulate discussion about commonly held assumptions about what students are learning and why.

Fourth, the PTP raised their fees, in recognition of their value as instructors, and of the ability and common practice of the medical schools to pay higher consultant fees. Fees were raised to $750 for the four sessions.

The issues addressed in the third protocol were hierarchy, sexism, fragmentation of learning skills, profit, and division between provider and consumer. By this time, the PTP had been approached by the other area medical schools, Tufts and Boston University. As had been predicted by the PTP, no medical schools wanted to implement this program. Reasons varied: it was too expensive; it discriminated against men. As long as the PTP fell within the acceptable range of innovations, exemplified by the "Simulated Patient" programs, it remained an acceptable program. When it confronted basic power relations and current assumptions about the goals of medical education, the PTP became unacceptable to current teaching programs. At this stage, in the summer of 1976, the PTP ended: women received inquiries and sent out the third protocol after that date, but have no longer taught sessions.

Discussion

What can we learn from the experience of the PTP? One way to evaluate it is to see in what respects the women successfully implemented a reform in physician education. The PTP demonstrated that a group of nonprofessionals could devise and implement a program. By example, then, the women demonstrated within the medical community that "consumers" can educate themselves and become active members in the medical community. The PTP established themselves as credible teachers to both medical students and physicians. By identifying themselves as feminists, the PTP openly brought political awareness and political issues into a teaching situation and confronted sexist attitudes and practices as they emerged in the teaching session. In addition, by emphasizing use of common language to describe medical procedures, and by demonstrating how a woman can participate in the examination, they focused on the distinction between provider and consumer and suggested ways that the consumer could gain more power in the encounter through knowledge and skills. They self-consciously went about channeling money into the women's health movement and got a good first-hand look at medical education. They created a need for feminists to teach pelvic examinations to medical students. They ac-

complished this both by their success in the first two phases, and also by their visibility in the women's health movement by doing this: medical students and health activists read about their success and the way that they went about teaching and meeting as an ongoing group, and saw by their example that it was possible.

The feminists wrote and circulated a manual for teaching pelvic examinations which is still in demand. The PTP gained considerable attention not only in the local medical and women's communities, but also nationally, through publications and networks. They continue to receive requests for protocols, for copies of their manual, and in general for information about how to implement pelvic teaching programs.(12)

However, in their own analysis, the PTP concluded that these successes were insufficient to outweigh the time and energy necessitated by the program. Their decision can be better understood if we turn to three issues: first, the PTP lacked a complete understanding of the history of "Simulated Patients" programs; second, the PTP evolved as a semi-autonomous group out of the WCHC, raising the issues of power and communication within a group of collective members and affiliated women, and between the PTP and the WCHC; and third, they carried on an ongoing dialogue about the advisability of instituting an interim reform.

In some respects, the task of the PTP had been made more arduous by their lack of complete knowledge and analysis of other programs. As we have seen, the development of the PTP occurred through its own experiences rather than being shaped by a vision of the eventual outcome.

When the feminists designed the protocols, it was without a historical analysis of the use of "Simulated Patients" and without a complete overview of contemporaneous programs (having only looked at what had been taught at Harvard previously and screened one videotape of a program in which a physician performed a pelvic examination on a "Simulated Patient"). If they had begun with a complete overview of precedents already set by other innovative "Simulated Patient" programs, they might have chosen other strategies with which to confront Harvard with an educated overview. The first two protocols followed essentially the same lines as "Simulated Patients" programs. What seemed to the feminists, at times, as risky and dangerous at Harvard, had already become institutionalized in other medical schools.

It was with the third protocol that the women were not only devising a better program, but were also explicitly challenging commonly held assumptions about medical care and explicitly stating some of their own political goals: to eradicate hierarchy and professionalism; to have women provide women's health care; to redefine the distinction between provider and consumer and to empower the consumer vis-a-vis the provider; and finally to challenge the monopoly over money and resources that medical schools have.

As a new program of the WCHC, the PTP was the focus of an evolving mechanism for implementing similar WCHC programs in the future. This process entailed working out problems and concerns raised during the course of the group about ways to facilitate communication and decision making in a semi-autonomous program; at times this process was frustrating and stressful.

In addition, the PTP was never wholeheartedly supported by members of WCHC. Not only were the women in the PTP constantly reexamining their goals and strategies, but they were shaped by the ongoing controversy in WCHC about whether to teach medical students. This contributed to a sense of frustration and exhaustion when the PTP evaluated the first and second protocols and drew up the third.

Finally, the task of initiating reforms in physician-training necessitates constant confrontation of the educational structures and individuals serving to oppress women. On the other hand, the struggle faced by the women to implement even the first protocol at Harvard demonstrates the threat they posed as feminist nonprofessionals entering the confines of medical providers. On the other hand, the ability of educational institutions to absorb and co-opt innovations is striking: teaching medical students ways to improve the pelvic examination for women was taken by them as a technique of managing their "patients" in sessions taught according to the first and second protocols. This ability was taken seriously by the feminists in their evaluations of the success or failure of the PTP, and must be recognized by others considering similar programs. What might appear to be positive reforms in theory might prove to be cooptations in practice, and hence not positive in the long run. Because the feminists paid close attention to the impact of their program during the process of setting it up and implementing it, they were able to evaluate it realistically.

In retrospect, we can see that the PTP was successful in some important ways and provides a thoughtful and politically responsible example of the ways in which health activists might institute change in the medical system. The experiences of the PTP also underline the necessity of an ongoing reassessment of the long range implications of short term reforms, not only in theory but in their practical application.

Acknowledgment

This article is a revised version of a presentation given at the fall conference of the Massachusetts Sociological Association on November 4, 1978. I would like to thank members of the Pelvic Teaching Program, the Women's Community Health Center, and the Science for the People Editorial Collective for their help and support in writing this article. Charlotte Weissberg provided sisterly criticisms.

Notes

†The term "patient" will be used in quotes to remind the reader of the debates over the definition of health and illness in society and over the power relations between provider and consumer of medical care.

*A person conducts a bimanual pelvic examination by inserting two fingers into a woman's vagina and feeling her cervix (tip of the womb or uterus, which extends into the vagina), and with the other hand presses down on her abdomen. In this way, the person doing the bimanual pelvic examination can feel the size, shape and position of a woman's uterus and cervix. A bimanual pelvic examination also includes checking a woman's external genitals.

A speculum is an instrument that is used to separate the walls of a woman's vagina to be able to visualize her vagina and cervix. By use of a mirror and light a woman can see her own vagina and cervix.

For complete information about what a good gynecological or pelvic examination should include, see *Our Bodies, Ourselves*, by the Boston Women's Health Book Collective.

References

1. For example, see the following: Kotelchuck, David, ed., *Prognosis Negative*, New York, Vintage Books, 1976; Dreifus, Claudia, ed., *Seizing Our Bodies*, New York, Vintage Books, 1978; Boston Women's Health Book Collective, *Our Bodies, Ourselves*, New York, Simon and Shuster, 1976.

2. Nurses, nurse practitioners and physician assistants also perform pelvic examinations. It is beyond the scope of this article to look at the differences among these professionals and between them and physicians.

3. Bart, P., Scully, D., "A Funny Thing Happened on the Way to the Orifice: Women in Gynecology Textbooks," *Am. J. Soc.* 78:1045–1050, 1973; Howell, M., "What Medical Schools Teach about Women," *N. Engl. J. Med.* 291-304-307, 1974.

4. Emerson, J., "Behavior in Private Places," in H. P. Dreitzel, ed., *Recent Sociology No. 2; Patterns of*

Communicative Behavior, New York, The MacMillan Company, 1970, pp. 74–95; Shaw, N.S., *Forced Labor*, New York, Pergamon Press, Inc., 1974.

5. Teaching hospitals and clinics associated with medical schools provide services and are also training institutions. Hence "patients" receive care and provide teaching material.

6. See the following for discussions of these programs: "Announcement: Using Nonphysicians to Teach Pelvic Examinations," *Contemporary Ob/Gyn.* 11:173, 1978; Billings, J.A., Stoeckle, J.D., "Pelvic Examination Instruction and the Doctor-Patient Relationship," *J. Med. Educ.* 52:834–839, 1977; Godkins, T.R., Duffy, D., Greenwood, J., Stanhope, W.D., "Utilization of Simulated Patients to Teach the 'Routine' Pelvic Examination," *J. Med. Educ.* 49:1174–1178, 1974; Holzman, G.B., Singleton, D., Holmes, T.F., Maatsch, J.L., "Initial Pelvic Examination Instruction: The Effectiveness of Three Contemporary Approaches," *Am. J. Obstet. Gyn.* 129:2, 124–129, 1977; Johnson, G.H., Brown, T.C., Stenchever, M.A., Gabert, H.A., Poulson, A.M., Warenski, J.C., "Teaching Pelvic Examination to Second-Year Medical Students Using Programmed Patients," *Am. J. Obstet. Gyn.* 121:5, 714–717, 1975; Kretzschmar, R.M., "Evolution of the Gynecology Teaching Associate: An Education Specialist," *Am. J. Obstet. Gyn.* 131:4, 367–373, 1978; Schneidman, B., "An Approach to Obtaining Patients to Participate in Pelvic Examination Instruction," *J. Med. Educ.* 52:70–71, 1977.

7. Information about the Women's Community Health Center (WCHC) and the Pelvic Teaching Program have been gathered from the following sources: Women's Community Health Center, Inc. "Experiences of a Pelvic Teaching Group," *Women and Health* 1:4, 19–20, 1976 (this is a reprint of the *Position Paper*, June, 1976, available from WCHC, 639 Massachusetts Avenue, room 210, Cambridge, Massachusetts 02139); WCHC, Third Annual Report, Cambridge, Mass., 1977; WCHC, "Letter to the Editor," *HealthRight*, 2:3, 2, 1976 (The address for *HealthRight* is 41 Union Square, Room 206-9, New York, NY 10003); WCHC, "Announcement," *Women and Health*, 1:1, 17, 1976; WCHC, "How to Do a Pelvic Examination," 1976; WCHC, "Proposals to Teach Pelvic Examinations to Medical Students," 1975 and 1976; Norsigian, J. "Training the Docs," *HealthRight*, 2:2, 6, 1975–76. Other sources have been informal and formal discussions with the PTP and the WCHC. As a member of both the PTP and the WCHC, I have drawn from my own experiences as well as from the above sources.

8. The development of the PTP could be analyzed from the point of view of the medical institutions as well as from its self-concept. This article will concentrate on the PTP from the feminist perspective.

9. The quote is from the *Position Paper*.

10. Through various networks, other women's health groups and publications heard about these sessions. *HealthRight, Women and Health,* and *Liberation News Service* published information about the program.

11. The PTP has refused to supply copies of their manual to any members of the medical profession out of context.

12. For discussions of the PTP written by members of the medical profession, see the Billings and Stoeckle article and the Announcement, listed in Note #6 above.

42   THE PRESBYTERIAN STORY: THE PEOPLE PULL THE STRINGS FOR A CHANGE

Peggy Gallagher

In 1984, at a time when the supply of hospital beds throughout the country was being carefully monitored. Presbyterian Hospital, a 1291-bed teaching and research center in northern Manhattan, received approval to spend about $500 million to renovate its current site and to build a new 300-bed community hospital. Its first bond issue to provide funds for the construction was, at $427 million, the largest hospital bond issue in history.

Presbyterian's proposal was approved, only months after New York State had lifted its one-year moratorium on hospital construction, because the hospital had said it would serve the surrounding community of Washington Heights/Inwood. However, the members of that community raised serious questions concerning the hospital's abilities to meet their needs.

Access to comprehensive quality health care has long been a concern of the residents of this community. Four out of five community hospitals have gone bankrupt and closed in the last 15 years. These closings have meant a loss of access to emergency and clinic services, hospital beds, and more than 1000 jobs. In addition, family practitioners were becoming increasingly scarce in the community and the average age of those remaining was 62 years. Consequently, residents were becoming more and more dependent on Pres-byterian Hospital, the only major health care provider in the area.

Community Spells Out Needs

When Presbyterian announced its expansion plans—and they went essentially unchallenged—a skeptical group of Washington Heights/Inwood residents decided to conduct their own health needs assessment to determine whether the plans were really relevant and appropriate. In September 1983, they started the North Manhattan Health Action Group (NMHAG), whose eight original members conducted a survey of the community, with technical assistance from the Community Service Society of New York City.

The group describes Washington Heights/Inwood as a diverse community—geographically, ethnically and economically—of about 200,000 people, with six distinct neighborhoods. In general, the neighborhoods to the west have an older population with higher incomes and relatively good medical coverage; by contrast, those to the east are young, poor and medically indigent. All but seven of the community's 32 census tracts are identified as Medically Underserved Areas, and a majority are also designated as Health Manpower Shortage Areas.

SOURCE: From *Health/PAC Bulletin*, vol. 16, no. 5 (June 1986), pp. 9–11. Reprinted by permission.

Map of Upper Manhattan
(showing sites of proposed, existing and closed hospitals)

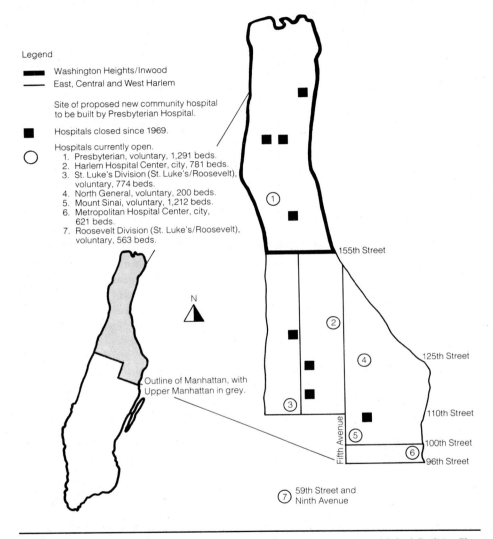

SOURCE: Community Service Society; New York City Health Systems Agency Medical Facilities Plan, August 31, 1983.

According to William Alicea, a NMHAG founder and cochairman, with Hildamar Ortiz: "Health was not an issue until recently—we had five hospitals—but we have lost all but one of our hospitals and we have seen a tremendous change in demographics in the last 15 years.

"In 1970, 20 percent of the community were from minority groups.

In 1984, however, the figure was 72 percent, more than half Hispanic, predominantly Dominican. In 1970, 10 percent of our community lived below the poverty level. Today it is 27 percent, and the number of residents living on public assistance is 60 percent higher than the New York City average. Consistent with this change, there has been an increase in the number of people who do not have health insurance, and who cannot afford to pay the high costs of health care."

For three months, the eight NMHAG members conducted interviews, in Spanish and English, of some 600 Washington Heights/Inwood residents, to determine their health care experiences and needs. Using a 10-page questionnaire, they found that 25 percent of the community's residents use hospital clinics as their primary source of care, compared with 9 percent citywide. Further, 12 percent of the respondents use an emergency room as their major source of care, compared with only 3 percent citywide. Not surprisingly, residents living in the insured, higher income neighborhoods reported having access to private physicians, while their poorer neighbors tended to rely on the emergency room or clinics for their primary care.

The group also conducted a physician survey in which they identified only 54 full-time-equivalent primary care physicians in the area. According to Alicea, this is fewer than one physician per 3500 residents, at least 25 percent below the state average. Forty percent of the physicians practicing in the area reported having no admitting privileges, and those who did were admitting mostly to hospitals outside the community. After reviewing all sources of care in the community, including the City Department of Health physicians and the Presbyterian Outpatient Department, NMHAG determined that at least 55 additional primary care physicians were needed in the community to meet the needs of its residents.

Health statistics for the area indicated that the most pressing health care concerns in northern Manhattan were distinct from those of the city overall. The average death rate is lower in this community than in the rest of the city for the usual leading causes of death: heart disease, cancer and stroke. However, disease rates for Washington Heights/Inwood are higher than those citywide for hepatitis, gonorrhea and lead poisoning; in addition, the birth rate, the percentage of women receiving late or no prenatal care, and the teenage fertility rate are all higher than those citywide.

Hospital Plan Bars Access

The North Manhattan Health Action Group issued a report entitled *Washington Heights/Inwood Neighborhoods: Assessment of Health Care Needs.* The report reviewed the community's health care resources, socioeconomic and other data, and concluded that community residents had needed better access to inexpensive primary and secondary health services. It looked to NMHAG as though Presbyterian's plan was not addressing these needs, and, in fact, would be excluding the community from such services.

Admission to a hospital is generally through one of three avenues: entrance through the emergency room, a referral from a hospital clinic, or admission by an affiliated physician. Plans for the proposed community hospital not only placed it in an area of least need, according to Alicea, but specified an undersized emergency room that could handle only 27 visits a day. Further, there were no clinics planned, thus barring access via that avenue.

The proposed community hospital was to receive most of its patients from private practitioners having admitting privileges. However, this method of entry would also effectively exclude community residents, as only three community physicians reported having admitting privileges at Presbyterian. Moreover, because hospital officials planned to use the same strict requirements for privileges at the new hospital that they use at the teaching institution, it was unlikely that many local physicians would qualify. Thus, local residents who would receive care from community physicians could not be admitted by them to the new community hospital.

According to Presbyterian's plan, the necessary link between local physicians and the new community hospital would be provided by the hospital's proposed Ambulatory Care Network Corporation (ACNC). The ACNC plan had been one of the things that helped to convince state and city planners of the suitability of Presbyterian's proposal overall. Presbyterian's planners had said that, based on a 1981 demonstration

project of need, they would "homestead" 50 physicians in the community; that is, loan them capital to start their own practices. However, since the ACNC's inception in 1981, it had not yet produced a single primary care site.

Community Pressure Pays Off

Presbyterian's expansion plans were approved by the state on the basis of proposed service to the surrounding community. The NMHAG investigation showed, however, that the hospital's plans were more focused on the interests of the institution than those of the community. The group determined to make Presbyterian more responsive to community needs and to make state regulators more vigilant in their surveillance of the hospital's contributions to community service.

They conducted an intensive, highly organized "bottom up" campaign that included the following:

- They decide to focus on the issue of primary care rather than the location or services of the community hospital, which they viewed as "after the fact." They wanted to emphasize prevention.

- At first, they met extensively with Presbyterian officials, whose strategy, Alicea says, was "to meet us to death. In response, we not only met with them, but requested more meetings, more documents."

- They also talked with residents wherever they could find them— in community groups and at schools. "We went to all community meetings," Alicea recalls. "We spoke to the interests of each group, and we made the strength and synergism of eight touch hundreds."

- When they felt they were not getting an appropriate response from the hospital, they decided to bypass Presbyterian and went to the State Commissioner of Health, Dr. David Axelrod. "We were encouraged by his response, at first," Alicea says, "but later, when he praised Presbyterian's plans, we felt he still did not understand how little those plans would actually do for Washington Heights/Inwood." They wrote a letter restating their position, but nothing much happened, and they wrote again.

- On May 25, 1985, with a grant from the state they had received after their first meeting with Dr. Axelrod, NMHAG held a public hearing in their poorest neighborhood under a banner that read "Let's Keep Them Honest." The hearing was attended by 300 people including their representatives from the State Department of Health and three from Presbyterian, led by its new president. A report of major aims and demographic statistics was issued, and 62 individuals and community-group representatives testified, over a seven-hour period, to their specific needs for improved health care services. As was true at all major meetings, discussions were bilingual, and day care services were provided. The proceeds were transcribed

and distributed, to repeat the messages again. "We had really 'out-organized' ourselves," Alicea says proudly.

- The hearing helped to get the action they needed. The group met for a second time with Dr. Axelrod, who subsequently directed Presbyterian to work with NMHAG to resolve the issues and to produce a model for primary health care in the community.

  "In effect," says Alicea, "Presbyterian wanted to cover the world—to consider its catchment area as global—but the state said 'If you want to use government money, you have to accept responsibility for the community in which you reside.' They even had to revise their mission statement to acknowledge that responsibility."

- A signed agreement was reached early in the fall.

Agreement Is a Major Achievement

"After all our research, we had decided to focus on the issue of primary care, and we had two major objectives," Alicea recounts: "To get primary care services consistent with the needs of the neighborhoods, and to get those services placed in areas of greatest need. As basic as those two principles are, they were hard to achieve."

The major points of the document provide for the following:

- Agreement on the general location, size and scope of services for four ACNC sites to be established in 1986.

- Agreement on a special-focus geriatric program in a housing development containing a large number of elderly.
- Agreement on the general nature and extent of the shortage of physicians and on collaboration to develop ways to redress that shortage.
- Agreement on the makeup of a steering committee to assure continuing community input into the Ambulatory Care Network Corporation overall; also, agreement to establish a consumer advisory group at each site, and to hold public meetings to obtain additional input.

Additional agreements addressed the composition of the primary care team, access to physicians, admitting privileges, the importance of health education and disease prevention, fee schedules, transportation—and one of the most important provisions, according to Alicea—adequate bilingual staff.

And what now?

"We will continue to serve as a research, planning and advocacy group for the Washington Heights/Inwood community," Alicea reports. "We have now grown to a membership of 300 individuals and organizations, we have just incorporated, and we are already working on our next projects—a birthing center and a comprehensive school health program.

"If more than four or five people are interested in some health issue, we'll listen," Alicea says. "We're not politicians, we're health advocates, and we're about work. We'll lend support, and we'll make it happen."

Section Fourteen

Reform and Change in
the Larger Society

The 1960s and 1970s provided an arena for *alternative* institutions in all segments of society, including health, schools, day care, work collectives, living communes, and political participation. These alternative institutions provided services and social relations that existing institutions either did not provide or provided in traditional ways. To be sure, not everyone involved in these alternatives had a vision of deep structural change in society. But many participants did, and their influence was quite large.

This notion of the integral connection between health reform and social change has become a powerful force for making democratic and progressive alterations to societies throughout the world. The articles in this last section provide examples from China and the United States.

In social revolutions, an entire society may be altered. When the Chinese Revolution finally succeeded in 1949, it led to a rethinking of many social institutions. Public health measures were seen as good in themselves, but in addition they were viewed as a way to reconstruct a humane society. Joshua Horn, an English surgeon, spent 15 years in China, from 1954 to 1969, providing medical care throughout the country. In "The Conquest of Syphilis in China" he tells how the campaign against syphilis was at the same time a struggle against prostitution, for the eradication of many forms of exploitation against women, for the elimination of poverty, and for the empowerment of ordinary people to take charge of major segments of their social lives.

Turning to the American scene, we find examples of health and social change that are not as all-encompassing as the Chinese Revolution, but that nevertheless illustrate our concern with the connection between political-economic structural change and health care. Self-help movements of many types grew in the United States in the activist period of the 1960s and 1970s. In the health arena, self-help groups provided countless people with new hope, both for their physical and mental maladies and for the social support needed to live with disabilities in a society that has little tolerance for disability. Irving Kenneth Zola, in "Helping One Another: A Speculative

History of the Self-Help Movement," writes about the social barriers to medical self-help. Because disabilities are socially stigmatized, the general cultural milieu mitigated against asking for help, and people often placed too much faith in doctors at the expense of their own capacities. Yet self-help proponents have overcome many obstacles and have developed a vibrant movement, particularly in the area of physical disabilities. Zola paints a picture of the United States as an aging society that will contain more and more disabled people. He argues that the discrimination and intolerance of difference and disability may, in fact, come back to haunt the perpetrators if and when they join the ranks of the disabled. In light of this possibility, the disability rights movement is actively changing deep-rooted cultural beliefs and behaviors in order to produce a more humane society.

As a final focus for this topic of health care and social change, let us look at one further area of recent concern. Environmental activism has been a major social movement in the last decade or so, and much of its effects have been directed toward environmental health issues. Phil Brown's article on environment health activism, "Popular Epidemiology: Community Response to Toxic Waste-Induced Disease," shows how people in Woburn, Massachusetts, worked out their own method of getting scientific knowledge and political power in order to deal with an epidemic of childhood leukemia, which they traced to corporate dumping of toxic wastes.

This discussion of social movements has taken us full circle, back to the first discussions of social epidemiology and the social context of health and illness. We have examined social constructions of disease and illness, and we have seen differences in lay and medical worldviews concerning health and illness. We have talked about the social nature of scientific knowledge, the inequalities in the overall society and in the medical encounter, and the problems of access to and quality of health care. We have developed a framework of political economy in which to study the distribution, composition, and function of the health care system. We have studied the convergence of economic factors and political forces in the relations between government and profit-making health industries and providers. We have analyzed professionalism in terms of the development of American medicine and in terms of lay-professional relations. And we have ended with a reminder of how the social nature of health and illness is once again reaffirmed in light of the importance of social movements in health care.

Throughout this process we have maintained a focus on the three major structural forces: political-economy, professionalism, and institutional structure. At the same time we have seen the dialectical (interconnected and interdependent) relationships between the micro- and macro-levels of health care, and have learned that we can never fully understand one end of the macro-micro continuum unless we are taking into account the other end.

I hope the material in this book leads you to pursue further study in the exciting field of medical sociology.

43 THE CONQUEST OF SYPHILIS IN CHINA

Joshua Horn

On a blustery day in December, 1920, a strange farce was enacted in the Town Hall in the International Settlement of Shanghai.

There had been some difference of opinion as to whether or not children should be admitted to the ceremony. Some had been against it lest it sully their pure little minds with unwholesome thoughts and cause them to ask awkward questions. But the majority had been in favour. 'After all,' they argued, 'there is little enough entertainment for children in this wicked city and Christmas is but four days ahead. The dear little innocents won't understand what is going on and it will give them a chance to plan their Christmas parties.'

There were no two opinions as to whether or not Chinese should be admitted. 'Let us fling our civic doors wide open,' declared the vicar magnanimously, 'Let us welcome spectators of all colours, creeds and denominations. Let us show them every courtesy and every hospitality. Some of them, inspired by the proceedings, will draw closer to us. Moreover, they will all pay the entrance fee and so assist our all-too-modest welfare fund.'

The wife of a High Court judge who had consented to draw the lots, took her seat beside the lottery drum. Her poise and grace contrasted with the evident embarrassment of the few brothel-keepers sitting at the back of the platform. No more than twenty had come out of the nine hundred who had been invited and they had not expected to be let down in this way by their professional colleagues. Neither had they expected to have those ridiculously huge paper roses pinned on to their lapels or to be showered with prayer books, religious tracts and crucifixes. Above all, they had not expected that the ceremony would take so long, for the festive season was approaching and they were busy men.

Her ladyship drew slips of paper from the drum and the moderator read out the names inscribed on them. At first, each name was greeted by a ripple of applause but soon the audience lost interest and a hum of conversation filled the chilly hall. When 180 names had been read out, a Civic Dignitary made a little speech in which he thanked all those who had participated and especially the 180 brothel keepers who were now in honour bound to close their establishments and free 1,200 girls by next April. He had prepared a much longer speech calling attention to the epoch-making nature of the proceedings and to the implications which they held for the moral and physical welfare of the Settlement, but he sensed that a long speech at this late

SOURCE: From *Away with All Pests: An English Surgeon in People's China*, pp. 85–93. Copyright © 1969 by Joshua Horn. Reprinted by permission of Monthly Review Foundation.

hour would not meet with universal approval.

Only one of the brothel keepers actually present had had his name called out and he took it remarkably well. He grinned sheepishly as his colleagues either sympathetically patted him on the back or hypocritically shook his hand in congratulations. He mopped his brow from time to time in spite of the cold, fidgeted with his rosette and the only thing at all unseemly in his behaviour was when he peeped into the drum to see whether it could possibly have contained all nine hundred names.

Not that he was worried. He knew perfectly well that most of the names that had been called out were fictitious. But he, having a reputation to keep up, wouldn't stoop to such a low trick. His establishment anyway needed redecorating and he would need only to change the signboard and install his brother as the proprietor. What queer notions some people had! To expect a brothel keeper voluntarily to close down a flourishing concern was like expecting the police to entrust the keys of the jail to the inmates.

But it was as well to play ball with civic big shots, time-consuming though it was. You never could tell when you would need their help.

The National Medical Journal of China at first hailed the event as a 'red-letter day for social reformers in Shanghai',[1] but later it editorialized: 'As we said in our last issue, we hope the French municipal authorities will come into line. With the present tendencies in world thought, civic authorities cannot afford to ignore the moral and physical welfare of millions of people *entrusted* to their care, *even though* they be of another race and nationality' (author's italics). The background to this sanctimonious gem was the fact that the French 'Concession', which accommodated slightly more than half of all the registered brothels in Shanghai, had not participated in this particular tragi-comedy.

Not that it would have made much difference if they had, since a conservative estimate of the number of prostitutes in Shanghai at that time was 50,000 registered and 100,000 unregistered.

The History of Venereal Disease in China

Until 1504, venereal disease was unknown in China, and this was not because it had not yet been correctly diagnosed, for at that time Chinese Traditional Medicine was already well advanced and hundreds of diseases had been accurately described in manuscripts which are still extant.

In that year, the old colonialists introduced syphilis into Canton and it soon spread widely throughout the whole land.

Syphilis is a 'social disease'—that is, a disease whose incidence and spread (and, as we shall see, its decline and eradication) are dependent on social and political factors. What were the political and social factors responsible for the hold it gained in China?

Firstly, imperialism and colonialism, the forcible occupation of her territory by invading countries, the subjugation of her people and the wrecking of her economy. In 1877, more than three hundred years after the introduction of syphilis into Canton, the British Admiral in Shanghai, concerned about the mounting incidence of venereal disease among the sailors under his command, summoned his Surgeon-Commander and between them they devised a scheme to protect them. They instituted a totally illegal system of compulsory medical examination of prostitutes with a fee for examination and a money fine for noncompliance. In the first year the revenue from fines and fees totaled 2,590 taels of silver. But the syphilis rate was unchanged.

Secondly, war, inseparable from imperialism and from the fragmentation of Chinese society consequent upon it.

Invading armies, and indigenous armies in the service of exploiters and oppressors, habitually loot, ravage and rape. They become infected with syphilis and they spread syphilis. The Kuomintang armies had a syphilis rate of about twenty per cent.[2] The incidence of syphilis in Chinese villages was directly proportional to the size and the duration of stay of invading US, Japanese and Kuomintang armies.

Thirdly, poverty, a result of feudal and capitalist exploitation and of the economic backwardness and insecurity they caused.

The editorial of the National Medical Journal of China for September 1920, entitled 'Vice, Famine and Poverty,' reads as follows:

'. . . The year 1920, will, we fear, be marked by much suffering, especially in the North where the long draught killed most of the crops and thus brought 20 *million* people to the verge of starvation. The present famine will swell the ranks of slave girls and prostitutes.'[3]

Fourthly, drug addiction. Until the British East India Company sent the first big shipment of Indian-grown opium into China in 1781, the drug was almost unknown in China. For many years before then, British merchants had bought Chinese tea, silk, cotton-textiles, porcelain and manufactured goods of a quality and variety unknown elsewhere, but in return, China imported very little. Replying to a proposal for wider trade, the Emperor Chien Lung wrote to King George III of England: 'We possess all things. I set no value on things strange or ingenious and have no use for your country's manufactures.' So the British merchants had to pay for China's exports in the silver which they had obtained by selling slaves in silver-rich Mexico and Peru. To halt this drain on their silvers the British East India Company extended the cultivation of the opium poppy in Northern and Central India and boosted sales to China. By 1820, profits from the sale of opium accounted for twenty per cent of the revenue of the British government of India. China's annual imports of opium rose from 2,000 chests (140–160 pounds in each) in 1800 to 40,000 chests in 1838, and silver flowed out of China at such a rate that, between 1832 and 1835, twenty million ounces left the country.

In self-preservation, the Chinese rulers had to act. On 3 June, 1839, Lin Tse-hsu, the special commissioner for Canton, forced the British and American opium merchants to hand over 20,000 chests of opium which he publicly burned. The result was the First Opium War ending in the humiliating Treaty of Nanking (1842) which ceded Hong Kong, opened the door wide to imperialist penetration and guaranteed a huge and exceedingly profitable market for the sale of narcotics.

'Legal' importation of opium into China continued until 1917 and after that 'illegal' importation continued until Liberation in only slightly reduced amounts and at a very much higher rate of profit.

Dr L. T. Wu, engaged in Narcotic Control in 1920, complained: 'What can Chinese government regulations do when advanced countries like Britain and the USA produce and export unlimited quantities of morphine and heroin without any question or supervision of their destination and when there are post-offices throughout China over which the Chinese Government has no control? . . .'[4]

Drugs and prostitution are co-partners in depravity. Most brothels were also opium dens and the girls, who had been sold into prostitution at an early age and who were not free to leave, also became addicts and lost their will to resist.

Fifthly, an attitude to women characteristic of class society which sees women as inferior to men, as their chattels and playthings. In feudal society with its polygamy, concubinage, child-marriage and a complete absence of legal and property rights for women, there was no attempt to disguise the inequality between the sexes. In Western capital-ist society, where the legal trappings of equality exist to a greater or lesser degree, the inferior status of women still persists in a concealed form, and organs for moulding public opinion, from glossy magazines to television, inculcate on obsessive pre-occupation with sex and present a picture of woman as little more than the sum total of her vital statistics.

World-wide Trends in Venereal Disease

We have seen that the spread of venereal disease in China was closely connected with policies pursued by 'advanced' imperialist countries.

What was happening within these countries themselves? In 1905, Paul Ehrlich, after 606 experiments, discovered the world's first chemotherapeutic drug, Salvarsan, which he named 606. It was thought that one dose would cure syphilis and it was hailed as a beneficent contribution to civilization. Some, however, were less enthusiastic. If veneral disease can be so easily cured, they argued, then this drug will become a license for lechery; venereal disease will disappear but fornication will flourish. They need not have worried. Venereal disease did not disappear. Neither did it after Penicillin, a much more potent drug, was discovered. It takes more than drugs to eliminate syphilis just like, as the Vietnamese are showing, it takes more than weapons to win a war.

Since 1957, syphilis has continually increased in the USA where there are at least 1.2 million *untreated* cases.[5]

According to minimal official estimates, the venereal disease rate among the invading US forces in Vietnam in 1966 was ten per cent[6] although other estimates put the figure as high as forty per cent. The incidence is still increasing, for in the first months of 1967, 46,561 *new* cases of venereal disease were reported among US troops in Vietnam as compared with 27,701 cases for the same period the previous year.[7] Venereal disease ranks highest of six major diseases among US troops in Vietnam.

There has been a huge increase in venereal disease in Australia in the past six years.

A Christchurch specialist, Dr. W. M. Platts, states that 'last year sixty per cent of New Zealand girls attending VD clinics were under the age of twenty—a proportion approached only by Sweden. . . . In 1955 the disease seemed to be under medical control . . . but since then the incidence of gonorrhoea has passed the peak reached in the 1930s. It had risen not only in New Zealand but in most parts of the world.'

VD in Britain, especially among teenagers has been rising alarmingly and is now the second largest group of notifiable diseases after measles. The incidence of gonorrhoea doubled in a decade and that of infectious syphilis trebled in the six years up to 1965. Venereologist Dr. Catterall of the Middlesex Hospital, London, describes the world-wide epidemic of venereal disease as 'one of the major health problems of the second half of the twentieth century'.

In 1963, Ambrose King and Claude Nichol, president and vice-president

respectively of the International Union against VD, stated:[8] 'Shortly after the Second World War there were high hopes that the venereal diseases were nearing extinction, and it has been a surprise to many that in a settled and prosperous society at peace and with potent therapeutic agents to hand, these diseases should be causing anxiety. In recent years there has been an increase in the incidence of syphilis and gonorrhoea in many countries. . . . At any rate, it seems that the problem of the venereal diseases is with us for the foreseeable future.'

The Incidence of VD in Pre-Liberation China

Since the Kuomintang health authorities left behind no reliable official statistics, estimates of its pre-Liberation incidence must be based either on figures published at the time by individual research workers or on conditions which were found to exist soon after Liberation.

In most National Minority areas[9] the incidence of syphilis was more than ten per cent. There were many reasons for this very high incidence including poverty, ignorance, superstition and oppression by their own feudal rulers, by Han landlords and merchants and by marauding warlords. Many of these National Minority societies were very primitive and, in some, slavery was only abolished after Liberation. Feudal lords and religious leaders (the latter nominally celibate) took what women they wished and spread venereal disease far and wide. There were no medical services to speak of and what there were, were beyond the reach of ordinary persons.

The offspring of the feudal or religious aristocracy were habitually put out to be wet-nursed by slave or serf women and, if the babies had congenital syphilis, they infected their wet-nurses.

In cities and urban areas, the incidence was five per cent and in the countryside it averaged between one and three per cent. However, in those rural areas ravaged by the Kuomintang armies, it was much higher.

When one recalls that China has a population of seven hundred million, the magnitude of the problem becomes clearer. There were some tens of millions of syphilis scattered throughout the country, most of them suffering from latent syphilis but many still potentially infectious.

The Present Venereal Disease Situation in China

The present position can be stated in one short sentence.

ACTIVE VENEREAL DISEASE HAS BEEN COMPLETELY ERADICATED FROM MOST AREAS AND COMPLETELY CONTROLLED THROUGHOUT CHINA.

This is a sweeping statement but I am convinced that it is true.

I now give some fragments of the vast mass of facts on which it is based.

In Peking it is impossible to find active syphilitic lessons to demonstrate to medical students. A generation of doctors is growing up in China with no direct experience of syphilis but this is of little consequence for the disease will never return.

At a conference held in the Research Institute of Dermatology and Venereal Disease of the Chinese Academy of Medical Sciences in January 1956,[10] specialists from eight major cities reported that a total of only twenty-eight cases of infectious syphilis had been discovered in their areas in the four years 1952–55. An investigation of infectious syphilis in seven major cities between 1960 and 1964 showed that by the end of this period, the early syphilis rate was less than twenty cases per hundred million of population per year; that is, it had very nearly reached the point of extinction.

In the National Minority areas, especially in those where the syphilis rate had been highest, a striking fall occurred in the ten years between 1951 and 1960. In the Wulatechien Banner of Inner Mongolia, where the syphilis rate had been nearly fifty per cent in 1952, not a single case of infectious syphilis was found among 3,158 persons examined at random in 1962. In the Jerimu Banner of the Djarod League, which had shown a sero-positivity rate of thirty-five per cent in 1952, ninety-seven per cent of the whole population was tested for syphilis and not a single new, infectious or congenital case was found.

Before Liberation, one of the harmful effects of the widespread syphilis in Minority areas was a progressive depopulation resulting from lowered fertility, a high miscarriage rate and the large number of babies born dead.

For example, the Ikechao League in Inner Mongolia, which had a population of 400,000 in the seventeenth century, was reduced to 80,000 persons by the time of Liberation. The Hulunbu League, which numbered 10,386 in 1933, had fallen to 7,670 in 1950 and an investigation of 2,334 nomadic families revealed that fifty-eight per cent were childless.

Following the anti-syphilis campaign this depopulation trend was reversed. In the Djarod Banner the population increased from 2,548 to 3,343 in ten years. In the same period, 390 herdsmen's families in Hulunbu League, Wusumu, registered increases of from 14.1 per cent to 21.6 per cent.

My friend Dr Ma Hai-teh, who has actively participated in the anti-syphilis campaign since its inception and to whom I am indebted for much of the material in this chapter, tells me of a Mongolian woman suffering from syphilis who had been married for five years but had not given birth to a live child. She was given a course of treatment in 1952 and the following year she demanded more injections because after the first course she had given birth to a fine baby boy and she wanted another. Tests showed that she had been cured and she was not seen again until the ten-year follow-up when she appeared with 8 children, having left one at home. This time she stated flatly that whatever the doctors said, she would have no more injections. She now had a big enough family and was satisfied!

In the rural areas, intensive search shows that the disease has been virtually eliminated. In Hsingku and Ningtu counties in Kiangsi province, a follow-up study five years after the anti-syphilis campaign revealed no new cases or recurrences. In 1960, a complete dermatological examina-tion of the entire population in Chaoan county (population 746,495) Kwangtung province, and Haian county (population 225,305) Kiangsu province, revealed only one case of secondary recurrent syphilis, and a re-survey of fifty per cent of the population of these two counties in 1964 showed not a single infectious case.

How the Victory Was Won

Since, as has been shown, the spread and persistence of syphilis in any country is due to social and political factors, it can only be eliminated by tackling these factors. That is to say, only an all-round political, as opposed to a purely technical, medical or legislative approach can ever solve the problem.

The conquest of syphilis in China within a few years of the conquest of power by the Chinese working class is an outstanding example of the decisive role of politics in tackling major health problems.

There were two essential preconditions for the elimination of syphilis from China. The first was the establishment of the socialist system which ended exploitation and made the oppressed masses the masters of their fate. The second was the equipping of all those involved in the campaign, whether lay or medical, with a determination to serve the people and help socialist construction, with the method of thinking of Mao Tse-tung, so that they would be able to surmount all difficulties confronting them.

The following measures were carried out on the basis of these two prerequisities:

The Elimination of Prostitution

Within a few weeks of Liberation, most of the brothels were closed down by the direct action of the masses. The vast majority of the people recognized that prostitution was harmful and that it constituted crude exploitation of the prostitutes who, for the most part, had been driven into prostitution by poverty or by brute force. Brothel keepers who were scoundrels, drug-peddlers or gangsters were dealt with directly by the angry masses or handed over to the Public Security forces. The few remaining brothels were closed down by Government order in 1951 when prostitution was made illegal.

The prostitutes were treated as victims of an evil social system. First it was necessary to cure the venereal diseases which affected more than ninety per cent of them and then to embark on their social rehabilitation. Those who had been prostitutes for only a short time were encouraged to go home and were found jobs. It was patiently explained to their family that no shame was attached to having been a victim of the old society and that now everyone who did an honest job was worthy of respect. Those who were deep rooted in prostitution were asked to enter Rehabilitation Centres where they studied the policy of the Government towards them, the nature of the new order, the reasons why they had become prostitutes and the new prospects which were opening up for them providing they themselves were willing to make a contribution. The flood-gates of the past were opened at 'Speak Bitterness' meetings which revealed reasons for their former oppression and degradation. At the same time they were taught a trade and spent part of the day in productive work for which they were paid at the same rate as other workers. They were free to leave whenever they wished and were encouraged to organize their own committees for study, work and recreation. Those who were illiterate learned to read and write. Those who could sing, dance, act or write plays gave performances in their own centres and in others in different parts of the country. Visits from family members were encouraged. When their rehabilitation was complete, they were either found jobs in the city or returned to their native villages where their economic security was guaranteed. One of them, Lu Shen Li, ex-prostitute from Kiangsu province, wrote a most moving letter in which she said, 'People in different societies have different fates. The old society made people into devils; the new society makes devils into people.'

Now the Rehabilitation Centres have all closed down for there is no further need for them. Some have been converted into factories and among their veteran workers are ex-prostitutes, most of whom have married and some have joined the Communist Party.

The Transformation of the Position of Women

The closure of brothels and legislation outlawing prostitution cannot, of course, be equated with the elimination of prostitution or with the complete emancipation of women. The only fundamental way to do this is first to change the structure of society and then change the thinking of those who comprise it. The first found expression in the Common Programme of the Chinese People's Political Consultative Conference of 1949 and the Marriage Law of 1950 which freed women from feudal bondage and gave them equal rights with men.

Changing the moral values and deep-rooted customs of millions of people takes a very long time and necessitates unremitting effort. Great progress has been made since Liberation and Chinese women are now approaching genuine equality with men. They occupy important posts in every sphere of governmental, political, productive and cultural work, and sex relations based on inequality are disappearing. Although it would be an exaggeration to say that they have already achieved 100 per cent emancipation, it can be confidently stated that history has never before witnessed such a transformation in the status of women as has happened in China since 1949.

The Elimination of Poverty

Although China is still a poor country, it is possible to talk of the elimination of poverty because poverty is relative and only has meaning in relation to the productive level and social system of a given country at a given time. Certainly a situation such as that quoted above, in which twenty million people were described as being on the verge of starvation and in which an influx of

girl slaves and prostitutes into the cities was regarded as inevitable, cannot recur. No one in China is allowed to fall below a subsistence level, to starve, to become homeless or to be without adequate clothing. No one is forced to beg or steal in order to stay alive. No one is burdened down by debt. Millions of new jobs have been created and a widespread system of social security is being built up. A clause in the Constitution reads: "Working people in the People's Republic of China have the right to material assistance in old age and in case of illness or disability.'

The economic roots of prostitution and crime have been cut for ever.

Mass Campaigns against Syphilis

The First National Health Conference in August 1950 adopted four guiding principles:
Health work should primarily serve the masses of the labouring people.
Chief emphasis should be placed on the prevention of disease.
Close unity should be fostered between traditional and modern doctors.
Health work should, whenever appropriate, be conducted by mass campaigns with the active participation of medical workers.

In the same year the Ministry of Health organized teams to investigate the venereal disease situation throughout the country and to work out plans for prevention and treatment. The following year an assault on venereal diseases in the National Minority regions was started.

In 1954, the Central Research Institute of Dermatology and Venereology was established to coordinate the field work and initiate appropriate research and training programmes.

In 1958, the Research Institute organized pilot projects in eight different provinces and when some initial successes have been scored, the Ministry of Health called a nationwide conference to study the experience gained in Ningtu county, Kiangsi. Characteristically, the conference was held in the little township where the work had actually been done and where participants could see it with their own eyes, discuss it with the local people and gain first-hand experience of its successes and problems.

Mobilizing an Army of Fighters against Syphilis

To find and treat millions of cases of syphilis and change the attitude of tens of millions of ordinary folk towards venereal disease, the existing corps of medical personnel was totally inadequate. A new approach was needed involving the mobilizing and training of thousands of paramedical workers and immediately a number of highly controversial questions arose. What sort of people should be trained? What minimal educational standards should they possess? How, where and in what should they be trained? Were qualified doctors from the old society able to train others or did they themselves need to learn more before they could teach?

In the course of prolonged and at times heated discussions it gradually became clear that to meet the challenge of eliminating venereal disease from the world's most populous country, the basic necessity was for medical workers to acquire a new philosophy, and a new style of work based on the thinking of Mao Tsetung.

At the same time, they needed to become familiar with the signs and symptoms of venereal disease, with the technique of blood testing and with methods of treatment.

This combination of political and professional qualifications is in China called becoming 'Red and Expert'.

Once agreement had been reached on these basic principles, it was easy to find the answers to the controversial questions concerning methods of training and recruitment.

As the work progressed and particularly as the formerly backward Minority regions caught up with the rest of China, the training and composition of medical teams underwent a change. For example, in 1952 when the first medical team went to Inner Mongolia, all its sixty members came from Peking, for there were not yet any modern Mongolian doctors. They lived and worked in yurts, a sort of felt-covered wigwam. In 1962, for the much bigger task of re-surveying the entire population, all but six of the team were Mongolians and they had access to first-class laboratory facilities in the newly-built medical school in Paotow. In 1962, there were 177,418 primary and secondary school students and 2,517 college students in Mongolia whereas, at the time of Liberation, ninety per cent of Mongolians had been illiterate.

The teachers had, for the most part, been trained in the old society as private practitioners and so they, together, with the trainees, studied politics and especially the 'Three Old Articles',[11] learned to mix with ordinary people and tried to get rid of their old feelings of conceit and superiority for, as Chairman Mao put it, 'To be a teacher of the people, one must first be a pupil of the people.'

Gradually, on the basis of a common political outlook, unity was established between teachers and pupils, between traditional and modern doctors, between the masses and the whole body of medical and paramedical workers, and this unity was further strengthened during the course of the actual work.

New Methods of Case Finding

To find the millions of cases of latent syphilis scattered throughout the country was an immense undertaking which could not be tackled along orthodox lines.

Opinions were divided as to how it could be done. Those with conservative, stereotyped thinking urged greater working efficiency, more personnel, better and speedier methods of blood tests and more expenditure. Theirs was a purely technical approach. Those who could think in a bold, revolutionary way urged a political approach, with reliance on the initiative of the masses as the key to success. The political approach won out, although not without a struggle. . . .

In a county in Hopei province, after prolonged discussions between political and medical workers, a form was drawn up asking ten questions, an affirmative answer to any one of which would suggest the possibility of syphilis. These ten questions contained 'clues' such as a history of a skin rash, falling hair, genital sore or exposure to the risk of infection. To draw up the questionnaire was one thing; to persuade tens of thousands of people to fill it in, honestly and conscientiously, was quite another thing. To do this intensive propaganda and education was carried out by anti-syphilis fighters who were able to make close contact with the people, give them the concept that they should liberate themselves, and enlist them as allies in the struggle. Propaganda posters were put up in the village streets, one-act plays performed in the market place, talks given over the village radio system and meetings, big and small, held night after night at which the purpose of the questionnaire was explained and the co-operation of the peasants gradually won. The opening talk would be brief and to-the-point and would go something like this: 'Comrades, syphilis is a disease that was bequeathed to us by the rotten society we have thrown out. It's no fault of yours if you have syphilis and no shame should be attached to it. It's only shameful if you cling to your syphilis when you can easily get rid of it. We've got rid of the landlords and the blood-sucking government that looked after *their* interests and now we have a government that looks after *ours*. We have a Party that speaks for us and shows us how to go forward. Now it calls on us to get rid of syphilis and we should seize the opportunity. This form asks ten questions and you should answer them honestly. We will be glad to help any of you who can't read or write. If you don't remember the answers to some of the questions, ask your friends and relatives. In fact, there's nothing wrong with friends and relatives jogging your memories even when they're not asked. This is *our* country now and we should all be concerned about the well-being of everyone else.

'Comrades, we're going forward to Communism and we can't take this rotten disease with us.'

At first in some places the response was slow; few villagers filled in the questionnaire and some of those who did so, concealed one or other of the 'clues'. More propaganda was done and more meetings were called at which the main speakers were those who had already been diagnosed as having syphilis and had been cured by a few injections. They told of the mental struggles they had gone through before admitting to the clues, and of their feelings after they had been cured. They recalled the brutality and indifference of the old days and contrasted it with the present.

The trickle of diagnosed cases increased until it became a torrent. News of the questionnaire, spread by political workers, attracted peasants from far and wide who came to the treatment centres eager to be diagnosed and treated.

All those having clues were given a blood test and it was found that one in twenty of them actually had syphilis. This reduced the problem of case finding to manageable proportions, but the skeptics were not convinced. They said this method was too crude, that it was not scientific, that politics couldn't diagnose syphilis, that it wasn't known how many cases had been missed. Accordingly, the Research Institute decided to test the method, improved in the light of experience, in Ningtu county, Kiangsi province, where the VD rate was known to be high.

The People's Communes assembled three thousand volunteers, some of whom, after suitable study, were given the political task of mobilizing the people to regard the fight against syphilis as their own fight. The remainder were given a seven-day course on the principles of diagnosis and treatment, at the end of which they examined some 3,000 people under the scutiny of experts, who checked on their results, questioned them, and watched them perform blood tests. Eighty per cent of the trainees passed this stringent practical and theoretical examination and thereby qualified to work independently. One old professor, who had been particularly skeptical, examined a trainee for twenty minutes without getting a wrong answer to his probing questions. He then graciously expressed his complete approval in the classical Chinese phrase, 'I bow to the ground with all the five points of my body.'

The campaign went on for two

months, covering not only syphilis, but also such diseases as ringworm of the scalp, leprosy and malaria. Forty-nine thousand cases were examined and treated.

Then the results were checked. Some 30,000 people who had been 'processed' by the trainees on the basis of the questionnaire were given a full clinical and serological examination by qualified doctors. It was found that 90.2 per cent of all sufferers from venereal disease had been discovered.

The value of the mass line method had been conclusively proved and the baffling problem of finding one case in a hundred or one case in a thousand among 500 million peasants had been solved.

In the National Minority areas, this method was not suitable and total population surveys were carried out.

In the cities, several case-finding methods were used including examination of collected age groups of service trade groups, of army entrants, of those about to marry, of pregnant women and of residents in particular lanes and localities. In some cities, the whole population was covered; in others, only those sections who were particularly at risk. In Shanghai, where the VD rate at the time of Liberation was as high as five per cent, the whole population was tested and to do this some 3,600 technicians were trained to perform the rapid fresh blood slide test for syphilis, which gives an answer of ninety-two per cent accuracy within twenty minutes and which requires only two drops of blood from a prick in the ear.

Active Treatment

Once the sufferers from syphilis had been discovered, treatment was a relatively simple matter although this, too, aroused some controversy around the question as to whether or not trainees with little knowledge and experience should be allowed to give treatment. Some elderly doctors with a strong 'closed-shop' mentality, argued that it would be unethical and unwise to allow such people to carry out treatment. But the Ningtu experience refuted their arguments and, moreover, it was obvious that for many years to come there would not be enough fully qualified doctors to carry the work load.

Penicillin was proved to be superior to all other forms of treatment and Chinese antibiotic factories were by now producing enough to supply all domestic needs, leaving a surplus for sending to improvised newly-emerging nations.

Criteria of Cure

The new approach to syphilis demanded a concept of cure which extended beyond the individual to include the whole community. The criteria for community cure were strict. They included the finding and treatment of all existing cases, a total absence of new cases appearing in the community, disappearance of congenital syphilis in new-born babies, and normal pregnancies and pregnancy outcomes in previously treated mothers. When these criteria had been fulfilled and maintained for five years the community was considered to be cured. This has already been achieved in most areas and soon, with continued follow-up measures to defect the rare case of recurrent or congenital syphilis, it will undoubtedly be reached throughout the country.

That it how China, once the so-called 'sick man of Asia', became the first country in the world to conquer syphilis.

Notes

1. *Nat. Med. Journ. of China, No. 6,* 1920, *p.* 226.
2. Lai, D. G., et al. 'Incidence of syphilis among Chinese Soldiers in Swatow.' *Chinese Med. Journal*, 42, 557, 1928.
3. *Nat. Med. Journ. of China, Sept.* 1920. *Vol. VI, No. 3.*
4. *Nat. Med. Journ. of China No. 6, 1920, p.* 66.
5. Clark, E. G. 'Untreated Syphilis and Natural Course.' *Proceedings* 12*th International Congress of Dermatology*, 2, 855. *Washington.*
6. *US News and World Report. May* 1966.
7. *US News and World Report.* 16 *October,* 1967. *p.* 37.
8. King, A., and Nichol, C. *Venereal Diseases*, ed. I, pp. 7–9, *Cassel, London*, 1964.
9. These are regions of the People's Republic of China where the majority of the inhabitants are of non-Han nationality. They have their own language, dress, religion and customs. Although they number no more than 6% of the Chinese people, the territories in which they have regional autonomy cover some 60% of the area of the Chinese People's Republic and 14.6% of deputies to the National People's Congress are members of National Minorities.
10. Dr Ma Hai-teh, *China's Medicine, No.* 1. *Oct.* 1966.
11. 'In Memory of Norman Bethune.' Mao Tse-tung, *Selected Works, Vol. II, p.* 337; 'Serve the People.' Mao Tse-tung, *Selected Works, Vol. III, p.* 227; 'The Foolish Old Man Who Removed Mountains.' Mao Tse-tung, *Selected Works, Vol. III, p.* 321.

44 HELPING ONE ANOTHER: A SPECULATIVE HISTORY OF THE SELF-HELP MOVEMENT

Irving Kenneth Zola

The roots of mutual-aid groups harken back to the frontier days of the United States. As early as the 1st part of the 19th century, Alexis de Toqueville noted the American penchant for joining groups,[1] and by 1900 a directory listed over 250 independent national voluntary lay organizations. For most of these organizations, be they men's service clubs, women's clubs, or others, the goal of helping, though often central to their avowed reason for being, was rather external to the members themselves. Those to be helped were the community in general or some specific cause or disease.

The shift from voluntary associa-

SOURCE: Reproduced with permission of *Archives of Physical Medicine and Rehabilitation*, vol. 60 (October 1979), pp. 452–456.

tions for helping others to mutual-aid organizations to help each other, was, however, not an easy one. Though some have found examples of such activities in early agricultural cooperatives,[2] the mass waves of immigration of the late 19th and early 20th century were the clearest stimuli to their proliferation.[3] Thrust into a nation in which there were few formal services to aid in their survival, the new arrivals turned to one another. Their response was the creation of mutual-aid societies where membership was based primarily on sharing some explicit social characteristic: race, religion, country of origin. Interestingly, by far the most "popular" of their services, though basic to life, came at the end of it: namely burial and funeral rites. A far-distant 2nd service was the lending of money. Thus, in these early self-help groups, the aid given to one another was of the most material sort. From this tangible kind of service, aid of a more social or psychologic nature was truly a giant step.

The difficulty of this step is illustrated in the history of that best-known of illness-oriented voluntary organizations: The March of Dimes. For here, where the rehabilitation problems of young children were enormous as well as controversial, there was no "coming together" of the afflicted. When it is remembered that polio patients were not isolated from one another and even had clinics, wards, and hospitals devoted to their exclusive treatment, then the fact that no support organization, however informal, ever arose or was encouraged is even more surprising.

In retrospect it seems that there was a kind of undertone that such activity might be considered inappropriate. Everything that could be done was being done *for* you. In a distortion of the recent slogan, "Do your own thing," it became, "Do your own suffering and managing, and keep your problems to yourself."

Three Barriers to Self-Help

From such examples I infer that there must have been a number of barriers which impeded the development of medical self-help organizations. Three barriers that seem most basic were: 1) the nature of the problems to which such groups were devoted; 2) the nature of the help required in dealing with the problems; and 3) the nature of the personnel best suited to give that help.

On several levels the diseases with which mutual-aid societies dealt were long considered socially unacceptable. Most concretely the groups dealt with issues of "loss" and "deficiency," from a missing body part or function—the ability to walk, to see, to hear, to speak, to urinate, to defecate—to the most taboo of psychologic traits, the inability to control certain aspects of one's behavior, such as gambling, drinking, drugs, sexuality, mental illness, obesity. There is no doubt a continuum of taboo problems, with several such as hearing, seeing, and walking, being far less stigmatized than others, such as facial disfigurement or colostomy.

But toleration for being less than perfect even in these respects is a very recent phenomenon. Only in the current generation of teenagers is the taunt, "Boys never make passes at girls who wear glasses," a ludicrous one. On the other hand we, the older generation, are still "hung up" on even the "most accepted" of handicaps: We speak louder to the deaf, avoid mentioning the beauty of scenes to the blind, and reprimand our children for staring at someone with a limp. All of this is complicated by our country's commitment to a belief that there is *no* problem that cannot be ultimately overcome. Thus unsolved problems or diseases come to represent a failure, and the bearers or survivors become constant reminders of this inadequacy. As such, a general response was to put them as far as possible out of sight and out of mind.

A 2nd barrier, the nature of the help that such problems entailed, was also threatening. For the idea of being in need of help is not an accepted theme in the Western world. No aphorism regarding help is known so well as "The Lord helps those who help themselves." Independence was the byword. Achievement against all odds and all comers was the measure of success. Horatio Alger was for many years the embodiment of the American ideal—a person who overcame his background to attain success. So too the folk heroes of chronic disease were not the millions who came to terms with their problems but those few who were so successful that they *passed*—the polio victim who broke track records, the one-legged baseball pitcher who made the major leagues, the great composer who

was deaf, the famous singer who had a colostomy. They were all so good that no one knew, and therein lay part of their glory.

In fact, it may be that the emphasis on such successes has done more harm than good for the majority of people with disabilities. For it masks the real kinds of help that the sufferers of chronic conditions need. Management in daily living does not involve doing dramatic tasks, but mundane ones. And these examples of someone overcoming a handicap once and for all certainly masks the time element required for such help. Most of this aid can neither be given nor utilized in a single encounter or short series of encounters. And the problem is not, for the majority, a temporary one but one that will last for *life*. That is what chronic means! How uncomfortable this makes people feel is frequently seen in the negative response to mutual-aid organizations which state this lifetime commitment explicitly, such as Alcoholics Anonymous, Synanon, Re-Evaluation Counseling, and the current Independent Living Movement.

The 3rd barrier to any widespread acceptance of mutual aid was the nature of the personnel involved in giving help—our enormous worship of the technical expert, especially the physician. For modern medical care has been, and to a large extent still is, the exclusive province of the physician. It has been hard enough for the physician to give up tasks, and inevitably some responsibility, to a growing army of allied health professionals. But these were at least nominally under his authority. Self-help organizations, on the other hand, were essentially lay groups and as such were largely outside medical control. As a result, any good that they could do was scarcely examined. Even when positive results of mutual aid were reported, as in group therapy and encounter groups, they were given little professional recognition and were dismissed as second-choice alternatives. At best they might be viewed as nice things for patients to do to keep themselves occupied and out of trouble. Such forms of help represented self-treatment and this, next to the use of chiropractors, was regarded by the ordinary providers of medical care as worse than no help at all.

Ameliorating Factors

With such formidable forces ranged against the mutual-aid organizations, how did they ever get off the ground? There is no single answer, but a number of events certainly pried open the door. For example, World War II had an enormous impact upon our ability to ignore the seamier aspects of life. Once and for all our insulation was broken. All of us, but particularly those in the Armed Services, confronted different cultures and thus different ways of defining as well as handling problems. In short we saw viable alternatives. Certainly one could argue that the civil rights movement truly got under way here as blacks and whites were forced to come to new definitions of themselves and others. (One might have expected this to have taken place much earlier with the great waves of immigration which inundated our country, but their influence was mitigated both by the vastness of America which permitted great isolation of most "natives" from these groups and by the philosophy of Americanization, which, accepted by the immigrants and encouraged by the residents, consciously attempted to extinguish all salient aspects of the heritage from which they came.)[4]

World War II, however, did more than this. It forced a confrontation with the most massive job of rehabilitation we have ever faced and this made certain kinds of physical handicaps no longer a personal but a national responsibility.

The A-bomb itself and its successor, the H-bomb, provoked the deepest questioning of who we were and what life was all about. At least one outcome of this searing of our social conscience was a financial commitment to the solving of life's problems. So in the postwar era, the National Institutes of Health flourished and some form of national health insurance became increasingly inevitable.

The change in the nature of help that might be needed was being challenged also by certain undeniable realities. With a host of infectious diseases coming under control, more and more people were surviving to middle age and beyond. Thus many latent or previously "numerically insignificant" disorders became more manifest—arthritis, diabetes, mental illness, heart disease, multiple sclerosis, stroke, cancer. Moreover, these were disorders which were more often disabling than immediately fatal, and for which no "magic bullet" either in prevention or in care was forthcoming. In short, they were problems which should require medical management for extended periods of time, some for life.

But there was something more to these disorders; they fundamentally altered the doctor-patient relationship. There was a shift from cure to care. No longer did treatment take place with the doctor doing and the patient receiving. To succeed at all, the patient had to help and, as in psychotherapy, to be an active participant. In short, treatment was something in which the patients themselves had a role—something that had to be recognized by them as well as their former "caretakers."

The Advent of Psychiatric Impact

The coming of age of psychiatry had another impact, for it made abundantly clear the importance of behavior in all aspects of disease— from how one gets sick to whether or not one recovers. In a sense it reemphasized the oneness of a person's mind and body—a phenomenon so evident in the almost ever-expanding category of disorders called psychosomatic. Thus, terms like "support" and "relationship" could no longer be something in medical care to be done if one had the time, but were at the very core of helping. And yet this was not an activity for which many health personnel felt trained or inclined. Even were they willing to actively undertake such a role, it is not clear that

numerically they would ever fill the need.

For given the current demand, the shortage of physicians is insurmountable and we are too committed to a line of scientific inquiry and specialization to ever turn back. No matter how many doctors now choose the path of primary care or community medicine, doctors in general continue to be more specialized rather than less. Thus partly by default and partly by delegation, many medical tasks—from history-taking to prescibing drugs, from giving injections to performing certain forms of surgery, from teaching to counseling—ultimately came to be done by people who were not MDs. The biggest jump, however, was not in the delegation of responsibility to less-trained personnel but in the taking over of many therapeutic tasks by people who had "been there" or were still "there." In short, the "expertise" of patients to help themselves and others began to be recognized.

The recognition of such expertise is at best a struggle. The world in general and the medical world in particular still too often feel they are in the best position to know what is in the best interests of the disabled. Often they contend it is their years of experience and lack of personal involvement which makes them see our needs more clearly. A personal experience shows how occasionally ludicrous this claim can be:

> I entered the workshop of a prosthetist who had been in the business for over 50 years. Noting that I had

had polio and use a cane to walk, he motioned me to come near.

He:

"I wonder if you'd try this cane." I did so.

He:

"Well, what do you think?"

IKZ:

"It seems solid enough."

He:

"Now watch this." He then proceeded to take the cane from me and pushed a little button about 3 inches from the handle, and out popped a 12-inch blade.

Before I could say another word, he went on: "This one is even handier; look!" Taking another cane, he also pressed a button and now brandished what might be called a 10-inch iron blackjack. "You know," he went on, "in times like these, crime in the streets and all, things like this self-defense cane should be pretty handy."

IKZ:

"Yes," (in my best tongue-in-cheek fashion) "particularly if the thief lets me lean on him for support while I dismantle my cane."

In a certain basic sense I feel that no matter how sophisticated or even understanding the unafflicted become, the sufferers will ultimately have to see to their own needs by banding together and pushing. This is not merely because the general public does not care but because, in a real sense, they do not know. It is not accidental that major changes in the architecture of public buildings have been pushed by paraplegics, reduction of drug maintenance costs by "mended hearts," extension of medical insurance coverage by ostomates, new speech therapies by the laryngectomies, or a new profession, enterostomal therapy, largely created and staffed by former patients. Thus public interest is not stirred by large numbers of "problem-bearers" alone. There have always been millions of poor, of black, and of consumers, as Michael Harrington has pointed out in "The Other America."[3] It has always taken something more to stir society to action.

Thus while there is some recognition of the legitimacy of the self-help movement and the people it represents, the acceptance of the voices of the disabled is grudging at best. Even with the greater attention to problems of chronic disease and disability, there is a way society speaks of them which perpetuates a separation and a distancing. It seems that, to justify rising health costs as well as the financial expenditure that it will supposely take to remove current architectural and programmatic barriers, we must quantify the extent of the problem. And yet in so doing we distort an important reality. By trying to find strict measures of disability we make into dichotomous categories what are indeed a series of blurry, continually changing continua. By agreeing that there are 20 million disabled or 36 million, or even half the population, in some way affected by disability, we delude ourselves into thinking there is some finite (no matter how large) number of people. In this way, both in the defining and in the measuring, we try to make the reality of disease, disability, and death problematic, and in this way make it at least potentially someone else's problem. But it is not, and can never be. Any person reading the words on this page is "at best" momentarily able-bodied. But everyone reading them will, at some point, suffer from at least one or more chronic diseases and will be disabled, temporarily or permanently, for a significant portion of his or her life.

That we persist in this denial means that the necessary steps to undo this process are likely to be difficult to acknowledge as well as to undertake. But at least 3 steps suggest themselves. First, we with handicaps and chronic disabilities must see to our own interests. We must free ourselves from the "physicality" of our conditions and the dominance of our life by the medical world.[6] In particular, I refer to the number of times we think of ourselves and are thought of by others in terms of our specific chronic conditions. We are polios, cancers, paras, deaf, blind, lame, amputees, and strokes. Whatever else this does, it blinds us to our common social disenfranchisement. Our forms of loss may be different, but the resulting invalidity is the same.

While organizing around specific diseases may have great benefits for raising research monies, it has divided our strength and pitted one disease group against the other. Not only has this led to an overspecialization of services but to underdevelopment of our consciousness. It has made us feel so dependent on others

(the medical world for treatment, the general public for money) and so personally accountable that it has made us feel that we have no the rights. We, patients all, perhaps the last and potentially the largest of America's disenfranchised, must organize on our own behalf. Cutting across specific disease entities, we must create advocacy, consciousness-raising, counseling, resource groups.[7] And wherever and whenever possible, staff members alike must have a chronic disease and/or physical handicap. I am not claiming that no one else can help or understand, but that, as with women and blacks, we are at a point in history where "having been there" is essential in determining where to go.

The self-help movement is, however, but one part of the struggle. It is a prerequisite for change, but neither the sole nor the sufficient avenue. We must deal as much with social arrangements as with self-conceptions; one, in fact, reinforces the other. Thus the problems of those with a chronic disability should be stated not in terms of the individual defects and incapacities affecting our *physical* functioning, but in terms of the limitations and obstacles placed in the way of our daily *social* functioning. What should be asked is not how much it will cost to remake a society completely, so as to be accessible to all with physical difficulties but rather why a society has been created and perpetuated which has excluded so many of its members.

There is a growing awareness that this exclusion is not an accidental byproduct of industrial society. There is an ideologic compatibility between the rise of capitalism and certain Western religions which have continually justified the hierarchical arrangements of people through "hard work" or "the grace of God." When the notions of religion and law were beginning to lose their power as absolute arbiters of important social values, Darwin, perhaps unwittingly ushered in the age of biologic determinism. One critic of the times realized the social import of his work by exclaiming in surprise: "Sir, you are preaching scientific Calvinism with biological determinism replacing religious predestination." The fixity of the universe and/or hierarchic relations once attributed to God was now being justified by scientific inevitabilities. In the ensuing hundred years, there has been an expansion of the influence of science in general and in particular of "medical science," until they have in some ways replaced religion and law. Where once a social rhetoric made reference to good and evil, legal and illicit, now it is to "healthy" and "sick."

We are now experiencing a medicalization of society, and with it medicine as an agent of social control. And while some have argued that this is a more humane and liberal way to deal with social problems, the notions of health and illness still locate the source of trouble and treatment in individual capacities, not social arrangements.[8]

In the most concrete terms, to have a portion of our population declared physically unfit serves many important social functions. In still another way it is important to recognize in this country that health occupations are the fastest growing category of employment, the medical world is in the highest income bracket, and health-related industries are amongst the most profit making.[9] Crassly put, "Some people are making money off of the sufferings of others." In these 2 ways, economic and political motives of the society have come to reinforce one another. And until the day that no one benefits economically, socially, or psychologically from someone else being beneath them, there will always be categories of exclusion.

Conclusions

Regardless of whether we join activist groups, support those who do, or seek in other ways to change the sociopolitical-economic structure of America, we must at the very least look into ourselves. For if morality or justice is not sufficient as a motivating force, perhaps personal survival will be. All of us must contend with our continuing inevitable vulnerability. Not to do so can only make us further unprepared for the exigencies of life. For when we grow old, and with today's technology "survive," sick and disabled, for increasingly longer periods of time, we will experience a triple sense of powerlessness: First, because of our very condition, we will indeed be more physically and socially dependent. Second, through our previous denial, we will have deprived ourselves of the knowledge and resources to cope. And third, from the realization of what we will have done to those who have "aged" before us, we feel we have lost our right to protest.

To the extent that we all feel we are receiving our "just deserts," it is very hard to demand any redress of the situation. We are left to the largesse of others to forgive us and to help us. Is it thus any wonder that study after study reports many of the elderly as feeling that their life has been worthless? A sour ending to any story cannot help but result in a depreciation not only of the present but of the past.

In this light, it is especially important to remember what Erik Erikson said[10] about society's continual denigration and isolation of the aged:

> Any span of the [life] cycle lived without vigorous meaning at the beginning, in the middle, or at the end, endangers the sense of life, and the meaning of death in all whose life stages are intertwined.

So too what we do to the physically handicapped and chronically ill, we do only to ourselves.

References

1. De Tocqueville A: Democracy in America, Heffner RD (ed). New York, New American Library, 1961
2. Katz AH, Bender EI: Self-help groups in western society: History and prospects. J Appl Behav Sci **12**:265–282, 1976
3. Handlin O (ed): Immigration as a Factor in American History. Englewood Cliffs, NJ, Prentice-Hall Inc, 1959
4. Glazer N, Moynihan DP: Beyond the Melting Pot. Cambridge, MA, MIT Press, 1963
5. Harrington M: The Other America: Poverty in the United States, New York, MacMillan Co Publishers, 1962
6. Illich ID: Medical Nemesis: the Expropriation of Health. New York, Pantheon Books Inc, 1976
7. Bowe FG, Jacoby JE, Wiseman LD: Coalition Building. Washington DC, American Coalition of Citizens with Disabilities, 1978
8. Illich I, Zola IK, McNight J, Caplan J, Shaiken H: Disabling Professions. London, Calder & Boyars Ltd, 1977
9. Health Policy Advisory Committee (ed): The American Health Empire: Power, Profits, Politics. New York, Random House Inc, 1971
10. Erikson EH: Insight and Responsibility, New York, NW Norton & Co Inc, 1964

45 POPULAR EPIDEMIOLOGY: COMMUNITY RESPONSE TO TOXIC WASTE-INDUCED DISEASE IN WOBURN, MASSACHUSETTS

Phil Brown

Residents of Woburn, Massachusetts, were startled several years ago to learn that their children were contracting leukemia at exceedingly high rates. By their own efforts, the affected families confirmed the existence of a leukemia cluster and demonstrated that it was traceable to industrial waste carcinogens that leached into their drinking water supply. These families put into process a long train of action which led to a civil suit against corporate giants W. R. Grace and Beatrice Foods, which opened in Boston in March 1986. On 28 July 1986, a federal district court jury found that Grace had negligently dumped chemicals on its property; Beatrice Foods was absolved. The case then proceeded to a second stage in which the plaintiffs would have to prove that the chemicals had actually caused leukemia. As this part of the case was under way, the judge decided that the jury had not understood the hydrogeological data that were crucial to the suit, and on 17 September he ordered the case to be retried. Because of this decision, an out-of-court settlement with Grace was reached on 2 September 1986.[1] The Woburn families filed an appeal against Beatrice in May 1987 on the grounds that the judge was wrong to exclude evidence and effects of pre-1968 dumping from the case.

This case has received much na-

tional attention and has had a number of important effects. It has focused public attention on corporate responsibility for toxic wastes and their resultant health effects. For some time now, civic activists have organized opposition to environmental contamination, and the Woburn situation provides a valuable case study which can help to understand, forecast, and perhaps even to catalyze similar efforts in the future. It has also demonstrated that the health effects of toxic wastes are not restricted to physical disease but also include emotional problems. The Woburn plaintiffs were one of the first groups of toxic waste plaintiffs to introduce such evidence in court. These data can expand our knowledge of the effects of toxic wastes as well as our understanding of the psychological effects of disasters and trauma.

Woburn also offers a valuable example of lay communication of risk to scientific experts and government officials. Citizens in other locations and situations have previously attempted to convey risks to appropriate parties. In Woburn and other

SOURCE: From *Science, Technology, and Human Values*, vol. 12, no. 3–4 (Summer/Fall 1987), pp. 76–85. Copyright © by the Massachusetts Institute of Technology and the President and Fellows of Harvard College. Reprinted by permission of John Wiley & Sons, Inc.

recent cases, however, a more concerted effort was made, which involved varying degrees of investigation into disease patterns and their potential or likely causes. I term this type of activity *popular epidemiology*.

Popular epidemiology is defined as the process by which laypersons gather statistics and other information and also direct and marshall the knowledge and resources of experts in order to understand the epidemiology of disease. Popular epidemiology is not merely a matter of public participation in what we traditionally conceive of as epidemiology. Lilienfeld defines epidemiology as "the study of the distribution of a disease or a physiological condition in human populations and of the factors that influence this distribution." These data are used to explain the etiology of the condition and to provide preventive, public health, and clinical practices to deal with the condition.[2] Popular epidemiology includes more elements than the above definition in that it emphasizes basic social structural factors, involves social movements, and challenges certain basic assumptions of traditional epidemiology. Nevertheless I find it appropriate to retain the word "epidemiology" in the concept of popular epidemiology because the *starting point* is the search for rates and causes of disease.

In order to develop the concept of popular epidemiology, I will first provide a brief capsule of the Woburn events. Following that, I will show commonalities between Woburn and other communities in popular epidemiological investigation. Finally, I will expand on the original definition of popular epidemiology by examining in detail five components of that concept.

Brief History of the Woburn Leukemia Cluster

In May 1979 builders found 184 55-gallon drums in a vacant lot along the Aberjona River. They called the police, who then called the state Department of Environmental Quality Engineering (DEQE). Water samples from wells G and H showed large concentrations of organic compounds that were known carcinogens in laboratory animals. Of particular concern were trichloroethylene (TCE) and tetrachlorethylene (PCE). The EPA's risk level for TCE is 27 parts per billion (ppb), and well G had ten times that concentration. The state ordered that both wells be closed due to their TCE and PCE levels.[3]

But town and state officials had prior knowledge of problems in the Woburn water. Frequent complaints about dishwasher discoloration, bad odor, and bad taste had led to a 1978 study by private consultants. They used an umbrella screen for organic compounds and reported a carbon-chloroform extract (CCE) concentration of 2.79 mg/L, while stating that the level should not exceed 0.1 mg/L. This Dufresne-Henry report led Woburn officials to ask the state Department of Public Health (DPH) to allow the town to change its chlorination method, because they assumed that chlorine was interacting with minerals. The DPH allowed this change and in the same letter told the officials not to rely on wells G and H because of high concentrations of salt and minerals. The DPH did not mention another important piece of information it possessed: In 1975 a DEQE engineer, who had been applying a more exact screening test to all wells in the state, found wells G and H to have higher concentrations of organic compounds than nearby wells. In retrospect, he stated that the level seemed high, but "at the time I was doing research only on the method and nobody knew how serious water contamination problems could be." Thus, before the discovery of the visible toxic wastes, both local and state officials had some knowledge of problems in Woburn water and specifically in the two wells in question.[4]

The first popular epidemiological efforts also predated the 1979 well closings. Anne Anderson, whose son, Jimmy, had been diagnosed with acute lymphocytic leukemia in 1972, had gathered information about other cases by word of mouth and by chance meetings with other victims at stores and at the hospital where Jimmy was being treated. She began to theorize that the growing number of leukemia cases may have been caused by something carried in the water. She asked state officials to test the water but was told that this could not be done on an individual's initiative. Anderson's husband did not support her in this effort but rather asked the family pastor to help her get her mind off what he felt to be an erroneous idea. This development led to one of the key elements of the Woburn story, since

Reverend Bruce Young became a major actor in the community's efforts.[5]

Another fortuitous circumstance occurred in June 1979, just weeks after the state ordered the wells shut down. A DEQE engineer, on his way to work, drove past the nearby Industri-Plex construction site and thought that there might be violations of the Wetlands Act. Upon investigation, EPA scientists found dangerous levels of lead, arsenic, and chromium, yet they told neither the town officials nor the public. Only in September did a Woburn newspaper break the news. At this point, Reverend Young began to agree with Anne Anderson's conclusions about the water supply, and so he placed an ad in the Woburn paper, asking people who knew of childhood leukemia cases to respond. He prepared a map and a questionnaire, in consultation with Dr. Truman, the physician treating Jimmy Anderson. Several days later, Anderson and Young plotted the cases. There were 12, with 6 of them closely grouped. The data convinced Truman, who called the Centers for Disease Control (CDC). The activists spread the word through the press and succeeded in persuading the City Council on 19 December 1979 to request the CDC to investigate. In January 1980 Young, Anderson, and 20 other people formed For a Cleaner Environment (FACE) to generate public concern about the leukemia cluster.[6]

Five days after the City Council request to the CDC, the Massachusetts DPH issued a report that contradicted the Young-Anderson map model of the leukemia cluster. According to the DPH, there were 18 cases, when 10.9 were expected, but the difference was not so great for a ten-year period. Further, the DPH argued that a cluster pattern was not present. Despite this blow, the activists were buoyed by growing public awareness of the environmental hazard and by popular epidemiological efforts in other places. In June 1980, Anderson and Young were asked by Senator Edward Kennedy to testify at hearings on the Superfund. Young hold the hearing:

> For seven years we were told that the burden of proof was upon us as independent citizens to gather the statistics. . . . All our work was done independent of the Commonwealth of Massachusetts. They offered no support, and were in fact one of our adversaries in this battle to prove that we had a problem.[7]

On 23, May 1980 the CDC and the National Institute for Occupational Safety and Health (NIOSH) sent John Cutler to lead a team affiliated with the Massachusetts DPH to study the Woburn case. This report, released on 23 January 1981, five days after the death of Jimmy Anderson, stated that there were 12 cases of childhood leukemia in East Woburn, when 5.3 were expected. The incidence of kidney cancer was also elevated. The discussion of the data was, however, inconclusive, since the case-control method failed to finds characteristics that differentiated victims from nonvictims. Further, a lack of environmental data for earlier periods was an obstacle to linking disease with the water supply.[8]

The conjuncture of Jimmy Anderson's death and the report's failure to confirm the water-leukemia hypothesis led the families and friends of the victims, along with their local allies, to question the nature of the scientific study. As DiPerna puts it, a layperson's approach to epidemiological science evolved.[9] The Woburn residents were helped in this direction when Larry Brown from the Harvard School of Public Health (SPH) invited Anderson and Young to present the Woburn data to a SPH seminar. Marvin Zelen, an SPH biostatistician present at the seminar, became interested. At this time, clusters of cancer and other diseases were being investigated around the United States, although the CDC did not inform Woburn residents of this heightened public and scientific interest in cluster studies. Moreover, the DPH issued a follow-up report in November 1981 which stated that the number of childhood leukemia deaths began to rise in the 1959–1963 period, before the wells were drilled. Assuming an average latency period of 2–5 years, the DPH report argued that deaths should not have started to increase until 1969–1973, when in fact the rate was lower than expected.[10]

In order to elicit more conclusive data, Zelen and his colleague, Steven Lagakos, undertook a more detailed study of health status in Woburn, focusing on birth defects and reproductive disorders, since these were widely considered to be environmentally related. The biostatisticians and the FACE activists teamed up in what was to become a major epidemiological study and a prototype of a popular epidemiological alliance between citizen activists and sympathetic scientists. FACE coordinated 301 Woburn volunteers who administered a telephone survey from April to September in 1982, which was designed to reach 70% of the city's population who had phones.[11]

At the same time, the state DEQE conducted a hydrogeology study which found that the bedrock in the affected area of Woburn sloped in a southwest direction and was shaped like a bowl, with wells G and H in the deepest part. The agency's March 1982 report addressed the location of the contamination: the source was not the Industri-Plex site as had been believed, but rather W. R. Grace's Cryovac Division and Beatrice Foods' Riley tannery. This major information led eight families of leukemia victims to file a $400 million suit in May 1982 against those corporations for poor waste disposal practices, which led to groundwater contamination and hence to fatal disease.[12] A smaller company, Unifirst, was also sued but quickly settled before trial.[13]

The Harvard School of Public Health/FACE Study

Sources of data included information on 20 cases of childhood leukemia (ages 19 and under) which were diagnosed between 1964 and 1983, the DEQE water model of regional and temporal distribution of water from wells G and H, and the health survey. The survey gathered data on adverse pregnancy outcomes and childhood disorders from 5,010 interviews, covering 57% of Woburn residences with telephones. The re-

searchers trained 235 volunteers to conduct the health survey, taking precautions to avoid bias.[14]

On 8 February 1984, the Harvard SPH data were made public. Childhood leukemia was found to be significantly associated with exposure to water from wells G and H both on a cumulative basis and on a none-versus-some exposure basis. Children with leukemia received an average of 21.2% of their yearly water supply from the wells compared to 9.5% for children without leukemia. The data do not, however, explain all 11 excess cases; the cumulative method explains 4 excess cases and the none-versus-some metric explains 6 cases.

Controlling for important risk factors in pregnancy, the investigators found that access to contaminated water was not associated with spontaneous abortions, low birth weight, perinatal deaths before 1970, or with musculoskeletal, cardiovascular, or "other" birth anomalies. Water exposure was associated with perinatal deaths since 1970, eye/ear anomalies, and CNS/chromosomal/oral cleft anomalies. With regard to childhood disorders, water exposure was associated with only two of nine categories of disease: kidney/urinary tract and lung/respiratory. There was no association with allergies, anemia, diabetes, heart/blood pressure, learning disability, neurologic/sensory, or "other" disorders.[15] If only in *in-utero* cases are studied, the results are even stronger in terms of the positive associations.[16]

The researchers conducted extensive analyses to demonstrate that the data were not biased. They compared baseline rates of adverse health effects for West Woburn (never exposed to wells G and H water) and East Woburn (at a period prior to the opening of the wells): no differences were found. They examined transiency rates to test whether they were related to exposure and found them to be alike in both sectors. Various tests also ruled out a number of biases potentially attributable to the volunteer interviewers.[17]

The report was greeted with criticism from many circles: the CDC, the American Cancer Society, the EPA, and even the Harvard SPH Department of Epidemiology. These criticisms demonstrate both legitimate concerns and clear examples of elitism and opposition to community involvement in scientific work. One of the legitimate concerns was the grouping of diseases into categories, despite their different etiologies. Similarly, the biostatisticians were criticized for grouping diverse birth defects under the broad heading of "environmentally associated disease."[18] The researchers argue, however, that they grouped defects because there could never be sufficient numbers of each of the numerous defects. Further, they claim that their grouping was based on the literature on chemical causes of birth defects. In fact, if the grouping was incorrect, they note that they would not have found positive results.[19] Some critics questioned whether the water model was precise enough, and whether it was independently verified.[20] Actually, the DEQE officials failed to release the water data in a timely fashion, making it impossible to obtain other validation. A more detailed model is now available, although it has been consis-

tently hard to get funds to conduct new analyses.[21] Critics have also noted that there were increasing numbers of cases even after the wells were shut down, and that these new cases were more likely to be in West Woburn than in East Woburn. If wells G and H were the culprit, such critics ask is it possible that there could be yet another cluster *independent* of the one studied?[22] In fact, given the chemical soup in Woburn, it is indeed plausible that this could be the case. Excavations at the Industri-Plex site produced buried animal hides and chemical wastes. A nearby abandoned lagoon was full of lead, arsenic, and other metals. A sampling from 61 test wells in East Woburn turned up 48 toxic substances on the EPA priority list as well as raised levels of 22 metals.[23]

The criticisms of most interest here are those that argue against the basic concept of public participation in science. Critics held that the study was biased precisely because volunteers conducted the health survey and because the study was based on a political goal. These arguments will be addressed below, as I develop the five elements of popular epidemiology. First, though, we will take a look at commonalities between several communities that engaged in forms of popular epidemiology.

Elements of Popular Epidemiology

Commonalities in Popular Epidemiology

Couto studied Yellow Creek, Kentucky, where residents identified problems of creek pollution caused by untreated residential and commercial sewage. Comparing this and other locations, Couto develops a model which is a valuable starting place on which I shall expand. Couto identifies three sets of actors. The *community at risk* is the community and people at risk of environment hazards. The *community of consequence calculation* includes the public and private officials who allocate resources related to environmental health risks. The *community of probability calculation* consists of epidemiologists and allied scientists.[24]

The community at risk is where popular epidemiological action begins. In Yellow Creek the shared evidence of obvious pollution was from fish kills, disappearances of small animals, and corrosion of screens and other materials. This "street-wise or creek-side environmental monitoring" precedes awareness of health risks.[25] My interviews with Woburn residents show the same phenomenon: People noticed the water stains on dishwashers and the bad odor long before they were aware of any adverse health effects. Love Canal residents remembered years of bad odors, rocks that exploded when dropped or thrown, sludge leakage into basements, chemical residues on the ground after rainfall, and children's foot irritations after playing in fields where toxic wastes were dumped.[26] Residents of South Brunswick, New Jersey, noticed foul tasting water and saw barrels marked "toxic chemicals" dumped, bulldozed, and ruptured.[27]

The next stage in Couto's model is *common sense epidemiology*, where

people intuit that a higher than expected incidence of disease is attributable to pollution.[28] As a result of such judgments, people organize and approach public officials. Another avenue, not mentioned by Couto, is taking the issue to court, for blame, redress, organizing and legitimation. When citizens organize publicly, they first encounter the community of consequence calculation, a community that usually resists them by denying the problem or its seriousness, and even by blaming the problem on the lifestyle and habits of the people at risk.[29] This is in part due to "environmental blackmail," whereby officials fear that plants will close and jobs and taxes will be lost.

The initial shock at the existence of the toxic substances gives way to anger at the public and private officials who do little or nothing about the problem.[30] This reaction is found in residents' attitudes toward corporate and governmental officials in Woburn and in numerous other sites.[31]

In Freudenberg's sample of 110 community groups, 45% claimed that government agencies blocked their access to data. Government resistance is often accompanied by governmental advice to people to alter their lifestyle in order to minimize the risks they face.[32] A Yellow Creek citizen who asked a state official about health effects on future children was told that it was best not to get married. When asked about threats to food gardens, the official advised residents to stop growing their own food.[33] New York state health officials recommended that Love Canal residents who were pregnant or parents of young children move, at a time when the state was not yet prepared to fund such relocation.[34]

The community of consequence calculation eventually challenges the community at risk to provide proof of a danger to human health in order to justify the cost of pollution cleanup or the consequences of a plant closing. This situation leads the community at risk to request help from the community of probability calculation, but this level of proof is typically very expensive, even if scientists are available to provide it. Often, in fact, they are neither available nor willing. University faculty, for instance, often consider such efforts to be outside the regular system of academic reward and prestige. In such cases, the community activists then may attempt their own study, sometimes focusing on *risk assessment* rather than classical epidemiological studies. Such research can demonstrate the existence of health risks and problems and can spur public investigation.

We can now build on Couto's work to generate a broader model of popular epidemiology. Although my examples often involve toxic waste-induced disease, the concept of popular epidemiology clearly extends into other areas.

Popular Participation and the Myth of Value-Neutrality

Popular epidemiology opposes the widely held belief that epidemiology is a value-neutral scientific enterprise which can be conducted in a sociopolitical vacuum. Directly re-

lated to this assumption is the belief that epidemiological work should not be conducted only by experts. Those who criticized volunteer bias and political goals in the Woburn study posited a value-free science of epidemiology in which knowledge, theories, techniques, and actual and potential applications are devoid of self-interest or bias. The possibility of volunteer bias is a real concern, of course, but in the Woburn case the care with which the biostatisticians controlled for bias is noteworthy.

Beyond the methodological and statistical controls for bias are a number of other important issues. Science is limited in its practice by factors such as financial and personnel resources. Without popular participation, it would often be impossible to carry out much of the research needed to document health hazards. Science is also limited in its conceptualization of what are problems and how they should be studied and addressed. Without popular involvement there might be no professional impetus to target the appropriate questions. These aspects of popular involvement are very evident in the history of the women's health movement,[35] the occupational health and safety movement,[36] and the environmental health movement.[37] These movements have been major forces in advancing the public's health and safety by pointing to problems that were otherwise not identified, by showing how to approach such problems, by organizing to abolish the conditions giving rise to them, and by educating citizens, public agencies, health care providers, officials, and institutions.

Without such popular participation, how would we have known of such hazards and diseases as DES, Agent Orange, pesticides, unnecessary hysterectomies, sterilization abuse, black lung, brown lung, and asbestos? Couto's discussion of the "politics of epidemiology" argues that the scientific assumptions of traditional epidemiology are not completely suited to environmental hazards. Epidemiologists prefer false negatives to false positives—i.e., they would prefer to claim (falsely) no association between variables when there is one than to claim an association when there is none. Epidemiologists require evidence to achieve scientific statements of probability, but this need exceeds the evidence required to state that something should be done to eliminate or minimize a health threat.[38] In this view,

> The degree of risk to human health does not need to be at statistically significant levels to require political action. The degree of risk does have to be such that a reasonable person would avoid it. Consequently, the important political test is not the findings of epidemiologists on the probability of nonrandomness of an incidence of illness but the likelihood that a reasonable person, including members of the community of calculation, would take up residence with the community at risk and drink from and bathe in water from the Yellow Creek area or buy a house along Love Canal.[39]

Indeed, these are the kinds of questions presented to public health officials, researchers, and government members in every setting where there is dispute between the citizen and official perceptions. These questions bring out the metaphors and symbols employed by lay citizens in risk communication, and they stand in contrast to scientific, corporate, and governmental metaphors and symbols.

Popular epidemiology obviously challenges some fundamental epidemiological preconceptions of a "pure" study and its appropriate techniques, such as the nomenclature of disease classifications and the belief that community volunteers automatically introduce bias.[40] Such disputes are not settled primarily within the scientific community. Professional antagonism to popular participation in scientific endeavors is common. Medical sociology has long been aware that such antogonism only occasionally revolves around questions of scientific fact; it usually stems from professional dominance, institutional dominance, and political-economic factors. Professional dominance in science plays an important role here. Professionals generally do not want to let lay publics take on the work that they control as professionals, a particularly ironic situation in the case of epidemiology since the original "shoe-leather" epidemiological work that founded the field is quite similar to popular epidemiological efforts. The Woburn residents' efforts are in fact reminiscent of John Snow's classic study of cholera in London in 1854. The scientific paternalism that holds that lay people cannot involve themselves in scientific decision making is a perspective quite familiar to analysts of health care, and which has been widely discredited in recent years.

Further, environmental health groups challenge the canons of value-neutrality and statistical reasoning, thus undermining the core foundations of professional belief systems. By putting forth their own political goals, they may challenge scientists to acknowledge that they have their own political agendas, even if covert, unconscious, or unrecognized. Corporate legal defenses may not be in collusion with professional dominance, but there is an affinity between the two in the courtroom. Corporate attorneys make much of the challenge that citizen activists are untrained individuals who are incapable of making valid judgments regarding pollution.[41] This affinity is due to the fact that popular participation threatens not only the professional-lay division of knowledge and power but also the social structures and relations that give rise to environmental hazards.

The Activist Nature of Popular Epidemiology

Popular epidemiology is by nature activist, since the lay public is doing work that should be done by corporations, experts, and officials. Popular epidemiology may involve citizen-propelled investigation of naturally occurring diseases for which no firm is responsible. With regard to the recognition of and action around Lyme Disease in Connecticut, where a tick-borne disease was the issue, citizen activists became involved because they considered health officials to be dragging their heels in the matter. Despite

such examples, however, popular epidemiology is particularly powerful when the issue is environmental pollution, occupational disease, or drug side effects. In those cases, persons and organizations are seen to be acting against the public health, often in light of clear knowledge about the dangers. The process of popular epidemiological investigation is therefore an activist one, in which epidemiological findings are immediately employed to alleviate suffering and causes of suffering.

Environmental health activists are by definition acting to correct problems that are not corrected by the established corporate, political, and scientific communities. Logically, the first step in protecting people from the hazards of toxic chemicals is appropriate corporate action, relating to the judicious use and safe disposal of toxic chemicals. It is well known that manufacturers are often lax in this sphere and frequently violate known laws and safe practices.

Given this situation, and given the fact that many corporations purchase land and factories about which they know nothing concerning their past use of toxic chemicals, public agencies present the next line of defense. These agencies include local boards of health, local water boards, state boards of health, state environmental agencies, and the federal EPA. Lay people often begin at the public agency level rather than the corporate level. As the case studies of Woburn, Yellow Creek, South Brunswick, Love Canal, and many other sites indicate, officials are often skeptical or even hostile to citizen requests and inputs.

Even when public agencies are willing a carry out studies, they often demand a different level of proof than community residents want. Further, agencies tend to undertake "pure" epidemiological research without reference to practical solutions to the problem. Moreover, even if they want to, many public bodies have no legal or effective power to compel cleanups, and they rarely can provide restitution to victims. Popular epidemiology emphasizes the practical nature of environmental health issues, and its practitioners are therefore impatient with the caution with which public agencies approach such problems. As with so many other areas of public policies, the fragmentation of agencies and authority contributes to this problem. Community activists cannot understand why more immediate action cannot be taken particularly when they are apt to define the situation as more of a crisis than do the officials.

Popular Epidemiology and Social Movements

Since the injurious products or actions are considered a result of corporate and/or governmental action and inaction, popular epidemiology seeks to place blame and responsibility on the appropriate parties and to obtain political, social, and economic redress. In many cases this local activism is linked to similar cases around the country and to a specifically focused political movement.

Popular epidemiological projects lead many of their practitioners to achieve a broader social understand-ing and to become politically active in other toxic waste issues on a national level. More than half the groups studied by Freudenberg cited accomplishments that extended beyond their local communities.[42] Activists do not necessarily start as activists but merely as citizens who notice that something is wrong. Their experience with the obstacles imposed by corporations, political leaders, and public health officials often turns them into activists. Frank Kahler from South Brunswick, Anne Anderson from Woburn, and Lois Gibbs from Love Canal are such examples. Not all participants necessarily reach this stage, any more than would be the case in other types of local activism. But even among those who do not expand their actions on a larger scale, there is a noticeable critical attitude in their thinking. Our Woburn interviews, for instance, show that there is a great deal of antagonism to large corporations and unresponsive officials. Residents who joined the litigation against W. R. Grace and Beatrice Foods hoped that their suit would place blame on the corporations and focus attention on their actions in order to avoid future recurrences of the types of problems faced by Woburn inhabitants. Public health officials do not share this desire to blame companies.

All social involvement has the potential to lead to greater politicization. What is distinctive about environmental issues, as has been the case with health issues for some time now, is that they have become salient to many people. In part this stems from breakdowns in the social system and in part from a new awareness. Environmental politics originated in natural resource protection but has shifted to greater emphasis on human health and safety. This change places environmental politics in the position of merging with the tremendous health politics of recent years, thus creating a major new social force in American society.

Lay-Professional Alliances

Popular epidemiology involves scientific, medical, and public health experts in varying degrees, but always in alliance with the citizen activists. Lay people can learn to utilize expert knowledge and acquire some of those skills themselves. There is, however, the problematic concern that high levels of epidemiological research will come to be the accepted standard, an unfortunate result because not all organizations would be able to marshall the level of research undertaken in Woburn.

Medical practitioners who criticize patient involvement in treatment often argue that such involvement is "antimedical," much as nuclear power proponents hold that antinuclear activists are "antiscientific." Such criticism is really a way to avoid dealing with the specifics of the situation, rather than a worked-out judgment on the merits of the case. Popular epidemiology is not antiscientific. Rather, it has a different concept of what science is, whom it should serve, and who should control it. As with the most astute health activists, environmental health activists wish to work with

professionals. They have shown their mettle in some very significant cases where their efforts in organizing resources and carrying out research have been invaluable assets. Freudenberg's survey found that 80% of the groups interacted regularly with scientists, and scientific experts were the main source of information for groups.[43]

As mentioned earlier, Woburn-type efforts should not be seen as the standard of proof. Yellow Creek neighbors conducted a more modest campaign which still buttressed their claims. By working in alliance with epidemiologists and other professionals, community residents can also educate those persons to different modes of analysis when indicated. And, as in the health care system, lay citizens can receive training in certain degrees of practice so that they are not completely dependent on professionals. Legator et al. have prepared a manual to enable lay groups to do just this; their book is *The Health Detectives' Handbook: A Guide to the Investigation of Environmental Health Hazards by Nonprofessionals.*[44]

Influencing Future Public Health Practices

Popular epidemiology can become a major influence on the future activities of public agencies that initially fail to do their work. In the case of the Woburn cluster, the first phase of DPH study in 1981 was the major impetus for reestablishing the state cancer registry. A registry had existed before, but it only utilized hospital data; the new registry was mandated to collect data on all tumors in the state.[45] The Woburn case also played a significant role in the passage of a Massachusetts law to monitor toxic wastes in water supplies. Many other Massachusetts communities have been spurred by the Woburn activism and have demanded fuller investigation and disclosure of environmental risks. A number of local groups have charged that the state Department of Public Health has failed to perform adequately. These groups have successfully obtained a state legislative order directing the DPH to release the names of nine sites currently being studied.[46] DPH officials previously had voiced concern that communities would be unduly alarmed by such notice. Agency delays contributed to the resignation of the Commissioner of Public Health. Further pressure is currently seen in legislative hearings regarding the allocation of significant sums of money for additional community health studies.[47] Woburn activism has also contributed to increasing research on Woburn itself: the DPH is conducting a major five-year study of the city, utilizing both prospective and retrospective data, and citizens have a large role in this process.[48] Environmental activism has led to shifts in EPA practices as well, even though the EPA remains weak in its mandate and often resistant to popular initiative.

Previously, environmental health hazards have been identified and controlled by two sources—scientific research and government regulation. But the environmental activism of the past decade has made commu-nity groups a third force in environmental hazard action. Freudenberg found that community groups believed that they had been successful in meeting their goals: 37% responded that they had been very successful, 46% that they had been somewhat successful. Almost half reported that they had eliminated or reduced their targeted hazard.[49]

Conclusion

By examining examples of popular epidemiology and by constructing a theoretical framework for it, we have shown it to be a highly politicized form of action. Popular epidemiology is also a form of risk communication by lay persons to professional and official audiences, and as such it demonstrates that risk communication is indeed an exercise of political power. In a growing number of instances, organized communities have been able to successfully communicate risk in such a way as to win political, economic, and cultural battles.

Yet there are some structural problems associated with such victories. Experts and officials may demand increasingly higher levels of proof, requiring field studies that are prohibitive in terms of time, skills, and resources. Concerted political action may win a case but not necessarily build up scientific credibility or precedent. People may fear such a result and begin to tailor their efforts toward convincing experts and officials, thus possibly diminishing the impact of their efforts on their communities.

Solutions to these structural

problems are not simple; community residents will have to find ways to work on several fronts simultaneously, and we should not assume that the task is theirs alone. Academics and health and public health professionals can play an important role in informing their colleagues and government officials that there are new ways to understand risk. The public as a whole needs to work toward more stringent and actively enforced environmental legislation and regulation as well as greater social control over corporations.

We are only in the earliest stages of understanding the phenomenon of popular epidemiology. Most research has been on empirical studies of individual cases, with a few preliminary stabs at theoretical and analytical linkages. The existing and future successes of popular epidemiological endeavors can potentially play a major role in reformulating the way that lay people, scientists, and public agencies view public health problems. This is an exciting possibility and one with which by definition we can all be involved.

Acknowledgments

This research was supported in part by funds from the Wayland Collegium, Brown University. This paper is a revised version of a presentation to the Boston Area Medical Sociologists meeting, 6 April 1987, where participants offered important feedback. Many of the ideas here have developed during a year-long faculty seminar at Brown University, where I have benefited from the interacting with Anne Fausto-Sterling, John Ladd, Talbot Page, and Harold Ward. Other ideas and data have come from my collaboration with Edwin J. Mikkelsen on a book about Woburn. Dorothy Nelkin and Alonzo Plough provided valuable comments on the manuscript.

Notes

1. Jerry Ackerman and Diego Ribadeneira, "12 Families, Grace Settle Woburn Toxic Case," *Boston Globe*, 23 September 1986; William F. Doherty, "Jury: Firm Fouled Wells in Woburn," *Boston Globe*, 29 July 1986.
2. Abraham Lilienfeld, *Foundations of Epidemiology* (New York: Oxford, 1976), p. 4.
3. Paula DiPerna, *Cluster Mystery: Epidemic and the Children of Woburn, Mass.* (St. Louis: Mosby, 1985), pp. 106–108.
4. *Ibid.*, pp. 75–82.
5. *Ibid.*, pp. 53–70.
6. *Ibid.*, pp. 111–155.
7. *Ibid.*, p. 161.
8. *Ibid.*, pp. 164–173.
9. *Ibid.*, p. 175.
10. *Ibid.*, pp. 176–199.
11. *Ibid.*, pp. 200–211.
12. *Ibid.*, pp. 209–215.
13. Jan Schlictmann, interview, 12 May 1987.
14. Steven W. Lagakos, Barbara J. Wessen, and Marvin Zelen, "An Analysis of Contaminated Well Water and Health Effects in Woburn, Massachusetts," *Journal of the American Statistical Association*, Volume 81, Number 395 (1984): 583–596.
15. *Ibid.*
16. Steven Lagakos, interview, 6 April 1987.
17. *Ibid.*
18. DiPerna, *op. cit.*, pp. 168–169.
19. Marvin Zelen, interview, 1 July 1987.
20. DiPerna, *op. cit.*, pp. 251–273.

21. Zelen, *op. cit.*
22. Allan Morrison lecture, Brown University, Department of Community Health, 25 February 1987.
23. Lagakos *et al.*, *op. cit.*
24. Richard A. Couto, "Failing Health and New Prescriptions: Community-Based Approaches to Environmental Risks," in Carole E. Hill, ed., *Current Health Policy Issues and Alternatives: An Applied Social Science Perspective* (Athens: University of Georgia Press: 1986).
25. *Ibid.*
26. Adeline Gordon Levine, *Love Canal: Science, Politics, and People* (Lexington, Mass.: Heath, 1982), pp. 14–15.
27. Celene Krauss, "Grass-Root Protests and Toxic Wastes: Developing a Critical Political View." Paper presented at 1986 meeting of the American Sociological Association.
28. Couto, *op. cit.*
29. *Ibid.*
30. *Ibid.*
31. Nicholas Freudenberg, *Not in Our Backyards: Community Action for Health and the Environment* (New York: Monthly Review, 1984).
32. Nicholas Freudenberg, "Citizen Action for Environmental Health: Report on a Survey of Community Organizations," *American Journal of Public Health*, Volume 74 (1984): 444–448.
33. Couto, *op. cit.*
34. Levine, *op. cit.*, pp. 103–104.
35. Helen Rodriguez-Trias, "The Women's Health Movement: Women Take Power," in Victor Sidel and Ruth Sidel, eds., *Reforming Medicine: Lessons of the Last Quarter Century* (New York: Pantheon, 1984), pp. 107–126.
36. Daniel Berman, "Why Work Kills: A Brief History of Occupational Health and Safety in the United States," *International Journal of Health Services*, Volume 7, Number 1 (1977): 63–87.
37. Freudenberg, *Not in Our Backyards*, op. cit.
38. Couto, *op. cit.*
39. *Ibid.*
40. DiPerna, *op. cit.*, p. 379.
41. Krauss, *op. cit.*
42. Freudenberg, "Citizen Action," *op. cit.*
43. *Ibid.*
44. Marvin S. Legator, Barbara L. Harper, and Michael J. Scott, eds., *The Health Detectives' Handbook: A Guide to the Investigation of Environmental Health Hazards by Nonprofessionals* (Baltimore: Johns Hopkins University Press, 1985).
45. Richard Clapp, interview, 14 March 1987.
46. Ken Cafarell, "Walker Lists 9 Ongoing Studies of Potential Health Problems," *Boston Globe*, 19 November 1986.
47. Larry Tye, "Budget Plan Would Boost State Funds for Local Health Studies," *Boston Globe*, 9 May 1987.
48. Lagakos, *op. cit.*
49. Freudenberg, "Citizen Participation," *op. cit.*

Appendix One

Sources of Data

Steven Jonas

This guide to the principal sources of health and health services data for the United States contains descriptions of the major data sources: who publishes them, how frequently they are published as of 1985, from whom they may be ordered, and what categories of data they contain.

Appendix I of *Health, United States 1984* [DHHS Pub. No. (PHS) 85-1232] contains very useful, detailed descriptions of all the common data sources, private and government. Appendix IV of the *Statistical Abstract, 1985* (U.S. Bureau of the Census, 1984) contains an extensive listing of sources of health data. The American Hospital Association's *Guide Issue 1984* contains a comprehensive listing of Health Organizations and Agencies, in Part C.

1. *Statistical Abstract of the United States*
   Published annually by the Bureau of the Census, U.S. Department of Commerce, Washington, D.C.,[1] the *Statistical Abstract* reproduces a vast collection of tables containing information from many different government agencies. They are accumulated under the following headings: Population; Vital Statistics; Immigration and Naturalization; Health and Nutrition; Education; Law Enforcement; Courts, and Prisons; Geography and Environment; Parks and Recreation; Elections; Federal Government Finances and Employment; State and Local Government Finances and Employment; Social Insurance and Human Services; National Defense and Veterans' Affairs; Labor Force, Employment, and Earnings; Income, Expenditures, and Wealth; Prices; Banking, Finance, and Insurance; Business Enterprise; Communications; Energy; Science; Transportation—Land; Transportation—Air and Water; Agriculture; Forests and Forest Products; Fisheries; Mining and Mineral Products; Construction and Housing; Manufacturers; Domestic Trade and Services; Foreign Commerce and Aid; Outlying Areas under the Jurisdiction of the United States; and Comparative International Statistics.

---

[1]Almost all U.S. government publications are to be purchased from the Superintendent of Documents, United States Government Printing Office (USGPO), Washington, D.C. 20402, rather then directly from the agency producing them.

SOURCE: Steven Jonas, *Health Care Delivery in the United States*, 3rd. ed. (New York: Springer Publishing Company, 1986), pp. 527–532. Copyright 1986 by Springer Publishing Company. Used by permission.

The *Abstract* also has its own very large "Guide to Sources," for all categories of data.

2. *U.S. Census of Population*
   The Bureau of the Census is part of the U.S. Department of Commerce, Washington, D.C. 20233. The Constitution requires that a census be taken every 10 years, at the beginning of each decade. The original purpose was to apportion seats in the House of Representatives and thus in the Electoral College. In modern times, in addition to the simple counts, a great deal of demographic data is collected by the Census Bureau. Hardcover compendia of decennial national census data are published periodically. Also available are special analyses for a wide variety of geographical subdivisions of the country. Many reports on the decennial censuses are published by the Census Bureau, but a good place to begin is in Section 1 of the *Statistical Abstract*.

3. *Current Population Reports*
   In addition to reports from the decennial censuses, the Census Bureau publishes seven series of reports on a continuing basis. These include estimates, projections, sample counts, and special studies of selected segments of the population. The seven series each have a "P" number. They are: P-20, Population Characteristics; P-23, Special Studies; P-25, Population Estimates and Projections; P-26, Federal-State Cooperative Program for Population Estimates; P-27, Farm Population; P-28, Special Censuses; and P-60, Consumer Income. Information on the content of each series is of course available from the Census Bureau. Subscriptions are not available for individual series but must be taken in two sets; however, single copies of reports from all series except P-28 may be ordered from the USGPO.

4. *Monthly Vital Statistics Report (MVSR)*
   MVSR is published by the National Center for Health Statistics of the Office of Health Research, Statistics, and Technology of the Department of Health and Human Services, 3700 East–West Highway, Hyattsville, Maryland 20782. It has several sections. *Provisional Statistics*, published monthly, contains the most recent data for the traditional "vital statistics"—deaths, births, marriages, and divorces. There is also a series of supplements, which appear on a semiregular basis and contain provisional final annual summaries of vital statistics plus technical information on methodology. *MVSR* may be ordered by annual subscription.

5. *Vital Statistics of the United States*
   This is the annual report of the National Center for Health Statistics (NCHS), concerning vital statistics. The address of the NCHS is given under *MVSR*, item #4 of this list.

6. *Vital and Health Statistics*
   This publication of the NCHS appears at irregular intervals. There are 14 series, not numbered consecutively, most of which report data from ongoing studies and surveys that the NCHS has carried out. Several series have been dormant for some time. The publication of some data shifts periodically between *Vital and Health Statistics* and *Monthly Vital Statistics Report*. In the late 1970s, a new publication appeared: *Advance Data from Vital and Health Statistics*. *Advance Data* presents data from such ongoing NCHS activities as the National Ambulatory Medical Care Survey (NAMCS), the Hospital Discharge Survey (HDS), and the Health

and Nutrition Examination Survey (HANES). Until the late 1970s, the NCHS published a useful guide, *Current Listing and Topical Index to the Vital and Health Statistics Series*. Presently they are publishing only periodic catalogs of their publications.

The 14 series in *Vital and Health Statistics* are as follows:

Series   1. Programs and Collection Procedures

Series   2. Data Evaluation and Methods Research

Series   3. Analytical Studies (primarily of mortality, stressing international comparison)

Series   4. Documents and Committee Reports

Series 10. Data from the Health Interview Survey (containing patient-perspective health, illness, and health services utilization data)

Series 11. Data from the Health Examination Survey and the Health and Nutrition Examination Survey

Series 12. Data from the Health Records Survey (reports data from two studies of nursing homes carried out in the 1960s)

Series 13. The data on Health Resources Utilization (includes hospitals nursing homes, and ambulatory care services)

Series 14. Data on Health Resources: Manpower and Facilities (health resources data appear also in *Health, United States* (#9 in this list)

Series 15. Data from Special Surveys

Series 20. Data on Mortality (reports of time-trend analyses for the United States)

Series 21. Data on Natality, Marriage, and Divorce

Series 22. Data from the National Natality and Mortality Surveys (different from Series 21 in that special studies are reported)

Series 23. Data from the National Survey of Family Growth

7. *Morbidity and Mortality Weekly Report (MMWR)*

This is a regular publication of the Center for Disease Control (CDC) of the USDHHS and is available on an annual subscription basis from the CDC, Atlanta, Georgia 30333. Following a large subscription price increase in 1982, *MMWR*, in the public domain, has been mass photocopied and circulated at cost by several organizations, including the *New England Journal of Medicine* (10 Shattuck St., Boston, MA 02115). In the past, it has been concerned primarily with the communicable diseases for which reporting is required by law. Most of the diseases covered are no longer of much importance in the United States and, for many of them, the reporting rates are poor. Nevertheless, it provides an important perspective on communicable disease in United States. Each week, case reports of specific outbreaks of communicable disease are reported; there are also occasional international notes, status reports on communicable disease control programs, and statements of official United States Public Health Service positions on various issues in communicable disease control. In recent years *MMWR* has acquired a broader purview, reporting on CDC, NIOSH, and USPHS activities in chronic disease control. Its value has increased significantly.

8. *Health Resources Statistics*

Health Resources Statistics is a former annual publication of the National Center for Health Statistics. It had three major parts: manpower, inpatient facilities, and outpatient and nonpatient health services. It was a voluminous work, reporting numbers, distribution, and some facilities and services utilization data. It was the major source of census data on health personnel and facilities in the United States, although the American Hospital Association and American Medical Association do, of course, report data on hospitals and physicians (respectively). Although not published since the late 1970s, it is still very useful for historical and comparative analyses.

9. *Health, United States*

The first edition of this work was published in 1976 under the title *Health, United States, 1975*. A combined effort of the National Center for Health Statistics and the National Center for Health Services Research, it has appeared annually since then. In earlier issues, there were several review articles on "selected health topics," but this feature was eliminated in the mid-1980s. Data are presented on Health Status and Determinants, Utilization of Health Resources, Health Care Resources, and Health Care Expenditures. It also contains a useful appendix, Sources and Limitations of Data. It is a boon to students and researchers in health care delivery because it provides one-stop shopping for most important health and health care data.

10. *American Hospital Association Guide to the Health Care Field*

This two-part publication of the American Hospital Association (840 North Lake Shore Drive, Chicago, Illinois 60611) appears on August 1 of each year. The first part, the *Guide Issue of Hospitals*, contains a listing of almost every hospital in the United States by location and gives basic data on size, type, ownership, and facilities, as well as a great deal of information on the AHA and the hospital supply industry. The second part, *Hospital Statistics*, contains a great deal of summary utilization and financial data on U.S. hospitals, by many different cross-tabulations. Some of the data are presented historically. The two parts together contain the most detailed available data on hospitals in the United States.

11. *HCFA Publications*

In 1979, the Health Care Financing Administration (HCFA) took over the responsibility of publishing annual health care financing data. This task was formerly carried out by the Social Security Administration. The *Health Care Financing Review* is a quarterly. It now annually publishes "National Health Expenditures" and "Private Health Insurance," which formerly appeared in the *Social Security Bulletin*. These summaries cover total amounts, where the money comes from, and where if goes. HCFA publications are available from the USGPO.

12. *"Datagrams" of the Association of American Medical Colleges*

The "Datagrams" appear monthly in the *Journal of Medical Education*. The AAMC is located at 1 DuPont Circle, Washington, D.C. 20036. Together with the annual issue of the *Journal of the American Medical Association* on medical education, "Datagrams" provides the principal source of data on medical education in the United States: schools, faculty, curricula, admissions, students, and the like.

13. *Center for Health Policy Research of the American Medical Association*

The center, which is located in AMA National Headquarters, 535 North Dearborn Street, Chicago, Illinois 60610, produces a variety of useful data on the physician work force from its own files. Formerly there were two annual publications, the *Profile of Medical Practice* and *Socioeconomic Issues of Health*. In 1984 there was one, *The American Health Care System, 1984*. The AMA also publishes periodic reports on special studies. Other major professional organizations are good sources of data on their own members.

Annotated Bibliography of Journals in Medical Sociology and Related Areas

This bibliography includes not only some journals from which selections in this book were taken but other journals as well. It is very informative to browse and scan journals in the library. You can get a good idea of the major issues, debates, and methods in medical sociology and in related areas. The categories in this list are in some cases overlapping.

THE MAJOR MEDICAL SOCIOLOGY JOURNALS

You can get a good overview of issues and debates in the field by regularly scanning these few journals.

Journal of Health and Social Behavior (American Sociological Association, quarterly)

This journal is published by the American Sociological Association and for many sociologists is the most respected journal in the field. For some, this journal has not always represented the whole spectrum of research in medical sociology. Articles are largely quantitative, though qualitative material has increased in recent years. This journal is widely looked to as a major source of research. It covers a wide range of topics, including a large amount on the sociology of mental health and illness.

Social Science & Medicine (Pergamon Press, 24 issues per year)

This widely respected journal, published in England, has a very international flavor. It is broadly multidisciplinary with sections on medical sociology, medical geography, medical anthropology, medical psychology, health economics, medical ethics, and health policy. The journal sponsors an annual international Conference on the Social Sciences and Medicine.

Sociology of Health and Illness (British Sociological Association, Section on Medical Sociology, quarterly)

Although it is the newest specialty journal in medical sociology, it has developed rapidly and is increasingly looked to. Reflecting the nature of British medical sociology, this journal is largely qualitative. It covers a broad range of topics, with strength in doctor-patient interaction, experience of illness, and theory.

JOURNALS COVERING A BROAD RANGE OF AREAS IN SOCIAL SCIENCE AND HEALTH

International Journal of Health Services (Baywood Publishing, quarterly)

This journal is multidisciplinary, covering health policy, political economy, medical history, medical ethics. It is quite international in context and includes diverse perspectives, but is particularly known for its strengths in political economy, Marxism, and radical analyses of the health care system.

Milbank Quarterly (Milbank Memorial Fund, quarterly)

Previously known as the *Milbank Memorial Fund Quarterly/Health and Society*, this journal is published by a foundation that sponsors medical research and education. The journal covers a broad range of areas, especially health policy, history, and medical ethics. Articles are often longer than other journals, and some are analytical and interpretive essays.

Journal of Health Politics, Policy and Law (Duke University, Department of Health Administration, quarterly).

This journal has a strong constituency among political scientists who study health. It covers a broad range of topics, with special emphasis on health policy, analysis of government health programs, government regulation, hospitals, ethics, and legal issues.

Journal of Public Health Policy (National Association for Public Health Policy quarterly)

This journal covers a wide range of policy issues, health planning, and public health interventions, with emphasis on social structural factors. Features interesting editorials on health politics, such as national health insurance and national health plans.

Women and Health (Haworth Press, quarterly)

This is the major source of journal-style research on women and health, though there are other sources such as newsletters published by advocacy groups. The journal covers a wide range of issues, such as sex differences in health, sexism in the health care system, and reproductive rights.

HEALTH POLICY AND CURRENT AFFAIRS

Other journals noted above provide more in-depth coverage of health policy. The following journals provide brief and very current analyses of policy, financing, and service trends.

Health/PAC Bulletin (Health Policy Advisory Committee, bimonthly)

This bulletin is published by a progressive research group, the Health Policy Advisory Committee, which formulated the term, *medical-industrial complex*. As would be expected, the journal has been a major source of information on the health care industry, on the growth of for-profit hospital chains, and of issues of access to care. It has also covered many issues of reproductive rights and medical ethics.

The Network News (National Women's Health Network, bimonthly)

This newsletter is the central information clearinghouse for the women's health movement. It contains news briefs and analyses of developments in pregnancy and childbirth, reproductive rights, health hazards affecting women, special health conditions affecting women, women health workers, pharmaceutical and surgical dangers, and health policy.

Disability Studies Quarterly (Brandeis University Department of Sociology, quarterly)

This is the leading source of current information on all aspects of disability. The main emphasis is on physical disability, although there is ample coverage of mental illness and mental retardation. It covers a wide range of topics in independent living, self-help, the disability rights movement, chronic illness, legislation, and policy.

MEDICAL ETHICS

Hastings Center Reports (The Hastings Center, bimonthly)

Ethics are covered in a number of other journals mentioned already, but this publication is the most central source of developments in the area of health ethics. It incorporates the work of medical professionals, social scientists, and philosophers, some of whom are resident scholars and visiting lecturers at the Hastings Center. It also includes coverage of ethical issues of health policies.

Journal of Medicine and Philosophy (Society for Health and Human Values, quarterly)

This journal includes articles on ethical issues, theoretical and philosophical concerns, the nature of medical knowledge, and client-provider relationships.

MEDICAL ANTHROPOLOGY

Culture, Medicine, and Psychiatry (D. Reidel Publishing, quarterly)

Although this journal includes research from a variety of disciplines, it is primarily a source for work in medical anthropology. The journal has a very international flavor, with special attention to cultural beliefs and health practices in third world countries.

Medical Anthropology Quarterly (American Anthropological Association, and Society for Medical Anthropology, quarterly)

This is a major source for research in medical anthropology. While it does cover international topics, it contains more American material than the above journal.

HEALTH SERVICES RESEARCH AND PROGRAM EVALUATION

Medical Care (Medical Care Section of the American Public Health Association, monthly)

This is a major public health journal featuring scholarship in research, planning, organization, financing, service provision, and evaluation of health services. It includes research from other countries as well.

Health Services Research (Association for Health Services Research, bimonthly)

This journal features studies of financing, access, utilization, medical practice, and planning issues in the provision of health services. It includes many studies of large data sets, including national surveys.

Inquiry (Blue Cross and Blue Shield Association, quarterly)

Covers health care organization, service provision, and financing. Lots of attention is given to Medicare, Medicaid, and private health insurers.

Health Care Financing Review (United States Department of Health and Human Services, Health Care Financing Administration, quarterly)

This publication emphasizes studies of the costs of medical services, forecasts for future needs and costs, and the impact of costs on federal programs. It often analyzes large national data sets, especially those involving federal programs.

MEDICINE AND PUBLIC HEALTH

New England Journal of Medicine (Massachusetts Medical Society, weekly)

This is widely considered to be the most important general medical journal in the United States. It features occasional articles on health policy, medical ethics, professional behavior, and client-provider relations. Since such articles reach a large public audience, they are frequently and widely cited.

The Lancet (Lancet, Ltd., weekly)

This is one of the two major medical journals in England. More than the *New England Journal of Medicine*, it features articles on public health concerns and health policy.

American Journal of Public Health (American Public Health Association, monthly)

This journal contains many clinical, epidemiological, and public health studies. Articles cover risk factors in health, preventive programs, large-scale surveys of disease, evaluations of treatment programs, and health outcomes of government health programs.

MEDICAL HISTORY

Medical History (Wellcome Institute for the History of Medicine, quarterly)

This is the major English source for medical history. It gives special attention to the evolution of scientific and social concepts in medicine. Articles deal with the history of medical practice, disease concepts, hospitals, and epidemics.

Bulletin of the History of Medicine (American Association for the History of Medicine/Johns Hopkins Institute of the History of Medicine, quarterly)

This is the major U.S. publication in medical history. The journal covers much of the same as the above. It also includes some work on the history of biological sciences.

Journal of the History of Medicine and Allied Sciences (University of Connecticut School of Medicine, quarterly)

This journal is similar in coverage to the above two journals, with perhaps more coverage of the history of science.

About the Author

Phil Brown is associate professor, Department of Sociology, Brown University and lecturer in sociology, Harvard Medical School Department of Psychiatry at the Massachusetts Mental Health Center. His research interests include mental patients' rights, mental health policy, treatment refusal, clinician-patient interaction, the sociology of diagnosis, and community responses to environmental disasters. He has written *The Transfer of Care: Psychiatric Deinstitutionalization and Its Aftermath* and has edited *Mental Health Care and Social Policy*. He is currently at work on a book, *No Safe Place: The Childhood Leukemia Cluster in Woburn, Massachusetts*. His articles have appeared in *Journal of Health and Social Behavior; Social Science and Medicine; International Journal of Health Services; Journal of Community Psychology; Mental Disability Law Reporter; Journal of Health Policy, Politics, and Law; Journal of Contemporary Ethnography;* and *International Journal of Law and Psychiatry*.